My
Little Bird

by Theresa H. Kulla-Klink

DORRANCE
PUBLISHING CO
EST. 1920
PITTSBURGH, PENNSYLVANIA 15238

Dorrance Publishing Co
585 Alpha Drive
Suite 103
Pittsburgh, PA 15238
Visit our website at *www.dorrancebookstore.com*

ISBN: 978-1-6366-1483-0
eISBN: 978-1-6366-1664-3

MY
LITTLE BIRD

I WAS BORN IN 1933 IN BERLIN, GERMANY, to German/Polish parents. Because they had grown up in a poor countryside area of small farms and were both from very large families—my father was the eldest of 13 children—they had left Poland in 1931 to come to Berlin to make a better living for themselves. My father wanted to study medicine at the famous Berlin University but because that course was so expensive he settled for Underwater Massage Therapy, which he loved. His dream was to work with Ferdinand Sauerbruch, a famous Berlin surgeon, which he later did and continued to do until September of 1939 when World War Two started.

They had a small apartment in the inner city and my mother was very homesick for her little village in Poland until I was born, when things got a little better. As I started out to be an only child I often wondered why I was alone: I also wanted to live in a big family, like my parents had done. When I asked my mother WHY, I was simply told to go at night to the window sill and put cookies out for the stork in the hope that we might be lucky enough to have it bring either a brother or sister for me. Well, I guess that was the end of my dreams to live in a big family!

For a while, growing up in a small family bothered me, especially as there were no children to play with in the whole neighborhood, but I did get used to it in a way. My parents must have noticed, however, and one day brought home a beautiful multicolored little bird for me to take care of. I was thrilled to have something to do and to have a responsibility but the feeling did not last long. It wasn't something I could play with and was mostly quiet and sat in a corner of the cage, so we both sat there and did nothing. It was summertime and all the windows were kept open and one morning when I went to feed it, the cage door was open and the little bird was gone. I never really found out what had happened.

There was, however, light at the end of the tunnel: my parents told me we were going to go on vacation to Poland to see my grandparents and so that my parents could help them with their work in the fields. I knew I had been there before but that was when I was very little and I did not remember. We took a train ride for about four hours to get there and I was a little scared by the new experience, hoping the train would not jump off its track. Every time the train turned a little to the left or right, I leaned over to the opposite side and lifted my legs up, which made people sitting across from us start to laugh and I remember being very embarrassed.

We made it safely to my grandparents and I loved it there; there was so much to do—I played with animals, visited my cousins and my grandmother showed me how to milk a cow. It was disappointing that they didn't have a horse but that they could not afford. There was only one thing that bothered me a lot. My grandmother had four geese which were constantly hand fed with a special feed to make them really fat and they were kept in a small cage where they could hardly move. This was done so that they got really fat and were worth more money in the market when my grandmother sold them.

Well, I felt so sorry for them that I felt I had to do something about it and one evening when everyone was busy I went to the cage, opened it, and let them out. The poor things could hardly walk but they made it to the nearest forest and disappeared and I never found out what happened to them. After she found out, my grandmother hardly spoke to me again but I felt great because I knew I had saved their lives. In a way I was glad to leave after three weeks and even though there was some sadness I still had to go home to prepare for school.

We made it safely back home to Berlin and in a way I felt safe and secure again being in our little apartment. One day when I came home from school, I noticed that a new store had opened in a building a little further down from ours, so I quickly went down to check it out. It was like a little clothing store with fur coats and nice dresses and suits and there was a big sign in the window which said that everything was hand-made and nothing had been done by factories! I was quite fascinated seeing all those pretty fur coats and dresses and while I was still staring at the window the door opened and out came a girl with a little boy. We looked at each other and smiled and said "Guten Tag" (Good day) and she asked where I lived. I told her and she said that was great and that maybe we could get together and play or go to the park. Her name was Hannah and the little boy was her brother, David, who she said she had to look after whenever her parents were busy. I was thrilled. I had found a friend! Hannah must have been a little older than I was and she was so pretty! She looked like I had always wanted to look with big brown eyes and dark curly hair. I felt like an ugly duckling next to her but I was just so happy to have found her. It was a Friday when we met and as I had to go home, we decided to meet again the next day when she again had to babysit little David.

I went home and told my parents about our meeting and, of course, they wanted to know who these people were. I really didn't like the idea my mother had which was that she would come with me the next day to meet them because I felt grown up having my own friends but I didn't say anything. That night I was so excited that I hardly slept at all! Well, we had such a good time in the park the next day and my mother seem to be okay as well and said that evening that they were really nice people. Hannah and I got along very well and I finally felt that I had a sister. We met almost every weekend and I was invited by her parents to go to their apartment where I could also play with little David. They had a nice, big, apartment with antique furniture and I guessed that they must be quite well off. There was just one thing I couldn't quite figure out about them and that was that when they were working in the store or outside in the street, they put things like white scarves around their sleeves on their shirts or jackets for everyone to see. One day I just asked Hannah what it meant. She looked at me with a shy little smile and said, "Because we are Jewish people the Government wants us to do that." I looked back at her and although I didn't know what she meant, I just pretended I understood and we never talked about it again. I did ask my parents though and they looked kind of strange and just said, "They are Jewish," and because I saw people on the street wearing the same thing, I didn't really bother with it. I guessed they were special people and Hannah and I were very close and had a lot of fun together. Then, one day, I got sick with the flu and had to stay in bed for a week. Of course, when I got up the first thing I wanted was to see Hannah but when I got to the store I almost fainted, Everything was boarded up, both on the store and the apartment windows and there was no one in sight; they appeared to have just vanished. I cried and ran home to tell my parents about it but they were silent and did not react. It wasn't until later that I knew what had happened. I continued to wonder what had happened to Hannah and her family but could never find anyone to talk about it and even my parents kept quiet.

There were other happenings in Germany at that time and people were in a turmoil. Ever since our Chancellor (Fuehrer) Adolf Hitler had declared war on Poland in September 1939, with his army taking over Poland in a very short length of time, people were scared and frightened about their future. In a way it made me happy because my grandparents were now living in Germany. At the same time, I was confused when I heard my parents talking to other people about the future and somehow I felt insecure even though, of course, I was still too young to really understand what was going on. I remember on one occasion we were very excited because we had a big sports event at school and our Fuehrer was supposed to come and greet us. He really did come and he and his bodyguards came marching in while we were standing in line to greet him. He even shook some students hands and I was so proud, I didn't wash my hands for a whole day. He looked so friendly and was so nice to us that I couldn't understand why he had invaded Poland and even more countries after that. My parents must have also been curious as they bought a little "Volksemp-faenger"—a little radio which was made for people to hear the news and alerts and to broadcast the success Germany's army had in capturing more countries. At the same time, there was also a scare by many people that all men might be called to active duty to become soldiers to fight on the front line, so my mother was very anxious about that too. I could not believe that my father would go to war and fight or even kill other men. A good thing we did not know what lay ahead of us for the next five years.

I could feel that my parents were getting really worried and with every day it got worse. Our involvement was increased because there was a young couple living across from our apartment and when the young man was called to active duty, his wife became very depressed about it and my parents helped her a lot. The lady was pretty big with a huge stomach and I had seen other ladies like that but I didn't want to ask her or my parents what was wrong with her. A little while later I heard a baby crying in her apartment and my mother and I went over to see the baby. It was tiny and not really pretty and I noticed that the lady was skinny again but there was no sign of a stork. I actually never saw a stork in our area and guessed my mother hadn't really been telling me the truth. This is when I realised that growing up you have to figure out a lot of things for yourself!

Months passed and my father was still waiting to be called for duty. I noticed there were more and more buildings boarded up and less people walking around with that white scarf around their sleeves. Our school was disrupted as well—one day we could go to school and the next day it was cancelled because something had happened. Our teachers had mostly been young people but more and more left for active duty and were replaced by much older ones, which made school much less fun than before.

Finally, one afternoon we heard a knock on our door and two soldiers in a fancy uniform were asking to talk to my father so we knew the day we were afraid of had arrived. He was told that within two weeks he had to go to the nearest "Kaserne" (barracks) to register for active duty. I started to cry and perhaps the soldiers felt sorry for me for they said that they didn't think my father would go to the front line and that because he spoke Polish and worked in the medical field, he might be put in a hospital to help wounded soldiers coming back from the front line. My mother and I were a little relieved and thought maybe he would have to go to a hospital in Poland. Of course, Poland now belonged to Germany and I so hoped we could go back and see my grandparents.

I suppose initially we were in shock but after a very slow start we realised there were only two weeks to go and very many things to be taken care of to get ready for my father's departure. He was told he only needed a small bag because he would be provided with a uniform, etc., but there were a lot of preparations to be made at home. It was hardest on my mother, really, because she had only ever been a housewife and it was my father who had taken care of all the other things like paying bills and taking care of all financial matters. I don't think my mother had ever even been to a bank. Finally, it looked as though everything had been done and that we were ready for my father to leave. In those last two weeks I think we hardly ate or slept.

Eventually, the day came and the three of us went to the nearest "Kaserne." There were a lot of other families there, mostly crying, and I think that until that moment no one really realised what was happening. The Kaserne was completely surrounded by fences and security guards were watching as we hugged each other very tightly and said goodbye. I saw tears running down my father's face and I think that was the moment I matured more than other children my age who hadn't been through that awful experience. We just watched as my father turned around, went through the gate and never looked back.

My mother and I went back to our empty apartment and waited and waited for a letter or something to find out where he had been sent. My mother and the lady with the baby became good friends and helped and relied on each other a lot. She had been told by the Government that her husband was on the front line but had no word directly from him. After what seemed like a long wait, we finally received a letter from the government saying my father had been put to work in a hospital in Poznan (now called Posen in German) in the western part of Poland, now Germany. We were relieved—at least we knew where he was and that he was alive—and I saw my mother smiling again for the first time in a long time. A little later we received a letter from my father telling us he was fine and that things were not too bad for him although he felt terrible for all the wounded soldiers being brought back to him from the front line, many of whom did not survive. He said he felt the war would soon be over. Little did any of us know then, thank God, that this World War 2 was the biggest and deadliest war in history and involved 30 countries.

One day, not long after we heard from my father, the lady with the baby received a letter from the government saying that her husband had been reported missing in action. The last time she heard from him, he had been fighting on the front line at the German/Russian border, but nobody knew for sure where he was and so she assumed he was a prisoner of war. There was a rumour going around that all German prisoners were being sent to Siberia, a vast Russian province, but no one knew for sure. At that time there were lots of rumours going around.

Whenever I could, I would listen to the little Volksempfaenger. I wanted to hear that the war was over or at least that what my father had written was true and that it would soon be ended, but mostly the news consisted of the Fuehrer giving endless speeches saying how proud he was of his troops and soldiers for invading more countries, meaning even more front lines. His idea was to consolidate all those countries into a big German REICH (empire), or at least that was what a lot of people thought. Sometimes he talked about the 1936 Summer Olympics which were held in Berlin and he made us believe that he had brought us that event, that he arranged everything. In the meantime more and more men were being called up for active duty and even some of the older ones were being called.

The lady with the baby told us that as she had no family in Berlin and still didn't know where her husband was, she was thinking of relocating to live with her parents in Muenchen (Munich) in southern Germany. She said that she would tell the government her new address so that her husband would know where she was when the war was over and everything was back to normal. Her decision was bad news for my mother and me as we had no one else close to us except for an old aunt who lived in the Berlin suburbs about an hour's travel away from us.

Perhaps because of this, we got the idea of relocating to my grandparents in that little village in the former Poland, now part of Germany. My mother wrote and told them of our idea and they were happy that we would be together as a family again. All we had to do then was to get permission from the government to leave, which wasn't too bad. The government officer just asked for our new address in case they needed to contact us and he even mentioned that it was a good idea to leave the big cities as it would be safer in the country. We were surprised but also happy and as we decided to keep our apartment until the war was over, we left all our furniture behind and just took our personal things. Unfortunately, my grandparents farm house was really a little too small for all of us, especially as my mother's two younger brothers were still living at home, but by luck we found a nice small cottage for rent in the next village. This was especially good as it was closer to my school. When we moved there, however, things had changed a lot and people were nowhere near as friendly as they had been before. In a way I could understand it: we were the ones who, by war, had taken away their home country and replaced it with another one. What little I knew!

It didn't take us long to settle into that little cottage—it was just a short 45-minute walk to my grandparents' and it was cute and also furnished, which was lucky as we'd left all our furniture back in Berlin. So far so good but I had to start school someday and that school was a little way down the road and also involved walking through cornfields, which sometimes scared me as there were hardly any people or cars around. At that time there were actually hardly any cars on the roads at all. My mother walked me to school for the first few days and then I started going by myself.

I started to feel uneasy from the first day when we registered at the principal's office. It appeared I was the only student from the old Germany and particularly from Berlin. All the other students were from the surrounding areas and mostly spoke in Polish even though everyone knew how to speak German as well. The school work was initially easy for me as they were behind in their studies at that school, so I just tried to fit in as well as I could. I also loved sports and was quite good but neither of those things made me at all popular with the other students, who gave me the nickname of "Berliner Bomben Scheisser" (Berlin Bomb Shit). There was nothing I could do and the teachers weren't really on my side either.

Then, one day when I was walking home from school through the cornfields, two older boys came running out of the corn, ripped my blouse apart and started to take off my skirt. I screamed so loudly that they must have been scared I'd be heard and they ran off, while I ran home as fast as I could and told my mother what had happened. The next day she walked me to school and talked to the principal, who promised to investigate but nothing ever happened and I don't think the boys went to my school. From then on my mother used to walk me to school and also picked me up at the end of the school day. Then, one day, a boy started to talk to me. He was two classes above me and asked what Berlin was like and told me he'd like to go there to study law when the war was over. He seemed very nice and was never bullying or making fun of me and I was glad to have someone to talk to. The best thing was that he also lived in that same little village and offered to walk home with me. When I told my mother about him, she found out where he lived and talked to his parents. They were really quite helpful and from then on I had my very own "escort." His name was REINHOLD MILDE. I never forgot his name.

Somehow, once I had that little "escort," life at school was much easier and I even made some friends, although of course none were like my friendship with Hanna. I talked about my feelings about friends to Reinhold and although he didn't say a lot, I knew by the way he looked at me that he knew more than I did. As he didn't say anything, I left the subject alone.

I was still listening to the Volksempfaenger almost every day, still waiting and hoping for the news that the war was over so that we could go back home to Berlin, but nothing like that came up, just comments on how great the German army was. Germany's young people adored the Fuehrer and so did I but I sometimes wondered why he wasn't satisfied with what he had achieved so far as Germany constantly grew larger with every country he invaded. Although there were no alerts to hear on the radio, there were rumours going around about air strikes by the United States and Britain against some of Germany's larger cities and, of course, Berlin was the largest city at that time. This worried me because, thinking that the war would soon be over as my mother said, I had left behind in Berlin the only doll I ever owned, thinking she would be safer there than in our little cottage. I remember I'd called her Edda and that she was quite tall and pretty and had big blue eyes.

One day, we received a letter from my father telling us that he would have one week's vacation but that he wasn't allowed to leave Posen because he had to stay close to the hospital in case something came up. However, we were allowed to visit him so we were really excited and decided to travel by train to Posen. From our little town of Namslau (Namyslow) to Posen (Poznan) was about 180 km or 110 miles and would take about two hours by train, so that was alright and my mother packed a small bag just for a week and off we went. We took the only taxi in town to the railway station and I still remember how proud I felt. It was the very first time I had been driven in a taxi! On the train I was pleased with myself too as I remembered not to lean to the opposite side when the train made a turn.

We got safely to Posen, which seemed to me like quite a big city, and I was so proud seeing my father in a nice uniform working in a hospital with all those doctors and nurses. My father found us a nice little bed-and-breakfast place to stay and the owners were really nice to us and gave us the very best food. Whenever we went out for a walk with my father we were fine but once when only my mother and I went for a walk, people call us "Berliner Bomben Scheisser" again and one young man even spat at us. Even now, I don't know how they knew we were from Berlin.

One morning while we were there, I woke up and felt quite sick. I wanted to go to the bathroom and fainted on the way and although I can't have been unconscious for very long, my father insisted on taking me to the hospital. The doctor checked me out but they could find nothing wrong and thought perhaps it was something like a little nervous breakdown. For the next few days I was given a small glass of red wine mixed with an egg yolk first thing every morning. It tasted horrible but it was only a few days before I felt better.

Very quickly the week was over and we had to leave again without even knowing when we would see each other again. The future seemed so uncertain that I cried almost all the way back to Namslau and I felt really very sorry for my mother who tried to be strong but who looked so very sad.

My mother also had a step-sister named Maria living in Namslau. Her husband and she owned the only service station in town and had three children with a fourth on the way. I never knew why but she and my mother had never been close and yet a few days after we came back from Posen, she turned up at our door crying so much that she could hardly talk. It turned out that her husband had been called up for active duty and was supposed to leave a few days later for the front line in France. She felt completely helpless and lost and my mother decided that as we were all family, we should help each other and so we started working together. In due course, my aunt gave birth to a little boy, so she now had three boys and a girl to look after and was probably too busy to think much about the war. Her husband had hired workers to help with the service station; there were two of them and they were prisoners of war captured by German troops in France and brought to Germany. They were held in a barrack in Namslau and during the day were sent out to work on farms and wherever they were needed.

One of them was very friendly to us. He spoke some German and whenever I was at the service station to help, we talked a little. His name was Julian and he told me he came from Paris where he was a waiter in a grand restaurant and that he also had a daughter about my age. He, too, believed the war would soon be over and we got along fine. One day when I was there he called me over and gave me two big chocolate bars which his wife had sent to him. Chocolate was really hard to buy in those days and I was very happy but when I showed my mother and my aunt they got upset and took it away from me, saying it might be poisoned. It made me really mad but I thought Julian might have been angry, so I never told him. I didn't get along very well with my three cousins. They were sort of stuck up and thought they were special because their parents were the owners of that service station, so we weren't together a lot. I still had Reinhold to talk to, but he was already making plans to go to Berlin after the war to study Law.

Lately, we'd noticed when listening to the radio that the speeches had become shorter and there seemed to be less happiness and enthusiasm in the reports. Rumours were going around that Germany's armies were being pushed back on almost all front lines and Polish people were hoping to get their country back.

My mother had started to worry about our apartment in Berlin and as she still had the address of our old aunt who was still living in the suburbs, she wrote and asked her if she would check it out for us. Our aunt replied that everything was alright with our apartment but the news wasn't all good as she also mentioned that on her way to see it, she saw of a lot of boarded-up houses and stores and also houses which had been burnt out by the now more frequent airstrikes. Even in the suburbs they had had a few airstrikes, though these were mostly caused by disoriented pilots who had lost their sense of direction.

We also received a letter from my father telling us that the doctors and nurses were having to work overtime at the hospital because of the number of soldiers wounded by the Russian fighting troops, who were starting to push back the German troops a lot faster than

before. When I read his letter I could actually feel his sadness. My grandparents were also having a very sad time as their two youngest boys—one was just under and the other one a little over 20—had been called up for active duty. That also meant that they didn't have any help on the farm and they were already feeling their age. The government sent some Polish workers to help them but they really weren't much help as they weren't interested in the hard manual farm work. There wasn't enough machinery to work with and most jobs had to be done by hand, to the extent that when it came to the potato harvest, even I had to help them out. Almost everyone knew it couldn't go on forever, even though the Fuehrer still talked about how well everything was going with the war.

One day my grandfather received a letter from the government saying that his favourite son, Franz, had been shot dead by snipers in the line of duty. Franz was the only son who had wanted to take over the farm, with the other boys not being at all interested in farm work. My grandfather started to cry and couldn't breathe properly, and we thought he was going to die. Fortunately, my grandmother had a bike and as fast as she could, she rode to the only doctor in the village, who immediately got on his horse and raced to help my grandfather. He gave my grandfather an injection in the arm and some pills to calm him down, then put him to bed with a drink, which I suppose was tea of some sort. The doctor reassured us that my grandfather wasn't going to die but did need to rest and be calm for a while. My mother was also very shaken and my grandmother asked us to stay overnight so that she wouldn't be by herself if she needed help.

In fact, we stayed a little longer than overnight because my grandfather was in a bad way. He didn't even know where his son was buried and I had the feeling that he didn't even think about the farm any longer. Eventually we went home and checked on Aunt Maria who seemed to be okay even though at that time there was still no word from her husband. Around this time I also talked a little with Julian, who really seemed to be in a good mood, smiling and saying that the war would soon be over. Maybe he knew more than we did.

Then, in the summer of 1944, we heard rumours about an attempt to kill the Fuehrer. We quickly turned on the radio and there was an alert saying that an attempt had been made to assassinate the Fuehrer, with more news to follow. This was really hard to believe, especially for the younger generation, including myself, who the media had led to believe that the Fuehrer was popular and kind and loved the children, only wanting a great future for them. We waited for hours to hear what had happened and if he was still alive.

It turned out that the person who was mostly responsible for the attack was an Army officer by the name of Claus Graf (Count) von Stauffenberg, who had been part of the attack on Poland and the invasion of the Soviet Union. His intention was to kill Adolf Hitler in his highly guarded complex at his headquarters in a forest in Ostpreussen (East Prussia). Since von Stauffenberg was both a highly ranked officer and a close friend of Hitler, so they thought, he had no problems walking through security checks carrying his briefcase containing the bomb intended to kill Hitler. He arrived at the office where a meeting was to take place with Hitler and some Generals and simply placed his briefcase under the table where Hitler would sit. He then quietly left the room, got out of the complex, and went back into the forest from where he heard the explosion. He then believed Hitler was dead but in fact Hitler had survived. There were some fatalities and that was the alert which we had heard. Claus, Philipp, Maria Schenk, and Graf von Stauffenberg died very shortly after the attack on Hitler in Berlin and although people were shocked, they were also glad that the Fuehrer was alive. For the first time, however, I was in doubt: was Hitler really the nice person we believed him to be? I discussed this with Reinhold but neither of us knew the truth.

We were uncertain about our future and the future of Germany but in some way we knew we would not win the war. My father's letters became less and less frequent and the way he wrote them had changed and didn't reflect the way he usually thought. Because he was suddenly required to not seal his letters, we assumed someone was checking his mail and therefore weren't able to write normally and ask him questions. At the same time, my grandparents were having a really hard time with the farm as they now had no help and most farmers were in the same situation, with their sons also away in the war. Fortunately, we were getting into the colder part of the year so there wasn't the same amount of field work to be done but the animals still had to be looked after and there was still a lot of work, which they somehow managed.

Another story came from my Aunt Maria and her service station. There was now not much help from prisoners of war from France like Julian. He could only go to help her twice a week and that was not enough so Aunt Maria decided to close the service station until the war was over. She heard from the government that her husband was stationed in France but never heard directly from him at all. One day when I knew Julian was supposed to be there, I went over to see her. Sometimes Julian and I had a hard time understanding each other, since I couldn't speak French and his German was limited, but mostly we understood what each other meant. I talked with him a little and he told me the authorities had other work for the prisoners to do digging trenches about three feet deep at the entrances of villages and in the fields so that the PANZER tanks couldn't drive over them and had to stop. This was hard for me to understand and I couldn't ask Julian to explain, so I went and asked Reinhold what he thought about it. We knew the Russian army was approaching the border of the former Poland, now Germany, and that Russia was quite quickly pushing back the German army but we thought that the trenches would hurt the German

Panzer, too, and so didn't understand WHY. We thought it must just be another rumour and that it couldn't be true that our German Army had been pushed back that far.

Something else that bothered the German people was that there were no longer as many speeches from the Furhrer even though he still assured us that we were marching forward to winning and that the world would be ours, and then the usual SIEG HEIL and HEIL HIT-LER greeting.

In the meantime, it was known that he had left his headquarters in East Prussia where he had almost been assassinated and gone to an un-known destination. At least, the destination was unknown to us and we tried to think where he could have gone knowing that Berlin was prob-ably not safe enough for him with the airstrikes there getting worse. It was possible he had gone to his Chalet Kehisteinhaus, which was also his retreat. It was located in southern Germany in the Bavarian Alps, a rough mountain group, above the Obersalzberg and close to Berchtesgaden, a very pretty mountain village. He used that chalet for meetings and to en-tertain highly ranked generals or good friends. It was quite hard to get there, as it was hidden in the mountain and heavily secured and guarded. But we really didn't know where he was and were just guessing.

More and more rumours were going around, particularly that the Russian army was pushing the Germans back faster and faster and were almost at the border of the former Poland. The prisoners of war really had to start digging those trenches then and because no one else was available, the women in the villages used to go into the fields to take them food and drinks. It was a slow process as it all had to be done by hand. One day I spoke with Julian and found I couldn't read his face—he looked both scared and also a little happy. Then he gave me a little piece of paper with his name and his address in Paris and told me that when the war was over and I was old enough to travel, I could go to France and visit him and his family anytime I wanted. I was really proud of that and kept that piece of paper securely hidden. Somehow I knew it would never happen, but miracles do happen sometimes.

One afternoon, I looked out of the window and saw all the prisoners of war marching by our house. I ran outside and there was Julian amongst them, waving and smiling. I couldn't think what had happened and when I asked my mother she told me that the government had decided to take the prisoners out of the little villages and put them somewhere else. It was said that they were being taken further into Germany but for them it was also closer to France and that was why they were smiling. We never found out where they had been taken.

Suddenly, people were talking about what would happen if the Russian army ran all over the former Poland and invaded Germany and whether we would then be living in Russia. If that was the case, we could never go back to our apartment in Berlin! My mother was worrying about it a lot and because we couldn't talk it over with my father, we decided to get the whole family together and make a decision about whether we should stay or leave and go back to Berlin. The main worry my mother had was that if we decided to go back to Berlin, we couldn't tell my father of our decision. She then realised, however, that my father would know where we were because his and our home had always been Berlin. When the family all got together to make decisions, my grandparents refused to leave their farm. It had been their home for generations and there was really nowhere else for them to go. Additionally, once the war was over, their sons would know where to come to. My Aunt Maria and her four children had distant relatives on her husband's side who lived not too far away from Berlin, so she decided to leave as well and to travel with us.

In the meantime the Russian army came closer and closer—we could even hear explosions and at night the sky was full of light like fireworks going off. That really scared us and we started to prepare to leave. As we didn't have any furniture and only our personal belongings, it was easy for us. Aunt Maria, however, had a whole house full of nice furniture which she had to leave behind and it was very hard on her. She also had to be strong for her children, especially her few-months-old baby boy, and eventually we left our cottage and moved in with her to help. Our little village got emptier almost every day. The younger women and children were leaving and going to wherever they knew someone further into the middle of Germany. Only the older people were staying and there weren't many of them.

We were almost ready to leave with just a few more days to go, when one evening we heard loud noises outside and saw a few Panzer in front of the house. We were scared to death when two soldiers came in but they were German soldiers who asked us what we were still doing there as we were already behind the frontline. The Russian army had pushed them so fast that now these soldiers were behind them and the front line was a few miles ahead of us. They assured us that they would be able to push them back again as it was just a small group of Russian soldiers who had cut them off, but it was really time to leave right now. Our immediate problem was how to get to the train station as there was only the one taxi in town and we couldn't think how to contact him. He wasn't living too far away from us but Aunt Maria couldn't leave the children so my mother and I ran as fast as we could to his house. On our way we saw a few burning houses and two Panzer shooting in our direction. We were in a panic and couldn't think at all, just ran to the taxi driver's house to find that although he was at home, he wasn't prepared to leave. He also saw the Panzer shooting but they were a little further away and we wondered if the German soldiers were right and had pushed them back a little more. We begged the taxi driver to take us to the train station so that we could leave and get somewhere safe even if only for a little while. Eventually he agreed and we drove back to pick up Aunt Maria and the children and then travelled on directly to the train station. The only words he said were "God Bless You. That is the last drive I can make as I haven't got any gasoline left."

I felt really bad that I wasn't able to say goodbye to Reinhold.

When we arrived at the railway station there was hardly anyone around and there we were—six scared people with no plans but hoping to somehow make it to Berlin. We hadn't received any letters from my father lately and didn't know if it was because the mail service had stopped or whether he had written a letter which we didn't receive because we'd left the cottage.

While we were waiting there for the next train to arrive, a few more people showed up, mostly women with children. Then, when the train arrived with some more people already sitting inside, it stopped and a voice came over the loudspeaker system telling us that this was the last train to Berlin. The voice then went on to say that there may be a few stops along the way but they didn't at the moment know where as we might be under attack from low-flying Russian planes. If this should happen, the train would stop and everyone should jump out and try to hide as close as possible to the train or even a little under it. When the danger was over, the train driver would let the passengers know by making a loudspeaker announcement and we would then all have about fifteen minutes to get back on the train before we continued on our way. We didn't really believe that anything like that would happen, but it did

The train was travelling quite slowly and there was hardly any light—just enough for the train driver to see—when about twenty minutes into the trip, the train stopped and the loudspeaker announcement came on that we were under attack and should get off the train and hide. Well, we jumped out and tried to hide as we had been told, which was very hard for the children as they really didn't know what was going on. Then the planes arrived. I believe there were about five of them and they were flying low over the train and started to fire on everything they thought moved. They must have known they were not shooting at soldiers and that there were only women and children. Then in a moment something happened which I'll never forget for the rest of my life. Not far away from us, hiding like us, was a young woman with a baby. The woman was suddenly hit by a bomb or a bullet or whatever they used to shoot and she was badly wounded, although the baby seemed alright. The only words we heard her saying were "Please take my baby, I am dying." Then the attack seemed to be over and the planes left but we were all in shock. An announcement was made that the train would leave in fifteen minutes and that everyone should now get back on board. What about the woman with the baby? We were all wondering when a young woman with an older child suddenly jumped up, picked up the little baby, and got back onto the train with it. The picture of it all happening stuck in my brain for the longest time and everything which happened after that experience is somewhat unclear. I remember that we weren't attacked again, probably because we were closer to Middle Germany and Berlin and out of reach of the Russian planes for a while. We had one more stop before we reached Berlin but I don't remember where it was. We were like walking zombies, but we made it to Berlin.

My mother and Aunt Maria decided that before anything else, we should all go to our apartment to recover from the trip and comfort the baby and that they would then try to contact Aunt Maria's relatives and try to decide how to get her and the children to their farm outside of Berlin. Getting to our apartment from the Berlin railway station, however, proved more than difficult. We used to take the U-Bahn (rapid transfer underground line) but were told it would be safer to get a bus or street car as part of it had already been destroyed and we might well get stuck somewhere. The buses no longer travelled to a timetable so we asked about the S-Bahn (rapid transfer system above-ground) which travelled in and around Berlin, but were told it was no longer operating because of the danger from airstrikes. We eventually managed to find a taxi which we all squeezed into by sitting on top of each other, and I think the driver only took us because he felt sorry for us. We probably looked desperate, completely run down and dirty and when we arrived he didn't even want any money from us. We saw a lot of destroyed houses in our area and people looked different from when we left Berlin. Everyone was rushing around looked scared and no one was really smiling any more.

When we got to the apartment, I was so happy—I had my doll Edda again, a little dusty but still alright. Our little grocery store around the corner, thank God, was still standing so we were able to buy some food and even though there wasn't as much to buy as there used to be, at least we had something to eat. While we were talking to the lady in the shop, she asked who Aunt Maria was as she hadn't seen her before and we explained the situation and that she had to get to a little village called Platkow, where her relatives lived. The shop lady then said that she knew of someone a few blocks away who, for a fee, sometimes drove people in and out of Berlin and that she would ask him if he could help and how much it would cost. This was a huge relief for us and we were only a little worried about the money as if we put everything together, we would have enough. My mother was really good at saving money and we still had some savings. The value of the Reichsmark (the German currency until after the war) was 10 Reichsmark = 1 US Dollar, but that changed after the war. Having got some food, we went home, where we had a bath and hand-washed some clothes, had a nice spaghetti dinner and all immediately fell asleep. Thank God there were no air strikes that night so we all had a good rest.

Because our apartment was really too small for all of us we hoped the shop lady wouldn't be too long letting us know about the person with the car and at noon she came and told us the driver would come that evening if we could pay 100 Reichsmark for the trip. As we had expected to pay more, we immediately said YES. We then helped pack the few things Aunt Maria had with her and waited for the driver to arrive. He had told the shop lady to tell us that he would rather drive at night than during the day because if there was an air-strike he could turn the car lights off and hide in a forest. As promised, he came shortly before it became dark but in a car which didn't look too good and we could only hope that they would make it to Platkow. Then they all left and we were all really very sad, knowing that our lives were changing and that we might never see each other again. There was still no letter from my father or from Maria's husband and, looking back, I realise that at that time everyone was trying to protect themselves, but my mother and I protected each other as well and our bond grew from day to day. I even forgave her the lie about the stork!

The night that Aunt Maria left was a really sad one for my mother and she both cried and prayed. I remember that we listened to the radio after Aunt Maria had left and there was news that the Russian army had almost reached the former border of Poland/Germany and were marching towards Berlin. In other words, Posen (Poznan) where my father worked in the hospital was now under Russian control, which also meant that my father was a prisoner of war for Russia and we had no idea where he had been sent. We also had no idea how Aunt Maria had got on and whether or not she had arrived safely. All of this combined to make my mother extremely worried. The lady from the store had promised to let us know how Aunt Maria's journey had gone and so we just waited and were still wondering the next morning when the car driver came to our apartment with a big bag of groceries. He had a huge stone-oven baked loaf of bread, two dozen fresh eggs, a giant piece of smoked meat and freshly made butter and sausage. It turned out that Aunt Maria's relatives had just killed a pig when she arrived and they wanted to share their food with all of us. There was also a note saying, "God bless you and try to be safe." We felt really blessed by all of it and couldn't thank the driver enough for helping us to take Aunt Maria to her family. Needless to say, we later walked around to the grocery store to thank that lady again for all her help.

None of us had really experienced an airstrike so we asked the shop lady what to expect and she told us that so far there had only been night airstrikes and none during the day. That sure changed later! She told us that the sirens would go off about an hour before the first wave of fighter planes arrived and that they would be travelling from the North Sea and flying over the north-western town of Hannover towards Berlin. She then told us that if the loudspeaker warnings mentioned Hannover, we should rush into the building's basement or any bunker if there was one close by because in that case the German FLAG (Anti-aircraft cannon) would start shooting, even though the FLAG was damaged and already had a hard time trying to stop the planes or even turn them back. Another person in the store joined the conversation and told us that the first wave wasn't too bad as they didn't drop bombs—they just dropped little burning lights to stake out the area, mostly in big squares, so that the wave of planes which followed would know where to drop their bombs and so flatten the whole area. These first planes then turned around and flew back the same way they had come. They called the little white lights "Christmas Trees" but at least we knew something of what to expect and how to act when the strikes happened.

The same person who told us about the airstrikes gave us the news that there would soon be information available through the Red Cross about how people could go about registering to find a missing person like my father. Apparently you could also register your own name and details so that if the missing person was found, families could be reconnected and this made my mother really happy, knowing there was a chance that my father would be found and put in touch with us. She straight away decided to register for my grandparents as well as we'd had no word from them and they were now under Russian control. This was the early part of 1945 and we were grateful to be able to talk to those people and to learn a little about the airstrikes and generally what was happening.

For myself, I sometimes had very sad moments thinking about Reinhold, wondering if he was still in Namslau or whether he had left as we did. Also Julian—as Germany had lost the war with France, was he back with his family in Paris? At these moments, I learned how to pray; it made me feel there was someone I could talk to and ask for help and somehow I suppose I felt better after a prayer. I also still thought about my friend Hannah and her family and wondered what had happened to them after they vanished. I'd heard rumours about Jewish people and hoped so very much that nothing awful had happened to them.

There were no airstrikes for the next few days so we enjoyed the good food sent by Aunt Maria's relatives and slowly recovered from that awful trip back to Berlin. There wasn't any school anymore and so I hung around all day mostly listening to the radio even though there were hardly any Fuehrer's speeches now and even the ones that came were short and dragging, just telling us how many planes had been shot down by the German FLAG. Again, there were rumours going around and this time they said that Hitler was in Berlin in the Reichskanzlei (Office of the Chancellor of Germany). It was said that the building was extremely strongly built and had an underground bunker, so it seemed most likely that he was hiding in there with his closest friends and his wife, Eva Braun. It was rumoured that she was twenty years younger than him and that they had married shortly before the war was over, but nobody really knew when and where they had married, just that it was probably in 1944.

I was getting used to staying at home and not going to school and sometimes even I started to wonder what the future would hold for me. I was still not an adult though and had my parents, or at least my mother, to worry for me, so I stopped thinking about it. Then one night it happened. We had gone to bed early and were woken up in the middle of the night by a very loud siren and an announcement saying, "This is an alert," that fighting planes were on their way towards Berlin and that we should be prepared to go down to the basement or the nearest bunker and to only take hand bags with essential medication. It was just as the grocery lady had described it and I was really scared. We made our preparations and then the second siren came on with an announcement telling us about the planes crossing over the city of Hannover and we remembered that now was the time to go. As there was no bunker close to us, we ran down the stairs into the basement to find a few older people were already sitting there almost motionless and then we heard the FLAG shooting start. One elderly lady realised we were new there and stood up to welcome us before saying that she was sure we'd see each other quite often from now on. She then said she would sneak out for a moment just to look out of the door and perhaps see where they had dropped the "Christmas trees." She returned quickly and said, "Thank God, we're not in the square: it's a little further down the area." We were heartened by that but then suddenly heard the roaring of planes over our apartment, followed a few minutes later by noises like fireworks and it sounded as though the FLAG had stopped firing. I felt as if I had stopped breathing but after about fifteen minutes the siren went off again and the loudspeaker announced, "ENTWARNUNG," meaning the attack and danger were over. Straightaway, everyone got up like robots, said goodnight, and left, so we did the same after thanking the lady who lived in the apartment building across from us—the one who had welcomed us when we first went into the basement.

Well, do I remember that we had a really hard time trying to get back to sleep for whatever was left of that night.

When we woke up the day after that first airstrike we were definitely still in shock but other people in the area seemed quite alright and when we went to buy some food in the grocery store and said,

"Wasn't that terrible?" the lady there looked quite amazed and said that it wasn't bad at all; that they had already had much worse strikes and it was only if you were in "the square" that you really had a reason to worry. I suppose our reaction was understandable considering that it was our first experience of a proper airstrike but then, all of a sudden, my mother looked seriously at the lady and asked her if the person who had taken Aunt Maria to her relatives in Platkow was still available for hire and willing to travel. This was so sudden that I looked at my mother in amazement—I could hardly believe what she had just asked. The shop lady said he was usually still available but that it might be a little more expensive now, and my mother turned to me straight away and asked if I would like to go and visit Aunt Maria and see how she was getting on. I couldn't have been happier about the idea and said that sure, I wanted to go! The shop lady said that she would go to see the driver and make the arrangements and my mother decided that the driver would take us there and then collect us after two days. I guess my mother just wanted to get away because of the airstrikes but, anyway, the next evening he again came and picked us up, though this time we had to pay Reichsmark 159.00.

Along the route to Aunt Maria's we saw a lot of PFERDEWAGEN (horse-drawn carts packed with people and personal belongings), travelling towards Berlin because they were being pushed out by the Russian troops. Like my grandparents, they had been living on their farms and then had to go, leaving everything they owned behind them. They had nowhere to go and just hoped to find someplace where they could stay. My grandparents had stayed back when we left and so far we hadn't heard anything from them. When we arrived at Aunt Maria's place we met her relatives and they all seemed to be doing alright—or as well as could be expected at that time. The driver left us saying he would return in two days but under the circumstances we had to worry that he might not make it back. Everyone was in the same situation and doing their best but sometimes promises couldn't be kept despite everyone's honesty and good intentions. Anyway, we had two wonderful restful nights with no sirens going on and off but heard on the radio that there had been another airstrike on Berlin.

By this time everyone was wondering what would become of us because by now we knew there was no longer any way we would win the war. My mother told Aunt Maria about the Red Cross and how missing people could be registered with the intention of then being able to make contact with each other and that we hoped my grandparents and Aunt Maria's husband would be registered.

As hoped, the driver came to collect us after two days and we set off back towards Berlin. Not long before we reached the outskirts of Berlin we noticed a wave of planes in the distance and the driver stopped the car and turned off the lights. As we sat there we saw a plane begin to tumble in the air and then it started to burn and within a few seconds it nosedived right down out of our sight into whatever was there beneath it. Again, that sight was something that no one who saw it could ever forget.

The driver waited a little longer there in the dark and then we continued towards the smoke which hung over our apartment in Berlin's inner city. It was good to be home but we were also still worried about when the next airstrike might come. The next morning when I looked out of my window, I saw two Flugblaetter (flyers or leaflets on a piece of thin paper) and when I went and had a look at them there was a message written in German saying something to the effect of "GIVE UP, THE WAR IS OVER, DON'T GET KILLED." They could only have arrived here if they had been dropped by the attacking planes together with the bombs and the lady in the grocery store agreed as she said they were always there after an airstrike. There were no more airstrikes the next night, though, and we all had a good night's sleep!

Then on February 3rd, 1945, we were listening to the radio and there was really no news at all and the day started nice and quietly until about noon. All of a sudden the alert came on, the sirens started, and the loudspeaker informed us that we were under attack from planes coming in from the direction of Hannover and that everyone should go to the nearest basement or bunker. My mother and I looked at each other in complete disbelief—it was daytime and not during the night when airstrikes usually happened. We very quickly picked up our small bag and ran into the basement where there were already three other people. We couldn't believe what was happening but then it started—the planes were flying over our area and dropping bombs all around us, making the concrete walls of our apartment building shake and wave backwards and forwards. It was absolutely terrifying and I can only remember that I really thought I was about to die. The noise and horror of it all went on for at least thirty minutes and then, suddenly and completely unexpectedly, there was complete and utter silence. No noise of planes or the FLAG—just nothing.

After some minutes one of the men slowly got up and opened the basement door to look outside. The street was filled with flyers of the sort I had seen earlier and the building next to ours was on fire. Our building was still alright but all the buildings were connected, which meant that at any minute the fire could jump over to our building and we realised we had no choice at all except to get out as fast as we could. My mother insisted there were things in the apartment we could still save and we ran up, grabbed a suitcase and she threw things into it. I still can't remember what she wanted or saved but at one stage she looked down and saw that our building had started to burn from the bottom up and that we had to get out immediately. We ran down the stairs and had to jump through the flames and the winter coat I was wearing caught fire but we were nearly back out on the street and managed to put it out. We had no idea what was happening to other people but it was horrible to see that almost every house in our street, indeed in the whole area, was starting to burn and we could only think of the nearby park where I used to play with Hannah as possibly being a safe place to go.

The park wasn't far away at all but on the way there we saw quite a few people lying on the ground, completely burned. They seemed to have shrunk to perhaps half their real size and the horror of it all made my mother start to cry. She must have stumbled across a BLINDGAENGER, an unexploded bomb, which then partly exploded, burning both of her legs. Her legs immediately looked like a huge, big blister and I had no idea what to do. She tried to sit down on the suitcase, then just looked at me and said she couldn't go any further, that she was going to die and that I should go on towards the park where there were people able to help me. I panicked, threw away the suitcase, grabbed my mother and half carried/half dragged her towards the park, screaming for help from anyone. I could see people in the distance in the park and finally two men in white coats came running towards us with a stretcher, put my mother on it and just picked me up. I saw that in the park they had two barracks, like little field hospitals and I saw female nurses there with white coats, and that was the last thing I remembered.

When I opened my eyes again, I could still hear bombs exploding and the air was thick with smoke and I realized I was still in the field hospital where I had collapsed and that my mother was still with me. She was lying on a stretcher with thick bandages around her legs but she was smiling at me, so I knew things weren't too bad. A friendly nurse came and explained that although I was completely dehydrated and exhausted, we shouldn't worry and that we were both going to be fine. We were apparently in the middle of the Christmas tree square and most of our home area had been flattened, including the grocery store, and we never did find out what had happened to the nice lady who worked there. So—we had lost absolutely everything we owned, including my doll Edda and that little piece of paper on which Julian had written his address in Paris.

The people in the hospital asked my mother if we had any friends or family living in the area around Berlin who might take us in. My mother's first thought was of Aunt Maria and her relatives but we couldn't travel that far and there were really enough people there already. The other possibility was that elderly aunt who lived in the suburbs of Berlin. She was my grandfather's sister and we thought she might take us in until the end of the war. We told the doctor about her but explained that we didn't know how we could get there as we doubted that the driver who had first taken Aunt Maria was still around. We were told to stay where we were overnight and that the hospital would contact the Red Cross people in the hope of finding someone who could get us there. We were worried about the whole situation as my parents had never really had a close relationship with her, but figured that in times like this, everyone had to help each other. There was no airstrike that night, thank God, but we had lost everything anyway and thanks to some medication from the doctor, we both had a good night's sleep.

The next morning the nurses told us that there were no street cars or bus service available but they had been lucky enough to arrange for someone from the Red Cross to come and drive us to our aunt's house. My mother knew the address and that the aunt owned a nice little townhouse where she lived with her daughter. I was curious to see the house as although I had been there, it was when I was too young to remember. My mother told me that there was a Catholic church across the street and that attached to it was a small hospital where I was born. The doctor then gave us, and especially my mother, a whole lot of medication to keep us going as there were hardly any doctors available. When we finally left, we drove past still-burning houses and there was nothing remaining of our apartment building except a mountain of ash and rubbish. It was terribly sad to see it all but my mother was alive and that was the most important thing for me.

The roads were badly damaged and crowded with people running backwards and forwards so it was a slow trip and took us almost an hour to get to the house and the difference compared with the city was almost unbelievable. Here we arrived to find a really cute, well-kept house with a fence around it and hardly any damaged or destroyed houses. My mother got out of the car and walked on her crutches to ring the doorbell, which was eventually answered by our aunt's daughter, who was about 30 and looked very surprised to see us. She recognised my mother and asked what had happened so my mother explained that we had just lost everything we owned in an airstrike and that we had nowhere to stay and nowhere to go until the war ended, and asked if we could stay. The daughter looked at us for what seemed like a very long time and then eventually said "of course" and invited us into the house. I had the feeling she wasn't too happy about the situation but we went inside and it was really nice. We were told we could stay in the guestroom, which was unfortunately upstairs and hard for my mother to get to on crutches, but it was really nice with two beds, a recliner chair and a fireplace. That was to be our home for quite a long time but we didn't know it then.

It was a really nice house but only had one bathroom and a small kitchen, which already had a bed in it with some other relative sleeping there, so it was difficult for my mother to cook. Those were hard times, though, and everyone was grateful to have any kind of roof over their head. The elderly aunt's name was Hedwig and the daughter was Elli and that first night we all had dinner together to discuss the situation and talk things over. Aunt Hedwig was quite nice about everything and told us we could stay until the end of the war, which by now we knew couldn't last much longer. The Russian troops were already advancing quite fast towards Berlin and the Allies were approaching from France and the North Sea in the opposite direction. We all hoped the Allies would be faster and would take over Berlin. Meanwhile, my mother and I had another problem in that we had lost everything in our apartment and didn't have any clothes to wear. Aunt Hedwig told us that clothing and linen and other things had been donated through the Red Cross and were available in the church and indeed we found nice clothes and shoes and even household items, so that problem was solved. The house was, however, a little crowded at times and Elli was really unhappy about the whole situation. Fortunately, it was her mother who owned the house and therefore she couldn't kick us out.

The days went by and my mother's legs were getting better all the time, so it was easier for her to get up and down the stairs. There was still no word from my father nor any news from the government of his whereabouts. There was hardly any news at all any more—very little on the radio and no shooting from the FLAG so the Germans were more or less left alone and everyone just tried to survive as best they could. Rumours went around that Adolf Hitler and his staff were in the Reichskanzlei in the bunker and perhaps there was no escape for him out of Berlin. We were already more or less surrounded and even the airspace was controlled as well.

It was March 1945 and there were rumours going around that the Allies would halt around the River Elbe and then let the Russian troops take over Berlin but nobody really knew what was going on. There were young boys and old men in uniform patrolling the streets at night and airstrikes still going on through what was left of Germany. Then, one night, I heard two young boys talking in front of the house saying that they weren't staying any longer and were going home and the very next evening there was on-one there at all. And then the alerts came on that the Allied troops had stopped at the River Elbe and that the Russian troops would take over Berlin. We were scared but just waited because there was nowhere else to go and it was impossible to prepare ourselves for what was to come.

Rumours were going around again that the Russian troops and Panzers were close to the outskirts of Berlin, which meant that they weren't too far away from us. We felt we had to be optimistic but at times it was really hard. One evening I looked out of the window and saw a horse tied to a tree a little further down the road. I wondered how it came to be there and thought that perhaps it belonged to some of the soldiers, so decided that the next morning I would take it some water. I got the water ready but when I got outside I couldn't see it, so assumed that maybe it was lying down and went to have a look. When I got to it I almost fainted. All that was there were some pieces of horse: the meat was all gone and it had obviously been butchered and the meat taken for food. It was a dreadful sight and I just ran home knowing that there was nothing at all to be done about it.

There were still some stores like the bakery, butcher and grocers, open in the neighbourhood and we still had some Lebensmittelkarten left (ration cards issued by the government in times of war to buy food and other commodities), so we decided we might as well use them up as we didn't know what supplies would be available or if we would still be able get them. Unfortunately, by the time we reached the stores there wasn't much left so we just took all we could get. As well as the ration cards, soup kitchens provided by the Heilsarmee (Salvation Army) had popped up and people could go to them and eat. They also sometimes provided butter and cheese, but I still always seemed to be hungry. Aunt Hedwig had a big basement in which she stored potatoes from her summertime garden and she also had some home-made sauerkraut in a wooden barrel as well as some smoked meat, so all that together with the ration cards meant that it really wasn't too bad.

I remember one day feeling really bad, though. Aunt Hedwig had cooked some dumplings and made five big ones—one for each of us living in the house—Aunt Hedwig, Elli, my mother and I and the other relative. I happened to look in the kitchen at a time when no one was around and I took one big dumpling out of the pot, took it into the bathroom and secretly ate it. When dinner time came around, of course, one dumpling was missing. Aunt Hedwig looked around and looked at me and my face must have been as red as a tomato so that she knew immediately that I was the culprit. All she said though was that she had thought one dumpling was missing but must have miscounted. From that moment on I really liked her and from that moment on I never again stole food from the kitchen.

One day we had an alert that we were only going to be able to use electricity for six hours a day because most of the power stations had been disabled by airstrikes and from then on everything was completely dark during the evenings and nights.

The days went by quite quickly and approaching March of 1945 everyone knew that the war would be over fairly soon. The Russian troops weren't far away from us then and people living in our area decided to put out white flags on a stick to show the Russian army that they surrendered. We used a white sheet and hoped that they wouldn't harm us and for the next few days things were pretty quiet. Of course, the German soldiers weren't defending us any more—there were hardly any troops left in our area and the German defence system had been almost completely destroyed. Once in a while we heard some shooting and also bomb explosions but we didn't know whether it was German or Russian troops who were firing, so we just sat there and waited. Then the sounds of explosions came closer and we knew troops were coming but not whether they were soldiers or Panzer!

Two days later we heard loud noises coming from the street, sounding like heavy machinery rolling by our houses. It was in the afternoon and when we looked out there were no people to see but there were the Panzer, driving slowly past. We couldn't see the drivers; there were just little holes in the front of the tanks so that the driver could see ahead. There was no shooting or stopping and they just kept driving slowly past us, presumably heading into Berlin's inner city, though no one knew for sure. We all just stayed inside expecting soldiers to come in but we later found out that that was the first wave and that they hadn't harmed anyone.

But the second wave was another story, they were the actual Russian troops in different vehicles. At that time there was yet another rumour going around that Joseph Stalin, the Soviet Union's leader at that time, had given his army a sort of incentive treat, saying that when they captured Berlin, they would have four weeks when they could do whatever they wanted with the German people. Whether this was true or not we didn't know but there were certainly four very bad weeks, especially for the German women. At this time only Russian troops could be seen on the streets—some on bicycles and some walking, but for a while there were no German people outside. Then, early one morning, my mother and I noticed that some of our neighbours were also walking outside and we decided to risk going out. We had made it just a little over one block to near the Church and the little hospital where I was born, when we heard the noise of low-flying planes and looked up to see two small planes right above us. One suddenly turned around and started flying directly towards us and we both immediately jumped under a broken-down bus to avoid being hit. There appeared to only be one person in the plane and I'll never forget that pilot's face with his big sunglasses nor will I ever know whether he was just scaring us or really trying to kill us but he then turned around and followed the other plane. The local priest had seen what had happened and we were still hiding under the bus when he came running out to take us into the church. Over the next days we heard about women being raped and people being killed, so maybe Stalin had given his troops that "treat," but of course we never found out for sure.

It took a little while before we dared leave the house and walk on the streets again but we realised that more and more German people were beginning to wander around to find places likes churches and also stores or anywhere else they could get what they needed. People who hadn't lost everything had things like household goods or bedding which they could trade for food and a little black market began to develop. Unfortunately, it was different for us as we had lost absolutely everything we possessed and we were just looking for donations and hand-outs. The hot item for bargaining was cigarettes; if you had cigarettes you could trade for almost anything.

One day when we were walking down the street and still nervously watching out for planes, we passed the huge cemetery next to the Church and hospital and noticed a young Russian soldier on a bicycle coming towards us. I started to shake like a leaf and he must have noticed because when he got near us he got off the bicycle and started to talk to us, although of course it was in Russian. He must have seen how frightened we both were because he started to try and speak a few words of German. He pointed to himself and said "Moscow" (the capital city of Russia), so we assumed he came from there and he then took a piece of paper out of his back pocket and wrote the number "19" on it, so we again assumed he was 19 years of age. So far the only strange thing about him was that he had about six watches in different sizes and colours on his right arm. We thought he must have taken them from people and only hoped it wasn't from people he had killed. Despite that, though, he had a nice smile and then he pointed to himself and his mouth and then to our mouths, which we guessed was asking if we were hungry. We nodded but by this time my mother was getting suspicious and we then turned and half-ran, half-walked back to the house, with him following us which was very scary because although we could do nothing about it, he now knew where we lived.

All that happened about noon and we had been in such a hurry when we got home that we forgot to close the fence gate, so it was left wide open. Later that afternoon my mother and I were outside putting out the garbage cans when the young soldier appeared again riding his bike and carrying a big bag. You would think that he would walk through the gate, but not him: he just jumped over the fence into our garden, walked up to us and gave us the bag, smiling and pointing to his mouth before leaving by simply jumping over the fence again. We went inside and opened the bag and there were two large loaves of bread, some sort of sausage we'd never seen, and also a big pot of soup which was something like Goulash. We really didn't know what to make of this and couldn't work out whether he wanted to poison us or was so kind that he would really bring us food for no reason. In the end we decided to try a few spoonfulls of the soup and wait a little while to see if it did us any harm and then after about an hour, we when we were still fine, we decided to eat it. It was really delicious and we were so very grateful to have it.

Over about the next week that young soldier came back four times bringing us food. He always just jumped over the fence even though the gate was open and then left again the same way. We never found out why he did it—he just smiled, gave us the food, jumped on his bike and then left. Then, suddenly, he never came back. We wondered what might have happened to him and thought that perhaps what he was doing for us had been discovered and that he had been punished.

Times became particularly hard for German women. There were constant stories of rapes and hospitals were offering special services so that women could be checked for diseases or possible pregnancies. Women tried their best to look as old as possible, even rubbing wood ash into their hair to make themselves look grey-haired, but they couldn't change their faces. Aunt Hedwig was genuinely old so she didn't have to worry that much and I was still not completely grown, but my mother and Elli also tried their best to look old and unattractive. The

Russian soldiers quickly caught on to what the women were doing and the famous words were "Frau,

komm" (Woman, come). Aunt Hedwig's house was connected to another house like a townhouse and two men were living there. We never talked to them and they kept to themselves but one night we heard a car stopping outside their house. Someone stepped out of the car and went into the next door house but there were still two uniformed Russian drivers in front who seemed to be waiting for the other one to come back out. We thought everything was alright and stopped watching but a few minutes later we heard noises at our door and there were the two soldiers from next door, just looking at us and kind of grinning. My mother jumped in front of me to hide me and I more or less knew what would happen but I couldn't even move. Aunt Hedwig kneeled down and started to pray but the two men took no notice at all and went into the bedroom where they started to drag three mattresses onto the floor. They almost had the mattresses sorted out when we heard a car honking outside and all of a sudden the men dropped everything, started really screaming at each other and ran out of the house to the car, where the other person was already waiting. They most likely thought they would have more time and it surely was a very close call. We were still afraid they might come back and even though nothing happened, none of us slept well that night. If it was true what Joseph Stalin had said about giving the soldiers their freedom for four weeks, at least those weeks were pretty much over.

We still hadn't heard anything from my father but we felt sure he must be either a prisoner of war in some country or that he was already dead. There was also no word at all from my grandparents and we worried because we had heard from others that some of the old Polish people had taken over the farms and then used the previous owners of the farms to work for them, and that would have fitted my grandparents' situation. But, before the war was over, there was no communication at all.

Early in April 1945, we were just living from one day to the next hoping that it would all soon be over and wondering what would happen—whether we would be under Russian control or that of the

Allies, though the Allies appeared to have stopped at the River Elbe and not advanced at all from there. Berlin was already under enemy control, so at last the airstrikes over the city had ceased, but there was no longer any leadership and although Germany was almost completely taken over, there was still fighting going on in some areas. We had little idea of what was happening and there was a lot of guesswork going on as even the radio was no longer working.

One day we went to the church, "Mater Dolorosa." I never forgot the name of that church even though I did forget the name of the priest—he was a very nice older man and every time we went there he had something for us. I suppose it was all stuff which had been donated and passed on as people cleaned out their basements after winter. Whilst we were talking he asked us where our relatives were and after my mother told him of our concerns about Aunt Maria and the grandparents, he said that he would try to get some information through other churches close to where they lived. He said that unfortunately he had no connections close to Posen (Posnan), so couldn't help with information about my father, but we were really happy that he would try and find out something about the others.

We then heard rumours that Hitler might be dead because all his possible escape routes had been blocked, but so far there was no confirmation. Like most young people, I found it hard to believe that the Fuehrer could be dead. I still remembered how he shook my hand and his nice smile and somehow thought that he alone couldn't have started the war and that maybe it was the fault of his generals as well? Anyway, maybe it was just a rumour.

A few days later the priest came to our house, all smiles and happily telling us that he had good news of Aunt Maria and her children—that they were all fine and there was a possibility that she might get a small farm house somewhere to the West where people had left. So far he hadn't heard anything of my grandparents because they were further away in the former Poland, but he was sure he would hear something pretty soon, which was great news for us.

It was almost the end of April 1945 and we noticed that there were far less instances of rape or torturing and killing being reported: maybe the rumoured four weeks were over??? Then, on April 30th, news was given out that Adolf Hitler and his wife of two days, Eva Braun, had committed suicide in the Fuehrer's bunker. So—it was true and not a rumour after all. The Battle of Berlin ended at the beginning of May 1945, with the complete surrender of the city to the Soviet Union.

On May 10th, 1945, Germany officially lost the war and surrendered to the Allies and the Soviet Union. The feeling amongst the German people is hard to describe: a feeling somewhere between being scared of the future but, at the same time, having relief that the war was finally over—in other words a huge uncertainty: would we become a part of Russia, the USA, Britain, or France, or perhaps even another, different, Germany later on? Once again, we could only wait from day to day.

My main hope was that my father would come back and that we could find another apartment. The idea of going back to school actually never crossed my mind. Everybody else was still at home and we, the young people of the day, felt so mature after all we had been through that we felt sure that the teaching we'd already had at school like basic reading, writing and mathematics, was enough to get by in life. Our worries were still getting enough food every day and having a bed to sleep in and for the next few months, nothing really changed. We were told that a lot of paperwork had to be completed and signed by the four winners of the war—Russia, the USA, Britain and France—but that was of little interest of any of us who just wanted to try and start a new life.

At this time, yet another new rumour was going around that Berlin was to be cut into four sections—one quarter each for Russia, the USA, Britain and France. It was hard to understand how it would all work and in which quarter we would be, so as we hadn't heard from the priest for quite a while, we went over to the church to ask him what he knew. We arrived to find him very quiet and serious-looking, though he seemed pleased to see us coming. He said the rumour might be true but also that he had some bad news for us, which he had received a few days before but hadn't yet worked up the courage to come and tell us. The awful news was that my grandmother had died shortly before the war ended. Apparently she couldn't handle the loss of two of her sons on active duty and the fact that the third one was missing in action, or perhaps a prisoner of war. She had died of a heart attack and her death meant that my grandfather was all by himself on his own farm but now working for other people. Our priest was trying to contact that church near him in Namislow and also the Red Cross, to try to get my grandfather out of there in the hope that he could be taken to Aunt Maria, who now had that farm house and would be able to take care of him if need be. The priest was still waiting for an answer but now, because my mother was my grandfather's closest relative, the priest asked my mother if that arrangement would be alright with her and she gladly agreed: it meant he would be out of there and even closer to us.

Meanwhile, we continued to wait and see what would happen with the arrangement of the four quarters. Gradually, we could feel a little more hope coming back into life. Berlin was still under Russian control but little stores started to pop up, people were trading items out of their houses and another rumour started that even the ration cards might come back, though no one knew anything for sure. One day the Priest came and told us that the division of Berlin into quarters was almost certain and that our region would be under American control. The Priest also told us that he had received word from the Church and the Red Cross that my grandfather had a very good chance of being moved from where he was and taken to Aunt Maria.

Yes—it turned out that we would be under the control of the USA and within a few days the Russian troops left and in came the American troops. We were, of course, both curious and nervous about what would happen next but it became apparent that the next wave of soldiers weren't the fighting sort as the tanks rolled through the streets without any shooting or explosions. Some of the soldiers in the tanks were even throwing candy and sweets, which definitely helped to convince everyone that nothing bad was going to happen. And so it happened that we started to hope and some even realised that the war really was over and that we could hope that one day there would be another, new, Germany. A few reports still came through about rapes but I didn't really believe it: the candies must have convinced me!

I did witness one incident which upset me a lot: two American soldiers were walking on the street and one of them was smoking a cigarette. The American soldier threw his half-smoked cigarette onto the grounds as a young German man passed by and when the young German bent down to try and get the cigarette, the American just stepped on his hand. Despite things like this, though, you could see an improvement in everyday life. The first TRUEMMERFRAUEN (women who helped to clear the streets of debris and tried to reconstruct some of the broken down and burnt buildings) were working and the Allies made it law that every woman between the ages of 15 and 50 had to register. My mother still had problems with her legs and I wasn't quite 15, so we were exempt, but others carried on and generally the German people were kind of happy and becoming hopeful again. Additionally, we'd heard from the Priest that the Red Cross had told him my grandfather was allowed to leave Namyslaw and could join his daughter, Aunt Maria, and that was really, really, good news.

Germany was divided into two—into East Germany and West Germany, and our fourth section of Berlin was situated in East Germany. It took a while before we caught on to the arrangement as there were always borders to cross. My parents had previously bought a plot of land which was now in East Germany and they had wanted to build a house for us there, a little over an hour into the countryside out of Berlin. They'd never managed to do so because of the war but the land was still there and my mother now hoped that when my father came home they could still build a house for us there. In our current situation, though, it was almost impossible to find an apartment or house to rent so we had to stay where we were. Gradually, buses and street cars started to operate again and although there was no timetable to organise them, we were still thankful for every little success and improvement.

At around this same time, my grandfather who was now living with Aunt Maria got word that his third son was alive and was a prisoner of war in Britain: he had lost two sons but the third was alive and would eventually come home.

We were so very happy that grandfather was now living with Aunt Maria but the terribly bad news suddenly arrived that Aunt Maria's husband had been on active duty in France when he was killed by a sharpshooter and was thought to have been buried in France, without any-body knowing for sure exactly where. Their baby was just one year old and Aunt Maria took the news very badly. My grandfather being there helped a lot and together they started to work on the farm again, grow-ing vegetables and keeping a cow and some chickens. All the time they had the worry of not knowing if the original owner would come back and claim it all but they hoped that would never happen or that, if it did, it wouldn't be for a long time. We made enquiries about going to visit them but there was still far too much uncertainly over train service schedules and whether we would be able to get there and back again, so we let that idea go for the time being. All the while, there was still no word from or news of my father.

1946 began and we could see an overall improvement in our cir-cumstances including the issue of food cards again, for which the USA authorities were responsible, and that helped a lot. As we were under US control, we joked that Harry Truman was now "our" President as well but we still hoped that one day we would have our very own "NEW" Germany. Lots of things were happening and the churches were very much involved with the younger people, including organising youth group meetings twice a month to get youngsters together to talk about their problems and socialise; they even provided music and whoever wanted to could dance, although it was more like jumping around than proper dancing. There was even talk about schools open-ing up again but I tried not to listen. The whole idea frightened me and I always used the excuse that I was needed at home to help my mother, though I knew I wouldn't get away with that forever.

Our situation at home wasn't the best. Elli definitely wanted us out of the house but there was nowhere for us to go. My mother had tried lots of different organisations but there was nothing at all available. Aunt Hedwig was alright but I imagine that she too would have pre-ferred us to move out. One day at a church meeting, a young man brought a chicken along and asked who wanted it. I assumed he was of-fering it up for someone to kill and eat it and so I said I'd take it. Well, I got the chicken and took it home and I'll never forget Elli and Aunt Hedwig's faces and them looking at me and asking what they were supposed to do with it, and I'm sure it didn't help a bit that I told them! I now think that at that stage I must have started my teenage years and begun to rebel a little! In fact, my intention was not to kill it as I thought it could stay alive and provide us with eggs. Anyway, we had a huge tree in the back garden with a bench underneath it, so I tied a long leash onto one of the chicken's legs so that it could happily run around and jump onto the bench to sleep, and we thus had an egg every day and, importantly, the chicken was still alive. Elli wasn't at all happy but when I looked at Aunt Hedwig's face I saw that her eyes were smiling: perhaps she still remembered the episode of that lost dumpling.

The American soldiers also started a youth group but unfortunately for me it was only for young people over the age of 18 because alcoholic drinks were being served. They also had much better music than the church groups and oh how I would have loved to go to theirs instead!

I did get used to my own group's meetings at the Church and the priest always tried to make it interesting for us. One Saturday a month was dedicated to dancing but there was always a trick or condition attached to attending. One of them was pretty mean—the girls had to crochet a nice shawl to wear and the boys had to crochet a small tablecloth or two coasters to put glasses on and if we couldn't show them then we weren't allowed to go to the dance. That kept us busy for most of the month but of course parents helped—especially the young men's parents.

At one of the meetings the priest came in with a young girl of maybe 17 or 18 who was carrying a few-months-old baby. She was introduced as Helga and her baby girl, Brigitta, and the priest asked if she could join our meetings and share a story which she had to tell. We all agreed and she passed the baby to the priest and then began to talk. She told us that when she was almost 17 years old she was raped by Russian soldiers and became pregnant. She said it took a while until she realised what was happening to her but she then told her parents and also our priest. She was checked at the hospital and they confirmed that she was pregnant but they also assured her that no disease was evident and that everything seemed normal and healthy. They explained her options, which were to have an abortion, have the baby and give it up for adoption, or have the baby and keep it herself. She started to cry a little but still went on with her story and told us that she had no pressure from anybody, not from her parents or from the priest, and that they said it was entirely HER decision to make. She said it was the hardest of decisions but that she wanted to keep the baby. We were almost in tears listening to her, realising how brave she was, and everyone gave her a hug and told her how welcome she would always be, including with the baby. She smiled and thanked us but said she would come on her own next time because it would be too much for the baby. She came to the meetings for a few months and was always happy and nice but was still different from us and not like a normal teenager. Then, suddenly, she stopped coming and the priest told us that she and her parents and the baby had moved to West Germany where there were relatives waiting to help them start a new life. We never heard from her again but I think I matured and grew up a little more after meeting her and hearing her story.

My mother and I had a little talk and I told her I was thinking about going back to school the next year, in 1947, and not only was she was really quite happy, but also I was proud of MY decision. So then we had to figure out when and where and which school and how to get there and back and how much it would cost us, which was now of some importance since we'd been told by Elli and Aunt Hedwig that we had to start paying rent for the little apartment we used.   .

My mother had heard from other women that if they hadn't heard from their husbands for two years and hadn't heard from the Government that they might be prisoners of war in some country, they could declare their husbands dead. If that claim was accepted, the women could then get a pension from their pre-war workplace or from the Government. It really hurt that my mother was willing to do that so that I could go back to school and I said that we'd do it next year and that perhaps if we prayed a lot in the meantime, he would be back before we started that process. After all, miracles do happen.

We were still trying to figure out this so-called "new situation"— the possibility of my going back to school and my father perhaps never coming back home, when my mother came up with the idea of trying to find out about the property which my parents had bought before the war. The big problem was that it was situated in Eastern Germany, which was still under Russian control, meaning we would have to leave West Berlin and go back into the Russian zone, but we decided to try it anyway.

We had to use a street car to get to the train station which wasn't too bad even though it was overcrowded, but when we got to the station we were told there might not be another train for about 90 minutes. We figured that as it was still early morning and the train usually took about 45 minutes to get to the village, that would be okay and so we waited but then realised that a lot of people were already waiting in line and even more were coming all the time. My mother asked the station manager if the train was going to be over-full and he answered that we'd be lucky to get on it at all. After about two hours, we heard a train coming very slowly into the station and I couldn't believe my eyes: there were even people hanging outside the windows holding on to anything and everything there was to hold on to. When the train stopped quite a few people got off but then people waiting got really rude and started pushing and shoving others out of the way to get onto the train. Well, we did the same thing and were just about inside the train but a lot of people didn't make it and they were either left behind or were hanging outside wherever they could. The train started to move again but only as slowly as it had been going when it arrived in the station and we had the feeling we could just as easily walk next to the train at the same speed.

Anyway, we eventually made it to the little village and walked to our property. It was very disheartening and my mother looked terribly disappointed: it was all a mess, with big rocks scattered around a burnt-out car and the fence was completely broken down. At that moment I felt so sorry for her as I think it was then she gave up all hope of ever having a house of her own there. She just turned to me and said, "Let's try to get home, we can never afford to live here." So we returned home the same way we had got there and even though it was late at night when we arrived, my mother had a hard time trying to get off to sleep. At least we had tried it out and gone to have a look and knew what the situation was.

At the next church meeting I told my story and everyone was glad that we'd come back, so that made me feel better. The young man who had previously given me the chicken came over and asked how the chicken was and whether it had tasted good. I looked at him with big eyes and told him rather angrily that we hadn't killed it, that it was still alive and giving us an egg every morning. He started to laugh and said he had hoped that was what would happen. He then said that he knew where I lived and asked if he could come over to see it some-day. I said I'd have to ask my mother first and he said alright—maybe he'd be able to come over after the next meeting. He wasn't good-looking and had a lot of pimples on his face, but he had a nice smile. His name was Wolfgang

When I later asked my mother if Wolfgang could come over to see the chicken she immediately agreed as, after all, he had given it to us. He then came over to our house after the next church meeting and was glad the chicken had found a good home but when Elli saw him, she went straight to Aunt Hedwig. Both of them then came back to ask me if my boyfriend was moving in as well. I was too embarrassed to say a word but Wolfgang seemed to understand the situation and just said goodbye and left.

I had begun to realise that my mother was really struggling to make a decision about what to do over declaring my father dead when some-thing good happened. Our priest knew our situation and one day he came over and asked my mother if she would be willing to help out in the church doing a little decorating and cleaning. He wouldn't be able to pay a lot but there were also sometimes basic foods and butter and cheese available which were donated by the Red Cross and Catholic charities. As he said, "Every little bit will help." My mother gladly agreed and for the first time in quite a while, I saw my mother happy again. She only worked a few hours a day but that and the food we re-ceived helped us a lot and things were generally a little better.

My mother also now had the opportunity to talk with other women and a few were in the same situation as we were with my father. Two of them in particular hadn't heard from their husbands or the government for two years. One of them had found out that there was an organisation which tried to find missing soldiers—it just required the family to go and see them and fill out some forms, putting down all the addresses where they'd lived and the last known location of the husbands. Accordingly, my mother and the women went and filled out the forms and my mother wrote down Poznan (Posen) as the last known location because that was where my father had worked in the hospital. The lady in the office who looked at the papers noticed "Poznan" and said there had been a lot of hard fighting around the CYTADELA there (the fortress on high ground protecting the city) and that lots of soldiers had lost their lives when the Russian troops surrounded the city and stopped everyone from getting out. She also told my mother that since her husband had been a medical person, the Russians might have needed him to treat their own injured troops, in which case there might still be hope that he had been treated differently from the soldiers. The people in the office told my mother to check back with them in three months so we made the decision to wait that long and if there was still no news, we would then both start a new life together.

The meetings at church continued and more and more young people were returning to school, as did Wolfgang. We talked a great deal during those meetings and one of the things he told me was that they had relatives in the United States and that his parents were thinking of leaving Germany and immigrating to the US with him. They wanted him to finish school in Germany first and as he was almost 17 he still had over a year to go in Berlin. I started to think that night and realised that if he left, I would miss him.

I started to look for schools and what they offered and found it more complicated than I had imagined. I was interested in languages, geography and biology as well as sports but wasn't really at all interested in mathematics or chemistry. I found two schools where the tuition wasn't too bad and which might have been suitable but they were both an hour away from us by bus, each way, and they were in the US sector of Berlin. I wanted to tell my mother about them but then I thought it over and decided to wait until the time when we would make a decision regarding whether or not my father was likely to return, which was already close.

At one of the meetings in church, Wolfgang asked me if I would like to go with him to the American youth club, but I knew we could only go if we were 18 or older and that we were both then too young. He told me that over the weekends young people between 14 and 18 were allowed to go there in the afternoon as long as they left by 7.30 P.M. and I agreed to go with him the next weekend as long as my mother approved. He said he'd come and pick me up on Saturday afternoon and I then had the problem of, firstly, telling my mother what I wanted to do and, secondly, deciding what to wear as my choice of clothes was extremely limited. Finally, two days before our so-called "date," I pulled myself together and just asked my mother. She looked at me seriously but was also smiling and said that she realised I was growing up fast and that Wolfgang seemed to be a nice boy who came from a nice Church-going family, and that I could go as long as I was home by 9 P.M. I was so happy that I hugged and kissed her and told her she was the best mother ever. We then went through my clothes and found a black dress which we had got from the Salvation Army—a little long but I didn't care. It was then that she told me that she had already saved a little money from her work so could now afford to pay for my tuition and that if, after the three months were over, there was no word from my father, I would have to go back to school. At that stage, I would have agreed to anything!

So the following Saturday, Wolfgang picked me up and we walked the thirty minutes or so to the club. When we got near we could already hear the loud music and it definitely wasn't church music! Then, when we got inside, I couldn't believe my eyes: there was a little screen with cartoons playing, a pool table and another for table tennis and so on. I felt as though I was in another world and so grown up. Wolfgang soon brought me a glass of something which I'd never seen before and said it was Coca-Cola—well, I gulped it down and didn't like it at all but didn't say so and that was my first experience of Coca-Cola! We seemed to spend the rest of the afternoon just walking around and talking to others and playing a few games; we were all so cool but the afternoon went by pretty quickly and all of a sudden the music stopped and a voice announced that it was 7.30 and time for us to leave. We had a little way to walk home so left straight away but I felt as though I was walking in a dream, especially when Wolfgang took my hand and we walked the rest of the way holding hands.

On the way home we talked a lot about the future and he explained his concern that he didn't know what would happen to him both because his parents wanted to leave Germany and because he wanted to study medicine and become a surgeon. When we got to my door just before 9 P.M. he thanked me for going to the club with him and said we must do it again and I, of course, agreed with him completely. Suddenly the pimples on his face didn't look that bad.

I told my mother all about what had happened that afternoon, except about the holding hands part (!) and she was happy for me but did say that I couldn't go every weekend, perhaps twice a month. She then also mentioned that she'd been told by the woman at the agency that they hadn't been able to track down her husband, so we really started to prepare each other for the worst. In addition to that I was thinking about going back to school, which scared me, but there seemed no other choice.

Strangely enough, it was only a few days after that while I was looking out of the window that I noticed a man standing by our gate in the fence. He didn't look very respectable or even very clean and had a beard and quite long hair and I wondered what he wanted with us, so called my mother to have a look. When she came and looked out, her face went as white as a sheet and she just ran down the stairs to the gate and she and the man both hugged each other. I really couldn't work out what was going on until they both came up the stairs and it suddenly hit me that this was my missing father. I hadn't recognised him because of the beard and the long hair and have to admit that at that moment I wasn't sure whether to feel happy or sad. My father and I also hugged each other and I saw tears running down both their faces. Alli and Aunt Hedwig came and joined us and I didn't know how they felt either with the possibility of yet another person moving into their home. They did the right thing though and prepared a nice dinner but my father's main wish was to have a bath. What to do about clothes was a problem as we didn't have any men's clothes but Aunt Hedwig looked out some things which had belonged to her dead husband and although they were old, they were clean and luckily they did fit my father, so at least he had something clean to wear.

My father told us he had been a prisoner of war in Denmark and that because we had lost everything we had in the city, he hadn't been able to find us until my mother registered with that agency. There was then the problem of where we were all going to sleep as the two beds my mother and I used would now be used by my parents. Eventually it was decided that I would have the recliner chair, which wasn't the most comfortable of places to sleep. At that time I wasn't at all sure how I felt or even if I really wanted my father back. My mother and I had got used to being alone and had developed a very strong bond during the last few years and now I felt I was being pushed back to being in second place. My thoughts frightened me—he was my father and we had waited so long for him to come back that now I felt disloyal. If only we could have been in a bigger place so that I could have my own bed, I might have felt better.

Then, of course, my father became the head of the family again and started telling me what to do, which was a whole new experience. He wasn't at all pleased that I wasn't already back in school and insisted that I had to go back straight away. At least he immediately found a job in the medical field, which was good, but a lot of things changed very quickly in our little family and my father and I disagreed and fell out about a lot of things. When I got older, I realised he only wanted the best for us, so I apologised and he understood, probably because he was basically in the same situation as I was at that time.

Meanwhile, at that time, I sometimes wished he hadn't come home at all and my feelings disturbed me so much that I talked to the priest about them. He assured me that it was quite normal that after all my mother and I had been through together while my father was absent, the bond between us was so strong without him that he now seemed like an intruder. I then registered to start school in the fall, so that was that worry taken care of but the only thing I looked forward to was spending time with Wolfgang when we went to the club meetings at the church once a month; he was the only person who seemed to understand me at that time.

The war and being a prisoner of war must have been very traumatic for my father. I did ask him about it all and what had happened—how he was taken prisoner and what Denmark was like—but he never answered me. He just kept very quiet and I guess he didn't want to talk about it. Perhaps he told my mother but she never said anything to me either. My father had a good job in one of the hospitals and that helped a lot. He was gone all day and my mother still worked at the church, where she liked being with other people she could talk to. With the money now coming in we could afford to pay for schooling for me and we easily could have paid for an apartment for all of us if there had been anything available. The fact that there wasn't anything meant I still had only my recliner to sleep on.

My father then got the idea into his head that perhaps we could clean up the property which we owned; that there might be a chance to repair the shack and live there until times got better. We told him the horror story of our trip there with people hanging outside the train but he had heard that was no longer allowed and that everyone had to be inside. Well, the decision was made that next weekend we would go there so that my father could have a look and see what could be done to make it somehow habitable. I looked at my mother and noticed that she had a hard time even thinking of the whole idea. I don't know if my father realised it or not, but his decision also meant Wolfgang and I couldn't see each other that weekend.

At least the train ride wasn't as bad as the last time and it was also much faster as the train could now travel much more quickly. However, when we got there my father looked absolutely stunned and obviously hadn't expected quite such a mess. He went over to talk to the neighbours as all the neighbours were living in broken shacks, trying to rebuild their houses, and they came to an agreement that they would help us to clean up our property. Just one of the problems was that there was no electricity and generators had to be used, which were hard to get at that time because everyone needed them. My father was relieved that there was at least a possibility of doing it, even though it was in Eastern Germany. Anyway, he promised the neighbour that we would be back soon and asked if he would start looking for helpers.

I was in deep shock at the idea of moving again. I had started back at school and was just beginning to get used to the students and teachers, most of whom were old, because the young teachers were either dead or still prisoners of war somewhere. We were allowed to study five languages and in the beginning I liked that and chose German, which of course was a "must," and then English, French, Latin and Russian. Thinking back now I must have been out of my mind trying to do all that and it wasn't long before I gave up Russian, which I was finding very hard to learn. With the others, I was willing to struggle on a little while longer, so it was devastating to think of leaving school again.

It took my father a little while to go back to the property; maybe he wasn't sure it was the right thing to do, but he didn't want to give up the idea. Anyway, it meant I was able to go to the club that coming weekend. My father didn't like the idea of me going and I think my mother must have convinced him to let me go and he told me to be home by 8 P.M. As always, Wolfgang and I had a good time and were walking home holding hands again when I realised it was already past 8 P.M. and worried about what my father would say to that. I mentioned it to Wolfgang as we passed our church and he just stopped and looked down at me (he was a lot taller than I was), put his arms around me and gave me a kiss. Well, I stood there like a zombie and neither of us said a word. Now I had had my first kiss as well as my first Coca-Cola. I noticed that at home there was a light in the window and that my father was looking out but I was no longer even afraid of being late, I just felt completely numb. When I got upstairs my father commented that I was almost 45 minutes late and that if it happened again I would get a "spanking."

I tried really hard to understand my father, realising that everyone who went through the war and its aftermath had changed in some way and that perhaps he was still visualising me as the little girl he had left behind when he went to war. I was almost sure that was the reason for the way he treated me and so I tried as hard as I could to be nice and to obey his rules. That helped a bit but our whole living arrangement made things difficult. Generally, things were getting a little better with more apartments getting rebuilt and repaired and also more people were leaving Berlin, some to move to West Germany, though the favourite place to move to was Canada. There were still long lines on the housing waiting lists but even so I think my father got frustrated with the property we owned as we only went there again twice. The neighbours hadn't had too much luck finding helpers anyway so he decided to wait a little while until times got better. That was great news for me as I had the weekends back and Wolfgang and I could go to the church meetings and once a month to the American club.

I was concentrating a lot on schoolwork but I had problems with Latin. I really blamed it on the teacher because he was already pretty old and also hard of hearing, but I just told him it was because it's an old language which nobody uses any more. Anyway, my grades dropped and I dropped Latin, which I regretted later in life because it's such an interesting language. But you don't think that far when you're young, especially when you're a teenager.

Wolfgang and I enjoyed our outings and started to talk about the future. He knew that his parents were seriously talking about leaving Germany to move to the United States when he finished his schooling. That would be in 1948 and it was already the end of 1947, so the time wasn't too far away. Our relationship had become much closer and we had such a strong bond that the matter became foremost in our minds. Both of us had a very strong Catholic background and although we were so very close, it was really a strong, platonic, puppy love. Even so, we started to talk about the future and the possibility that as soon as I finished school in Berlin, I would go over to the States and we would get married. They weren't sure yet where they would go but thought that he would probably start university somewhere on the east coast of the U.S. The future started to look bright and made us really happy and although we agreed to keep our plans to ourselves for the time being, we started to look forward and even our school grades got better.

One weekend we went to the US club as usual and even started to dance a little—he was much better than I was and I kept stepping on his feet, so we just started to get closer and danced so that we wouldn't step on each other's feet. Well, when we left the club it was already late and I knew I wouldn't be home on time but that didn't make us walk any faster and we carried on, still talking about our future and hugging each other. Of course, I was late and my father was standing in the window when we got to my house. When I got upstairs he told me he was going to give me that spanking, then took off his pants belt and started hitting me with it across the lower back. It was really hurting until my mother stepped in and pulled him back. I was shocked and ran into the bathroom, locking myself in and really crying and I swore to myself then that if I ever had children, I would never, ever, hit them. Eventually, my mother knocked on the door and came in and hugged me and she tried to explain that my father didn't know how to raise children and that perhaps he, himself, had been treated like that when he was young. Somehow I understood and when we went out of the bathroom my father was obviously feeling very bad. He said he was sorry and that it would never happen again and in fact it never did. He tried to be nicer and we never mentioned it again. I knew he loved me very much but was just unable to express himself. Wolfgang's parents were very loving and I didn't tell him what had happened.

With everything that was going on in my life, I wasn't aware of the tension developing between the Allies and the Soviet Union. Rumours were going around that the Soviet Union wasn't satisfied with just the quarter of the city which they now controlled and that they were preparing to take over all of Berlin. That would mean the whole city of Berlin would be under Russian control, since it was situated in East Germany anyway. Stalin wanted to push the Allies out of West Berlin and back to West Germany, so that he could control the whole city and the idea of all of us belonging to East Germany under Russian control was a scary thought. We were just entering the year 1948 and we all thought we were working towards a new future and now this was happening. Nobody was really sure what to do: we were just recovering slightly from World War 2 and we definitely didn't need another war.

Wolfgang and I were also worried about how it would all affect us as he would finish school in the summer and then most likely would be leaving for the U.S. with his parents. Sometimes he picked me up after school so that we could be together and have time to talk and one day he came up with the idea that maybe we should get married while he was still in Germany—just a civil marriage, not a church marriage. His idea was that when I finished school it would be much easier for me to enter the U.S. because firstly I would be his wife and secondly, he would already be there. At first I was speechless but very happy, although there were obvious problems in that although he was 18 and therefore an adult, I would need permission from my parents in order to marry and I wasn't at all sure I'd get it. Wolfgang also agreed that that could be a problem and in any case he still had a few months schooling to complete, so we decided to wait to see how long it would take his parents to complete all the paperwork in order to immigrate to the U.S. I must admit the thought of leaving my parents behind in Germany made me very sad, but we still had time to think about it.

Over the next few weeks the situation worsened; there were meetings and then more meetings in the city between all four winners of the war, but no news came out. Then, as spring started in April 1948, the Russians closed all highways, railroads and canals from West Germany going into West Berlin with the result that nobody living in West Berlin could get out of West Berlin and, also, nobody could get in. It was complete chaos. The Russians believed that by closing off entrances to West Berlin, people living there wouldn't be able to get food, gasoline, medical supplies, coal, or almost anything at all, and that would result in the Allies pulling out of West Berlin, meaning that the Russians would be able to take over the whole city.

We were informed that all of West Berlin only had supplies to last about six more weeks and nobody knew what would happen after that: perhaps we would all die. Only West Berlin was affected since the Russians already controlled East Berlin anyway and people there, including Aunt Maria and my Grandfather, were fine. We also lost our property to East Germany. As well as everything else, even electricity was cut off most of the time and there was nothing left for us to do except pray for a miracle and hope the Allies would try to help us.

Wolfgang and I decided not to ask my parents for their permission for me to get married as his parents now weren't able to leave West Berlin anyway and we were still going to be together.

The Autobahn, the highway connecting West Germany to Berlin, was also closed and as that was the main highway in and out of Berlin, that was when the "Berlin Blockade" began. Rumours were spreading quickly that American President Truman was saying the Allies were not withdrawing from West Berlin because if they did, the Soviet Union would take over all of Germany and with that, the Cold War began. Now everything started to happen very quickly. There was no regular air traffic allowed in the area but the air space to and from West Berlin was still open for military purposes and the Allies decided to supply West Berlin by air with everything we needed. The Americans called it "AIR LIFT," we called it "AIR BRIDGE" but whatever the name— American, British and French cargo planes started to fly into West Berlin and every minute a plane landed with supplies at one of the three airports we had in West Berlin. For the Americans it was Berlin-Tempelhof, for Britain it was Berlin-Gatow, and the French used Berlin-Tegel airport. Despite the supplies, gasoline and electricity were rationed and our life in West Berlin wasn't easy but at least we weren't living under Russian control and the situation had to end eventually.

Wolfgang and I really started to look forward to leaving Germany when it was all over. We told my parents of our plans and they agreed and we all even agreed that eventually we would bring them over into the U.S. as well, and that made me very happy. Wolfgang kissed me then, saying, "Since you are my wife already." The time for him to leave school had almost arrived and there was still no sign of the Air Bridge being over, so Wolfgang decided to look for part-time jobs after school so that he was earning a little and not constantly having to ask his parents for money. All of us just lived from day to day and it felt like sitting in a cage. We still went to church meetings but the US clubs were almost ready to close.

At the same time, the black market started to bloom and although my father didn't smoke, he was sometimes given cigarettes by patients and we were able to sell those on the black market in exchange for food. We also had a new currency: on the west side we had the DEUTSCHE mark and East Germany together with East Berlin had the OST Mark (East Mark), so there was already a positive split to see.

Then suddenly Wolfgang's graduation was over and he was out of school. Quite a few young students and friends told him that they felt there was really no future there for young people and that after the blockade was over they would leave Berlin and go somewhere else. I couldn't wait to graduate too, but I still had to wait another year. In the meantime, Wolfgang had found a part-time job in a hospital cleaning rooms and helping some patients. It didn't pay a lot but at least he had a little spending money. Christmas 1948 was a quiet and kind of hopeless holiday but we were all thankful to be alive and not under Russian control and Wolfgang and I were glad to have each other to talk to and to belong to each other.

By the spring of 1949 the Allies were clearly succeeding and they were delivering more cargo than ever before to the just over two million people living in West Berlin. Luckily we weren't aware of it at the time but it was a very dangerous situation. We were later told that the Allies had stations in West Germany and Great Britain with Panzers, troops, and also fighter planes ready to start fighting for Berlin if Joseph Stalin, the leader of the Soviet Union, made any moves like shooting at the cargo planes flying over Eastern Germany into West Berlin.

My parents had the good news from the housing department that we were almost on top of the waiting list for re-housing. Maybe in a few months we would be able to get a one-bedroom apartment, which meant I might even have my own bed. One evening after a church meeting when Wolfgang and I were walking home he gave me a little white box and told me to open it there and then. In the box was a small golden ring like an engagement ring for me to wear. I really cried and of course he put it on my finger! He smiled though and said it wasn't gold, just cheap gold metal and that he had got it on the black market, but to me it looked like a 2-carat diamond. In a war-torn city, you're blessed if you have a person to whom you belong; it makes you feel secure and safe.

All in all the air bridge situation started to look a little better and everyone hoped it would soon be over—except perhaps for me because I was still wondering what would happen when Wolfgang and his family left. His parents had told us they would leave as soon as the danger was over but I still had to finish school. At least Wolfgang now knew where their distant relatives lived, which was in Washington, D.C., but he had no permanent address yet.

The recliner probably had something to do with it, but I was having many sleepless nights worrying about how things would be in a foreign country, living with strangers and speaking a different language. Yes, I'd learnt English at school, but was that enough? Someone told me that "school English" is quite different from that spoken in English-speaking countries. And then there were my parents as well; except for business lines, there weren't any phone connections in Berlin at that time, so we would be completely cut off.

I discussed all this with Wolfgang but he couldn't foresee any real problems. He would be there and he knew his parents would always help us, in addition to which his relatives were supposed to be quite wealthy. He said as long as I was with him, I'd be fine and that if he couldn't go to college straight away, he'd find a job to support us and that, after all, we were still German citizens. Because of my worries, though, I hoped that air bridge situation would go on a little longer; I must have been the only person thinking like that in the whole city.

Even though everything went very smoothly, still some problems came up—the three airports being used for the cargo flights soon became too small and wear and tear set in with the result that even more cargo had to be flown in. It was mostly building supplies but more people also had to be hired and even a lot of volunteer workers came to help, with some of them working 12 to 15 hours a day. Additionally, the winter of 1948/'49 was very cold—much colder than usual—so even more coal had to be brought in but everything was organised almost perfectly and the Allies let all of us know that they would support us for as long as it was necessary.

Then Spring arrived properly, that lovely time of year, and Wolfgang and I were outside most of the time, walking and talking about the future and the more we talked about it, the safer I felt. Just a few more months of school to go and I already felt I was ready to leave. Finally, the Soviet Union realised the blockage of West Berlin was a failure and in May 1949 the Soviets lifted the blockade and re-opened the roads, canals and railways into West Berlin. With that we were somehow free again and out of our cage even though the allies were still flying in some cargo, just to be sure that everything had started working again.

Wolfgang's parents now really started to get ready to leave. All the forms had been filled out and there were only a few more preparations to make. I was happy that Wolfgang was still in Berlin and was with me at the graduation, which was bittersweet for both of us. His parents still had to wait until scheduled air flights were available for the public and it would be perhaps two or three months before they could fly out of Tempelhof to Frankfurt/Main and then on to New York. Wolfgang was still working and I decided to take a six-month course in bookkeeping and secretarial work, just in case I was able to find a job there and start working so that I could help with the money. Our plan was for me to be there in Washington, D.C., by Christmas.

When we went to our church and told the priest about our plans, he laughed and said, "All that because of a chicken!" He also told us about Helga and Brigitta, the girl who had her baby because of a rape by the Russians. It turned out that she had found a nice young man, an American soldier, and that they were getting married and also leaving for the U.S., which was really nice to hear. My parents had been told they might possibly get that one-bedroom apartment in November which would make them busy moving while I was still in Berlin and able to help them. So everything was looking really great. I thoroughly enjoyed the course I went on and learned a lot from it and even my father was feeling better and hoping he could get back our property located in East Germany.

We were busy during that summer of 1949. Wolfgang was working and I had my secretarial course, but we enjoyed the weekends of what was supposed to be our last summer in Germany for quite a while. The Allies continued to fly some supplies into West Berlin until September of 1949, stockpiling supplies just in case the blockade was reinstated. It was still a tense situation and none of the people in West Berlin thought the Russians would give up that easily so it was still a kind of cold war situation between the Allies and the Soviet Union. Germany was now divided into two with Eastern Germany under Russian control and West Germany under the control of the allies and although Berlin was situated in Eastern Germany, it was still the capital of both Germanies.

September arrived quickly and with it, Wolfgang and his family received the date for their departure. It was Wednesday, October 26th, 1949—a date I never, ever forgot. We could feel the uncertainty ahead of us but assured each other that we would only be apart for a few months and that if we were lucky we might even be spending Christmas together in Washington, D.C. Wolfgang's parents even said that maybe their relatives over there, who were American citizens, could pledge for me, which would make it a lot easier for me to go.

Well, we went to say goodbye to the priest and he wished us all the best and blessed us; he really liked us. Then the inevitable last day arrived, the 25th October, and we spent nearly all day together while Wolfgang packed all his things together. I had decided not to go and see them off at the airport and just wanted to say goodbye to him alone so I said goodbye to his parents and wished them a safe flight and said that we would see each other again soon. Wolfgang then took me home and we were both terribly upset and emotional. We could hardly let go of each other but eventually we said we hoped to see each other again soon and then he just kissed me and turned around with tears rolling down his face. He never looked back and it reminded me vividly of when my father had left for active duty at the beginning of the war. I was a complete nervous wreck and even my father gave me a hug, which was very unusual. That night I hardly slept at all and felt so completely alone that I could have been the last person on earth.

Wolfgang had promised to write to me as soon as they arrived in Washington as we didn't have any phone connection. They might have a phone overseas but we in Berlin still didn't have one so there was only mail delivery, which might take two weeks or more. Somehow I got through the days until his first letter arrived telling me that they had arrived there safely but he wanted to come back to Berlin. Even so, he liked the area where they were staying with his relatives, where he had his own room in a big house. He said everything was so very different from Berlin and that everyone seemed so rich compared to us. He was hoping to talk to his relatives about me over the next few days so that we could start preparing immigration papers and, if need be, to ask if they would sign the pledge. I was once again hopeful and happy and couldn't wait for his next letter.

In the meantime, my parents got the good news that they would be getting an apartment and could move in starting from the 1st of December. Then, about a week later, I received the next letter from Wolfgang telling me he liked the area where they were living but there was such a big difference in their lifestyle compared to what he was used to in Berlin that he was seriously thinking of coming back to Berlin. He hadn't told his parents how he felt yet and his other relatives were away on a week's vacation. He said he wasn't planning to register for the University yet and that he would look for a job first and hopefully work until I was there, which probably wouldn't be before Christmas. He went on and on about how much he was missing our lifestyle compared with the one in Washington, D.C. Well, it wasn't the news I had hoped for but perhaps if he came back to Berlin, it might be even nicer, so I told him that in my next letter. Now that my parents knew they were getting that apartment, they started to look for affordable furniture. I had told them the recliner was NOT moving to the apartment and fortunately they understood!

As there were still a few weeks left until Christmas when we thought either Wolfgang would be back with us or I would be in the States, we decided to visit Aunt Maria and my grandfather, neither of whom we'd seen since January 1945. They, however, were now living in East Germany and it wasn't as easy as we had thought. My father knew that some patients of his were driving people around and acting like taxi-drivers (but at cheaper rates) like the one we used to have in the inner city who knew the grocery store lady, and he found one who would take us. That driver warned us that it would take a while to get there because although it was usually just an hour's drive away, we were West Berliners trying to enter East Germany and we would have to go through several checkpoints. The first one was to get out of West Berlin, which wasn't too bad, but getting into East Germany was kind of tricky and worse than going through any airport security check. Additionally, after checking us out completely, we had to pay a fee before we could continue on.

At that time we could already see the difference between East and West—people in the West were trying to rebuild and repair their houses and roads but that wasn't so in the East where most of the roads had deep potholes. Anyway, we made it there and found it was a nice, clean, little farm house with some acreage and with chickens running around. Grandfather, of course, missed his former farm and my grandmother but he was alright and a big help for Aunt Maria and her four children. We were glad to all be together again and stayed two days before we returned home. When we got there, there was a letter from Wolfgang telling me he had found a job in a hotel and was starting to save money for his fare back home. Like me, he was his parents' only child and they didn't like the idea a lot, but he was now an adult so they reluctantly agreed. I was now kind of confused as to whether I would be leaving Germany or not but the one thing I realised was that I would be in Germany for Christmas and that meant I would be moving into the other apartment with my parents.

Because of our move to the new apartment my mother was suddenly very busy so stopped working at the church and I asked the priest if I could take over her old job, to which he readily agreed. For me it was the best thing that could happen as it kept me busy and stopped me from mulling over my own situation. So in the morning I went to secretarial school and in the afternoons I helped the priest and he even paid me the same as he'd been paying my mother. It was good to be there and see all those people again: quite a few had already left Berlin but there were still some old faces. It was also actually the first Christmas since the war and the air bridge so we tried to decorate the church with whatever we could find and with whatever donations came in. With everything I was doing, I was busy all day and tired at night but still I found myself unable to sleep. My parents had found some nice furniture—it was all used stuff but we didn't care as long as we were within our "four walls," as we called it. I still didn't have my own bed! My parents used the only bedroom and I had a nice sofa-bed in the living room, which I suppose was alright as we didn't have a lot of visitors anyway and I could go to bed whenever I wanted.

About ten days after his last letter, I had another from Wolfgang saying he was still very determined to come back to Berlin. He also mentioned that he'd come to like the job he had at the hotel and was meeting a lot of people and because he had to travel quite a long way to get to work, his parents had said they'd buy him a car. He still needed to get a driver's licence, but reading between the lines, I could tell he was excited about it all. He just mentioned in passing that his relatives there and his parents had told him they would be filling out my immigration forms at the beginning of next year, so it might take a little longer for me to get there. I had to agree as there was nothing else I could do anyway. He also told me he had sent me a little Christmas present to my new address.

I talked to the priest about what was happening in my life and explained that I might not be leaving as soon as I had expected. He didn't say a lot—just that Wolfgang was a very nice boy and that sometimes things take longer than we expect. I now started to like our new apartment. It was wonderfully quiet—we even bought a radio so that I could listen to music and now that the terrible stress wasn't there any more, my relationship with my father just got better and better. Even so, I still missed Wolfgang terribly and was still hoping that we'd be together again soon.

My mother was talking to neighbours and found out that things were much cheaper in East Berlin, especially if you pay with your West Mark. One neighbour in particular was a dressmaker and did a lot of sewing of dresses, blouses and even men's clothing and she confirmed that everything in East Berlin was cheaper. As there was now a bus service available, my mother, father, and I decided to go there and check it all out and found it was all true: everything was a lot cheaper, including food prices and even hairdressers. So while my parents went food shopping, I went to a hairdresser and had my hair cut and also permed. What a disaster it was having that perm done: my hair looked as though it had been burned and I almost lost it all: that was my first and certainly my last try at the hairdresser!

Anyway, we returned home and had a lovely Christmas together. We had a letter from Wolfgang and his parents wishing us all a Merry

Christmas and then my present arrived a little later. It was a lovely blue sweater in my favourite colour and also a little necklace with a tiny cross. I really liked it and hoped so much that we would be together again soon—even more when I put the necklace on and saw a little "W" engraved on the back of the cross.

I was completely overwhelmed by the present and wrote to Wolfgang straight away thanking him and telling him that whatever he wanted to do, whether it was him coming back to Berlin or me going to Washington, was alright with me. Because I thought it might help him to make a decision, I filled in some of the news for him which was that West Germany and West Berlin were really improving. We now had our first Chancellor for the West, Konrad Adenauer. He was being called the Father of the New Germany and was responsible for "Das Deutsche Wirtschaftswunder" (The German Economic Miracle). The future now looked quite hopeful and even though there were still problems with the East Germany/Soviet border checks, it still looked a lot better than the year before. My father had also started to mention that since the air bridge was now over, we would be able to travel to East Germany to have another look at our property there.

The next letter from Wolfgang took longer to come and when it did he told me they we all very busy over there. A coworker from the hotel was teaching him to drive so that he could take the learner driver test to get his permanent driver's licence, which was hard because the traffic conditions in Washington were completely different from those in Berlin. He said they were hoping to start on the paperwork for me soon but at the moment his relatives were completely involved in their own problems and his parents couldn't do anything as they still only had German documents. There wasn't much I could say or do so I didn't tell my parents anything at all. My secretarial course would soon be over and for the time being it was only me who had to know when I could leave. Whilst on my course, though, I had made friends with another girl. She was a little older than I was and her name was Rita. She had a boyfriend called Jonathan who was an American soldier from Florida and I found I had someone I could talk to about Wolfgang and me. She told me that she would never leave Germany but I argued that

Wolfgang was also German and that made all the difference if we were both prepared to leave for a foreign country. She just said that the American way of life was so different from ours and with us in Germany just recovering from the war and all the trauma and everyone being poor, most people just wouldn't be able to handle the move. I still defended Wolfgang and his choice.

With hindsight I think that deep down inside me I almost realised we wouldn't see each other again; maybe he was one of the ones like Rita had described who couldn't handle the new lifestyle, but I kept that thought to myself. One good thing was that the chicken had died a while ago because otherwise it would have constantly reminded me of the times we'd had together. It was now almost two weeks later that I received another letter from Wolfgang telling me that his relatives had filled out my immigration forms and were ready to send them off to wherever it was they had to go. But, they warned him, it might take a few months as a lot of German people wanted to immigrate to the States. As far as I understood the situation anyway, there were only a certain number of people, like a quota, allowed to immigrate to the States and I would have to have someone pledge for me. Reading his letter, it suddenly hit me that perhaps they really didn't want to do it but I still had some hope left that after finishing his driver's license, Wolfgang would concentrate more on my situation but I didn't mention it in my next letter to him. In his latest letter he told me a lot about getting his driver's license and how happy he was but there wasn't one question about what everyone at home was doing or how they were getting on. Another thing he told me was that he'd smoked his first cigarette with his coworker and that he hadn't like it at all—he got dizzy and coughed a lot and wrote that he'd never try one again.

After this letter I again had a few sleepless nights but I decided to use my time and to extend my secretarial course for another six months, until the fall of 1950. The course fees had to be prepaid so, if my papers should arrive sooner, I could leave at any time. One day when I was working at the church the priest showed me a wedding picture: it was Helga and her husband and the little girl (from the Russian soldier) and they looked really happy. I was happy for them but it did hurt me a lot.

When the priest asked how I was doing I explained that I was still waiting for the paperwork and he just commented that sometimes things take a little longer than expected.

So, I extended my course and Rita was staying until the fall so it was good to have her around. Just looking at me, she knew I had no good news but she didn't say a word. One day my mother gave me a hug and asked how Wolfgang was doing and I knew her feelings and that she didn't want to lose me. I told her about the paperwork and she just told me not to worry and that we would make it eventually. It was then close to three weeks since the last letter had arrived.

After Wolfgang's last letter I almost gave up hope of seeing him again. He apologised for not writing sooner but his excuse was that his parents and his relatives had flown him to New York for a three-day visit. He told me all about this trip and how they had taken a tour to the Statue of Liberty and then gone to Chinatown in the evening for a Chinese meal. For him everything was new and I had to wonder if his relatives weren't doing it all on purpose to make him forget Berlin and, possibly, me. He still told me how much he missed his old life in Berlin and me, as well, but I guessed I was coming in second in his thoughts. He was so involved in his future and everything he was seeing and experiencing for the first time—rather like me and my first Coca-Cola in the American Club—and even said that if he passed his driver's licence when they went back to Washington, his parents had promised they would buy him a car. His only fear was the heavy traffic in Washington.

He promised to write more often and sooner and asked me if I still wore that necklace. He now also asked about the priest and how I liked my new apartment with my parents and that gave me a little hope again, but—to be honest—only a little hope. The next day I saw Rita and told her all about it and she was still very sceptical and simply said that it probably wasn't his fault. She explained that his relatives, and also his parents, probably didn't want me to go over to the States and would prefer that he married an American girl. In my heart I realised that his feelings and plans were changing a bit and in one of his letters he had even mentioned that he wouldn't, after all, mind living in New York. I just thought que sera sera, and whatever will be will be because it was really the only way I could handle all my emotions.

I then had a break from thinking about it all when our priest asked me if I would join a few other ladies and accompany a small group of children around the age of ten on a trip to West Germany for about a week to have a little holiday. Because of all the trauma they had been through, some of those children really needed a break from their routine and a holiday. He was thinking of going to Muenchen (Munich) by bus, which meant leaving West Berlin and driving through East Germany to get to West Germany and so on to Munich. I was quite looking forward to the trip as I'd heard a lot about Munich and the Bavarian Alps.

It was now over three weeks since I'd heard from Wolfgang so that night I decided to be decisive and write to him telling him that I really wanted to know what his intentions were—whether he intended to stay in Washington, or even New York if he preferred it there, or whether he still planned to come back to Berlin and that I needed to know how he felt and what his intentions were.

It only took a little over a week before I received a letter from his mother and even though I knew before I'd even opened it that it wouldn't contain good news, I knew that I had to know the truth and couldn't go on as I was at the moment. She simply said that she was sorry to write and tell me that Wolfgang was being torn between his future and me and she pleaded with me to let him go. She explained that she felt our relationship had been perfect when we were still so young and going through those terrible times and that although we had then needed each other's support, our feelings for each other were now holding him back. She then offered me money for leaving him and somehow I wasn't even shocked. I think I'd almost expected it but I was very deeply hurt and felt as though I was being bought. I never answered her and after that I returned two letters from Wolfgang without ever knowing if he knew about his mother's letter to me.

The next evening I took my metal "golden" ring and also the necklace with the cross and I went to the cemetery behind the church. I then made a hole under a tree and buried them both.

I told my parents everything that had happened and I know they felt sorry for me. I think my mother must have already guessed that something was wrong and she just reiterated that we would all be fine; that I had my whole future ahead of me and that as there was usually a reason for everything, perhaps Wolfgang and I were just not meant to be together. I guess they were also both happy that I'd be staying at home. The fact that I had been offered money to let him go really hurt both of them as well, especially as we were only poor because we'd lost everything because of the war and not for any other reason. When I went back on my course I told Rita the whole story and she also thought that it wasn't entirely Wolfgang's fault and that his relatives were probably most responsible as his parents had to do more or less what they wanted. Listening to her talk helped a little and she also said that whenever I was ready to go out to eat or on a date, just to let her know and we could go together. I knew that would take a while as for the moment I felt I needed a wall around me to protect myself and my feelings. When I told the priest the whole story, he thought the same thing—that it was probably because of the relatives.

The priest then also mentioned that he was ready to retire and that a new, younger, priest would be arriving soon so he really didn't know if he would be going to Munich with us—depending on when the other priest arrived. Nevertheless, we started to get everything prepared for the trip for the nine children, three ladies, the priest and myself. It was planned that we would stay on a farm with lots of animals because most the children were growing up in the inner city and hardly ever saw a live animal, so it would be a great experience for them. We were only planning to make the one trip during that week in Munich but since we'd been lucky enough to get a lot of donations, we may be able to have more trips to other places in West Germany, because we weren't allowed to stay in East Germany. Even though the war was over, as well as the air bridge, things still weren't completely right and there were always incidents happening at the border, now even more of them happening between East and West-Berliners. We were pretty sure the Communists were behind the trouble but overall West Berlin tried to make people's lives easier.

When the day arrived for us to go on the Munich trip, we all met at the church. The new priest had already arrived and was quite an energetic sort of person and the children were all hugely excited, so we all got quickly onto the bus and drove off to the border of West Berlin and East Germany to get onto the Autobahn. We were checked out for weapons and told we could only drive at a certain speed—there would be no racing on the Autobahn anyway, because of the bad road conditions. We had a lot of fun with the children on the bus, telling stories and playing little games and were lucky that the driver liked children! When we arrived at the border of East Germany going into West Germany, we suddenly felt a kind of FREE feeling and could drive faster with no speed limit at all.

It still took us a few more hours to reach the outskirts of Munich and the road to the farm and then suddenly there it was—a beautifully fenced farm with horses, goats, chickens and a large, pretty guesthouse for all of us. The farm owners had a nice little house for themselves with a farm-worker's cottage attached and quite a big kitchen. The children slept on the floor on mattresses, the priest had his own room and the ladies and I had a room with bunk beds. Within ten minutes of arriving, the children were all asleep. That evening I missed Wolfgang very much and thought how much he would have liked it there. I knew he liked being outside. Or maybe not, anymore.

Many years later I heard from mutual friends from that time that Wolfgang joined the U.S. Air Force Academy, married a wealthy girl from Boston and had a daughter. They lived in New York, the city he seemed to love. He was then drafted as a pilot into the Air Force and onto active duty and was shot down during the Vietnam war and killed. I sometimes wondered if he ever thought back to that poor girl in Berlin.

When everyone woke up at the farm in Muenchen the next morning, everyone was pretty hungry but we got the best breakfast ever: pancakes, bacon and eggs and fresh milk, which was really enjoyed by both us and the children. We decided not to go into the city of Muenchen that day and to just let the children enjoy the farm life so they went horseback riding with the farm helper on the two ponies, watched the cow being milked and even searched for eggs in the chicken's nests—all of it a first experience for those children. They had a wonderful day and so did I just watching them, as it reminded me of my grandparents' farm in Poland. By that evening everyone was exhausted so the priest decided to give them another farm day tomorrow. We did realise that one day we must see Muenchen, the capital of Bavaria, which is located by the River Isar in the south of Germany. It has many old buildings with museums and castles and is famous for the Marienplatz (St. Mary's Square) located in the old town of Muenchen with its "Glockenspiel" (clock tower) and, of course, famous for the "Octoberfest." We wanted to show them at least a little of the city and as it was all donated money, we were obliged to provide some degree of education because we were planning to make trips like that to other cities in Germany.

When we told the children about the trip into the city of Muenchen, they weren't too happy because they preferred to stay on the farm, but after the priest had explained that we wouldn't get money for other trips if we didn't do this one properly, they gladly agreed. The next day we went hiking, which they loved, and the next day was the trip to the big city of Muenchen. I really loved that trip, even though I was still hurting a lot. I felt there must have been a reason for what happened and that perhaps I should have opened those last two letters in case there was an explanation for his behaviour, but it was too late now.

Because our driver wasn't familiar with the roads in the inner city of Muenchen, we left early in the morning but in fact everything went very well and we got to the Marianplatz quite early. While we were walking around there, the children overheard some people talking in another language and asked the priest if they were speaking English, as they pronounced Muenchen differently, sounding like Munch. The priest tried to explain that it was English and that the names sounded different because the German language has "Umlauts" (groups of sounds) such as a, o or u with two little dots on top of each letter, or ae, oe or ue could also be used like Muenchen = Munch or Koeln = Cologne, and there are more cities with the Umlauts in Germany. I wouldn't have expected the children to understand, because I didn't either, but they certainly looked as though they did. While we were there we had a nice lunch of Schnitzel (a thin slice of veal or other lean meat coated with breadcrumbs and fried) and noodles and applesauce, and it was all delicious. After that the children went off to gift shops to buy souvenirs for their friends and families. With three of them we had to take extra special care as they were emotionally unstable, with two of them having lost their fathers in the war and one who had witnessed the rape of his mother. Most of the reason for the donations we received was so that we could take trips like these and help to make them forget the horrible things which had happened.

All in all, the day was a success and when we got home to the farm, dinner was ready and waiting for us—just cold cuts since we'd had the big meal at noon. Everyone was dead tired but it was a happy tiredness and we still had three days left at the farm for the children could do what they wanted. Of course, they chose to play with the animals and it was so rewarding to watch them. When the day came for us to leave and go back home, we thanked the farm owners and helpers, all of whom had been really great and treated us so well, and into the bus everyone jumped. We left West Germany to get to the East German border and then somehow that FREE feeling left me. Leaving West Germany wasn't too bad but getting into East Germany was never easy and we were all searched by the East German police, who even went through the children's souvenirs. It gave us a strange feeling: we were all Germans and yet in quite a short length of time we had been divided into two. It makes one wonder if that's all or whether something else will happen again. Anyway, we made it back onto the Autobahn and into West Berlin once again.

Even though we'd really enjoyed the short holiday it was quite nice to be home again and to start planning the next trip, which the priest said would be in about two months. It was going to be a different sort of trip with only seven children of around 12 or 13 years of age and we'd be travelling to Hamburg, a major port city in Northern Germany which was connected to the North Sea by the Elbe River. It would be quite different from the farm in Muenchen but with different children as well and we were looking forward to it.

Back on our course the next day, Rita wanted to know everything about the trip. We had now become quite good friends and I liked that as we had a lot in common and a lot to talk about. The only bad thing was that Rita smoked and I started as well. At that time we had no idea how dangerous smoking was nor how addictive and my father had also started smoking after we didn't have to sell cigarettes on the black market for food. At that time almost everyone smoked and I thought it was sort of "chic" to smoke while enjoying a cup of coffee. Rita and I talked about what we were going to do after we'd finished the secretarial course and we knew we'd have to look for work. Rita said she might leave for West Germany as it would be safer there. I still loved my hometown of Berlin very much but it was still in the middle of East Germany and the way the East Germans were behaving towards West Berliners at the borders, we really couldn't trust them. Sometimes I felt as though I was sitting on top of an active volcano which was ready to explode at any moment and Rita felt the same way. Even my father couldn't bring himself to start building or cleaning up our property in East Germany. The banks had started to give loans for property building but my father said that even if we put all our money together and took out a small mortgage, the same things could happen again and we would lose everything all over again. And how right he was! So, we waited and decided to just save our money for the time being.

It was almost a year since Wolfgang had left and I still had bad days but being busy with both a job and with my course definitely helped me to get my mind off him most of the time. Rita was a little more mature than I was and being with her also helped me. One evening she asked me to join her for a meal in a small diner close to the secretarial school. She said it would just be the two of us and I liked the idea so having decided to meet on a Saturday at 7 P.M., we met at the diner, found a nice table and had a cigarette and a coffee while we started looking at the menu. I noticed that she was smiling a lot that evening and then the door opened and in walked her boyfriend, Jonathan, and another young man and they both came straight to our table. I then realised why she'd been smiling but probably looked really stupid when Jonathan introduced his friend, Michael, to us. I glared at Rita and was quite mad at her but she explained later that she had to trick me like that or I would never have agreed to go.

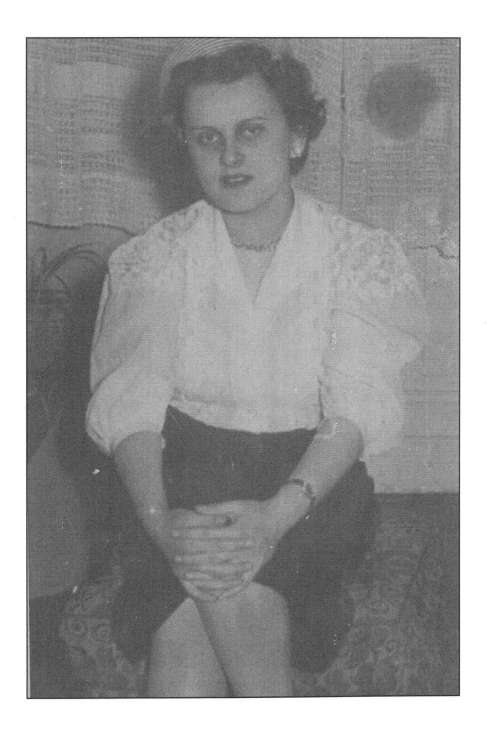

Well, I had to admit that Michael, who was a young soldier from San Francisco, was really quite good-looking. However, Rita's English was much better than mine as she was used to only speaking English with Jonathan and I found I had quite a hard time trying to talk to them in my broken "school" English. Even so, we had a nice dinner and talked a lot about the war and the States. Sadly, sitting and talking with them reminded me of what had happened to my doll, Edda, because of the American bombs and fighter planes and I felt strange sitting there talking to the two of them. I didn't say anything about it, but it bothered me. Maybe I still wasn't over my German puppy-love. As we were going in almost the same direction to get home, Michael walked with me but it only reminded me of walking with Wolfgang and holding hands. When we arrived, he thanked me for my company and asked if we could meet again soon along with Rita and Jonathan and I agreed, telling him to just let Rita know, but that evening was not one of my best-ever evenings.

I thought a lot about why I was behaving and feeling the way I was and I even tried to talk to the new priest about it but he was different from the other one and much younger and seemed to have other things on his mind, so Rita turned out to be a better listener. She explained to me that she wasn't in Berlin when it was bombed and taken over by Russian troops and had instead been in a little village in West Germany when the Allies took over West Germany, so her experience had been a lot less traumatic than mine had been in Berlin, the capital of Germany. She came to Berlin after the war ended to take care of her grandparents so she only really experienced the Air Bridge, which she thought was horrible. Our experiences had been very different and what with that and the shock over Wolfgang I would say I had post-traumatic stress disorder as the doctors would have diagnosed it in later years, although at that time the science hadn't been developed and what I had was just described as "shock." Maybe that was why I was trying to put myself behind a protective wall.

Anyway, Rita asked me how I'd enjoyed the dinner date with them and I had to agree that it was really nice and that I'd be prepared to do it again. She suggested that perhaps in a couple of weeks we could go and see a movie but because the movie was in the American Club where I'd had my first Coca-Cola with Wolfgang, I found I hesitated for a few minutes before I could agree to go. I then promised myself that I would fight that feeling of reluctance—after all, there was nothing I could have changed and I had to realise that it was all in the past. When the day of the movie came, Rita and I went to a thrift store to try and find something nice to wear. We found some really cute clothes and this time the dress wasn't too long, as the one had been when I had that date with Wolfgang. The three of them came and picked me up at home and Michael gave me a little bouquet of flowers, which was another "first" for me and made me feel special. The way we walked to the Club was pretty familiar as I'd walked it a lot before but our arrival was very different because since we were with uniformed American soldiers we didn't have to identify ourselves. That really impressed me as when I'd come to the Club with Wolfgang, we always had to show some kind of identification.

We watched the movie, which was some sort of war film and afterwards had a hotdog and a Coca-Cola before playing some games and walking home. Shortly before we reached my home, Rita and Jonathan went their own way, mostly I guessed because they wanted to be alone, so just Michael and I went on. He told me a lot about California, especially San Francisco where he'd grown up, and that he had two younger sisters and a father who was selling real estate, and he missed them a lot. He had two more years to stay in Germany and said with a smile that he hoped to stay in Berlin. When he left he said good night and gave me a kiss on my cheek then turned as he walked away and said, "Buenas noches, carino!" I wasn't sure but thought that was probably Spanish, so looked it up when I got home and found that, yes, it was Spanish, and meant "Goodight, sweetheart." I couldn't help laughing—he was behaving like a Spanish man and they're known for their charm! The next week on our course, I told Rita about it and she laughed as well and confirmed that his grandparents had immigrated from Spain. She said she had known it would take someone charming like him to get me out of my shell.

As it happened, we were busy at the time with our preparations for the trip to Hamburg, so when Rita suggested another date with the boys, I refused and let her know that although I'd like to go on another date with them, it would have to be later on when I got back, and not now. When Rita heard that she really laughed and said it would be a new experience for Michael to have someone refuse a date with him.

When we left our course the day before the trip to Hamburg, Rita asked me what time we'd be leaving in the morning and I told her we'd go about 8 A.M. as the distance to Hamburg was shorter than that to Muenchen, and she wished me a safe trip. Then, the next morning when I got to the church just before 8 A.M. and everyone was there ready to get onto the bus, an American jeep driven by a young soldier came around the corner and drove right up to the bus. I thought I wasn't seeing right but, yes, it was Michael and he jumped out and walked towards the bus and introduced himself to the priest saying his name was Michael and that he was also a catholic and came from San Francisco. He said he just wanted to give something to "that lady" for the trip and I was so embarrassed I could have crawled under the bus. It was a good thing the old priest wasn't there any longer. Anyway, he came over to me and gave me a hug and a small package, wished me a safe trip and jumped back into his jeep and drove off. Of course, everyone wanted to know what was in that package, including the priest, so I opened it and found there were crackers, Hershey's Kisses, and eight packets of cigarettes. As the priest was a heavy smoker, I gave him some of the cigarettes and he smiled and said, "Thank you," and that made me laugh because he said it in English and not in German. Even though I was embarrassed, I defended myself by telling myself that there was nothing wrong with what had happened and that it was just what friends do for each other. Was that Spanish charm tricking me into thinking like that?

We then left and the bus went through the same procedure of leaving West Berlin, entering East Germany, getting onto the Autobahn and then on to Hamburg. Hamburg and Muenchen are quite different—Muenchen is surrounded by mountains, the Bavarian Alps, and the famous port of Hamburg is on the North Sea. We were taken to a hostel where we were to stay for the week and although it wasn't as nice as the farm in Muenchen, it was quite an interesting area. It was decided that the next day we'd take a tour of the Hamburg harbour to look at the huge ships and tankers which gave the city the name "Gateway to the World" because from there you could cross the Atlantic Ocean and get to the East Coast of the U.S.A.

It was amazing to see it all and we stayed for lunch, which was a specialty of Hamburg—a fish sandwich with pickled herring. I loved it but although they ate it because they were hungry, our teenage group wasn't that excited by it. We filled the week in taking tours and looking at some of Hamburg's amazing architectural buildings but decided that perhaps it wasn't really the right sort of area for our teenagers and that our next trip should be more into the mountain region again. Anyway, the week was successfully over and we went back to West Berlin and home.

By this time Germany was officially divided into two nations: West Germany was the Federal Republic of Germany and had Bonn as its capital city and with that decision made there was no hope of any negotiations to reunite East and West Germany. Bonn is located on the river Rhein (Rhine) and is also famous for being the birthplace of composer and pianist Ludwig van Beethoven. The Soviets reacted quickly and they officially declared East Germany to be the German Democratic Republic with Wilhelm Pieck, a politician and a Communist, as their first President. All this meant that Berlin was no longer the capital city of Germany but it was still divided into East and West with East Germany now sitting in a separate nation. At least we had the first Berlin International Film Festival in June 1951 with the opening of Alfred Hitchcock's film *Rebecca*.

When we went back onto our course, we talked a lot about the future of West Berlin and with that about our future as well. The existing situation could go on for years, perhaps forever, and Rita didn't know what to do either. She felt she couldn't leave her grandparents alone but taking them to West Germany would be unbelievably hard as well as they were now already in quite advanced old age. It was all a worry, but something immediate that we had to look forward to was that Jonathan and Michael had asked us out for dinner the next weekend.

When they picked me up, Michael gave me a hug, saying, "Hola, mi novia" (Hello, my sweetheart), and "¿Comestuvo tu viaje?" (How was your trip?), so I looked at him and very politely asked if he would please stop talking Spanish; otherwise I'd have to walk around with a dictionary hanging around my neck so that I could answer him. He started laughing and just asked what language, then? I really liked the way he laughed but suddenly thought, *Oh, God, that's all I need—to start really liking him!* I sarcastically said how about Latin and he laughed again saying it was never his intention to become a priest but he answered in German that perhaps we should stick to English. I found I was really confused about his attraction as he was completely different from Wolfgang, not only was he always in a good mood and happy-go-lucky but he was good looking, as well.

We walked again to the club and although there was no movie this time, there was a little dance floor and as everyone was 18 and older, we could all dance. The boys had somehow ordered a bottle of Sekt (champagne), which I'd never drunk before, so I was quite giggly and laughing and when the music started we got up onto the dance floor straight away. We were dancing slowly and quite closely but the other couples were dancing the same way, so I didn't give it any thought. Then it was after 10 P.M. and we were on our way home and the boys were saying that on our next date we should go somewhere else to a nicer restaurant or bar. Like last time, Jonathan and Rita went their own way, so just Michael and I went on to my house. When we arrived, he looked at me quite seriously and gave me another kiss, but this time not on the cheek, and told me I was very nice and very cute and then he left.

I found it hard to get to sleep that night, constantly thinking about Wolfgang and Michael and how different they were. Yes, Michael was a little older than Wolfgang but, more importantly, they had grown up in completely different lifestyles. Wolfgang and I both grew up in wartime and Michael had been in safe surroundings even though his parents had divorced and he and his two younger sisters lived with his father. The way he explained his growing up, money wasn't an object and although his mother had remarried they were all on good terms. I started to think then that perhaps Wolfgang's relatives and parents had meant well in not letting me go to the States—perhaps thinking I was too young to handle such a different lifestyle and even possibly worrying that I would miss my parents too much. Whatever their reasons, it made me feel a little better about them.

The priest was planning the next trip which was to be with emotionally disturbed children, but then word came through that donations weren't coming in like they had before, so we couldn't afford to take the trip for the time being. We were all disappointed and the priest even mentioned that it would be a good idea for us to look for some other part-time jobs. As our secretarial course was almost finished anyway, I decided to start looking for a job. Rita was in the same position and as we talked about it we realised it probably wasn't too hard to find a job at that moment because a lot of younger people had left West Berlin to go to West Germany, Canada or Australia.

The tension between the Soviets and the Allies was growing so there wasn't a great future for West Berlin, even though West Germany and West Berlin were developing much faster than the East. Because of that and because of the better living conditions on the West side, sometimes people from the East tried to move over to West Berlin but were stopped at the borders and sent back. This resulted in hate and anger developing in the East and a pretty unstable situation altogether. Rita was quite unhappy with the overall outlook and the only joy we had was when the weekends came and we could go on those dates and have fun, dancing and laughing.

The next weekend was different. Jonathan had asked Rita to tell me that he was on a training exercise in West Germany for the next three weeks, which surprised me even though I had noticed on our last date that Michael was behaving differently. Rita and Jonathan asked me to join them for dinner anyway, but I declined because I knew it was the only time they had to themselves. I occupied myself writing resumes and helping at the church as a volunteer and generally keeping as busy as possible, but I smoked more! Two weeks went by and Rita and I were still trying hard to find a job after the course finished. I hadn't heard anything from Michael, but then I couldn't really as we had no phone and the mail wasn't the fastest, either, even if he had my address—which I wasn't sure of.

It was then only a week to go until he was supposed to be back from West Germany or wherever he was, when I went onto the course and Rita gave me an envelope with a single red rose. She said Jonathan had given it to her to give to me from Michael. I opened the letter and it was written in German saying he missed me. I was totally confused but Jonathan just said he'd be back soon.

When the three weeks since I saw Michael were up, I asked Rita if we were all going out that weekend and she said yes, as far as she knew and that Jonathan had said Michael was able to get the jeep, so we didn't need to walk and could even go a little further to find a different restaurant or bar. I wondered if Michael would actually come or whether he'd found another training he had to do but Rita reassured me and said she was sure he'd be coming.

During that week a met a former classmate of mine who had met her American boyfriend shortly after the war was over. He was an African-American who came from Texas and he told her all sorts of stories about what a nice house he had along with his cars and a good job. She believed him, of course, because we weren't aware of the American lifestyle and anything was better than living in Berlin. Anyway, she followed him to Texas and that was the last I heard of them until now when here she was with the cutest little girl and I asked her if she was back on holiday. She just looked at me and said no, that she'd come back to her parents in Berlin because her boyfriend's stories had all been lies. There hadn't been a proper house—more of a shack without even any running water and he also didn't have a job and just hung around with his friends drinking beer. She had then discovered she was pregnant but her boyfriend didn't want to get married so she did the only thing she could and wrote to her parents begging them to get some money to her so that she could come home. Her parents had been against her going in the first place but were very understanding and sent the fare money straight away so that the baby could be born in Germany instead of in the U.S.A. Stories like hers were heard quite often but despite it all, she was just so happy to have the little one.

That week I received two job offers—one as a secretary on a Workman's Compensation Board and the other as a cashier at a Health Insurance Company. I was really happy, particularly about the Health Insurance one, which also paid more, so I thought I'd go for that one. At the same time, Rita found a job too as a secretary in the bookstore. That was a really great week!

On Saturday, the "date day," I started to wonder if they would come because they usually came about 7 P.M. and when it reached 7.30 I had just about started to give up hope when I heard a car honking and there they were. There were also a lot of people looking out of their windows—they'd never seen the jeep and their big question was who the American soldiers were about to pick up. Well, I had to go out of the house somehow, but you could see their disbelief when Michael jumped out of the jeep and opened the door and gave me a hug and all the heads turned away from their windows while Jonathan and Rita sat in the back, laughing. We drove a little further away this time to a nice, cosy restaurant and bar where they even had live music. Michael and I didn't talk a lot and I didn't ask him how the training had gone, we just enjoyed a great dinner with a glass of Sekt and also really enjoyed the music. We were dancing to a slow Foxtrot and could hardly move when all of a sudden Michael asked me, "How is my little bird doing?" and again he laughed, or rather—smiled—maybe he knew how much I liked his smile. I was so nervous I could hardly talk and I'm sure he noticed because he held me even closer than before. I was relieved when the dance was over, said I had a really bad headache and asked them if they'd mind taking me home. I don't think they minded so we left and dropped Rita and Jonathan off where she lived with her grandparents. Now Michael and I were alone in the jeep, just driving home and I couldn't think why I was such a nervous wreck. I suddenly started to cry and we just looked at each other and Michael called me his "little bird" and said that everything was fine and we'd see each other the following week. He said we'd be alone and that he had something to tell me, then gave me a kiss on the cheek before I got out and he drove off. I didn't know what he meant and couldn't wait to see Rita and talk it over. Anyway, the next week at the course, Rita gave me a letter from Michael. This is the letter:

"Darling,

Told you on our last date, I have to talk to you alone. I am completely honest with you, never intended to date you. Rita and Jonathan told me about you and what you went through during the war and with Wolfgang. They asked me if I would take you out on a date, but not to tell you about the plan. I agreed but mentioned not for too long since I am dating someone else right now.

"But I fell in love with you after dating you a few times. You are so different from the girls I knew before, especially American girls, you are so innocent and sweet. I am promising nothing, marriage, money, etc. I love you and I want to be with you. I saw in your eyes that you care for me too.

"I will be at your house next Saturday to pick you up. I stayed away from you for those three weeks to find out my feeling for you.

"If you will be there next Saturday, I will be very happy. If not, it wasn't meant to be.

"Michael."

After reading that letter, I cried and cried and demanded to know why Rita had done that to me. She apologised and explained that she and Jonathan had felt very sorry for me, had come up with the idea to make me laugh again. Jonathan knew Michael from the barracks and he was known as a very charming guy and a bit of a womanizer, but was sure to make me laugh again even though he was dating another girl. In the meantime he had dropped her, which they thought was wrong, unless of course I did care for him. I just nodded.

I read the letter over and over again and couldn't wait for the next day so that I could talk more to Rita about it but to my surprise Jonathan was there as well. They obviously felt very bad about the whole situation and hadn't thought Michael would react like he did if they talked to him. Or, perhaps he was just playing a role for whatever reason. I told them to look at the letter and asked why he was mentioning that he wasn't promising marriage or money—I didn't want money, or marriage for that matter—maybe it was just another Spanish trick of his to get what he wanted. I said that in my eyes he was just a spoiled brat and that I felt sorry for the girl he had dropped, if indeed it was true that he had dropped her. Rita and Jonathan then told me that he'd just said in the letter about marriage and money because he knew that's what had been offered by Wolfgang and his mother, and of course I had no answer for that. Rita then asked if I would be meeting Michael on Saturday and that was another question I couldn't answer. She kept reminding me that nobody knew what would happen to us in West Berlin—we might be overrun by the Soviets again, ending up under Russian control, or in Siberia, some concentration camp, or even dead—and that we should try to get some happiness while we had the chance as nobody knew what tomorrow would bring. She pointed out that Michael wasn't a bad guy and that he liked me a lot; also that they thought I liked him just as much. I thought about it and then told Jonathan to tell Michael that, okay, the "little bird," as he called me all the time, would fly out of the house on Saturday at 7 P.M. to talk about the misunderstanding. All the time I was saying it, I was just thinking to myself, *Please, Dear God, don't let Michael smile at me again.*

As it was only Monday and we had the whole week ahead of us, Rita made the suggestion that we go to the thrift store to see if they had any nice clothes, saying I needed something pretty for my "misunderstanding date" and she needed something too, for her Saturday date. So we went and I found a very pretty blue dress which fitted me perfectly. I thought it was a little daring with its deep neckline but Rita loved it and said it looked fine. We also found a pair of white shoes with a little heel and although I'd only ever worn sneakers before, Rita convinced me that they looked very pretty and I should have them. When I walked, I felt I was walking like a duck but I bought them anyway and Rita also found something nice to buy.

When Friday came around my mother saw the new clothes and asked me if we were going somewhere special. She knew about our Saturday dates and I explained that Michael had the jeep and we would all go a little further afield—maybe to Lake Wannsee. That was a really nice area and was also in West Berlin, which it had to be because Jonathan and Michael, being American, were not allowed to enter the East. I didn't tell her that only Michael and I were going. On Saturday afternoon I got ready and at 7 P.M. said goodnight to my parents and told my mother I might be a little later tonight. She looked at me and said, "I love you very much, my little baby girl," and I realised she somehow knew we were going alone.

When I looked out the window, Michael was there already, this time wearing his uniform. He looked handsome, very handsome, and I was scared to death walking towards him in my white duckling shoes. I made it safely to the jeep though and, yes, he smiled and that was all I needed. He gave me a red rose again and asked if I knew the Wannsee Complex, which I'd heard about but being a German citizen, wasn't allowed to enter unless I was with an American escort. I started to talk about his letter but he countered by saying it was rather stupid of him to have written it and asked if we could discuss it over dinner. It took us quite a while to get to the complex but it was lovely—located right on the lake with a cosy restaurant and a bar with live music and with a small hotel in the background. It was all very beautiful but mostly I had to concentrate on those duckling shoes so that I didn't fall flat on my face.

As soon as we went in, I realised why Michael wore his uniform as no Germans were allowed in, perhaps because we lost the war. It was a very exclusive environment and pretty dark, too, but I saw quite elegant ladies sitting there and felt about 15 years old, which I think Michael realised because when I looked at him I had the feeling his eyes were smiling at me. I started to talk about the letter but he interrupted me again because he'd ordered a bottle of Sekt and somehow I had no chance to bring it up again. The way he behaved and handled everything made it seem as if he'd just grown up with it. The music started to play and he asked me to dance and I somehow managed to ignore the blisters which had already appeared on my feet and have one dance before our dinner came. I don't know what it was but I could eat very little and had to pretend that my stomach wasn't feeling very good.

All of a sudden he asked me why I never wore a wristwatch and when I said, "Because I don't have one," he produced a small box and opened it and out came the most beautiful wristwatch. "This is for you, little bird," he said—"from now on you'll always know what time we meet." I didn't know what to say and really now felt like a little bird trying hard to hide in the nest. I said I needed some fresh air and suggested we walk a little and at that moment I think I really fell in love with him. Getting up and leaving the restaurant reminded me of my duckling shoes, the blisters and the pain, so I just took them off and started to walk barefooted. Michael looked at me, took me in his arms and said, "My little bird, I really love you; please stay with me tonight," and I knew I didn't want to go home.

Driving home the next day, I realised how beautiful the whole area was and that just across the lake was Eastern Germany that was so hard to get into.

Michael said that he wanted to apologise to my parents for not taking me home last night and although I wasn't sure it was such a good idea, he insisted on coming in with me. It was Sunday morning and my father had gone to church, so it was my mother who answered the door and let us in. Michael introduced himself in broken German and tried to explain why I hadn't gone home last night, saying he'd had some Sekt and didn't want to drive the jeep in case he was stopped and checked by the military police. I'm sure his smile helped a lot because my mother just smiled back at him and said, "Okay." We knew it was a white lie and I'm sure my mother did, as well, but she didn't say anything then and in fact never talked about it again and I was so grateful to her. Having got that over with, Michael drove off telling me he'd stop by the college tomorrow.

The next day at the course Rita just asked me if I was alright and if everything was okay, and I just said that yes, everything was fine. She mentioned that her grandfather wasn't feeling well and that she might go home early if I'd be alright on my own. I said I'd be fine and just mentioned that Michael might be dropping by later. She did go home early and when Michael arrived he smiled and looked quite happy. I told him about Rita's grandfather and he asked if there was anything he could do but I really didn't know either. He then had an idea and asked me if I knew about the PX Stores. (The PX Store is an all-'round store selling most things, but mostly food and accepting only US Dollars.) It was there for American soldiers, or rather the Allies, and no Germans were allowed in except with an American escort. I told him I'd heard about it and he suggested that when I'd finished we could go to one which was just around the corner and buy something for Rita so that she didn't have to cook that day. I really liked the idea so later on we drove there and it was huge. They seemed to sell almost everything and it was also cheap. The food tended towards the American style but they did have German food as well and we bought fried chicken, macaroni salad and a few other goodies and took it all over to Rita. We were surprised to find Jonathan was there as well and he'd done the same thing, so Rita and her grandparents had plenty of food. Rita had called the doctor and said he would be coming the next day to look after her grandfather.

With that, we left and Michael asked me if we could do the same thing for my parents as well—perhaps go shopping once a week or so and then he could eat a typical German meal with me and my parents if my mother would cook it for us, which I thought it was a great idea. When we got home Michael said he didn't know what day he'd stop by as he had to go to the British sector to deliver some papers but that I should tell my parents about the PX idea and perhaps we could go on Friday. He also said that Saturday was "Date Day" with or without Rita and Jonathan and I really felt I didn't understand the world any longer—but in a very happy way.

Rita came to college a little later the next day because the doctor had been in to check on her grandfather. He hadn't been able to find what was wrong and thought it might be his heart, so he had to go to the hospital to be checked. With all of that going on, Rita was pretty busy, so I helped her as much as I could. As there were only a few weeks of my course left, I made the decision to get the job with the health insurance people and Rita decided on the job at the book store, so at least that was taken care of.

The night before I'd talked to my parents about Michael's offer to buy some food at the PX. They felt embarrassed but I convinced my mother that she would be working for it as she was the one who had to cook for us and so she eventually agreed. I told Michael their decision the next day and we went to the PX Store. Michael was buying a whole lot of food and I had to stop him, explaining that we didn't have a refrigerator and couldn't store all that food without it going bad. It was hard for him to comprehend that we didn't even have an icebox and he slowly began to understand the two completely different lifestyles we had. I guessed that he'd spent quite a bit of money and asked him if a soldier's pay was that great because if it was I would apply for a job at the barracks, but he just said his pay wasn't that good but his father helped him out a lot. My mother was really overwhelmed with all that food and wanted to know when we would like her to use it and we decided to wait until sometime the next week, as tomorrow was our "Date Day." We stopped by at Rita's after the shopping but, sadly, she wasn't able to join us because of her grandfather's condition and because she couldn't leave her grandmother alone.

Michael then told me about his trip to Gatow saying it was a very pretty place in the south west region of West Berlin at the Havelsee Lake and was surrounded by forests and beautiful parks. Gatow Airport was under British Control and had played a big role during the Berlin Airbridge when the allies were flying supplies into West Berlin. I told Michael I'd never been there because it was quite a distance away and with no one there to visit, I'd had no reason to go. He then mentioned that they also had a Gatow Complex, like the one we stayed in at Wannsee Complex, only available to the Allies and their escort, if any. He didn't look at me while saying this but suggested perhaps we should have dinner there tomorrow. He said his only problem was what to tell my parents when he took me home: could he say the same thing had happened and he was unable to drive me home because he'd had too many drinks again?

The next Saturday he picked me up a little earlier and his face was so serious that I couldn't help laughing. I told him not to say a word, and that I had told my parents and talked to them properly for quite a long time the night before. They had already known what was coming and didn't approve or disapprove and I really thanked them for that.

All Michael could say was "Oops, thank God!" Years later my mother told me that they had been glad for me and that made me laugh all over again. Michael had picked me up earlier because it was quite a drive to where we were going and it was really similar to the Wannsee Complex with almost the same atmosphere except that this time I wasn't such a nervous wreck. Michael ordered a bottle of white wine which I liked better than the bubbling Sekt and the music was nice so we were able to dance a little more, especially as I was wearing better shoes and not those duckies. Michael ordered steak and I had fish—he was surprised I didn't order steak as well and I explained that I wasn't used to eating a lot of red meat; that we only ate red meat on Sundays as there wasn't much available during and just after the war and then I only had a little piece as my father had the biggest portion. He was a very good listener and what I was saying was all new to him, the same as the way he treated me was completely new to me, and he slowly became my best friend.

It was a lovely weekend and with Christmas approaching, it was already getting chilly and wouldn't be long before the beginning of another year, though Michael and I both avoided talking about it because it would most likely be his last one before returning home to the States. I just reminded him that he was going to experience a German Christmas which would be different from those he'd known before. On our way home from Gatow we stopped by at Rita's and found Jonathan was there too. Her grandfather was improving, so might be coming home fairly soon. I was reminded of my own grandfather and Aunt Maria and wondered how they were doing in East Germany. Rumours were going around about revolts in East Germany and people were unhappy with their living conditions compared to West Berlin and West Germany. The inspections and security checks at the borders had become stricter and Michael said even the security around the barracks had tightened up. Luckily, he was still able to use the jeep if needed and we needed it a lot while we all tried to help Rita and her grandparents. I applied for the healthcare job and was told that for the first three months, it was only for half a day. That was alright as I knew I had to start somewhere and it was arranged that I would start at the beginning of the new year.

We had arranged for the German dinner at home to be on the Wednesday of the next week and I asked my mother what she was thinking of cooking. She thought she would make Rouladen, which is tender rolls of sliced beef filled with pickles, onions, mustard and bacon, cooked with red cabbage and potato dumplings and with homemade applesauce for desert. It would be different for Michael and I wondered what he would think of it. Wednesday duly arrived and so did Michael with a nice bouquet of flowers for my mother and a bottle of wine for my father, while I got my single rose. The table was set and we were ready to eat and my father, as usual, said a short prayer in German while Michael just sat quietly. I was surprised how much he ate and he told my mother how good it all tasted but there wasn't a lot of conversation as Michael just had his broken German and my parents couldn't speak a word of English. Despite that, though, nobody felt uncomfortable, which was the most important thing. After dinner Michael looked around and seeing that there was no dishwasher, he joined in and helped with the washing-up.

We then went for a drive and Michael started to talk about how good he felt sitting with a family. He had grown up not having a real family, as his parents divorced when the children were still little and with his mother gone it was just him and his two small sisters. His father had girlfriends but never remarried. It was much as I had expected so I was glad he liked our little family. We talked for a long time and one of the things he said was that he couldn't believe what he was told when he came over to Germany: that we were their enemies and not to be trusted, that the Allies had won the war and the Germans should more or less do as they were told. I told him that I hated them because we'd lost everything through them, even the only doll I ever owned, Edda. I think he might have felt a little guilty at that moment but he understood and all these talks we had brought us very close together.

I also talked to him about my grandfather and Aunt Maria and her four children and he said he'd like to visit them but not in East Germany with him being an American soldier. He suggested perhaps we could meet them in East Berlin instead of East Germany and wondered if it would be possible for him to get a permit by saying they were his relatives.

I wrote to Aunt Maria telling her our idea and that Michael, an American soldier, would also come—the idea being that we would meet somewhere in East Berlin and I asked her to let me know what she thought. It took quite a while for her to answer and when she did she said that she didn't think it would work, partly because my grandfather couldn't make it for health reasons, and partly because the children might say in school that they'd met an American soldier—in other words, she was scared. It was then that I realised the system was working and there was a definite split between East and West, even amongst relatives. Michael asked his Commander about visiting East Berlin and was told he would be allowed to go but that I couldn't go along with him. The Commander also said that he didn't recommend going, anyway, as there were sometimes problems at the border and so in the end we decided it was too dangerous and that we wouldn't go.

As the weeks went by we were approaching the Advent, one of the nicest times of the year. Michael experienced a cold Christmas for the first time and unlike California, we thought we might even have snow on Christmas Day. We hoped to get a nice Christmas tree but there wasn't much to buy in the way of decorations so we decided to check out the PX Store for those and were lucky enough to find a small tree and also decorations. I had to explain to Michael that we celebrated Christmas Eve—going to church late in the afternoon and then opening presents when we got home and also that we actually had two days of Christmas. I then asked him if he'd like to join us and he said he would and that it would be very special for him. I was hoping he would join us at church—the Mater Dolorosa Church—so that I could show him where I was born. My mother would then cook the meal and after opening the presents we'd all sit down to our usual Christmas Eve dinner of potato salad and wiener sausages. I told my mother our plans and she agreed. We also told Rita and Jonathan our plan since Michael had invited Rita and Jonathan to Complex Wannsee for a big Christmas party being held for American soldiers. It sounded great; we only hoped it would snow a little.

I couldn't decide what present to buy for Michael and when I mentioned it to Rita she said she was buying Jonathan a sweater, so I decided to buy one for Michael as well. The only store we could think of was the Thrift Store and we were lucky enough to find two pretty good looking sweaters, one in white for Michael because he had dark hair, and a blue one for Rita to give Jonathan, who had light brown hair. We never told them where we'd bought them! The day before Christmas Eve Michael asked what time he should pick us up to go to church so I realised he was really coming to the church with us. We said about 4.30 because the service started at 5 P.M. I then decorated the little tree, put Michael's present under it and also some chocolates for my mother and some cigarettes for my father. The next day Michael picked us up as arranged and we drove to church, where all of us were quiet. I was remembering Wolfgang and Michael seemed to know that and just held my hand. The Mass was short and afterwards I showed Michael where I was born before we continued back home. It was all very new for him. When we got home we opened our presents—my mother got a beautiful vase, my father a bottle of Whiskey, and I got a beautiful pair of earrings shaped like a heart with a tiny, tiny, diamond in the middle. We then had dinner while our little radio played Christmas music and although he didn't say anything, I don't think Michael really enjoyed the dinner at all. Also, my father had never had a whiskey drink, but regardless of all, it was a Happy Christmas and after helping with the clearing up, we left to pick up Rita and Jonathan.

We gave Rita's grandparents lots of sweets and then all drove off towards Complex Wannsee. It was now getting quite chilly and we all hoped it might snow. When we arrived there was a huge, very American, party going on and it was the first such occasion for Rita and Jonathan, who loved it. The music was wonderful, too—American Christmas songs and I really liked "White Christmas" by Bing Crosby. I remember wondering to myself what kind of Christmas next year would bring and while we were dancing, Michael told me he'd written Christmas cards home to his father and sisters and he'd told his older sister that he'd met a little bird in Berlin.

When he told me that, my mouth dropped open. I didn't dare ask him what she'd said but of course he wouldn't have got a reply yet. It was a lovely Christmas and Rita was happy again, too.

The next week was a busy one: Michael had changed duties with someone else and was off-duty and as there was a little snow on the ground we went to Wannsee, which is a little hilly, and tried to get a sleigh. We had wanted to go sledding but gave up before breaking our legs and decided on sightseeing instead. We went to see the Kurfuerstendamm, which Berliners call the Ku-Damm, Berlin's famous shopping boulevard, which was still showing war damage but had been slightly repaired and cleaned up by Berlin's "Truemmerfrauen." Close to the boulevard was the Kaiser Wilhelm Gedaechtnis Kirche (Emperor Wilhelm Memorial Church) one of West Berlin's famous landmarks, with its damaged church tower a sad reminder of the destruction caused by war. We walked all around there and ahead of us was the Berlin Zoo. It was lucky that all those famous landmarks were located in West Berlin so at least we were able to visit them.

Also at Christmastime, they have a Christmas market where they serve Gluehwein (Glow Wine) for people who have started to get cold because you definitely start warming up and glowing after a few small glasses of it. It's mostly drunk in December when it's cold; I don't think anyone could handle it when the weather's warm. It's made out of warm, dry red wine which is combined with some sugar, whole cloves, cinnamon sticks, and anise, and it's optional to add Rum or Amaretto into it, which would make you glow pretty fast. It's a German tradition, a bit like eggnog in the States. Michael couldn't believe all of it and he behaved like a little kid—too many Glow Wines, maybe? Thank God, he left the jeep at home! We had so much fun and to make it perfect, it snowed.

There was still a lot to do before New Year's Eve. One of Michael's friends had a German girlfriend whose parents owned a house in the Wannsee district, which, although damaged, was still livable and they allowed us to celebrate the New Year there. We were about sixteen people, including Rita and Jonathan, and everyone had to bring something to eat and drink, but no fireworks were allowed. For that the PX Store was perfect and everyone was looking forward to the party with nobody trying to think of the year ahead. We got there early and were able to decorate a little and even had a record player with some American songs to dance to. None of us knew each other so we introduced ourselves, which was easy as the girls were all Berliners, then someone started the player and we could dance. Michael said, "The last dance of this year belongs to me, baby bird," and then we were all talking, dancing and laughing but I did notice that Michael was flirting a lot. Whenever I looked in his direction he noticed it and smiled that famous smile of his. When they announced that the last dance of the year was coming up, I wondered if he would remember and yes, he came over and asked me to dance—the song was "Because of You" by Tony Bennett. He asked me if I'd been jealous to see him flirting and I said of course not, that I hadn't even noticed but he answered that he wished I had been jealous and I had to laugh because I was. Then it was midnight and the New Year had begun, and a lot of tears with it!

That first day of the New Year was beautiful—cold but with a blue sky and snow on the ground and Michael and I decide to go out and walk a little. The way Michael had been really flirting the night before was still bothering me and although so far I hadn't said anything, he must have noticed how quiet I was. I suppose he knew me pretty well by then and just asked me outright if it was his flirting last night. When I answered "yes" he said he'd done it on purpose to test my reaction and see if I'd do the same thing. I thought I was hearing wrongly but then he said there was a reason for it, because if I really cared for him he wanted to ask his commanding officer if he could get an extension to stay in Berlin for another year. I asked what would have happened if I had done the same and he just said, "Don't ask," so apparently I passed the test! He said it would give us a chance to get to know each other better but he already thought I really liked him. He said another reason was that before he came to Germany he'd heard it said that German Fraeuleins were easy to get and not to get serious with them. I didn't know what to say and wondered if that extension could really happen but apparently his father and his commanding officers were good friends from San Francisco and that was the reason he had so many privileges like getting the use of the jeep and getting off duty whenever he had to. Anyway, if it happened it would be a dream come true so in a way we were both glad he'd flirted that night.

That New Year's Eve there was some shooting not too far from where we were—apparently two men from East Germany tried to flee and were swimming to get to West Berlin when they were caught and shot. Because of that there was tension all over West Berlin and talk about whether that could start another war. West Berliners were already getting used to sitting in a "cage" without much hope of the situation ending.

I finally started my new part-time job as a cashier at the healthcare studio and found actually working was quite different from going to school. Not much could be done electronically with calculators or type-writers and I really had to use my brain; a good thing it was only for half a day. There was nothing like online banking or just sending a cheque by mail, the members had to visit in person to pay their monthly dues in cash. Sometimes we had lines of people waiting and the worst thing that could happen was that if you had more money left at the end of the day, it meant you'd cheated a member. If you had less money at the end of the day, you were okay as they just took the money that was missing out of your paycheck. It was sometimes frustrating. Rita's job at the bookstore was easier as not so many people were coming in to buy books. Even though the first week went by quite quickly, everyone was looking forward to the weekend and the four of us decided to go back to Complex Wannsee again just to have dinner and relax a little. When they picked me up on Saturday, Michael told me he'd spoken to his Commander about his extension and was straight-away asked, "German Fraeulein?" When Michael said yes, the Commander said it could probably be arranged for one year and then also said they were having a party in two weeks' time, that Michael was invited and why didn't he take me along? Right away we knew it was a test to judge me, but we had to go and after Michael smiled at me, I knew I could do it. Meanwhile, the weekend was lovely again and we were rested enough for the coming week and I also still had two weeks before the devastating dinner party at the home of the commanding officer and his American wife, who Michael said lived in the upmarket district of Dahlem, close to the American Embassy.

Everybody was busy during the next week; it was always the week-ends which were the highlight, especially as I hardly even talked to Rita now that she had her full-time job. Michael had stopped by the apart-ment telling me he'd pick me up on Saturday at the usual time and then we could decide what to do and then when he picked me up, Rita and Jonathan were too busy to join us, so we went again to Complex Wannsee. He mentioned that he'd had letters from his younger sister and his father and that neither of them had mentioned me, which didn't bother him as his older sister might not have told them about me. All that week I was thinking about what I was going to wear to the dinner party. My clothes were all from the thrift store, though Michael didn't know that. In the end I just asked Michael and he said he'd been thinking about it too and that if I liked he'd pick me up from work on his day off and we could go and look for something. That really took a load off my shoulders as I wanted to look pretty, but not to look or behave like a "German fraeulein," especially after what I'd heard said about us.

Rita knew I was nervous about the dinner party and on Monday evening she came by to see how I was doing. I told her about going shopping for something to wear and that I was worried about how to pay for it, but Rita said that perhaps Michael would help out with that. Rita knew me well and knowing how much of a nervous wreck I could be, she mentioned that her grandmother had some prescription medication which she took if she got nervous or upset and suggested that if she got one of the pills for me, I might be more relaxed. We laughed a lot over the idea and thought perhaps I should just try half a pill on the Thursday as an experiment and then if I was okay, I could take the other half before the dinner party.

On Tuesday Michael picked me up to go shopping and I warned him I didn't have many Deutsch Mark to spend, to which he replied that he had a few dollars left and we could use those if I promised to wear the heart-shaped earrings he'd given me for Christmas, so the deal was done. We headed towards Kurfuersten Damm and I thought to myself, *Oh my God, nothing is cheap there*—but then remembered that in some stores you could pay with American dollars or Deutsch Mark. Michael was wearing his uniform and the sales ladies were very friendly and helpful to us because we'd most likely be paying in dollars and I felt so much like a "German Fraeulein" that it was embarrassing for me. Michael was alright though and not embarrassed; perhaps he was flirting but if he was I didn't see it. In the end we bought a very nice simple winter dress and a beautiful winter coat—both simple but quite elegant and I had to admit that I liked myself in them.

Then Thursday arrived and with that the trying out of the half pill, which I took after I got home from work. Perhaps an hour later I started to feel calm and relaxed and that lasted somewhere between four and six hours before I was back to myself again and quite nervous. Nevertheless it was a great feeling that I could take the other half before the party and would be alright. I told Rita the result on the Friday and she just laughed and said he hoped her grandmother wouldn't miss the one pill.

Michael picked me up on Saturday evening and told me I looked really pretty. I don't know if he meant it or not but it really didn't bother me as I was under the influence of that half pill. He had bought a beautiful bouquet of flowers and some wine for his boss. When we arrived at the house, security guards opened the gates for us and I thought to myself what a difference it made whether you won or lost a war, then a maid opened the door for us and his boss, Mr. Daniel McCallister, asked us in. He must have been in his late forties and I felt his eyes looking over me but it didn't matter as I'd swallowed that pill, thank God. He took us into the living room where the furniture was out of this world, at least to me who was used to so little and things like my recliner bed. There were three or four other couples and Mrs. Elena McCallister. She was beautiful and a little exotic, perhaps in her mid-thirties, and when Michael introduced me as Theresa, she asked where I was from. I explained that I was actually Polish but had been born in Berlin and she said she had been born in Buenos Aires in Argentina and had met and married Daniel there before moving to the States to California. She then introduced us to the other guests but I felt a complete outsider. Somehow Michael managed to always be close to me and fortunately they had a buffet-style dinner, so at least I could pick out the things I knew. Daniel's family had originally come from Ireland and he was a nice man and easy to talk to and I hoped I'd been accepted by him and the others. After about three hours everyone was ready to leave and Mr. McCallister said we must get together again and that Michael should bring me along as I was a nice girl. Mrs. McCallister also said goodbye to us and, to Michael, that it was nice seeing him again. Their eyes seemed to lock for a moment but I could have been wrong: maybe the pill was just wearing off.

At least the dinner party was over and the fresh week had begun but I hadn't heard from Michael since he took me home that last weekend. Rita stopped by just wanting to know how everything went and how I'd got on with the pill but I ended up telling her the whole story. I said how pleased I'd been to have the pill and also mentioned my suspicion after seeing the look between Elena McCallister and Michael, even though perhaps I was just being over-suspicious. Rita was quiet for a moment but then reminded me that Michael was known as a womaniser and that I'd have to either accept it or leave him. Apparently even Jonathan was surprised how long our relationship had already lasted even though all they actually knew was that Michael had been or perhaps still was going in and out of the McCallister's house even when Daniel was away on business trips. Rita pointed out that it was my decision alone and that I had to do whatever I could cope with. She didn't say any more but what she'd already said was really enough.

My parents' main doctor's office was near where we lived and when my mother had her next appointment there, the doctor asked her if I would be able to babysit their two small children from Friday night to Saturday night as his wife and he had to go to a convention on the other side of town. I jumped at the opportunity as it would give me time to think about what to do. On Wednesday Michael stopped by where I was working, it seemed just to see me and we went to a little café for coffee. We were both quiet to begin with but then he asked me if I'd enjoyed the dinner and what I thought of the McCallisters. I had to say something so just said what a beautiful woman Elena was and that the dinner was fine but not really my scene at the moment and that I had felt out of place. He didn't comment on Elena but just said that we wouldn't go any more if it made me feel uncomfortable. He also said he'd heard from his older sister, who asked him to say hello to me, and also that Daniel had told him the one-year extension had been granted but that, if need be, he would be able to leave at any time. It seemed he knew exactly how to handle me and just carried on by asking what we were going to do over the weekend. When I told him about my baby-sitting commitment he just smiled, said, "Okay, little bird," and that he'd stop by on Friday.

That night my father came home from work and told us about a lot of tension and revolts at the borders and that someone had told him that if it didn't stop they'd probably build a wall surrounding West Berlin so that neither East Berliners nor people from East Germany would be able to get out and enter into West Berlin or West Germany. Even though it was just a rumour, it was making Berliners jittery because then we would be really caged in, which would be terrible. The cold war between the Allies and Russia was escalating and we wondered what kind of future was ahead of us. When Friday came around, Michael picked me up and gave me a little package to open—inside was a crystalline little bird with a small piece of metal hanging around his neck saying "I love you." Well. At that moment all my suspicions went away. And he knew it.

The babysitting went well but while I was there the doctor told me the same story about the wall as my father had told. The doctor, however, said it couldn't be done—that you can't cage people behind walls. That night I'd had a lot of thoughts going through my mind. I was almost certain I couldn't leave Michael but, on the other hand, maybe he just wanted the extension in Germany because of Elena and not for me—perhaps I was just a cover-up. Even though we never talked about it, I think both of us knew what we were thinking. There were so many questions and I was glad to be by myself that night even though I still didn't come to any sort of decision. It was like looking at that little bird and thinking, *Shall I keep it? Or throw it out?* And that night there was another shooting at the border.

After thinking, rethinking and thinking again, I finally felt I was ready to talk with Michael. I somehow felt it was my fault as well because I'd always been that shy introverted little bird but I realised that was just the way I'd been raised. When I looked at my mother I saw that she was just like me and believed the man of the house was the boss: even if he was wrong, he was always right. My parents had been born and raised in a little Polish village and didn't know any other way and so they raised me exactly the way they'd been brought up themselves and even coming to a big city like Berlin couldn't change their upbringing. Being brought up that way, though, and then finding different lifestyles and influences like Michael was confusing and hard to understand and I felt I couldn't keep up with them and more than a little bit lost. It was obvious that I had to change my way of thinking and become a little more of an extrovert and more self-confident so that my nervousness would disappear. Maybe my brain was just developing its first "equal rights" movement but whatever it was, I knew I had to change. I had a long talk with Rita about how I felt and she completely agreed with me.

As there wasn't much time during the week, I took the next chance I had at the weekend and when Michael suggested spending the weekend at Complex Wannsee, I replied that I'd rather go to Complex Gatow and he agreed to it even though he looked surprised. That was my first try but what I really wanted was to talk to him about Elena because that situation was bothering me a lot. When I thought about it, whenever we were invited to a party, I'd have to worry if there was someone there he'd had or was having an affair with and I really couldn't cope with that, so whatever came out of our talk that weekend, I was ready to leave him and that thought felt good.

He picked me up that next weekend, smiling and happy-go-lucky as usual and looking very handsome but I wasn't nervous and even that "little bird" thing didn't bother me that much. On the way to Complex Gatow we were laughing and singing and I had the feeling he was glad I was his little bird again, but of course he didn't know what was on my mind. He told me his sister Janet had written again and told me to watch her big brother in Berlin and he showed me a picture of her—she looked beautiful and I could see a lot of resemblance to Michael. We arrived and got a nice table for dinner and because I just wanted to get it off my chest, I asked him outright if he was having an affair with Elena. He looked at me as if he had expected the question and immediately answered that, yes, he had had an affair with her, that she was the girl he mentioned in the letter—the one he had dropped because of me. He asked who'd told me and I just said I could tell from the way they'd looked at each other at the dinner party. He told me that from his side his affair with her was just passion but that she was still a bit shattered by the break-up and that's why he'd tried to stay close to me at the dinner party to avoid any problems. I still wasn't sure whether Daniel knew about it or not but I was relieved to have it out in the open between Michael and myself and since I was quite sure he was telling the truth, I felt I had a better chance of coping with it and even Michael felt relieved. I knew I still had to work on my self-esteem but also that things like that take a long time, sometimes a whole life. When I told Rita everything that had happened, she smiled and said I must really be something pretty special to him. For a little while we forgot the tension of the cold war.

Our lives suddenly became quite hectic with Rita's grandfather becoming ill again and having to go back into hospital and then my own father being diagnosed with diabetes, which meant he had to eat a special diet. Food for diabetics wasn't cheap at that time and Michael and I went to the PX Store quite often to get what he needed and our relationship grew a lot, especially as most misunderstandings had either been resolved or, at least, were out in the open. Then, also in March 1953, Joseph Stalin, the leader of the Soviet Union, died. It was he who had been their leader when the Russian troops took over Berlin and now a power struggle began in Russia with Nikita Khrushchev finally becoming the First Secretary of the Central Committee of the Communist Part of the Soviet Union. With that yet another scare and more tension developed within West Berlin, with everyone wondering in which direction Russia would go after Stalin. Of course, West Berliners were only living on rumours and even Michael didn't know anything concrete. The only thing we had left were our weekends, to talk and somehow regroup, and we even started to talk a little about our very uncertain future. About this time, Michael's sister Janet and myself started a correspondence between ourselves with just a little letter once in a while. She sounded really nice and had told her father about Michael and me but he hadn't commented in any way—either good or bad.

One day Michael came over and told me that there was another gathering coming up at the McCallisters'—a sort of spring celebration—and that he thought we should go if I could cope with it. After thinking about it I asked him if we really had to go, to which he more or less said "yes" so as I was feeling strong enough, I agreed to go—to which he smiled and said, "Okay, BIG bird." I then had two weeks to prepare myself emotionally for it and although Rita was a big help in guiding me along, there was no pill offered this time! When the time came, it was a beautiful spring day with "Lilac" (Flieder in German) one of my favourite spring flowers, out in full bloom. At the house everything was the same—security guard and maid at the door and Daniel there to greet us. He looked really tired and stressed out and the political unrest was obviously taking its toll but he was very kind to me and even gave me a hug, making me feel quite secure especially with Michael right there next to me.

The house was decorated like a flower garden and there she was—Mrs. Elena McCallister—as beautiful as ever. I would even say more beautiful than the last time and when she came right over to greet us I didn't even dare look at their faces. She said, "Well, there she is—your little Theresa—how nice to see you again," and as the music was playing she took Michael off straight away to the dance floor to start dancing. Daniel came right over to me and asked me for a dance and I guess he knew more about his wife and Michael than we had realised. He was really nice to talk to and asked me how we had got on when the Russians took over Berlin and whether anyone in our family had been hurt. I was able to say no to that but did tell him about the airstrikes and how we'd lost everything we owned because of them and he was very understanding, especially about the loss of my only doll, Edda.

Michael and Elena were dancing on the other side of the room but he kept looking in my direction and smiling when our eyes met and it was a very different situation from the last time. And I wasn't nervous. Well, maybe just a little! When the party came to an end we said goodbye and Daniel told us to stay in touch but Elena was nowhere to be seen. When we were in the jeep, Michael held me and said his little bird had become a big bird today but made me promise that I would always be his "little" bird. I couldn't remember ever having felt so happy and safe and secure.

Yes, I tried to be the BIG bird with the world but I was still a "little bird" with Michael. I received a letter from Janet telling me a little about their family, including the fact that Michael was always the favourite son and very spoiled by his father. Since their mother left, their father had taken care of almost everything and he was very proud of his son, whom he wanted to take over his Real Estate business. She also told me that, at school, he'd been very popular with the girls and I couldn't see why she would tell me that—was she warning me or was she just telling me the truth?

Janet also told me she was in college and wanted to become a nurse and also started to tell me a little about San Francisco. She told me about Alcatraz, a federal prison about 1.5 miles off shore, an island of 47 acres which was used only for notorious bank-robbers and murderers and which had once held Al Capone amongst its famous inmates. It was used for 29 years and rumours said that escape was impossible. 36 prisoners had tried but all of them were caught, killed, or drowned. She mentioned the Golden Gate suspension bridge—almost 1.75 miles long which connected Francisco with the Pacific Ocean and went on to say that if you wanted to eat fresh fish, Fisherman's Wharf was the place to go, and she even included pictures in her letters. To me it all sounded like a fairytale and I wished I could see all those pretty places—you could feel how proud she was to be living in such a beautiful city. When they were younger, Janet and her younger sister and Michael had travelled all over the United States with their father and I enjoyed reading about it all in those letters. She was my age and had seen most of the world, whereas we were just sitting in a cage.

Michael hadn't told me about all of what was in those letters, but for him it might not have been special because it was just the way he'd grown up. Our relationship was a very close and happy one and I just got used to seeing him look at any pretty girl who passed by. He spoiled me a lot and I believe that in his way he really loved me. The part-time part of my job was almost over but I decided to stay working part time for longer so that Michael and I could spend more time together. Rita also started only working part time in the bookstore because her grand-father by then needed a lot of care. It was a beautiful summer and as Michael could get a whole heap of time off duty, we spent quite a lot of it being outside at Lake Wannsee. Maybe Daniel was glad to get him away from his house and his wife! It was hard to understand how Michael had so many privileges compared with his comrades but maybe his father had just asked his good friend Daniel to take care of him. Sometimes we started to talk about our future but it was a subject that scared me and I really didn't enjoy those conversations even though Michael did—for him it was real, but not for me.

Politically, nothing had really changed that much with the power struggle still going on in the Soviet Union and still with disturbances going on at the border and in East Germany.

In June of 1953 construction workers in East Berlin took to the streets to protest for an increase in work schedules by the communist government of East Germany and there was rioting as the crowd swelled to between 30,000 and 50,000 workers. They called for a general strike, the resignation of the communist East German government and free elections. Soviet troops struck quickly and without warning and the army, supported by tanks and armed vehicles ploughed through the crowd of protesters who mostly fled, though some of them tried to fight back resulting in about twenty deaths and a hundred wounded. Most of the protesters had tried to reach the Red Cross in West Berlin and the Red Cross offices there opened up in support. The Soviet commanders declared martial law and by night time the protesters were shattered but it showed the world that East Germany and East Berlin weren't happy with their regime. Everyone in West Berlin believed another war would break out soon or that the rumour about the wall wasn't just a rumour.

Michael stopped by that afternoon for just a very quick visit and told me that all the Allies' soldiers and Officers were on high alert. He was very serious and maybe also a little scared and gave me US$100 in case I needed food or anything. Without him I wasn't able to go to the PX Store so now had money to buy on the black market as people were always happy to get dollars. I think both of us were scared but he promised he'd be back as soon as the danger was over or at least that he'd somehow let me know what might or would happen. That night it was very quiet and I think most people were even afraid to talk. I thought of Janet and how nice it must be to live in freedom and be able to go wherever you wanted, whenever you wanted.

Well, a few days passed by and everything was quiet. Rita and I met up but she didn't have any news of Jonathan either. Then, towards the end of the week, I was at home in the late afternoon when I heard Michael's jeep stopping and there he suddenly was, telling me the danger was over and so was the high alert as both the Allies and the Soviet Union were keeping quiet in order to avoid another confrontation which could lead to the possibility of another war. We took a long walk, not talking a lot but just being happy to be together. Jonathan was also back with Rita and as the weekend was coming up, the four of us decided to go to Complex Wannsee to celebrate being together. It was such a nice evening in June and we all wondered why people can't just live in peace. We had a nice dinner but it was somehow different from our other dates and even Rita felt the different atmosphere. Nevertheless, it was the most romantic and sweet evening for all four of us, with none of us knowing what the future would bring.

Following the uprise in East Berlin there was mass immigration to West Germany via West Berlin and riots and protests were starting in East Germany with general dissatisfaction characterising public life. The Soviet Army used military force to suppress the rioters and support the East German regime. In response the United States under the leadership of President Dwight D. Eisenhower, started to support the uprising with a food relief programme for East Germany which they called "The Eisenhower Package." Through it, the United States pledged to distribute millions of food packages to East Germans through East Berlin from distribution centres in West Berlin. The packages contained lard, peas, flour and pasteurised milk. In response to those "Food Packages," the East German government cut off rail and bus traffic to West Berlin, which led to even more tension, and tried to prevent people getting to the distribution centres to collect food. The "Eisenhower Package" ended in October 1953. That was another hit against West Berlin; we sometimes called it "Tense City" but mostly we were able to go to one of the complexes just to feel a little bit of freedom.

One night, Michael stopped by just to tell me that there was the possibility of him being able to stay one more Christmas in Berlin— from 1953 to 1954—but that would really be the last one. He gladly accepted that all we could do was to live from day to day, hoping for the best. We then received a letter from Aunt Maria telling us that grandfather wasn't in good health and that she and some friends who all had little farms in East Germany might move to East Berlin. Living conditions on the farms were bad and with grandfather unable to help her and with the four children to support, she was no longer able to handle the farm work. She thought she might get a job in the city to try and support them all but we couldn't think how she would handle all that having never lived in a big city. My father wrote back and said that if she did need to move, he would try and get a permit to go over to East Germany to help her but the way things were looking, he wasn't sure he'd be able to go there. Aunt Maria replied that with us being West Berliners, it might not be a good idea anyway and that really got me thinking of the damage a war can do—not only splitting countries and cities, but also families. Sometimes when I couldn't sleep at night, I thought back and wondered about people I knew: what had happened to Hannah and her family and whether they made it out of the country to safety or died in some concentration camp somewhere; or Julian— was he back in Paris again? And Wolfgang—was he happy with his new lifestyle? There were so many memories. A few weeks later, Aunt Maria wrote again saying that grandfather had died. And we couldn't even go to his funeral.

My mother had a hard time over not being able to attend her father's funeral, especially since they hadn't seen each other for a while. At the same time my father was still trying to find his parents whereabouts. He didn't know if they were still in Poland, or rather now Russia, on the little farm or if they'd been able to get out of there before the Russian troops took over Poland/ Germany. He'd done all he could and registered them with the Red Cross in the hope that someday they'd find us. West Berlin had calmed down a bit but there were still lots of riots and uprisings going on in East Germany. The borders had been tightened up even more but still people from the East tried to get into West Berlin any way they could. The Easterners used a new way to check for refugees in West Berlin and also going into West Germany: vehicles had to drive over a large board which had mirrors attached so that the police were able to check underneath the vehicles for people hiding there. Nobody trusted anyone and most of the West Berliners were saying they couldn't continue to live like that for the rest of their lives.

There were still a few months left before Christmas but what would happen after that we didn't know and actually didn't even care. Michael said he was just happy to stay for another Christmas with lots and lots of Gluehwein. Then one day he came over and told me his father might be getting married to a widow (apparently quite wealthy) who was also from San Francisco and had two grown-up children. Michael was really surprised and I didn't think he really liked the idea and then a few days later I received a letter from Janet telling me the same story and, reading between the lines, I got the impression she also had problems accepting the idea. I was getting along with Janet quite well as even though we were from such different backgrounds, we seemed to have a lot in common. I did wonder though why I always met well-to-do people when it was so exhausting for me to keep up the conversation and behaviour. At least I was trying to be the Big Bird to the outside world and that Michael found amusing and charming. The next big surprise was when Michael told me that after getting married in the fall, his father and his new wife planned to visit West Berlin—his father wanted to see Michael and, I had the terrible feeling, to check me out as by that time he knew about me. The Americans were able to fly into West Berlin on American more or less military planes and I figured Daniel had probably arranged that part of things. So, here I was again, getting ready for another test. When I said that to Michael he just laughed, saying Big Bird should know how to handle it by now. But nothing was set in concrete yet and there might still be changes.

I told Rita about it and right away she said, "I guess you'll need another pill if it happens!" In a way I was sad: why couldn't people just accept me as I was? When I talked to Michael about it he just commented that they meant well and were just trying to get to know me. Anyway, nothing was definite yet so I stopped worrying about it. We were still enjoying the summer weekends with long walks and lots of conversations and even the thought of Daniel and Elena's next get-together, which was coming up soon, didn't scare me anymore as long as I knew Michael would be next to me.

It was a pretty quiet week with nothing really drastic happening—just the routine shootings at the borders and riots in East Germany—I guess you get used to living in a war zone. Michael and I opted for Complex Gatow for the weekend, mostly because it was such a pretty drive to get there. We talked about his father getting married and he really hadn't got used to the idea. He was used to his father's girlfriends but they weren't living with them and now, being married, they would all have to live together. I think he was so used to being the number one that he was more than a little jealous and it was then that I realised that being an only child wasn't such a bad thing—you were always number one.

The music was really nice and I remember they played the song "That's Amore," sung by Dean Martin. I really liked his voice and as we were dancing I wondered if it really was "amore" or just that the situation of living in a war zone made one look for security and love. Michael must have read my thoughts because he looked at me and said, "No, it is real." The weekend was over much too fast but it gave me enough recreation to start the new week. At that time you didn't hear of people being overweight or obese or addicted to any kind of drugs, they were mostly skinny, depressed and hopeless and very fearful of the future. I received a lovely letter from Janet, saying how much she would like to meet me and I thought she was struggling with the thought of her father's marriage. At least she never tried to test me and I was glad she just accepted me the way I was.

The next weekend there was to be the get-together at Daniel and Elena's house and I was surprised that for the first time he invited Rita and Jonathan as well and I wasn't sure whose idea that had been. Anyway, Rita and I were very happy that we would have each other to talk to and

Rita found a very pretty outfit to wear at the thrift store and looked great. Our arrival was the same—security guards, maid at the door and Daniel there to greet us. He was such a nice and friendly guy, also giving Rita a hug and taking us straight out into the garden where a buffet-style dinner had been set up and this time I noticed that a few more people had been invited. Rita and Jonathan were introduced to the lady of the house, Mrs. McCallister, who was as beautiful as ever and charming to everyone, although I just got the remark "Oh, hi, Theresa, back again?!" I wasn't able to reply so Rita just said, "Yes, and we are very honoured to be invited." Elena kept looking at Michael who was chatting with Daniel then went over and gave him a big hug and I was afraid to look at their eyes. They started dancing straight away and only Rita looked at me to see how I was taking it. Then Daniel asked me for a dance, just like last time, and he mentioned that another couple had been invited—a German girl whose name was Barbara and her partner called Andre. Andre was a friend of Daniel's and about Daniel's age and was also a commanding officer, but from another army station. He took me over to their table and introduced me to them while Michael was still dancing—yes, with Elena. Just like old times, I thought.

Barbara, Rita and I started talking and it turned out that Barbara and I had a similar background as she was also in Berlin when the Russians took over, so there was quite a lot to talk about. She'd lost her father in the war and her mother had declared him dead so she would get the pension to enable her to survive with Barbara. Suddenly she said that I must know Michael, because she'd seen me arrive with him, which made Rita and I really look at her. I told her that I not only knew him but that he'd been my boyfriend for almost two years and she smiled and asked how I'd managed that and how many affairs he'd had in those two years. I must have been as white as a sheet because as soon as the music stopped, Michael came over and asked me to dance—he must have been watching us and noticed something. I didn't say anything and he held me quite close and started to ask me if Barbara had said bad things about him and that he wouldn't be surprised if she had, but I didn't answer him and from then on he never missed a dance with me. During the evening, Daniel talked to me about Michael's father getting married and said that they might be visiting him on their hon-eymoon so that he could see his son, but that it would all depend on West Berlin's political situation. I liked Daniel a lot. He was a nice man and I could talk to him and be myself. He'd even admitted that after Michael first told him about me, he'd wanted to meet me and judge if I was one of those German Fraeuleins, so at least he was honest. He just said I was good for Michael.

It was a lovely evening so after taking Rita and Jonathan home, we went to the park for a walk and I asked Michael why he was still with me—that everyone I talked to mentioned his affairs and was surprised that he hadn't dropped me like the others. He got serious again and said, "Don't you remember? I told you when we met, you're so different from the others—that's why I love you and haven't had any affairs since we've been together." I believed him again!

My father received good news regarding his parents as the Red Cross had found them both living in a Retirement Home in Salzwe-del, a little town in East Germany. It was good to know we'd found them but the problem now was how to get them out to West Berlin. As it turned out, it wasn't too difficult as they were both old and only costing East Germany money, so all my father had to do was to fill out a whole lot of paperwork. Unfortunately all the Retirement Homes in West Berlin were filled to overflowing and the only way forward was for my father to fill out all the forms and then have his parents stay with us until there was room in a West Berlin Retire-ment Home, which basically meant waiting for someone else to die. There went my sofa bed in the living room but since the living room was quite roomy, we could fit another bed at the other side of the room for me. It wasn't ideal but I loved my grandparents a lot and really had no choice. Once my father had completed the paperwork, he was told it might take about two weeks and that then an ambu-lance from East Germany would bring them to our apartment. We were warned that it would be quite expensive but they were my father's parents and were so very happy to be coming to us. I told Michael about it and he was worried about the situation, though nothing could be done at the moment.

Michael had also received a letter from his father saying he and his wife were planning to arrive with us at the end of November and would stay at Daniel's house for a week or two. He showed me a picture of them—his father looked as handsome as Michael, only older, and his future wife looked pretty flamboyant, which I almost expected. I wondered to myself if there were only rich people living in the States. Michael and I still had our weekend coming up to relax and just be together and we went to Complex Wannsee again which was so very pretty at that time of the year with fall approaching and the leaves changing to their red colouring. Almost another year over and still no sign of the cold war ending. If anything, it was even worse. While we were there Michael suggested I stay at the McCallister's big house until my grandparents could get into a Retirement Home but he understood when I explained that that was all I needed—knowing Elena would treat me like an unwanted maid. Anyway, it was a very nice weekend and I was ready again for the coming week. We'd bought a simple bed, which was fine, and were now just waiting for my grandparents to arrive.

One evening, Rita and Barbara stopped by our house, asking if I'd like to join them for a walk, which was a great idea as the three of us were in almost the same position. We went to our little coffee shop and started talking and Barbara apologised for what she'd said about Michael at the last dinner party, saying she hadn't realised we were in a relationship and had just repeated the rumours that were going around about Michael. She then just said that if you have a good-looking guy, you never have him all to yourself. I told Michael about the meeting later on and I didn't think he was too happy about it but he didn't say anything. My father then suddenly got word from the Retirement Home in East Germany that my grandparents would be brought to us by the end of the following week.

All of us were really happy and were waiting for the grandparents to arrive and tell us how they'd got on leaving their farm in Poland. Michael was on duty almost all week but he really wanted to come and greet them as well: sometimes he surprised me—he could be so different at times. We were told they'd arrive sometime on Friday afternoon, so I told Michael and also warned him that my grandfather was almost blind, so not to wonder about his reaction. By noon they'd already arrived—both very tired but very happy to be with us and we didn't ask too many questions so that they could rest after their journey. I was my grandmother's favourite grandchild and always had been. She had twelve children and of course quite a few grandchildren and I never figured out why I was her favourite. She was very openminded for that time and for her age so I hoped to get along well with her as long as they were staying with us. After a while Michael arrived with two cute little flower bouquets, one for my mother and one for my grandmother and when he gave my grandmother her flowers and a hug, she had tears in her eyes. I don't think anyone had ever given her flowers and I think that watching it was one of my happiest moments. I had told her about Michael and she just said "Hello" to him, which she thought was "Thank you" and then we left to spend the weekend at Complex Wannsee. Grandmother waved us off and I was so proud of Michael for what he'd done for them.

During one of our long walks at the lake, he told me how lucky I was to have a family like that—that he'd never met his grandparents and never even visited Spain. He could be so heartwarming at times. He told me his father was preparing for the wedding, supposedly a big event in San Francisco, and how much they were looking forward to seeing him here in Berlin. At that time there weren't too many uprisings going on in East Germany so they might be lucky and things would be normal. Well, maybe not normal for them, but normal for us.

When I got home my grandparents were already settled in but my grandmother was still very talkative, telling us about their journey from Poland to East Germany. It had been a Polish family who took over their farm and my grandparents had to work for them, eating and sleeping in a tiny room on their own farm. It must have been very hard for them but grandmother was very religious and that helped her over the hard times they went through. Then slowly my grandfather became blind and grandmother had a difficult time walking, so they were no longer of any use to that family. They were asked if they had any relatives in the West, the Red Cross was contacted and then through them they found us and were shipped out of the country with nothing left except the clothes they were wearing. It was sad, but they were now happy, especially my grandmother, and although it was a little crowded at home, we all managed.

Michael showed up in the evenings twice that first week and seemed to enjoy my grandparents. I really had to laugh—what a combination it was: old Polish people, a young girl from West Berlin and a well-off young man from the United States and they all got along nicely. Why couldn't the world be like that? The way he felt about us changed my opinion of Michael somewhat: maybe he now knew that I wasn't a German "Fraeulein" after all and didn't need to be tested all the time.

As it was his day off, Michael came to pick me up from work on the Wednesday and since there was so much restoration and construction work going on everywhere, we decided to go and see a movie at the Kurfuerstendamm (Ku-Damm). We watched a film called *The Man In-between*, starting Clare Bloom and Hildegard Knef, which turned out to be a film about war-torn Berlin and smuggling people from East to West, and we surely didn't need to watch it as we were actually living with it already. Close to the theatre was the Berlin Zoo, which had been badly damaged by the war and animals had been removed because of lack of food. Now they were trying to rebuild the zoo and even the animals were being replaced and it was a good feeling to see the progress being made. Michael was looking for the little stands which sold Gluehwein, but no—that was only at Christmas, so he had to wait! It had started to get chilly in the evenings and fall was here in full force and even though I usually liked the fall, there was something about the trees without their leaves which sometimes reminded me of dying and, of course, reminded me that another year would soon end.

I felt sad that evening without any apparent reason but Michael was still happy-go-lucky and didn't want to go home, so we went to visit Rita. Barbara was there as well and so was Jonathan—all drinking German beer and having a good time. Jonathan would be going back to the U.S. next year as well and Rita was being pushed to make a decision about what to do: whether to put her grandparents into a Retirement Home in West Germany and go with Jonathan to the States, or to stay with them. It was a hard decision for everyone who was in a relationship with American army personnel and although we had a few months left, sometimes there were days when you felt like the sword of Damocles was hanging over your head. Barbara was ready to leave Germany with Andre, but Andre was older than the rest of us and perhaps she felt more secure than we did. Even with those worries, though, it still turned out as a nice get-together. Michael told them all about his father getting married in October and then coming over to see Michael with his new wife and I thought his father getting married again was still bothering him, the same as it was bothering Janet. The fact that they'd be staying with the McCallisters bothered me a lot but Barbara assured me that it would be fine, even with Elena there. I was still having trouble getting over that. When it was time to leave we got in the jeep and went off but decided that all six of us would meet up the next weekend and think of something to do.

Michael seemed to be quite happy that evening but I still felt sad and sort of alone in the world—maybe it was just the ending of the year and the uncertainly of what would happen the following one. We were planning our next weekend and then he dropped me off at home and when I got in my grandmother was still up. I wondered if she was actually waiting for me to come home and I was glad she was up. She was sitting in a big chair which we'd bought for her and when I came in and tried to give her a hug, she just stroked my cheeks and said, "Moia mata mvszka" ("My little mouse" in Polish). I reminded her that despite being fluent when I was small, I'd lost my Polish language and so she continued in German, telling me that my eyes were glowing. There was so much love in her words that I just sat cuddled into her lap and must have fallen asleep.

Yes, I had fallen asleep, and when I woke up hours later my grandmother was still sitting in the same position, still awake and just holding me. The next day I found I felt better—perhaps I'd just need that comfort of being held unconditionally. I received a letter from Janet saying that everything was in full swing for the upcoming wedding and that she would prefer to be with Michael and myself as she'd met the two grown-up children belonging to her father's bride-to-be and that they were quite arrogant and demanding. She also mentioned that she thought her future stepmother must be quite wealthy. Again, I felt quite "little" but everyone called me little anyway—Michael called me little bird, my grandmother little mouse, and even my mother called me little baby.

On the weekend Rita and Jonathan were busy doing something else so it was just Barbara and Andre and us and after dinner we went to Barbara's house. They'd been lucky and their home had only been damaged but not lost. Barbara's parents were away over the weekend so she invited us to stay overnight—there was plenty of room and we could have something to drink without having to worry about driving afterwards and we thought it was a great idea. They even had a record player and quite a few nice Perry Como records to dance to. Barbara was a lucky girl: Andre was a nice guy, perhaps partly because he was older. He told us he'd lost his wife to cancer three years ago and for some reason I wondered if Barbara was the right girl for him—she was young and carefree, but weren't we all at that time. Michael and I danced a lot that night, perhaps because there was really no one else to flirt with, though sometimes I had the feeling that Barbara wouldn't have minded. Maybe that was just the wine making my mind think like that. Anyway, all of us had a good time and Michael even started to sing those Perry Como songs: he couldn't hide his Spanish heritage.

The next week was another busy one at work and also at home trying to help my parents take care of my grandparents. It was just a few days before the wedding in America would take place and Daniel asked Michael to come over on the weekend so that we could discuss his father's arrival and what to do and show them and also how to handle the situation as they weren't American military. I really didn't want to go but had no choice. I knew Elena would belittle me again but promised myself I would be the "big bird" to the outside world. All Saturday, I had that sad feeling again of being all alone and Michael obviously noticed it when he picked me up. All he said was that I shouldn't be afraid of Elena and that they were now only friends.

This time Elena stood at the entrance and, seeing Michael, her eyes lit up—certainly not in the way that a good friend's eyes would do. She took us in to Daniel and little snacks were served, but no music to dance to this time. They discussed all the arrangements for November and because it was his father they were talking about, even Michael got excited. Daniel started to talk to me and asked how I felt about it all and as there wasn't much else to say I just looked at him and said, "SCARED!" He started to laugh and said, "You don't have to be, little girl," and there it was again—that word "little," which made me slowly start to feel like a dwarf, even though I knew he hadn't meant to hurt me. I also realised that evening that Elena wasn't over that relationship with Michael but because Daniel didn't pay any attention to them, I wasn't sure if he knew anything or not. Anyway, everything was planned and we all hoped nothing bad would happen in the political situation while they were there. Michael took me home and all of a sudden, for no reason at all, I started to cry. Perhaps it was the stress I was under with his parents coming and the situation with Elena but I felt totally overwhelmed. Michael just held me, telling me everything would be alright.

I knew I had to pull myself together and took the next week off work, partly for that reason and partly because my grandfather had to get an eye check-up and my help was needed. With my father working, my mother found it hard to handle things like that, though luckily Michael offered to drive my grandfather to the doctor in the jeep. My grandfather was quite nervous as I don't think he'd ever driven in a jeep or even a car for that matter, only in that ambulance from East Germany to Berlin, and then they were put on stretchers in the back. Michael was driving and grandfather was supposed to sit in the passenger seat but we had a problem getting him to sit down. Because the roof was open and his sight was so bad, he insisted that he wanted to stand up so that he could see better. He looked very cute standing there looking like a General or some other dignitary waiting to wave to his greeters but in the end we calmed him down and told him it was against the law to stand up in a moving car and that the police could arrest him for that, and that convinced him!

The wedding in San Francisco for David Mendez and his wife-to-be, Gloria, was set for the weekend and shortly after that they'd be on their way to Berlin. I'd heard from Janet that they were planning to completely re-decorate and re-design their house and she and her younger sister Joanna, were really upset about it. It looked as though their father was planning to start a completely new life with Gloria. Daniel and Elena were asking Michael if we were able to help them to prepare and clean up their guestroom for the visitors and whilst Elena could easily have found some other helper, she insisted it had to be us— or rather, Michael—and because I was with Michael she couldn't leave me out. We went there on Saturday the next weekend and I ended up mostly being the cleaner while Michael was kept busy arranging flowers and entertaining Elena. We were invited to stay for dinner and drinks afterwards but Michael declined because we had already arranged to meet Rita and Jonathan to go to Complex Wannsee. It was clear from her face that Elena didn't at all like the fact that a "little" like me was able to get Michael away from her but we left anyway and picked up Rita and Jonathan and had a great time there until that sad feeling caught up with me again.

When Rita and I went to freshen up in the ladies room, she said I looked unwell and asked if I was alright and I told her how sad I was sometimes feeling. She suggested I see a doctor and offered to come with me but I said I thought I'd be fine as soon as all the stress over the forthcoming visitors was over. I pointed out that I'd have to make an appointment and really didn't have time right then but that I'd go and see one if I was still feeling that way later on. Rita didn't make much comment, just asking me to tell her when and if I was going, and then I forgot all about it, at least for that night. My only wish at that time was for the whole wedding event and everything connected with it to be over and done with.

Well, we knew the coming week would be hectic and as Michael was off-duty on the coming Tuesday, he wanted to pick me up from work and go shopping at Ku-Damm again, insisting that I needed a new wardrobe for the big Gala Dinner for his father and his new wife. I still had that beautiful winter coat he'd bought for the first dinner party with the McCallisters, so all I needed was a nice dress. He'd found out from his father that their most likely arrival date was Tuesday, November 3rd, but because they were travelling on an American military plane, there was no set schedule as the planes flew when needed. They would fly from New York to Frankfurt, Germany, and then on to West Berlin arriving at Berlin-Tempelhof Airport, which was controlled by the United States and also played a big role in the air bridge operation when it was used to fly food and almost anything else into West Berlin. So, their scheduled arrival was set for Tuesday but we knew that could change. They were leaving right after the wedding ceremony and I still couldn't find out how Daniel McCallister was able to arrange their flights into West Berlin, as even though he was a high-ranking commanding officer, I thought even they had rules to work by.

The last weekend we were ordered to stop by at the McCallisters' to check if everything was in order for those important guests. Elena seemed to be satisfied with everything and she didn't pay any attention at all to me, which was great. The plan was that the McCallisters were going to pick up the newlyweds from the airport, along with Michael, and take them to their home to rest, so nothing was planned for that evening. The next day was to be the big Gala Dinner and probably the next test was waiting for me. I had to take time off work again and I didn't think the company was too happy about it, but I was only working parttime so it didn't really matter too much.

Everything was perfect and the visitors arrived almost on time. Michael had promised to stop by at our apartment to tell me all about it and when he came later it was a beautiful fall evening so we went for a walk around the park. He seemed happy to see his father again but wasn't sure about his new stepmother, Gloria. He said she had cold eyes but was very beautiful and his father seemed to be happy. We talked about the next day's celebration and when he would pick me up, etc., and he knew I felt a very little bird again. Even his famous words that "Everything will be fine" didn't help me this time. When I got home my grandmother was still awake and waiting for me, just looking into my eyes and waiting for me to sleep in her lap again. I was exhausted and overwhelmed but glad to be home with no plans to make or worry about now that everything was perfectly arranged.

Well, the big day arrived—November 4th—and I was NOT ready to meet Mr. & Mrs. Mendez but I had no choice. Rita took half a day off work so she could come over to help me get ready before Michael came to pick me up around 6 P.M. She brought some mascara with her which she'd bought on the black market "to make you beautiful," she said. I actually wasn't feeling that great anyway and as it showed, I had to promise her I'd see the doctor as soon as the guests left, and then of course I started to worry myself, hoping I hadn't got cancer, though in fact I was sure it was only the stress. Rita did a great job with the mascara and with the new dress which we'd bought, I truly did look beautiful and it made me feel really good. When Michael arrived he was surprised and proud of how I looked.

At the McCallisters', Daniel greeted us at the door and from there we could see into the living room where Mr. and Mrs. Mendez were standing. Daniel gave me a hug and said, "Theresa, you look beautiful," and I couldn't believe what I was hearing—what a change of opinion and I noticed I hadn't heard that word "little," which immediately made me feel a foot taller. Even Michael laughed and I realised he was as nervous as I was. Daniel realised what I was going through. He was such a kind man and I felt Elena didn't deserve him, especially as she only had sparkling eyes for Michael. I guess Daniel knew more than he let on and that was why he was so friendly to me. Now came the test— saying hello to David and Gloria Mendez. Michael introduced me to them, saying, "This is Theresa, who I've told you about," and they looked so graceful I felt like bowing my head. I just welcomed them to Berlin and said it was nice to meet them but there was no emotion in their faces when we shook hands and I was just relieved to get that particular part of the evening over.

Dinner was then served and when we were all sitting down Mrs. Mendez started a conversation with me, saying, "Oh, you come from Poland?" I replied that my ancestors had but that I was born and raised in Berlin. She then kept asking if I knew Auschwitz and I became almost stiff with awkwardness.

(Auschwitz-Birkenau was a concentration camp, built and operated by Nazi Germany in occupied Poland. There were almost 40 concentration camps built but Auschwitz was called the largest killing centre ever and was also called Death Camp Auschwitz. The Commander was Rudolf Hoess and it operated from 1940 until 1945.)

It took me a few seconds to be able to answer her but then I said that, yes, I'd heard of it but that when it started to operate I was too young to understand. All I'd known was that my best friend's parents, who had owned a dress and fur shop in the inner city of Berlin, had disappeared overnight and that only later did I find out they'd been taken to Auschwitz and most likely killed. By then I knew what Auschwitz meant. Maybe Mrs. Mendez genuinely wanted to know about it but if she wanted to embarrass me, she certainly managed it. Daniel came to my rescue by putting some music on and asking everyone to dance but before I could catch my breath, Elena grabbed Michael for the dance. At least Mrs. Mendez stopped asking questions!

Daniel came and sat down with me and said, "I am sorry," and I thought perhaps I reminded him of his daughter. Michael then came over and asked me for the next dance but I declined; I felt sick to my stomach and as dinner was over, Michael offered to take me home. He then asked if I'd prefer to go to see Rita or even drive to Complex Wannsee and I opted for Wannsee, just to get completely away from everyone. We stopped by my house to tell my parents where we were going and then carried on. That night I really did feel sick so Michael decided to tell them I had the "flu"—if nothing else, that would give me time to rest until the weekend. After that, I decided to go back to work for the next couple of days. I'd already missed too many work days and as everyone was busy sightseeing, I wasn't needed for the visitors. Our next meeting was planned for the coming weekend when Michael wanted to show them another landmark—the Glienicker Bruecke (Glienicker Bridge), also known as the Bridge of Spies, and I was supposed to go along for that, with dinner arranged to be at the McCallisters' again. This bridge had first been built out of wood in the early 1900s, and spanned the River Havel connecting Berlin Wannsee and Potsdam, a very old and historical little town and actually a border town between Berlin and the State of Brandenburg. The bridge was constantly being rebuilt and renovated to keep it in good condition and Potsdam itself was also called the Land of Gardens, Palaces and Royal Parks for the Kings of Prussia, now East Germany. These days the bridge was mostly used by the Allies as a link between their West Berlin sections and the military mission in Potsdam. In other words that bridge connected West Berlin (State of Wannsee) and Potsdam (East Germany). It was also unique in that it was the only checkpoint fully controlled by the Soviet Union as all the other checkpoints between West Berlin and East Berlin and East Germany were under East German control.

Michael picked me up that afternoon and we drove to the McCallisters' to collect them, but after first having a cup of coffee. That went fine and then I had to use the restroom, so I was the last one to go outside and to my surprise, there were two jeeps. Daniel was driving one with Mr. & Mrs. Mendez, and Elena was sitting in Michael's jeep, leaving me the option of sitting with Daniel and the Mendez couple in one jeep or getting into Michael's jeep with Elena. I was having a really hard time deciding what to do and then Daniel jumped out of his jeep and told his wife to get into their jeep. It was a very tense situation and there was no point in arguing so Michael and I didn't say a word about it. I was feeling so frustrated with the whole situation that I felt I could just leave and walk home. The viewing of the bridge, however, was really interesting for them and Mr. Mendez in particular seemed to really enjoy it.

Then that evening dinner started off with cocktails and appetizers and everyone was making the usual small-talk when Mr. Mendez tried to get my attention from across the table by pointing his finger at me and saying, "What was your name again?" I said my name was Theresa and he nodded and just said, "Oh, yah." I think I became something like a zombie as I just started to talk and said I had something to tell him. I told him that he hadn't lived through a war fearing for his life almost every day, being shot at by low-flying planes and tanks and going to bed hungry most of the time, as I had. I told him my mother almost lost her life and that I was almost raped at 13 years of age. I had to stop for a minute to take a deep breath, but I wasn't able to stop talking and carried on to tell him my father had been a prisoner of war, that I grew up without a father, lost five of my immediate family members without even knowing where they were killed and that my family had lost everything they owned except the clothes they were wearing. I pointed out that we weren't poor because we were bad people but because of the war, which none of us had started—and all of that even though my family and I had never killed or harmed anyone on earth.

There was complete silence in the room and I then started to cry and tried to leave but Michael and Daniel held me back, with Michael holding me even in front of his stony-faced parents. I had totally lost control at that point and Michael took me out to get some fresh air and to try and calm me down. I told him to get me home, that I didn't care if Elena sparkled at him or not or if Mrs. Mendez wanted to try to embarrass me, I just wanted to go. I didn't know if Michael understood how I felt—that rich, spoiled kid from California whom I loved with all my heart. He asked if I'd like to go somewhere where we would be alone but I insisted that I just wanted to go home to my grandmother, who I knew was waiting for me. I asked Michael to apologise to everyone for my behaviour and to tell Daniel that I said thank you, and Michael just said he'd see me first thing in the morning, Sunday morning.

I slept very well that night—maybe I needed that confrontation with them to blow away my stress. At 8 A.M. I heard a little knock at the door and when I opened it, there was Michael with his famous smile, which immediately made me laugh. He had bought two bottles of Sekt—one for my mother and one for my grandmother, and also some cigars for my father. Perhaps because my grandfather was always so quiet, Michael had completely forgotten him but my grandmother just said, "Well, I'll give him a glass of my Sekt!" Michael then asked if I would like to go to church with him that morning so after a cup of coffee, off we went to church. He was wearing his uniform that morning and I knew how people were going to react but I didn't care. As I expected, all the heads turned to us when we walked in, but the priest was smiling.

So far no one had mentioned yesterday's incident with me and when I asked Michael about it, he said that as far as he could remember, nothing was said about it but today he had a hangover. He always made me laugh. I asked about plans for the day and he said he'd like to stop at Rita's and say hello and that Daniel had arranged a relaxing meal at Complex Gatow for that evening, and would I please go? Michael's father was trying to make a reservation to leave Berlin on Wednesday, November 13th, if they could get on an American military plane to Frankfurt, where they wanted to spend two or three days. That would mean only three more days to go! Rita was happy we'd stopped by and I told her everything that had happened. She said she was proud of me as we didn't deserve to be treated the way we were and it wasn't only me—

a lot of German girls were being treated like that by their American in-laws. She also reminded me that I had to make that doctor's appointment and with the Mendez couple leaving next week, I thought I'd make an appointment the next week with the doctor whose children I sometimes babysat.

We went to the McCallisters' house to meet them for our trip to Gatow and I must admit I felt a little scared about what their reaction would be. Daniel opened the door and I started to talk about it but he quickly put me at ease saying it was alright and that everyone understood. What a relief that was. The trip to Gatow was nice but the weather had changed into a typical November day in Germany with grey skies, drizzling rain and even the occasional snowflake. When we reached the clubhouse, however, there was a fire already going and it was lovely and cosy. The Mendez' were still stony-faced but no questions were asked. Elena was kind of quiet as well, just looking in Michael's direction once in a while. Michael, though, was very affectionate to me, even holding my hand in front of everyone and I thought maybe I'd done the right thing, after all.

Because Daniel had a busy day ahead trying to get the Mendez' flight arranged and Daniel was on duty and I had to work, we started home not too late but it had turned into an enjoyable evening after all. They were planning one more dinner together and Michael would let me know the details.

I had a good night's rest again but still didn't feel quite right, so I decided to make a doctor's appointment after work, if I could get one. Michael stopped by while I was at work to tell me that dinner had been arranged at the McCallisters' for Tuesday evening, which would be the visitors last dinner before leaving for Frankfurt. The only available flight had a stop-over in Munich, and Daniel had managed to arrange seats for them. That evening, Rita stopped by and we talked for a long time. She was under a lot of pressure as well as Jonathan had to leave in January and she still didn't know what to do. I didn't think she was ready to leave Berlin.

When Michael had stopped by at work he had given me a letter from Janet, who wanted to know how everything had gone. She said there were a lot of changes going on and that Gloria was supposed to move in with them and was selling her own house. Janet felt as though she was losing the home she'd grown up in and it was quite hard on her. When I wrote back I told her everything that had happened during her father's visit and then waited for a reply.

After Rita left, I walked over to our doctor's office to make an appointment and there was one available on the Friday. At that time, there were hardly any specialists; your doctor was your house doctor and took care of you by checking you over and if he found something wrong, he would send you to the hospital. I made the decision to see him and really hoped I was alright and wouldn't have to go to the hospital. I didn't tell anyone about my appointment, not even my mother. We then had a nice evening at home. Mother and Grandmother had a glass of Sekt and Grandfather had one too but I don't think he liked it that much, perhaps because he just wasn't used to it. My father had decided to stop smoking cigars because more and more the news was saying that it really wasn't good for your health. Looking out of the window, I saw it was snowing. It looked pretty but I had that sad feeling again that the year was coming to an end and I started wondering again what would happen next year and where I'd be in a year's time, even possibly still caged up here in West Berlin. It didn't look good with the cold war still going on and still more unrest at the borders.

Michael stayed with his parents at the McCallisters' house and I wondered how Elena was behaving. The thought that scared me was that if we should ever get married and Michael travelled on business trips alone, would I always worry about what was going on. Janet had told me in one of her letters that her father was untrustworthy like that and her mother couldn't handle it, hence the marriage breaking up. I had to wonder if Michael would be the same. I was making myself even more sad and had to stop thinking about it.

On Tuesday evening, Michael picked me up for the farewell dinner. I had the feeling the Mendezes were ready to leave and that perhaps they had expected something different in Berlin and not that half damaged city. It was a nice dinner and even David and Gloria were smiling at me. Elena still couldn't control her feelings for Michael and although there were a few glances at each other, I still didn't know how he felt. After dinner the visitors had to get packed up for an early morning departure from Berlin Tempelhof, so we all said our farewells and the Mendezes shook my hand, wished me all the best and said we might see each other again. Michael then took me home and said we'd have a nice quiet weekend together, just the two of us, wherever I wanted to go. He was then going back to the house to stay the last night with them and going to the airport to see them off the next morning. Wednesday he was on duty, so we were supposed to meet up again on Thursday, which was fine with me. I had the feeling that I had to be alone.

When we met on Thursday we went over to see Rita who still had a lot on her mind over her very hard decision about whether to leave her grandparents and go to the States with Jonathan or to stay behind in Berlin. We talked a lot about the future and what to do and also what would happen in Berlin as rumours were still going around about a wall being built around West Berlin. If Rita went to the U.S. she would be secure with Jonathan but what about our parents and grandparents— what would happen to them? We'd grown up in a war-torn environment and didn't know how it felt to be free and secure and it turned into a very intense conversation.

As the next day was Friday Michael and I planned to go to Complex Gatow and spend a relaxed weekend there. It was also the day of my doctor's appointment, which I'd only mentioned to Rita in confidence. Michael was on duty until noon and my appointment was in the afternoon, so I was a little nervous at work and sincerely hoped that there was nothing wrong which would entail a visit to the hospital. For a day in November, the weather was nice so I got ready and told my mother

I was going for a walk and might stop by at Rita's. I told her Michael was picking me up later and we'd be going to Gatow, which she was used to by then, so if he arrived before I got back, she should tell him where I'd gone and that I wouldn't be long.

When I got to the doctor's there were a few patients waiting so I registered at the front desk and waited until my turn came. When it did, the doctor asked me if there was anything wrong or whether I was just visiting him and I really didn't feel like joking. I tried to explain my symptoms and he checked me out thoroughly and when it was over we both sat down and he just asked me if I didn't know I was pregnant. I felt like a stone, just completely numb. When I got my voice back I said that wasn't possible as I didn't have any signs of being pregnant. He explained that everybody is different and he thought I was about six weeks pregnant. He asked me if my mother knew, which of course she didn't since I didn't know myself. He said everything was fine and that I should go and tell Michael and then return to see him with Michael in two weeks' time. Then I found myself standing outside and not able to move—not to home or to Rita's; I wasn't even able to think. For a start, I had no idea what Michael's reaction would be to be becoming a father at 25 years of age.

Slowly, I started to walk into the park where people walking by were looking at me strangely, perhaps thinking I was drunk. I was still walking when Michael caught up with me and asked me about the doctor. I asked him how he knew I'd been to see the doctor and he told me that when he was looking for me, he couldn't make out what my mother said—just that it was something about the park and Rita, so he went to see Rita and, because she was worried about me, she told him about my appointment. He just looked at me and asked, "Is it a little bird?" and when I nodded, he just smiled and said, "Thank God. I thought you were sick." He said it wasn't the way it should be but that it was our little bird and asked if I felt the same way. I just nodded and he said we should go and tell my parents that we were going to spend the week at Gatow, because there was a lot to talk about. Indeed, we talked the whole weekend—there seemed endless questions to answer. Rita and Jonathan stopped by on Saturday, wanting to know what had happened to me, and Rita said she almost knew I was pregnant. I could see from Jonathan's face how lucky he would have felt if it had happened to Rita.

Somehow the world felt different. I hadn't expected Michael's reaction and he told me he was almost expecting something like that because I'd been more erratic and behaving differently from the way I usually did. The way he treated me, I think if he could he would have put me into a shell so that nothing could happen to me. It showed me how much he really loved the idea of a family and must have missed being part of one when he was growing up. We decided not to tell my parents until we'd been to see and talk to the doctor again in two weeks. There were a lot of questions to be answered: should be get married before Michael had to leave for the States? If we did, it would be easier for me to get into the States and the baby would be an American citizen, or should we wait in Germany, so that the baby would be a German citizen? I knew my parents would probably prefer that but they were questions I'd never thought of. We were in a completely different situation and for a while the cold war didn't seem such a big problem any longer. In a way Rita was kind of sad and I thought that maybe pregnancy was what she wanted as well; she knew Jonathan would be very happy about it.

That week went by very fast and Daniel had asked Michael if we'd go over for dinner the coming weekend. It was our first free weekend since the Mendezes had left, as the previous weekend we'd been in Gatow thinking over the news from the doctor. He even invited Rita and Jonathan as well and we all gladly accepted. When we got there, the procedure was the same and another couple was there—also a German girl and an American soldier. I hadn't realised there were so many Berlin girls in relationships with American soldiers, but then I wouldn't have met Michael had it not been for Rita's relationship with Jonathan and her trying to act as matchmaker. Elena was quieter than usual and hardly talked to us and I wondered if she knew something. I asked Michael if he'd told Daniel our news and he grinned and nodded, so I knew then that she did. Not that it mattered any more but I did notice that she was drinking a lot.

The girl from the other couple started a conversation with me and asked me if that was Michael Mendez I came with and I asked if she knew him. She started to laugh and just said, "What girl doesn't!" She said he had lots of girlfriends but mostly only short-lived relationships and that put the question into my mind again—would he turn out to be like his father? She then said that lately he'd hardly been in the barracks and that no new girl had shown up, so that helped me a bit. When Michael came over to us and gave me a kiss, the girl just couldn't believe it, asking me if he was my boyfriend. Michael answered for me, saying, "Yes, this is Theresa, my girlfriend," and then started to laugh when he looked into her amazed face. That was certainly the end of that conversation!

Elena was getting a bit drunk and Daniel got her out of the room. In a way I felt sorry for her as knowing about me must have made her give up hope. Daniel told us his parents had got home safely but that instead of Frankfurt, they'd stayed in Munich for two days and had fallen in love with the city. Of course, it hadn't been damaged as badly as Berlin and if the weather was clear, they'd even have been able to see the Bavarian Alps, which would have been a very pretty picture.

So, all in all, the future didn't look that bleak at that moment and I hoped the Allies and the Soviet Union would come to some arrangement to stop fighting over Berlin and let it be one city again instead of a city with checkpoints on every corner. That would certainly make it easier for us if I should leave Berlin and my parents and grandparents behind. It was a nice get-together and I couldn't quite believe that by the summer of next year we'd be a family. Even Michael's eyes were looking kind of dreamy. We were looking forward to Christmas—not this coming one—but the one after that when there would be one more little bird with us and it was a lovely warm feeling.

Some days I didn't feel that great but at least I knew I wasn't dying of cancer. The two weeks were now up and we had that appointment with the doctor, after which we wanted to talk to my parents about it. I wasn't really too worried because my bond with my mother was so strong after all we'd been through together, that I knew she, at least, would understand. Michael picked me up on Thursday afternoon and I think he was even more nervous than I was. The doctor had met Michael before and when we went in he just asked us to sit down so that we could talk. So: there the two of us were—sitting in the chairs, holding hands and most likely looking like ten-year-olds who expected to be punished for doing something wrong. In fact, the doctor was very nice and asked us what our decision was—whether to keep the baby or give it up for adoption, as abortion was completely out of the question. We said we would definitely keep it and that we'd tell my parents over the weekend and he was happy with our decision. He said that everything looked alright so far and that the baby was probably due sometime in June next year. At that time medicine wasn't very advanced, so that the date was only approximate, but at least we knew what would happen. He then gave me another appointment to see him the next month and that was the first hurdle over, with the next one to come on Saturday.

We stopped by at Rita's to find her grandfather's health had taken a turn for the worse and they didn't know what was going to happen with him. Rita just said, "One comes, the other goes." It was sad because if something should happen to him she only had her grandmother left and that would make it even harder for her to leave. She had never talked about the reason, but she had been raised entirely by her grandparents and leaving her grandmother completely alone would be terribly hard.

We couldn't plan anything for that weekend because of our plan to talk to my parents, so Michael dropped me off at home. I then talked to my parents to ask if it would be alright to invite Michael for dinner on either Friday or Saturday and my mother said Friday would be best because my father had some meeting to attend on Saturday. It was alright but my mother had a strange look on her face and I couldn't make out what she was thinking. My grandmother was also there and she was smiling—she always smiled and was still smiling after raising twelve children. I told Michael the dinner would be on Friday, so we still had the weekend to ourselves and on Friday he arrived with flowers, chocolate and a bottle of whiskey for my father. I don't think he'd even finished the last one Michael brought over. Grandmother got a hug, which she really enjoyed and I had the feeling that these two really liked each other. Everyone liked my grandmother: she seemed to understand everything and always had good advice.

My mother cooked chicken noodle soup for dinner and it was so delicious, I think even Michael liked it. Then we somehow had to start the conversation, which meant I had to start because otherwise we wouldn't be able to understand each other. It took all the energy I had but I just said, "Mama and Papa, you will be grandparents next year." Silence. Then my grandmother smiled; she looked at me and reminded me of the night I got home and slept on her lap—she said my eyes were glowing and she knew I was pregnant; she could see it in my eyes. What a wise woman she was. That took us over the silence and the one thing my father did was to get up and pour a glass half full of whiskey. I'd never seen my father drink hard liquor, or—at least—not that amount! My mother didn't say a lot, just asking when the baby was due and if we would be getting married here and in church. I explained that we'd just found out and wanted to let them know first; that we'd talk about it more in the days to come. I thanked my parents for being so understanding and when I went to the kitchen, my mother followed me and gave me a hug, telling me that whatever happened I would always have them behind me and that we'd all get through this. That meant just so very much to me.

Michael's only comment was that I had a wonderful family and at that moment I felt very blessed having Michael and my family behind me. After dinner and that conversation, we left to see Rita and Jonathan and asked them to come with us to Wannsee. Rita really needed a break and asked her neighbour if she would please stay and watch her grandparents so that they could come with us.

It was almost the end of November and the weather had changed to snowing and chilly but nothing else had really changed except that now, for me, the border revolts became of secondary importance with my priority concern being completely for myself. Michael was on active duty for most of the week and he only stopped by on Friday to tell me we had dinner that evening again at the McCallister house. My old mistrust about Elena and Michael came up again and I really didn't understand why it was always at their house, though I realised we couldn't meet up in our crowded apartment. Anyway, we went there on Friday and I was hoping we would have the weekend to ourselves. There was quite a crowd there again, with dance music playing mostly Latin American songs. Elena was back in action again, as beautiful as ever, and Daniel was as friendly as ever. The song "When I Fall In Love" by Nat King Cole started to play and Michael knew I loved that song, so he started to come over but Elena was faster and grabbed him as he went past and off they went onto the dance floor. As it happened that wasn't the last dance they danced together. I think she would have done anything to get me out of the way, but I had the feeling Daniel controlled her.

Daniel and I talked most of the evening and one of the things he said was that he'd always help us get into the States if need be. I was mostly seeing Elena and Michael, who were drinking quite a bit, and as I didn't have a driver's licence I wondered how we'd get home. Daniel noticed and just said, "Don't worry, Michael's not driving tonight; I've already taken the keys from the jeep and you can stay in our guestroom tonight." I couldn't help remembering the letter Janet had written to me saying that although his father loved his family very much, he just couldn't control his affairs. It looked like Michael would be following in his footsteps and that would be one thing I couldn't handle. It made me very sad.

Slowly the evening came to an end and when people were already leaving, Michael came over. He was having a hard time walking in a straight line and Daniel told him, like a father, that he wasn't driving any more that day and he could stay in the guestroom with me. He looked quite shocked but right away agreed. I'd already left the room to go to the guestroom and had the same feeling I'd had before—that I didn't care if he was with Elena or not, I just wanted to be alone. It wasn't a good feeling to have, especially now, in my situation. A little while later Michael came in as well. He was a lot clearer and said he'd had some coffee but also mentioned that Elena wasn't over their affair and we must somehow try not to be there in the house so often. Was he also not over his passion for her, I wondered, but I didn't ask as he'd already fallen asleep in the chair. Despite everything, it made me smile as it reminded me of the days that I, myself, had spent sleeping in a chair. But one thing I was sure of—I had a lot of thinking to do before we could get married or before I left Berlin.

Of course, he had a bad hangover the next morning and he felt embarrassed in front of Daniel. Elena was nowhere in sight—I imagine she must have had a hangover as well, or perhaps she was just mad that I'd stayed there too. At that moment I felt ten years older than Michael: he just looked like a little boy. I thanked Daniel for everything and he just said that Michael was lucky to have me and then said with a smile that he wished he could go back to being as old as Michael was now. Michael took me home and just told my parents that we were going to Wannsee as we had some talking to do.

On the way we stopped at Rita's as I wanted them to join us that evening if they could. Rita saw that something was wrong and said Jonathan would be arriving later and they would take the bus together to Wannsee, as Jonathan didn't have the privilege of having a car or jeep like Michael did. Michael gave her money to take a taxi instead of waiting for the bus, which might or might not come or even be very late as there was no set schedule, and I was happy they would be coming. I wasn't feeling like talking about the night before but Michael started to apologise over and over again about his drinking and behaviour with Elena. As he'd mentioned before, he broke off the affair after meeting me and she knew it was just an affair—he'd told her that from the beginning, and she'd said it was okay because she was already married and also ten years older than him. Maybe she really had fallen in love with him, he said. He knew he shouldn't have started the affair but said he was kind of impressed with her and a MAN and that she was beautiful with a lot of South American temperament. He believed Daniel knew something was going on, or at least he guessed something was. He told me all that and said, "It wasn't love, little bird. I love you and we'll be a little family next year." It sounded so nice but like Janet said—her father loved his family very much and still had affairs. Maybe he'd told his wife the same story: that it wasn't love. What a similarity.

It wasn't snowing and the air was nice and clear, which I felt I needed, so we walked around the lake and when we got back to the club house Rita and Jonathan were already there. Rita asked me what had happened and I told her the whole story about the night before. She didn't say very much—just that I had a lot of thinking to do but luckily

I had two strong women behind me, my mother and my grandmother and that I wasn't alone. She said I would just have to make my own decision about Michael, adding that he wasn't a bad guy at all and he'd most likely spoil me and never leave me. She added that sometimes it is the woman's fault and that he was very good looking and, as he'd said, also a man. We all had a nice dinner together and everyone seemed to somehow relax. They had a record player for dance music and the place was pretty full of dancing people. We also were dancing when Michael started to very quietly sing Spanish love songs, or anyway very romantic sounding songs, perhaps ones sung by Perry Como, into my ear and with every song my distrust went further away. At that moment I realised I would always be too weak to handle his powers of persuasion. Just as Janet had told me in one of her letters, that's what happened to their mother and in the end she had to leave their father. Again, what a similarity.

There were so many maybes I had to deal with: Maybe he knew at the moment what my thoughts were, maybe he didn't: Maybe he was like his father, maybe he wasn't. There was definitely no maybe about the fact that he knew for sure that I loved him. It was a very emotional evening: maybe my brain was giving me the wrong signals, maybe not. We were all still sitting at the table when I felt so tired and exhausted that I just put my head on Rita's shoulder and must have fallen asleep. When I woke up, I was lying in bed and wondered what had happened. Michael told me that he and Jonathan had carried me out into the hotel room—luckily at that time nobody really had weight problems.

Well, the weekend was over without anything really being accomplished. The McCallisters were having a Christmas party in about two weeks and I had promised Michael that I would go, so I was stuck with that, then at the end of the year I had my next appointment with the doctor, which would bring me back to reality. We still hadn't come up with any plans. As far as he knew, Michael had to leave in March but I kept pushing that thought further and further into the background. For now it was just Christmas to get over. I had to keep asking myself why I went on that blind date to meet Michael in the first place; he was exactly the type of man I liked but, of course, nobody could have known that in advance and certainly I'd never expected to meet anyone like that. Now I had met him and didn't know what to do with him! During the week we hardly saw each other but had planned to go to Gatow on our own on Friday as Rita and Jonathan were otherwise occupied. I had told my parents I would make a decision after Christmas and was relieved that they weren't pushing me.

At the beginning of the week I'd sent Janet a letter telling her a little about us but not the BIG news yet, just asking her to tell me a bit about Michael's teenage years and something about his two years of college. That was all he'd done as his father wanted him in his real estate office so that he could teach him and have him take over his business after his military time was over. I hoped to find out something that would help me to decide once and for all what to do but she hadn't answered yet and probably wouldn't until next week or nearer to Christmas.

Anyway, it was just the two of us to go to Gatow. I loved that drive: it was so pretty even in the wintertime with no leaves on the trees and Michael was happy-go-lucky without a care in the world. How I wished I'd never met him! That was what my mind told me but my heart thought differently. When we arrived it was kind of crowded again and Barbara was also there. She was the girl we'd met at the McCallister's party who asked me if I knew Michael Mendez, since I was with him when we entered the room. She recognised us right away and waved us over to join her and a friend who was with her though I didn't think it was the same friend as last time. As there were some empty chairs, we went over but I thought, *Oh, no, not again*, because she was somehow at ease and, I thought, Michael's type of girl. She asked if we were still together as though she couldn't believe it and Michael answered that yes, we were and would continue to be so. She started to laugh and asked if he told that to all his ladies. He laughed as well and answered, "Of course, and they all love it," and then he asked me for the next dance. I really wasn't ready for jokes like that at that moment and again I felt like a midget or an ugly duckling. Michael saw that I wasn't happy and asked if I needed some fresh air, so I nodded and we went out onto the porch. He smiled and said they were only just joking and I understood—maybe my hormones were just playing with my emotions.

We had to get back in quite quickly because the porch wasn't heated but all those incidents weren't helping me make my decision. Or maybe they were. Barbara and Michael were dancing quite often and I saw her trying to get quite close to him and I just sat there and smiled; at least I had learned that already rather than reacting to it. It then looked as though the place wanted to close up and the music stopped and people started to leave, so we all did the same but as we said good night, Barbara asked us if we had anything planned for Saturday night. She said if, not, perhaps we could meet there again and enjoy the evening together. I didn't say a word but Michael said it was a good idea and that we'd see her tomorrow, after which we went to our room.

He stretched out on a chair and said, "See, she finally let go of me, now I'm all yours." I knew he was joking but part of me thought maybe he wasn't. I asked him to tell me something about his teenage years and college and whether he was always so popular with the girls. He grinned and said, "Mostly, yes," but that there had never been the right one. I also asked him what type of woman he liked most—was it mostly those from south of the border, Spanish and South American, and he agreed, so I asked him what he wanted with me then as I was completely Eastern European and didn't have those hot temperaments and traits. He was silent for a moment then asked if I really didn't realise how special I was or how sexy I sometimes looked and that he'd also heard that women from Poland are mostly beautiful and also renowned for their hospitality. As an example, he pointed out how my parents had taken him into their lives and how happy my grandmother was when he'd given her a hug, and how beautiful that was. He said, "Darling, I really love you and our little bird," and he wasn't smiling or laughing. His eyes were very serious and with that he won me over yet again. So, was he telling the truth? Maybe not and once again I was unable to make a decision except to think, *Que sera, sera*, until after Christmas.

That evening I was too tired to even think about making a decision anyway—after talking and talking I was just too tired and after putting my head on his shoulder I fell asleep again, just like I had that night sitting on my grandmother's lap. The next morning was a beautiful day for November, still kind of chilly but not enough so to stop us walking around the forest. We talked about a lot of things and he asked about how things were when the Russians took over Berlin, things he hadn't even heard about. I told him how I hated the Allies, since they destroyed the only doll I'd ever owned and he smiled and said, "See how it is when you love one, that's how things can change." He told me a little bit about his family and how he missed having had a complete family and how he thought maybe that's why he was kind of wild as a teenager and young adult, but he also admitted that most of the Mendez men were good looking and that's when I interrupted him, said, "Also, MEN"; he really loved that. But it was a nice conversation and for a little while I forgot I had to make that decision about whether to leave Berlin or to stay. If I left it would be a real life change—a complete life change—and that scared me. Even with Michael at my side, he couldn't always be there and I would otherwise be quite alone.

We had an early dinner and then Barbara and her boyfriend or friend or whatever he was, were already waiting for us. Somehow that didn't bother me too much even though Barbara kept looking at Michael and I thought most likely she was just waiting for the music to start. When it did, it was the romantic songs which started to play and she very quickly jumped up and asked Michael for the first dance. It gave me a chance to talk to her boyfriend, who seemed to be quite nice but came from the barracks in Gatow, so must have been British. He wanted to dance as well but I declined saying I was tired after walking in the forest and I realised that lately I was usually tired, probably because of my body changing. He told me he'd met Barbara a few weeks ago at another dance party and liked her a lot in the beginning before he realised she was too much of a German Fraeulein and that he was thinking of saying Adios to her. He also warned me to watch out for my guy as she could be pretty persuasive when she wanted something. I told him I'd already noticed that and we both had a good laugh. We didn't stay that long, much to Barbara's dismay.

The weekend was over and we had to return home and Michael was on duty until Wednesday so except for my work until noon it was pretty quiet for me. Then Michael picked me up on Wednesday and we went to check on Rita. Her grandfather had been admitted to hospital again and her grandmother had "flu" and I was afraid to stay because of the possibility of catching her "flu." Michael was unusually quiet so after we left I asked him what was wrong. He told me that Elena had stopped by at the barracks that day to give him an invitation for the "first" Christmas party next weekend and told him that another one would follow for a party shortly before Christmas. He said he only had the one invitation for one person and that the reason given had been that I couldn't be invited as I might be carrying the "flu" bug. I found it all hard to believe so asked him what he intended to do and he said that if I wasn't invited, he wouldn't go and added that perhaps another reason she'd gone to the barracks to invite him was so that Daniel wouldn't know about it.

I was really thankful he'd told me about it, otherwise perhaps it would have been another stroke on the negative side, and we decided to wait and see if another invitation came for me, otherwise we wouldn't go—or at least I hoped it would go like that. He also gave me a letter from Janet which had come through the mail with the other papers from the States and said he'd let me know tomorrow about the invitation, which gave me a chance to read Janet's letter. It was such a sweet letter. She said she felt she didn't belong in the house any longer since Gloria had changed everything around and I felt I'd found a sister because we seemed to have so much in common. I'd asked her about Michael's younger years and she answered that he'd had a cute girlfriend from Mexico for quite a while before he left for Germany and everyone had thought she was "the one," but that after he left there were just a few letters and then nothing else. She said that must have been about the time he met me. She also said that most of the Mendez men were like that—most of them had affairs even though they loved their families.

After reading Janet's letter didn't feel a whole lot better but she was telling the truth and meant well. I had a hard time getting to sleep and kept thinking about the Christmas party and not being invited and I started to get suspicious about why Elena would tell Michael I had "flu." Firstly, I didn't have "flu" and secondly there were only three people who knew about Rita's grandmother's "flu"—Michael, Rita and Jonathan—and why Elena went to the barracks to give him that single invitation. I hated myself for the suspicious mind I'd developed and really wanted to change how I felt. Was the "flu" just an excuse not to invite me, I wondered, but it was only Michael who was in contact with Elena. I decided not to say anything about it to anybody as another invitation might still come and if it didn't, Michael had promised not to go on his own. It was only if he found an excuse to go without me that I would have reason to worry.

He didn't come by on Thursday but came on Friday evening and we went to a little coffee shop for a snack. He didn't come up with any news about the Christmas party and when I asked him, he said, "Oh, yes, she brought the second one for you, as you're not sick." There was nothing suspicious in his behaviour and I felt kind of stupid for thinking that something was going on and that I must definitely change my way of thinking. He arranged to pick me up the next afternoon and I had a much better sleep that night. The next day my mother asked me for the first time if we'd made up our minds what we were going to do about our situation. I understood she just wanted to know what would happen and I felt sorry for her but had to just say, "Mama, let's wait till after Christmas."

Michael collected me to go to the party and I wasn't worried about going. I promised myself I wouldn't ask stupid questions as there must just have been a misunderstanding. Not too many people had been invited, which was nice, but I didn't know any of them. Elena was there looking beautiful and charming as always and I pulled myself together and tried to act the same. Michael noticed it and I could see in his eyes that he was inwardly laughing. Maybe he was happy about it, or maybe not? Everything was beautifully decorated and very Christmassy and pretty with lots of candles and if you hadn't known you were caged up in a war-torn city, you wouldn't have believed it.

Michael got side-tracked and was talking to the other couples he knew from his barracks and Elena was serving drinks to them and I was kind of standing by myself until Daniel came over. He was very sweet again and finally said, "Sweetheart, are you finally over your 'flu'?" I felt that stony feeling coming over me again but tried to hide it while I told him I'd never had the "flu" and that it was Rita's grandmother who had been ill. He was surprised and said that when he'd given Elena the invitation for Michael and myself, she said I wouldn't be coming because I was ill, but he'd given her the invitation anyway telling her I might be better by the time the day of the party arrived. I felt as though someone was hitting me over the head with a stick but I tried to be calm despite my suspicions apparently being right—that Elena was the one and maybe Michael as well. I knew she would do anything to get me out of the way, but would Michael? I looked over to where everyone was standing and saw they were having a good time, with Michael at the centre of attention as always.

I began to feel dizzy, very much as I had when I passed out during the airstrike when I tried to save my mother's life, and I hoped it wouldn't happen again. Daniel, who knew I was pregnant, noticed something wasn't right and realised I wasn't feeling well. He gave me a glass of water and asked me if I'd like to lie down the guestroom for a while, which I thought was a good idea. Luckily there was a bathroom attached as my stomach was hurting and I started to vomit, thanking God that I'd been left alone. I was lying down again when Daniel came in to check on me. I didn't have to tell him what was wrong, he already knew. He brought me some more water, sat down in a chair and we started to talk. I told him how different and difficult it was with Michael and I coming from completely different backgrounds and lifestyles and he understood. He told me that when he and Elena met in Buenos Aires, she came from the poorest part of the town, that he'd been blinded by her beauty and had fallen in love with her. But, he said, she adapted to the new lifestyle. Too fast, he said, and we both knew what he meant. I was very sure he felt the same way about Elena as I did about Michael; we loved them dearly.

It took a while before Michael noticed I wasn't in the room any longer and he came looking for me and found us in the guestroom. He seemed to be pretty worried and came dashing in asking what had happened. I just told him I wasn't feeling well and didn't mention anything about the invitation. I decided not to ask or tell anything about Elena anymore. Daniel just said we could stay overnight so that I could have a rest and he wouldn't have to take the keys from the jeep again. I was very happy about that because it meant I didn't have to return to the crowd again. Michael just said, "Go to sleep, little bird, and I'll come back here soon." Daniel smiled and said, "Sweetheart, I'll watch Michael for you."

I was glad they'd left the room. I needed to be alone and started to enjoy that room—the space, the lovely decorations, that spacious bed compared to mine in the apartment. From the bed you were able to look out of the window and it was a lovely clear, cold, December winter's night with stars shining. I felt guilty thinking like that and comparing this room with our apartment because my parents had done everything possible to make it a home and it wasn't their fault there was a war or that the war was still affecting so many things. There were still many upheavals at the borders with no sign of the two Germanys ever being reunited.

Sometimes I could hear some laughter and music coming from the other side of the house. What a different lifestyle it was! I must have fallen asleep but was woken up by the smell of liquor mixed with perfume. Because of a shining moon and the windows being decorated with lights, the room wasn't completely dark and I saw Michael was there next to me, but not sleeping. He seemed to be wide awake and just said he'd missed me. Since I'd made a promise to myself not to ask anything I tried to joke and said, "Well, I'm glad you found me, since I haven't been too far away from here," but he wasn't joking back, which was unusual for him. He answered, "I was watching my little family sleeping." That word "family" hit me—was I falling into that category already? Like Janet had said—the Mendez men all loved their families but there were always affairs involved in some way. It certainly looked as if here was another one like that. I wondered how that perfume smell got into his hair but I didn't ask and he was unusually quiet, making me think that somehow something must have happened at the party. I would so much have liked to know about that invitation but wasn't prepared for another lie. I really wanted to sleep; put my head on his shoulder and fell asleep.

When I woke up the next day I felt better and Michael came in with breakfast. That was the first time he'd done that, so we had breakfast in bed—just like in the movies. That scale of "yes" or "no" was even again, actually tending a little to "yes." When we went into the living room, only Daniel was there reading the paper. He seemed to be just the same but Elena was missing and all in all it was a strange atmosphere and I asked Michael to take me home. Daniel saw us out and told us that the last Christmas party would be in about two weeks and that he'd give that invitation to Theresa himself. Now I knew what it was about.

We wanted to stop at Rita's to see how she was doing and on the way there Michael suddenly asked me whether I wanted to know what happened last night. I replied that if he wanted to tell me that was fine, but it was also fine if he didn't and he looked surprised. He then told me that Elena didn't use the invitation Daniel gave her, she just made one out for Michael and told Daniel I wasn't coming. Then, when Michael told her I wasn't ill, she made out another one to include me. Michael then said that Elena was thinking of filing for a divorce. That really bothered him since he'd told her from the beginning that their relationship was nothing serious or emotional and was only an affair. He was worried that if she went through with it, Daniel might blame him. The only thing I could say was that we should wait and see. She might change her mind as she wouldn't easily replace the life she now had and, anyway, Daniel would win in the end as she was the one who had cheated on him.

Daniel agreed with me but was still worried about how far Elena would go. The only thing I could tell him was that he'd played with fire when he started that affair, and he knew it. I asked if that was his first affair with a married woman and he stayed quiet before then answering, "No, but the other was very brief." I told him that this time he'd caught the wrong one and he argued that when he'd had those two affairs he wasn't in any relationship. I decided there was no sense in talking about it so stopped answering him and we continued on to

Rita's. Her grandmother was doing better, which was good news, and I told her about the Christmas party last night. She said she thought I should stop going there, that it wasn't good and was too much stress for both the baby and for me. Slowly it was sinking in that I had to think about that as well and I made my decision not to go to the next party, even if Daniel gave me the invitation himself. We didn't stay too long; another week was coming up and my next doctor's appointment, which was on the 29th December. I wondered what the doctor would say.

Michael was on duty until Wednesday again, so there was no stress and I could stay home with my family. My mother was trying to prepare for Christmas, she loved it when everyone was at home. We made a list of things to get from the PX Store but as we weren't allowed there ourselves, we'd have to wait for Michael for that. I wrote a letter back to Janet but didn't mention anything about Elena. Janet had told me in her last letter that she was looking for an apartment—that she wanted to move out of her home and that her father would pay for everything. After that there would only be Joannah left and when she finished school, she would most likely leave the house as well.

On Wednesday evening, Michael showed up and we went for a walk around the park. It was cold but nice and clear. Michael seemed somehow changed, and was hardly joking any more, telling me that the next weekend would be the last one we could enjoy at either Wannsee or Gatow, then it would be the last Christmas party before Christmas and the New Year, and then the year would be over. He suggested that maybe next weekend we could start making plans for ourselves and I thought it a good idea, as much as anything so that I could start talking to my parents about our future. I thought maybe wild Michael was becoming a little more mature, which surely would be nice, and of course he knew that March of next year now wasn't that far away.

I must admit that it was a pretty sad feeling to know that everything would be changing next year. He must have had the same thoughts as both of us were looking at each other and just hoping for the best; somehow we felt very close but both of us knew it wasn't going to be easy. He took me home, took the list for the PX Store and arranged to pick me up on Friday afternoon so that we could get the things my mother needed for Christmas before we left for Wannsee. He just gave me a hug, but it felt different—almost as though he'd really grown up in the last three days.

It was Friday when we went to the PX Store to get the things my mother needed for her Christmas preparations and we also found some beautiful candles and little ornaments to decorate the apartment. Christmas is such a special time of year and it was fun doing it and seeing my mother so happy that she was able to do all that decorating. After that we asked Rita and Jonathan if they would join us but they were already busy doing something else so we went off by ourselves. Michael seemed a little more relaxed than last time and I asked him if he'd had some good news. He smiled and said, "Yes, maybe," and that he'd spoken to Daniel at the barracks and Daniel had told him that Elena wanted to spend the holiday with her family in Buenos Aires and would be leaving the next week, even before the second Christmas party. No wonder he was relaxed and he asked me if I wasn't happy about that news but I got kind of irritated and told him, "Listen, I wouldn't have come anyway. How does Daniel feel about it?" Michael said he didn't know and we weren't even sure if Daniel knew about their affair. It was a relief for Michael but he didn't know if she would come back to Berlin or stay in Argentina for good or even go back to San Francisco.

I joked about it and told him to watch out next time he met a beautiful married lady. "Okay," he said, "thanks for the advice," but that he'd already found one almost married. Well, at least he was already joking again. I can't say I was so enthused about it, of course, as I could have lost Michael, but it was not meant to be. We had a lovely dinner and could somehow feel the tension leaving us. We did our walk around the lake again and it was cold but beautiful. It was strange to see some houses which still hadn't been fully repaired after the war but had still be decorated a little showing that people were hoping again for a better future, as were we.

When we got back to the complex and started to make plans, in a way it was very romantic but also SO scary. Michael was supposed to leave in March and the last time I'd seen the doctor he'd said that the baby would be due sometime later in June. Michael suggested having a very small wedding with just my family, Rita and Jonathan and Daniel (with or without Elena) at the Registry Office. H would then fly back to the States and then return for the birth of the baby. He told me to talk to the doctor and ask if that was a good idea as he was afraid it would be too much stress for me to fly over pregnant into completely new surroundings in a new country and with new doctors, etc. After the baby was born, then we would have a church wedding, which my parents would love. It sounded almost too perfect but sometimes miracles do happen.

We left it like that and finally we had a plan. I wondered if Michael wanted to include his parents in that plan and when I asked him about it he just said they'd be invited as well if they could find the time between parties and cruises. He did mention that he'd like to bring Janet with him and knowing the connection Daniel had to the military, I supposed it could be possible. That would be the best Christmas I could look forward to. It was a lovely weekend and we felt like little children; I promised Michael I'd go to the last Christmas party with him, especially as Elena wouldn't be there. When we got home on Sunday, I told my other we were almost ready with our plans and that made her very happy, too.

Michael was on duty until Wednesday but stopped by every evening so that we could go for a walk in the park. On Tuesday he told me Daniel had said that Elena left that day. There were some places available on a plane flying out of Frankfurt to New York and then somehow on to Buenos Aires. Daniel hadn't said what had happened between them and I couldn't work out how Michael felt about it, but he seemed to be okay. On Wednesday we went to see Rita, since Rita and Jonathan were also invited to the second Christmas party. Daniel said that with Elena gone it wasn't going to be a great event and that there would just be a few people, which sounded really good to me. That reminded us that Christmas was next week; it was a bittersweet feeling.

We were really looking forward to the party and hoped there would be NO stress. Michael had arranged to pick me up on Friday afternoon so we could buy some small gifts for Christmas, go to the party and maybe still go to Wannsee over the weekend and when he arrived we went to the PX Store. I got a nice pair of warm slippers for my grandmother, which I knew she would love, and some little nick-knacks for the rest of my family. For my mother we bought a pretty set of crystal wine glasses, which she would be very proud of.

We then picked up Rita and Jonathan to go to the party and arrived to find only two more couples were there. Everything was still decorated for Christmas and for dinner we had pizza—what a change from the last party when Elena was still there. Daniel seemed relaxed but was quieter than usual and just told us that Elena and he had to work things out as their marriage had been shaky for quite a while. He looked at me and I guess he knew what had happened between Michael and Elena but it turned into a very nice evening anyway and we were able to take Rita and Jonathan home and still drive on to Wannsee.

We talked about Christmas and thought we'd go to church Christmas Eve and eat at our apartment and open up the gifts. We then still had two days of the Christmas holidays to plan for since our apartment was too crowded for all of us. Everything seemed so relaxed and easy to plan; I really wasn't used to that. Would we really have a future together? This weekend was, I would say, the nicest we ever had together—could Elena really have had that much power or control over him? I didn't dare ask and was just happy the way things were. When we looked out of the window, it was snowing. Just in time for Christmas.

Well, the Christmas week began and the weather was still nice—cold but not too much so for us to have our walk in the park. I'd been having some back pain recently and was waiting to see the doctor, but the pain wasn't really bad. My family had bought Michael a very lovely black sweater with BERLIN on the front—they'd bought it in one of the souvenir shops that had recently opened at the Ku Damm. When Michael came over on Wednesday he told me that Daniel had asked if we'd go over to his house after we finished dinner and spend the rest of Christmas Eve with him. He said we were welcome to stay there as Complex Wannsee and Complex Gatow were both closed over the holidays. I think he must have been quite lonely and we both said, yes, of course we would. I really felt quite sorry for him and it was also good for us as we had a place to be together and I loved that guestroom anyway! He told Michael he would order dinner from the barracks and maybe two more of his friends, like ranking officers and their wives, would come over as well. So, that was all planned and everything seemed too good to be true.

On Christmas afternoon Michael arrived with presents and my grandmother was smiling because she loved to have a big family get-together. My parents and the two of us went to church and I was so proud being with them all and I think Michael liked it as well as he wouldn't let go of my hand. It was so emotional for me and I was just so proud of my family. Later on, after having our traditional Christmas Eve dinner of sausages and potato salad, we started opening the presents. Grandmother had her warm slippers and she almost cried and again said "Hello" to Michael, which we all knew meant "Thank you." My mother really liked the set of wineglasses and for my grandfather and father we'd bought cotton handkerchiefs, winter socks, warm gloves and chocolates and other sweets. Then it was Michael's turn and he loved the sweater—tried it on immediately and didn't take it off again. I was really happy and he looked awesome in it! Then it was my turn and I opened a little box to find the most beautiful golden-green opal ring with two little rubies on each side. I couldn't believe it and it fitted perfectly. Even my parents looked astonished and when Michael asked me if I liked it, I couldn't even reply. Michael's eyes were full of love and he cried; it was such a very emotional Christmas for me that I never, ever, forgot it. For Michael—maybe it was my family or maybe he'd never experienced anything like that. After wishing each other Merry Christmas, Grandmother got a hug (she was already wearing her warm slippers) and she thanked him again by saying "hello." Maybe she wanted another hug? And with that, we went off to go and see Daniel

Two other couples about Daniel's age were already there and they were waiting for the dinner to arrive. Everyone liked Michael's sweater and, of course, they all admired my ring and when Daniel shook Michael's hand and pointed to my ring, I felt like royalty. Then dinner arrived—it was only turkey, green beans, mashed potato and apple pie but it tasted much better to me than the fanciest dinner in a five-star restaurant. The other two couples were really nice. We talked a lot about the war and the aftermath and they asked me a lot of questions but it was all in a nice conversational way and nobody was trying to embarrass me or treat me like a German Fraeulein. As the evening went on, my back was beginning to bother me a little and I just wanted to get into that guestroom and enjoy it so Michael and I said goodnight and both left the table. When we reached the guestroom we gave each other the biggest hug and I believe we BOTH had tears in our eyes.

It was a wonderful Christmas Eve. I loved my ring, which must have cost a fortune, and I wondered where Michael had got the money from—I was sure his parents hadn't helped him buy it. The next morning, we had a nice breakfast and Daniel asked us to stay on for the next two days of the Christmas holiday, saying that on Sunday he had to be back in the barracks anyway. It was such a nice offer we felt we couldn't refuse and honestly didn't want to, either. Daniel must have been very lonely but I didn't dare ask him outright about Elena as I felt he most likely wouldn't want to talk about it.

Over the holiday we went and checked on my family to make sure everything was alright. My grandmother (whom I still called Oma sometimes) was all happiness; I don't think she took off her new slippers even when she went to bed. She asked me if we'd be there on New Year's Eve and I told her that we most likely would be, but not all evening. Then she whispered that I'd have to teach her how to say "Thank you" in case Michael brought her anything again and I said that I would when I went back on Sunday. Her eyes were bright and shiny. My little Oma, she was so sweet. In the afternoon we stopped by at Rita's. I wanted to show off my ring and she was amazed by it, but Jonathan had given her a beautiful necklace, so she was also really happy.

On our way back to Daniel we started to have a walk in the park where lots of people were walking about in new clothes—probably all Christmas presents as well—but my back bothered me again so we stopped and drove back to Daniel's house instead. Michael asked me about my backache but I said there was nothing wrong and we weren't really worried about it as my doctor's appointment was the following Tuesday and I would tell him about it then. Daniel was cooking when we got there and we had delicious spaghetti with meatballs—a lovely peaceful evening and we talked a lot. I got the impression that Daniel felt he was with family and that we were both his grown-up children. He had another year to stay in Berlin and then he would also be going back to the U.S. but we didn't let negative thoughts get in the way as everything just seemed too perfect at that moment. Daniel also invited us for New Year's Eve along with Rita and Jonathan and a few more people who were coming. It should be a wonderful end of the year with no scary thoughts for the next year. Then suddenly it was getting late and Daniel seemed tired and I also couldn't wait to get into that guestroom. Once we were there I told Michael about my Oma, how much she loved her slippers and that she wanted to learn how to say "Thank you." I said I thought she had a crush on him but although he just laughed, I got the feeling he wanted to say something else about women, perhaps something like "Yes, young and old love me," but he didn't say anything so maybe I was wrong, but I knew his sort of jokes by now. Anyway, I kept quiet and the next morning we had a great breakfast and as Daniel had some paperwork to do and I was feeling better, we were able to have that walk in the park. In the evening we made some sandwiches and went to bed early and then next morning Christmas was over and Michael had to be back in the barracks. It was Sunday and he dropped me off at home saying he might stop by on Monday evening.

My family was happy to have me staying at home that night and my grandmother begged me to teach her how to say "Thank you" in English. It was actually pretty easy and she said, "Now I can say the right words to Michael. He's such a nice man, and good-looking as well." She got really excited talking about him and I had to laugh and said, "Oma, Grandfather can hear you saying those words." In reply she just brushed it off, saying, "Oh, no, he's also hard of hearing!" I told my mother about my appointment with the doctor on Tuesday and she wanted to come with me but I said I'd prefer to go alone. Then it was bedtime and how I missed that guestroom of Daniel's, but looking around and seeing my family, I felt blessed to have them.

Michael did stop by on Monday evening and brought me a letter and a Christmas card from Janet wishing me all the best for next year. There was also a little box containing a bracelet with a lot of little hearts hanging from it. She told me that she'd most likely be moving out in January because her stepmother's grown-up children were gradually moving into the house. She'd found a one-bedroom apartment near Fisherman's Wharf which she liked and had told her father about. She said he had nothing against it and perhaps he would be glad when she was gone; I could feel the sadness in her writing.

Michael and I went for our walk in the park but it was chilly so we ended up going into a little coffee shop for a cup of coffee to carry on talking. I told him I'd see the doctor tomorrow and then on Wednesday we could maybe get some little gifts for the last day of the year. Daniel would get a bottle of whiskey and we thought my mother would like a handbag with a fitting purse. My father was still smoking and making all kinds of excuses why he couldn't stop, so we thought we'd buy cigarettes for him and that my grandfather would love a new pipe. Grandmother was praying a lot, so we thought she'd love a rosary. We planned to do all that on Wednesday afternoon and then Michael would come over on New Year's Eve and bring everything before we went to pick up Rita and Jonathan for the New Year's Eve party at Daniel's. Everything was perfectly planned and Michael said he'd try to come over on Tuesday to find out what the doctor had said.

When I went for my appointment, I was a little nervous and hoping that everything was alright. The doctor checked me out and when I told him about my back pain he said that it wasn't unusual but mostly happened later in pregnancy so asked me to see him again during the first week in January. He said he might ask for a hospital test as he didn't have the right equipment in his office, but that I shouldn't worry. I told my mother what the doctor had said and told Michael the same when he turned up, and he seemed relieved. In the afternoon of the next day we took care buying the presents we'd planned and then he had to get back to the barracks.

Thursday was the last day of the year, so Michael came in the afternoon with all the presents for my family. My mother was delighted with the handbag with the fitting purse and Grandmother almost jumped out of her chair when she saw the rosary. Michael gave her a hug again and she finally said, "Thank you." It was in rather broken English, but we understood her and she was so excited that she started talking and talking but in Polish and we all really had to laugh. After that we left, picking up Rita and Jonathan and driving off to Daniel's house.

Daniel or someone else must have worked hard to take down all the Christmas decorations, because it was now really nicely decorated for New Year's Eve. There were sandwiches and snacks placed everywhere and also a record-player for dance music but no firecrackers were allowed because of the cold war situation. There were other people there already and it was a lively crowd. Daniel was happy, perhaps a little too happy I thought, but maybe he really missed Elena. I didn't dance much, just a few dances with Michael and he was so sweet and romantic that I thought maybe that was what being in heaven felt like. There were quite a few pretty girls in the crowd but Michael wasn't even flirting; what a relief.

Before we knew it, it was 10 P.M. and only two hours to go until the New Year. I couldn't help wondering what the next year would bring—it was a happy thought but also a little scary. Daniel brought me a cup of coffee suggesting I stick with that for a while and then it seemed like only a few minutes were left before it was 12 A.M. and the New Year was there. Everyone hugged each other and I guess Michael and I were the only ones that were not really laughing, just holding each other and knowing that we had a rough year ahead. When Michael returned, we wanted to check up on my family but promised Daniel we'd stay those two days with him since everyone had to be back in the barracks on Monday. My family was fine and everyone was happy, so we went for a walk and then back to Daniel so that he wouldn't be alone. We had a lot to talk about—I had another doctor's appointment and we also had to find out what we needed for the registry and had to make an appointment for the small wedding we planned. Daniel had already made plans for the three of us to go to dinner at Complex Gatow, which was now open again.

Sometimes I watched Michael and he looked kind of distant and I wondered where his mind was—was it really here in Berlin or was it in Buenos Aires? That thought scared me a lot but I kept quiet. If Elena knew Michael would be back in San Francisco in March, I would have lost. I felt and knew it, but there was no way to find out as even Daniel didn't know. I tried to push all those negative thoughts out of my mind again, trying only to have happy thoughts. We had a lovely dinner at Gatow in a very relaxed atmosphere and when we got home we played cards and then went to bed as we were all still tired after the New Year's Eve Party.

Nothing really happened the next day, we just walked again, had dinner and went off to sleep because the next day was Sunday and they had to be back at barracks. Michael was listening to some music from a little radio which was in the guestroom and they were still playing Christmas songs and everything was peaceful as I fell asleep. When I woke up in the middle of the night, I saw Michael out on the alcony smoking a cigarette, which he seldom did. When he saw that I was awake he came inside and fell asleep again but I didn't: so many thoughts were going through my mind and I really felt pretty alone and like a little bird again.

The first day of the New Year. What an overwhelming feeling!. Rita and Jonathan had stayed overnight as well, so Daniel made a great breakfast and then Michael had to drive Rita home because the neighbour who looked after her grandmother needed to get home. I stayed back with Daniel and he looked so lost that I just asked him outright about Elena. He admitted missing her despite all the problems they'd had. He said that he more or less knew when he'd married her that he wouldn't be the only one because he was older than her, maybe too old. I knew how he felt. He said that so far she was still in Buenos Aires and he didn't currently know what her plans were but that if she was still thinking she wanted a divorce, she could have one because he was getting tired of her affairs and didn't think she'd change. Oh, how I understood him. He said again that if I ever needed help in any way, I should just contact him and I felt I'd found a friend—or better, a second father.

I finally must have fallen asleep but when I woke up my pillow was wet so I must have cried in my sleep. Michael was still next to me and noticed but he only said that everything would be fine. He would also have a hard time leaving me alone in March but would be back in June. He'd told Daniel already that since he wouldn't be in the military any longer, there'd be no problem, and Daniel had said he'd see to that. He also told me that next week he'd find out what we had to do at the registry office and that made me feel a lot better. I made a promise to myself there and then not to have any more negative thoughts. Michael took me home that Sunday afternoon and promised to stop by whenever he could find the time.

My family was happy I was staying at home, especially my grandmother. Whenever I looked at her she was smiling again and I thought she could look right through me and most likely knew me better than I knew myself. I thought about what my Oma went through—she'd raised twelve children without any running water or electricity. She'd had a broken ankle because a cow kicked her and because there was no money for a doctor, she'd just gone to a sort of medicine man in her little village in Poland with the result that the broken ankle never really healed properly. As a result, she'd had to limp for the rest of her life and still didn't complain, even when they had to leave their home with nothing except their clothes. She was still smoking and smiling, so why was I complaining when I had so many people who loved me? I should be happy and smiling all day long.

I managed to write a thank-you letter to Janet that night and wished her all the best with her move into her new apartment and said that if everything went well, we'd see each other this year; I was really looking forward to meeting her. I slept pretty well that night.

The next day after work I went to see the doctor. He didn't check me out, just asked me about my back pains and I told him there was just a little bit of pain sometimes. He then told me to go to the hospital in the afternoon of the next day, saying he would be there and would use some different instruments to do a better check-up, which was fine with me. When I got home I told my mother about it and she really wanted to come with me but I really rather wanted to go alone. Michael also showed up for a few minutes and I told him the same story. He also wanted to come but he understood how I felt.

After work the next day I went to the hospital, which was quite close by. It was more like a clinic but it was much better equipped than the doctor's surgery. The doctor was already there when I arrived, along with two nurses and by then I was pretty scared. He examined me and then told me that my female organ, the uterus, was lower than it should be—almost like it would be later in pregnancy—so it might be pushing against my lower back. I asked if there was any danger and he said there wasn't but that I should avoid a lot of stress and also avoid lifting anything heavy. He said I wouldn't be able to fly to the States with Michael, so I told him I'd stay in Berlin until the baby was born. He told me to go and see him again in two or three weeks and I felt better even though I didn't really understand all of what he'd said.

Michael was already waiting when I got home, so I told him everything and he agreed to stay in Berlin. At least we knew now that there wasn't anything seriously wrong and for the first time in a long while I saw Michael laughing again: no more negative thoughts and no scare about Buenos Aires. That I didn't tell Michael. My mother felt better as well and as we still had a little time left, we went to see Rita to see how she was getting on. I told her about my hospital visit and she told me to be careful; also that her grandfather wasn't doing too well, which was very hard on her. We told them that next weekend we'd take them along to complex Wannsee to relax a little, then Michael gave me two kisses—"one for you and one for our little, little bird."

We were planning to pick up Rita and Jonathan on Friday to go to Complex Wannsee for a nice weekend and Rita's neighbour had offered to look in on her grandmother. I was really looking forward to it. Michael stopped by on Thursday telling me that Daniel had found out by talking to someone from the registry office that there were registration papers to be picked up and that it would then take about four weeks before an appointment was made. That would take us to around the end of February, which would be perfect, and Daniel and Michael would take care of all of that and pick up the papers. Because we had two citizenships, though, maybe I would have to go along as well. I guessed that both registries were at the same place. Everything seemed so perfect and sometimes that can be scary.

When we picked up Rita and Jonathan, Rita asked us if we could stop at the hospital where her grandfather was as she wanted to check up on him. It was near the Ku dam, like a real hospital, so we went to look for him. We were told that he had heart trouble and they had put him into the Intensive Care Unit, and things didn't look too good. I felt sorry for Rita but as she said, one goes, the other comes, and all we could do was hope for the best. On our way out we could see the newborn division and both of us had teary eyes. I have to admit, I prayed a lot these days, like my Oma did. It calmed me down as I still had those back pains, but the doctor said that just happens sometimes.

After the hospital we went on to Wannsee. It was snowing again and looked really pretty outside. Even though I hated the war and all that came with it, I realised that without it I would never have met Michael, that spoiled kid from the USA. There must be a reason for everything, I thought. Sometimes I thought back and wondered what Wolfgang might be doing, living in New York in the city he loved at first sight. We didn't stay up too long. Everyone was tired and emotionally exhausted, especially Rita because of her grandfather. Before bed, we looked out of the window and watched the snowflakes and Michael commented that we wouldn't have snow in San Francisco, did I think I could handle that? I was half asleep already, but very happy.

On Saturday after breakfast we took our walk around the lake and when we got back saw Daniel's jeep parked in front of the complex, which didn't look like good news. Daniel was sitting at the bar with a coffee and saw us coming in and went straight to Michael telling him he'd had word that David, Michael's father, had had a mild heart attack. I never knew how they did that as no one really had a phone connection, but perhaps the barracks had phone connections. Michael just said he could see it coming as his father's lifestyle wasn't the best, with too much stress, partying and smoking. But Daniel told him it wasn't really that serious and David said he just had to change his lifestyle and lower his workload. Michael wasn't that concerned, or if he was, he didn't show it, but I was wondering whether his father would let him come back in June or whether he'd have to start at the office straight away. I just kept quiet. Daniel stayed with us the whole day and I guessed he didn't want to be alone in that big house. I still pushed all negative thoughts aside and hoped for the best for everyone.

We walked a lot that day, then had dinner and all of us went to our rooms. We knew it would be a rough year but promised each other we'd do our best to make it through alright. Both of us were pretty emotional and had a hard time getting off to sleep. Michael blamed Gloria, his new stepmother, for lots of things and said she was pushing his father too hard with all those parties and social gatherings. Finally, we fell asleep and although my back was bothering me again, I kept quiet.

On Sunday we dropped off Rita and Jonathan and Michael took me home, but he wanted to come inside and say hello to my family. I believe he was still bothered about his father. Grandmother was really happy to have her big family again and Michael stayed for a little while. When it was time to back to the barracks he left and I missed him already. Grandmother, of course, just looked at me and knew I was sad, so she waved me over and I slept again in her lap.

The week began with good news when my parents got word from the Senior's Centre that my grandparents might get their own little apartment within the next three months. It would be a relief for my parents as our apartment was pretty crowded even though I wasn't home all that often, but I was very sure my grandmother wouldn't really like the idea. She loved her big family and in their little home on the farm in Poland, not everyone even had their own bed, with some of the children having to share. When my father told her, her face dropped, but it wasn't long before she started smiling again. The only wish she had was that we should visit them if we had time. "But bring along Michael," she said. I explained to her that he had to go back to America fairly soon and she said, "Oh, yes, I've read a lot about America and New York and know how far away it is." I was really surprised by Oma and she said, "I like to read at night if I can't sleep." She was an amazing woman. We had the good news but the bad news then came that Rita's grandfather had taken a turn for the worse.

When Michael came on Wednesday, he brought along the forms to fill out for the registry. It wasn't that hard to do—just as you would do if you eloped. We planned to fill them out over the coming weekend at Daniel's house so that all being well we could be getting married in the middle to end of February. Rita asked if Michael could drive her over to the hospital to check on her grandfather and when we got there the doctor told her that his heart was very weak and there wasn't much hope for him. Again, we passed the newborns' section and it gave me a really warm feeling and reminded me that I had to see my doctor again in the coming week. I hoped everything was alright as I still had those back pains.

Michael had changed quite a bit after Elena left the country and even though he still looked whenever a nice-looking girl passed by, it didn't bother me anymore. I guess we all do that if someone nice looking passes by, no matter whether it's a man or a woman. I always tried to think positively now.

Michael told me he'd spoken with his father from the barracks and that he seemed better and was trying to change his lifestyle and looking forward to seeing him in March. We assumed he didn't know about our situation or our plans. Michael hadn't told him anything and apparently neither had Daniel and Janet didn't know yet. His father had just mentioned that Janet and Gloria didn't get along very well, so Janet was moving out and that bothered him somehow since Gloria's two grown up children we still moving in. Michael said he wanted to give him our news face to face in March and I kept quiet even though I had a bit of a problem with that. Maybe in my next letter to Janet I'd tell her a little bit about our plans—maybe she would be thrilled to be becoming an aunt.

We had arranged to stay at Daniel's house over the weekend to fill out the forms, so Michael picked me up on Friday afternoon. I was also supposed to see the German Police to get my identity confirmed, whilst Daniel would confirm for Michael, and I'd also made an appointment to see the doctor again the coming week, so it looked as though we had everything under control.

Daniel had invited some people I didn't know to his house; it seemed he couldn't be alone. Michael was very talkative and had a little too much whiskey, so Daniel and I had time to talk. I asked him about Elena and he said he'd heard from her, that she was still in Argentina and had told him she wouldn't come back to Berlin. There was no mention from her about a divorce, so he would have to wait and see what she would do but he said he was thinking that he might file for divorce himself, as he didn't see any hope of saving their marriage. The way he said it was sad, but he was right.

Michael started dancing with one of the ladies and seemed to be becoming the old Michael again but I kept on smiling and stayed quiet, trying not to have negative thoughts. Then one of the girls who really looked and behaved like a German Fraeulein, came over and asked me if I was Theresa. When I nodded, she said she'd had a brief relationship with Michael shortly after he came to Berlin and asked what I did to keep him for so long. She said, "You better watch out, he's hard to keep," and then left laughing. Michael must have seen her because he then came over with a cup of coffee and asked me for the next dance, but I declined—suddenly I wasn't feeling that great. I started to wonder if it would always be like that. When we were married and went out somewhere, would girls still show up telling me they'd had an affair with him? I didn't think I could handle that. I noticed Michael had stopped drinking and thought Daniel had told him to.

When everyone had left, I was glad because I could go to my favourite guestroom again. I didn't mention what that girl had said and Michael didn't ask but he was very kind and told me that Daniel had invited us for dinner the next day in a great restaurant near the Ku Damm. I really didn't care at that moment, I just wanted to close my eyes and sleep. Michael was listening to music and then went out to the balcony to smoke a cigarette. I wondered what his thoughts were—was he afraid to get married or afraid to go back to the States? I then remembered my mother saying that they loved me and would always be behind me and that made me happy enough that I fell asleep.

The next morning Daniel made a great breakfast, after which Michael and I went for a little walk and checked up on my family. They were all well and had received a letter from Aunt Maria telling us they were all doing fine, including grandfather as well, but you could sense the distance already between east and west and she didn't mention anything personal, perhaps fearing that the letter might be opened and she could then be in trouble. As long as they were healthy, that was all that mattered. We then went back to Daniel's and had a nice afternoon before going out to dinner and everything was fine again as long as we didn't mention the subject of last night.

Daniel said he would feel strange going back to the States in a year but that as he would still be in the military, they might send him off somewhere else, he didn't know yet. He then mentioned Elena, the first time in front of Michael, who didn't react at all; maybe he knew more than we did. I had to remind myself not to have any negative thoughts, but sometimes I did have trouble trusting him completely. Maybe it would be better when we were married and the baby was born. I was always fighting against my negative thoughts and Janet's words popped into my mind that the Mendez men love their families but that there are usually some affairs involved.

That evening was really nice and we all retired early as Daniel had paperwork to complete. Michael and I were sitting on the couch and dreaming about our future together and he was talking really seriously. He knew I'd see the doctor next week and we both hoped everything would be alright. What an irony it is, I said, that the people (the American soldiers) who destroyed everything we owned through airstrikes, also provide the man I love the most. He really had to smile at that. I said we had to thank Rita and that blind date and told him that I hadn't really wanted to go when Jonathan first asked me to. He replied, "But you are mostly Polish and I've read that the Polish are sensitive and lovable." I guess he was right on that! It was a lovely evening.

The weekend was over too quickly and we had to leave Daniel's house on Sunday afternoon so that Michael could be back at the barracks again. I had a busy week coming up before going to the German Police and then to see the doctor and it was the middle of January already. Michael took me home and came into the apartment to give my grandmother her hug; he really liked her and I guess he missed having his grandparents around when he grew up. As there was still some time left, I wrote a letter to Janet telling her my situation and a little bit about our plans, hoping she would be happy for us.

I had some back pains that night and because they were starting to make me nervous, I decided to try and see the doctor the next day after work. I was lucky that there weren't too many patients so I could see him in the afternoon and I told him again about the back pain I was having. He repeated that it was too early for those pains as the baby shouldn't be due until the end of June or the beginning of July and he also mentioned that I hadn't gained enough weight for that stage of my pregnancy. He asked me to go to the clinic again sometime during the week for a better check-up and gave me some vitamin pills because my appetite was poor. It frightened me a little but the doctor didn't seem to be worried, so it couldn't be too serious.

Michael stopped by in the evening to find out what the doctor had said and I told him everything was fine, just that I had to stop by the clinic again for another examination. I gave him my letter to Janet to mail and told him that I'd mentioned a little about our plans and my situation. Perhaps it was my imagination or negative thinking again, but his eyes seemed to change for a moment while looking at me before he said that was fine and that he'd been going to do it himself that week. Maybe I should have kept quiet, I hated those moments of not knowing if I was right or wrong, so I just said that if he wanted to tell her himself instead of me doing it, then just not to mail my letter. He started to laugh saying "no" and that I was too sensitive and of course it was just fine but I couldn't get over his changed look. Perhaps I was wrong; he was probably right.

It was a cold night so we stopped over at Rita's to find there was no change in her grandfather's health. Jonathan was there too and he was very kind and warm towards Rita; I was so happy for her. The two boys were talking and I was able to tell Rita about the doctor and my back pain. She said she was worried about me as I looked very pale and not as if I was pregnant at all. She wondered how Michael felt about it all. I told her about my letter to Janet and Michael's strange look and she just said, "Take care of yourself." I tried not to show it but I was feeling confused that evening. Michael took me home and was kind and very lovable, so I felt it was my imagination again and that perhaps he'd just had a busy day in the barracks and also a lot of things on his mind to do with his father. When I got home my mother looked at me and said I looked very tired, that she'd make a cup of tea to calm my stomach but in fact I fell asleep before she bought the tea.

At least I had a good night's rest, so after work I went to the police station and took care of the paperwork to identify myself. Michael was unable to come and said he'd come on Wednesday, so I decided to see the clinic on Wednesday so that I could tell him what was going on. When I got there, the doctor was already waiting for me. He couldn't find anything wrong but said it was too early for back pains and that the location of the baby was too low. He said I might have some problems at the end of the pregnancy, but we'd take care of that when we got there. He reassured me that there wasn't any danger so far, so at least I could tell Michael what was going on.

When he picked me up on Wednesday, I have him the form from the German police station and told him what the doctor had said. It made sense to him but I felt he was a bit absent minded. There wasn't anywhere else to go and talk, only Rita's, so we went there. They were glad we'd come—there wasn't much news about her grandfather except that he wasn't able to walk unaided, so there was no way he could come home. I talked to Rita about my doctor's visit and she just said that she hoped everything would be fine right up to the end. When we left, Michael said he wouldn't have time to see me on Thursday but that he'd pick me up on Friday to spend the weekend at Daniel's.

We were going to stay at Daniel's again the whole weekend and I hoped that perhaps I'd have a chance to talk to him about Michael and what I thought was his distant behaviour. I had some time to think: was it a repeat situation like I'd had with Wolfgang when he left and his relatives influenced him not to get in touch with me and even offered me money not to contact him? Yes, we were very young then—I understood that, but this situation was different as we were older and more mature. But whatever I thought, there was no real answer so I had to wait and see if I would get any sort of information and advice from Daniel.

I had time to think until Friday but really came to no conclusion. I even talked about it with Rita because she was almost in the same situation with Jonathan. She now really wanted to go to the States with him—I suppose she'd fallen in love with him even though in the beginning she didn't really care for him that much. But if her grandfather should die, what would she do with her grandmother? She still had some relatives living in West Germany, so maybe something could be worked out so that she could live with them, but overall it was still a very emotional decision for her to make. Also, Jonathan was not Michael; you could really trust and depend on him.

On the Friday Daniel had also invited some other guests but I hoped to get a chance to talk to him alone and I got my chance when Michael was busy talking to the others. He must have known I wanted to talk to him because the first thing he asked me was whether there was anything wrong and I just bubbled over and told him my worries. He thought for a little while and then said that I now knew Michael well and also his way with women, that his father was the same when he was young. Then he said that he thought I most likely knew about Elena and Michael, that he had more or less known but hadn't expected it to get that serious on Elena's side. He said he was almost ready to give up and then Michael turned up with me and the so-called affair ended. He didn't think Elena ever forgave Michael for that. "You really have to make your own decision," he said. "If you marry him, you'll have a good life; I know he does love you—but you'll have to be prepared to accept affairs. If you can handle that, you'll be fine, he's not a bad guy." Now I had to find out if I would be able to handle that.

Michael asked me what Daniel and I talked about and I just said I'd tell him later. We danced a few times and he was almost like the Michael I knew, charming and tender, and I felt relieved as I couldn't handle a lot of stress right now. The party ended reasonably early and we could leave for my favourite room. I told him what Daniel and I had talked about and even told him that Daniel knew about his affair and he replied that he thought he would have known. I just told him everything that was bothering me, that I was scared of leaving the country, scared he might have affairs, his parents not liking me, something wrong with the baby, and so on and on. He was listening and then also started to talk, saying he hadn't wanted to come to that first blind date because of Elena but that he'd wanted to help Rita out when she told him about me. Then he said, "You know the rest," and I could feel that he was very emotional as well.

Michael also said that he was afraid of how his father's health would affect his plans but he smiled and said, "We'll make it." That really reassured me and I hadn't felt so good for a long time. We were still caged in Berlin and there was no hope in sight of anything changing in the near future but people were getting used to that and had started to live their lives on either side of the divided Berlin. People from the Eastern side still tried to get over to the West but most didn't make it. A lot of families were torn apart by living in that cold war situation but we all hoped that someday it would change, for better or worse. I really felt great that weekend, maybe we'd really needed that talk and we felt quite close. Daniel was happy for us; he was such a great guy. He had got all our papers together and wanted to go to the Embassy for an interview and to talk things over and because he was such a high-ranking officer, he shouldn't have a problem. We were therefore hoping that by next week we would get a date for the wedding ceremony. The only sadness I had then was with regard to my parents and what would happen to them when I left, but I couldn't talk about it at the moment. The weekend went by so quickly and we hated to leave our special room.

The new week began and Michael stopped by every night just to say hello to us. After our talk the weekend before, things were much more relaxed between us even though we realised time was moving very quickly. Daniel had already told Michael we'd probably get a date for our marriage between the middle and end of next month and then in March Michael had to leave, though we hadn't yet got a date. We hardly talked about it and tried to avoid the subject. He spoke with his father through the military connection and he was doing better and said he couldn't wait for Michael to be there. He didn't yet know anything about us but Janet spoke with Michael as well and she was really happy for us and looking forward to meeting me.

Janet had now moved out of the house into her own little apartment and was dating a young man from her gym classes. I had to admit that I was really looking forward to meeting her as well. Since Michael's stepmother, Gloria, had rearranged almost the whole house and her two grown up children had moved in, Janet said the house she'd grown up in just wasn't the same house anymore. Michael agreed that he'd feel the same way and told me that we'd probably have to get an apartment as well. That didn't matter to me as I always lived in an apartment and as long as I would be with Michael, I'd be fine. Sometimes when I was thinking, I realised how far I would be from Berlin, the only city I really knew as the other places had all been little villages, but I kept that to myself and didn't tell anybody.

Those back pains were still bothering me. The doctor had said no stress and no heavy lifting and whilst the no lifting wasn't a problem, the stress was pretty bad. My whole life was changing. My grandparents were moving into the Senior's complex, which meant I got my bed back, but I lost grandmother and although I could visit them, I couldn't sleep in her lap when I was feeling down and exhausted. There were so many "ifs," "buts" and "maybes," it was hard to handle them all and if I'd known all that, I don't think I would ever have gone to that first blind date. Especially as I didn't even like him because of his attitude and arrogance. He said it too about me, how could I compete with Elena, that beauty from Argentina. Maybe it was meant to be. Yes, another "maybe."

On Wednesday he was off duty in the evening so we checked up on Rita to find her grandfather was much the same and the doctors didn't have much hope. The coming weekend we were staying at Daniel's house again because there weren't too many weekends left to stay there. Daniel told Michael to bring Rita and Jonathan along for a night, saying they could stay in the office overnight. Rita was happy to get out of the house for a few hours as she had a lot on her mind, not least of which was that if her grandfather passed away and she wanted to leave for the States, she had to find a solution for her grandmother. So, one way and another, we were all looking forward to the coming weekend.

On Friday Michael picked me up and we then went to pick up Rita and Jonathan to go to Daniel's house. Rita was feeling a bit depressed because she'd been told by the doctors that her father hadn't got long to go; his heart was getting weaker and there was nothing that could be done. Daniel got some pizza from the barracks but everyone felt a little down and I noticed that Daniel was pretty quiet as well. I suppose he realised it would also be his last year in Berlin. There was uncertainty for all of us. We talked about the war and how long it would be before Berlin was divided as the tension continued to grow between East and West and the rumour about the wall was still around. That would result in an even more caged feeing for West Berlin. As long as I could remember, I'd been living in some kind of war right from childhood up to becoming an adult. Daniel understood but Michael didn't really because when he was sent over to Germany they knew they were going to former Nazi Germany and for them we were still the enemy who lost the war. Maybe that was why some of them had that attitude; I understood that. We had quite serious talks that night but it showed that winner and looser were still able to communicate and get along with each other. Daniel seemed tired so we all retired early for the night. It was very emotional being in that room which we both loved and where we'd spent very happy but also very sad moments together. It would soon be over but we tried to be optimistic and knew we'd find another place in which to be just as happy or sad.

At the beginning of next month, I had to see the doctor again and lately I'd started to wonder whether it would be a little girl or a little boy. I told Michael what I was thinking and he laughed, saying, "Of course it'll be a little boy and as handsome as his father." That was a typical Mendez answer but it made me happy. It was a wonderful evening and made me proud that I was going to be his wife and for a while I forgot all the "ifs," "buts" and "maybes"!

The next day, Saturday, we took Rita home and went driving around in West Berlin as much as we were allowed to, trying not to get too close to the borders because Michael was wearing his uniform. It was a beautiful cold January day and Michael told me to enjoy it as I wouldn't have that in San Francisco; that once we were there we'd have to go to the Canadian mountains to experience cold and see the snow. Michael wanted to walk around the park but I told him my back was bothering me. I also felt something like a pulling sensation in my back but I didn't tell him that. Instead, we went back to Daniel's house and I lay down for a bit until the feeling went away. I was worried, though, and decided to see the doctor on Monday. We didn't do a lot that Saturday—just talked; there were so many things to talk over—and then Michael went back to the barracks to get something to eat. Even Daniel noticed that I was worried and told me just to stop work for a while and take it easy. I wished Michael could stay in Berlin a little longer but even Daniel couldn't do any more as he'd already extended his stay.

Once again, the weekend was over too fast! After work on Monday I stopped by at the doctor's and got a chance to talk with him and tell him about the strange pulling feeling in my back. He told me there was no reason to send me back to the clinic again but that there was a possibility I might not be able to carry on a full-term pregnancy. It was only a possibility and might not happen but that I should have all the rest I could get and maybe take a few days' vacation. He said I had a lot going on with my forthcoming marriage and then Michael leaving, and that I should stay away from stress as much as possible. He knew my nervous system was a mess anyway and suggested I buy some relaxing tea as he couldn't give me any medication. He also told me to see him again straight away if I felt anything was wrong. I begged him not to tell anyone what was going on—not my mother, nor Michael for that matter—and he promised he wouldn't.

When I left the office, I realised that deep down I'd expected something like that right from the beginning because I'd looked in some books and realised things didn't seem quite right. I felt that maybe we were blessed and all would be well and that's why I didn't want to tell anyone about it yet. If I had a chance, I would talk to Rita. When Michael stopped by later I told him the doctor had said everything was fine, that I just had to eat a little more, but when grandmother looked at me earlier when I got home, she'd known something was wrong. I told my mother I was taking a vacation from work as January was a quiet month anyway but I don't think she believed me.

Michael and I saw each other on Wednesday, his day off, and we checked on Rita as usual. She was now almost waiting each day for her grandfather to go, so I didn't say anything about my doctor's visit. When Michael dropped me off at home, I asked him if he'd talk to Daniel and see if we could stay in "our" room over the weekend. "Of course we can," he said, "he'd be happy if we'd live there!" but, of course, I wouldn't have wanted to leave my parents alone. I also told Michael I was going to take a few days' vacation and he thought it was a great idea. February was about to start and we were waiting for our marriage date sometime between the middle and end of the month.

On Friday evening we went to Daniel's house and he was happy not to be alone. We had canned chicken noodle soup from the PX Store and I tried to eat as much as I could. Michael looked surprised and commented that I didn't normally eat that much but good-hearted Daniel smiled and said, "Well, she's eating for two now." It was such a relaxed atmosphere and I felt good.

A few days ago, Daniel had spoken to Michael's father who'd said he had to have some kind of operation but was going to wait until Michael got home so that he could start taking over the business with David's partner. Now Daniel asked Michael whether he'd told his father anything yet about our plans and Michael replied, "No, I want to tell him face to face." Daniel looked surprised and I kept quiet. Later, when it was getting late, we went off into "our" room. In there I felt safe, as though I was caged in but a happy "caged in." I asked Michael what he'd do if his father wasn't happy about our plans and he replied, "He wants me to be happy, I'm his son, so don't worry—it'll be fine." I kept quiet but started to pray, like my Oma always did, and looked out into the cold January night and hoped for the best while Michael slept.

On Saturday morning after breakfast we drove to Rita's and she asked us to drive her to the hospital to see how her grandfather was. His health hadn't improved and he was now on life support because he couldn't breathe on his own and as we stood beside his bed, I didn't think he even recognised Rita. The doctor came to talk to Rita and asked her if she knew what his wishes were—whether he wanted to prolong his life through life-support or not. Rita said he'd once told her that as soon as he couldn't live on his own without machines, he didn't want to continue, so the doctor gave her and her grandmother a few days to think about it and then let him know what to do. Rita told us that she'd tell her grandmother it would be best to let him go and asked Michael if he would drive them so that her grandmother could say goodbye to him. Michael of course agreed and said he'd do that on Wednesday, when he had the afternoon off duty. This time we stopped at the newborn section and looked in. Michael put his arm around my shoulder and I felt so safe, but Rita had tears in her eyes; it was a very emotional moment for all of us.

We checked on our parents and they were all alright. I think Grandmother was having a hard time dealing with leaving us to go to the Senior Centre, and she always had her rosary, the one Michael gave her, in her hands and was praying. I really admired her; she was a very strong woman. We then had some lunch at Daniel's house and he told us he'd invited a few people around that evening. It would be a pot-luck dinner so we could stay at home and no one had to cook, which was a great idea. Michael wanted to walk in the park a little and I didn't want to say no but I was already tired. I told him an idea I'd had that next weekend perhaps we could go to Complex Wannsee—it would be the last time for a long time and just the two of us, like a celebration, and he happily agreed. As he wouldn't be in the army, he might not get in again after March and that was where our relationship had begun.

Our walk over, we went back to Daniel's and although I kept it to myself, my back was hurting quite a bit. People were coming in with all kinds of food—we had enough for a whole army—and Michael was the perfect entertainer again. I was already getting used to it, or at least I acted as though I was. Daniel came and sat down; he knew I wasn't feeling good and he just said, "It's not in our hands what will happen." I asked him if I could go to the guestroom and lie down and of course he agreed, so I went and lay down and must have fallen sleep because I woke in the middle of the night and Michael was there—but no smell of smoke or perfume.

I couldn't get back to sleep straight away, too many thoughts were running through my mind: next week Rita and her grandmother had to make the decision regarding grandfather's life-support and Michael and I were preparing for the wedding ceremony and then after that it would

already be March and he would have to leave. What would happen if
there were problems with his family, or with the baby? I also had the
strangest feeling about Elena and wondered if she knew Michael would
be back in San Francisco in March. That was the thought which scared
me the most and I thought I'd try to ask Daniel tomorrow if he'd heard
anything from Elena about her future plans. That thought calmed me
down a little because I always tried to have a "Plan B" and in my situation right now, I wasn't able to find "Plan B" yet. I was so much looking
forward to next weekend at Complex Wannsee for our little celebration.

I finally fell asleep and when I woke, Michael must have already
been in the kitchen as I heard talking from there. We had breakfast and
then Daniel said that the wedding would be a little more towards the
end of February unless there were any cancellations, but there was still
time. Then, when Michael went out to clean the jeep, I asked Daniel if
he had heard from Elena. He just nodded and said she'd contacted him
to ask for some money and as she'd had time to think things over, she
wanted to talk to Daniel and didn't want to file for divorce; that she
planned to go back to San Francisco in April. Daniel said he wasn't
ready for that and was still thinking about filing for divorce himself. In
any case, Daniel would have to take some time off to meet her in San
Francisco. I asked him if she knew Michael would be there as well and
he said that he didn't know and hadn't said anything to her. Were my
thought right? Could Michael have told her? Were they still in contact?
It was a terrible thought but with that I had "Plan B," which I decided
not to tell anyone about.

In the afternoon, we drove home and since I was on so-called vacation, I would take it easy until Wednesday when we had to take Rita
to the hospital. I was looking at Michael and couldn't believe he would
deceive me but with so many "ifs," "buts" and "maybes," anything could
happen. He wasn't happy leaving me alone and promised to stop by the
next evening, also saying he was so much looking forward to the next
weekend. Grandmother was smiling when I got home and I knew I'd
be sleeping in her lap again.

Yes, I slept on my Oma's lap! Next morning, I thought about the
conversation with Daniel about Elena and got cross with myself. There

were my negative thoughts again. It didn't have to be Michael who'd said he was coming back in March, they had friends in common through Michael's parents and they could have told her too, but I felt so helpless when it came to Elena. I really had to work on those negative emotions. Anyway, I didn't have to work that morning and it was nice being with my family again. My mother asked about the wedding date and I told her. I also told her a little of what the doctor had said and she said she'd thought something was bothering me. "Be careful," she said, "that's why you're an only child: I had problems as well." Now I finally understood that, too. She then said that they loved me whatever happened and that we're a family and I had to promise her that if I had any problems I'd tell her right away so that we could go to the clinic.

Michael stopped by in the evening and I almost apologised, but of course he didn't know my thoughts. It was nice just being with him again and we went to the coffee shop together and discussed our next weekend in Complex Wannsee. We were both excited; there was a possibility it might be the last time we would be spending a weekend there together. On Wednesday Michael was taking Rita and her grandmother to the hospital to say goodbye to her grandfather and I decided not to go in; it would be too hard. I was so happy that night, maybe I really did need a good rest. Michael took me home but couldn't come the next day, so it would be Wednesday when I next saw him. I wanted to look really pretty for that coming weekend, so I got out that one dress we'd bought for the first meeting with Daniel and Elena, the earrings he'd bought me, Janet's bracelet and of course the beautiful ring. The dress was already a little tight but there was a reason for it and when I looked at myself in the mirror, I thought I looked really pretty.

Michael came on Wednesday to pick us all up. Rita's grandmother was a little sedated to say goodbye to her husband and Michael and I waited in the hallway outside. They didn't want to see the doctors actually pull all the plugs, so they didn't stay with him very long. We drove to Rita's home very quietly. She now had to decide where her grandmother was going to go as Rita was ready to leave for the States with Jonathan. Michael offered to help with the funeral arrangements but we didn't stay too long as both of them needed to rest.

Then the weekend came and Michael picked me up on Friday with a rose—an artificial one as there were no roses in the wintertime—and he looked at me and smiled and said I looked beautiful. That was all I needed. He also told me he'd spoken with his father again and his father was drawing up all the paperwork for Michael to start working right away. I asked him if they asked about me and he looked away and said, "No." I knew they were making trouble for him but thought we would be able to work through that. That night we had a wonderful dinner, very romantic with candlelight, but I had back pains again and also that pulling feeling on my back was there, but I kept quiet.

The next day was stormy and chilly so we decided to stay inside and talk and relax. It was fine with me—I needed plenty of rest anyway, doctor's orders! We started to talk about our years of growing up and he told me about his youngest sister, Joanna, who lives or lived with his mother after his parents' divorce and with whom they'd hardly had any contact. I asked him if he ever had the feeling I was a German "Fraeulein" and he replied, "Never," saying that if he had, we wouldn't have been together very long. I knew what he meant as I'd heard that from others already—just a short relationship. The only worry he'd had after he broke up with Elena and met me, was that he suspected Daniel knew about the affair and that Daniel would be very strict with him and maybe even send him back to the States. That was why he decided to take me along to the first party at Daniel and Elena's house, hoping he would accept me and that would show Daniel the affair was over. We were lucky, or at least Michael was, that Daniel accepted me the way I was. Daniel later told Michael that it was my eyes which caused him to accept me, since it was always obvious what my feelings and thoughts were. Like that saying, "A person's eyes tell you more than their words." Michael said he felt the same way and he even told me that at the beginning of our dating, he had a lot of fun acting arrogantly because he liked the way my eyes looked at him when I was angry with his behaviour. I really laughed at that.

As I grew up during the war, there wasn't much to tell him about my upbringing, so he carried on. After he finished high school, his father sent him to college in San Francisco to study communications, because he was going to have to communicate well with people when he took over his father's real estate business. Well, he didn't mind studying communications but not only the sort the teachers taught, there were other sorts of communications to learn, and he grinned. His father got tired of paying a lot of money out for the college and sent him into the army and off to Germany instead. And here in Berlin, he liked it. We also talked about our hobbies and, like me, he loved animals. Another interest we shared was travel. For me it was a dream so far but I hoped one day to be able to see more of our beautiful planet. For him, it was different as he'd seen more already and had been to Canada, Mexico and places within the States. I hoped one day I could travel to South America but told him he couldn't come with me unless he was chained to my leg, otherwise he'd be running off with some South American beauty queen, and he really laughed at that. I was slowly discovering that by joking with people and making them laugh, you don't have to show your true feelings: like a clown—you never know his real feelings—and I believe I used some of that joking technique all my life when I was pushed into difficult situations. I really enjoyed that day. In the evening we went to a little bar where we had a bite to eat and Michael had a few beers and then we went back and listened to some music. At least Michael did. I was so tired I fell asleep but it had been a wonderful day.

I woke up in the middle of the night to find the music still playing but the chair was empty and Michael wasn't there. I looked outside but the jeep wasn't there, either, so he must have gone out. At that moment, I didn't know what to think; where could he have gone in the middle of the night? I didn't know what to do and started to cry and shake and thought I was going to faint. It was almost the same feeling I'd had after we had the airstrikes during the war, when we lost everything and the streets were burning and my mother sat down on the street, saying she couldn't walk any further. I remember she wanted to die because her legs were all burnt and I dragged her along to the new hospital tent and then collapsed myself, feeling completely alone. Then I heard a car driving into the parking lot and it was Michael. When he came into the room he saw I was crying and completely messed up and then he became frightened, wanting to know what was wrong. I told him how I felt when I'd found I was all by myself and he showed me the packet of cigarettes in his hand and told me he'd only been gone a little while to look for a cigarette machine because the store was closed.

He felt so sorry and kept apologising over and over again and held me very tightly until I'd calmed down. There was really nothing to it—he couldn't have known that I'd wake up at that time; it really wasn't his fault at all but it wasn't what I needed just then. Later in life I experienced more of those attacks when I felt all alone in the world. It was then called a Panic Attack or Post-Traumatic Stress Disorder but at the time nobody knew what it was. It wasn't life threatening but I had to guard against those feelings which were all left over from the war. I was also scared of fireworks, which reminded me of the noise of the exploding bombs and the fear never went away completely. Slowly, Michael started to understand what the war really meant to us. After a while I was fine again so we tried to get back to sleep; he must have forgotten to smoke, since the package was still unopened the next morning.

Michael was still worried the next day and told me to rest until we left at noon and then the weekend was over again. Perhaps during the coming week, he would find out from Daniel about our marriage date. We stopped at Rita's on our way back and were told that her grandfather would be cremated and that they would collect his urn from the mortuary on their own as her grandmother was finding it too hard to talk to people. We understood. Michael came with me into the apartment to say "Hi" to my family. He still felt bad but it wasn't his fault at all, or anyone else's—just very unlucky timing. Yet again I was feeling those back pains and the pulling feeling and I went to bed early.

On his way out, Michael told me he'd come and check on me every evening if he could as there was no way of getting hold of him if I had any news. I thought that was a good idea but hoped that having made it so far, we would be alright and nothing bad would happen. I had a good night's sleep, but on Monday that pulling in my back was a little stronger than last time. I still had time off work because the doctor had given me a note, telling them I was ill, so I took it easy and wrote a letter to Janet asking her how she was doing. I told her a little about us and that I had some small problems with the pregnancy, intending to give it to Michael that night to be mailed. I wasn't feeling great that day—tired and listless and I noticed my mother was watching me.

That night, Michael dropped by and I gave him the letter to mail and he said he had some good news for me. He and Daniel had been talking and Daniel said he'd try again to get a little extension for Michael. He couldn't promise anything but it made us quite happy anyway; we just didn't know how Michael's father would react to that news. I believe that Daniel also wasn't that happy with the thought of his so-called "little family" breaking up for a while, but we'd have to wait and hope for the best. After that, Michael drove off telling me he'd stop by the next day as soon as he could.

I wanted to go to bed early and get as much rest as possible but I had a hard time falling asleep because that back pain just wouldn't go away. It was past midnight when I noticed I was experiencing abdominal pains coming and going and some tightening in my abdomen, which somehow scared me. It then went away for a while and then returned. The only thing I could think of was to write a note to Michael in case I had to go to the clinic, as if he came to the apartment there'd be no one there to tell him what was going on, whether I was with the doctor, at the clinic, or even the hospital. When I'd done that it was already morning and my father was ready to go to work but I pretended to be asleep. When he'd gone, my mother came to see me and I told her what was happening... I thought she would panic but, no, she was very calm: she said she knew all that and was sorry, that I should get dressed while she ran over to the doctor to ask him what to do. I showed her the note I'd written for Michael and we decided to leave it on the kitchen table. My mother then ran for the doctor and I started to really hurt. My grandmother was still sleeping, thank God.

The doctor and my mother came back after about an hour; he did a short examination and said it looked like false labour and early con-tractions. I was in the 4th month of pregnancy. I hardly understood what all that meant, all I knew was that I was frightened. The doctor said he'd take me to the hospital in the hope that something could still be done and that my mother could stay home and wait for Michael to arrive. I asked him if I would lose the baby and he looked at me and said, "I don't know. We'll do everything we can, that's why I'm taking you to the hospital and not to the clinic." I more or less crawled into his car and we went to the hospital, the same one in which Rita's grandfather had died.

I was in a lot of pain when we got to the hospital and the doctor put me straight onto a stretcher and wheeled me into a room. The doctor told me he had to go back to his practice and tell his office to close until noon and then he'd be back. After an hour, he was back in the hospital talking to some other doctors about what to do as it really looked as though they couldn't stop the contractions, despite the injections they'd given me. The doctors decided there was nothing more to be done and so it was that I miscarried and lost my baby. The doctor put me under a little sedation and then talked to me, saying that he knew how I felt but when things like that happened, the chances were high that the baby wasn't developing normally and somehow the body feels it and just rejects the baby. He said he knew it was very painful not only physically but also mentally but that a disabled baby would have been hard both for me and for the baby—that there are things between heaven and earth which we just cannot explain. He wanted to keep me in hospital overnight because I was running a slight temperature and the doctor said he'd see my mother and tell her what had happened and that as soon as Michael got there, they'd come and see me. I felt very tired and couldn't remember a lot about what happened after that except that I was taken into another room.

When I woke up and saw my mother and Michael standing by my bed, my mother cried and Michael looked terrible and had obviously been crying before. My mother just gave me a hug and told me she knew how I felt because she'd been through it and Michael just gave me a kiss and said, "I'm so sorry." We didn't talk a lot, I was just too exhausted, but Michael said he'd take my mother home and then come back. I was too tired to think but I remembered the doctor's words and they somehow made sense to me. God didn't want that child to suffer through life and he took it back for whatever reason. When Michael came back I told him how I was thinking and he felt the same way. I asked him if he knew if it was a boy or a girl and he thought the doctor had said a little boy but he wasn't sure. We were just holding hands and Michael told me he was thinking about when he picked me up tomorrow and wondering if my parents would allow me to stay at Daniel's house for a few days until I was feeling better. He'd already told Daniel what had happened and our apartment was so crowded they were both worried I wouldn't have enough rest at home.

I said they wouldn't mind and then Daniel said he'd see to it that Michael could stay with me instead of sleeping in the barracks. Daniel had also had the news that Michael could stay in Berlin for four more weeks, until the end of April, but Daniel had to sign some papers agreeing that there would be no extension after that. At least that meant there would be less stress and we could make better plans and with that I must have fallen asleep.

I suppose because of the medication, I must have slept at least ten hours and when I woke up the doctor was standing beside my bed. He took some blood to check but although I was still weak, my temperature was right again and the doctor told me I could go home. I remembered that it was Wednesday, so Michael's day off, and assumed he would come at noon anyway to find out how I was. When the doctor came back he said my blood levels were normal except that I was a little anaemic, for which he gave me some medication, and that yes, it was a little boy. Even though I was very sad, I thought, *There's a reason for everything*, and even if I didn't know that reason, it made it easier to deal with. I waited for Michael and he came with my mother about midday and were told they could take me home. We tried not to walk past the newborn section.

While driving home, Michael got me to ask my mother if it would be okay for me to stay at Daniel's for a few days until I was stronger. When I asked her, I could tell she wasn't completely happy with the idea but she knew it was better for me and did agree so we drove home so that I could get some of my things for a few days. My father was home from work and he was also very down because he'd been through the same thing with my mother, and not even grandmother was smiling.

Michael promised my parents we'd stop by every day to see them and then we drove off to Daniel's. Like everyone, he was also pretty sad but pleased that he had his little family a bit longer. He made it clear that this was Michael's last extension and we promised him we'd let him know our plans and retired once again to "our" room. I was very tired but had to admit that some of the stress was gone, even though I felt bad thinking like that. Michael went and got some whiskey; I guess he needed it that night, but we agreed not to do any more thinking or planning right then, and that we'd make a new start the next day. I thought he'd probably have a little too much whiskey but I didn't care, I felt I was at home again and had no more pain.

I didn't sleep that well and kept waking up—maybe reality was settling in and I started to realise what actually happened and that there was another life-change ahead of me, or rather us. I realised Michael had taken it pretty hard. For him—spoiled, well off—he hadn't been faced with a lot of disappointment or responsibility and life was always, or mostly, fun and now he was experiencing that life can be pretty tough at times. I decided that we should start talking about our future the next day and that maybe my parents and Daniel could help a little. It was great that we had four more weeks until Michael had to leave and with those thoughts, I fell asleep again.

The next morning, we had a good breakfast and Daniel told Michael that he would give him the rest of the week off so that we could work out what our plans were as the wedding date was coming up. He had to leave for the barracks but would be back in the afternoon. First, we had to go to Rita and tell her. She was sad as well but commented that she was almost expecting something like that as there were too many abnormalities from the beginning, and I had to agree with her. She, too, wanted to know our plans and we told her we still hard to work on that. I was still quite tired but we quickly stopped by at the apartment to say Hi to my mother, who was happy I was feeling a little better. Grandmother wasn't smiling her usual smile and just said, "Now you have a little one waiting for you in heaven."

When we got home, we made some lunch and were waiting for Daniel to come home. I told Michael I'd write to Janet and tell her what had happened and that he would come at the end of April instead of in March. I then asked Michael if he had any thoughts about the wedding and there was silence. I asked what he thought of the idea that instead of getting married now, we could plan a nice wedding later with all our relatives, either here in Berlin or even in San Francisco. I was sure his family would love to come here to Germany or my parents could come with me to the States for the wedding. Michael was quiet for a few minutes then said, "Let's wait to see if Daniel thinks it's a good idea and if he does, then we'll just get engaged before I leave." We agreed that this way neither his family nor mine had any reason to get upset or feel left out as they'd all be there together. It sounded like a good idea but a lot of communication would have to be done. When Daniel got home and had thought about it, he said it didn't sound like a bad idea, so why not try it?

Daniel also said he'd spoken to David about Michael coming in April and that David wasn't upset but had just sounded tired. That was big progress for one day and we said goodnight but in our room we kept on talking. He asked me a very sweet question: "But we will have children, right?" That made me cry but I said that of course, we would. It was particularly touching for me, who had always wanted a big family. I was tired and lay down while Michael sat in the chair listening to music and after a while he said he'd ask Daniel to cancel the wedding and then get in touch with his father and tell him that we'd be getting engaged before he left Berlin. That was the best news ever. Maybe this was "There's a reason for everything."

Since there now wasn't really any rush, the next day we asked Daniel to cancel the wedding date and he agreed. He said he also thought it would be a good idea for Michael to talk to his father first about what was really going on and Michael asked if he could go to the barracks the next day to use the army connection to talk to his father, so that was taken care of. As I had to see the doctor the next day anyway, it was good timing. We also needed to go to the PX Store to get some food for Daniel and us, so might as well get something for my family as well while we were there. I could feel that I was getting a little stronger every day; the physical pain was going away but the emotional pain was still pretty much alive. However, the thought that the baby might have been ill and suffer for its whole life helped me a lot to accept what had happened.

We got all the food, including for my parents and when we dropped it off I told my mother a little about our new plans and could see that she liked them. I also told her that after Michael had left I would be back at home again and since we'd had word about my grandparents getting a little apartment, it wouldn't be so crowded. She liked the idea of us getting engaged first and then deciding where the wedding would be after Michael came back. I could see she really liked it because it meant I wouldn't leave after the baby would have been born. On our way back we stopped at Rita's and I told her a little about our new plan and it liked it a lot too, saying the first plan had been very hectic but this one made more sense. She'd been in touch with her other relatives in West Germany and told them the situation with her grandmother and was hoping one of them would perhaps take care of her as a caregiver, then Rita, too, would be out of that Berlin "cage." So far everything looked well under control but we'd had that before and then all those other things had happened. I was trying only to have positive thoughts and so was Michael.

We made a late lunch for Daniel and ourselves and then talked some more. Daniel offered to let me stay at the house after Michael left but I wouldn't have felt comfortable being there by myself, so I declined that offer saying that I'd already told my parents I'd be back at home but that if I needed any help, I would ask him. I looked at Michael and thought he looked somehow relieved and I had to laugh inside myself. I thought, *Now you know how it is with those affairs*, but in fact I felt as though Daniel was my second father. Later he told me that he had a thought that Daniel would like to start an affair with me, like Michael had done with Elena, but I didn't think that at all and I got a good laugh out of it.

Later that evening we started to talk about our engagement date. He was leaving at the end of April, and when we checked the calendar, we found that Easter was the 18th and decided to set that as our engagement date. We only wanted to be alone; no big party or celebration, just the two of us and we only had to find somewhere to go. It sounded really romantic and that was how we wanted it. I also told Michael I was thinking of quitting my present half-day job and going back to the workmen's compensation full time job as I felt I needed to work and be busy rather than sitting around and getting depressed. I also wanted to talk to the priest to say that if he needed any volunteer work done over the weekends, I would be available. Michael said he'd know more tomorrow after talking with his father.

It was getting late and we were both tired so went to our room. We were happy with our decisions and there were still weeks left—almost ten—so there was time to relax a little and with some of the stress gone, our relationship had become calmer. We only hoped his father was alright with Michael's decision and I privately wondered how long it would take him to get things settled in San Francisco. I remembered Janet telling me he left his Mexican girlfriend behind when he was shipped to Germany, so I asked him about her. "Oh, you mean Juana," he said. "She's a nice girl, quite shy, but you met my father—you know how he thinks and she was Mexican, you know what I mean," and, yes, he laughed, adding that she was very pretty. I thought that wasn't really what I wanted to hear, but maybe it was. I decided to change the conversation as he usually knew what I was thinking and said he could see in my eyes exactly what my thoughts were. I said in future I'd have to close my eyes when I asked him something but he smiled and said he'd still know.

The next day, he dropped me off at the doctors and went to the barracks for that talk with his father. I had to wait quite a time to talk to the doctor and he then quickly examined me and said everything seemed to be alright again. He asked me if I still had those back pains and when I replied that they were now very little, he said that was normal and that now only my mental health had to heal, adding that I was still young and would have more children. I told him about Michael and my new plans and he also thought they were much better.

After a bit of a wait, Michael came to pick me up and I saw him coming. He looked fine and told me his father was alright with April and that after hearing about our new plans, had said he had expected I would be Michael's wife when he went back. How wrong we were; he must have noticed how we felt about each other when they were here in Berlin. Well, that was good news. On the way home I decided it would be a good idea to stop by at the workmen's compensation place and ask if anything was available and they gave me some application forms to fill out saying there might be a vacancy later in the year. It was almost afternoon when we got home, again as happy as could be after accomplishing a lot again that day.

For the first time, we tried a little walk in the park and it wasn't bad but I was glad to be back in the house again when we returned. Daniel was already home and we had sandwiches for dinner and I told them my doctor had given me one more note for the coming week, so that I could stay home from work. Michael had to be back at work but the upcoming weekend we were still able to stay at the house. Daniel said he'd invited a few more people for Saturday, so there would be a little party and we had to get some food and alcohol to get ready for it. Daniel loved his so-called "little parties" but I didn't really care for them because I was always afraid I'd meet some girl who'd tell me she'd had an affair with my boyfriend. But, I thought, he wasn't in Berlin long enough to have had that many and that was my first positive thought for the day. I was proud of myself but couldn't look at Michael as he was already smiling and I hoped he couldn't read my thoughts.

It was a quiet night and I only filled out my application for the new job which I hoped to get, so that we could drop it off on our way to the PX tomorrow. Apart from that we sat and listened to music and for the first time in a long time, I had a cigarette. Michael looked at me and said, "Don't smoke; it doesn't look good on you." I'd smoked when I first met him but somehow he'd changed his mind about it and I remembered that he really didn't care too much about me back then as he was just doing a favour for Rita and Jonathan. He might have seen it then as being a very short relationship. Anyway, I didn't smoke another one as I'd been raised in the old-fashioned way to believe the man of the house was the boss and what he said had to be done, even if he was sometimes wrong. I'd seen it with my parents—my mother did the same thing—but with my grandmother it was different and she was the boss of the house, that little rebel. I was tired and told Michael I'd go to bed like an old married couple and he said, "Couple, yes, but far from old."

Next morning, we dropped my application off at that office, went to the PX Store to get what Daniel wanted and also had a look in at Rita's. She looked fine so far and was sincerely hoping her grandmother would be able to go to West Germany to stay with those relatives and have a proper caregiver. After we'd dropped off the food, we tried another little walk and the air was nice and I felt better walking. Later, Daniel came home and told Michael that he'd talked with his father, who sounded a little different. He asked Michael why he hadn't talked to him about our relationship earlier and Daniel said he hadn't wanted to stress him out because of his recent heart attack. Daniel had even told him about the loss of our baby and, most importantly, that it had been a little boy, and said he'd sounded sad. It was hard to believe he'd changed that much, but miracles do sometimes happen and I felt more confident.

We started to prepare a little for the next day as people would show up early evening. I thought to myself what a change it would be, being in the apartment again compared to this house but thinking positively, I thought maybe it would be sooner than I thought before I could have my own home. In the morning we again tried a little walk and it felt good just holding hands and talking. I noticed Daniel was acting a little differently, as though something was bothering him, but I didn't ask and we prepared for the coming guests and forgot about it as the first ones were already arriving. Daniel said there might be six or eight coming and Michael was in a good mood—maybe it was the whiskey that caused that. When the last ones arrived, I couldn't believe my eyes—there was that same girl who'd told me she had a short affair with Michael when he arrived in Berlin. We looked at each other and she looked in disbelief at seeing me still there. "Are you still here with Michael?" she asked me and I said, "Oh, yes, and I will be with him for a long time." She laughed and said, "Well, wait until his affairs start," and like last time she went to have a dance with him. Michael danced with her and she tried to get pretty close and then he looked at me and his eyes were cold. I surely hoped that coldness wasn't meant for me.

The music stopped and the dance ended and he came to my side of the room; his eyes were still cold but he asked me for the next dance. While we were dancing I asked him what had happened, that his eyes were so cold that even I could see it. Then he started to smile and said, "I hate it when girls try to make a pass, like the last one." I interrupted him, saying, "Well, you had an affair with her, right?" and he agreed, saying it was just when he'd first come to Berlin, so why was I mad when she tried to be friendly to me. "It's very different," he said. "If a girl like her is that easy to get, a man has to make a lot of effort being nice and romantic to try and win her over for a romantic relationship, if you know what I mean. If that relationship is missing, a man loses interest very quickly." I knew what he was saying: "German Fraeulein," that was the name they were given, but I kept quiet. He said that when he'd met me he thought I was the same until, after a few dates, he'd noticed I was always sarcastic or even rude to him, so he really had to try hard to win me over and that slowly he'd fallen in love with me and noticed that I started to like him, too. I agreed and said, "Yes, you were an arrogant and sarcastic person who even tried to speak Spanish with me when you hardly knew the language yourself." We really had a good laugh over that and I realised we were flirting with each other. I liked that, it was really funny, and I had a good time that evening.

I remembered Daniel had been somehow quiet earlier that evening, so I tried to talk to him. He told me he'd been contacted by Elena for more money because some of her relatives had become ill and needed medication and he felt used. He added that she still wanted to come to San Francisco in April. But: that was his problem and I couldn't give him any advice on that. He then said again that his offer still stood—if Michael had gone and my family apartment was crowded, I could stay here in the house any time. I didn't know quite what to make of it but thanked him again for the offer and told him I was going to have a full-time job and also be busy being a volunteer at the church over the weekends until Michael came back to Berlin again.

Somehow I wasn't so sure about Daniel anymore and remembered Michael's relieved face when I declined Daniel's offer to stay there. Maybe he wasn't so wrong thinking Daniel wanted revenge for what Michael did with Elena, but I didn't say anything to Michael about that conversation because I didn't want to make problems with Michael's boss, who even had the power to send him back earlier than planned. I tried not to think about it but it would make sense. When it was getting late, the guests began leaving, including "that" girl, who was slightly intoxicated. She made me feel somehow ashamed of being a German girl—the German Fraeulein I'd tried so hard not to be.

When we retired to our room and carried on talking, we agreed it had been a very nice evening and talked about our engagement date, deciding we had to find a nice place for the two of us to celebrate. It couldn't be at Daniel's place because he'd make a big party out of it but there were a few small German hotels opening up and perhaps we'd try to find one of those. Then I was asleep on the couch with my head on his shoulder.

I woke up pretty early while Michael was still sleeping and last night's happenings came back to my mind. After we went to that first party at Daniel's house and Elena was still there, Daniel was very friendly to me and I was surprised how quickly he forgave, or pretended to forgive, Michael for his affair with his wife, just because he'd brought me along as his so called "ew" girlfriend; all of a sudden it didn't make sense to me. I really liked him as a so-called second father but was there more behind it that I didn't know about but Michael did?

I kind of brushed it off as negative thoughts but then when Michael woke up I just blurted out, "Am I a German Fraeulein too?" He looked at me sleepily and said, "No. You're my little Polish bird." I then said that I couldn't be a German Fraeulein as I'd only had one good friend, Wolfgang, who was German, and that Michael knew about him when we first met. I added that Michael was my first encounter with an American and look what had happened: nothing but problems. Michael couldn't stop laughing. "See," he said, "that's what I like about you— your temperament and still being naïve. That's why I like your grandmother, too—she's the same as you." I had to laugh as well and then we heard Daniel in the kitchen, so it was time to get up and make breakfast but I somehow felt uncomfortable, though perhaps it was just my imagination.

We hung around a little longer and Daniel asked us where the engagement party would be, then insisting that it should be there in his house. We told him that we wanted to celebrate alone—just the two of us—and he just said we'd talk about it later and immediately ended that discussion, leaving us feeling like fifteen-year-olds or at least, I did. We didn't say anything, partly because I was afraid that if we did, Daniel might get mad and send Michael away earlier or even take the jeep away from him. We had to think of something and I suddenly had the idea that I could tell Daniel that as I was an only child, if we had a party, it would be considered a family affair and I would have to bring my parents and grandparents along. I loved my parents and grandparents dearly but on this occasion I might use them, thinking that because they couldn't speak a word of English and with my grandmother's bubbling personality, it would be an occasion which Daniel would find very hard to handle. Michael couldn't stop laughing, saying I was also sneaky and he loved that. I just told him that when you grow up in a war, you use every trick you can to survive.

We left after lunch and went to check on Rita and Jonathan. They were very happy and hoping everything would go well with Rita's grandmother so that Rita could go with Jonathan. I saw the love in their eyes and felt so happy for them and I so hoped that Michael and I would be together very soon as well. The way he treated me, I felt very secure and happy being with him but we still had a long way to go. He dropped me off at home and told me he'd come again tomorrow and as it was his day off, we could do something nice together.

It was then nearly March and the Senior Centre had told us that my grandparents might be able to move in in March, so I decided to help my mother clean up the apartment a little. Grandfather's eyesight had worsened a bit and it wasn't now easy for him to get around without help, so he would now actually be better off in the Centre where help was always available. The start of March also meant Michael's departure was getting closer. If we hadn't lost the baby, we'd be married by now and the baby would still be on its way and although physically I was doing fine, I still had to fight my emotions. I talked to my mother about the problems she'd had with miscarriage and she'd experienced it twice—once at almost the same time as I lost the baby and the second time the baby had been stillborn about six months into the pregnancy. As I was the first and nothing was wrong, no one really understood why and at that time science wasn't far enough advanced to find out what the problem was. I just hoped I hadn't inherited that particular problem. My father had wanted a son badly and sometimes I believed he wished I was a boy.

In the evening, Michael stopped by and we had our little walk. The weather was clear and beautiful and still chilly but it wasn't spring yet so we still had some beautiful days ahead. I sometimes thought I smelt a breath of spring flowers and when I told Michael, he just smiled and said, "You're very romantic and I like that so much," and his eyes were warm and glowing as he looked at me. We went to the little coffee shop and talked for a little while but he had to be back at the barracks tomorrow and couldn't come, so I wouldn't see him again until his day off on Wednesday. We wanted to go to the Ku Damm to look for a place for our engagement celebration for the two of us and also to buy rings. He asked me how I wanted the little diamond set and I explained that I didn't want a diamond ring because I already had that other beautiful Opal ring he gave me for Christmas. All I wanted now was a very small golden ring which I could wear alongside the other ring and I suggested he could get the same ring for himself, also very tiny. He looked at me and said he'd never heard that before and that he'd expected another answer—a large diamond ring—and he laughed and said that wasn't how women in the States wore their rings. I said, "Well, I'm not in the States yet and maybe later you can buy me a huge diamond ring." He really laughed and gave me a very romantic kiss.

We still weren't sure about Daniel and his so-called big celebration. I knew my family would never come so we had to think what to do and because Daniel seemed to be behaving strangely lately, we didn't want to make a mistake. Michael had to go so we decided to talk more on Wednesday and he dropped me off back at home. He started to drive off but then turned around and blew a kiss at me—that was a "first," he'd never done that before.

Michael being like that made me so happy and I hoped he'd be able to take care of all the work he had to do for his father's business so that we could start our life together.

I was busy doing things in the apartment and talking with my grandmother. She wasn't that happy but she understood that grandfather needed help and she wasn't able to do it because she had problems herself with her legs. She also realised I would be going in a few months and although it was hard on her, she was a strong woman.

When Michael picked me up on Wednesday, he brought me a letter from Janet. She said she was so sorry about our loss and the only thing she wanted was to come to Berlin with Michael to pick me up. She was very happy herself with a new friend from her gym class. His grandparents came from Italy, his name was Stefano and it looked like it was developing into a romantic relationship. I was glad for her. There was also a picture of him in the letter and he was very good looking. I showed the picture to Michael and said, "Thank God, you've got competition." He just laughed and answered that the Mendez men never had competition, they were always better looking. I wasn't sure if he really meant it or not, but hoped he was just joking.

We then went off to Ku Damm to look for a small German hotel, but most of them looked more like bars, so we weren't quite sure: maybe Complex Gatow or Wannsee again would be better. We also looked at plain golden rings but Michael didn't like even one of them, so we had to keep looking. I almost said, "Let's try the thrift store," but I bit my lip—I didn't even know if he knew what a thrift store or secondhand store was.

It was almost a "must" to stop by at Daniel's every Wednesday, so we did and found him sitting in his office doing paperwork. He asked us if we'd thought about the engagement party and we said we hadn't yet as there was still a while to go. He then said, "But I have. We'll have a nice, big party with live music, good food and nice people, right, Theresa?" I didn't know what to say and just nodded and Michael didn't say anything. "Okay then," he said. "I'll work on that then." After that he said we'd have a little get-together at the weekend and that if we wanted, we could bring Rita and Jonathan along. As it was getting late and Michael had to be back in the Barracks, we started to leave and Daniel said, "See you at the weekend." We drove off and couldn't understand if all that had just been Daniel being friendly or whether there was something else behind it, and if so—what? We'd have to ask Rita and Jonathan if they were able to come on the weekend but they'd have to ask their neighbour to keep an eye on Grandmother again, so we decided to do that tomorrow. I really didn't know what to do about that big engagement party.

The next day we stopped at Rita's again and told her that she and Jonathan were invited the coming weekend, suggesting they came on Saturday afternoon and stayed in the office again overnight and they gladly accepted as going to Daniel's parties was special for them. They didn't normally go out a great deal as Jonathan had no jeep to use and Rita didn't have a car and that was why we took them with us whenever we could, but Rita was also wondering about all the parties Daniel had, saying maybe he was just lonely. My parents had word that my grandparents could be moving any time after the 15th March and that was perfect as Michael would be able to help us move them. There wasn't much to move but even driving us and my grandparents to the Centre would be really helpful.

Daniel told us to come on Friday afternoon. There was nothing to cook as he'd already ordered food to be delivered to the house—most likely through the military. When we drove there, Michael and I were talking about Daniel and I told him about my thoughts about revenge for Michael's affair with his wife. Michael didn't really believe it could be so and even if it were true, wondered how he would do it and I had to then say, "Just through me, perhaps." Michael looked at me and said, "You wouldn't have an affair with him, he's more than double your age," and I replied that I wouldn't start an affair with anyone for that matter, it was just that it all of what was happening didn't make sense to me and Daniel's strange behaviour had only started recently, just as Michael was about to leave.

After we got there we were chatting and I deliberately told Daniel my grandparents had found their own senior apartment to move into, so our apartment wouldn't be so crowded any longer. I did it because Daniel always talked about our crowded apartment but he didn't really pay any attention to what I'd said. As it was getting late, we retired to our room and were really happy and thankful to Daniel that he gave us that chance to be there together in his house. I wondered if maybe we should go there less often, but the chance would be over soon anyway. Michael started to light a cigarette and looked at me but I just laughed and shook my head. He said, "Good girl," but I really would have smoked one too if I hadn't been told growing up that the man is always the boss in the house.

It was a quiet evening and I thought about picking up Rita the next day and wondered how the party would turn out. I was a bit anxious and hoped "that" girl wouldn't be there—the one Michael had the affair with and was so mad about. I was getting frustrated with myself; there seemed hardly anything else to talk about except affairs and parties but right now I couldn't do anything about it. I also wondered if Michael's father and stepmother would come here to Berlin if we got married here and was afraid my parents would be too scared to fly to the States because none of us had ever flown; it was all something to be dealt with when the time came.

I had trouble getting to sleep that night because there was really no one to talk things over with except Rita, and she wouldn't be there until tomorrow. The only solution I came up with was that if Daniel really wanted to hurt someone because of the affair, it could only be Michael or me. I decided that I'd be friendly but distant to everyone, except Michael, of course. As the saying goes, "Kill them with kindness." I didn't know if I'd succeed but I'd certainly try and with that thought I finally fell asleep.

The next day was a beautifully sunny winter's day and we walked a little. I didn't mention anything to Michael about my thoughts because I didn't think he would understand and maybe I was wrong, anyway. I wasn't used to worrying about things like that as I'd always had other things on my mind. Daniel seemed in good spirits, which was nice, and in the afternoon we picked up Rita and Jonathan. Rita looked lovely and very happy and I was so glad for her—she really deserved happiness and Jonathan was so proud of her.

When we got to the house, the food had already been delivered—mostly American food of course because it had come from the military, and there was also plenty of liquor. I didn't get a chance to talk to Rita so I was just friendly and charming. There wasn't any live music, just a record player with romantic love songs, quite a few in Spanish. Rita just passed by me quickly, whispering, "Don't worry, I'm behind you," and I felt good knowing she was there for me. We decorated the room nicely with candles all over and artificial flowers and then the first guests arrived—two couples, both American soldiers with their German dates and when we introduced each other they seemed very nice. Then two more American soldiers came without company and I was already feeling a little bit relieved when the door opened and there was "that" girl with two more of those. I felt Daniel looking at me, as did Rita, but I didn't show any emotion, just a friendly smile. Michael was in the kitchen and hadn't even seen them and the girl waved at me and loudly asked me if I already lived there, saying that was smart as I could watch my boyfriend better, even though he'd be gone pretty soon anyway. I didn't answer and wondered how she knew all that; I was very sure it wasn't from Michael.

Then Daniel was nowhere in sight but Rita came over and sat next to me and the three girls went over to the bar and helped themselves to drinks. The music started and Daniel came back into the room and so did Michael. When he saw that girl, he stopped for a minute, looked at me and then got himself a drink. One of the unaccompanied soldiers came over and asked for a dance and I couldn't decline as I had no reason to, so we danced and he told me he was new here and came from Florida but so far liked Berlin a lot, as I knew most of the American soldiers did. Michael was dancing and laughing with one of the three girls but I was dancing too, so there was nothing wrong in that, and Daniel was just sitting on the couch and watching everyone. I was getting sick and tired of these "watching parties" and wouldn't have minded going home to our crowded apartment and then Michael started dancing with "that" girl and apparently didn't mind dancing pretty close. Perhaps it was the whiskey; I didn't know.

After that dance he remembered me and came over and asked for the next dance. Well, we danced to a lovely Spanish song and he was the same charming man as he always was to me. I told him I needed some fresh air and would go outside for a little while and he said he'd be right there. I got fresh air but instead of Michael, Daniel showed up and said, "Well, Theresa, do you like the party?" I said, "No, I do not," and he replied, "That will be your life if you marry Michael, think about it." I turned around and went into the guestroom and cried. I couldn't figure out how Daniel had meant it; maybe he really meant it well. Rita came and checked on me and said Michael was having a good time, but not to worry—that it was just the whiskey.

I was lying on the couch when Rita came back and brought me half a pill—the same pill I took from her grandmother to calm my nerves when I first went to Daniel's party with Michael and was so nervous I could hardly talk. I told her what Daniel had said to me about the parties and she couldn't really understand what he meant either, but it seemed to me that it wasn't meant in a bad way. Rita left again and I went to sleep almost immediately. I woke up in the middle of the night when Michael came into the room and although he smelt like a whiskey bottle, he seemed pretty sober. He asked why I was there sleeping instead of at the party and I told him about waiting outside for him but said he must have forgotten as he hadn't shown up. He said he'd gone there but nobody was outside and as Rita wasn't there either, he'd assumed I was with Rita somewhere in the house. I could see he felt uneasy and he apologized—I could see that he really was sorry and I didn't mention that I'd had that talk with Daniel. I said it was alright as long as he'd had a good time and he said that he had but that he'd missed me. "Well, if you missed me, you could have looked for me," I answered and he smiled his famous smile, saying that yes, he should have but that I knew how it easy it was to get sidetracked at a party. It didn't make a lot of sense to argue with him—he'd always win and he knew it.

The next morning, we had breakfast—or at least, I had breakfast—as Michael was still sleeping. Daniel and I were in the kitchen together and were quiet for a while before he then apologised for what he'd said last night about the party. He said he'd just wanted to let me see how my life would be with Michael—that there would be lots of parties like that because his father's company was well-known in San Francisco and lots of well-off clients would have to be entertained. He said he'd had those parties to show me that, because he liked me a lot and looked on me a little bit like a daughter he'd never had. He said there was nothing else, like most of us had thought. I felt really embarrassed about how wrong we were and he also mentioned that there would be no big engagement party if we didn't want one, that he could see we wouldn't like it and should find a nice place just for the two of us, which would be better for Michael as well. I thanked him so much and said he'd taken a load off my shoulders but I still hoped Michael would change his womanising ways when he had a family. Then Janet's words came into my mind—that the Mendez men love their families, but also those affairs.

When Michael got up we took Rita and Jonathan home and then had our little walk and last night's party wasn't mentioned. It seemed as though he had to do a job last night entertaining people and had done the job well. I did tell him what Daniel had said about not having the big engagement party and after thinking it over he said he thought it would be nicer for us if we just celebrated alone and that now we really had to look for a place. When he took me home, we talked to my parents and they asked if he could take us to the Senior Centre on Wednesday to have a look in case my grandparents would need some small pieces of furniture or other little accessories. He then gave me a big hug, telling me how happy he was and how proud of me; he always knew the right words to turn me around—maybe not completely, but 75% for sure.

Before leaving, he told me there was a possibility that he wouldn't be able to stop by on Monday and Tuesday because of work at the barracks but promised that on Wednesday he'd take us to the Senior Centre to check it out. I said that was fine, but in reality it wasn't, since I didn't really trust him completely any longer, but there was nothing I could do about it.

I had a good night's rest and on Monday afternoon I went over to Rita's because I knew she was on her own. We talked about Daniel and his parties and letting us off the big engagement party and Rita was pretty much convinced that Daniel was telling the truth—that he was just trying to somehow show me how life in the States could be, because we knew nothing of that lifestyle having grown up during the war. We promised each other we'd always try to stay in touch when we were living in the States, so we'd each know how the other was handling life in America. We both knew it would be a big challenge but that we could make it and with those positive thoughts, I walked back home. My mother was still up and in the kitchen and we sat down and talked, with her telling me how hard it had been for her leaving the little village where she'd grown up and moving to the big city of Berlin. She said she was so homesick that it took her a while to get settled and even then she never really felt at home.

I didn't sleep that well because my thoughts were running wild. If only I could feel more secure with Michael—he was a good guy and flirting was just like doing a job, so that was okay, but how far can a job go? I knew I had to let go of all those negative thoughts or I'd be unhappy all the time and I at least had a good rest and felt better the next day when I went shopping with my mother. We had a little grocery store nearby—nothing compared with the PX, but enough for our basic food and it felt really good being with my mother again. Even so, by evening I really missed Michael and hoped he would have time to just stop by for a little while.

There was nothing much to do so I sat in the kitchen and was listening to music when I heard a car stopping in front of the apartment and, sure enough, there was Michael's jeep. I quickly got dressed and ran out and was so happy that he'd come. When I got in the jeep, I smelt whiskey and asked him if he'd had a drink. He said, "Yes, after work a few of us went to the bar next to the barracks and had a drink." He'd never done that before and then he kept telling me how sad he was feeling about leaving Berlin and going back to the States. He seemed distant again so I gave him a big hug and immediately smelt just a very little perfume-like smell on his overcoat. I didn't comment but just asked if there was dance music in the bar and he said yes and that you could actually dance there too, so I asked if there were girls as well. He said, "Yes, there were, but I didn't dance," and smiled. I said, "Maybe we could go there one day and you can show me the bar," but he looked at me and said, "No, there's nothing for you there." Well, he'd said enough and I more or less knew what kind of bar that was—not a place to entertain well-off clients, that was for sure. He then said he had to go back to the barracks but would return the next day and with that he drove off and there I was, again, not knowing what to do or what to think. Like quite a few times before in my life, I stood there without a clue what to do and then realised I was getting cold, so went inside. Maybe I was over-reacting again, so the best thing to do would probably be not to ask anything, but what kind of relationship was that?

The next day Michael came early in the afternoon so that we could all go and check out the Senior Centre apartment. It was kind of cute but not very big and all they needed was bedding and some towels and once we'd got those, we could take my grandparents there the following week. I realised I would miss them, especially my grandmother, but there was a sofa-bed in there too, so I'd tell my grandmother I could always stay there overnight if she wanted me to. All in all, it looked cosy.

After dropping my parents off at home I suggested a little walk. Michael was pretty quiet and after a while he said he felt bad about the way he'd talked to me last night but that that place was really not for me—he said.

"There were lots of easy girls, you know what I mean," and I said, "Yes, German Fraeuleins," and he just nodded and said that was where he'd met "that" girl. I didn't argue with him; I would have lost anyway but I also felt I had no right to argue. He turned my head, looked at me and smiled and I had lost again. We then talked some more about a place for our engagement celebration but had no new ideas so far. He did say a colleague had told him about a little antique store in a small side street off Ku Damm, which carried all kinds of things and that perhaps we could check it out over the weekend. He always found the right words to make me smile again.

Michael also mentioned that he'd spoken to his father, who had sounded tired and still wasn't feeling completely well. His father also said he missed Janet—who would have thought of that! With the weekend coming up, we decided not to stay at Daniel's house and instead perhaps go to Complex Wannsee again as there weren't too many weekends left. The thought somehow made me sad and for the first time I asked him how long he thought it would be before he could come back again. He told me that was also the question he'd asked his father, who'd said it all depended how soon the paperwork took to wrap up as he knew Michael wanted to be back in Berlin as soon as possible. His father said at the latest it would be in the Fall, so approximately five months and at least that gave me some idea of the timeframe. We finished our walk and stopped at the coffee shop so that we could talk a little more but the decision for the coming weekend had been made and we would go looking for those rings and stay at Complex Wannsee.

I went to the workmen's compensation office to check the availability of a job but was told there wouldn't be anything available before June, so couldn't think what I would do all day. I then went to see the priest and told him my situation, explaining that I'd have time to spare during the day. He said there was always something to do there—watch children or maybe go and visit elderly people and help them at home. "Don't worry," he said. "We'll find something for you, but I can't pay much." I didn't care, I just wanted something to be busy with until Michael came back so that I was occupied and not just sitting around. I also told the doctor that if he needed a babysitter again, I'd be available day or night. When Michael stopped by that evening, I told him what I'd done and he laughed, saying, "That's great, at least you won't be off visiting bars and dancing." I didn't find that funny but most likely he'd never had to look for a job. Sometimes lifestyle and upbringing make it hard to laugh at certain situations and although Michael didn't have to worry, for me it was very important to have work to do for a living. Most likely, he'd never have to look for a job but I didn't say anything as I didn't want to start an argument. He told me he was really looking forward to the coming weekend in Wannsee—that we could relax and talk for hours and then he laughed and said, "If you want, you can even have a cigarette." Sometimes I really didn't find his jokes funny but I laughed anyway.

On Friday afternoon we went to try and find that antique store and finally found it. It was a pretty store and because Michael was wearing his uniform, the storeowner immediately showed us the most expensive items first. There was nothing I really liked but Michael found two rings, a little wider than I wanted, but one fitted Michael perfectly. The ladies ring was also wider and had some tiny diamonds on it and that was the one Michael wanted for me. I tried to explain that I couldn't wear that ring with the opal one and he said, "Then wear it on the other hand." The store owner, of course, agreed with Michael as he wanted to sell the rings and in the end I had no choice and we walked out with both rings. What Michael wanted; Michael got. In the jeep he asked me if I liked the rings and as there was really nothing I could say, I just said, "Yes, they're nice," and we both laughed because we both knew I didn't care for them too much. Maybe he just wanted to show me that he was the man of the house, because I'd told him about my father being the boss and the rest of the family having to do what he said. Whatever, we had the rings and we went on to Wannsee, where we had a lovely dinner and I was allowed to smoke a cigarette. Sometimes he behaved like a macho man, but still, I loved him dearly and I was very sure he knew it.

We realised that weekend that there weren't that many left—perhaps six at the most as although he didn't have an exact date yet, Michael knew he'd be leaving around the end of April. I had to give him my mailing address as there was no phone connection and I was sure I couldn't use the barracks connection. We'd had so many favours already through Daniel, so had to be thankful for that.

The next day we did our walk around the lake; I liked that walking so much and knew I'd miss it terribly. Hopefully, I'd have a lot of little jobs to keep my mind busy with other things so that I wasn't only thinking about who Michael was entertaining or whether he was flirting with well-off clients. I told myself the five months would pass quickly; positive thinking! We then drove around Wannsee a little—a lovely place with lots of forests and little lakes and Michael noticed I was quiet and wanted to know what I was thinking. When I told him, he put his arm around my shoulders and said, "Everything will be fine," and I remembered that I'd heard that quite often before. We still had a nice Saturday and then had to leave on Sunday afternoon anyway.

We thought maybe on Wednesday 17th, the next week, we could move my grandparents into their new little apartment if the jeep was available. We'd been told they could move in after the 15th and having the jeep would be a great help so when we got back to the apartment, Michael came in with me to talk about the move. My grandmother wasn't smiling that much recently but still always had in her hands the rosary which Michael had given her. When we told her about the move, she had teary eyes and I felt so sorry for her, but there was really no alternative and I would visit them as much as I could. Michael then left saying he'd be back the next evening and we tried to put some things together ready for Wednesday's move but it was emotional for all of us.

When Michael came late in the afternoon the next day he had something in his hands and said, "Look what I found behind the barracks, I know you like them," and he had three blooming lily of the valley plants, usually a sure sign that Spring is coming. I had tears in my eyes—he knew I loved Spring and also flowers. That was why I loved him—he could be so thoughtful and tender and that made me forget that sometimes there was another Michael, cold and sarcastic. He didn't behave like that to me but I saw him treating others that way. Anyway, that was the nicest gift he could give me and I cherished it more than a big diamond ring. When I told him that, he smiled and said, "You're so different—not at all like the girl in the saying 'Diamonds are a girl's best friend.'"

On Wednesday we were ready for the move and when Michael came to pick us up, my grandparents and my father were the first ones he took to the centre, then he collected my mother and me. It was a really big help having the transport since Grandfather was almost blind and really didn't know what was going on. Grandmother told him what was happening but he still seemed to be a little confused and I felt so sorry for them. If only we had a larger place so that they could have stayed with us. The centre had caregivers as well as nurses and a doctor on duty and they were all really nice and helpful. It wasn't a big facility, just about forty people, so that was nice, and from the window you could see the garden and trees, which must look very pretty in the summer when the leaves were on the trees and everything was blooming. We were really lucky to have found that place, which apparently had something to do with my father working in the hospital. The doctor came in and introduced himself and told us that in a few days they'd check my grandparents out and do some tests, because they hadn't seen a doctor for quite a while. In a way I was happy for them but I knew I'd miss my grandmother; where would I sleep when I was feeling down? Even Michael looked sad and took my hand because he knew the story about me sleeping in her lap. Hopefully, I wouldn't need that anymore!

As it wasn't too late, we still had time to go to the coffeeshop and talk. In four weeks, it would be our engagement day and in five weeks Michael would be leaving. I had to stop thinking about it, otherwise I would have cried. Daniel had talked with Michael earlier and wanted us to come over on the weekend—not for a party but just so that we could spend time together and Michael asked me if I wanted to go. Knowing the situation with Daniel, I said that I thought we should and Michael agreed. He also told me that Daniel had said if we didn't find a nice place for our engagement celebration, we could stay in his house and he'd move out and stay with friends for the weekend. I thought that sounded pretty good and that we might even take him up on that offer and Michael thought the same, so it looked as though we were getting some control over our plans.

It was nice just sitting together holding hands and we didn't need to talk at all. I think reality was setting in with Michael and that he now realised this easy-going part of his life would soon be over. I wished I could go with him and help him with whatever he needed to do, but maybe not going with him would make it more realistic. Anyway, he had to go, so dropped me off and held me really tight, looking as though he was scared. He told me that we'd be at Daniel's house over the weekend and would most likely take up his offer for our engagement if we hadn't found anything else. When I got into the apartment it looked empty and then I saw my bed and had to smile, wondering how long it would be that I'd have that bed for myself.

Again, I didn't get a lot of sleep that night as I had so many thoughts running through my mind. One decision I made was to see the doctor the next day and tell him I wanted to quit my part-time job because I felt I wasn't concentrating enough to handle a cash register and might make mistakes, which wouldn't be fair on the clients. I had enough little jobs lined up to keep me busy until I was able to start the full-time job and, honestly, I just wanted to spend as much time as possible with Michael before he left. I was honest with the doctor and he really understood and gave me a note to take to work saying I had to quit for health reasons. When I went and talked to the boss, he understood—or at least he said he did—but I had the feeling he was glad I was leaving and I understood as I hadn't been the best employee, always a little absent-minded. My parents were okay with it as they knew what I'd been through, but Michael didn't know about it and I thought I'd tell him that evening when he'd promised to stop by. My mother and I cleaned up the apartment a bit but it still felt empty even though we knew it was best for my grandparents that they'd moved.

When Michael came over that evening, I was surprised to see him wearing the top which we'd given him for Christmas with "Berlin" written on it; he really must be having a hard time leaving! I had to smile when I saw it but he didn't, so I didn't make a joke of it which I'd wanted to do when I first saw it. When I told him I'd quit my part-time job he said, "Oh, great, if we're really friendly to Daniel on the weekend, maybe he'll give me a few days off, like a vacation before I leave." I had to laugh and told him he was sneaky as well—like when I'd tried to trick Daniel out of having that huge engagement party.

All of a sudden, he asked me if I'd like to go and visit my grandparents—just the two of us—and that the next day he'd have more time and would take all of us to visit them. I was so happy to see grandmother and they looked fine though grandmother had teary eyes again when she saw us. She noticed Michael's top, pointed at it and said "Berlin" and smiled. I thought she was lonely, but she never complained. When we went back to our apartment, we told my parents that we'd seen Grandmother and Grandfather and my father said that they wanted to go tomorrow and would take a taxi. Michael must have understood what my father meant—maybe he just understood the word "taxi"—so he told my father in his broken German that he would take us. We still had a little time left so went for a walk and decided to get something nice to give Daniel over the weekend. Michael suggested whiskey and looked at me with that famous smile, but I told him it was supposed to be a present for Daniel, not for him. He really had a good laugh over it and I loved to joke with him. It had to be something special for Daniel, especially as we wanted to get a few days of vacation for Michael, so we decided to think about it overnight and after a big hug, he drove off.

He arrived earlier than I expected on Friday because he wanted to go to the PX Store to find something for Daniel before we drove to see my grandparents. We found two very nice whiskey glasses—the sort made for tourists with "Berlin" written on the side and, of course, that bottle of whiskey, since Michael insisted that the bottle went together with the glasses. I was used to it by now—what Michael wants, Michael gets. After that we picked up my parents and drove to the centre. Everyone looked fine but I could tell my grandmother had lost quite a bit of her smile and I hoped so much that she'd get used to her new little apartment. We stayed for a while because my father had to sign some paperwork. Because they were refugees, my grandparents were entitled to receive money from the state to live on and also contributions to pay for the centre and to help my grandfather because he was disabled because of his sight and hearing problems.

When all that was done, we took my parents' home and continued on to Daniel's place, where we gave him the glasses and the bottle of whiskey. He looked at us laughing and asked what we wanted from him and we both said, "A little more time for Michael." He explained that he'd signed the paper for Michael's one-month extension and that there was nothing more he could do, but he promised he'd try to get him a week's vacation so that we could spend more time together and that made us very happy. We had some pizza for dinner and the two men poured a glass of whiskey. I wanted to have a taste of it and had a sip which, to me, tasted terrible and I never drank whiskey again; I just didn't like the taste of it. We talked for a while and Daniel told us he wanted to visit Ireland, where his ancestors came from and that he hoped to do that while he was still stationed in Germany. He didn't mention his wife and I didn't want to bring her name up. I was so glad that everyone was wrong in thinking Daniel wanted an affair and he became my second father again.

We talked about a lot of things and then Daniel took the bottle away saying it was his present and made us a big pot of coffee instead. He really treated us like his children, which in a way was very nice. At the end of the evening when we were all tired, we went off back to what I thought of as our little hideaway and talked some more about our future. San Francisco would most probably be our home because of the real estate business and I felt I knew a lot about San Francisco already after reading a book about it. It all sounded so perfect—perhaps too perfect to be true but I pushed that thought away as being another negative thought and those were my last thoughts of the night.

On Saturday all of us had a late start and when I opened the window, for the first time this year it felt like spring. Next week, though, was the last week of March which meant that at the most we had four weeks left. When I realised Michael was standing next to me he said, "Yes, we have four weeks left," he must have read my mind. He said it was just goodbye for a little while and that everything would be fine after that and somehow that wording sounded familiar. While we were having breakfast, Daniel told us there was a little spring festival going on behind the barracks—"not a big party," Daniel said, and smiled at me, "Just some music and some food. It should be nice, why don't you come over too?" It sounded nice and we thought we should try it, so had our little walk again and then after lunch we drove over to the barracks.

I'd never been to the barracks before because, of course, no Germans were allowed unless you were accompanied by someone in the US military. As Daniel and Michael were with me, I had no problems, especially with Daniel being a high-ranking officer. I wasn't allowed to go into the barracks, but outside was fine. Nice music was playing and there was Coca-Cola, of course, which made me remember my first Coca-Cola with Wolfgang in the American Club; how long ago was that? I had to smile and when Michael asked me, I told him the story and he laughed too, saying I was stepping up—first Coca-Cola, then yesterday my first whiskey, what will be next? And I answered, "Flying in a plane!"

We found a nice table and were just sitting and watching people when Daniel went into the barracks. Michael showed me where he'd found the lily of the valley flowers, but there were none left—someone must have found them and picked them. We danced a few dances and then she came in—"that" girl with a few others and she waved at us and in her loud voice called out, "You two are always together, like glue." Neither of us reacted to her—it was embarrassing for her but apparently she didn't realise it. When Daniel returned, he brought us some hotdogs and Michael asked me if that was a first as well but I told him I'd already had them in the American Club. Daniel mentioned that there was a possibility Michael would get his week's vacation, he just had to find out when it would be, and that was great news for us.

It was a lively group of people—dancing and singing to welcome Spring but at ten o'clock the festival ended and we all left, but it had been such a nice evening. At Daniel's house the two of them had a whiskey and I was allowed to have a cigarette. Michael's order. In our room we talked about the flight and he thought he would fly from Berlin-Tempelfot airport to Frankfurt, West Germany, then on to New York and on to San Francisco, as that was the way he'd come over. He said it was a very long flight and as they were military planes, they weren't too comfortable either. I told Michael I must remember to write to Janet to get her new address as I didn't know if I'd be able to write to Michael at his father's address, where he'd be living. Only four more weeks. I tried hard not to think about it after such a lovely day.

I woke up several times that night with my heart racing and hoped those stress attacks weren't coming back. I decided to see the doctor about them and see if there was any medication available to calm my nerves. With the weekend almost over again, on Sunday afternoon we got ready to go and see Rita and Jonathan again before Michael had to be back at the barracks. Rita and Jonathan were fine—they knew what they wanted and her grandmother had agreed to move in with relatives in West Germany, which was great as Rita really deserved a little happiness. Before Michael left for the barracks we walked around the lake and stopped at the coffeeshop; it was hard to let go of each other as if every minute was precious even though we still had four weeks left and even a week of vacation. For the first time in our relationship, I had the feeling Michael really cared for me, which made life a little easier but all the "ifs," "buts" and "maybes" didn't disappear at all. Michael promised to stop by the next evening; it was the last week in March.

The next day I saw the doctor and told him about my sleeplessness and he gave me some Valerian tablets, a natural remedy made from Valerian roots, and which is good against insomnia and anxiety. It's an old German household remedy called Baldrian and I'm very sure it's still being used today. I then went home and wrote to Janet even though I wasn't actually sure if I'd already written or not, but she would understand the emotional state I was in. I told her how bad I felt about Michael's departure and losing the baby and how I hoped he'd soon be back. I gave her my mailing address and asked for hers as I wouldn't be able to mail letters to her through Michael anymore, and I asked her to stay in touch with me until I'd be able to see her in person, hoping that she would understand and help me.

I talked a little with my mother about what she and my father intended to do after I'd left. She didn't know because my father still had a while to work before his retirement and there was uncertainty about being caged in West Berlin. Our property was in East Germany, which we couldn't go to even though that was where my father wanted to build so that they could retire to their own house. That hope seemed to be gone. Also, I didn't believe I would ever move back to Berlin after Michael and I were settled in San Francisco and that talk was quite emotional for both of us. We realised that whatever happened was meant to happen and that there was nothing we could do about it. I took two of those Valerian tablets and slept a little better. The next evening Michael stopped by for a little while and told me Daniel was saying that his week's vacation would be the first week of April and that we should do something special every day. The problem was that there wasn't much to do in West Berlin and we'd have to think of something; maybe Daniel would have some ideas. Meanwhile I gave Michael the letter to mail to Janet and with that, he had to leave.

The fact that it was the last week of March kept running through my head most of the time. On Tuesday our priest stopped by in the morning to ask me if I'd have time over the next couple of days to help decorate the church with flowers for the coming weekend when there was a little celebration going on to mark the beginning of spring. It was the time of year when everyone was happy the cold was almost over and there were lots of little celebrations going on and I was glad to get out of the house and do something other than think about Michael's departure all the time. On the way to the church we passed the cemetery and I remembered burying Wolfgang's presents under the tree there. It was a very negative thought and I sincerely hoped I didn't have to do the same with Michael's. That thought really scared me and I made myself start to think positively again.

Being at the church was really nice. I even saw some of the people I'd worked with before when we drove the children into West Germany and everyone told their stories. They, of course, wanted to know about Wolfgang and could hardly believe what had happened, but people do change. After a few hours, the church started to look really pretty and after lunch the priest suggested we finish it off the next day. One of the ladies said why didn't I go over on Saturday for the little spring festival and take my boyfriend with me—the American soldier who she said she'd seen me with when we went to the church at Christmas. I wasn't sure as I didn't know quite how it was meant, that maybe it would be just to put him down because a lot of West Berliners still had an attitude towards the Allies. I would probably have done too, if I hadn't met Michael.

When Michael stopped by later that day, I told him about going to the church but didn't say anything yet about that little spring festival. He brought me some more lily of the valley flowers which he'd found in another place behind the barracks. He mentioned that he'd talked to his father who told him that he'd had lunch with Janet who was very happy with Stefano and it looked as if the relationship was quite serious. "It seems," Michael said, "that my father is mellowing out." We decided that the next day, on Wednesday, Michael's half-day, he would pick me up from the church at noon and we could have a short visit with my grandparents. We still had time for a little walk but I felt that every day was getting harder emotionally for both of us. Because we couldn't find a nice place for our engagement celebration, we'd decided to stay at Daniel's house since he'd been kind enough to make that nice offer, and we decided to tell him that the next day.

On Wednesday Michael came to the church to collect me. The priest was there as well and, of course, everyone was looking at us and I wasn't sure what their thoughts were of me having an American soldier as a boyfriend. I felt a little uneasy, especially after Michael put his arm around my shoulders, and I'm sure he did it on purpose as I could see his eyes laughing. Some of the elderly ladies turned around and walked away but the younger ones and the priest came over and tried to talk to Michael—they in broken English and Michael in broken German. It was a funny communication but everyone understood what was being said. I was really proud of the way he handled the situation and how charming he was but that was his trademark, being charming and flirtatious. And he really was good looking! Before we left, the priest asked Michael to come over on Saturday for that little spring festival and he promised he would. I was glad the priest had asked him and I didn't have to.

Then we went to Daniel's house and when we got there I had the feeling he'd had a little too much whiskey. I might have been wrong as he was drinking a cup of coffee, but even the coffee smelt like whiskey; maybe he'd put some in the coffee. We told him we'd come to him over the weekend but that on Saturday we were going to that church festival. He liked the idea and said that if he didn't have any other arrangements he might join us as he hadn't been to church for quite a while. I didn't think the priest would mind but I was a little nervous about what the parishioners would say, but I kept quiet.

The next week was Michael's weeks holiday. From now on it would be pretty busy with Easter coming up and our engagement. Michael hadn't had a date set for his departure so I just hoped it would be the last day in April and was thankful anyway for the extra month we'd had. When Michael drove me home we ended up sitting in the jeep just sitting close and holding hands and watching the stars; it was now getting harder and harder emotionally every day and we both hoped it wouldn't be too long before we were together again.

Before he left, Michael told me he didn't think he could come the next day, Thursday, as he'd swapped shifts with another soldier, but from Friday we'd have the whole weekend, so on Thursday morning I went shopping with my mother. I also helped around the house and we had time to talk. I knew my parents would miss me terribly but my mother told me their house would always be open if I had any problems in San Francisco. I knew that and although I loved those mother/daughter talks, I was on an emotional rollercoaster. In the afternoon I reread that book about California and especially San Francisco, so at least I wasn't completely uneducated about Michael's past or the area where he grew up.

By the early evening I needed some exercise and walked over to Rita's. She was really happy to see me and we talked about what would happen. She was planning to leave Berlin with Jonathan at the end of the year and wanted to get married in the States as with her grandmother having gone to West Germany, she wouldn't have any relatives here in Berlin. Rita looked at me and told me that she really wished me all the best and hoped Michael would treat me like a princess and I felt as though I had a knot in my stomach—it wasn't that far away. There was a knock at the door and when Rita opened it, Michael was there smiling. He said he hadn't had to change shifts so he went to see me and my mother had just said "Rita," so here he was. That made my evening. I really started to trust him as he could have gone to that bar next to the barracks and I wouldn't even have known; maybe everything would be fine, like he always said. He could see how happy I was and said, "See, I'm not that bad"—of course, he knew what I was thinking.

We stayed a little while and then went for a drive in the jeep. He told me he'd been told that his departure would be between the 27th and the 30th of April. Well, we had to face it but we still had about four weeks ahead of us. As always, we were sitting close together in the jeep, holding hands, and we both smoked a cigarette. He had to leave but it was only until tomorrow and then we had the whole weekend for ourselves. When I got home, my mother looked at me and said, "You look so happy; you must love him very much," and I just nodded. That night I didn't need those Valerian pills.

I really slept well and felt rested the next day, so my mother and I baked some sugar cookies—nothing fancy but they tasted really good and I decided to take some to my grandparents and then to Daniel as well. So, when Michael picked me up on Friday afternoon, I asked him to stop by at my grandparents and he asked me where the cookies had come from. When I told him, he said, "Well, you can bake; that's another plus for you," and so we joked around.

My grandparents were okay so far. My grandmother told me they'd been checked over and there was nothing serious wrong with them, just a little pain here and there, mostly old age related, so that was good. I could feel, though, that they were lonely, particularly my grandmother. She'd had twelve children and now only had my father, who was her oldest child, around; the rest had spread all over and nobody was in West Berlin or even West Germany for that matter. She didn't complain but her eyes told more than words. She really enjoyed the cookies and Michael told me to tell her that he had baked them for her. She laughed about that and he gave her a big hug, but that special smile of hers had gone. It was sad.

We then went to Daniel's house and gave him the cookies and he really enjoyed them too but he was different again even though there was no whiskey smell. Michael left to get us some pizza for dinner so I just asked him if there was anything wrong. He replied that Elena had contacted him from San Francisco and was asking for money. "Yes," he said. "She's still my wife but I'll be broke if she keeps on asking for money." He said the amounts she asked for weren't small and he didn't know what to do, whether to file for divorce or not. He'd heard through friends that she most likely had a new boyfriend and was supporting him. He said if he filed for divorce he might not even pay for her support as he could prove she'd been unfaithful to him quite a lot. I somehow believed he still cared for her and I felt bad because I was just wondering whether, if she has a new boyfriend, she'd be running after Michael, but of course I didn't tell Daniel that.

Michael came back with the pizza and then Daniel asked us if it would be okay for him to come with us the next day to that church spring festival. We said it would be fine. I knew the priest wouldn't have anything against it and as for the parishioners—well, anyone can go to church. After dinner we still went for a little walk and I did tell Michael about Elena being back in San Francisco with a new boyfriend and waited for his reaction. The only thing he said was that she would never change and that Daniel should get rid of her so that he could start over again. That could mean a lot of things, so I stopped talking about it. It was a really pleasant evening and a lot of people were out walking but I could see from some of their expressions that they were looking at Michael and me and wondering how I could do that—a German girl out with an American soldier. In some ways I could understand that but what would West Berlin have done without the Allies supporting us with everything through the air bridge for nine months; perhaps we'd even have been under Soviet control. Not all Germans thought like that, though, and my thinking of course was influenced by mixing with American people. It bothered me a little but when I looked at Michael I didn't think he even saw their expressions and certainly didn't pay any attention to them.

After getting home, Daniel said he was tired and went to his room and we went to ours, talking about what special things we would do for our little engagement celebration. Maybe we would cook something completely different at the house and we thought it would be fun. It was only three weeks from now and we thought it would be pretty romantic and something we'd always remember.

The next morning, we woke Daniel up and I had the feeling he'd had too much whiskey the night before; he was going through a rough time just then. He seemed alright after breakfast so we decided to go to the PX Store, which was open all day on Saturday, and get some little snacks to take to the church festival. We bought quite a few things to snack on, so the people there could taste some American food, which I was pretty sure they wouldn't have tried yet. When we got there, quite a few people had already arrived and then the priest came over and greeted us and Daniel gave him an envelope. I assumed it was money, since the priest thanked him and smiled and I thought how nice that was of Daniel. We took out our treats and people tried them—some liked them and some didn't but, well, it's like that all over the world, but overall it was a nice get-together and something different from big parties.

Michael's vacation started the next day, Sunday, March 28th, and would last until April 4th, which meant he didn't have to go back to the barracks at night and we could be together all the time. The problems we had were whether my parents would allow me to stay away from home for a week and also where we were going to stay. The only thought we had, which I didn't think my parents would mind, was for us to stay in Daniel's house for the week so when we got back from the church festival, we asked him outright, feeling rather like homeless people. He laughed and said he knew what we were asking and that, yes, we could stay but a condition was that we cook dinner on at least three days of that week. We then had to ask my parents but I was sure they'd allow me to go—after all we were both over 21, or at least 21—so that was our plan and when we asked them, they agreed on condition that I promised to check in with them and say hello. I wished we could have gone to Aunt Maria, but that was East Germany and not safe enough.

During that week we wanted to get some little presents for Michael to take to his family in San Francisco and to just drive around and be together. It sounded so perfect that it almost scared me. We had to get food for the three days when we had to cook and it sounded like fun even though neither of us were the best cooks. I suggested we get a German recipe book from my mother so that we could cook some German dishes and we wondered how Daniel would like them. My mother also offered to bake more sugar cookies, and all that stopped us constantly thinking of Michael's departure, which was now set for April 28th. I felt Michael was also having a hard time thinking of that day but it would only be goodbye for a few months and we'd have to make the best of it.

That Sunday evening, we went over to see Rita and Jonathan and told them our plans. Rita had stopped working at the shop and had become her grandmother's caregiver for the rest of the time they'd be in West Berlin, and for that she got paid by the State. It wasn't a lot but meant she could stay at home and take proper care of her grandmother. We decided that one day during that week the four of us would get together and go downtown to do some window shopping and maybe find a little café where we could eat. We then drove back to Daniel's but he was already in his room because he had to get up early on Monday morning, so we listened to some music and just enjoyed each other's company until I fell asleep on the couch—again without those Valerian pills.

On Monday morning we had breakfast together and then Daniel had to leave for the barracks. We talked about the menu for the coming week and had decided to cook on Tuesday, Thursday and Friday, the big question being what we were going to cook. Eventually we decided that on Tuesday we'd have an easy meal of chicken noodle soup with barley and lots of vegetables in it, possibly with some kind of pudding as desert. Friday was to be Bratwurst with Sauerkraut and mashed potatoes, which was easy to make. For Thursday, however, we opted for meatballs and red cabbage with dumplings and a mixed salad followed by ice cream, and for that we needed help with the dumplings and the meat balls, so we went to see my mother and told her our plan. She was delighted to help with the meatballs and red cabbage and told us to just give her all the ingredients and she'd cook it for us. That week was during Fastenzeit (Lent), which usually starts at the end of February and lasts forty days until Easter. During that time Catholics are not supposed to eat meat on Fridays or do a lot of other things—even not smoking if you usually do that. As my mother was a strict Catholic, I didn't think she'd be too happy about us having the Bratwurst on Friday, so we told her we'd have fish, which we were allowed to eat. She gave us a cookbook, just in case we needed it and all we had to do then was to get all the ingredients from the PX Store and give my mother what she needed. It was a lot of fun, though we probably just looked like two silly teenagers.

In the afternoon we stopped at Rita's and asked her if Wednesday was a good day to go downtown and walk around and she said she'd be glad to come with us, so it looked as though we'd be busy the whole week. When we finally got home, Daniel was already there and had brought some hotdogs from the barracks. We told him we'd organised our cooking plans but didn't tell him what we were going to cook. The weather was still nice so we went out for our little walk and then with not much to do that evening, everyone went to bed early. Tomorrow was to be our first cooking day, but that was easy as we had all day to cook chicken soup and we really laughed about it. It was quite a while since I'd laughed that much and it helped us push out any thoughts about Michael's departure. That evening I again didn't need my Valerian pills; I just put my head on his shoulder and went to sleep

We got up early to start making the chicken noodle soup so that everything would be ready for dinner when Daniel got home. First we cut up the chicken and looked for the largest pot in the kitchen. It was a stewing chicken which we'd been told would take a little longer to cook than a frying chicken, but that the taste would be better. Well, it certainly took a lot longer to cook, but we had time to spare, so while we waited for it to soften, we cut up the vegetables. We eventually started to wonder if perhaps we should have bought a different kind of chicken but it was too late for that now so while the chicken cooked we listen to some music and even danced in the kitchen. It was then lunchtime, so we thought we'd have to do something and decided to take the chicken out of the pot and cut it up into smaller pieces with a sharp knife. The taste of the soup was really good, so we dumped the vegetables in along with the barley and the smaller pieces of chicken We unfortunately hadn't realised that the barley would swell up and, as we'd used the whole bag, the soup was getting thicker and thicker and we had to add more water into it until the pot was almost overflowing and we then had to add another pot. It almost looked like a field kitchen and was a complete mess. In a way it was funny but the worst part was that the soup had almost lost its chicken flavour because of all the water we'd had to dump in it to dilute the swelling barley.

We sat down and tried to think what to do and decided the best thing was to be honest with Daniel, go to the PX Store and just buy some chicken noodle soup in a can. We did that but left the mess of our own soup for Daniel to see so that he'd know we really had tried. We both decided that cooking probably wouldn't be one of our hobbies. When Daniel got home we told and showed him everything and he had the best laugh ever, but the canned chicken noodle soup was delicious. All in all, it was the best day ever and the only worry Daniel had was what would happen with our meal on Thursday but we were safe on that as my mother was cooking it for us. I will never forget that chicken soup day. After dinner, we walked for a while and it was so nice doing that together. The next day was to be our day of going into town with Rita, which should be nice as there was no cooking involved and that evening Daniel opened a bottle of champagne saying that that chicken soup needed a celebration.

It was such a nice evening I wished that time would just stand still. Daniel was in a better mood and told us he was thinking about filing for divorce while he was still young enough to start over again, and we thought that was a good idea. We told him our plans for the next day, confirming there was no home cooking, and as it was getting late and we were already looking forward to the next day with Rita, we retired to our room. Pretty soon that room would be over too, so we just enjoyed every minute we could of being together. Thinking back to our blind date, both of us had to smile about how unfriendly we were to each other until we slowly fell in love. Michael interrupted that I did first and although that was true I wouldn't admit it and then, realising that we were getting emotional again, we changed the subject. It wasn't easy but it was only going to be goodbye for a few months and for the fourth night, I didn't need those pills.

Rita was already waiting for us when we got there the next day and we went looking for little souvenirs for Michael to take back—maybe a Berliner Baer, which was and is the symbol of Berlin, for his father and a top with "Berlin" on it for Janet; we thought that would be nice and we were lucky and found just what we wanted. Some little sidewalk cafes were opening up and it was already spring and if you didn't know it, you couldn't imagine that just a little further on there was a checkpoint and the border of a free city, while we were caged in. It's amazing how fast people get used to that feeling of not living in freedom. We had lunch in one of the little cafes, sitting outside and watching people, but couldn't do it for long because it was still chilly. We then walked around a little and noticed little stores and bazaars opening up and it looked as though West Berlin was becoming its own little city. We really enjoyed that and had what we wanted—to do something new every day while Michael was on holiday. Even Rita said she thought she'd miss Berlin: how true that was and I was so sure that I would as well but we didn't let any of those negative thoughts take over.

We finally took Rita home and stopped by at my mother's to ask her what time we should stop by to collect our dinner and she said any time tomorrow afternoon. While we were in the neighbourhood we also looked in on my grandparents and they were fine apart from being lonely. I felt so sorry for them but there was nothing we could do about it. Getting home, Daniel was sitting in his office drinking a cup of coffee which smelt more like whiskey, but we didn't say anything except that we were tired and going into our room. I was worried Daniel would become an alcoholic and I blamed it all on Elena but I didn't tell Michael what I was thinking as he had enough on his mind just then. All in all, we had a successful day, and I loved every minute of it.

Well, we were glad it was Thursday—our day to cook—but luckily my mother was doing it so we were sure it'd be done in time and taste good as well. When we got up, Daniel had already left and we just hung around the house trying to clean up a little and waiting for noon so that we could go and pick up the food. The weather wasn't that great so we couldn't even go out walking and we just started talking about growing up and how different everything was. He told me about his holidays in Mexico and Canada and visiting different cities in the U.S. He liked Mexico a lot—he said that the people were friendly and that he liked their temperament as well as their music. That made a lot of sense to me—the Mexican girlfriend he'd left when he was transferred to Berlin, then Elena—that must have been his Spanish blood, sort of blood related, while I was more from the Eastern side. The only thing I could tell him about was Poland since I hadn't been anywhere else. It was too bad we didn't have any pictures to share because our lives were a complete contrast; maybe that's what made it so exciting.

When it was time to collect the food, my mother had everything ready and it smelled so good. We were very sure Daniel would like this kind of food. When we got home it was late afternoon and luckily Daniel wasn't there, otherwise he would have known someone else had cooked for us. When he did arrive, he had pizza with him, saying he wasn't sure if there'd be anything to eat and when he saw our food he laughed and asked who had cooked it. The kitchen was clean and he knew right away that we hadn't cooked it. We told him the whole story and it was fine—he really liked the food and so did Michael, and that was the main thing. He'd spoken with Michael's father who said he was doing alright so far but he was complaining about his wife, Gloria, spending a lot of money. He'd also seen Elena and her new boyfriend in downtown San Francisco. They hadn't talked, just said hello, and her new boyfriend looked quite a lot younger than her—well, we all knew that story. I didn't think it bother Michael at all as the look on his face didn't change a bit. Daniel had been told by his boss that he'd also most likely have to go back to the States by the end of the year, and that would be a change for all of us, but as Michael always said—everything would be fine. The dinner was a great success but as it was late again, we all decided to retire for the night.

Tomorrow would be the Bratwurst day, there wasn't much we could do wrong, and so far we were enjoying that week of vacation. We knew that as soon as he left there would be a lot of work for him and also for me. Thinking back, I asked him if he ever regretted having met me. He said he hadn't regretted it but just that in the beginning it had been a waste of time as I wasn't really friendly. "But that changed very fast," he said, and laughed. Well, that wasn't really what I'd expected but he was right—I wasn't friendly because he was so arrogant—but it was a relaxed conversation and brought us again one day closer to his departure.

It was Friday, the Bratwurst day, but that wasn't bad and we had time because the Bratwurst had to be cooked in the afternoon, otherwise it would be cold and I didn't imagine Daniel would like cold Bratwurst. Only a week to go before it would be Easter and our engagement. The weather had cleared up and we were able to go walking and we could see spring had arrived with the buds on the trees ready to open and some lilies of the valley in the forest and it all looked so beautiful that we enjoyed the walk hugely, but we also had to face the reality of what the passing time meant for us. We'd come so far together that we knew we'd make it as long as we stuck together.

It was already afternoon when we got home and we started getting dinner ready, then as soon as Daniel got home we fried the Bratwurst. He liked the dinner but I didn't think Sauerkraut was his favourite, but at least he tried everything. Later on, he told us that he'd invited his friends over for dinner the next day—the ones he'd be staying with while we used his house for our engagement celebration, so that should be nice. Daniel said he'd bring some food home from the barracks—apparently he didn't trust our cooking skills that much! We talked a little about the overall situation with West Berlin, nobody wanted to pull out of Berlin, either East or West, and rumours were still going around about a wall being built because more and more people were trying to leave the Eastern part to get over to the West. Some were even talking of leaving Germany altogether and immigrating to other countries, like Canada and Australia, but that would be a long process. After that we retired and all of a sudden, Michael said that if there should be any problems, we'd just elope and get married in Las Vegas. I didn't quite understand what he meant but didn't ask him again and we finished off the evening listening to music and dreaming until we fell asleep.

The next morning, we cleaned up the house a little before Daniel's friends came and then Daniel went to the barracks to get some food for an early dinner. I asked Michael if he knew those people but he'd never met them either. Well, everything was nice and clean and we had some candles burning and it was really cosy and then we heard Daniel's voice talking outside and he came in with his friends. I thought I wasn't seeing properly: the couple was a man with an African-American lady. She was very pretty but except perhaps in pictures, I'd never seen an African-American person before. I think Michael gave me a little nudge in the side, telling me not to stare, and Daniel introduced us, so the ice was broken. I felt so dumb but apparently those two hadn't seen my surprised face, or at least hadn't mentioned anything. They were really nice people, older than us and they came from New York—the man was one of Daniel's bosses and she was his wife.

We had a nice conversation and I was glad my English wasn't still that school/broken English—because of talking to Michael and Daniel most of the time, it had improved a lot and it turned out to be a very interesting evening. When we were in our room again, Michael asked me if that was another "first" for me—meeting an African-American person, and I nodded. "Yes, you looked as if you were seeing a ghost," Michael said. I was really embarrassed but he just smiled and gave me a hug, saying it was fine, they understood.

Although Michael said they understood, it still bothered me a lot as there always seemed to be a "first" of everything for me. Yes, I was the youngest out of our group and I knew I had so much to learn, but my self-esteem was pretty low right then and I just started to cry and couldn't stop. Michael tried to calm me down; he might have understood, he might not, I really couldn't tell and I had to take those Valerian pills again to calm down. Well, that was the last day of Michael's vacation and from now on time would run quickly but we still had next weekend for our engagement celebration. When I felt a little better, Michael told me that after our first few dates, when he started to speak Spanish to me and he saw how upset I got at not being able to answer, he felt really bad, so stopped doing it. Then he laughed and said he actually really liked it when I got mad because then I couldn't hide my feelings and my eyes told him how I really felt. He said that he really did speak Spanish fluently and with that he won me over again and I felt better, but it didn't really help my self-esteem.

I realised that the next day he had to be back in the barracks again and after that would be the last week before our engagement, and after realising that, I stopped thinking. I apologised to him for my silly behaviour but he just held me and I felt safe again. I remembered the doctor saying I would always have a weak nervous system and that possibly it was inherited as my mother was the same. We listened to some music after that but I fell asleep on the couch again.

I slept really well and Michael woke me up with a cup of coffee on Sunday, which was very special. It looked like a beautiful morning and the sun was out so we were sure we'd have a good walk. While we were sitting on the couch, Michael looked at me and said, "I'll teach you some Spanish words every day now and I want you to repeat them to me at least once a day. The first words are 'Te amo' (I love you). Will you do that for me?" I had to laugh. "And how about you?" I asked him. "Well, I said it already," he said. He always had the right words to make me laugh. I packed up all the belongings I'd used that last week and then we had breakfast with Daniel and talked about last night's little get together. Daniel said they were a really nice couple—she a high school teacher in New York—and that they had two children. He said they had problems early in their relationship because of her African-American heritage, but that they'd stuck it out, and my positive thought for the day was that we could, as well.

We started our walk and the air felt good and lots of other people were also walking around like us, holding hands. I looked at him and said, "Te amo," and he smiled; of course, he knew that already. After we picked up our belongings, we decided to say hello to Rita. She was busy doing things for her grandmother but just looked at us and said how happy we both looked. In a way we were but our thoughts had to stay in the present and couldn't go too far into the future. Michael was saying that when I got to San Francisco I should take some courses in business administration and communication because that would help if I worked in the Real Estate office. He said perhaps I could help him as he had the feeling his father would like to retire and his partner was elderly as well. I wasn't so sure about that idea and didn't know if my English was good enough, but he said, "You only learn a language properly when you live in that country." There was still time to think about that.

When we were home we sat in the car for a little while but then he had to go and he promised he'd stop by the next day. My mother was happy to have me home again and in a way I was happy to be there, too, but I missed Michael already and was wondering how I'd be able to get through the first days after his departure. I sincerely hoped that full-time job would start in July and hoped that at the latest Michael would be back in October to get married—either here in Berlin or in San Francisco or Las Vegas, I really no longer cared where it would be.

Our priest showed up the next morning and asked if I had a few hours to spare as an elderly lady from the church had fallen and broken her left hand and needed help for a few days this week. I gladly agreed as Michael wouldn't come until later anyway, so I had time to kill. He told me where she lived and it was close to the church so I got ready and walked over. I told my mother that if Michael came earlier than expected, just to tell him "church" and then he'd know where to find me. Her daughter opened the door and I knew her from church. She told me she just needed help for a few days as she was going to take a vacation from work and then she'd be able to take care of her mother herself. I was just glad I had the opportunity to get out of the house and be busy.

The lady I was helping was lovely and I tried to help her as much as was needed. We started talking and she'd seen me in church with Michael, so I told her a little about our plans and that I was having a hard time now because of his forthcoming departure. She understood completely and then she said something I really valued. She said, "God won't give you more than you can handle." She told me she'd lost one of her sons during the war when he was on active duty and she didn't even know where he was killed and buried. She showed me pictures of him—he was only 19 when she got the news "killed in action"—so I thought, *Why am I complaining?—we're both alive and we'll get through this too.* It got later than I thought and told her I'd go back and help again tomorrow and she gave me 20.00 Deutsche Mark, which was a lot of money at that time, and thanked me for listening to her. I then walked over to the church where I saw Michael's jeep in the parking lot and assumed he must be inside talking to the priest. When he saw me, he came out and said, "Buenas noches" (good evening)—my second Spanish lesson—and then asked me if I remembered yesterday's lesson. I really had to laugh—"Yes, te amo," and we both laughed.

As I had that money I invited him to the coffee shop for a bite to eat. He said he thought he'd seen a letter from Janet in his room but had forgotten it and would bring it tomorrow. We had a nice time and when the bill came, I took it and paid it and felt good about doing it. He laughed and said, "Okay, now you're becoming independent. You should have told me you were paying, I would have eaten the most expensive meal on the menu." It felt good to be joking around. We still had to get some things to eat and drink for our engagement and Michael looked very serious when he said, "I hope I don't forget the rings, please try to remind me the day before." He looked so serious that I believed him until he laughed and told me that I looked completely confused when he'd said it. If I could just change my behaviour so that people couldn't see my feelings in my eyes! But I guessed it was probably only Michael who could do that.

It was a lovely evening and I was looking forward to going to help that lady so I told Michael I'd show him her house so that tomorrow if he wanted to, he could pick me up from there. He liked the idea and with that he had to leave. He just said "Adios" (goodbye) and that was my third lesson in Spanish. It occurred to me that if we went along with one sentence a day, it would take years until I could speak Spanish.

When Michael took me home that evening, I said, "Te amo and adios." I think he liked it. I later talked to my mother and asked her if she would do us a favour and bake something for our engagement. I knew she would love that and asked her for a "Schwartzwaeldkirschtorte" (black forest cake). I knew they took time to make and if you bought one at a bakery they were quite expensive. The cake's like a sponge cake filled with whipped cream and cherries. She hesitated for a moment but, of course, she said, "I'll try my best," which made me very happy.

I had been looking forward to the next day, got up early and told my mother we'd get her all the ingredients for the cake from the PX Store. On the way to the lady I was helping, I discovered that the lilac tree close to the graveyard was just about to start blooming. Some varieties start to bloom early and they mostly stay in bloom for six weeks. I used to steal those beautiful smelling lilac branches for Mother's Day; most teenagers seemed to do that; and yes, I did it—I stole a branch from the tree and took it with me to the lady. She was so happy and I saw teary eyes and when I told her they were my favourite flowers, she admitted that they were hers, too. I cleaned up again and prepared a little lunch, but mostly we were talking as she talked constantly. I felt she was probably lonely but it didn't bother me—she was a little bit like my grandmother. She told me she'd recently lost her husband and that she still missed him every day and I told her about my grandparents, saying how lucky they were to still be together. How true that was.

I told her Michael would be picking me up in the afternoon from her house and she said that was fine and that she hoped he could understand a little German I told her he spoke broken German and she laughed and said, "We still have hands and feet to help us." I really enjoyed her company and later, when her daughter stopped by and told us that she might be able to take over in two days, I almost told her that it was fine, I could stay on. I kept quiet, though, as I thought she might not like it. A little while later Michael showed up at the door and Mrs. Bohn (that was her name) called out for me to just let him in. Well, I did, and in came Mister Charming and introduced himself and the two of them then started to talk, like she said—hands and feet included—and she really liked it. She pointed to the lilac flowers and pointed towards me, so he knew I'd brought them. But it was getting late and we had to leave, and shaking hands, I found another 20.00 Deutsche Mark in my hand. It was nice but I felt completely overpaid—but she probably paid me for listening to her.

In the jeep, I told Michael about the black forest cake and that we had to get the ingredients for my mother to use tomorrow and explained that this cake was a specialty in Germany. He asked me if I liked the lilac flowers and I said, "Very much." He looked at me and said, "Te ves guapa" (You look beautiful) and that was lesson number four for Spanish. Tomorrow would be Wednesday and his half-day off, so I could only stay until noon and we had to go to the PX store and also had to visit Daniel to see how he was doing, so we both said Adios and he drove off. I really enjoyed that day.

I was really looking forward to Wednesday and going shopping for our engagement celebration the coming weekend. Because I could only stay until noon, I got up early to help Mrs. Bohn and she was happy to see me that early, so we had breakfast together and I told her about our engagement the coming weekend. She wished us all the best and said Michael seemed like a good guy. She also said that if she were young like me, she would leave Germany as well as there was no future there for young people. Her daughter was available to start helping her on Friday, she said, but that I could go over any time as she loved talking to me.

So, at noon, Michael came over and collected me. He finally remembered to bring Janet's letter with him and she'd sent a lovely congratulations card with a pressed flower inside the card. I thought it was an orchid but as I'd never seen one except perhaps in pictures, I didn't comment. She also included her mailing address so that we could stay in touch. We went to the PX Store to get what my mother needed and still had no idea what to buy for ourselves but we were definitely going to have that black forest cake. "We'll think of something," Michael said, and he bought two bottles of champagne and some crackers with cheese and some nuts.

We then went to Daniel's house and he seemed to be fine but said he'd made up his mind and was going to file for divorce so that he could start anew. It was sad, but for him the best thing to do, especially as there were no children involved. He told us he'd leave on Friday at noon and would be back on Sunday at noon, so that we had two days to celebrate. Michael and I still had time left for a little walk before he had to take me home and when he dropped me off, I told him, "No Spanish lesson today, otherwise I'll mix them all up," so we just said "Adios" again and he left saying that he'd pick me up again from Mrs. Bohn's house the next day. It would be my last day with her, which was really too bad.

My mother said she'd looked at all the ingredients and thought it would be a super cake. I went to bed but couldn't fall asleep—I just had too many thoughts running through my head and hoped that full-time job would start in July so that I'd be busy. My mother heard me tossing around and brought me some tea, telling me again that they would always be there for me, no matter what happened. I fell asleep eventually and then it was already morning so I had to get up for my last day helping Mrs. Bohn. When I arrived, we had breakfast together and she got up and gave me a beautiful locket with a key to close it up. She said, "This you can have to keep and you can even lock it up; it's for sentimental items." *Yes*, I thought, *I don't have to bury anything under the tree at the graveyard, like I did with Wolfgang's presents*, but now I could even smile about it. I really thanked her for that and loved it at first sight.

I wasn't able to do any work; I just had to sit and listen to her telling me all the good and bad experiences in her life. Then Michael arrived and she started all over again. I felt sorry but told her we had to leave then. She understood, wished us all the best for our engagement, and told me to stop by at any time. When I showed the locket to Michael, he really liked it—he looked at me and smiled and said, "Maybe we can put our baby's first tooth in there." It was a bittersweet feeling, because in about three months that baby would have been born. Michael said, "Our second baby's first tooth."

It was an emotional subject for me so we changed the subject and talked about Friday. He said he'd pick me up on Friday afternoon but it might be a bit later, then we'd get the cake and try to find something for us to eat, thought we still didn't know what. I had an idea, "Why don't we just buy hotdogs? And the PX Store has some delicious macaroni and potato salad." He laughed, saying, "What a combination!" but that it was a great idea and that's what we'd do—problem solved. I just jokingly reminded him not to forget the rings and he smiled and said it was a good job I'd reminded him as he would have forgotten for sure. With "Te amo" and "Adios," he drove off.

I showed my mother that lovely locket from Mrs. Bohn and she loved it too. I was really looking forward to our weekend and our engagement and decided not to wear that opal ring but only the golden ring; that would be enough. Before we'd leave for Daniel's house, I wanted to see my grandparents and find out how they were but in the meantime I put a few things together for my two days away and I could see that my mother was kind of emotional as well, though she tried to hide it. She had put the final touches on the cake and it looked delicious and my mother was really proud of it.

It was almost four o'clock before Michael showed up and I was a little disappointed even though he'd said he'd be a bit later, but I didn't say anything. By then it was too late to see my grandparents but perhaps we could do that tomorrow. My mother showed him the cake and he was amazed at how it looked. We very carefully put it in the jeep and I could see that my mother had teary eyes as she wished us all the best. We then went to the PX Store for the hotdogs and drove on to Daniel's house.

When I opened the door, I smelt the beautiful fragrance of lilac flowers and going into the living room, saw two huge vases full of lilac (Flieder) flowers. I couldn't believe it. "See," he said, "that's why I'm late—I couldn't bring myself to steal those flowers out of people's yards so I had to go to a flower shop and buy them." I was speechless and we almost forgot to bring in the cake. I asked him how he knew I liked them and he said because Mrs. Bohn had said I loved them. He then asked me what we should do now—eat first or the rings and as I wasn't even hungry I said, "Maybe the rings first." "Okay," he said. "Let's open a bottle of champagne first, that goes with the rings and the engagement." I didn't know what to say or how to say it and he went to get the rings. He gave me his ring to put on his left hand finger and then he gave me my ring and when I looked at it there was a small diamond in the middle with little ones all around it. He put it on my finger on my left hand and I looked and him and ask him when he'd done it. He gave me a hug and said, "You don't have to know everything, little bird."

All I could say was "Now we're engaged," and he laughed and said, "Looks like that." It was a hugely emotional moment for both of us and I now felt that we really belonged together. He opened one of the bottles of champagne and we had champagne and hotdogs with black forest cake, after which he turned on the music and we danced until the bottle of champagne was empty. I didn't even regret that headache the next morning.

Well, on Saturday morning when we had breakfast, Michael asked me how I'd liked our engagement, "Mrs. Future Mendez?" I answered, "It was great, but maybe too much champagne," and he told me that we'd emptied both bottles and that he'd almost emptied one himself and laughed and added, "But we'll never forget that food combination!" It sounded strange—"Mrs. Mendez"—strange but lovely. I admired my ring again and everything seemed perfect and Michael said, "There's another first again, this time for me, too."

We had to clean everything up and then we wanted to see my grandparents and also Rita and Jonathan, hoping we could do something together later in the day. My grandparents were fine. I showed my grandmother my ring and she asked me if we were "verlobt" (engaged) and I just nodded. She wanted to give Michael a hug as she saw his ring as well but I had the feeling she wanted that hug more for herself than as a congratulation. She clapped her hands and said she was happy for us and I had the feeling they were getting used to their new place. Grandmother had met another elderly couple at the dinner table who also spoke Polish so she was very happy about that as well. We also stopped at my parents' house and my mother admired the rings though my father was kind of quiet, as he had been recently. I had the feeling he didn't care too much for Michael and most likely would have preferred a German man so that I would stay in the country, but it was too late for that now. We told my mother how good the cake tasted and that made her very happy.

From there we drove on to Rita's and they also admired the rings and wished us all the best. Michael had the idea of inviting them for lunch and as Rita's neighbour had agreed to look after her grandmother, they said they would and the four of us went to Ku Damm where we were lucky enough to find a cute little restaurant in a side street and had Wiener Schnitzel and fries. Michael told them about our food combination the day before, which caused a big laugh, and then as we still had some black forest cake left, we decided to go back to the house and have coffee and cake there. Rita of course knew black forest cake but it was a first for Jonathan and he really enjoyed it. Since all the champagne was gone, we had to take a bottle of wine, just for a toast. Suddenly it hit me that there were only ten days left until Michael's departure but I didn't let anyone know, still trying not to think negatively. We listened to music and danced a little, so all in all it was an enjoyable evening until the time came when Michael had to take them home.

After coming back to the house, we carried on listening to music and dreaming about the future. We knew Daniel would be home at noon tomorrow so we needed to clean up but decided to do that tomorrow morning. "Don't worry," Michael said, "everything will be fine, little bird." He must have read my mind and I realised I could never lie to him; he would know right away. I found it difficult to fall asleep that night and had to take two Valerian pills, which I hadn't needed for some time.

I had a restless night even after taking the Valerian pills but I knew I had to get used to the idea of being alone for a little while. I was never happy being alone but I knew I had my parents and friends there if I was lonely and I was glad when the night was over and I could get up. Michael was still sleeping, so I made coffee and this time I was the one who took it to him which really surprised him even though he certainly liked it. Once we were up, we cleaned up a bit and went for a walk. We still had one more weekend before us before his departure and I noticed those emotions slowly creeping up on me again, but I had to fight them. After our walk, we were sitting and waiting for Daniel to come home. We still had a little piece of that cake left for him to try. I asked Michael which airport he was flying out of and it was Berlin-Tempelhof, the same one the allies had used to support us with food through the air bridge. Michael said he'd leave on Wednesday, April 28th, but he didn't have a time yet. When I asked him if it would be possible for me to go along and say goodbye at the airport he said Daniel would pick me up and we could then meet at the airport. That would be the third goodbye to people I loved—first my father, then Wolfgang and now Michael. I thought Michael would be the hardest one but told myself everything would be fine.

Then, Daniel came home and he couldn't believe his eyes when he saw all those flowers. He congratulated us and looked at the rings, saying, "They came out beautifully," so he'd known all about it. He then invited us for lunch as there was hardly any food in the house except that one piece of black forest cake, which Daniel ate even though he said he'd had one before. We had a great lunch and then came back and collected our belongings, ready to leave. Daniel said he'd try to give Michael an afternoon off this week so that we could still have some time to do things together and then Michael and I drove around a little before he dropped me off at home saying he would come again tomorrow afternoon. We would also have the coming weekend, our last one, and had to decide where to go. When Michael had driven off and I went inside, my mother looked at me and saw how emotional I was, but I knew I had to go through that alone.

I thought it over and realised that if I wanted to keep my sanity I had to accept that what would happen would happen and that I couldn't change it, as much as I wanted to. The thought calmed me down and I slept. Next day I helped my mother a little with the housework as I knew Michael wouldn't be there until the afternoon. I then took a walk over to the church because I wanted to thank the priest for arranging the job with Mrs. Bohn and he told me there was a possibility I could be helping Mrs. Bohn again for a few days because her daughter had a hard time with her mother. I gladly accepted and just told him to let me know but not to arrange anything for next weekend as it was my last weekend with Michael. He told me there could be more jobs like that in the future and I hoped so as they would keep me occupied until that full-time job started and then, hopefully, Michael would be back in the Fall. I felt a lot calmer after that.

On my way home I met Michael so we just drove around and he told me he'd spoken with his father who told him he was planning a three-month business course for Michael so that he would at least have the very basics needed. That would go on until the end of July and then he could start just doing simple things like visiting clients as he was such a "people person." That sounded great but somehow I felt it would take longer than until October, but we had no choice. Michael didn't say anything to that so it must have been alright with him. We talked about our last weekend together and felt complex Wannsee would be the best choice as that was where we'd started. After that weekend there wasn't much time for anything since there were only three days left until his departure. As far as he knew, he would have to leave late in the afternoon to get into the States the next morning, because of the six-hour time difference. He promised to write if he could almost every day and also to keep in contact with Daniel and I had Janet's address as well as Michael's. We tried not to talk too much about it as everything seemed to be under control but it was still emotional. On Wednesday we wanted to get some more little things for him to take back.

As we had some time left, we walked around the park and stopped at Rita's. She was also starting to plan now as she had to cancel the rental agreement for the apartment because her grandmother was leaving as well. In a way she was sad to be leaving the country but was also happy to have a better future to look forward to. We couldn't stay as Michael had to get back to the barracks, so we left and just sat in the jeep for a while, not saying a lot but just being together. On Wednesday we had to go and see Daniel, since it would be the last chance to be at his house before Michael left and we realised that now things were the other way around—it wasn't the "First" time things happened, it was the "Last," which was harder to handle. He said he'd be back tomorrow and with a big hug, he drove off.

That Tuesday Michael came a little early so we could go and visit my grandparents. My grandmother looked a little happier since she had met the couple who also spoke Polish, but you could still feel her sadness sometimes. My grandfather wasn't any help to her at all since he was almost blind by then and his hearing had got worse, too, but at least they were still together. When she saw us coming she looked almost like the old grandmother again, I think mostly because of Michael, who she seemed to like a lot. I had the feeling he reminded her of someone special but she never said anything. I thanked Michael a lot for being so nice to her but somehow he must have liked her as well.

I had the idea of having a picture taken of the two of us together and we tried to find a shop which would do that. We decided to go to the Ku Damm because there was a place there which did photography and we thought they might take one. Well, we went over and found the little shop which did all kinds of thing, including selling pictures and picture frames—a really neat little place, so we went in and asked the man in there about taking pictures. He said they usually didn't do that sort of thing but seeing Michael in uniform, he must have thought it was something special, and he smiled and said, "Okay, how many do you want?" They were quite expensive but we asked for two—they would be about three times as big as a passport photo—so he took the pictures and told us they'd be ready to pick up the next day. That was great as Michael had the Wednesday afternoon off and we could pick up the pictures and also say hello to Daniel as it might be the last time we were in his house.

We still wanted to drive to Complex Gatow, just to say goodbye, as we'd never be able to stay there again because when Michael came back he'd no longer be in the military and therefore not allowed to stay there. We talked about him going back to his parents' house and how different it might be now with Gloria and her daughters living there and I felt it did bother him in some way. He even told me he might be looking for his own place and when I got there we could live in an apartment for a while until he made enough money to be able to afford a house. I really didn't care, as long as we could be together again. I could feel an uncertainty about him and perhaps even a little fear as well as he'd really never lived alone and had always had someone who cared for him. Yes, he might be even more uncertain and I, as I hadn't left my home yet, but as long as we were together, I felt we would make it.

It was already getting dark but we still walked a little way in the park and then, after driving home, we sat in the jeep for a while and I noticed that he was having a hard time leaving to go back to the barracks. He just held me and told me that if I needed anything, to let him know and he would send it to Daniel, whatever it might be. Then the idea of Las Vegas came up again and he said that would be our decision and nobody else's. I wasn't too keen on the idea but if there was nothing else, I would do it. At that moment I felt I was being stronger than he was and I didn't know whether to be happy about it or whether to be scared, but time would tell. Certainly, he was very emotional that evening.

After Michael drove off, I felt a little confused because to me he had always been the tall tree and whenever I was down and depressed I could lean on his shoulder for protection and everything was fine. That night I saw a different Michael—uncertain and even a little scared. When I got home, I talked with my mother about it and she just smiled and told me that was usually the case because women are stronger than men. She added that we shouldn't let them know it because they like to be the leader even if they're wrong and I remember that she'd told me that before. I still had to think that over for a long time as Michael, to me, had always seemed to be the stronger one—though now I felt a little differently, but I wouldn't let him know that. Even so, I felt I had a little more self-esteem and I had a pretty good rest that night.

When Michael picked me up on Wednesday noon, he was the old Michael again, charming and on top of everything and I had to smile to myself. It was a beautiful spring day and we walked around the park and even though a week from today was his departure, I had the feeling I could handle things, even with Michael being gone for a while. As the weather was so nice, we decided to drive to Complex Gatow to say Adios and the drive through the forests and past the little lakes was really lovely; I always enjoyed that drive. We walked around and looked at everything, mostly for the last time, thinking about what nice memories we had there—good ones and sad ones as well, but we were able to smile, which had to be a good sign.

We still had to say hello to Daniel and wanted to talk things over with him but explained that for our last weekend together we were staying in Wannsee, where our relationship had started. He just smiled and understood. He told us quite a few soldiers were going back as their three years had been completed, but the next pack would be coming soon. It looked as though a lot of the soldiers liked it in Berlin and quite a few were already married to German girls or engaged like us. It was just so sad that we had so many problems because of the cold war. We then drove off and thought we'd go and also say goodbye to the priest and he could bless Michael for his trip home. We were then just sitting in the jeep, not saying a lot because somehow we seemed to have accepted the idea of our separation. We were so much looking forward to our weekend and we wanted to make it really special. We'd collected our pictures and were looking at those—they'd come out very well and we were glad we'd got the idea. Well, actually, it was my idea but I let Michael believe it was his, trying out what my mother had said, and Michael was so happy it was HIS idea!

Friday arrived and with that our last weekend together—and with that, our separation, for however long it would last. Michael arrived at noon with a pretty flower arrangement for my mother and some cigarettes for my father as he still hadn't been able to give up smoking. He didn't have to say goodbye yet as he'd be taking me home on Sunday and he could do it then. Spring had arrived and it was really beautiful and we got ready to drive to Wannsee. There wasn't much talking between us—we both had our own thinking to do as our lives were about to change drastically and we didn't know what direction we'd go in so had to hope for the best.

When we arrived at Wannsee, Michael went into the back and gave me a bouquet of 24 yellow roses. He knew I loved yellow roses but where he got that from I didn't know; they were beautiful. We got our few belongings for the weekend and checked in and everyone admired the roses, including me. We were given a really cosy room and they were all very friendly to us and I guessed Michael must have talked to the manager when he made the reservation, telling him it was a special celebration. It was still lovely outside so we went and walked around the lake, discovering the first swans of the season on the water. Everything looked so peaceful and it was relaxing, just walking, holding hands and not even talking.

When we got back, we got ready for dinner and found the restaurant was almost empty. Perhaps it was too early for most but we got a nice table overlooking Lake Wannsee and the dinner was awesome with steak and all sorts of fish; there was something for everyone. Also, nice music, which all in all made it an event you would never forget. Michael ordered a bottle of champagne and looked at me and laughed, saying, "Just one bottle today!" Everything was perfect and the music lovely and we danced a lot that night, not talking much but just holding on to each other until 11 o'clock came and the restaurant closed down.

When we were back in our room we started to talk about the time we met on that blind date when he was only thinking about Elena and I hated his arrogance and sarcasm. He admitted thinking I was a German Fraeulein, since those were the only sort of girls he'd met since coming to Germany. We talked about how we then slowly fell in love and, yes, I admitted to starting to like him first. With all we'd been through I had the feeling this might be adios for ever but those were negative thoughts and I pushed them aside. We talked and talked until we fell asleep. The next morning was another beautiful day so we walked back around the lake and watched the swans. As we had the whole Saturday ahead of us, we drove around and visited Rita and Jonathan, but nobody mentioned Michael's departure. We decided to go for lunch to the Ku Damm area and took Rita and Jonathan along and I noticed Rita was watching me. I told her I was fine, that the time would go quickly and that we'd be together again. She, too, was happy with her decision to go with Jonathan back to the States and we all had a good time together. We even talked about next year when we were all settled, saying perhaps we could meet up in the States somewhere, but of course those were just dreams—but nice dreams and it was good to be looking forward to something.

As it was late afternoon, we wondered if we could still go to church to say goodbye to the priest and so that I could find out how soon I could go back to Mrs. Bohn. When we got there Saturday evening Mass had just started, so we went in as well and joined the Mass. Michael was wearing his uniform again and some people looked at us as though they were disgusted, but I was now used to that. After the end of the Mass, we went to the priest and asked for his blessing, mostly for Michael as he was the one who needed it most, and he also blessed our rings. He was very kind and wished us all the best and also told me that Mrs. Bohn was waiting for me to start as soon as Michael had gone. Her daughter wasn't able to handle everything as her office needed her as well and Mrs. Bohn might need me for about four more weeks until she was able to take care of herself. That was wonderful as it meant that if I'd be able to start the full-time job in July, I'd be busy and not getting bored at home, so that seemed under control.

On the way back to Wannsee we stopped at my grandparents' place—Michael wanted to say goodbye as there wasn't much time left before the 28th. We found them at dinner and also met the other Polish couple and they all seemed to be getting along very well, which made me really happy. I told my grandmother about Michael's departure and she looked at me sadly but told me that if I ever felt down, I could go over and sleep on her lap. "Remember," she said, "the way you did before." That made me very emotional and I had to leave the room for a little while but Michael came and took me back in and my grandmother knew how I felt, though I don't think my grandfather knew what was going on.

It was still a little light outside when we drove back to Wannsee and we started our little walk, knowing it was our last night together. You can fight against your emotions as much as you want, but this time it was quite hard, mostly for me, so there wasn't much talking; just holding hands. Anyway, we saw the swans again, graciously swimming across the lake—pictures you never forget, those really special moments. Michael was so confident that he'd be back at the latest in six months and that then all the anxiety and stress would be over. That night I had problems with that and the words from "that" girl popped up: "Wait till he starts his affairs." I kept quiet and didn't want to remind him of that affair so we had a nice dinner and listened to the music until the restaurant closed down. Back in our room, we listened to more music and watched the stars through our window and then tried to sleep, wondering how things would be a week from now when he would be thousands of miles away.

We hardly slept that night but now we had to go through with it, we had no other choice and there was still the hope that we'd see each other in five months. After breakfast on Sunday morning we had our walk around the lake and, yes, it was pretty certainly for the last time. We then packed our belongings and I took my roses as well as they were still beautiful. My mother had once told me that if you want to keep roses, wait until they start to die and then hang them upside down on a wall so that they dry out, and then you could keep them for a long time, so that's what I wanted to do with them. We wanted to stop by at Rita's so that Michael could say goodbye to her—Jonathan he'd mostly likely see in barracks. That was emotional as well, as she had the original idea of the blind date. Michael jokingly told her it was all her fault but Rita couldn't even smile; she was really upset to see him leave.

We also went by Daniel's and I looked into OUR room, most likely for the last time as well, as I wouldn't come here again after Michael's departure. Daniel told us he'd pick me up on Wednesday and take me to the Berlin-Tempelhof airport and then take me home again. Michael would have to go with the other soldiers and couldn't come with us. That was fine, as long as he'd take me home so that I wouldn't be completely alone. They also arranged that as soon as Michael arrived in San Francisco, they would be in contact through the military and Daniel would let me know. From then on we could communicate through the mail as I had Janet and Michael's mailing addresses. Unfortunately, I wasn't allowed to go into the barracks, even with Daniel, but there were talks going on about the post offices working on phone connections to the U.S. so that people could go to the post office and fill out an application for a call to be made to the U.S. There would then be a wait at the post office, perhaps for hours, until your call came through but I had their phone numbers, just in case, even though that talk was all for the future. Michael still had to say goodbye to my parents and we wanted to do that today as the next two days were completely full, so we went home and Michael gave my parents a big hug and told them they'd see each other again in five months. My father was okay but my mother had teary eyes.

Afterwards, we sat in the jeep for a while, somehow feeling a little relieved that this part, at least, was over and that now we just had to work on the next part. He told me again that I should let him know if I needed anything and I just joked that I wouldn't need anything except maybe him, but he wasn't even smiling. We still talked and talked about anything and nothing, just to kill time and stay together for as long as possible. He said he'd pack his bags the next morning as there wasn't much he had to take back except for the gifts from Berlin and that he'd come by tomorrow in the early evening so that we'd be able to go for a walk. It was a special TE AMO that night and with that he drove off.

Well, I knew there were at least three hard days ahead of us until Michael's departure, but then that was over and a new episode would begin; we just had to go one day at a time and I somehow felt a little relieved. My night wasn't the best but those Valerian pills helped a little and on Monday morning after breakfast I walked over to see Mrs. Bohn. I told her I'd be able to help her for the next four weeks until her hand had healed and she was delighted. She asked if I could also work at weekends and I hadn't really expected that so told her I'd do a half-day on weekends and her daughter could do the other half. I had the feeling she overplayed her disability a little because of not wanting to be alone, and of course that I understood completely. I told her Michael would leave on Wednesday and that I would start with her on Friday because I'd need that one day to recover and she agreed.

It was a blessing to have those four weeks of work. I knew she paid very well and also I'd be occupied while I waited for the full-time job to start. I decided to start saving the money I made for the Fall, so that I could contribute as well and that idea made me feel better. I knew I'd be able to save because I didn't have to pay any rent. When I got home I told my mother about it and she agreed completely. I felt somehow exhausted, probably because of lack of sleep and all the tension of the last weeks, so I decided to take a nap in MY bed. Mother came and covered me up and it was a lovely feeling, like being a baby again without a worry in the world.

I had a good rest until Michael showed up for our little walk. I guessed I'd miss that walk the most but I could still go by myself, with the summer ahead and the evenings quite long. After the walk we went to our little coffeeshop and had some coffee and a sandwich and I told him about Mrs. Bohn's offer, which he thought was great. He said his father had called him earlier in the day telling him how happy he was that he'd soon be seeing his son. He also mentioned that he had registered him for that Real Estate business course, which would go from May 15th to August 15th. I didn't say anything but thought that was pretty close to October, even though actually it was nearly two months before. Well, one month longer wouldn't be that bad. He would live in his father's house, so back in his old home. After we finished the coffee, he had to get back and we again sat in the jeep for a while. We seemed a little more relaxed now and he said we'd do the same thing tomorrow and then it would be the last time, at least until he came back. I looked at his hand and he was wearing the ring; I guess he noticed and he smiled and said, "Don't worry, it's not coming off. So," he said, "I'll be back tomorrow and we'll walk again and then the next walk will be in five months." He was really thoughtful and tender and that night I slept a little better.

I got up early the next morning and went to do a little shopping with my mother and then just sat around waiting for Michael to show up. He came a little earlier, so we had time to walk around the park and also to have coffee. Michael told me he'd spoken with Daniel and asked him to take care of me while he was gone. Daniel asked him if it would be okay with him if he had a get-together at his house and invited me, saying he would take me home afterwards and I wouldn't stay in his guestroom. Michael had nothing against it but I told him, "Not right now," and that I had to think about it. "There are so many memories," I told him, "memories about us, so right now I don't think I could handle it." He just smiled and said, "I trust you; if you want you can go, but don't stay overnight." Yes, that was our last evening together. Daniel would pick me up the next day at noon and take me to the airport where we would meet Michael. That night I needed an extra Valerian pill and prayed like my grandmother had taught me to.

I didn't get much sleep that night—April 28th, 1954—the day of Michael's departure back to the U.S. I could hardly eat any breakfast, my stomach was in knots, and I was glad my father had gone to work as I was sure he wouldn't really have understood and it was easier with just my mother and myself. Daniel had promised to collect me by noon, so I just sat around and waited. The song, sung by Doris Day, "Que Sera Sera," crossed my mind; how true it was: what will be, will be. There was nothing we could do; it was up to a Higher Power. We heard the jeep stopping in front of the apartment and then Daniel knocked at the door and I realised he'd never been up to the apartment before. I told my mother I didn't know what time I'd be back as we didn't know what time the plane would leave because there wasn't a schedule for military plane departures.

We didn't talk a lot on the way to the airport and as we arrived, we saw Michael standing there at the fence already waiting for us, so Daniel stopped and let me out. Michael said we didn't have a lot of time because the plane would leave in an hour but there wasn't much to say and we both found we could hardly talk anyway. But, as the saying goes, "Eyes say more than words," and those were very intense moments with both of us hoping to see each other in five months. "Daniel will tell you how and when I get home," he said, "I'll write as often as I can," and I promised him the same thing. Time was over, a last kiss, a last hug and the words "Te amo, little bird," and with that he turned and walked away and never looked back. It was de-ja vu for me—my father, then Wolfgang, and now Michael. I wanted to wait and see the plane taking off but Daniel came and took me back to the jeep. I felt like a zombie, too tired to even cry.

In one way I felt good: that part of leaving was over and hopefully his return would be a joyful occasion. Daniel wanted to go and have a cup of coffee but I declined and asked him to take me to my grandmother; I felt I just needed her. He dropped me off and told me he'd be back in two hours to take me home and I agree to that. When my grandmother saw me coming, she smiled and said, "I knew you were coming. I know how you feel because many years ago I went through almost that same situation. I thought it must have something to do with my father and me but I didn't ask; I was too tired and just fell asleep." Two hours later, Daniel woke me up and took me home as arranged and he told me that as soon as he heard from Michael, he'd come and tell me.

That night I sat down and wrote a long letter to Janet, telling her everything about my feelings and emotions and asking her to stay in touch with me at least for the next five months, as I knew she was the only one in the family who would tell me the truth. I kept the letter to give to Daniel to mail as I didn't trust the post office with that letter—it might take much longer to get there or even get lost. My father saw me sitting there and crying and he brought me a little glass of whiskey saying that it didn't count as liquor that day and was more like medicine. He really did care but couldn't show his emotions like my mother and I could and after drinking that "medicine," I didn't even remember falling asleep.

When I woke up the next morning, it took me a few minutes to realise the extent of the happenings of the last few days and then I had that feeling again, as I had with my father and Wolfgang, of losing the person I loved and being left behind. Again, I felt all alone on this earth and as though the earth had stopped turning but I fought hard to get rid of those feelings since there was hope that we'd see each other again in a few months. I thought about Michael, who must already be in the States, at least on the East Coast, so by tomorrow at the latest I should hear something from Daniel. I tried to relax and put the dying roses upside down on the wall above my bed and then gave my mother the address of Mrs. Bohn, just in case Daniel came to our apartment to tell me about Michael.

By the afternoon I needed some fresh air and went over to Rita's. She knew I'd be coming and we talked and talked, which helped me a lot, especially as she felt sure Michael would be back at the end of the year. Somehow she felt guilty about bringing us together but how could she have known what would happen. When it started to get dark I felt I'd have loved to take a walk in the park but I didn't feel ready yet to be alone doing that, so I went home and listened to some music. Tomorrow was my first day back with Mrs. Bohn, so I went to bed early but still had to take those Valerian pills. The next morning, I got up early and took the letter I'd written to Janet to give to Daniel to mail. I sincerely hoped Daniel had some news from Michael.

Mrs. Bohn was really glad to see me, so we had breakfast together and I did some little jobs, like the laundry and her dishes, but was mostly talking with her. I could understand why she had problems with her daughter, as she really did talk a lot! Finally, I had a chance to talk to her about Michael, saying that he'd left on Wednesday and must almost be home by now and, yes, I started to cry. She was very helpful and understanding, telling me he'd be back and that I shouldn't worry.

After lunch, quite late in the afternoon, I heard a jeep stop and Daniel arrived. He was smiling, so I knew it was good news, and he came over and told me he'd just had a call from Michael; that he'd arrived in San Francisco and was already home and wanted me to know that everything was fine, he'd had a good, quick, flight and would write to me tomorrow. That made my day; at least that part was over and he was safely at home. I gave Daniel the letter to mail to Janet and he wanted to take me home, but I still had a little longer to stay with Mrs. Bohn. He offered to take me to dinner over the weekend but I had to work the half-day, so suggested we do it another time, which was fine with him.

Once home, I sat down and wrote a long letter to Michael saying I hoped he was fine and that I missed him a lot but I kept the letter until the next time I'd see Daniel to give it to him to mail. I went to bed early again, so that I'd be ready for the next day with Mrs. Bohn, even though it was just a half-day. I tried not to take any Valerian pills, and I slept pretty well.

The weekend arrived, the first weekend without Michael, but I still had that half-day with Mrs. Bohn, so that was good. I realised it would be pretty lonely from now on as there had always been something to do while Michael was around, especially at the weekends staying at Wannsee or Gatow or Daniel's house. Well, I'd been spoiled and would just have to get used to the new situation as because of mostly being with American people, I now had hardly any German friends. However, it was only until October and I knew I could live through that. I went to Mrs. Bohn's to keep her company until noon and then her daughter came to take over.

When I got home, Rita and Jonathan were waiting for me to take me for a walk. It was so nice of them as they knew how much I loved to walk but that I had problems going by myself, so we walked and talked almost all afternoon about the courses our futures were taking. Their future was much more set than mine but I was ready to fight for our future as well. Our walk was much longer than Michael and I usually had but it was what I needed. We also went to the little coffeeshop where Michael and I usually went and it was emotional but I knew I had to get through it. Rita said, "You'll hear from Michael next week for sure," but Jonathan didn't say a word. I was tired when I got home so just listened to some music until I went to sleep.

On Sunday morning I had another half-day with Mrs. Bohn. She really loved to talk to me and in a way it was perfect because my mind was occupied with other things. Walking home, I decided to go to church with my parents in the evening, and then the first weekend alone was over. Because I was working all day next week, I stopped at my grandparents' and could see that my grandmother was expecting me. I didn't want to ask her why: there must have been something she'd experienced in her past, but I wondered why I would be her favourite granddaughter when she had so many and thought I'd ask her one day in the future, if I had a chance.

Arriving home, I saw Daniel's jeep in front of our apartment and found he was waiting for me. When he saw me, he got out and asked me if I'd like to go to dinner with him. I didn't know what to do or what to say; I knew Michael wouldn't have anything against it as he was like a father to us so I agreed, asking that we not go to a fancy restaurant like some at the Ku Damm, but just a little one would be fine. I remembered the letter I'd written to Michael the other day and made a note to give it to him to mail and he said he'd mail Janet's letter as well but, thinking about it, I thought maybe I'd mail the letters to them through the regular mail, just in case Daniel forgot to mail them or even lost them.

Anyway, I told my parents I'd be gone for a little while and they just said, "Be careful." He drove to the Du Damm and found a recently opened little restaurant which mostly served American-style food. He said he'd just wanted to get me out of the house for a little while, which I though was a nice idea, and then mentioned that he was planning a little get-together the next weekend. He said that if I wanted to go I'd be more than welcome but I knew straight away that I wasn't going. I wasn't yet ready to go to a party, especially not at Daniel's house, but I told him I'd think about it. Those words "German Fraeulein" all of a sudden came to mind—I was engaged and not a party girl. I thanked Daniel for the dinner and asked him to come right away if he had any word from Michael or Janet, but thought to myself that I had to find out if there was another way of communicating with them and that maybe tomorrow I'd check with the Post Office. At least that first weekend was over.

As he'd promised Daniel to write the next day, I hoped to hear something from Michael this week. I realised how convenient it had been driving around in the jeep: now there was a lot of walking necessary as the bus service was bad in our area and taking a taxi was too expensive. It would have been easier to use a bike but I didn't have one and buying one would be expensive and mean I couldn't save for the Fall. Monday was a quiet day at Mrs. Bohn's because she wasn't feeling that great and slept a lot, which wasn't too bad as she had a lot of books and I loved to read. I didn't expect any news from Michael but hoped to hear from him the next day so when I'd finished I just went home, listened to music and then went to bed. The same thing the next day but by Wednesday I really expected something. Mrs. Bohn was still not feeling well, so her daughter stopped by to check on her and thought it was just a common cold. I really hoped so as I hoped to keep earning some money to save.

I was ready to go home when I saw Daniel coming and he smiled and gave me a letter from Michael saying, "Let's go and have a cup of coffee." First I sat down and ready the letter. It was so nice and he wrote that he was missing Berlin and me so very much and was almost ready to come back but had promised his father he'd at least go on the course which started on Monday, 17th May, for three months. Maybe after that he could convince his father to let him come back to us so that we could get married. He said he didn't even care for San Francisco any more as all his old group was split up; some were married, some had moved away, and so he was lonely just like me.

As we went for a coffee, I couldn't go to the post office, but it looked as though this arrangement might work. Daniel asked what Michael had written, so I told him and he seemed to be glad. I told Daniel I'd write another letter tonight and asked if he would mail it again as Michael couldn't have received the first letter I'd written. I was also waiting for a letter from Janet. After the coffee, Daniel asked if I'd decided about going to the get-together on Saturday and I declined, telling him I might have to stay at Mrs. Bohn's place overnight since she wasn't feeling well. I could see he wasn't really pleased with my answer and didn't want him to get mad with me because of mailing the letters, so I thought that as Jonathan received mail from the States as well, I might ask him to do that for me—otherwise we would have to go the regular way with our own addresses. When Daniel dropped me off, he only said, "I'll see you on Saturday, you might change your mind": he knew it was only normally a half-day's work on Saturday.

The next day I stopped at Rita's on my way home from work and told her about Daniel's invitation and also talked about the mailing of the letters. The first thing she said was that I shouldn't go to the party and then added that we'd talk to Jonathan about mailing letters. That made sense, but we would have to tell Michael and Janet to use Jonathan's address at the barracks. Whatever, we would find a way.

That night I wrote a long letter to Michael again, telling him what had happened since I last wrote and I was planning to give that letter to Daniel on Saturday. I also mentioned Daniel's invitation for the coming weekend and told him I wasn't going. There were so many things to tell him: mostly that I missed him and that I was waiting for a letter from Janet, and I also mentioned the possibility that his and Janet's mail could go either through Jonathan or even by direct mail, so that we didn't have to go through Daniel any more. We had our own mailing addresses, so I asked him to let me know what he thought we should do.

When I got to work on Friday, Mrs. Bohn seemed to be a little better but I asked her if I could stay overnight anyway so that I had an excuse not to go to the party. She was glad to have me help out, so I arranged to stay overnight from Saturday to Sunday. Coming home from work I took the letter to Michael along with me to Jonathan to ask him if he could mail it from the barracks but when we talked about it, he said it would be better if I could mail that letter from my own post office to Michael's home address, and the same with Janet. That way, nobody at the barracks would know about our communications, including Daniel, who otherwise was able to see what mail came in and went out. Rita said she had to go shopping and would mail my letter directly and that way we'd be sure it went out and Daniel wouldn't need to stop by and deliver any replies. Maybe I was wrong about Daniel, but I had the feeling a long time ago that he wanted something else and now that same feeling was back again. That evening, I told my parents about staying overnight with Mrs. Bohn because of Daniel's party plans and they completely understood and were glad I didn't want to go to the party.

I had a restful night and on Saturday morning on my way to Mrs. Bohn I saw a few lilac branches on that tree in the cemetery. I couldn't help myself and broke some off for Mrs. Bohn and had to smile about Michael's remark about stealing them instead of buying. Yes, that was the hard part: always remembering some words, laughs or smiles. Mrs. Bohn really enjoyed the flowers and said it was a good thing not to go to that party—that anything could happen and then Michael would be sad and disappointed.

Daniel arrived in the afternoon and brought two letters, another one from Michael and also one from Janet, and then he looked at me and said, "Well, baby, are you ready to come?" I looked at him and said, "No, I have to stay overnight at Mrs. Bohn's place as she's ill and alone." His eyes were cold and he said, "Well, maybe next Saturday—make sure you ask Michael for his permission." That scared me a bit and in a way I was almost certain he wasn't the good second father that he'd always pretended to be. Not to make him mad, I said, "Yes, I'll try my best." I had to think of something and decided that if he got really insistent, I would ask if Rita and Jonathan to come with me and if he wouldn't allow that, then I wouldn't go.

I started to read the letters. Janet wrote that she couldn't wait for me to go to San Francisco in the Fall and also said Michael was very lonely and still wearing the ring—that he never took it off. She said he was really missing me and couldn't wait to have me over there. "Don't worry," she wrote, "I'll watch him for you." Then I read Michael's letter, which was so beautifully written that it made me cry and I knew I had to write again that night. When I told Mrs. Bohn about the letters she was really happy for me and we had a lovey dinner. It was out of a can but with a glass of wine and we were both really comfortable and had a very relaxed evening. She didn't even talk that much and I had time to write a letter to both Janet and Michael, addressed to their home addresses. When it was getting late and Mrs. Bohn was tired, I went into the other room and turned on some music on her little radio and just started to dream. Michael's course would start in eight days and time seemed to be going really fast... and that was the last thing I remembered of that evening.

It was Sunday, so a half-day, and when Mrs. Bohn and I had breakfast together, she told me that if I ever needed to use her as an excuse for something, she'd be happy for me to do it. I guessed she'd rather do it than be alone but it was nice of her. At noon, I walked home but wanted to stop at Rita's on the way to ask if she had mailed the letters to Michael and Janet. For no particular reason, I was having an emotional day but it was now almost two weeks since Michael had left, so I supposed I was going to have good days and bad days. I tried to pull myself together, but it wasn't easy. Rita was glad I'd stopped by and told me she'd mailed the

letters. The post office had told her it could take up to ten days to the States but the schedule for planes was getting better and it might not take that long. I wondered what Daniel would say if he noticed there was no mail coming in and that I wasn't giving him any to post, but Rita said, "Just tell him you didn't want to bother him and give him more work than he already has," and that sounded fair to me. She had also thought that Daniel wasn't that kind and friendly guy he pretended to be and had had the idea that he wanted revenge for what Michael did with Elena, and I was the best target. There was nothing to prove it but I felt better after talking with Rita.

That evening was quiet and I went to bed early and Monday was quiet as well. On Tuesday evening I was ready to leave Mrs. Bohn when Daniel stopped by and brought a letter from Michael. He seemed in a better mood and offered to drive me home, then asked if I had a letter to mail. I said, "Not today," and that I'd write that night. "By the way," he said, "I talked to Michael today and told him about the little get-together and that you didn't come. He said you need to get out of the house and that I should tell you that." I didn't believe one word he was saying but he kept on talking and said he'd have another little party the following Saturday and that I could make it to that one. I was too scared to say no, so I answered that I'd see and my thoughts were to ask him to invite Rita as well.

So, he took me home and I read the letter from Michael saying he really missed me but that the course would start on the 17th, so he'd be busy then. The next day after work I went to Rita and told her the story and she was okay with it so I would tell Daniel when I saw him. Sure enough, he came on Friday to pick me up from work and had a letter from Janet. I hoped that was the last letter through Daniel and that maybe the next ones would come to my address. Of course, he asked me about the party on Saturday and I tried to explain that I'd like to take Rita and Jonathan along as I wouldn't know anyone there. He just said, "Don't worry, there are also Fraeuleins there and, by the way, Jonathan is on duty this Saturday but Rita can come if you really want; the more the merrier." I was a little shocked and hoped Rita would come and said to Daniel that I would go if Rita went with me but that we wouldn't stay overnight. He said he'd pick me up at my apartment at around six the next evening and dropped me off.

I went straight to see Rita and told her what he'd said and she said she'd almost had the feeling that something like this would happen as Jonathan had let her know that day that he was on duty over the weekend. It could have been coincidence, or on purpose, we had no way of knowing, but she said she would come with me and that we could then keep an eye on each other. She said she'd arrange for her neighbour to watch her grandmother and that she would be at my apartment at five o'clock, just in case Daniel arrived earlier, and I really thanked her for that.

Saturday, the day of the party, arrived and I went home from work at noon. I still didn't really feel good about going but with Rita with me, it should be alright. I hoped the letters I'd written to Michael and Janet's addresses would be there soon, then they'd know where to mail their next ones. There was still the possibility that one or two would go through Daniel but I couldn't have done it any other way.

Rita was there at five as she'd promised and, yes, we were right— very soon after Rita arrived, Daniel came as well, even though he'd said six. He looked surprised when he saw Rita there already but as he'd invited her as well there was nothing he could do about it. When we got to the house, there was loud music and quite a bit of alcohol so Rita and I decided that when we were ready to leave, we'd look for a taxi to take us home as it didn't look as though Daniel was going to be sober enough to drive. Because of the American families living there, taxis in that area were always available.

When we went into the house there were quite a few people running around and it didn't look like the same sort of get-together at all. Of course, "that" girl was there and I was ready to turn around and leave but she saw me and came over. I expected a few nasty remarks but to my surprise she started to talk with us like a civilised person and even asked how Michael was doing and when he'd be back. She was actually quite nice and wished us the best for the future. People started to dance and Daniel invited me and there was nothing to do but dance with him. He was dancing pretty close and asking me about my full-time job starting on July 1st. He also mentioned that Michael would start his course the next week and said, "So it's time to meet other people again," adding that it might be a while until he learned enough about his father's business to take over. Everything he said seemed negative towards our relationship. I told him I needed to rest a little if he could look for another dance partner for a while and he just smiled but didn't say anything and instead of dancing he had a few more drinks.

It wasn't long before the other guests started getting louder and louder and Rita and I decided to leave and knew we had to find a taxi to take us home. I had to let Daniel know we were going and he'd started dancing with "that" girl, so we just said goodbye and I saw "that" girl smiling. Daniel looked sort of surprised but only said, "Thanks for coming." We waited a little until we found a taxi to take us home but were we ever glad to be out of that house! My mother was still up when I got home and I could see how relieved she was to see me home. We talked for a little while but I had another half-day with Mrs. Bohn the next day, so went to bed. My thoughts were of Michael starting his three-month course next week and that for me it was a little over four weeks until I started my full-time job.

Well, I expected Daniel to come over and apologise for his behaviour on Saturday but Sunday came and went and nothing happened. I was disappointed but he used to be Michael's boss and still was Jonathan's boss and I felt I had to keep quiet and not do anything about it. But I did write a long letter to Michael that night telling him what happened and my mother promised to mail it to his father's address. I hoped Michael and Janet would soon start sending letters direct but there might still be a few coming through Daniel, though slowly that would stop. The next day Michael was due to start the business course and I really wished I could be there with him. I hoped he'd tell me all about it but I knew that because he'd be busy there wouldn't be too many letters arriving.

Monday was a quiet day with Mrs. Bohn. She had somehow changed in the last weeks and her spirit seemed to have slowed down but I didn't dare ask her if something was wrong. Sometimes I had the feeling she had lost her will to live but I could have been wrong and there were only two weeks left until my time with her would be over. Unusually, there was no sign of Daniel but I'd done what he wanted and hoped that he'd show up the next day as I was waiting for letters from San Francisco. My mother mailed the letter to Michael, so I started a letter to Janet. I really missed them both and even though I'd never met Janet, we'd found out through writing that we had a lot in common.

Finally, on Tuesday afternoon, Daniel showed up with a letter from Michael. He said, "I hope you got home alright, you should have stayed longer. It was a really fun party and you could have stayed in the guestroom with Rita." I had the feeling he just wanted to hurt me because Michael and I had so loved that room. He also asked me if I had a letter to mail and then I had to tell him that my mother was now mailing the letters direct to the States because he was so busy and we didn't want to burden him. I couldn't make out what he was thinking but he didn't offer me a ride home and I enjoyed walking home even more.

When I got home my mother had a letter from the workmen's compensation board, telling me there was the possibility of starting my job earlier, on June 15th, and asking me to stop by. That was such good news and the next day I explained to Mrs. Bohn and asked if I could have a few hours off to go there. She agreed right away so I set off for the bus. From our apartment I'd be able to walk but from there it was a little too far. So, that was it and I got there. It was my first real job and, yes, I was nervous. I got to the front desk and showed them the letter and the receptionist took me into the visitor's room where, after a few minutes, another elderly lady came and interviewed me. She asked me if I knew how to use shorthand and I confirmed that I did. I'd learned it on my business course and now I was proud that I had. The lady was pleased and explained that the boss dictated letters and that

I'd have to be fast because he sometimes spoke very quickly. Because there were no calculators or electric typewriters or any other electrical equipment available, she also asked if I was good with numbers and I knew that I was.

The lady seemed satisfied with my answers and told me I could start on June 15th, a Tuesday, and that I would have a three-month probation period. I didn't tell her about my plans to get married that year and leave the country but so many things could happen in the meantime, so I kept quiet and was just happy I had the job. The lady then said that office hours were from 8 o'clock in the morning until 4.30, that I would have thirty minutes for lunch and that they also had a Kantine (canteen) for lunch and snacks. I was so proud and happy to have that job. When I got home that night I told my parents about it and even my father smiled and I then wrote to tell Michael about it. It was my third letter in four days and my mother would mail it the next day.

The next day when I saw Mrs. Bohn, I told her about my new job and she was very happy for me but asked that if she had any kind of emergency before June 15th, I would come and be there for her. I said that of course I would, and that even if I was working full time after June 15th, my weekends would be free if she needed help and that, too, made her very happy. After work I went to Rita's and told her everything about the job. We hadn't had a chance to talk about that last "little" party and agreed that it sure was strange, but more and more we were coming to the conclusion that Daniel wasn't really the good boy he pretended to be. Jonathan came over as well and mentioned that Daniel was as friendly and nice to him as always, so it must have been me for some reason. The next weekend was coming up and I hoped that everything would be okay.

On Friday afternoon Daniel showed up at Mrs. Bohn's place and brought another letter from Michael. He seemed in a good mood and even offered me a ride home and I was somehow relieved. He then asked if he could take me out to dinner on Saturday and I was caught again so told him that if nothing else came up, I would go, and he seemed to be fine with that; I had no other choice. I had a quiet evening at home and read the letter from Michael. He said he was ready to start the business course because he wanted to get it over with but he hadn't received my letter yet telling him to mail everything to me at my home address. That day his first week on the course would be over so his next letter should tell me more about it, though of course I wouldn't get that until next week. The end of next week would also be my last week with Mrs. Bohn, then I had two weeks to get ready for my new job. In a way I was excited but I was also a little scared as it would be a different environment again, and I also assumed everything would be spoken in German rather than English.

I had a talk with Rita about that dinner date with Daniel on the weekend and she didn't know what to do either so I decided that if he showed up I would go to dinner but take enough money with me to take a taxi home. If need be, I could pretend to use the bathroom and just leave since I was very sure we would end up somewhere at the Ku Damm. I was only going because of Jonathan, since he was still his boss. That evening, I told my mother about it and she seemed a little worried, but I assured her nothing could really happen.

Late in the afternoon on Saturday, Daniel stopped by at the apartment so I went out and he seemed fine and even asked me where I'd like to go. I said Ku Damm would be fine as I knew there were quite a few people around, so we went there and found a nice little restaurant. He ordered a drink for me but I declined saying I had some stomach problems and would rather not. He was fine with that and carried on to tell me that lately he hadn't really been himself because he'd filed for divorce from Elena, that it was a tough decision and that he knew she would fight it or want a large amount of money. That must have bothered him a lot and maybe that was the reason for his behaviour. He smiled and said, "I wish I was 20 years younger," and I knew what he meant. He also told me that he'd spoken with Michael's father, who seemed happy, and that Michael was attending the course. We had a nice dinner and soon afterwards he took me home. I was very relieved and it looked as if the situation was under control. I was glad everything had gone well with Daniel and dinner—a little less stress.

On Sunday I only had half a day with Mrs. Bohn but her daughter showed up in the morning and told me she was a little worried about her mother and we decided she should see a doctor the next week, which was also my last week. I recommended seeing our doctor; he was very good and if he wasn't sure he'd send patients to the clinic to check them thoroughly, as he'd done with me. The daughter asked me to make an appointment the following week so that I'd still be able to help them. When I left that afternoon, I went through the cemetery and passed the tree where I'd buried Wolfgang's presents and I had to smile as I thought back to those days which were even more chaotic than now since it wasn't so far away from the actual war going on. The way things looked now, everyone had more or less accepted the divided Berlin and it could even take years before Berlin's fate would be decided as people from the Eastern side were still trying to flee East Germany to come here to West Berlin. Thoughts like that went through my mind and even though I loved my hometown, there was a lot of uncertainty that came with it. While I was with Michael and his friends I'd never realised that I was still living in a war-torn city.

I decided to say hello to my grandparents as it had been a few days since I'd seen them and I found them fine. Grandmother asked me how Michael was doing and I told her what was happening but her happy smile wasn't there anymore. After that I decided to go home but somehow it was a sad day as I was missing Michael very much and felt really alone, so I decided to try a little walk in the park instead of going straight home. It was my first time alone and I hoped that lonely feeling would go away but instead it got worse. For the first time my mind wondered what would happen to me if Michael should never come back and it was such a strong feeling that it really scared me. It was now almost four weeks since he left. By the end of August, the course was supposed to be over, but then his father might have something else in mind before he could come back to Berlin. Well, next week I should hear from him and find out how he was doing, so before I made myself sick with worry, I went home. My mother made me tea and I took two Valerian pills and went to bed but still had a hard time falling asleep.

My last week with Mrs. Bohn started and I promised her daughter I'd see our doctor to make an appointment for her mother so left a little early to do it. When I got there, the doctor was glad to see me and was asking about Michael so I told him everything I knew, which of course wasn't too much, but I hoped to find out more this week. I also told him about my earlier start at the full-time job and he said I'd find I felt better as I'd be tired at night. He had an opening for Mrs. Bohn on Thursday afternoon; it would be good for her to be checked out. It was such a beautiful late May day that I didn't want to go home straight away, so stopped by at Rita's and instead of sitting inside her apartment, and as Jonathan wasn't there either, we decided to go for a little walk.

She knew how I'd been feeling lately and tried everything to help me. I even missed the PX Store, so we decided that next time Jonathan was there, we'd go and buy all the things we bought when Michael was still around. I was also worried about being able to handle that shorthand, as it was a while ago that I was on the course. Rita had a great idea and said that from now on, we'd practice a little every day to find out exactly how much I needed to catch up and after that I felt better and although we walked quite a distance, it felt great. When we got home, Jonathan was already there and Rita told him about the PX Store, and he laughed and said, "You're half American already if you miss the hotdogs!" We decided we'd go there on Wednesday to buy some food, which meant I had time to ask my mother if she wanted anything, as well.

On the way home, I so hoped to hear from either Michael or Janet with some news from San Francisco, but it all depended on how long the mail took. My father was already sleeping so it was just my mother and me and it was always nice to have a mother and daughter talk. We talked for quite a while as my mother had the idea of applying for a permit to go and see her father and Aunt Maria in East Germany. With Michael not there, it might be easier as we were all only Germans, whereas if we were married, then I would be an American and that might create problems. We would have to go to the Town Hall and find out what we needed and I really would have liked to go since it had been a while since we'd seen each other, so we decided to try it out during the two weeks after I'd finished with Mrs. Bohn.

I wished we had a phone so that Michael and I could talk to each other. When I'd been at the Workmen's Compensation Office, I saw there were phone connections and wondered if maybe I'd be able to make a short call but when I'd asked the lady she smiled and said that the connection was just for use inside the office. Good thing I didn't mention a call to the U.S.A.!

When I went to work the next day, I was really hoping to get something from Michael or Janet, or maybe both. It was a quiet day at Mrs. Bohn's and she slept a lot so I was able to read. When I told her about her appointment with the doctor on Thursday, it looked as though she was glad to be getting checked out. Late in the afternoon, shortly before I was due to go home, I heard Daniel's jeep stopping, which could only be good news, meaning mail. I dashed out and he had a letter from Michael. He must not yet have received my letter about mailing direct to my address but I more or less expected that and thought it might take a few more days before they would know. Daniel asked me if I'd like to have a coffee with him and, well, I thought it would be alright but told him I had to say goodbye to Mrs. Bohn and read my letter first, especially as there was something else in it, perhaps a picture, and Daniel said he would wait.

I went inside and opened the letter and there was a picture of Michael, looking so different from when he was here as he was wearing a shirt with "San Francisco" on top and shorts and slippers. I couldn't believe it but he looked so handsome and in the background you could see the Golden Gate Bridge. He wrote that Janet had taken the picture, then he told me a little about his course saying it was kind of stressful and that because it was a private course there weren't too many people attending. He said that next time he wrote he'd take a picture of all the students. He added that almost two weeks had already passed and he'd be happy when it was over and he could come back to Berlin for me; he was getting along quite well with his father but not with his stepmother and stepsisters. I showed the picture to Mrs. Bohn and she smiled, saying, "He sure is a good-looking guy." Yes, I knew it was true but really couldn't decide if that was a good thing or bad. I said goodbye and went out to Daniel and also showed him the picture. He only smiled and said, "Yes, he's something else," and I really didn't know the meaning of that.

Anyway, we went to the little coffeeshop and he told me he'd received a letter from Elena's lawyer telling him they were starting the divorce process and drawing up the settlement agreement, so it looked as if she was mostly after the money. I didn't know how the courts in the U.S.A. worked but I didn't think she had any right to a settlement as she was the one who'd been unfaithful but I could see from Daniel's reaction that he was worried. When we'd finished our coffee and he'd taken me home, I showed my parents the picture and my mother commented that it looked very different than here in Berlin. I even thought I saw palm trees in the background, though I wasn't really sure. It was California, though, and I knew palm trees did grow in California. Well, I'd find that out when I was there. It was a really nice day and I sat down and wrote to say thank-you and also told him I'd be going to the PX Store with Jonathan the next day since I missed the hotdogs. I thought he'd get a laugh out of that. I was tired and so happy and didn't need any Valerian pills that night.

I had such a good night's sleep that my mother had to wake me up the next morning; it must have been the letter. She then gave me a list she had written for the PX Store for that night; it wasn't much, just some fresh fruit and vegetables which were much cheaper there than in the German stores and I took some of my saved money to pay for it as I didn't have to pay for anything else at home. Mrs. Bohn was actually looking forward to her appointment with the doctor and I had the feeling she was a little afraid she might be ill and wouldn't be able to take care of herself any longer. Apart from that it was another quiet day and I looked forward to going to the PX Store later to get the food with Rita. When we went to the store we realised we had to carry what we'd bought by hand as there was no jeep waiting to drive us home—it looked like I missed other people as well as Michael, but we managed.

We had hotdogs for dinner and although I didn't think my parents really cared for them much, they didn't want to spoil my fun. My mother had been to the Town Hall and brought home a lot of papers to fill out for our hoped-for trip to see Aunt Maria and my grandfather in the coming week, after my work with Mrs. Bohn was over and until 15th June. We hoped it wouldn't be too expensive. After dinner I listened to some music and was looking at both those pictures—the one we took when Michael was still here and this new one from San Francisco and I wondered how my life would be next year. Maybe we'd have a baby next year; that would be so nice; and over those thoughts I fell asleep and woke up the next morning with both pictures still lying next to me.

When I arrived at Mrs. Bohn's, she said her daughter would be there at noon and that we could then take a taxi and drive over to the doctor. She had packed everything already as if she would be gone for at least a month, but that was Mrs. Bohn—everything had to be in order. Her daughter came at noon and we travelled by taxi but then had to wait a little while before the doctor showed up. He checked her vital signs and they all seemed okay but he ordered a blood test at the clinic next week, so I'd have to be there one more day to help them, which was alright as I needed the money anyway. After the doctor's we drove home and I started to go home as well but decided to walk a little in the park. It wasn't as bad being alone as the first time had been and I actually relaxed just walking by myself and dreaming and thinking that if I was lucky maybe by the end of the week there would be some mail from San Francisco. I hoped that it would come by direct mail, if not this week, then definitely the next. I started to run to tire myself out a little in the hope of sleeping better.

Then it was Friday morning, almost the end of May and my last full day at Mrs. Bohn's. The first two weeks of Michael's course were over and my full-time job would start in two weeks; it was kind of an important day. I still had to go to the doctor's and make the appointment for Mrs. Bohn at the clinic and when I got to Mrs. Bohn she seemed a little better and asked me if I had a bicycle. When I said no she mentioned that she had one in her basement, not new but still in very good shape, and as she couldn't use it anymore, I could have it if I wanted it. She said her daughter didn't care for it and would rather take a taxi. I was delighted, never having owned one, and told her that would be wonderful as I might be able to use it to go to work and also for shopping. I went down into the basement and looked at it and found it was almost like new because Mrs. Bohn took really good care of her belongings and it was perfect for me. I had a nice day and that night I would drive home on my bike. I would really miss that lady; she was so kind and understanding. She also told me that if I saw something in her house that I liked, I could have it as she was thinking of possibly selling the house and going into a senior's home and if she did that she wouldn't be able to take everything with her.

Late in the afternoon I brought the bike out of the basement and when I saw Daniel coming, I showed it to him. He really liked it and told me he used to have one too when he went to school and that he'd had a lot of fun with it. Then he gave me two letters, one from Michael and one from Janet. He also said that he was going out for dinner with the African American couple I'd met at his house and that If I wanted to, I could go with them. I agreed since I really missed those nice dinner dates with Michael. He said that he'd pick me up at my apartment in the afternoon and that I'd be able to drive in the jeep—I wouldn't need to go to the restaurant on my bike. Sometimes he could be really funny.

I read Janet's letter first. The way she wrote was so nice, saying, "Why don't you just come, leave everything behind, Michael really needs you." How I wished I could have done it but there were too many "buts" involved and I had to wait until Michael came here and not the other way around. I'd have to explain it to her in my next letter as she wasn't familiar with the circumstances here in our divided city. I then read Michael's letter and could read between the lines that he missed me. He even sent a poem and even though I thought he'd probably found it in some book rather than having written it, I still loved it.

"I may be far for a minute, for an hour, for a day, for a month, but I always will be there for you and I will never say Good Bye."

It was so beautiful, I cried.

I said goodbye to Mrs. Bohn, took the bike and drove off and was so proud when my parents saw me coming. They couldn't believe it but they were also glad that I wouldn't have to walk or take the bus. That night I wrote back to Michael and Janet saying that, yes, I really missed Michael so much but that time was going fast and I remembered that in four or six weeks we'd have had our little baby if everything had gone well. But there's a reason for everything. Maybe we would find out, maybe we never would, but I needed two Valerian pills that night.

The next morning, I rode my bike to work. It was only a half-day because Daniel wanted to pick me up later on to go to dinner with that African-American couple. I was actually looking forward to it. Yes, I'd been so spoiled by going out while Michael was there and always having something to do over the weekend. I talked with Mrs. Bohn as the next day was my last day working there and the only thing I had left to do was to make an appointment with the doctor at the clinic, which I wanted to do on Monday. I found a few little things to take for our apartment but still had time until next week. When I got home I started to get ready for the dinner and looked for a nice dress to wear and those beautiful earrings I'd got from Michael, and when I looked in the mirror I found myself looking pretty.

Daniel picked me up late in the afternoon and also gave me a compliment and somehow it felt good. We drove to a nice restaurant near Ku Damm where the other couple was already waiting and I got more nice compliments from the lady. She looked very elegant; well, maybe living in New York did that. They asked me about Michael and I told them about the baby we lost and that we're engaged and that he'd be back in October—well, the whole story—and they said that anytime we were in New York we'd be welcome to stay with them. Those were all dreams for me at the time but it was nice to dream. We had a fish dinner with shrimps and other kinds of fish but I had a problem with the shrimps: I wasn't used to eating like that but I tried the best I could. I could see the lady was smiling and looking at me and I was so embarrassed but she just whispered, "Don't worry, honey, you're doing fine. I know that feeling, I've been through that too," and that made me feel better. It was a lovely evening and I enjoyed it too and had the feeling that if we went out for dinner in San Francisco and ate like that, I'd know how to handle it. We talked on for a little while longer before we left and Daniel took me home saying that he'd come to the apartment as soon as the next letter arrived. I just hoped the next letters would be direct to my address.

I had a restful night and the next morning I went to work with Mrs. Bohn for the last time and, of course, rode my bike. I found a few little things I wanted to take and if I saw Daniel again I'd ask him if he could put them into his jeep and drive me home with them. Then, after finishing, I told Mrs. Bohn I would see the doctor and let her know about her next appointment. I took my bike and rode off, showing Rita and Jonathan my new transportation on the way. They had a good laugh about it but I just told them they didn't have one and I did! Rita reminded me that next week we'd start find out how my shorthand was and I realised that was very important: only two more weeks to the new job. I even went to the park and rode around a little until I got tired and went home, where I listened to some music and thought about San Francisco. I knew there were nine hours' time difference so it must be Sunday mid-morning there and I wondered what Michael was doing there now and looked at the picture he'd sent me with the Golden Gate Bridge in the background. Again, I had the feeling of being all alone on the planet and sometimes even had the feeling that I'd never see him again, which was a very terrifying thought.

On Monday I woke up and actually felt unemployed. Indeed, I was—but just for two weeks. After breakfast I saw the doctor about Mrs. Bohn's visit and there was an opening at the clinic on Thursday afternoon, so I had to see her and tell her that. She seemed alright with it and asked me if I'd found anything to take home so I showed her what I liked and said that Daniel would pick it up with the jeep. I didn't stay too long as I'd promised Rita I'd go and try out my shorthand. Well, it wasn't too bad but did need improvement, so we decided to do a little bit every day. There was something else we had to take care of and that was some decent clothes for the new job, so we did the only thing we could and went off to the thrift store. It had been a while since we'd shopped there and decided to try and go that afternoon. When we got there, it looked a little nicer than the last time and they also had more merchandise and, after looking around, I found a few nice things to wear to the office and at pretty good prices. I was glad to have that behind me but wondered if I could use my bike to get there. Maybe not: if the weather was nice I could walk and if it was raining I could take the bus and by wintertime I wouldn't be here anyway.

Rita was busy, so I left but went to the park on the way home and drove around a little. When it was time for supper I went home and my mother was waiting at the door to give me a letter from Michael, so finally the change of address had worked. There were a lot of stamps on the envelope and perhaps he'd paid more postage to get a faster delivery but it didn't matter—the first letter had got safely to the right address. I opened it and there was a picture of an older but very nicely decorated building and even a picture of the students, all nicely dressed people who I guessed were between 20 and 40 years old. He confirmed that he now knew where to send the mail and that Janet did as well, but said he missed me terribly and thought we should have gone to the States together, married or not. I could read between the lines that he was really down and sad and felt that maybe we should have done that, but now I couldn't leave the country—or if I could, I'd never get into the U.S.A. because I was a German.

I wrote a long letter back and this time I reassured him that everything was going to be fine. Only four more months but I started to worry a bit as it wasn't in the least like the happy-go-lucky Michael. As soon as I heard from Janet I would tell her the same, since she'd also said I should just go over and leave everything behind, but at the moment I couldn't do anything. I told my mother about it and she also agreed that I should have gone with him and wished they'd told me that at the time. The next day my mother and I planned to go to the Town Hall to try to get a permit to see our relatives. I couldn't sleep for a long time, so I took two Valerian pills. The doctor had told me that they weren't chemicals, just herbal, so it wasn't bad to take them. I looked at the dried-up roses and had the picture and must have fallen asleep.

After breakfast my mother and I walked to the Town Hall to find out about the papers we'd filled in to go to East Germany to see our relatives. There was a long line of people waiting to be interviewed and we asked how much it would cost us, per person, to get there and someone told us 50 Deutsche Mark, so my mother decided that, as my father was working anyway, just she and myself would go. We would have to pay for transportation as well and didn't know what to take, whether a taxi or a bus. We waited almost two hours until we finally reached the end of the line and were able to speak with an employee who looked through our papers. We had to identify ourselves and were then told it would take two or three days for someone to look at all the papers, so we should come back by the end of the week and with that, we left. If everything was alright, we'd be able to drive over the following week and although I would be glad if we could go, I was also a little afraid of going into the Eastern side.

We had lunch at home and then I took my bike and went to Rita's to practice my shorthand. It was already going a little better because what I'd been doing was that whenever I saw a few words, I used my hand and tried to write those words in the air in shorthand and it actually helped. I still had almost two weeks to improve. Rita and I talked again, as always, about the future. Rita was pretty confident and said that even if everything failed, she could still come back to Germany, meaning West Germany, because here in Berlin she would be alone because her grandmother would also be in West Germany, so for her that would also be a goodbye to Berlin. The situation wasn't really stressful, but definitely uncertain. She also told me she was worried about me, as it was such a very big lifestyle change because of Michael and the way he lived, which I wasn't used to—though most likely it would be easier than the other way around.

It was almost supper time and I took my bike and drove around in the park a little before going home. It was a quiet evening so I was just listening to music and, yes, starting to write another letter to Michael, which I felt was the closest to talking to him. I told him everything that had happened that day but it felt like talking to the wall: there was just me sitting at the table and writing and nobody else there. Yes, it would be easier if there was a telephone, but there was none. My mother noticed that I was still up and brought me some tea and I tried to sleep but I was so worried Michael might be falling into his old behaviour with women and that was my biggest fear. There was absolutely nothing I could do right now but I decided I would write to Janet the next day and tell her about my worries; I was just too tired that day.

I didn't get much sleep that night so next morning I felt down and tired but I needed to see Rita because of my shorthand practice and if

I was early enough I wanted to pass by Daniel's house to ask him if he would bring those little things I wanted from Mrs. Bohn's to our apartment. I was in luck: he was still at home and we decided to move them later in the afternoon, which meant I was able to do the shorthand and also get my stuff home. At Rita's, we practiced and I was fine: getting better. Rita asked me how everything was going so I told her my worries and she completely understood but had no solutions either. She still felt sorry for bringing us together on that blind date but, of course, she'd meant well since Michael is really not a bad guy except for the problem with women and maybe that would change if he was married. Not that that helped me at that moment.

As Rita was busy, I left and drove around in the park and also intended to mail my letter to Michael. My mother made lunch and I told her Daniel would deliver those little things from Mrs. Bohn later on and I then had the afternoon free to write a letter to Janet. I told her everything I was worried about and asked her to please tell me the truth. I then had those two letters to mail but decided to do it when Daniel came with the jeep. I was so tired I felt I had to have a nap and slept for almost two hours, which made me feel a lot better. When I woke, I had a strong cup of coffee and then heard Daniel's jeep arriving and I asked him to drive first to the post office so that I could mail the letters. We then picked up my things, which fitted perfectly into his jeep and, of course, he asked me to join him for a cup of coffee. That wasn't a bad idea as it meant I could talk about my worries. When I did, he was quiet for a moment and then he started to talk about why he'd had all those little parties to show me how my life would be with Michael. He also admitted that he liked me more than just as a friend but realised he couldn't force anything so he gave up that idea and wanted just to be friends. I really liked that—him now telling me the real truth. He also said that with Michael I had to be very open, but one thing for sure, he said, "He really loves you." That didn't help me at that moment but at least now I could also talk to Daniel about my problems. He had his own problems with Elena fighting over the settlement, but he had a good lawyer so hoped it would turn out alright. When he drove me home, we unloaded the things we'd collected and he drove off, telling me he'd stop by and check on me once in a while. My mother also liked the stuff from Mrs. Bohn: cute little pictures and pretty vases and a very nice windchime. Maybe tomorrow I'd have another letter from Michael.

There was nothing really to do that day, just my shorthand practice and preparing for the next day to take Mrs. Bohn to the clinic for her check-up. I hoped that, maybe in the afternoon, the mailman might bring another letter from Michael, but I doubted it. As it was a beautiful day again, I took my bike and rode to the park and even sat on a bench for a while thinking about our future, as I always did. A lady with a stroller passed by and also sat down on the bench. She had a really cute little boy and somehow we started to talk. She told me he wasn't quite a year old and that she had two more children only a year apart and that this one wasn't even supposed to be here but that they were so happy to have him after having two girls.

I started to tell her about my baby and how I came to lose it and she felt sorry but told me that there's often a reason for something like that—that perhaps it was ill or something else was wrong and yes, I knew she was right but it was still hurting. She lived in the next block, not far from us and we got pretty friendly with each other so I told her that if she ever needed help with the children, just to come over—that I wouldn't want any money and playing with the children would be pay-ment enough. She was very happy about that as she said with three small children, things weren't easy and they did cost money. She told me her name was Helga, so I'd found a German friend, and when she had to leave I went with her to show her where I lived, so that if she needed help, she could just come and tell me. That would be great and I'd be with little children, which I really loved.

I then went to see Rita for a little practice and told her about it, and she liked the idea as well. Rita also wanted to catch some fresh air, so we went back to the park and walked around and more and more I could see that she was looking forward to leaving Berlin and getting married and starting her own little family with Jonathan. I was happy for her and sometimes a little jealous, for her life seemed to be more under control than mine. When it was almost supper time, we went home and my mother showed me another letter which had arrived from

Michael. That was great: two letters in a row and when I opened it I found it was quite a long one. He told me that on 15th June he would have to be in the office with his father for about two hours each day, just to start to get used to incoming clients and that he liked the idea as he enjoyed talking to people. Maybe his father wanted to speed everything up so that he could come sooner. I wrote back to him telling him about my new friend Helga with the baby. It was a long letter as well but it seemed a little brighter. It was then getting late and I knew I had to be at Mrs. Bohn's the next day so I went to bed and slept pretty well.

After breakfast in the morning I took my bike and went to Mrs. Bohn's to find she was almost ready and although her appointment wasn't until early afternoon, she insisted on leaving at noon so I had to go to the taxi stand and order a taxi to get to the clinic. Mrs. Bohn was satisfied but I knew we'd have to wait once we got to the clinic. We duly waited until the taxi came and took us to the clinic where, of course, we did have to wait. The doctors checked her out and took a blood sample, saying the results of the test would take a few days but that she looked alright, only her lips seemed to be a little blueish. After that we drove back home and she was glad it was over. At home, I told my mother about Helga and the visit with Mrs. Bohn and also Michael's new job with the real estate company, and all in all it had been a nice day.

On Friday, we had to go to the Town Hall to find out about the papers for our planned trip to Aunt Maria and we left early, just in case there was a long line of people again, but to our surprise there was hardly anyone there. The employee told us our papers were fine and that the permit would expire in four weeks, but we intended to go the next week anyway as it was my last free week before my full-time job. We paid our 100.00 Deutsche Mark and took the permit and left and now had to find out how we could get there. We thought we'd have to spend the money on a taxi as getting a bus or streetcar would make it quite a long and stressful trip, so we went to the taxi stand and asked one of the drivers. He wanted to know exactly where it was and thought it would cost us about 40.00 Deutsche Mark each way, so it was cheaper than the permit and we told him where to pick us up on Monday of the next week. Well, it was expensive, but we didn't know when we'd see each other again.

My mother and I ate lunch at home and then I took my bike and went to see Rita. When I looked at the calendar, the 15th of June was on a Tuesday, so on the Monday I'd still be unemployed. We did some shorthand training and with every day I felt more secure. We then wanted to get some fresh air, so we went for a walk in the park for a little while and then when I got home my mother made supper and we talked about our trip to East Germany. I'd heard from someone that there was a shortage of bananas, so we decided to buy a lot of bananas to take with us, hoping maybe my cousins would like them. After that I was just listening to music but felt like talking to Michael so I sat down and wrote a long letter telling him what had happened. For him as well, June 15th would be the start of a new schedule—his few hours at the office. I just wrote everything down as though I was talking to him and it felt good.

I wondered what I'd do this weekend and remembered our weekends had always been nicely planned and there were always nice things to do; sometimes just walking and holding hands. Perhaps tomorrow I'd go over to my new friend Helga and play with the kids. It was hard for me to invite friends over to our apartment because it was small and my father needed his rest after the stress of the working week but since the weather was nice I could ride my bike and I also had to mail Michael's letter but for the moment I also needed rest, so I decided to go to sleep.

I didn't have much planned for that weekend except perhaps to write another letter to Michael, but first I wanted to see Rita for my daily shorthand training, so I rode over to see her after lunch. Since the weather was nice again, we walked around the park and I told her about our planned trip to East Germany to see my relatives. She didn't like the idea a lot but there was nothing wrong with us politically and we didn't have any arrest history or any other kinds of warrants against us, so we didn't foresee any problems. We did our shorthand practice and I was already doing fine, so as Rita was busy, I decided to go and see my grandparents. Grandmother was fine but Grandfather seemed sort of distant, which wasn't surprising as he was blind and also hard of hearing and there wasn't much for him to do. Ever since they'd moved out of our apartment, my grandmother had lost some of her spirit. She just seemed lonely and although she had her new Polish friends, they only saw each other at dinner time as all four had a problem walking. Even so, I was glad to have said hi to them.

After seeing them I went home and my mother told me Daniel had stopped by and wanted to talk to me. He said he'd come back later but couldn't tell them what he wanted because of those language problems, so we had lunch at home and I started a letter to Michael until I heard Daniel's jeep stopping. I went outside and he asked me if I'd like to go to a little Festival behind the barracks, like the one I went to with Michael when we picked those lily of the valley flowers, the first sign of spring. Yes, I wanted to go; there were so many memories involved with that place and, also, Daniel and Jonathan were the only connections I had to speak English and mix with Americans. I told my mother about it and she smiled and said, "I thought you'd like that."

I looked out the prettiest summer dress I owned and I liked myself again and when Daniel picked me up, we drove there to that lovely setting with music playing and a dance floor on the grass. There were no Lilies of the Valley any longer but, anyway, it was a familiar surrounding and again with lots of food but no alcohol, thank God, just Coca-Cola and other sodas. There were a few people I remembered from when I was there with Michael but I'd never really talked with them. I really enjoyed it and found "that" girl was also there, although she'd somehow changed and looked decent and wasn't so very loud-mouthed anymore. She came over to us and introduced us to a nice-looking soldier who she said was her boyfriend and that they'd been together now for quite a while. Maybe that was what had changed her. She asked after Michael and I told her the story and she really wished us well but couldn't hold her tongue, saying, "He doesn't deserve you." Daniel started to laugh and said, "I told her so, too," but well, it had happened. We danced a few times but mostly I was sitting and watching people, and I really liked that.

When it was getting dark, we had to leave and Daniel took me home. I was really thankful for what he'd done; I somehow missed that life I had with Michael, but we'd have it again. Daniel asked me if I wanted to go with him to Gatow, where he had to pick up some paper, but tomorrow was Sunday and I had to get my papers together for our trip to East Germany. I told him that and he understood but said, "Be very careful." That night I finished my letter to Michael telling him everything that had happened and even about "that" girl, but I must have fallen asleep writing as my mother woke me up in the middle of the night.

The next morning, I really didn't remember how I got home the night before, it must have been all the memories I had of the festival. Anyway, after breakfast I drove over to Rita for my shorthand practice and spent a little time in the park but the rest of the day we spent putting our stuff together for the next day when we'd leave to see our relatives in East Germany. The taxi driver picked us up quite early as it would probably take us around two hours to get there. Everything was packed and we had some problems with the load of bananas, but we managed. At the border points we were checked out and although it wasn't too bad, it felt a little scary and it was hard to understand that we were all Germans.

When we arrived at my aunt's, they were all really happy to see us; it had been quite a while. Of course, they all loved the bananas and it was only Grandfather who looked old and tired. They were planning to move out of East Germany into East Berlin because Aunt Maria could no longer handle the heavy work on the little farm and they thought they might take an apartment in the city as that would also be better for the children finishing school. If you were looking around, you could definitely see the difference between East and West and looking at the houses and roads, nothing was really in good condition. In a way, I was glad to live on the West side, even though we were caged in. They weren't really caged in there since they had East Germany around them and could move around. We had a great time together and were happy that we'd done it even thought it was expensive, and then late in the afternoon the driver picked us up again to face the same thing with check points and then on to home.

My father was already home when we arrived and he was a little worried about us and glad we were back. He gave me a letter from

Janet; that was really nice and I sat straight down to read it. She told me how everything was going—that her relationship was getting quite serious and they were most likely going to get married the next year. She also told me Michael missed me a lot and was looking forward to his new schedule of seeing and talking to people instead of just sitting inside a schoolroom. He seemed to be okay, she wrote, but pressured me to come as soon as possible. Well, I wrote back saying that I'd love to be able to go tomorrow but that we had to stick to our plan and I was sure she'd understand. Only one week and one weekend and then my full-time job was available and Michael's new schedule would also start. I was really tired that day so went to bed early.

The last week of free time began and I had to start preparing for the new job and see Rita every day for my shorthand practice, but there were no really important things to do and just waiting for letters to come from San Francisco was excitement enough. On Wednesday there was another letter from Michael telling me how he was doing and also saying that he'd met one of his old friends from before he came to Berlin, so at least he had one friend from the past. That friend was also engaged and he also said he was getting along pretty well with Stefano, Janet's boyfriend, who he really liked. So I then again had to tell him what was new in Berlin and it was like a diary for both of us. The next day I would have to mail that letter and I also decided to see Helga, thinking maybe I could help her with something and I thought I'd also stop by at Mrs. Bohn's to see how she was and whether she'd had the results of her blood tests. Well, it was still only late afternoon and I had some time to kill so thought I'd do that right then and took my bike and rode over to her. She looked better and had also had her test results. They said she was borderline diabetic and had to take medication for it and stay away from sweets. She had a sweet tooth, so would have to fight that, but there was nothing serious wrong, so she was glad. We talked a little bit and she said most likely she would sell the house and move into a place for senior living.

After Mrs. Bohn's I left for home and Daniel showed up to check out how I was so we went to the coffee shop for a snack. I told him all about East Germany and how everything had gone and he told me about Elena, saying his lawyer told him she wanted half of his assets and that if she got that settlement she would go back to South America. My first thought was that if she did, that danger would be gone and Daniel smiled; I was very sure he knew what I was thinking. It was nice being with an American again and he mentioned a little festival at his house that weekend and asked me to go, saying he would pick me up and take me home. This time I was glad to be asked; I'd missed those get-togethers since Michael left. I told him I would go and he just smiled and said, "They are addictive, right?" and I had to agree. He also mentioned that he'd spoken with Michael's father who had said he was happy with his son, who was doing quite well. Of course, that was Michael's favourite occupation—talking with people. After that he took me home and, saying, "Until Saturday afternoon," he drove off.

After that I was just listening to music and reading about some of the culture and lifestyles in the U.S.A. and found there was a lot to study. I wondered how our wedding would be. I thought just something very small and we could still do something larger later on, but for now that would be fine and I thought it would be easier for everybody. I would have to tell Michael that in my next letter and with those thoughts I went to bed.

Apart from the shared housework and waiting for mail from San Francisco, there really wasn't anything much to do and except for seeing Rita for the shorthand practice, I was just waiting for Saturday for that little get-together. The exception was on Friday afternoon, when I went to see Helga and her three children. I felt sorry for her as there was so much to do and I noticed quite a few empty beer bottles lying around. She must have seen my look and sort of apologised for the mess but said that her husband usually drank a few beers at night when he came home from working as a carpenter. She said he also repaired damaged buildings and it was a stressful situation, especially as she wasn't able to help by working because of the children. I helped her to clean up a little and even though the apartment had just two bedrooms and was quite small, it was pretty hard to keep everything under control. I felt lucky not having had those problems and even though I loved children, I re-alised that maybe I didn't appreciate how much work it was to take care of them with no help. I again offered to help her but it would be hard in the future, though there were always the weekends when I'd be free.

Going home, I decided to write another long letter to Michael telling him about my idea of having a small wedding, and that it would be so much easier. Seeing Helga's family, I really missed him a lot that evening. He only had two months of school and maybe two months of office work and would be able to come in October, which would make it the best Christmas ever. It was a long letter and I told him everything: all my thoughts and emotions, just as if he were sitting next to me. That night I had to take the Valerian pills.

I woke up pretty early. It was Saturday and I was looking forward to the little festival but first I wanted to go to the post office to mail Michael's letter so that it would leave that day and not sit there over the weekend. We then had some lunch and in the afternoon Daniel came and picked me up. He said that quite a few people would most likely turn up but that didn't bother me anymore as I was used to those parties and by then my English language was

My mother made lunch pretty good. When I got to the house at least twenty people were already there, including that African-American couple. I was really happy to see them as I somehow liked the lady. She told me her name was Rebecca and that she had grown up in Harlem, a district in New York City, and also had a rough time growing up but that she had always wanted to become a teacher and had worked very hard to be one. We had a lot to talk about sharing our growing up experiences and she was very interested to hear my story of the war and the time went by very quickly. Daniel and I danced a few times and I noticed that he wasn't quite sober any longer so I started to worry about how to get home as I didn't have any money with me for a taxi. Rebecca noticed I looked worried and wanted to know what had happened, so I told her and she just said, "Don't worry, I'll take you home." She said she didn't drink, that she was an alcoholic but had now been dry for years after becoming one as a teenager when she was mixing with the wrong kind of people. I was so relieved that she would take me home and we continued to enjoy the music and our talking and even though she was older than I was, there was never a big difference between us ladies and she was relaxed and understanding since she must have gone through a lot.

When it was getting quite late and although people were still dancing and drinking, including Daniel, I was getting tired so Rebecca wrote a note to Daniel in case he wondered where we were and then drove me home. She gave me their address in Upstate New York, where they lived, and said if we didn't see each other here in Berlin again, I could go and visit them any time in New York. It had been a great evening and even though Daniel's behaviour hadn't been correct, I realised he was going through a hard time just then and I understood and it had worked out fine. Tomorrow I would write another letter to Michael and tell him everything.

All in all, it was a nice evening and I really enjoyed Rebecca's company and hoped we would get a chance to visit New York City one day so that we could visit her. Well, Sunday was coming up and I wanted to pack my things together for Tuesday for the new job and even though I went to bed late, I woke up early and decided to go to church with my parents. The priest was happy to see us together again and wanted to know everything about how Michael was doing. I told him the story again and I could see that he really wanted us to get married in church. If we could keep it small, we could even manage a small wedding.

My mother made lunch and I went to Rita's for my last shorthand practice. By then I was doing pretty well so I wasn't worried. She wished me good luck for the new job and I hoped it wouldn't last longer than five months. I went back to the park and rode around a few times but it looked as though a thunderstorm was coming so I went back home, remembering that I still had to finish the letter to Michael about that little festival. When I got there my mother told me Daniel had been there and she'd said "Rita," but we'd missed each other while I was still in the park. He'd said "Back" to her, so I knew he'd return and just as I started to take a nap, I heard his jeep stopping. There went my nap, because I was quite sure he wanted to invite me for dinner to apologise for his behaviour the night before. When I met him outside, he really did feel sorry and apologised, but at least he was sure I got home safely with Rebecca. And, yes, he invited me for dinner so we went back to

Ku Damm and found another just-opened little Italian restaurant. Since the mail now came directly to me, he asked me how Michael was doing. He knew from his father about the new schedule but didn't mention anything about it. I told Daniel that from now on my time would be limited because of the full time job and he just said, "Maybe a little get-together will still be possible," and after that he drove me home, so I still had time to finish Michael's letter. It was a long one again, full of hopes, emotions and a little fear, but he would understand; and I then went to bed because I was then really tired and tomorrow would be my last unemployed day.

I slept quite well and there were still a few things to take care of the next day, like getting my clothes together and also some paper to take along. I didn't know what I would need but was sure they'd tell me. The day went by fast and the next day work would start at 8 o'clock in the morning. I wasn't sleeping that well, so got up early, had a little breakfast and left for the bus but arrived about thirty minutes too early when everything was still closed, so I just waited for the first ones to arrive. Eventually the lady from the front desk saw me there and told me to come in. I was nervous and my knees felt shaky but everyone was nice and friendly and at 8 o'clock when everyone was there, we went into the meeting room and she introduced me, saying, "This is Theresa Klein, our new employee." Well, there were about thirty employees and she introduced them to me by name but I didn't remember one of them. She then told me that our boss was Herr Seefeld and that we also had a company car, a Volkswagen Beatle, and the driver was Herr Kinds. Well, it was all overwhelming but Frau. Scjneider, the lady from the front desk, just smiled and said that it would take a while but that I'd remember all of them in due course. That first day wasn't bad since I was able to just get to look at everything and remember how to find my way back to my room after coming from the bathroom.

When it was lunchtime Fraeulein Karin Lorento, my so-called roommate asked me if I wanted some lunch as well and took me across the street where there was a canteen. I wasn't hungry and just wanted to see what everything looked like but as there were some sandwiches and also soups at a very reasonable price, I just got a cup of chicken noodle soup. Not too many of the employees were there and I think most of them took their own lunch. It was so strange; there wasn't one word of English, of course—it was a German company and we were still living in Germany. In the afternoon I had to write a few letters. The typewriters were, of course, all manual, and typing was something else. The letters on the keyboard had to be pushed down very hard and if you wrote a few letters a day your fingertips were hurting by the end. There was nothing electronic, everything was manual and I surely hoped I would get used to it, but that was the good old times.

Fraeulein Lorento was quite nice and she helped me a lot. She was a little elderly and told me a little bit about everybody in the office but it was my first day and I had no idea about whom she was talking. She asked me if I was engaged and I told her about Michael and that he is, or rather, was, an American soldier. I didn't think she was really excited about that but she didn't say anything. She told me that the next day we'd get long lists with the payment amounts from the insured clients and that we had to be fast to add them all up. My head was spinning already, but everyone made it and so could I—even without adding machines and just by doing it all in my head. I have to say, I was glad when the first day was over and I decided to walk home to clear my head. Most of the employees took the bus, walked or had a bike. I thought about Michael, today was his first day as well on his new schedule and I felt very sure he'd had a better day than I had, though I told myself it would get better tomorrow.

That walk home was great and I decided that I'd write to Michael when I got home to ask him about his first day. I guess my mother knew how I was feeling because she cooked one of my favourite dishes—pork steaks with mashed potatoes and a mixed green salad; it was so good. I sat down to write to Michael but had only written a few lines when I fell asleep on the table and my mother had to wake me up. And yes, I didn't need any Valerian pills.

The next day I took the bus again but not so early and arrived shortly before eight, just as everyone else did. I was still tired from my first day but having coffee helped. Fraeulein Lorento was a little late and I was told she was mostly late, so I sat down and waited to see if anyone would come and tell me what to do. Frau Schneider, the secretary, came and brought me lists with numbers to be added up and said they had to be done by noon. She must have recognised my scared look and said, "If it's a little later, don't worry, you are new, but be sure everything is done without any mistakes." I wondered what the rest of the employees were doing and if everyone had to work that fast but anyway, started as fast as I could and was finished by noon, just hoping all the numbers were correct. I took it to Frau Schneider, who was surprised that I'd finished by noon, and then I went back to my room. When we were ready to go to the canteen for lunch, Frau Schneider came to me and told me everything was correct and I was pleased and also glad I wasn't too slow. We had potato salad and sausage for lunch and I decided that from next week on, I'd take my own lunch. In the afternoon we had a few more letters to write and the second day was over.

I was too tired to walk home and decided to take the bus, which would also leave me time to write that letter to Michael. Two more days and my first week would be over and in my head was the thought that maybe Daniel would come and suggest something for the weekend. I had dinner and started to write to Michael telling him everything which had happened and that I really missed him and this time I didn't fall asleep and wrote a long letter. I hoped that maybe the next day I'd have one from him and I was also expecting a letter from Janet. My mother came and asked me how the first two days had been, so I told her and she could see that I wasn't really all that happy. "It'll get better with time" was all she said.

There were only two days of my first week left and I was happy that it would soon be over. When I arrived on Thursday morning, I realised I'd forgotten to take any lunch to work so thought I'd start with that the following week. There wasn't much difference in the work from the day before and I slowly started to get to know some of the employees, but still had a problem remembering all the names. Fraeulein Lorento, my roommate, suggested I call her Karin, so that was easier as well. After lunch Frau Schneider came over and told me our boss, Herr Seefeldt, would most likely call for me the next day as he had some letters to dictate. Well, I knew it was coming and I found myself ready for it.

That evening I decided to walk home again as I needed fresh air and when I arrived my mother had two letters waiting for me, one from Michael and another from Janet. I read Janet's first and she really didn't have too much news, just that Michael was looking forward to working in the office for a few hours and she told me again, "Come as soon as possible," but she apparently couldn't understand that being a German citizen, I couldn't enter the United States without a Visa or Passport. I then read Michael's letter and for the first time I felt a little sad. He seemed a bit better, more relaxed, perhaps because he was looking forward to his new schedule, but I should know more about it the next week as this was the first week for him, too, just like me.

My mother cooked dinner but I wasn't really hungry, so I took my bike and rode over to Rita's, where I told her a little about my new experience and we even practiced a little shorthand for the next day. I was very much missing speaking English and hoped Daniel would come and have a little surprise party. When it was getting late I went home and got ready for bed but I really didn't feel like writing a letter to San Francisco and although it took a while until I fell asleep, I was up early the next morning. I had something to eat, took the bus to work and was right on time and then mid-morning we got a call on our internal telephone from our boss, asking me to go to his office with a shorthand pad as he had some letters to dictate. I felt a little shaky but had to go and it took a few moments before I found his office, knocked on the door and went in. It was a big office and he was sitting at the far end behind his desk. Everything was so big that I felt like a midget and even Herr Seefeldt looked like a giant but he was very friendly and told me not to be scared; that he would speak slowly. He really didn't talk very fast, so it wasn't too bad and after finishing the three letters, he told me I could go and that if anything was wrong, he would call me. Karin asked me how it had gone as she'd never written for him, and we were waiting to see if he would call me. It took about thirty minutes and then he called back, asking me to go to his office. I was pretty shaken up when I got to his office but he smiled and told me that everything was correct so far except that I'd forgotten all the punctuation marks. He told me he'd done them himself but that I should concentrate on that, so that wasn't too bad, though I was really glad when the day was over and again I decided to walk home.

When I was close to home, I saw Daniel's jeep in front of our apartment and I had to admit I was glad to see him. He laughed and asked me if I was ready for a little get-together the next day. "Yes," I said, "I am," and he mentioned that he promised to only drink coffee. I was really looking forward to that and when I told my mother that, she answered, "See, now you're back to German living again." It was still early, so I started to write to Michael and told him about the little party since I knew he wouldn't have anything against it especially as this time I would take some money with me just in case there was too much drinking going on. I finished the letter and decided to mail it the next day and was then so tired that I fell asleep pretty quickly.

I woke on Saturday morning and felt rested and was looking forward to today's get-together so I helped my mother with a little housework while waiting for Daniel to pick me up. The next week I felt sure I'd receive more information about Michael's new schedule. There was just the one thing bothering me—the fact that Janet always said in her letters that I should go over as soon as possible, even though she knew our situation. Well, I didn't worry too much about it as she probably just meant well.

Daniel came to pick me up in the afternoon and we went to get some treats from the PX Store. I loved that store; they had such awesome things to buy. Daniel asked me about the new job and how I liked it and I told him it was okay for the amount of time I'd be working there. He didn't say anything to that but mentioned that he'd spoken with Michael's father and that Michael was doing well now that he had his favourite hobby of communicating with people. There were quite a few people gathered around, most of whom I didn't know, but it was still fun, talking and dancing. I wondered if the life in San Francisco would be like that and asked Daniel and he said, "Not quite as hectic," but added that since they had the real estate office, there would still be clients who had to be entertained. Well, I was pretty sure I could handle that. Daniel kept his promise and only had coffee, so he was able to take me home and he then asked if I'd like to go for dinner the next day because there was the next week ahead and it was almost the end of June. It hit me then that the end of June was when our baby would have been born, so I sat down and started to write to Michael. It was a very emotional letter and I wondered if he had thought of that, too. Maybe I'd made a mistake and should have gone with him, married or not, but it was too late now. That evening I had to take those Valerian pills.

The next day we went to a nice little restaurant where they served Italian dishes and it seemed that more and more little restaurants were popping up now. It was a really relaxed evening and there were now only two more months left before Michael's course would be finished; then if we were lucky he'd be back in October, or at the latest in November. Daniel took me home since the next day was already the beginning of the new week and I didn't want to be too late to bed. I hoped the week would be better than the last one and the next morning I took the bus again and, of course, forgot to take lunch with me but the prices at the canteen were very affordable.

Karin came in a little late as usual but we then started to talk a little about our personal lives. I asked her if she'd been married before and she replied that she'd been engaged during the war but that her fiancée was killed in France and she didn't even know where he was buried. I could then understand her reaction when I told her I was engaged to an American soldier. After being with Americans for so long, I almost forgot that they used to be our enemies and that we were the losers in that war. I met some other employees that day but still had problems remembering their names. If anyone asked me if I was engaged, I just said yes but nothing more and I was sure Karin wouldn't say anything. That day went by quickly and when it was over I found myself walking home again. I met Helga and she asked me if it would be possible for me to go over the next day as they had a parent-teacher meeting for their oldest daughter and she'd like me to look after the other children. I said I could and warned my mother not to wait for me after work as I'd be with Helga's children. Lately I seemed to be having emotional days, maybe it had something to do with our baby or perhaps it was doubts about Michael's coming back, but I knew I had to push the negative thoughts away.

The next day, the boss again asked me to write a few letters so I had to go into that huge, hardly furnished, office. This time he spoke a little faster but I tried to follow as fast as I could, also not forgetting the punctuation marks. Again, he said he'd call me back if anything was wrong. As it was getting to the end of the month, we had long lists of numbers to add up for the bookkeeping department and I forgot about the boss possibly calling me back if something was wrong, but he didn't so everything seemed to be fine. That was a relief. The day went by quickly and I remembered I had to go and help Helga with the children that evening.

When I got out of the office, the bus had just left so I had to hurry, almost running, and our company car, the Volkswagen Beetle, stopped and Herr Kinds, our driver, asked me if he could give me a lift home as he could see I was in a hurry I really didn't want to talk to anyone, so I thanked him for his offer and just said that I was running for exercise. I arrived just in time, before they left, and the children were running around. I collected a few empty beer bottles and Helga told me there was pizza for when the kids got hungry and also a bottle of milk for the baby. I really didn't know where to start first but the baby was crying so I started to feed that first and then concentrated on the other two by feeding them the pizza. The whole apartment was a mess but poor Helga had no help and obviously couldn't handle it all. My wish had always been to have six children, because I was an only child, but at that moment there with three children, I reduced my number to three and decided that would do just as well. I was glad after two hours when Helga and her husband came back. When I got home I was exhausted and my mother had a good laugh, saying that was just the beginning—just wait until they become teenagers! I didn't need any Valerian pills; I was too tired.

Well, nothing then really happened until Friday when I got a letter from Michael telling me about his new schedule. He seemed to really like it and he had his first dinner appointment with potential buyers, an elderly couple who wanted to buy property on Lombard Street. There was hardly anything available as that crooked street was more like a tourist attraction and a one way street where they had busses going in and out all day, so Michael convinced them to look for another property and they were happy that Michael had actually explained all that to them. They came back to him and Michael was so proud and I was proud of him, too. He also mentioned that he couldn't wait for his school time to be over so that he could be full time in the office. That was the first time he didn't mention coming back to Berlin to get me but I was so sensitive when it came to our life together.

It was the weekend again, so I hoped Daniel would show up with some idea for the weekend. We had breakfast and it was a hot day so I didn't want to ride my bike and just listened to music and rested after that hectic week. It was already my second week of work and next week it would be the start of July. I heard Daniel's jeep stopping, so I went out and he had a huge bouquet of dark red roses in his hand. I felt embarrassed but he smiled and said, "Don't worry, they're not from me. I spoke with Michael's father yesterday and Michael was on the phone as well and asked me to get you these roses because your baby would be born about now and he loved you very much." I really couldn't stop crying. So he did remember and I was convinced he really cared for me. Daniel said he'd be back in the afternoon and that Rebecca, the African-American lady, had invited Daniel and me and another couple for dinner that evening. I was glad to be getting out of the house, otherwise it would have been a lonely night. When I got into the apartment with the roses my mother asked if they were from Daniel so I told her the story and she said, "I would have been a grandmother by now," and she had tears in her eyes.

Daniel picked me up and we went to a really nice restaurant which had just opened in Wannsee. Rebecca and her husband and another elderly couple were also there and we had a great dinner of baked trout with mashed potato and a mixed salad. Rebecca already knew about the baby I'd lost and I told her about the flowers from Michael. She said, "He seems to be a good man," and when Daniel drove me home, he mentioned that he was happy Michael had remembered. He said the next day, Sunday, he'd come over and think of something for us to do so that I wouldn't be alone. When I got into the apartment I saw the other dried bouquet and thought that when this one was dying, I'd hang it next to the first one. I felt happy and listened to some music thinking that I'd write a thank you to Michael the next day.

Well, my parents went to Church that Sunday morning but I really didn't feel like going so I sat down and started that thank-you letter to Michael. I knew it would be an emotional letter to write and for the first time I asked him if he had any idea when he would be back in Berlin. The next week would be the start of July and his course would officially be over in August and

unless anything changed, by October or the beginning of November we'd still be on schedule. I also told him about my job, but of course that wasn't as interesting as his was in San Francisco and in the end I had to stop the letter as I didn't want to push him or just be complaining, so I kept quiet—which was always my way when dealing with emotional problems.

I decided to get some fresh air and to go and say hello to Rita. I told her about the flowers Michael had sent me and she really liked that and we had a nice conversation before I had to go home for lunch as I was expecting Daniel in the afternoon. I was thinking about work next week and also the fact that we were getting paid the next week—it was just a half-paycheck but I was proud of it and thought I could save some and also maybe could send some little presents to Michael and Janet as well as pay for some food for my family and those thoughts made me feel good.

Recently there had been quite a few things happening at the border which made one realise we still lived in a divided city. In the afternoon, Daniel came to get me as he had to drive to Gatow because of some paperwork and he knew I loved the ride there with so many memories. We talked a lot about our future since his was as uncertain as mine and although he knew he had to be back in the States by the end of the year, I got the feeling he wasn't really looking forward to it. Coming back, we stopped at the Ku Damm and had some dinner and another weekend was gone. I then listened to some music and reread my letter to Michael before going to bed.

The work week started as always with a lot of typing and adding up of numbers but on Wednesday we got paid—it was a little less than I expected but I could still manage what I'd planned. My plan for the coming weekend was to ask Daniel if he wouldn't mind driving me to Ku Damm to look for some little presents for Michael and Janet and when I got home on Thursday, my mother gave me a letter from Janet, including a picture of her with Michael and Stefano They all looked so happy and I wished I, too, could have been in that picture but time was moving so quickly that soon I'd be there as well.

When work was over on Friday Daniel was standing there with the jeep waiting for me. I felt embarrassed as most of the employees were leaving and when they saw me with an American soldier they must have thought he was my fiancée, not only an American but also much older than me. I just smiled, though, and got in the jeep—it was my life and not theirs and I could always explain to them later. We went to the coffeeshop and had a little snack and when I asked him about my plan to go to the Du Kamm over the weekend to buy some presents, he said he'd be glad to do it. When I got home there was a letter from Michael waiting for me. He told me all about his office work, which he really loved, but there was nothing asked about my job, which in a way made me sad. I knew that was just Michael but I didn't feel like answering straight away, especially as I'd just mailed that emotional letter to him a few days before. I thought I'd answer over the weekend and was tired anyway, so went straight to bed.

I was really excited when Daniel picked me up to go to the Ku Damm to get some little gifts for Michael and Janet. I looked at Janet's picture again: she was small and I figured a medium size would be fine as I wanted to buy her a shirt, maybe in white with black letters saying BERLIN on top. For Michael I wanted to get a desk set for his office so that he could write notes on it with a pen with a little Berlin Bear on it; which I was sure he would like. I asked Daniel to look for gift-shops and we found quite a few. One in particular I liked, so we went in and I found exactly what I was looking for; the shirt for Janet was very nice and there was also a desk set. It was more expensive than I expected which meant I couldn't save anything but I'd given my mother money for food and it was my first paycheck, so it didn't matter to me.

Daniel and I decided on an early dinner and then across from the store there was a newly opened bar where Daniel said he just wanted to have one beer to check it out. Well, I didn't completely agree but he did so many favours for me that I couldn't refuse and it turned out to be a really fancy bar mostly occupied by Americans in uniform. They had nice music and a small area for a dance floor but everything was pretty pricey. I had a glass of white wine and Daniel had his beer and we really enjoyed the atmosphere, the only thing missing was Michael. I believe Daniel noticed how I felt and we left but it was a really relaxing Saturday evening. When he dropped me off at home, Daniel mentioned that Rebecca and her husband were coming for an early dinner the next day and Rebecca had asked him to tell me to come, too, saying she really liked me. I thought it was a good idea and I liked her too, so Daniel arranged to pick me up early the next afternoon.

I showed my mother the gifts I'd bought and she really liked them too and we started to talk a little. I liked those mother/daughter talks, they made me feel secure and safe, and afterwards I listened to music and looked at the latest pictures from San Francisco, thinking how lucky I was because of the life I was going to have, but mostly of course, because I'd be with Michael again. It was then already late and I decided to pack those little gifts the next day. I must have had a good night's sleep and when I woke up in the morning my parents weren't there, most likely having gone to Church, so I had a cup of coffee and started packing my little gifts. I was really proud of them.

As my parents weren't home and it was a beautiful day, I took my bike and rode over to Helga to check on her but when I arrived I found her with her eyes all swollen and her husband half sitting and half lying on the couch with a beer bottle in his hand even that early in the day. She must have cried a lot but we couldn't really talk much and I promised her I'd stop by again over one of the coming days. While I was in the neighbourhood I went to see Mrs. Bohn to see how she was getting on. She was really glad to see me but looked a little run down because she was trying to sell the house and there was a lot of work for her to do. I felt bad not being able to help her but she understood that during the week I came home late from work and that I didn't want to give up the weekends because of Daniel and his lifestyle. I knew it was selfish and I also promised her I'd stop by again over the next few days.

My mother made lunch and I was getting ready for the early dinner at Daniel's and looking forward to talking with Rebecca. I realised that the next week was already the second week of July and that Michael's course should be finished by August 15th, which made me very happy. Daniel came early so that we could prepare a simple supper and spaghetti was the fastest and easiest so the four of us enjoyed home cooked spaghetti with meatballs rather than restaurant food. Rebecca and I always had something to talk about and she told me that they, too, had to leave by the end of the year and that although she looked forward to being back home, she would miss Berlin which she thought a special city. I didn't really feel like that since I was born and partly grew up there, but yes, it was HOME. Daniel took me home not too late as another work week started the next day and I just felt I had to give my mother a big hug, which of course she liked a lot.

I wasn't really looking forward to the next week at work but guessed I'd get used to it. I felt as if I was living in two different lifestyles but, of course, that would soon change. I was expecting mail from Michael, at least two letters, so I'd soon know how things were developing over there. It took me a while to fall asleep lately but I tried to manage sleeping without the Valerian pills. On Monday morning I took the bus to work as I was already a little late and didn't want to be like Karin, always a little late. Since nobody mentioned anything about Daniel picking me up on Friday and being an American soldier and older than me, I didn't say anything either, so only Karin really knew. The day went just like any other day; the boss dictated some letters and since he never called me back, he must have been satisfied with my work. Karin mentioned that on Friday there would be a summer party in the park for all our employees and that they'd done that for the last three years since there'd been a place for it. Karin said it was a lot of fun but most of the time there were a lot of drunken employees and since no one owned a car anyway, they had to either take a taxi or Herr Kinds, the driver, had to make several trips to take people home. I wasn't really that interested in it but Karin said, "You'd better come, so people cannot gossip about you," meaning that somehow they knew that my fiancée was an American soldier.

At the end of the day when I left the office it started to drizzle and the bus had already left, so I tried to walk home. When I was halfway there it started to rain quite heavily and then there came our company car and Herr Kinds stopped and asked me if he could take me home. Since it didn't look as if the rain would stop soon, I thought maybe I should go with him. He said, "I am Karl Heinz," and wanted to know where to take me. He told me he lived on the other side of the office with his mother and sister but I didn't want to ask too many questions and just told him my name and where I lived with my parents. It was quite different driving in a jeep compared to a Volkswagen. When we arrived home, I thanked him for the ride as it was then raining heavily. My mother saw me getting out of the Volkswagen and asked me who that was so I told her he was our driver. There was nothing much to do that evening and as it was raining hard I didn't go anywhere, just took a book and went to bed hoping to have the next letter from Michael soon. Before I went to bed I told my mother about the office party on Friday in the park and she laughed and said, "You're going to a German party?" and we both had to laugh.

Nothing was really happening that week except for the party on Friday after work at 5 P.M. On Wednesday, Daniel came and picked me up from work and also saw the faces of the employees. Maybe I should tell Karin to tell all of them that he was the boss of my fiancée, who was currently in San Francisco; maybe they'd feel better if they knew that. Anyway, we went to the coffeeshop and had some sandwiches and when I told Daniel about the office party on Friday, he smiled and asked if he was invited too. I told him it wouldn't be such a great idea but he was just joking and asked me to try to keep the weekend free for us.

When I got home, there was a letter from Michael and I opened it before doing anything. He also agreed to a small wedding and told me all about his communications with clients. He really liked it and had already closed a deal for the people who wanted to buy at Lombard Street, known at the "crooked street" in San Francisco. It was quite a big deal and his father was really proud of him but he actually didn't ask how my job was going and he hardly asked about us in Berlin. He mostly knew from Daniel but he could have asked me too and in my next letter to him I decided to ask him straight if he had forgotten Berlin already. I couldn't write back that evening, it would have been too emotional so I just took two Valerian pills and tried to sleep.

Even though I slept all night, I was still tired the next morning so I took the bus again instead of walking. I guess Karin must have told a few people from the office about my engagement and that this was not my fiancée but the boss of my fiancée and somehow they looked a bit friendlier but I was still glad when the day was over and I took the bus back home. I knew I had to see Mrs. Bohn and Helga but I didn't feel like seeing or talking to anyone, so I started to write the letter to Michael, of course telling him everything about home and finally asking if he already had any idea when he would be able to come back to Berlin, so that I could start making plans as well. Since his course would be finished by the middle of August and if he then stayed in the office two more months he should be here in November. Well, I finally had that off my shoulders, so I would just wait for his answer.

I really felt tired and tomorrow was the office party. We could leave at noon, to have time to change and be there at 5 o'clock. I didn't feel like going at all but couldn't not go so I dearly hoped it would rain cats and dogs. Next day it was a beautiful morning, no rain in sight; well, the office party was on. We got out at noon but not everybody was coming as some of the more elderly people didn't care for it and so we just needed one van to transport the rest of us. As it started at five, I figured if I stayed two hours it would be enough, so I could walk. When I got there, the boss had brought a little radio and about twenty people showed up; there was a lot of food, a lot of wine and beer, and quite a few were happy already. I saw Karin so I went and sat next to her and although I wasn't really hungry, everyone started to eat so I had some Bratwurst and potato salad and a Coca-Cola. The boss came over and told me my work was going very well, including the punctuation. Karl

Heinz stopped by as well and told me that if I liked, he could take me home later as he had to drive back and forth with the others and I told him that if it didn't take too long, it would be a good idea.

It was past eight already when the first ones started to go home, so Karl Heinz was getting busy and he took the first ten home and then came back for the rest of us. He drove around, dropping everyone off and I was the last one so we started talking a little. I told him about my engagement to Michael and marriage at the end of the year and then our plans to leave for San Francisco. He only said, "You are so lucky, if I could I would leave Berlin and Germany tomorrow; there's no future here for young people." and I was somehow surprised to hear that. He then told me that he'd lost his girlfriend a year ago because of a lung disease and that they'd wanted to get married as well. At that time medication for those kinds of diseases were hardly available. He showed me a picture of her; she was beautiful and only 19 years old when she died and I showed him a picture of Michael, to which he replied that he was a handsome young man. He didn't really like working as a driver but that was the only job he could find at the moment. When we were home, I thanked him for the ride and he said again how lucky I was to be leaving the country.

My mother was still up and I told her about the party and Karl Heinz and what had happened to him. I hadn't asked him how old he was, most likely in his middle 20s, about Michael's age. I thought it over and, yes, I was so lucky to have Michael. After all, the evening wasn't all that bad but very different from American parties and I was still looking forward to the weekend as I was sure Daniel would find something nice to do.

I had a good night's rest and was waiting for Daniel to show up. He arrived early in the afternoon and told me about a little party at his house, which was fine with me as I could really relax there and since the weather was nice, we could sit outside on the porch. Of course, he asked me how the party at the park was and when I told him about it he smiled and said, "Different from ours, right?" and I had to agree to that. "That" girl was at the party as well; she was also engaged and ready to leave Berlin. She became quite friendly and was asking about Michael and said, "Yes, he's a good-looking guy; if he could only be faithful," and she admitted that she'd had a hard time after he became disinterested in her. "Well, either you can handle his affairs or better leave him"—she wasn't the first one who told me that. It wasn't too late when the party ended and Daniel took me home and just mentioned that he had to drive to Gatow again and that if I liked, I could go with him. Since I liked that ride and the weather was beautiful, it seemed like a good idea.

At home I still wasn't too tired so I listened to music and compared the two parties and I had to admit that I liked the American one better, but of course I was more used to going to American parties. Sometimes I felt bad because Germany was my home and yet I was drawn to the so-called winner over Germany, it must have been because of Michael. I finally went to bed but had to take two Valerian pills. On Sunday my parents went to Church and I checked on Helga and her family. She seemed okay so far but her husband had gone to the "Fruehschoppen"—a meeting in a pub or tavern for late morning drinking, especially on Sundays. She said that if it didn't stop she would leave him and go to her parents in West Germany and I told her I thought it would be best, especially for the children.

After that I went back home and we had some lunch before Daniel picked me up in the early afternoon. The drive to Gatow was wonderful going through the forest and it brought back a lot of memories of driving to Gatow with Michael. We even stopped and walked a little in the forest and some people were walking around looking for mushrooms. I used to do that with my mother after the war but you had to be careful and know what kind of mushrooms you were looking for since some of them were very poisonous. My mother knew all of them because she'd collected them when she grew up in Poland. It was a nice afternoon and on our way back we found a nice little restaurant and had a light supper. Daniel was waiting for the papers from his lawyer and the offer they would make for the divorce settlement and I could see he was more relaxed about the divorce now because he could start out anew.

When we arrived home, he told me he'd come by in the middle of the week and after that I talked a little with my parents and started to listen to some music. I remembered that next week was the middle of July and Michael's two-month course and my one month of work were already over, so if everything went well, he'd be back in October. I really did miss him and I expected some letters the next week. Maybe Janet and Michael had already received my little package, the shirt and the desk set. I somehow had an emotional evening and was so hoping that everything was going well.

Getting ready for the coming week meant getting a good night's sleep so I went to bed early but Monday was really nothing to talk about, just a regular workday so afterwards I went home and got my bike and rode a little in the park. I really didn't want to talk to anyone; those old feelings had come back of feeling all alone in the world but I knew if I went to the doctor he would say it was just a little depression so I had to try and get over it myself. But lately I had to take those Valerian pills to get even a little sleep. When Daniel checked on me on Wednesday, he noticed I was quiet and not bubbling like usual so I told him how I felt—that it was the end of Michael's two-month course and my first work month and I really couldn't make any plans. He understood what I meant but no one could really do anything about it. We went again to the little coffeeshop for a snack and he mentioned that we'd have to do something special over the weekend to make me smile again.

What really bothered me, too, was that I hadn't received a letter from San Francisco that week and the week was almost over. Perhaps tomorrow I'd have two letters but on Thursday I only received one from Janet thanking me for the shirt, which she was very proud of, but she didn't mention a lot about Michael except that he was very busy driving clients around and showing them properties. At least I had something and maybe tomorrow I'd have a letter from Michael. On Friday after work, Daniel stopped by just to tell me we'd go out for dinner on Saturday and he'd stop by Saturday afternoon. When I got home, my mother gave me a letter from Michael and for a moment I was scared to open it in case it held bad news but in fact it was a nice letter telling me how busy he was with the clients. Also, inside in a piece of foil, there was $50 and a note saying "Get something nice" and a P.S.

saying "I almost forgot to thank you for the desk set; it's really nice." I was happy about the letter but not so happy about the $50, which somehow reminded me of how Wolfgang's relatives had given me money to give Wolfgang up, and that wasn't a happy feeling. I had a bad night thinking about the $50 he'd sent me; I felt cheap somehow—if he'd sent a little present it would have been lovely, but money; I was earning my own money now. Maybe I was being too sensitive but I wasn't telling my parents anything about it.

It was a beautiful Saturday morning again so I decided to visit Rita and see how she was doing. They were all okay and Rita and I went for a little walk around the lake. I told her about the money and she also felt the same way as I did but we finally came to the conclusion that he really meant well and even though I always had in my mind not being a German Fraeulein, I finally pushed those negative thoughts aside.

We had some lunch at home and I wanted to start a thank-you letter to Michael and Janet but couldn't find the right words so decided to do it the next day and in the meantime Daniel stopped by and we went to the Ku Damm area, doing some window shopping. I told Daniel the money story and I felt for a moment that his face changed but he didn't say anything except that it was nice of him to do that—he knew I liked little presents and maybe he was too busy to get one so he just put the money in, and that made sense to me. We found a little diner and had some supper and he told me he wasn't able to come later as he had a lot of paperwork to do, mostly divorce papers to be signed, and that Elena would most likely get half of his assets and that would be the end of it. I felt sad for him but finally he could start anew. After he took me home, I started to write a letter to Janet but thanking Michael was a different story, at least for me as I had a problem doing things I was emotional about and found it hard to express myself without hurting anyone so, after thinking it over, I felt I needed a night to sleep on it and that's what I did.

I did a lot of thinking that night and in the morning I was still tired but it was Sunday and Daniel wasn't coming, so I had all day just to relax. I started to write to Michael but somehow I couldn't find the right words so thought I'd get some fresh air and took my bike and rode around the park. There were the swans again, reminding me of seeing them last when Michael was still there. The fresh air felt good so I went home and had lunch and started to finish the letter to Michael. I thanked him for the money and also told him of seeing the swans, wondering if he still remembered. Lately my emotions were really mixed up and it bothered me a lot that I couldn't start making any plans. There wasn't a lot to do that Sunday, so I started reading again and listening to music. Pretty soon it would be the end of July and in August Michael's course would be over; maybe by then he would know more and finally we'd be able to make some plans. I really needed that day to rest and get ready for the next week at work and I decided I would take the bus to work from now on as it would be easier than walking or taking my bike.

On Monday it was mostly a quiet day at the office and since I'd again forgotten to take my lunch, Karin and I went to eat at the canteen and found Karl Heinz was there as well. He asked me if I already had a date to leave Berlin, but of course I didn't know. He mentioned that he had thoughts about leaving for Australia but that was just a thought, he said, and also mentioned that he had a friend who was possibly leaving for Canada. It was amazing how young people from the caged-in West Berlin just wanted out.

Well, not a lot really happened during the week except on Wednesday when Daniel showed up and we had our little coffeeshop meeting and the promise that we'd do something over the weekend. He said he'd pick me up on Saturday afternoon; that was the highlight of the week. On Friday afternoon I really had to see my grandparents as I already felt guilty. They were fine or at least, Grandfather was, but my grandmother had really lost her smile and the glow in her eyes. She was asking when Michael would come back but I couldn't give her an answer. She knew I was sad but only said that it wasn't in our hands what was going to happen. I so wished they could live with us, then I would still have a chance to sleep in her lap if I needed it.

I was glad the work week was over, but no letter from San Francisco this week; maybe something would come on Saturday and, indeed, Saturday morning the mailman brought a letter from Michael. As usual, he told me a lot about how much he liked the job but also missed me a lot, but no mention of making any plans. In about two weeks his course would be finished, on August 15th, but so far nothing had been said about how long his father wanted him full-time in the office, it had been said until the end of October. It was a sweet letter but somehow I felt the distance between us.

I was glad when it was afternoon and Daniel picked me up for dinner in the Ku Damm area. He told me he'd spoken with Michael's father the night before and that he was very pleased with his son's performance. They took clients to dinner in San Francisco's China Town, which is a famous part of San Francisco and used to be the largest China Town in North America. Daniel said he must be doing quite well since he was able to close two deals already and although I didn't say anything to that, I felt like a very little bird at that moment. Would that be my life? Would I fit into that life? I couldn't answer that and I didn't think Daniel expected an answer, either. Well, we had a nice dinner and when Daniel was taking me home he told me they had a barbecue behind the barracks the next day and he would come and get me. I thought he knew how I felt. Getting home, I started to think about it: well, it was Michael's job, not mine, so I really wouldn't have to have anything to do with those sophisticated parties until I was more used to it. I fell asleep thinking about those simple barbeque get-togethers.

It was a beautiful Sunday morning and also the beginning of August and I was looking forward to the barbeque behind the barracks. During that period of my life I really didn't know which country I loved more, my home country of Germany or my dream country, the U.S.A.; I was torn between those two. We had a little lunch at home and I waited for Daniel to pick me up. When he arrived, he looked tired; maybe he was feeling the same way as he'd once told me he wouldn't mind going back to Ireland, where his ancestors came from, and where he still had relatives. Maybe it was as if people who had to pull up their roots to go to different environments and lifestyles never really felt at home anymore. Daniel didn't say a lot and I guessed he'd had some not-so-good news, but I didn't ask.

The barbeque party was great and I enjoyed every minute of it. Sometimes I had the craziest idea that if I liked Daniel a little more than as just a friend, I would have a very safe and secure life, but that was only when I was sad and down about Michael. Going through a terrible war, not knowing if you would survive the next day, makes one look for security and safety most of the time but I'd also heard from some people who went with their boyfriends or already-husbands that they were quite disappointed and sad about the different lifestyles in the Golden Land, and who had returned back home. Well, I thought, time will tell and by the end of the year I would know more about where I was. In Germany in the summertime it can be light outside until ten o'clock and as it was almost getting dark and tomorrow was the start of another working week, we had to leave. After looking really lost earlier that evening, Daniel looked a little more relaxed and told me he'd be back on Wednesday. Lately I'd had to take those Valerian pills almost every night.

The first day of the August month started out pretty quiet, or maybe I was getting more at ease in my new working place as even writing for our boss wasn't scary anymore. In two weeks, Michael's business course would be over and hopefully we could somehow make plans. The days went by quite quickly and on Wednesday Daniel showed up for our midweek coffee date. He looked somehow more relaxed and told me the divorce papers had been sent to his lawyers and he'd agreed to giving Elena half of his assets and nothing further, so it would be a clean break. He'd spoken with Michael's father again and he was so proud of his son. The coming weekend, Michael had to show clients a property which was located about a four-hour drive out of San Francisco, so they decided to stay there overnight. I didn't pay too much attention to that since I was sure Michael would tell me about it. When Daniel took me back home he mentioned that he'd plan something for the weekend, so we had something to look forward to.

On Friday I received two letters, one from Janet and one from Michael. Janet's was sweet as always and always with that same sentence: "You should have come with Michael; you could have stayed with us for a while." I thought that next time I wrote I had to ask her why she always told me that. Michael's letter was kind of emotional, telling me how he missed me, though it sounded like it was an excuse for something—or maybe it was my suspicious mind. Yes, it was time for us to be together again. There was no mention of anything about an out-of-town trip but actually he might not even have known about it when the letter was written. Well, we'd made it so far, we would survive the rest as well. I rode around a little in the park and watched the swans and thought about the weekend and what Daniel had planned, then went to bed early with another week having gone by again.

Before I fell asleep, I remembered that Karin, my coworker, had invited me and some other office workers to her 40th birthday celebration on Sunday in a local restaurant, because her apartment was too small. I had almost forgotten and she'd asked if I wanted to bring along a guest. I had the crazy idea of taking Daniel, as she hadn't said "Germans only" and I knew Daniel had always wanted to go to a "Germans only" party. When he picked me up on Saturday, I told him about the birthday party and he really liked the idea as he loved German beer. "The worst thing that can happen," he said, "is that she can kick me out." Well, we went for dinner that evening and I told him my worries about Michael and he just said, "Set an ultimatum; he needs that." Maybe he was right and I decided to do that in my next letter to Michael. It was a nice evening and afterwards I couldn't find the right words for Michael's letter, so I thought I'd do it the next evening.

For the party, Daniel said he would take a taxi, otherwise he wouldn't be able to drink beer and he arrived on Sunday with a beautiful bouquet of flowers from the PX Store, ready to go to an original "Germans only" party, only we didn't know if Karin would let us in. When we arrived, I went in first to talk to her about Daniel and she grinned and said, "Bring him in." Quite a few guests were there already and they were either walking or were taking a bus so that they, too, could have some beer. I waved Daniel in and he was smiling and gave Rita that beautiful flower arrangement. Karl Heinz and a few colleagues from the office seemed a little surprised about Daniel but nobody said a word. For dinner we had Eisbein (a German specialty dish of pickled ham hock, usually cured and lightly boiled. In Southern Germany it is known as Schweinshaxe and usually roasted) and it is eaten with Sauerkraut and mashed potatoes; a heavy meal and quite fatty and, of course, requires a lot of beer. I was surprised that Daniel liked it, maybe because of the "lot of beer," but it became a nice lively group and Daniel even bought a round of beer for everyone, which helped, too. Looking around, I realised that winners and losers of a war can be friends as well. All in all, it was a nice evening, despite a little too much beer for someone. Then it was getting late and tomorrow was the start of another work week, so everyone went home. Daniel called us a taxi and he thanked me a lot for taking him to that German party, saying he'd really enjoyed himself. He also reminded me to be a little stricter with Michael and told me he'd be back on Wednesday for our coffee date. That evening I was too tired to write to Michael, so planned that for the next night.

On Monday in the office, the people who were invited to Karin's party came into the office and were quite surprised how great that party was with an American there, "just like they are real people," so we had a good laugh about that. When we went for lunch, Karl Heinz was there as well and he also liked last night's party and thought Daniel was a great guy. He knew Daniel used to be Michael's boss so he just mentioned that when Michael came back in the fall, maybe he could meet him too. It looked to me that he liked Americans; maybe he wanted to have some contact with them because his plans were also to leave Germany.

That night I started a letter to Michael. He must be back from his out-of-town trip and this week, the middle of August, his three-month course was finished so I asked him, in a very friendly way, if we could now start making plans for his return and our wedding. I didn't want to push him, but I had to know, and after doing it I felt relieved. I asked my mother to mail the letter the next day and then had a good night's sleep after that.

It was just another week starting, only this week Michael's course would end, so it was an important week. On Wednesday, Daniel came over for our midweek coffee date and I told him about giving Michael an ultimatum but that I hadn't heard anything so far since he'd hardly received my letter yet. I hoped to hear something from San Francisco, maybe from Janet and Michael, by the end of the week. Daniel said he didn't want to be alone so was planning a little dinner party at his house for the weekend and asked me to take Rita and Jonathan along because they were hardly able to leave the house. Rita still had to make plans for her grandmother to be sent to her relatives in West Germany. Daniel told me he'd pick us up on Saturday afternoon and that I should let Rita know, so on Friday after work I went over to them and told them about the dinner party. They loved the idea and also the thought of getting out of the house.

On Saturday morning the mailman delivered a letter from Janet telling me Michael was happy the course was over and then she mentioned that she was kind of worried about him lately as he was drinking a little too much. She wrote that perhaps I should mention it to him in my next letter so that he would know I knew about it. It worried me a lot. Maybe I would be able to talk some sense into him but I actually doubted it, even though I would certainly try. I knew that combination of Michael's—liquor and women—and it made me quite sad. Somehow I made it through the night and was glad Daniel had that party otherwise I would have been pretty down at home. I didn't mention anything to my parents about it but was glad when Daniel came and picked me up. He saw something was wrong, so he stopped before we went on to Rita's and I just got pretty emotional and told him about Janet's letter and Michael's drinking. He said he knew about it as his father had told him but he hadn't wanted to tell me and that I shouldn't worry. In a way I was glad Daniel hadn't told me about Michael's drinking, so I hadn't needed to worry, but if I had known earlier I could have deal with it better and maybe talked to Michael about it. Either way, I had to deal with it now and I decided that the next day I'd write a long letter to him and more or less beg him to think about our future together.

Well, we picked up Rita and Jonathan for the house party and although I didn't feel at all like having a party, it was better to be there than just sitting alone at home and being depressed. I told Rita about it and she seemed a little concerned as well, as we both knew how Michael could get when he drank. I wasn't feeling that great but pretended to have fun. At least Rita and Jonathan enjoyed it, and that was nice. When it was getting late and Daniel took us home, we started to have a little conversation after dropping them off. Daniel wasn't as concerned as I was but my thoughts were more a combination of drinking and affairs. As Janet once told me, the Mendez men love their families but, well, it was hard for them to fight those temptations.

As Daniel was busy the next day, I had enough time to write my letter. It wasn't easy to find the right words but I managed to write a long letter, saying that Janet had told me about his drinking a little too much and also telling him all about here, what was happening, etc., and I asked him to write back soon, saying how I was waiting for him to come back by the end of October or beginning of November. That was all I could do. I was very tired and also emotionally tired and with a new week of work ahead, I went to bed early.

Karin's birthday party with Daniel was still the talk of the office and some asked me if we could arrange another one. I told them it depended on whether Daniel would come again but I was very sure he would love it so when Daniel picked me up, I'd ask him if he'd come to another German party. In a few days, August would almost be over, which meant that in about two and a half months at the most, Michael would be back. Somehow I was very happy but also kind of scared. Karin and I had become quite good friends and talked about it and she said that although the West Coast of the U.S. was a long way, I'd be fine as soon as I settled down.

When I got home, I wrote to Janet telling her that I'd written to Michael about the drinking, so that she knew, but then nothing interesting really happened and the most exciting event was waiting for the letters from San Francisco. Daniel picked me up on Wednesday and I told him about maybe having another German party one of these days, perhaps in the same restaurant, and he was all for it so I promised I'd arrange it with my coworkers and let him know.

Finally, a letter from Michael arrived telling me all about his out-of-town trip with clients and also saying that he'd talk with his father very soon about how long he had to stay in the Real Estate office to get experience and then he'd tell me about our plans. There was nothing mentioned about too much drinking, but of course he hadn't received my letter yet. Those last months there was only waiting for letters and writing letters but that was the only communication we used to have at that time. In the meantime, Karin and I organised the German Party for the coming Saturday and then one evening when I was going home from work I checked with Mrs. Bohn to find her house was almost empty. It was also for sale and she looked somehow sad but told me she'd found a nice apartment in a Senior Housing block. It made me think how lives were changing and how the old ones have to leave for the young ones to start. There was no letter that week, so I told Daniel about the coming party on Saturday at five P.M. again and how everyone was looking forward to it.

On Saturday, everyone decided either to walk again or to take a taxi because of the beer. Daniel picked me up in a taxi and we were a lively crowd of about twenty people. It was amazing how everyone was trying to start a conversation in broken English and Daniel in broken German. Karl Heinz was there, too, and made conversation with Daniel as his English wasn't perfect but better than most of the others and he told Daniel of his plans for leaving the country as well. Daniel made it pretty clear that it wasn't easy for a German to immigrate to the U.S. or Canada, that you have to take any job you are offered even if it's completely different from the one you are used to. He told Karl Heinz it would be easier for him to immigrate to Canada first and then try to enter the U.S. from there but that some people couldn't handle that and went back to Germany because it's not easy to start completely anew. I didn't say a lot to that but it got me thinking.

When supper was ready it was another German specialty "Sauerbraten" (a beef or lamb roast pickled for about three days in a sweet and sour sauce with cloves and onions) served with red cabbage and dumplings. Daniel really enjoyed this one, I thought better than last time's Eisbein and then of course the beer. I really enjoyed seeing them trying to communicate with each other and I was glad I could pay back something to Daniel after he'd done so much for Michael and me and now, with Michael gone, helping me. After ordering another round of beer, it was time to leave and we ordered a taxi again. I saw Karl Heinz starting to walk home; he most likely didn't have enough money for a taxi, and I asked Daniel if we could take him home as well. Daniel called him over and told him to jump in the taxi and he said his drive home was a little out of the way but Daniel said it didn't matter. I'd hardly been in that neighbourhood. It still wasn't fully repaired and you could still see traces of airstrikes. Karl Heinz thanked Daniel for the ride and seemed a little embarrassed and told Daniel that that wasn't where he grew up, that where he'd grown up everything had been flattened during the war. I could see Daniel become quite serious and driving home, he looked at me and said, "You must have had a terrible time during the war." I didn't answer and then, arriving home, he asked me if the next day, Sunday, I'd like to go for a ride in our small part of West Berlin. He also wanted to get in touch with Michael's father, so maybe he'd have some news for me and, of course, I agreed.

Lately my thoughts were going wild and sometimes I really wanted to end this situation either way. It was so stressful and my life was only existing by waiting for the mailman or going to the post office and mailing letters; somehow my life was out of order. Daniel arrived at noon for that joy ride and told me he'd spoken with Michael's father. He'd admitted having some problems with Michael and his drinking and his father didn't understand why he did that; his course was over and he'd done well and was also doing well with the real estate. They were talking about him coming to Berlin for me but his father had told him he had to stay until the end of October; well, at least I had some plan. Daniel continued by telling me that Michael was looking for an apartment, he wanted to move out. Well, I saw that as a good sign and thought maybe he did that for us to live there at the start and thought he'd probably tell me about it in one of his next letters. I felt a lot better.

We had a lovely ride and Daniel told me he'd had word from his boss that most likely he'd have to ship back to the States before Christmas. I couldn't see how he felt about it but it would be another life change. We found a little diner and had some sandwiches and then we drove back home since another work week would start the next day and I was sure that one day next week I would hear from Michael about his plans. If his father kept him there until the end of October he would be back here in November, so it would only be around eight more weeks and that night I slept without Valerian pills.

The third week of August started with a lot of rain and thunderstorms; a good thing we had the bus station close to our apartment. Office work was as usual and when I told Karin about Michael's search for an apartment, she was really happy for me. The weather was so bad I couldn't even go for a ride on my bike. When I told my mother about the apartment she was somehow worried about the timing and the fact that there was nothing really to prepare for—even if the wedding was very small, we would have to register at the town hall and I had no specific date to show. My mother was right; I hadn't even thought of that and I decided to write a letter to Michael that night asking for more information.

When Daniel stopped by on Wednesday, he'd spoken with Michael's father but more about military happenings than Michael's apartment, but he would still be there until the end of October. I had the feeling Daniel was trying to avoid talking about that subject but mostly, perhaps, had negative thoughts, and could only hope that by the end of the week I would know more. Daniel told me he had a lot of paperwork to do on Friday and Saturday because he had to start preparing for his return to the U.S. before Christmas, but he said we'd definitely do something on Sunday. That was fine with me as it would give me time to catch up with personal things like going through my wardrobe and working out what I would need to buy as well as giving me some time to see my grandparents.

On Saturday the mailman brought a letter from Michael; it was short but sweet telling me how much he missed me and that he'd spoken with his father about coming to Berlin and that he could leave by the middle of November—but still no comment about the drinking or looking for an apartment. By that time, I didn't know which letters had gone back or forth or whether he'd received them or forgotten to answer and decided the best thing would be to talk to Daniel tomorrow to see if he could call again and find out more. Everything was very much confused.

I hardly slept that night until I finally decided not to make any plans at all; there was no sense in planning with hardly even a little clue of a timetable and when I told my mother about my decision the next morning, she agreed with me. When Daniel stopped by at noon on his way to Gatow, I went along and I also spoke to him about my decision. He also agreed and promised he'd call San Francisco to find out what was going on. At least I had a plan now, now Michael had to come up with his decision.

It was a beautiful ride again and as the weather had cleared up we were even able to have a little walk in the forest. Summer was almost over and pretty soon the leaves would turn yellow—a beautiful sight—before eventually falling off the trees. I liked the fall with all the nice colours but it was only a few weeks before everything looked empty again and the branches were bare until next spring when everything started to grow and bloom again. We found a little diner, this time near Gatow, so we had some supper there before driving back home. It was a nice evening and mostly I had a plan. As usual Daniel said he'd stop by on Wednesday and I hoped by then he'd know something from San Francisco, or maybe I'd have a letter.

That week was the last one in August and Karin called in sick so I was alone in that office, which was quite nice. Someone knocked on the door and it was Karl Heinz telling me that as soon as his friend and his family left for Canada, he would most likely follow them as Daniel had advised as the Canadians were looking for carpenters. That wasn't his occupation, he was a car mechanic by trade and so was his friend, but they said they would do any kind of job. He was pretty excited but said it might take a while. His friend had told him it could take over a year but he was willing to wait since he wanted a better future and we didn't know what would happen to caged-in Berlin. He asked if I knew yet when I'd leave and without saying anything about my uncertainty, I just said most likely by the end of November.

I couldn't wait until Wednesday to hear some news from Daniel and when he stopped by we were on our midweek coffee break. He told me he'd spoken with Michael's father and so far nothing had changed, the plan still seemed to be for Michael to come in November. I told him about Karl Heinz' decision to go through Canada first and he said, "Tell him I said good luck." For the weekend he'd planned a little get-together in his house and mentioned that time was passing quickly before he too had to go back. Our little group seemed to be falling apart and it made me sad; we'd developed good friendships. He then took me home saying he'd pick me up on Saturday afternoon.

I was still hoping until the end of the week to hear something from San Francisco and there was nothing else really happening, just work and waiting and nothing came from Michael, just a letter on Saturday morning from Janet. She always wrote such sweet letters and I hoped I'd meet her in person soon. She told me Michael had apparently found an apartment and he was planning to move in sometime in September. It was in a nice neighbourhood but not too close to his house where his father lived. She also told me he'd changed a bit; he'd become distant from his family and she'd try to find out what was going on. She said she'd tell me the truth because she felt I should know, so at least I had someone on my side watching out for me.

When Daniel picked me up on Saturday afternoon, I showed him Janet's letter and he said, "Yes, Janet's a real nice girl, she's always very helpful," and that made me happy; someone I could trust. The get-together was a really nice group but I hardly knew anyone. Daniel introduced me as Michael's fiancée and one guest looked at me and said, "You mean Michael Mendez, that spoiled kid from San Fran?" I just nodded since his face looked as if he felt sorry for me. I didn't say anything as there was really nothing to say but I felt like a little bird again.

Daniel was embarrassed about that remark and said, "He didn't mean it in a bad way, but that was Michael's nickname in the barracks: the spoiled, rich kid from San Fran," and I remembered when I met him how arrogant and sarcastic he could be. The next week was the first week of September and I was certain I'd know more either from Janet or Daniel or from Michael himself. Karin was back at work, so everything was back to normal again and my work didn't scare me anymore. My shorthand had improved a lot and even my counting of long lines of numbers was pretty good and I felt kind of proud about it. Slowly I felt my life was getting a bit more organised; only the plans for Michael's return to Berlin were somehow disorganised but a decision would be made pretty soon now.

Daniel stopped by on Wednesday as usual but hadn't been able to talk to David as he and his wife, Gloria, were out of town, so I was just waiting again. Daniel was planning something for the weekend but he was almost running out of ideas and it would most likely be a little get-together at his house as that was the easiest for everyone. He suggested I ask Rita and Jonathan to drop by as well and also said Karl Heinz from the office might like it as he's also interested in immigrating to the States. I thought it was a good idea: most likely Daniel was feeling pretty lonely and he was always so happy with a lot of people around, so we decided the get-together would be on Saturday and I would inform them.

On Friday afternoon when I got home from work, I found a letter from Michael and he mentioned that he'd found a nice two-bedroom apartment to move into and that he'd do that in the middle of September. There was still no mention of approximately when he would be coming but I assumed the apartment was meant for the two of us. There was still no mention of his drinking. Well, at least he or we had a place to stay for the first time. He said that he missed me so much and that I should have gone with him in April, but it was too late now.

I told Karl Heinz about the invitation to Daniel's house party and he was really excited about it, but Rita and Jonathan weren't able to come because Rita's grandmother wasn't feeling well and nobody was free to stay with her. I needed to tell Karl Heinz how to get to Daniel's house but instead just told him to be at my house at about four o'clock so that Daniel could tell him where he lived or even let him come with us. On Saturday, right on time at four P.M., Karl Heinz showed up at our apartment and Daniel wasn't even there, but he was always either a little late or too early, so I went outside and both of us waited for him. We explained that Karl Heinz didn't know where Daniel lived and I wouldn't give him the address in case he didn't like me giving it out, but Daniel just told him we'd take him along. Karl Heinz thanked him and said he had money for a taxi to get home, as it was out of the way.

Well, it was quite a big group and this time I knew a lot of them as most of them were there when Michael and I were, but they were all new to Karl Heinz, who did a pretty good job trying to communicate in his broken English. Some of them kept asking me about Michael so I told them what was going on and although some might have believed it, I could see on their faces that some of them didn't and it didn't even bother me anymore; I'd done everything I could. There was no dinner but we had nice snacks and then when it was getting late and the beer supply was almost gone, everyone started to leave and Karl Heinz called a taxi—you could see he was proud to pay his own way home. Daniel took me home and told me he'd try to get in touch with San Francisco the next day and would come to see me in the afternoon and I started to relax a little since I really had tried everything and just hoped to get more news next week. Maybe Janet would know something.

On Sunday morning I went to church with my parents and the priest sure was happy to see me and asked about the wedding and if I had any idea when it would be. I could only tell him that I didn't know at the moment and he obviously understood that I didn't want to talk about it. Late in the afternoon Daniel stopped by and told me he'd got hold of David and talked about Michael, who was already moving out little by little, so he didn't have any news and there I was, waiting again for the next week and some news.

At the beginning of September, nothing really happened until Wednesday when Daniel stopped by, but even then there was no real news. Daniel hadn't been able to get in touch with San Francisco and there was nothing for me to do but wait. Karl Heinz thanked me again for that evening and said he'd really enjoyed it; at least someone was happy. When Daniel and I went for our midweek coffee break, I told him I was only waiting this week and if I didn't hear any REAL news, I might cancel the whole wedding arrangement; I couldn't handle this situation any longer and I really believed Daniel understood. I wasn't mad at Michael if he'd changed his mind, but I just wanted the truth.

Well, on Friday when I came home from work there was a letter from Janet and, yes, I was afraid to open it; maybe I'd now find out the truth. I sat down at the kitchen table with my mother and opened the letter. Janet wrote that she was so sorry to tell me but that she'd seen Michael and Juana, that Mexican girl he'd left behind when he was shipped to Germany, coming out of Michael's new apartment. She'd confronted them and asked him what was going to happen to me and Michael wasn't able to say a word and Juana acted as if she knew nothing. After a few minutes silence Michael said they were only friends, nothing else, and that he would fly to Berlin in November. She added that that was all she could find out at that moment then said that she hoped I would find out more from him if he was going to be honest and that he was still wearing our ring; she felt so sorry but she thought I should know.

Yes, I was shaking but deep down I almost expected something like that. I told my mother and she kept quiet but I felt better—at least I knew a little and maybe they were still only friends, but I very much doubted that. Yes, the Mendez men loved their families but there were the affairs, would that happen to me as well? I wanted to wait for the weekend and talk to Daniel about it, maybe he could get in touch with Michael since I had to know the truth, one way or the other. Even after hearing that news from Janet, I felt we'd finally be able to straighten out our problems. I decided not to say anything to anybody in the office until I was sure what had happened.

When I left the office on Friday, Daniel was outside waiting for me, which was unusual, but I got in the jeep and Daniel started to talk. He'd been in touch with Michael's father and they'd had a long conversation. Janet was right: Michael and Juana had been seen together on and off since July and that must have been the reason for Michael's drinking and moving out. Apparently ever since Juana found out Michael was back, she'd showed up at the office and at the house and, knowing Michael, I didn't think it took him too long to start an affair. Apparently he seriously wanted to come back to Berlin since he was still wearing our ring but Daniel told me I'd have to contact Michael to find out exactly what his intentions were. Daniel felt really sad telling me all that but there were rumours going around already. I could somehow imagine Michael being married to me and still having Juana. The only thing I could suggest to Daniel was to ask if it would be possible to talk to Michael over the phone from the barracks and Daniel said that as it was a family emergency, he would find out.

He wanted to know what we should do over the weekend but I said

I just wanted to stay home but that if he found out anything about that phone call, he should come over, and he understood. When I got into the kitchen, my mother saw something was wrong. I wasn't able to cry and felt for a moment that the world had stopped turning. When I told my mother what was going on, she only said, "There's a reason for everything, but wait until you've talked to him; maybe it's not as bad as it looks right now." I was glad to be alone, just looking at the pictures and the dried flowers over my bed, and I promised myself at that moment that whenever I had the chance to leave caged-in Berlin, I would fly all over the world and visit wherever I wanted.

That night I hardly slept, trying to decide what to do. Even if we were married, it could always happen again, it was like a disease with Michael. Finally, I fell asleep and the next day I went to see Rita and told her about it. She only said that she'd seen it coming but she was also very sad since she and Jonathan were the ones who started it, but I assured her it wasn't her fault we fell in love on a blind date. When I'd calmed down a bit I got on my bike and rode around the lake telling myself I had to talk to Michael first.

When I got home, Daniel was waiting for me, telling me his boss had said that as it was a family emergency, I could have permission to talk to Michael in San Francisco and that he'd called to tell Michael he had to be in his house on Sunday morning at 8 o'clock, which would be 5 P.M. here in Berlin. I was so excited to be calling long distance for the first time and as we had a nine-hour time difference, Berlin was nine hours ahead of San Francisco. Then Daniel asked if I wanted to go and have a glass of wine someplace, saying it would be good for me and I thought he was probably right so I went with him. He asked me what I'd do if Michael really had or still has an affair and it was a hard question to answer because I actually had no answer. We talked about the end of the year when Daniel would be back in the U.S. and so would Rita and Jonathan as well; but whether Michael and I would be there was the big question. Our little group had been together for quite a while and all of a sudden they were leaving in different directions of the world and that thought really hit me hard: for me it was like a security blanket having those close friends. That glass of wine really was what I needed and I felt I was ready for the talk the next day with Michael; it was almost five months now since we'd spoken, otherwise it had only been letters. Daniel took me home and said he'd come to fetch me the next day at noon, then we'd drive to the barracks and wait for the call.

I had a bad night but realised that the truth would come out and whatever it was, it would be easier to deal with when I knew. On Sunday morning I wasn't hungry at all but my mother urged me to eat at least a little because she knew about the forthcoming call and she made some pancakes. Without my mother I would be totally lost; she really understood how I felt. Daniel showed up at noon and we drove to the barracks. It was a strange feeling going inside with all the security checks but with Daniel with me, I had no problems. By then it was four o'clock so we still had an hour to wait and I was quite shaky so took two of the Valerian pills which I had with me; I didn't want to faint while I was on the phone.

The phone rang a few minutes before 4 o'clock and when Daniel picked it up, it was David telling Daniel that Michael was coming on the phone, so Daniel gave me the phone and left the room. I took it and asked, "Michael?" and after a few seconds of silence, his voice came on saying, "Yes, I'm here." Neither of us said a word and then suddenly, "Hi, my little bird." I had a hard time not to cry but somehow we found a way to start talking. He told me honestly about Juana, how she was following him and how they'd then met in a bar, that they were both drinking and it just happened. I wasn't saying anything so he kept on saying how sorry he was, how much he loved me, and that he'd come in November so that we could start our future together.

There was silence again, then I could hear his emotion in his voice when he said, "But I have to tell you something else." Somehow I knew what was coming: "Juana is pregnant." For seconds I couldn't talk and Michael kept on saying, "Are you okay?" I just asked him what he'd do now and I felt my whole body was numb. Michael answered that the child was his responsibility and he would take care of it but said, "You and I will have our family and our children. You are my family." The only thing I could say was, "Michael, I love you very much, but I have to think how to deal with this," then I started to cry and hung up the phone.

Daniel came back in and said I looked as white as a sheet and asked me if Michael had told me everything. I nodded and he said, "I knew about it, also about Juana, but I didn't want to tell you." Michael had told Daniel about it and also that he would provide for the child; nothing else except that he would come in November and marry me. I was too numb to say anything and just asked Daniel to take me home. I told him I'd call in sick for a few days off work and I told him I'd make a decision over that time. He just said he'd come by the next day to check on me.

I hardly remembered that evening and night. I told my parents everything about the phone call and I had the feeling they somehow expected something like that but they didn't ask me about my decision, for which I was very thankful. I asked my mother if she'd go into my office to tell them I was ill and would be off for a few days. I now had those two options—to call everything off or to still marry him and start our own family but I knew there would always be a connection between Juana and Michael because of the child since Michael loved children. The big problem wasn't the child at all, but Juana would be and I knew I had to make that decision on my own, that nobody could help me.

Somehow I made it through the night and next morning my mother took a taxi and went to my office to tell them I was ill but I didn't think they believed it. I also called a taxi, took some money from my savings for the wedding and went to complex Wannsee. It was a beautiful day and there were benches to sit on, so I sat there remembering the beginning of our relationship which started there, hoping to make the right decision and I think I sat there for hours. I then realised I had to get home since I hadn't told my mother where I was and when I got home my mother was terribly worried, not knowing where I'd been. I was still numb and I suppose I'd started to put a wall around myself so nobody could get close to me and hurt me again.

Daniel showed up late in the afternoon asking if I wanted to drive around a bit and I agreed and told him what I'd done today, going to Wannsee. He thought it was a good idea and I still had a few days to decide. I started looking at Daniel in his uniform and realised he was an American soldier, just like Michael, and I saw him differently from before. It was just a crazy thought: those Allies destroyed everything we owned and then I trusted them and got hurt. My mind was going wild and I really had to pull myself together. I didn't know if Daniel noticed what was going through my mind and hoped not. When he took me home he asked me if he should stop by tomorrow but I said Wednesday would be fine. I planned to write to Janet over the next two days and to write to Michael with my decision by the end of the week but I was then too tired to think anymore and just wanted to sleep so decided to write to Janet the next day. My parents were really worried but I was a fighter and whatever I decided, I knew I'd be fine and that I just needed some time.

I actually slept almost ten hours but was still tired the next day. I wrote to Janet, telling her I'd spoken with Michael and that he'd been very honest and told me everything and I also told her about Juana expecting a baby, since I didn't know if she knew about that. Then, after finishing the letter, I went to the post office and mailed it, also deciding to see Rita as I had to tell her. Jonathan was there, too, and seeing him in uniform made the same feelings come up as when I'd looked at Daniel and that really scared me. Rita almost cried after I'd told her about Michael, asking me what I would do. Right then I didn't know and Jonathan left so that we could talk. I asked her what she would do and she said, "Honestly, I would break up with him; he'll never really stop it and you'll always be full of stress. He would never leave you," she said, "but what kind of life is that?" Yes, those were my thoughts, too but I was still hoping my mind would change. I would wait for tomorrow to have another talk with Daniel and maybe then I'd be ready to make a decision. I went home and was listening to music but was so tired again that I went to bed. That night would have been the night when I'd sleep in my grandmother's lap.

When Daniel stopped by on Wednesday evening and we went for our coffee break, he told me David talked to him yesterday about Michael, saying he now drinks almost every night, and Daniel asked me if I'd made up my mind. I almost had the feeling it was my fault he was behaving like that but he was the one who started that mess and that helped me not feel so terribly sad and brought me closer to making my decision, so I told Daniel that I'd tell Michael what I'd do pretty soon and Daniel seemed to understand.

When Daniel took me home, he asked what I wanted to do over the weekend and I just told him I didn't want any partying, so he suggested that one day, maybe on Saturday, he'd pick me up and we could drive around and if the weather was nice, we could even have a walk in the forest. I knew he meant well, since he must have already known what my decision would be and that was fine with me. It took me another day to sit down and write to Michael with my decision and it was then the middle of September when I wrote that Dear John letter:

"Michael, it took me a while to write this. I still love you very much but I've made my decision to let you go and am breaking off our engagement. I'll tell you why: we come from different backgrounds and lifestyles and I don't believe we would be happy together.

"Also, you have a baby coming and I know how much you love children. I don't even know if I'm able to have children after already losing our baby through complications and my mother told me she has problems as well, which is why I'm an only child.

"I'm sending back your ring. Maybe we just met at the wrong place at the wrong time and I wish you all the happiness in the world. Have a great life. I will never forget you. Your little bird."

I then took off my ring, put the letter and the ring in a little box and mailed it to him the next day. My parents didn't say anything, for which I thanked them, and that evening I wrote a letter to Janet telling her of my decision with Michael. I asked her to please not send any pictures of Michael but hoped she and I could stay in contact because I'd really like that. That letter I mailed the next day and with that I had to start a new life again.

On Saturday Daniel stopped by. It was a nice afternoon and we were able to walk in the forest and I told him what I'd done so that he knew in case San Francisco should call He looked at my hand and said, "You sent the ring back, too," and I just nodded. I couldn't cry anymore; there were no tears left.

Daniel was busy on Sunday, which was fine with me, and I spent most of the day with my grandparents, mostly of course with my grandmother and she was so happy I was there. I told her everything and I felt she was the only one who really understood me. "Time will heal everything," she said. "I know how you feel," and she had tears in her eyes. I had the feeling she'd been through something like that herself but I only found out many years later. I eventually had to leave since I had to be back at work on Monday. Our doctor had given me a certificate of illness but not for the real reason, so that was good.

I removed the pictures from the wall above my bed but left the dried flowers. I still had the locket Mrs. Bohn had given me, so I put the pictures in there and also the earring, watch and other jewellery Michael had given me over time, and locked it. I then gave the key to my grandmother and she kept it for me together with the rosary she was still using. Only my mother knew who had it and where it was, just in case something happened to my grandmother.

So, on Monday morning a different kind of life started for me. It was a strange feeling; everything was the same only my life was completely changed and there was no more dreaming of living in the "Golden" land, as the U.S.A. was sometimes called. I guess reality hadn't really set in. When I reached the office, most of them weren't there as I was early and that way I didn't have to answer too many questions. Karin arrived on time, so I talked with her about what had happened and she was really sorry but, thank goodness, didn't want to talk about it in detail. I didn't tell anyone in the office and decided I would only tell them if someone asked me. That was my new life now, working all week and resting over the weekend to get ready for the next week's work. Yes, I realised how lucky I was all that time.

On Wednesday, Daniel stopped by for our coffee break but there was no news from San Francisco and Michael mostly likely hadn't received my letter yet. It was a good thing Daniel was still there but he told me he had to leave by the end of December so would most likely stay over Christmas and then leave. He more or less ordered me to at least have dinner one day over the weekend, most likely on Saturday, and said he would let me know. I agreed.

That week went by pretty fast but there was no mail from San Francisco. When Daniel stopped by on Friday just to tell me he'd pick me up on Saturday afternoon so that we could decide where to go for dinner, he said he hadn't heard from San Francisco either. I knew I should go and visit Rita but, being honest, it bothered me seeing Jonathan and Rita together, especially when Jonathan was in uniform. With Daniel it wasn't too bad since he was alone and I was alone, but I had a problem with couples.

My thoughts were running back and forth wondering what my future would be; for a long time, my future had been living in the U.S., now I might be caged in West Berlin for the rest of my life. I'd heard from someone that some girls were applying as nannies to go to England; maybe I should look into that. Then I remembered Rebecca telling me that whenever we were in New York I should visit them, but of course then it was still Michael and me. She'd given me her card with her address but I was sure I couldn't find it anymore and I knew for certain that Daniel had a card from them, so I planned to ask him the next day.

It was Saturday afternoon when Daniel picked me up, telling me that David had called him wanting to know about my decision since Michael was almost getting out of control—it wasn't only Juana, but he was hanging around with the wrong crowd as well. Daniel had told him everything and that my letter was on its way. I started to feel sorry for Michael; always spoiled and taken care of and now experiencing how tough life could be. I asked Daniel about Rebecca's address and he promised to look for it. We had a nice dinner in a small restaurant near Ku Damm and driving home Daniel said that if he had time he'd stop by tomorrow, if not then on Wednesday, or if he had any news from San Francisco. I was thinking about that plan I had; it would be for a year only, but I had a goal.

I didn't tell my parents anything about my new plan; they would have been terribly worried at the thought of me leaving all by myself. Maybe that idea I had about leaving Germany by myself was just to show Michael and his family that I didn't need them, that I could make it on my own, but whatever it was, it helped me to get over that situation a little faster. Daniel didn't show up on Sunday because he was busy and there was no news from San Francisco so I had a quiet day. I started to read about Au Pair girls as that sounded even better than nannies, since those girls lived with the family and got to know the culture and I knew that for me it would be either Great Britain or the U.S.A. as it would help to have learned the language and I decided to find out more. Maybe it was wounded pride, but I still had very bad emotional days when I was ready to let Michael know he should come back and that we'd get through this together, but I knew it would happen again and again.

So a new week started and I was waiting for Daniel to show up on Wednesday so that I could talk about my Au Pair plan, but he showed up on Tuesday at work to tell me he'd spoken with Michael, that Michael was not marrying Juana and that he still wanted to come back to Berlin. Michael was thinking Juana had tricked him into this and although he'd completely take care of the baby, he wanted me to change my mind. There I was again between love and reality and I just told Daniel I'd let him know the next day when he came around.

I thought I was slowly getting over it but now I had to decide again, which I hadn't expected, and I knew that I wouldn't get much sleep that night. My heart said YES but my mind said NO because I knew it wouldn't stop with this affair; that there would always be other ones with different excuses, and I also knew I wouldn't be able to handle it so my mind won over my heart, but only very narrowly. The next day when Daniel came, I would tell him my decision that if Michael called again he should tell him my decision was final and that he shouldn't come to Berlin. I knew it was most likely that if he did, then my heart would win.

Daniel stopped by in the afternoon and when I told him everything he only said, "I hoped you would do that. Michael is a great guy, but women are his downfall." Nobody knew that better than I did. Daniel had to deliver paperwork to Gatow again, so we went my favourite way and somehow I lost some of my stress knowing that whatever happened in my future, it was meant to be; that I wasn't able to change it and I really didn't want to. September had nearly arrived and for Daniel it was time to organise his return back home. There wasn't too much to prepare, only his personal belongings, because the house in which he lived was fully furnished for use by the American Majors or Generals. He hadn't heard from his lawyer about the divorce settlement, but "no news is good news." When I asked him what he intended to do when he got back, he said he really didn't know yet, but then smiled and said, "Unless you come with me." I smiled back at him and said, "We're great friends, but that is all." Of course, he knew that.

That Sunday, Daniel was busy so I had time to rest and think. Thinking was my main work those days and so far I was just running in circles, though I was sure that I'd hear something from San Francisco the next week. The work week began as always with nothing out of the ordinary and then on Wednesday Daniel told me he'd received a call from a very calm-sounding Michael to tell me a letter from him was on its way. Maybe it would arrive by the end of the week. We had our mid-week coffee break and Daniel wanted to know if I would go with him to buy some things he wanted for his return, like little souvenirs, and I knew I'd really enjoy that.

On Friday when I got home from work, there was that letter from Michael, so I sat down and very slowly opened it. It was a very sweet and mature letter and he wrote:

"I haven't received your letter but I know what is in it. I am not using any excuses for what has happened and have had sleepless nights thinking about us. I know if I came to Berlin, I would win you back but maybe you would feel pressured, so I do not want that. I still love you very much and maybe we'll have another chance later in life, you never know what life has in store for us. Let us stay in loose contact. Janet has said the same. I will never forget you. Michael."

I couldn't talk or think or do anything. The only thing I was happy about was that there were no bad words or accusations and no fighting; it was a friendly "Goodye" and at least both of us were now able to start anew, even if it was hurting badly.

I sat there for a while and my mother saw me and just came over and gave me a hug and held me; she knew and didn't need to say anything. I realised, maybe for the first time, that there was no Michael

Mendez in my life anymore, no one close to me except my parents and grandparents of course, and no wedding, no starting a family and no living in the "Golden Land." Maybe in the background my brain was still thinking about "if," "perhaps" and "maybe" but it was over now; it was a clean break-up and I had to deal with it and accept that the past was gone, that only memories were left and that I had to face the future.

When Daniel came over at noon on Saturday, he saw that I'd received the letter and suggested that we went out for a little dinner and that I then stayed over in the guestroom at his house, saying maybe it would help me, that room which Michael and I used to love. I thought about it and knew it was wrong but I was free now so I told him I'd do it. When I told my parents, I saw that they didn't like it but they didn't say anything so we left and had dinner close to Wannsee before driving to the house. Actually, there wasn't much talking between us. Maybe Daniel was thinking about Elena and Michael and how he felt then, most likely the same thoughts as I had that evening. He opened a bottle of wine and we started to talk and he promised to find out more about the Au Pair situation through Rebecca in New York and said we would definitely stay in touch. It was then getting late and the wine did the rest, so I retired to the Memory Room.

I looked out of the window and watched the stars as we'd done so many times before and said goodbye to Michael and the past, as I knew I'd never come back here again. I must have fallen asleep in the chair but thinking back it really had helped me; it was like a closure. In the morning Daniel came in with a cup of coffee and asked if I was feeling a little better and I smiled and said, "Yes, I think I do; this was a good idea." He then took me home and I started to write a letter to Janet telling her everything and also saying I'd be happy if we could stay in loose contact, after which I prepared for the next week's work and also for the start of my new life.

There wasn't much change at the moment except that the wait for the mailman was gone. September was almost over and I was somehow afraid of what the New Year would bring as this one wasn't going to be my favourite. As long as Daniel was still there, it wasn't too bad and I felt there was still a connection to Michael.

The week started alright except that Karin had some health problems so she missed two days of the week and I had to go by myself to the canteen. One noon Karl Heinz was there too; he was on vacation for a week. He asked me when I was leaving and I didn't have to say a lot, he just saw it. He felt very sorry but was polite enough not to ask for any reason. He then mentioned that his sister, Brigitta, had applied as a nurse's aide to go to Eltham, England, a district southeast of London, and was really hoping it would work out. He, himself, was still waiting for his friend to get all the paperwork together and leave for Vancouver British Columbia, in Canada after being told the West Coast of Canada was prettier and also warmer than the East Coast. As soon as his friend was settled there, he would leave for there as well but he said it might take a year or even a little longer. He was willing to wait, though, as he saw it was a good opportunity to save money and thought maybe if the situation in Berlin settled, he might come back and start his own business. At least he had a goal.

Well, my life had just changed and I had to get over that first and then think about my own goal. I knew Daniel would help me to find something on the East Coast of the U.S.A. The West Coast would be much further away from home but of course being with Michael there would have been different.

As there wouldn't be a mailman coming anymore, there was no rush to get home and I just had to accept that and only maybe hope for a letter from Janet once in a while. We were approaching October and the weather was still nice so I mostly walked home from work, which felt good after sitting in the office all day. I thought about my 21st birthday coming up in November: a big thing because being 21 you're considered an adult and aren't dependent on your parents any longer. Usually there were big parties as you could then drink openly but I wondered if anyone would even remember my birthday. I really had to stop those negative thoughts. The only highlights I had were those midweek coffee breaks with Daniel and the weekends. Slowly, everyone in the office knew about my engagement breakup but hardly anyone asked me what had happened and that was great. The only one who mentioned it was our boss and he just said he'd heard about it, "so you're staying with us then." When I nodded, he smiled and said, "That's nice," so my shorthand couldn't have been that bad.

About two weeks after I'd written to Janet she wrote back telling me that Michael had broken up with Juana, was living alone in his apartment and was working a lot but still drinking too much. She said he was giving Juana money every month until the baby was born, around April, and then he would make a payment plan but he would have joint custody. Janet was most likely going to be engaged to Stefano next spring; it was so nice of her to tell me all that and it made me feel as if I still belonged with them.

One weekend when it was almost the middle of October, Daniel and I were together and he told me he wanted to have an Octoberfest party at his house and asked me to help organise it. I was very excited about it and he said we'd talk more about it on Wednesday, which I really looked forward to. When Wednesday came, he said he wanted to invite around 25 people, including Rita and Jonathan and also Karl Heinz, and that we needed to order food from the PX store the next day. It was a nice thought, going to the PX Store again and when we went we ordered Schweinebraten (roasted pork), Schweinshaxe (roasted ham hocks), Wuersti (sausages), Brezen (pretzels), Knoedel (potato or flour dumplings), Sauerkraut and, of course, a lot of beer; it was quite an order. I thought of Michael; he would have loved it.

When I invited Rita and Jonathan and also Karl Heinz, they were really happy about it. A German Octoberfest in an American household, the only things missing were a Dirndi (a traditional female dress worn in Bavaria at the Munch Octoberfest) and Lederhosen (men's Octoberfest outfits of knee-length leather pants). Of course, those items we couldn't get in the PX Store and anyway they were too expensive and mostly only worn in Southern Germany and Austria, but not in Berlin. Daniel told me to get everyone to help with the setting up when the food arrived on Saturday afternoon and that he'd pick me up. I could see in Karl Heinz' eyes that he had problems with getting there and since I had money saved for the wedding, I told him I would lend him the money for a taxi and he could pay me back whenever he could and I could see he was relieved. Rita and Jonathan would take a bus; it wasn't that far. So all of us were waiting for Saturday; it would be my first party get-together without Michael.

The food was promised to be delivered to Daniel's house at around five in the afternoon, so everyone had to be there to help with the setting up. So far there were about fifteen people and that included us but there was a huge amount of food so we hoped all the invited guests would come. If not, then we'd have a lot of leftovers—but everyone would be happy to take some home. Everything was put on the tables and the party officially started with Daniel having made sure the beer was reachable by everyone.

Altogether we ended up with 20 people and, to my surprise, THAT girl came as well, but alone. She saw me and came over and asked me how Michael was, so I had to tell her what had happened. She was really sorry and not pretending and said, "That's Michael, you would never have him for yourself." I then asked what had happened to her and could see she didn't want to talk about it but she said it was a similar story. We stopped talking about it and were concentrating on the food, which was delicious, when the music started to play and some people started to dance the Polka, which originated in the middle of the 19th century in Bohema, part of the Czech Republic. It was a pretty lively dance and well known all through Europe and although not all of them were in good shape for dancing, it was really fun to watch them. Rita and Jonathan tried it too but gave up after a few minutes.

I watched Daniel and his favourite German beer, and had the feeling he wasn't going to be able to drive me home. I wasn't willing to stay in the "Memory Room" again, since I'd said farewell last time, but there was the possibility that I could share a taxi with Rita and Karl Heinz; we'd find out. At the end of the party there was still lots of food left and we told everyone to take some home and it was all gone in minutes. I then talked with Daniel about taking me home and he said he couldn't but that I could stay in the room. I explained that I could share a taxi and he felt really bad but understood so the four of us called a taxi and started the drive home. We dropped off Rita and Jonathan first and then me, with the last one being Karl Heinz who lived a little bit out of the way. Karl Heinz had really enjoyed the Octoberfest and I thought he must not have had a very good home environment. I remembered Karin telling me his father went missing in action and that they never found out what happened to him.

I felt sorry for Daniel in the way he was left with all the mess in the kitchen and thought maybe the next morning I'd grab a taxi and go over to help clean up. I'd saved the money, at least it was good for something. I could have taken my bike but the weather was changing as it was already Fall and pretty soon it would be November, the month I didn't like at all because it was always grey and windy and raining; we called it the dying month. I thought a lot about Michael that night; I'd really missed him at the party. He could be happy as a child and serious the next moment. As my grandmother said, "Time heals all wounds," but I wasn't sure how long that time would be, maybe even forever.

I got up early the next morning and my mother was happy about the leftovers I'd taken home and agreed when I told her my plan to go and help Daniel, so I called a taxi and went. Daniel was sitting in the kitchen looking quite helpless and when he saw me coming he had to laugh. He excused himself for not taking me home but, he said, "That German beer is dangerous." It didn't take us too long to clean up and everything was soon in order again and he was glad to have experienced an original German Octoberfest. We talked for a little while before he took me home until our next midweek coffee break and I spent the time sitting and listening to music and wondering when or if I would hear again from San Francisco.

I met Karl Heinz in the canteen on Tuesday and all he could talk about was the Octoberfest. He also asked about a Christmas party and said it would be nice if I could find something out so I tried to explain that Daniel would be leaving Berlin right after Christmas and might be too busy, but I promised to ask him. Daniel stopped by on Wednesday and we had our little midweek snack. He'd talked with David, Michael's father, the day before who'd said that Michael was doing excellent work but living a pretty isolated life right now and that although Juana shows up at the office quite often, Michael hardly pays any attention to her. I knew how he could be if for him an affair was over. I told him that Karl Heinz would love to do a Christmas party and Daniel smiled and said he wasn't sure since he'd be leaving the week after Christmas. He also told me that he'd had word from his lawyer that Elena was accepting his divorce offer of half his assets and that his problem now was to decide whether to take out a large mortgage on his house and pay her out or sell the house and do it that way; neither was an easy decision for him.

By the end of this year all my American friends would be gone and I was wondering what would be in store for me; it had turned out to very different from what I hoped it would be a few months ago. At least I had a good job and hopefully my plan for a chance to become an Au Pair would work out. While taking me home, Daniel mentioned that he had to drive to Gatow again at the weekend and asked me to go along, which was nice. Then, smiling, he said, "Well, November will be here next week and also your 21st birthday will be in November, have you made any plans?" I was so surprised that he remembered and he said he'd written it down, "Let's plan a surprise party." That made my day. I thought everyone had forgotten about it and we said we'd talk about it over the weekend.

The next day I told Karl Heinz that Daniel would think about the Christmas party but that there was also a Christmas party in the office and we still had a few weeks to go until Christmas. The week went by pretty fast and Daniel showed up on Saturday noon on the way to Gatow. He wanted to know what I wanted to do for my birthday and as my birthday was on a Friday, we decided I would celebrate with my parents and visit my grandmother and grandfather and then we could use the Saturday for a birthday party at Daniel's house. That sounded perfect. We would invite Rita and Jonathan and Karl Heinz—that was a must already as I had the feeling he just wanted to get out of his house. Then we'd invite a few of Daniel's friends who I also knew, and that was it—I didn't want a big thing since if everything had been alright, Michael and I would have been married already as my birthday was at the end of November. Daniel would take care of the birthday cake and the food we'd order from the PX again; everything was settled.

Somehow I had a sad feeling that everything was coming to an end—all my friends were leaving Berlin and only I was left behind in the caged-in Berlin. That poem came into my mind—that there is a reason for everything—but whatever the reason was, I sure didn't like it. We had a nice dinner at Gatow and Daniel was also quiet, perhaps thinking what the new year would bring him. On our way home he told me he was busy on Sunday, so we'd meet again on Wednesday unless anything came up, in which case he'd stop by and tell me.

So, I had the Sunday for myself and could go to Rita and tell her about my birthday party. She was really happy to come and told me her relatives from West Germany would come and get her grandmother at the beginning of December. She had teary eyes and again it hit me what a war can do—splitting up families and relocating a lot of people, causing a lot of heartache and anxiety with it. There was still no hope of putting Berlin together again and reuniting Germany.

I promised Rita I'd help her pack up her belongings. There wasn't much and after her grandmother left, they were also going to try to get out; in other words, they wouldn't even be here for Christmas. Jonathan had to leave on a military flight and Rita needed special permission, since they were also engaged, to fly with a regular flight out of West Berlin (Tempelhof Airport) via Frankfurt/Main to New York, where they would meet up again. That was all she knew at the moment and it sounded pretty adventurous to me, but she had no other way of doing it. As far as she knew, from there they were driving to Florida, where his family lived, and he then had a few weeks' vacation before deciding if he wanted to stay in the military or get out and look for a job and that was all she knew so far. At that moment I somehow felt more secure here in Berlin but if Michael and I were married I could have gone with him and he would be out of the military already, but that was past now.

When I got home that evening, I told my parents about my birthday plans and they were really happy I was spending my official birthday with them and having the party the next day, which was the last Saturday in November. When I went to work I saw Karl Heinz and told him about his invitation to my birthday party at Daniel's house and you could really see how his eyes were sparkling. I gave him the date since we were just at the beginning of November and it was still a while away.

I would have invited Karin as well but she wasn't really that fond of being with the so-called "winner" of the war.

Almost every night my thoughts were far away in San Francisco and I was wondering if they (Janet and Michael) would remember my birthday. Yes, I knew I was behaving like a child looking forward to Christmas, but some days were pretty hard. The week went by quickly and Daniel and I had our midweek coffee break and Karl Heinz gave me back half of the money I'd lent him for that taxi ride. He also had to give his mother money, like rent money and money for food, so he always seemed to be broke. That coming weekend Daniel only had one day free as his time before leaving became shorter and shorter as well, so we decided to have a little dinner at Wannsee on Saturday, which would give me some free time to help Rita with her packing.

Everyone could feel the tension rising, and time was moving quickly, especially for Rita and Daniel. Rita's relatives were supposed to come at the beginning of December to pick up her grandmother and I could see tears in Rita's eyes because of leaving her grandmother. It also wasn't easy for her grandmother—first losing her husband after 57 years of marriage and now relocating again to a place she'd never lived before. I felt good that my grandparents still had each other. When I got home that evening, my mother was still in the kitchen and we started a mother-daughter talk and for the first time she asked me how I was feeling. I tried to tell her some of my emotions and there was that poem again, that there's a reason for everything. She must have seen on my face how I felt and she stopped talking about it; she was very good at that. Instead we talked some other things over including what we'd do on my birthday and decided on nothing special, just going to see my grandparents to have some coffee and cake, since we had the birthday party at Daniel's house the next day.

I got my things together for next week's work and went to bed. The last few days had been pretty emotional, maybe because of the Christmas season and also the fact that my best friends were leaving. Nothing really happened at work. Daniel was there on Wednesday for our midweek break and we talked over ordering the food for the party, which we'd do at the weekend.

When I got home on Thursday, there was a letter from Janet and that made my day. She wrote with all the news from San Francisco: Michael's father had gone to hospital with an apparent heart attack, but it turned out to be a bad anxiety attack and the doctor told him to take it easy, which was great but meant more work for Michael. She wrote that Michael was working almost day and night and that his drinking wasn't so bad, which I was really glad to hear and thought I'd have to tell Daniel about on the weekend. I sat down almost immediately and wrote back. I so wished I could write Michael a letter, too, but I knew it wouldn't do any good.

Over the weekend Daniel and I met and we had to decide what kind of food we wanted since we had to order the coming week for the end of next week delivery. We did it all through the PX; he could even order the birthday cake. We still couldn't decide what kind of food and then I had the idea—why don't we just order American hamburgers with French fries, because I was very sure I wouldn't have hamburgers again for quite a while. Daniel thought it was a great idea and for me it was a great birthday present so we had it all done and settled and when I told him about Janet's letter, he was really happy for me.

The week started out busy as the boss had a lot of letters to dictate and I was tired when I got home which was good as it stopped me from thinking. The weather was like a typical November—fog, rain and wind and sometimes even a snowflake. Daniel came midweek for a short coffee break; he had a lot of paperwork and there were only about four weeks left before he had to leave. I had a hard time believing that and with Rita leaving as well, I'd be back to my traditional German lifestyle. I still hoped to get an Au Pair job, but for that I had to wait until Daniel was back in the U.S. as I'd decided I wasn't very interested in England but did want to go to the U.S. Daniel told me he'd already ordered the food and the cake for the next week but wanted to check that everything was in order over the weekend, so our next meeting would be on Saturday.

I saw Karl Heinz in the canteen again and he more or less reminded me about my birthday party the following Saturday. In a way how he acted was cute; maybe he was afraid we might forget him. I told him that, yes, I did remember my own birthday and for him not to forget to be on time. On the weekend we check the order at the PX Store and everything was fine and as Daniel had a little time, we went job-riding and he told me he'd most likely sell his house and share the proceeds of the sale with Elena and start anew. He was also thinking of leaving the military and even San Francisco and moving further down to Southern California. He promised again to find something for me and then he smiled and said, "And if I find something in San Francisco, would you go?" I didn't have an answer to that.

That night, I thought a long time about the question Daniel had asked me: would I go to San Francisco if there was a job. The emotions I'd been through lately, I would, but in reality it wouldn't work.

I promised Rita I'd go again on Sunday to help, which was a good idea. She told me Jonathan wouldn't be able to come to the party on Saturday as he also had a lot to do, so Rita and I would take a taxi to Daniel's house, since most likely Daniel wouldn't be able to take us home. We got it all done and Rita was almost ready to leave with all her personal things packed but for the first time she told me she was scared, mostly because she knew no one except Jonathan. We promised each other we'd stay in close contact and if anything should go wrong, she could come back to Berlin. She also had some money saved and she was selling the furniture in the apartment, so she should have enough money for a return ticket and I also had some money saved which I could lend her, and all that made her feel more secure.

With all that settled, I went home and was preparing for the big next week of becoming an adult. My mother asked what I wanted for dinner on my birthday as my parents weren't used to going out for dinner. She knew I liked pork chops and potato salad and she made the best potato salad ever, so that's what we would have and she said she'd bake a "Streuselkuchen" (a German crumbcake), for which she was famous. It made me feel at home and safe which I hadn't felt for quite a while.

The week started quite busy again; there was a lot of paperwork to do as we were getting towards the end of the year. Karl Heinz told me he'd also take a taxi on Saturday and you could see he felt as if he belonged to the group, which I really had to smile about. Daniel stopped by very briefly midweek and I told him not to pick Rita and me up on Saturday, that we'd take a taxi because he loved that German beer too much and he just laughed about it.

On Friday morning, my mother gave me a present—a very pretty purse. I could see it was from the thrift store but I didn't say anything and I really loved it, and my mother. At work, hardly anyone knew it was my birthday, which I loved, and only Karin wished me all the best. Karl Heinz stopped by and told me he'd give me my present the next day and when I got home everything was ready to eat. I hoped there would be a letter from San Francisco but there was nothing. After dinner we went to see my grandparents and grandmother gave me a candle and said it was a special one which had been blessed in her hometown church in Poland, which really did make it special. We took my grandparents some of the crumbcake as my grandmother really liked sweets, and it was a nice evening.

At home afterwards we all had some cake and I thanked my mother for all her work and she gave me a big hug, which she always did when she became emotional. When I lay in bed I was happy and sad as well; happy because I had such a loving family and sad because there was no letter from San Francisco. My thinking was wrong, Michael wasn't even my friend anymore.

Saturday was a beautiful Fall day, a bit chilly but a blue sky. I'd told Rita I would be there by early afternoon with the taxi to pick her up. Yes, I was waiting until noon, hoping the mailman would stop by but noon came and went and I even saw the mailman passing by. *Well*, I thought, *maybe it's better like that.*

I called the taxi and picked up Rita and she gave me a beautifully perfumed body spray. When we got to Daniel's he told us only eight more people were coming, which was fine with me, and that I had to follow him into the living room, where he had something for me. There were two cards on the table and something wrapped from a florist. One card was attached to the florist's paper, which I opened first and there was a beautiful dark red rose and the card. I couldn't believe it: on the card was a little bird which looked as though it was flying and a "Happy

Birthday" and signed Michael. I was speechless and, yes, I was crying. I looked at Daniel and he explained that Michael had send the card a week ago and asked him to get the rose for the party. I felt like running home, packing my suitcase and jumping on a plane straight to San Francisco. Janet also sent a beautiful birthday card and then Daniel came with his gift—a pair of leather gloves. I didn't know what I felt, whether I was happy or sad; most likely both.

We then had to run outside as the food was arriving and also Karl Heinz. Karl Heinz gave me a little package with the cutest little Berlin Bear in it and then he said, "It's not really a birthday present but I bought it when you told me you were leaving for the States and as that didn't happen, I'm giving it to you now." I thought it was a unique idea. All the guests were there and we had the best birthday dinner ever, American hamburgers. Yes, I was happy, Michael had seen to that but how could I forget him if he kept doing that. Karl Heinz asked me where I got that beautiful rose from and I told him the story. "Yes," said Karl Heinz, "he must be a great guy, too bad it didn't work out for you." I thought to myself that if he started with that poem now:.. "there is...." I wouldn't talk to him anymore, but he didn't. We were right to get a taxi; Daniel and the German beer were best friends and when it was getting late and we tried to say goodbye to Daniel, I didn't think he'd remember it the next day. Karl Heinz asked if we could maybe just take one taxi and each pay a third as it would be cheaper, and that's what we did. I told Rita I'd stop by the next day and Karl Heinz thanked me for the invitation and also said that if he had some kind of party with his friends in the future, I could also go.

I looked at the rose at home and thought about the first one he gave me. I really wasn't over him at all and as soon as this Rose dried up, I'd hang it over my bed with the others.

Well, my birthday was over and I was a year older but my emotions were still there and still the same, so nothing had changed so far. I was sitting there and looking at the rose, remembering the time with Michael and thinking about the baby; it would have been almost six months old by now. Someone told me once that life is a test and I felt I had been tested quite a bit so far. That evening was not one of the happiest in my life and I needed double the amount of Valerian pills.

The next morning my mother looked at me and knew how I'd felt last night. I told her I was going to Rita's to help her and if Daniel showed up she should just say "Rita" so he knew where I was. Rita had received word from her relatives that they would be in Berlin to pick up her grandmother around the 10th of December, so neither of us were in the best emotional state. We talked about last night and Michael's present and she said, "It was really nice of him, but hard on you." We discussed if I should send him a thank-you card or just write to Janet and thank them both in one letter. Rita said it was my decision but thought maybe I should write him a thank-you and we both came to a decision. We then saw Daniel stopping outside and he came in, apologising for not taking us home but saying the beer was stronger than us and we could understand since he was under quite a bit of stress as well. He took us to lunch and then we took Rita back home.

While driving around a little afterwards, he asked me about Michael's present and I told him my thoughts and asked him too about thanking Michael for it. He immediately said, "Write him a personal thank-you card, he's also had a bad time. I have some nice Berlin souvenir cards at home, let's get one." We found one with Lake Wannsee, it was so pretty and I chose that. He told me he'd leave between Christmas and New Year, so at least he'd still be here for Christmas. After taking me home, he said he'd try to stop by on Wednesday but he wasn't sure. In the evening I sat down with that card to thank Michael but I had a hard time finding the right words so all I wrote was "Thank you Michael for that beautiful rose," and at the bottom of the card I wrote, "Tesknie za Toba"—"I miss you" in Polish, hoping he didn't find out what it meant. It was a really silly thing to do but I did it anyway and had the excuse that it wasn't written in English.

The week started busy again and it was also the first week of December when everybody was busy and I'd also promised Rita I'd help her sell the furniture from the apartment. Her relatives were coming from West Germany by driving on the Autobahn to West Berlin with a van, which wasn't that great as the Autobahn wasn't in great shape and had never really been repaired. It still had a lot of potholes but using a van meant they were able to take some furniture along for Rita's grandmother. We were busy almost all week selling stuff out of the apartment and the relatives had told Rita they would most likely arrive in Berlin on Saturday, December 11th, stay overnight in Berlin and then go back with her grandmother. It was like an ambulance journey and they needed a permit for it but everything had been taken care of. The same week that they left, Rita and Jonathan were leaving Berlin as well and although Rita didn't know which day yet, it was definitely before Christmas. Daniel had helped Jonathan with the arrangement and offered that if Rita had to stay a day or two longer, she could stay in his house as her apartment would be empty by then.

Daniel wasn't able to come to see me on Wednesday so we'd see each other on the weekend and in the meantime I was thinking about the letter I'd mailed to Michael, wondering if he'd already received it. I'd been really over emotional at that moment and not thinking clearly: of course he could find out what it meant, he just had to look it up in the dictionary since he knew I was Polish and that was the only other language I knew well but it was too late now. I was glad that week was over and there was a day or two when Daniel and I could still do something if he had time. I also had time to write a thank-you letter to Janet and also to think about a little Christmas present for my family and my few left-over friends; I still had a hard time thinking about next year with everyone gone.

Christmas is always the most hectic time of the year but this year it was especially hectic because of everyone leaving at different times. That weekend Daniel had to go once more to Gatow and I was going with him as for me it would most likely be the last time as well. Of course, that ride was full of memories but I still wasn't able to smile thinking about them.

I told Daniel Rita's relatives were coming the following weekend to collect her grandmother and he said that would be great as he'd arranged for Jonathan to leave on the 15th December and for Rita to go on the 17th December. That meant Rita would stay two days at Daniel's as he'd offered and I asked him if it would be okay if I stayed there those two days as well, saying I would go to work as usual and come back at night and he agreed. Also, there was to be no Christmas party at Daniel's house as it would be too hectic but Daniel wanted to go to dinner with Rita and Jonathan and he also included Karl Heinz; we just had to choose a day. At least a little bit was in order. I was afraid for Rita: it was her first flight out of Germany and she'd be landing in New York, such a big city, but Daniel said there were a few more experienced people on board and they would take care of her until she met Jonathan at the airport in New York, and that made me really happy.

That weekend went by too fast and the second week of December started. I met Karl Heinz at the canteen and told him there was no Christmas party at Daniel's house but that we'd go out for dinner before Jonathan left on the 15th December, which made him smile as well. He then told me there would be a small Christmas get-together in the office on 22nd December. By the end of that week it would already be two weeks since I'd mailed the thank-you card to Michael and I was now wondering if I would hear something back from him this week.

Finally, the week arrived when the relatives were coming to pick up Rita's grandmother. Rita was a nervous wreck and Jonathan couldn't be a great help because he was at the barracks most of the time. Poor grandmother; I had the feeling she really didn't know what was going on. Since we were all kind of confused, Daniel gave me his plan for the next few days. After the relatives left on Sunday, December 12th, Rita would stay with Daniel until Friday December 17th—a little longer than expected as Jonathan had to stay in the barracks the last few days before he left on December 15th, and I would stay with Rita until she left on Friday December 17th. We now all understood what would happen and on Monday, December 13th, we were going to that dinner for which Karl Heinz was already waiting. We hoped we had everything under control but it was kind of chaotic.

At the end of the week, when I got home from work, there was a letter from Michael. Was I ready to smile about it? No, I was not; my eyes were teary as I opened the letter and there was a card with little hearts and small red roses and handwritten was "I miss you, too." Of course, he'd found out what the Polish words meant. At that moment

I wasn't able to write back and I wanted to ask Daniel if it would be possible to put a phone call through over Christmas and for me to talk to Michael. That gave me a little time to think about it because I didn't feel able to handle long distance love letters.

So far everything was going well and the relatives arrived on Saturday. They were really nice people and told us all about the check points they had to go through to get to West Berlin and then the next day, on Sunday, they said goodbye, took grandmother, and left for West Germany. I then took almost broken-down Rita by taxi to Daniel's house while he was still in the barracks working. He arrived home pretty soon and also brought some food from the barracks. The house had three bedrooms so Rita slept in one but not in OUR room. Daniel took me home and I told him about Michael's letter and asked about the phone call at Christmas, to which he said it should be possible and he'd work on it, and we then decided to meet again at his house the next day at about 6 o'clock for that dinner with Karl Heinz and that I'd take Karl Heinz with me after work. I was so tired that evening that I fell asleep in the chair.

The next day, Monday, Karl Heinz was already waiting outside after work and was really excited about going to dinner with us. He had a bag with six beer bottles as a present for Daniel and while we were waiting for the taxi to come, he told me his friend had received some paperwork to fill out from the consulate regarding his application to immigrate to Canada. He said it might take a while but Karl Heinz was willing to wait as long as it might take. His sister, Brigitta, was also waiting for a reply to leave for England and his younger brother, Horst, who was 17 years old, had applied to the U.S. to be an exchange student for a year. That Kinds family seemed to be falling apart but most young people from West Berlin felt there was no future for them and wanted to leave.

The taxi came and we were on our way to Daniel's. Daniel thanked Karl Heinz for the beer, but said, "Am I that bad?" Rita looked a bit better and more relaxed and was just waiting for a telegram from her relatives to say that everything had gone well on the trip back. Daniel decided to take us to a nice restaurant around the Ku Damm area which had great food, like steak and fish and chicken, etc. I'd never really cared for steak, possibly because I wasn't used to eating it, but I loved fish like Forelle (trout). Karl Heinz ordered a huge steak and I wasn't sure he'd ever eaten one but the speed with which he ate it, he must have liked it. The plan was that after Jonathan left on Wednesday, I would stay over until Friday and see Rita off and most likely I would have to take that Friday off work but so far our plan was working fine. That evening, Daniel took Karl Heinz and me home and Daniel told me he would try to arrange a phone call with Michael on Christmas Eve.

The next day was the last one to say goodbye to Jonathan as he was leaving on Wednesday, so after work Karl Heinz offered to take me over to Daniel's house in the company car, though he had to go back straight away as he wasn't allowed to use the car for personal use. Jonathan was already there, looking very tired and stressed out as there was a lot of un-certainty ahead for them both, so we just talked a bit before he had to go back to the barracks because he was already on standby for the American military plane. I hated goodbyes, they always hurt, so I just gave him a hug and told Rita I'd be back the next day after work to stay with her until she left on Friday. Daniel took me home saying he was going to find out what time he could arrange for me to speak with Michael.

That rose I'd received for my birthday slowly started to die and I wished my emotions would do the same, but they didn't. I thought about the New Year when my closest friends would be gone and won-dered how it would be. I told my mother I'd be staying with Rita until she left on Friday and that I'd then come home and she was okay with it. When I came from work on Wednesday evening Rita told me Daniel had told her that Jonathan left at noon for Frankfurt but that he was on standby again for New York. I slept with her in the other bedroom, not in OUR room, and the next morning Daniel took me to work and said he'd pick me up as well since on Friday I was taking the day off from work. Rita received a telegram from her relatives saying every-thing had gone well and that her grandmother was alright, which made Rita feel better and she had some closure.

That Thursday night no one was actually hungry and we just had a few snacks as we realised it would be our last time staying there together, that Rita was leaving the next day and Daniel only had about two weeks left in Berlin because he was supposed to leave right after Christmas. Rita and I hardly slept that night. We shared addresses but even if Rita had a phone I couldn't call her because Daniel would be gone by then as well, and Rita couldn't call me either. I'd been told that if you went to the post office you could apply or register for a phone call but it might take you hours and would be quite expensive so that was out and we had to think of something else but after living in a war-like situation you mostly could find a way of doing things.

Rita had to be at the airport between 10 and 11 on Friday morning as she was on standby for Frankfurt, so Daniel dropped us off at Tempelhof Airport and went back to the barracks to check for news. Quite a few people were waiting for the flight to Frankfurt, mostly Americans, and Rita knew three of them through Jonathan, so she was practically hanging on to them as it was her first plane flight and she was really scared. Daniel came back with the news that Jonathan had arrived safely in New York and would be waiting at the airport for Rita. Since both were flying into America with sort-of military carriers and both flying from Frankfurt/Germany, there was just the one arrival gate and most likely they couldn't miss each other.

Around noon time there came the announcement for the passengers for that flight, that they would soon be boarding and should get ready as all the standbys had made it. Yes, a big hug and off she dashed, and no looking back. I was used to that behaviour already but it still hurt. Daniel kind of smiled and said, "So I am the next and last one," and I had the feeling again of being alone and forgotten. I always had that feeling even in later years; it must have been the war I went through and I could hardly handle fireworks because of the airstrikes and gunshots and dead people; I'd seen too much of it.

Daniel was getting hungry so we went and had some lunch and I then felt very tired and just wanted to get home so he took me home and told me the phone call on Christmas Eve was fine, he just needed to get the exact time, and that Michael knew about it already. He said he'd come and get me tomorrow afternoon and we might go out for dinner. I was so happy for Jonathan, that he'd made it safely back home, and then I was sitting on my bed and looking at the dried flowers and I really missed Michael.

That weekend was quiet. Daniel stopped by on Sunday afternoon to tell me that he'd spoken with Jonathan and that Rita had arrived safely in New York after a rough ride with lots of turbulence over the Atlantic but they were fine now. That made me happy for them because now they could start their life together. We had a nice dinner at Wannsee and Daniel had found out that the call on Christmas Eve was on that Friday at five in the afternoon, so pretty much everything was settled. We had our little office party on Wednesday, so Daniel said he'd show up on Thursday and maybe there would be some news. I still had no little gifts but I just really didn't care. I thought of beer for Daniel and that I'd just give my mother some money so she could buy herself what she wanted or needed. I almost forgot Karl Heinz, who I knew would give me something, and decided that as he was smoking, I would give him some cigarettes because at that time we didn't know how dangerous smoking was for your health. The only wish I had was to get Christmas and New Year over as fast as possible.

We had that little Christmas get-together at the office and it was quite nice. Karl Heinz gave me a pretty white wool scarf with matching gloves and they were new, not out of the Thrift Store. He asked me if I liked them and I really did so I felt embarrassed about my cigarette gift but I guess he knew how I felt. The next day, Thursday, Daniel stopped by for a little break and told me Rita and Jonathan were on their way to Orlando, Florida. I had to admit I was a bit jealous but I also wished them luck; they deserved it. That evening I had to take those Valerian pills again; tomorrow was Christmas Eve and the call with Michael. We only worked half a day so I had a little time to think over what to say to Michael.

December 24th, Christmas Eve, was always special for me and it was a nice sunny but cold day. I remembered when I was a child and was outside on Christmas Eve it was so still and even the air smelled different; it was a special night. Karl Heinz had the company car and was able to take me home that noon and I had the feeling he was waiting for an invitation for the two Christmas holidays, but I wasn't able to do that because I didn't know myself what would happen since Daniel was leaving the following week as well. I just wished him Merry Christmas and said I'd see him next week at work. He seemed a little sad but didn't say anything. I told my mother about the call but said I'd be back after that so we could have our Christmas dinner of potato salad and sausage. My mother also asked me if I'd go with them to church on Christmas Day and she was very happy when I said I would.

Daniel came around four that afternoon for the call to Michael and surprisingly I wasn't really nervous about it, so we just waited for the phone to ring and it was shortly before five when it rang and Daniel answered it. It was Michael so he gave the phone to me and left the room. I said, "Michael," and he answered, "Yes, Theresa," then silence again, so I wished him a Merry Christmas and he kept on talking about his life there and how sorry he was but that he could understand my decision. I had to promise him I'd stay in touch with him, "You never know what life has in store for us," he said, and that Janet had said the same and that I should get in touch if I needed help. His voice was getting emotional and I promised him and with that the call was over. I knew he was serious, otherwise he would never have called me by my first name, always lovely romantic nicknames. Somehow it was a part closure and he was right, you never know what life will throw at you.

Daniel took me back home; he'd been invited to one of his friends' home, so he wasn't alone. I told him I was going to church with my parents the next morning and he asked if he could join us. I said of course and that church would be at 10, so he said he'd be at my apartment at 9.30. We had a big hug and he wished us Merry Christmas.

My parents gave me a nice vase for Christmas; they knew I loved flowers. When we had our traditional Christmas dinner, I told my parents Daniel wanted to come with us to church the next day and my mother smiled but I didn't know how my father felt—he went to the bathroom and I thought he didn't like the idea too much although he didn't say anything. My parents went to bed quite early so I sat and listened to music and looked at our tiny Christmas tree and, of course, my thoughts were far away wondering what Michael would be doing that night. In a way I was glad about our arrangement to stay in loose contact as that way I still belonged a tiny bit to Michael and wasn't all alone. I thought my feelings didn't want to give up completely and maybe he felt the same way. Just one thing bothered me: as soon as Daniel had gone there was no phone connection possible although I still had to find out how much a call would cost and maybe it wouldn't be that expensive. I was really proud of my smart ideas; I think your mind gives you all those ideas to make it easier to go on. I even had to smile thinking about that spoiled kid from San Francisco.

Daniel was on time for Church the next day and I'd hoped he wouldn't be wearing his uniform, but he was and I could already see the parishioners' faces at another American as they wondered what happened to the last one and noticed that this one is much older as well, but I couldn't do anything about it. My parents had gone along already and didn't wait for Daniel; I knew it was my father because my mother wasn't like that and was friendly with everyone no matter who they were or where they came from. Anyway, Daniel got me and we drove to the church in the jeep and the church was so overcrowded with people that nobody really paid any attention to Daniel. My parents walked home afterwards and I told Daniel I'd have lunch with my parents and then in the afternoon I'd like to say Merry Christmas to my grandparents but that after that I'd have time if he wanted to do something. I think he was waiting for that so he agreed and also told me that he'd be leaving on December 29th, Wednesday the following week.

I had lunch with my parents that Christmas Day and I asked my mother why they'd walked to church instead of waiting for Daniel so that we could have all gone to church together. She was quiet for a second, then she said, "You know Papa. He was embarrassed you came with someone else. They didn't know about Michael." I knew he was like that but I loved him anyway. I was surprised when Daniel showed up right after lunch. He said he had nothing else to do at home and he knew I wanted to see my grandparents, so he wanted to take me over there and I knew I shouldn't ask my parents to come, so I went alone. Grandmother was happy to see me but grandfather was getting more and more distant, which worried me. Grandmother was the same and still bubby and still praying with the rosary Michael had given her, but the sparkle in her eyes wasn't that bright any longer. I so wished I could be more help to them but they were in a good place and well cared for and as I knew Daniel was waiting, I left and told them I'd be back soon. Grandmother had tears in her eyes; she was like me—overemotional.

I told Daniel about the call with Michael and the plan we had and he thought that was good but said, "Don't be in each other's way if you find someone else; life's too short to wait for years." I knew that, but it helped me right then. We drove around and ended up in Gatow, had a nice dinner and made some plans for the last three days he was still there in Berlin. He would leave on Wednesday morning so I would say goodbye to him on Tuesday evening but there would be no way for him to let me know how and when he got to San Francisco until he could write a letter. I could hardly believe that this episode of my life was over; it had been a very long and eventful one and a lot of "buts," "ifs" and "maybes" lay ahead of me. While we were driving home he said he'd stop by the next day for a short visit and then on Tuesday evening we'd say goodbye. So, Christmas 1954 was almost over. I still had to get over New Year's Eve and Day and then would have to see what the New Year would bring.

On the evening of Christmas Day, it started to snow quite heavily and looked really pretty. My parents went to bed early so I just started to write a letter to Michael; I think I used him as a diary and told him about Christmas Eve and about Daniel leaving on Wednesday; maybe it was just an outlet as there was no one left to talk to about old times. I asked all kinds of questions as if he was sitting next to me and I felt better for doing it. I wouldn't mail the letter yet as I wanted to tell him about Daniel leaving. Finally, I felt tired and, hoping he would like the way I wrote, thought maybe he would do the same and tell me how his life was going, not thinking that way did not make any sense at all.

When Daniel stopped by the next day, we just had a short lunch break and then he went back to the barracks to clean out his office because on Monday he had to finish his office work and then there was only the Tuesday evening left to say goodbye. That evening was the same as the last one but I didn't write to Michael, I put my stuff together for the next day's start of the work week. A lot of people call in sick on Monday—most of them just wanting a few extra vacation days for the last few days of the year and even our boss was so-called "sick." I met Karl Heinz at the canteen and he asked me when Daniel would leave and when I told him the plan he wanted to come to the airport with me to see him off but I told him I wouldn't be going to the airport and would say goodbye on Tuesday. "It will get kind of lonely then," he said. "Maybe we should start speaking English to each other so you won't lose the language and I'll learn more." He smiled, since everything which had to do with English was of interest to him.

Well, that day I walked home after work. It had stopped snowing but the air was still smelling like snow and that evening my mother made my favourite dish of pork chops, but even they didn't taste that great. She'd also found Valerian tea in the store, which she boiled for me and put in some honey. It tasted quite good and made me really sleepy; maybe it was the warm honey. I felt really rested the next morning, so after saying goodbye to Daniel that night, I could finish my letter to Michael and it could then be mailed.

On Tuesday morning I told my mother I might be home later as Daniel would pick me up from work, that it was his last day in Berlin and so we'd go out for dinner and she was alright with that. Karl Heinz came in the office and asked me what time I'd be meeting Daniel as he had something to give him. "He'll be outside to pick me up," I told him and he said, "Okay, I'll be outside too." The day dragged on since most of the work was done for the year but finally it was over and when I left, Daniel was already waiting and so was Karl Heinz, who gave Daniel a little box with a tiny beer bottle with "Germany" written on it, which could be used to hang on a car key. It was really cute but he didn't say where he'd got it from. Daniel didn't say a word but you could see he loved it and then they gave each other a hug and said goodbye.

So, we went to Wannsee and had dinner and, yes, I realised our transportation would go away when Daniel did. I would probably be so busy changing my lifestyle that I'd have no time to get emotional. Daniel told me he'd try to send me a telegram from wherever he could when he had time and also find something to get me to the States, then he drove me home and gave me a big hug and a kiss. I wished him a safe trip and, yes, said, "Say hello to Michael and Janet," and then he drove off, of course never looking back. It was a good thing my parents were already asleep as I behaved like a zombie. I sat down, took out the letter and started to write, telling Michael that Daniel had just left and that now I had to get back to my German lifestyle and that I hoped I wouldn't forget the English language, like Karl Heinz had said. I mailed the letter the next day.

When I went to work on Wednesday morning, it was a different day altogether. I didn't know what time Daniel would leave but it really didn't matter anymore; he was just gone and I so hoped he would be able to find some kind of work for me over there. I decided that just to fill the evenings, I'd talk to our priest as there was always some kind of work to do, visiting handicapped people at home or going to hospitals and life care centres to talk with them, like I'd done with Mrs. Bohn, or watching children in the evenings if parents were unable to be there. I was also wondering if I would get an answer from Michael and Janet, my mind would not let them leave.

I met Karl Heinz in the canteen and he asked how I was; he knew I was having a hard time but there wasn't much to say and he then asked me what I was doing on New Year's Eve. I thought to myself, *What a silly question*, but said, "I'll go to bed at eight in the evening." I knew he meant well and I apologised for my rude answer but he understood and just said that he and some friends were having a Silvester Party (a New Year's Eve party) in one of the local restaurants there and that I could meet his friend as well—the one who was preparing to immigrate to Canada. His sister, Brigitta, would be there as well so I wouldn't be all by myself. I told him I'd think about it and would let him know.

I'd actually never been to a German Silvester Party as I'd always been with my American friends and before that I was too young, so it was then mostly church get-togethers. I'd heard rumours that there was mostly a lot of drinking going on but thought I'd talk to my mother when I got home and ask for her advice. She knew about Karl Heinz and that he was my coworker and he belonged to the same church as we did, so she said it might not be a bad idea as they would go to bed early and otherwise I'd be sitting there all alone. "But," she said, "be sure to come home after midnight and don't let anyone drive you home if they've been drinking. Take money with you for a taxi." I had to smile—there was my mother talking to me as if I was ten years old; she'd never said anything like that when I was with Michael. I almost had the feeling that she thought they were the winner of the war and we were supposed to do what they said but I never found that out. After thinking it over I decided I would do it, but only by taxi. And when I went to work the next day and met Karl Heinz in the canteen, I told him I would go to the party but would use a taxi to go home. He liked it and said, "I can pick you up, then, as I have the company car and the boss isn't in Berlin, and that will make it cheaper, just one way," so that was fine.

I wanted to see the priest that night and ask him about any little jobs but it was quite cold and I was just tired and wanted to go home, so thought I'd go next year, which was just a few days away anyway. My mother asked me what I was going to do and when I told her, she seemed glad that I wouldn't be alone. I started to write another letter to Michael; my idea was to write a few lines every day as if I was talking with him, and then mail it later.

Karl Heinz picked me up on Friday, December 31st, at around 6 o'clock and I took a bottle of wine with me. It was California White Wine which Michael and I had bought at the PX Store and when Karl Heinz saw that, he was proud to show it to the others. When we reached the restaurant, you could already hear the loud music and people singing and we still had five hours to go to the next year. There were about twenty people looking at us when we walked in, which was different to what I was used to, but Karl Heinz took over and said, "This is my new friend from work, her name is Theresa." Everyone clapped their hands and I felt accepted and then Karl Heinz introduced me to his so-called "Canadian friend." His name was Walter and his wife was called Monika; a couple in their 30s who seemed really nice. We found a table and Karl Heinz produced that California wine and those two were impressed. His sister hadn't been able to come, so Monika and I started to talk about Vancouver and looking forward to leaving Berlin. They had friends there already, so it would be easier for them but the problem was the long waiting period. Monika told me she'd start working there as well and that most women immigrating from Germany went housecleaning and got paid one Canadian dollar an hour, which would help the family a lot.

By talking and eating and drinking, the time went by pretty fast and it was very different from the parties at Daniel's house with other sorts of discussions, like who was having an affair with whom. I didn't think Karl Heinz had told anyone about Michael, which was good. Then shortly before 12, everyone was watching the clock, then came a big bang and everyone was screaming, "Prost Neu Jahr" (Happy New Year). Some people were crying but everyone gave each other a hug and a kiss and it was 1955. I stayed a little longer but by then a few people were already falling asleep so I told Karl Heinz I'd get a taxi and go home. He understood and said, "Now you know a German get-to-gether, but this one was different since it was New Year."

As I'd promised myself I would use the letter to Michael as a diary, when I got home I wrote a few lines, just telling him about the German New Year's Eve party. I wondered what he would do for his New Year celebration because it was still 1954 in San Francisco.

The first day of the new year was mostly quiet as everyone was tired from celebrating and I needed fresh air so I decided to walk over to my grandparents. Grandfather was sleeping when I got there but my grandmother was up and walking in the hallway and smiled when she saw me. There was a cafeteria there, so we went for a cup of coffee and I noticed the kitchen staff were so shorthanded they could hardly handle things and I had the idea that if I could work there as something like a kitchen helper, perhaps just for some hours in the evenings or on weekends, then I would see my grandmother and also make some extra money and wouldn't be hanging around at home. I asked one of the servers if I could talk to the manager and he sent me to the office where I explained what I wanted. The manager was silent for a minute and then said, "Yes, we could do with some part time help but we can't pay a lot of money, maybe 2 or 3 Deutsche Mark an hour. If you could do that, you're hired; I know your grandparents and they're lovely people."

I was so happy. It wasn't only the money, it was more because I wouldn't be sitting at home every evening, so that was a great start on the first day of the new year.

When I went home and told my mother about it, she understood me completely. I then wrote in my letter to Michael telling him what had happened and decided that was enough for now and that I'd mail it the next day and wait to hear from him; maybe he wouldn't even answer it. I got my things ready for the next day—the first week in the new year—and hoped I would hear more from the manager soon. Slowly the "sick" people returned to work and the regular routine resumed. I also hoped I would hear something from overseas that week, at least maybe from Daniel and Rita. Life was so different now: everything was still in the same place but for me it looked different.

On Tuesday I received a telegram from Daniel. It had taken him almost six days to get to San Francisco but he was now in his house and thinking of putting it on the market, perhaps even through the Mendez Realty Company, and as soon as it sold it could finalise his divorce with Elena. He'd seen Michael, who was living alone in his apartment and had asked how I was doing and told Daniel that he'd written a letter to me the other day, so that would arrive soon. They were expanding their company to include the Los Angeles area, so sometimes he had to go down the California coast if there was a potential buyer or seller. His father had partly retired, so it was Michael and another hired agent working there now. It would have been nice living there but as Michael had said, you never know what life throws at you and although I couldn't wait for that to happen, I could dream about it.

On Wednesday, the manager from the Senior Centre came over and asked me if I could come to work on Friday and Saturday for about three hours each day between six and nine as there was a little celebration for an 85-year-old gentleman and he was allowed to invite some guests. I gladly accepted and if I'd receive that letter from Michael this first week in the New Year as well, that would be a good sign.

After the manager left, I realised it was Wednesday and that my midweek coffee break with Daniel had gone as well; so many changes but as long as I had a little contact with San Francisco, it was fine—

maybe Michael was right and we'd see each other again, maybe in fifty years. I was happy to have that kitchen job over the weekend and be able to make my grandmother happy. When I went home the next day, there was the letter from Michael. He was happy about our arrangement and treated his letter as a diary as well and told almost the same stories as Daniel had and for the first time he mentioned his baby being born in April. He said he hardly had contact with Juana except for when she came to the office to pick up her monthly allowance and he hardly talked with her. I knew how Michael could be if he lost interest in someone and how cold he could be. He ended the letter saying we'd keep it as a diary and mail twice a month; it was quite a silly situation but it helped me and maybe him, too.

On Friday I met Karl Heinz in the canteen and he asked me what I was doing over the weekend, so I told him I was working and he said I was working too much because Walter and Monika (the Canadian/Vancouver couple) wanted to invite us for coffee and cake on Saturday afternoon. I couldn't go because I started work at six and when he said there was still Sunday, I replied that I had things to do on Sunday and might be tired, so he suggested maybe the next weekend and I agreed.

When I got to the kitchen there were a lot of people and I put on my white uniform and started—in the kitchen, out of the kitchen, cleaning tables and washing dishes and it was pretty hectic. I saw my grandmother sitting at a table and just overheard her saying to her neighbour that I was her granddaughter, and she looked so proud. I was pretty tired when my hours were finished and it was snowing and cold so I spend the money I'd earned that evening on a taxi to get home. My mother had Valerian tea with honey ready but I actually didn't need it and had no emotional thoughts; I just wanted to sleep. Waking up the next morning I remembered it was another kitchen help day but wouldn't be too bad since there was no office work before it, but I was still tired so I took it easy all day until I had to start at six in the evening. It wasn't too bad that night as there was no birthday party like the day before and I had the feeling I would get used to it and that for the time being I wouldn't look for another job. The kitchen helpers were all friendly and helpful and of course nobody knew my past.

When I was ready to leave I decided to take the bus and not spend my hard-earned money on a taxi but before I left the manager came and asked me if I liked the job. Well, I didn't really like it, but it was a job. The manager asked me if I could also work Thursday, Friday and Saturday, as his kitchen helper had told him it was a lot easier now that another kitchen helper was there. I thought for a minute and then told him that as long as Sunday was off, I'd try it. When I got home and told my mother, she was a little worried and said, "But don't work Sundays too." I started the next letter to Michael, telling him about the new job, but got really sleepy and remembered the next day was Sunday and I had all day to write letters. I wrote a lot in my diary for Michael and also wrote a letter to Janet and to Daniel before I packed my office stuff for the next week and then listened to some music. That week went by really fast and the emotional thoughts came up that Michael's baby would soon be born and that mine would have been one year old in June; I needed my mother to make a cup of Valerian tea with warm honey that night.

I was glad I'd finished all my letters and just kept the diary one to Michael and mailed the others to Janet and Daniel. The new year started and with it the work increased. When I met Karl Heinz in the canteen, he reminded me about Sunday's coffee and cake and I told him about my new work schedule of three days now, but he insisted I still had to go on Sunday: he'd have the company car over the weekend because he had to wash and clean it and do some work on the brakes. "I'll let you know," I said.

Thursday and Friday weren't too bad but Saturday was pretty hectic and I was almost ready to call a taxi when I saw Karl Heinz waiting outside with the car—he now knew my schedule and where I was working. I really had to laugh about that; he seemed to be quite stubborn but he caught me at the right moment to tell him I'd go to the coffee and cake appointment the next day but only if he picked me up and took me home. He had a good laugh about it because he'd won but it was only because I was so tired that night. He said he'd be there at 4 o'clock the next day and then my mother saw me getting out of the car and asked me if that was Karl Heinz. I told her the whole story and also about the coffee invitation and she was pleased that I'd be getting out of the house. I wrote a few lines in the diary again, telling Michael about the invitation as I felt kind of guilty, even though it wasn't a date and just an invitation for coffee with a coworker. I then had my tea and was gone.

On Sunday, after my parents and I had breakfast, my father asked about the work in the kitchen; he never asked how Michael was doing. I just did some reading, of course about California, and this time I concentrated more on things about Los Angeles and Southern California; my mind just wouldn't give up. When Karl Heinz picked me up, I wanted to get some flowers for Monika and it hit me that all the German stores were closed; not so the PX but I couldn't get in without an American and we had none—I had to remember that next time. Walter and Monika saw us coming. The apartment complex wasn't the best but their own apartment was very nice and comfortable. She'd baked her own crumb cake, which tasted delicious, and we talked about their trip, or rather their one-way ticket to Vancouver. They were hoping everything would be approved this year and if they were settled, Karl Heinz could also leave in 1956. It would be faster for him because they would vouch for him the same way their friends had done for them. It was so nice to look into their faces and see the hope they had for a better future and I wondered if I would ever make it to the U.S. When Karl Heinz took me home, he mentioned that it was a nice evening and said we should do it again. I only smiled, but it was nice. Different, but nice.

I wrote some more in the diary about the coffee party with Karl Heinz; maybe I shouldn't have done it but Michael and I weren't in a relationship any longer so there was nothing wrong with that. Another hectic week was before me, so I just went to bed. Lately it had been snowing pretty heavily and it looked so lovely with little children sitting on their sledges and sliding down the little hill we had close to our apartment. If I'd had a camera I could have taken pictures to send to San Francisco but things like that were a luxury and quite pricey so we couldn't afford them.

I saw Karl Heinz in the canteen and he was grinning and I knew immediately that he had another coffee invitation for the weekend. He told me that his oldest sister, who was already married, had a little boy and that if the snow was still on the ground we could go and play in the snow and maybe have some sandwiches in the evening. I couldn't help but laugh and asked him what plans he had for the weekend after that, at which he smiled and replied that he'd find something.

The week went by pretty quickly and even the kitchen days weren't that bad anymore and then at the end of the week I received a letter from Daniel saying he'd listed his property with Mendez Realty and there were two potential buyers. He said he'd been too busy up to that moment to do anything for me but now that the property was up for sale, he'd have more time. Michael and he had been out for dinner a few days ago and he thought he was single and somehow that made me feel good. Karl Heinz had the company car over the weekend, maybe he'd convinced the boss that the car needed more repairs: he was pretty good at convincing people. It was just too bad; the snow was almost gone; there were only the sandwiches left at his sister's apartment.

As there was no playing in the snow, we went straight to see his sister, Christina, whose apartment was a little out of the way but in a nice neighbourhood The building belonged to the University of Berlin and they had a pretty nice apartment at the bottom of the building with a huge garden surrounding the property, of which her husband, Werner, was the caretaker and it seemed a pretty good deal at that time. I didn't know if Karl Heinz had told them about Michael but nobody spoke about it. Those two were the only ones in that family who were not interested in leaving Berlin; the other three couldn't wait to get out. I wasn't sure about the mother but the speed Karl Heinz was going I was sure I would meet the mother the next Sunday for some very important happenings.

We talked a lot about the war and everything that happened and as they were a little older than me, they had different opinions. Christina and Karl Heinz were not in Berlin when the Russian troops invaded Berlin—they were somewhere walking between Poland and Berlin, trying to hide in churches overnight. Christina had been raped twice before she reached Berlin and her husband was a prisoner of war of the Allies and had been shipped over to the U.S. for two years in a working camp until he was released and sent back to Germany and on to Berlin. Of course, the building where he lived with his parents had been flattened but the Red Cross helped him to find his parents and also Christina, who he had known since high school. Well, I couldn't say too much as I wasn't sure if they knew I'd been engaged to be married to an American soldier. We had good tasting sandwiches and a glass of homemade wine; I didn't understand how it was made but the taste was really good even though I didn't like wine that much.

They were really down-to-earth people and couldn't understand why Karl Heinz couldn't wait to get out of the country, saying things would get better and Germany would be united again, and "it's our home country." When Karl Heinz took me home, we talked about it; maybe they were right. I looked at the diary I was writing to Michael and was looking for words since I was sure it wouldn't interest him a lot: he'd grown up on the other side of the fence. I still missed him a lot and decided that I'd leave it until tomorrow to write about my day.

I put my things together for the next work week and realised January of the new year was passing quickly. I hoped to hear something from San Francisco that week. I hadn't seen Karl Heinz all week; maybe he was sick or couldn't find a coffee invitation idea but I wouldn't have gone anyway. I felt a cold coming on so needed a rest and I also wanted to write the diary telling Michael about what was happening here so I needed that Sunday free to rest and write some letters.

When I left work on Friday, I saw Karl Heinz waiting outside with the company car, so at least I got a ride home although he also had a bad cold and there was nothing new planned. He said the boss had told him that if he wanted to take the car home over the weekend, that was alright but that during the week it had to stay in the garage at the University. He told me he was thinking about taking a course in English at the University and wondered if I could help him a little, so I told him I would if I had the time.

I dragged myself through Saturday but I took a taxi as I felt really lousy and then I was glad I could stay home and finish my letter to Michael and also write to Janet. I wrote more than I wanted to, even asking Michael if he'd decided on baby names. There was no sense in all of that but I had the feeling he was still in my life. I had a little talk with my mother as well and she asked me if I'd heard from Michael so I told her my story and she said, "This is harder on you; you'd do better to break it off and not drag it on." Maybe she was right.

I was really glad I could stay home that Sunday; lately I liked being at home, where I felt secure and safe. Two more weeks and January would be over, it was unbelievable how quickly the time was passing; maybe if Daniel could find something for me over there, I could leave in 1956. I was wondering how Rita and Jonathan were doing in Florida as we hadn't heard anything from them and there was no way to find out, since I hadn't even got the address of their relatives.

Very, very slowly I was turning into a German again and in order not to lose the English language, I decided to go along with what Karl Heinz wanted to do and that whenever it was possible, we should speak English with each other. Also, I would try to help him with the English course so that when he left for Canada he'd be able to talk some English. I felt better and when I went back to work again and met Karl Heinz in the canteen, he felt better as well and I told him that if he wanted to take that English course, I would try to help him. He was so excited and wanted to find out when it would start, how long it would last and, most importantly, how much it would cost. The good thing was that it was held at the university where Christina and Werner were living.

The week went by quickly—no letter from San Francisco but I'd just mailed one, so for sure next week. As I'd thought, on Friday evening there was Karl Heinz with the company car, picking me up from my kitchen job. He was grinning and said he'd "found" another invitation for Sunday; he could be very funny at times. He said, "Since my mother has heard a lot about you, she wants to meet you too, so maybe I could pick you up on Sunday for coffee in our apartment." As I already knew it was coming, I agreed and it was arranged that we'd see each other on Sunday. He told me he couldn't drive the car around too much as the boss might look at the mileage and then there was the gasoline as well, which was expensive, and I decided that the next time he drove me around I'd have to give him some money for the tank. That was another "new" for me, as with Michael we didn't care: it was paid for.

Luckily, Karl Heinz had bought a little flower bouquet and, as his mother smoked, a few packets of cigarettes, which he gave to me saying they were for me to give to his mother. Yes, I should have bought something, but I forgot. When we reached the apartment, I remembered that I'd been there before with Daniel when we dropped of Karl Heinz. Their apartment wasn't big but very nicely decorated and homely. His mother opened the door and let us into the living room and I felt her eyes all over me like an examination. I knew that feeling of being tested by my American friends before being accepted, so now I was being tested by my own German people. While we had coffee, we started to talk and his mother, who was a very bubbly person, said that she was also a "Truemmerfrau" (ruins-woman or rubble woman, a name for the women who in the aftermath of the war, helped to reconstruct the bombed city of Berlin). She said it was hard work but they were proud to do it and it made me think how lucky I'd been, being with my American friends at that time. Her husband went missing in action and the last letter they'd received came from Poland. He wrote to them saying that he didn't know what would happen, that they were surrounded by Russian troops and tanks and might not get out of there. That was the last letter they received and he never came home so after a few years of struggling, she had no other choice but to declare him dead so that she was able to get the pension from the company he worked for.

Horst, her youngest, also came and joined us. He was also a very bubbly teenager, who was already approved as an exchange student to go to the States in the summer for a year. He didn't know exactly where—either Pittsburg/Ohio or Columbus/Ohio, and—of course—he couldn't wait. It was a really interesting afternoon and I was glad I'd gone to hear other people's stories. When it was already getting late and tomorrow being another work week, I asked Karl Heinz to take me home. His mother said it was nice meeting me but I wasn't sure if she meant it as her eyes weren't friendly. Maybe Karl Heinz had told her about my past. While he was driving me home, I asked him if he'd told his mother about Michael and he said, "Just a little but she approved of you." I looked at him and asked him, "Approved of what?" but there was no answer.

It was an awkward situation at that moment; usually Karl Heinz was able to get out of tense situations as a winner but there he was quiet so I just thanked him for the invitation and went to our apartment. My mother was still up and asked me how it went, to which I just replied, "Well, okay," so she knew I didn't want to talk about it. I sat on my bed and a lot of thoughts went through my mind, including my suspicion that Karl Heinz most likely wanted more than a co-worker or good friend but when I looked at the dried flowers over my bed, I knew I wasn't at all ready for a relationship although a good friend to talk with would be great. I definitely would have to talk with Karl Heinz about it. I liked him: he was funny, smart and really great to talk with but I supposed my brain wouldn't let go of my emotions and feelings for Michael.

The next week started and I was glad it was quite busy and I didn't see Karl Heinz at all; he might have been avoiding me, but that was alright. On Saturday when I left the kitchen job to go home, he was there with the car to pick me up. He grinned and told me he wasn't able to find an invitation for the next day but that if I wanted to, we could drive around a little and maybe walk in the forest. We were having beautiful winter weather, cold but sunny. He didn't say anything about our last meeting and I was too tired to start a serious lengthy conversation. Apparently the boss hadn't checked the mileage, otherwise he would have said something. At home I thought about it: there was nothing wrong in having a good male friend and as I'd mailed Michael's letter a week ago, I could start a new one, but I was getting tired and decided to write to him tomorrow after my talk with Karl Heinz.

When Karl Heinz came over on Sunday at noon, I gave him some money for gasoline. At first he didn't want it but I convinced him to take it since his mother had to watch every penny now because her youngest, Horst, would be leaving for the States and would need new clothes and with Brigitta leaving for Britain as well, it was all pricey. She was working half a day in a laboratory but the pay there wasn't the best either. We started towards the park and I realised too late that it wasn't the best idea, because Michael and I had walked there a lot as well.

As he didn't mention it, I asked him again—"Approved for what?" He didn't look at me and didn't immediately say anything but then said, "You know what I mean, why would I always invite you and look for you?" The only answer I could give him was "I like you but I'm not ready for a serious relationship." He was quiet for a minute and then said, "I understand you; let's be friends," so that was settled and I felt good about it. At the end of the park there was a little stand which must have been new and they sold warm Gluehwein, so each of us had a glass but we split the cost. It was a nice afternoon and we both now knew the status of our friendship. New week he wanted to go and find out more about the English course.

Arriving home, I started that letter to Michael, telling him about Karl Heinz and that he was my coworker and how we only speak English to each other, which was partly true, so I wouldn't forget the language and he would learn more English since he wants to immigrate to Canada next year. I then got ready for the next work week and January was gone already.

I still couldn't find the right words for Michael's diary/letter, so as I thought there was sure to be a letter from him this week, I'd wait for that to arrive. Nothing really exciting happened but Karl Heinz found out more about the English courses: they had a three-month course for 125,00 Deutsche Mark twice a week from 6 P.M. to 7 P.M. Tuesdays and Fridays and a six-month course for 200,00 Deutsche Mark, also twice a week on Mondays and Thursdays from 6 P.M. to 7 P.M. and the courses were sponsored by the University of Berlin. The good thing was that they were held at the place where Werner and Christina lived. I asked him what he wanted to do as one course would start in February and last till May and the other one till August, so if he was going to leave for Canada in 1956, it would be perfect.

I saw in his face that he was uncertain and I was pretty sure it was because of the money so as I still had money left from the wedding account, I told him if he took the six-month course I would lend him 100,00 Deutsche Mark towards the tuition. It wasn't too bad for me, since I didn't need to give my parents any money for rent and food and I had two jobs and I told him that. He was embarrassed but I convinced him that if he gave me back 20.00 Mark a month he'd have paid it back before the course was over in August. I thought it made him happy and that anyway most likely that was the reason why he wanted to leave Germany for Canada—because he could earn money there. The next day I gave him the money to register as next week was February already. He also told me his sister Christina wanted us to go over on Sunday as she'd found out her brother would take that English course. Well, that was fine but everything was going very fast with getting to know the Kinds family.

When I got home on Friday there was a letter from Michael; a nice long diary/letter and he wrote that he hadn't given up completely on us but wanted to wait until the baby was born, take care of all the formalities and then start anew. It sounded so nice but for me it was like a fairy tale, even though I hoped for it. He even told me what names he was thinking of for the baby—for a girl maybe Bianca and a boy maybe Christopher. I really liked Bianca, it sounded so romantic, but of course Romance was Michael's trademark. He also wrote about his job: how much he loved it and how proud of him his father was. There was just one thing missing: he hardly asked how we were doing. It sounded more and more as if he'd turned back into the Michael I met on the blind date, but I still missed him terribly sometimes. I had the feeling Michael was falling back into his old lifestyle because their company was expanding and they almost belonged to San Francisco High Society but maybe I was just imagining things, since his letters were so lovable. I was hoping against hope we might still have a chance as he'd written that after the baby was born, he would start anew and, otherwise, why would he tell me that? So, after a few days of writing, I could send my letter too.

The next day, Saturday, I was able to sleep a little longer since that kitchen job started later and Karl Heinz would most likely take me home, and it was almost noon when I woke up. I'd needed that rest. It was a nice day again, so I took the bus to the kitchen job and I was early so I went to see my grandparents. Both of them had pretty bad colds so that's why I hadn't seen grandmother walking around lately, but otherwise they seemed to be fine. That evening was fairly hectic as there was another party—a 50th wedding anniversary party—and those two looked so happy. Whenever there was a party like that, we got good tips, so I didn't mind but I was glad to leave and Karl Heinz was waiting to take me home. He said he'd registered for the course, which would start on February 14th and last until August and I could see he felt good about it. Out of the blue he asked me if I was still in contact with Michael, so I told him the truth but there was no answer. Anyway, tomorrow afternoon we had the invitation to Christina's. I was so tired I didn't read the letter again, which I normally did. I told my parents about the invitation and my father said, "Oh, that young man who picks you up; next time tell him to come in and say hello." I knew what he was thinking: that he was one of "us" and not like Michael, belonging to the winners of the war. It made me really sad, but he was my father.

The next day we went to Christina and Werner's apartment which was also the place for Karl Heinz course. We'd talked about the money for the tuition and decided not to tell anybody. Well, Christina asked about the course and how much it was costing, so Karl Heinz told her the story and you could see on her face that she didn't agree with it but she only said that there were more important things to pay for than that. Karl Heinz just replied that it was very important to him that he already knew the language when he went to Canada.

Karl Heinz seemed a little irritated with his sister about her remarks about the course and since it was already late and another week was starting the next day, we decided to leave. Werner let us out and apologised for her behaviour, explaining that she was pregnant and moody, so we understood. The week ahead of us was February already and we'd be busy with work and, for Karl Heinz, preparing for the English course.

I received a letter from Janet and finally a letter from Rita in Orlando. Janet was as friendly and happy as always and told me she would most likely get married by December of that year and would let me know when she knew more. Rita's letter wasn't so convincing and I could read between the lines. She wrote that everything was so different from Berlin, that there were palm trees and it wasn't as cold as in Berlin, which she missed very much. Most likely she was too busy with other things and wasn't trying to find out what was coming to her but she didn't mention Jonathan at all, which was strange, and I hoped she'd settle down after a while... I started the diary/letter to Michael again and we even talked about the baby, but he never mentioned Juana and somehow I felt sorry for her. She loved him and I didn't think she'd tricked him into anything. All I knew was that the baby would always be cared for.

On Saturday, Karl Heinz picked me up after the kitchen job and we tried to figure out the best way for me to help him—there would only be Sundays as during the week it was almost impossible and we needed to find a place where we could work. We decided that as Werner had keys for all the University, we would just use a room there, which would be perfect. The next day was the last so-called "free" Sunday so we'd just walk a little and drive around a little. He couldn't spend a lot of money as he'd paid his 100.00 Marks and had to pay back my 100.00 Marks, but at least there was a plan.

We still had to see Werner and Christina to ask them if we could use a room on Sunday to do some work and that went fine and Christina apologised for her behaviour, saying she wasn't feeling that great because of her pregnancy. There was now a lot of work ahead of us for the next six months and that was great because there wasn't time to think. Karl Heinz started his course and he really liked it, so we started to speak English to each other.

Almost every night I wrote some lines in the diary even though I knew it wasn't of great interest to Michael and it seemed we wrote to each other about two completely different lifestyles. In his last letter he'd written that he would most likely have to fly to Los Angeles for a realtor meeting and that he would write from there. Some days I wondered if there was a reason for doing that as most likely we'd never see each other again, or was he only using me as a side-burner, just in case everything went wrong. He knew I'd most likely take him back and I was very sure I would do that.

Time went by quickly and Karl Heinz had his first week behind him so on Sunday we did some homework. The teacher was quite good the way he started the course; he used short but whole sentences, mostly questions, and the homework was to answer them. I enjoyed it as well and it was definitely worth the money. Sometimes we had lunch or dinner with Werner and Christina and then the Sunday was gone.

The following week, February was over and I received a letter from Michael from Los Angeles; very sweet and lovable and all the emotions were back again—I missed him and started all over again to fight it. He wrote that he'd been on Rodeo Drive, which was very famous for pricey and extravagant stores used by Hollywood stars and starlets but didn't say if he'd bought anything there. It was so different compared to my life now. He wrote that there would be something in the mail for me and I thought that in my next letter to Janet I'd have to ask her why all that.

The way Michael acted bothered me and although I was sure he didn't mean to be unkind, I just couldn't understand it. March arrived; it was still deep wintertime and only the thought that spring would soon be here made you feel good. Karl Heinz was doing really well with his course and if he kept going like that until August, he'd be better than me with our second language—at least, that's what he told me!

I wrote a letter to Janet trying to explain how I felt about those long-distance love letters, hoping she would understand and maybe talk to Michael about it. His baby would be born next month and he'd left at the end of April, so that would be almost a year now and mine would turn one year old in June. That year, 1955, would be full of memories but time heals all wounds, as my grandmother would say. I hadn't heard from Daniel lately; he must be busy with his house sale. Janet told me in one of her letters that Elena and her younger boyfriend had gone back to Argentina.

I received Michael's little package on Friday when I got home from work and it wasn't a letter—it was a beautiful light blue long-sleeve T-shirt with "Los Angeles" written on the top in white; it was stunning. My mother saw me unpacking it and couldn't believe her eyes but my first thought was that I could never, ever wear it here anywhere I might go. I still loved it; I could pin it on my memory wall together with the dried flowers over my bed. It must have been very expensive and most likely had been bought on Rodeo Drive; whenever I had my emotions a little under control, something like that seemed to happen and there was no one I could talk to about it.

The next day, Saturday, Karl Heinz picked me up from the kitchen job and he gave me the first 20.00 Mark back saying that next month he'd give me 40.00, so that I could have my money back earlier. I felt bad, as if I was playing a double game, but Karl Heinz was just my good friend. That evening I felt very tired so we just went home and, anyway, the next day would be another study day for his course. My mother was still up and asked about the T-shirt and when I said, "Don't worry, I won't wear it," she seemed relieved. I decided to just write a short thank-you to Michael for the T-shirt and wait for a response either from him or from Janet before I replied. I looked at the beautiful shirt on my memory wall and it looked really pretty between the dried-out flowers. I hoped Karl Heinz really didn't need a lot of help with his homework the next day and that if I gave him some money for gasoline, we could drive around a bit but I was too tired to think of anything else and fell asleep.

When Karl Heinz stopped by the next day, I asked him if he needed a lot of help and he said no but his friends, Walter and Monika, had asked us to stop by so they could show him the kind of papers they'd received to fill out. So, that was nice and something else to do. When we got there and looked at the papers, there was a lot to fill in but it looked as if they were pre-accepted. There was no date set yet, mostly likely in the Fall, but there were also a lot of costs involved. They were going by boat from Bremerhaven, West Germany, which is a port city on Germany's North Sea coast and the emigration centre for those who left Germany for America and Canada. From the East Coast of Canada they had to take a train across the country to Vancouver on the West Coast—a long trip and also expensive but they saw no future for a United Germany for them and their ten-year-old daughter and it mean for sure Karl Heinz would be able to follow them in 1956. What an adventure, but they were determined to do it and since Walter's friend had sent him a letter of employment as a carpenter, it made immigration easier. I wasn't sure if Monika was so happy about all of that, but it was her family.

As it was already late and tomorrow the start of another work week, we started home and all of a sudden Karl Heinz asked me if I'd heard anything from Michael. I don't know why, but I felt I had to lie and I said, "No, just from Daniel and Janet," and that was the whole conversation. At home, I just wrote a short thank-you note to Michael and was then waiting for Janet's letter to see what she would say to that.

March was already here—Spring, the favourite season of the year—even though it still actually looked like Winter. I saw a few snowdrops, which even grow and bloom when the ground is still frozen. They're the first sign of Spring and, yes, I remembered seeing them blooming behind the barracks last year; there were so many memories and it was a good thing I was so busy that sometimes I didn't find the time to remember. I wanted to contact Rita as I was worried about her and had her return address from the envelope. I also wanted to check out the post office to see if I could register for a phone call to the U.S. and find out how much it would cost me.

Karl Heinz was doing great with his course so there wasn't much for me to help him with on Sundays and we had some time to talk. We had almost the same background and he was even born in the same hospital as me, only four years earlier. They had also lost all they owned in the airstrikes and were sent to Poland until the Russian troops pushed us back towards Berlin. My mother and I had been lucky and were able to use a train but they mostly had to walk and the distance between Pozna (Posen/Poland) was roughly 270 km or 160 miles. It was quite a way to walk especially with most of the streets and railways destroyed, and that's why they didn't make it to Berlin before the troops took over Berlin. They were actually behind the front line and he also told me that his mother was raped while he was with her. It made me almost understand the way he was and why he didn't care too much for his life in Berlin. He had also lost his father and I was lucky that my father had come back and that even though we'd lost everything as well, we were still healthy. Maybe that put a slightly different opinion in my mind about the way I felt towards the Allies, but deep down I still felt the same about Michael. All the same, overall Karl Heinz and I had a lot in common.

Nothing much really happened then, just work and on Sundays Karl Heinz and I would go for walks if the weather was nice or visit some of his friends. I'd written a letter to Rita and was waiting for an answer and I hadn't heard from Daniel either, which was a little disappointing. I could understand as he had his old life back and with his divorce from Elena and the sale of the house, he was probably pretty busy. Going to the post office to try and find out about a phone call didn't make sense, either, as there was actually no one to call. I didn't have a phone number for Rita and although I could call Janet or Michael, that wouldn't make any sense either, so I just waited for a letter from them.

I realised that April 10th—next month—would be Easter already and also one year since Michael had left Berlin. Finally, I had a letter from Janet and I had teary eyes reading it; like me she was over emotional but couldn't or wouldn't give me advice and I had to decide for myself. She said Michael was still somehow depressed about our situation and most likely he expected me to understand but I knew Michael's thinking and handling of temptations and for sure it wouldn't be the last time. The only other thing she said was that he was so much waiting for his baby, which would most likely arrive next month, and that he'd written to me and that letter should arrive soon. It looked as if neither of us could let go.

My life right there and then was less stressful, even if I was always working. We had an invitation from Karl Heinz mother to a more or less "farewell for a year" party for her "baby," Horst, who was leaving, to go as an exchange student to Columbus, Ohio, in a few weeks. She asked me if I would like to go with her to a department store to get some items he needed and I agreed even though I wondered why she had asked me when she had two daughters. She was fun to be with and we went and bought him some winter clothes and also some boots as he'd been told Columbus gets very cold in the winter. At first I wanted to tell her about the thrift store but I didn't know if she knew about it and I didn't want to tell her I used to buy there before I met Michael. I gave her some money for him, but asked her only to give it to him the day he left, otherwise there'd be none left.

Finally, Michael's letter arrived; it was so lovable the way he wrote about our past and how happy he was that when, next month, Bianca or Christopher would be born, our new life would begin. I wasn't sure what he meant by OUR life will begin and felt as though I was living in two different parts of the world.

As Easter was the next week I decided to wait a little and not write back to Michael straight away, then at the end of March I had the letter I'd written to Rita returned marked "Name Unknown." That really shocked me and there was no way to find out what had happened, but I would try to write to Daniel and find out if he knew where Jonathan was. I was contacted by the priest asking if it was possible for me to stop by at the church as they needed some help with decorating for Easter and also preparing an Easter egg hunt for the children and when I told Karl Heinz about it, he was all for it since he belonged to the same church. I had to take one Saturday off from my kitchen job and then Karl Heinz and I went and helped with the decorating and the Easter egg hunt. At the beginning of April, I wrote to Michael wishing him a Happy Easter and asking him to let me know when his baby arrived. I knew I shouldn't do that, but I just did it. I also sent Easter greetings to Janet and Daniel, asking Daniel if he knew what had happened to Jonathan.

That Easter week I got a letter from Janet wishing me Happy Easter and also an Easter card from Michael with a $50 bill inside, saying I should buy the biggest Easter egg I could find. It made me feel as if I was receiving care packages, which was happening at that time with churches, hospitals and children's homes receiving donations and clothing from the U.S. Somehow I had to stop that, but how? Of course, my heart jumped every time I received a letter; I'd have to do something after the baby was born; deep down I knew it was an excuse but I pushed that thought away. I told Karl Heinz about the card and the money and already felt I was doing something to stop it but he showed no emotion and just said, "That's nice of him."

Our Easter was really nice, mostly being with the children at the Easter egg hunt at the Church. The weather was nice and we were able to take some nice walks but I noticed Karl Heinz being a little different and quieter and although I knew what it was, he actually had no right to be mad at me: we were only good friends and I'd told him that from the beginning. Maybe after the holidays I'd talk to him about that. Well, we made it through Easter and the care package from Michael. I told my mother about it and she didn't have much to say either but I felt she also wanted me to stop that contact. The more they were against it, the more I defended what I was doing but I realised something had to be done. First of all, there would be the talk with Karl Heinz, maybe the next time he picked me up on Saturday evening after my kitchen job but there was the possibility he wouldn't come any more.

However, he was there the next Saturday, grinning when he saw me, so I knew the talk wouldn't be too harsh. After I got into the car, he apologised for acting like that saying he knew I had a hard time after Michael left and that I most likely still did have; he'd had a hard time after his girlfriend died, so he understood. I really liked that about him and our friendship was back to normal again. For being so understanding, I invited him for dinner in a nice restaurant and he laughed at that and said, "But don't tell Michael what you did with the money he sent you." I was happy we had our friendship back.

It was almost the end of April and still no word from San Francisco and then on Saturday, April 30th in the morning, the mailman knocked on the door and gave me a telegram from Michael, saying Bianca was born on April 29th. Yes, it hit me like a rock, even though I expected it, and my mother knew without me having to say a word. My kitchen job started in the afternoon but before then I had to go for a walk. So, Bianca Mendez, his first child. I wondered how she looked as I'd seen a picture of Juana once: she was beautiful and Michael wasn't bad looking either—that little girl must be gorgeous and I wondered if I'd ever see her. I had to pull myself together so nobody would notice anything at work. It was a good thing it was Saturday and that Karl Heinz would pick me up from the kitchen job: the way our friendship was now, I could tell him about it.

Finally, the work was done and Karl Heinz was waiting outside. He saw right away that something was wrong and I told him what had happened and, of course, I cried, but he just held me for a while until I calmed down. It was great to have someone to lean on in bad times but finally it was over and somehow I felt good. Michael and I just had to make a decision about how our lives would go on.

I also received a letter from Janet telling me that Bianca was healthy and Michael very happy and then she told me something which made me sad—that Michael and his father were planning to try and convince Juana to give up her rights to their child for a certain amount of money in a lump sum so that Michael could have full custody of Bianca. Their reason was to give that little girl the best in the way of education and upbringing, which Juana wouldn't be able to do since she'd grown up in a different lifestyle from the Mendez family. It reminded me very much of me: would it be the same situation if my baby had lived? That thought scared me and I didn't feel that great after reading the letter, but perhaps Juana would reject the offer. I still wanted to send a card and congratulations to Michael, so maybe he'd tell me about that or just not mention anything. I wasn't going to tell Karl Heinz, it was too shocking for me. I bought a nice congratulations card and a little cross, went to our priest and had it blessed, and then put it in the card to send to Michael for his daughter, telling him that the cross had been blessed by our priest as he knew the priest and our church well. For the moment that was all I could do except wait for his reply.

It took a while until I received a letter back from Michael. He told me everything about his plans, saying it was with the lawyers now and Juana had accepted the money offer, though he didn't tell me how much it was. He said he would keep me posted, that it might take four to six weeks, and then we could make our plans. Yes, we would make our plans, but they might be different from how he thought. In the meantime, Daniel wrote saying the only thing he knew was that Jonathan had been released from the army and that he didn't know where he or they had gone. There was nothing I could do except just hope they were okay.

May was almost over and the weather was beautiful and Karl Heinz and I were able to take long walks. The next month, Horst would be leaving for Columbus/Ohio and I had now been waiting almost four weeks for Michael's reply, which finally arrived in the first week of June.

The baby was home with the Mendez family and Michael had moved back to his parents' house as Gloria, his stepmother, was hardly home and her two daughters had moved out, so there was enough room. He wrote that everything was going well with Juana, she was signing the papers and he'd hired a nanny for Bianca for the time being. He liked the cross a lot and he'd bought a little frame for it and hung it over her bed: so, he also had a memory wall then. It had started to get a bit like a fairytale, a little unreal, but whatever Michael decided to do, he went through with it; it might take four more weeks and everything would be done. I could not write back and decided to wait until he told me what his plans were, and maybe there would be another Dear John letter on its way.

Karl Heinz told me that Horst would be leaving for Columbus, Ohio, the following Tuesday and asked if I would go to the airport as well. Of course, I said I would as his mother was taking it quite hard—it was the first time he'd left home and would be away for a whole year. I thought a lot about Michael those days. I still missed him badly some days, but most likely it was emotional and not reality; just like Juana - neither of us were made for that kind of lifestyle. Maybe she loved her child so much and she knew she'd have a better life with her father than she, herself, could give her—there were a lot of "maybes," "ifs" and "buts" involved but actually it shouldn't involve me at all.

I had to take Tuesday afternoon off from work as Horst was leaving in the afternoon from Berlin-Tegel airport. Everyone was there—the whole family—and Horst was not the bubby teenager, he was quite serious and after hugging everyone he had teary eyes, turned around and walked on and, of course, did not turn around.

The end of June arrived and there was still nothing from Michael. In a way I was glad but I was also sad; in other words, I was being pulled back and forth about making a decision. I didn't know if Karl Heinz noticed anything but if he did, he didn't say anything, which I was thankful for as even I, myself, didn't have an answer. We didn't see each other that often, only when he picked me up on Saturday night after the kitchen job and on Sundays. He was also busy helping his mother with little chores around the house because she had a hard time after

Horst left and I was fine at home during the week when the only thing to be doing was sleeping. At least I didn't need the Valerian pills anymore. I felt I had to answer at least Janet, though I more or less gave up on Daniel helping me with a job overseas. I could understand him because for those soldiers stationed there in Berlin, it was more like a vacation and they were not really in action—it was fun for them—so I felt I had to try by myself. I decided to talk to Brigitta, Karl Heinz' sister, who was leaving for Britain by the end of the year. Maybe she could look for something for me—anything except helping dying people: that I couldn't handle and I actually had problems with that all my life, a reaction left over from the war.

Finally, Michael sent me a letter. I was so afraid he'd put in a picture of Bianca but he didn't. Well, I wanted to see her but I was also afraid to see her—that was the emotional state I was in. He wrote that it was almost done and that Bianca would have his name, Mendez, and they'd just put Juana and her last name onto the birth certificate as her mother. Well, he'd told me that already, but finally he asked me how I was doing and if I needed anything and his last sentence was that then we have to talk about our future. I wondered how many papers I would have to sign should we get married, saying that everything is his as I didn't own anything. At least he gave me a little time to think about it but even with all that, I missed him.

I was still waiting for any news from San Francisco, otherwise nothing exciting was happening and half of 1955 was almost gone. It wasn't a very exciting life, just working, but I liked it and I loved the long walks we took around the lake on Sundays. Finally, I received a letter from Michael and, yes, I was scared to open it because I still wasn't quite sure what I wanted to do. The letter was sweet and lovable as always and he mostly wrote about his daughter. He told me he was so busy with work and Bianca that he was thinking it would be hard for him to come to Berlin to get married and would rather I go to San Francisco by myself and we got married over there. He would take all the necessary steps for me and it would be easier on him as because his father wasn't really involved in the business anymore, he was more or less the boss of the company now. They had a staff of eight agents so he had a lot on his mind and I really could understand that. He sounded really happy and cheerful and very much looking forward to our life together but that would not be my life. I was supposed to let him know how soon I'd be able to settle everything at home so that he could start with the preparations.

Well, now the moment of truth was here, deep down I'd known for quite a while what my answer would be, but now I had to say it out loud and be clear. I needed a few days to sit down and leave behind all my emotions before writing a "Dear John Letter" for the second time. The letter wasn't too long and I just told him his life wasn't my life and that what we had in Berlin was a fairytale, at least for me. I told him he'd always have a special place in my heart, and I really meant it, but somehow it was not meant to be. I wished him all the best for himself and his daughter and for his future, and that was all I could say. I closed the letter and asked my mother to mail it the next day because I didn't trust myself not to change my mind on the way to the Post Office. And with that letter, one of the most emotional but also very happy episodes of my life ended.

When I met Karl Heinz at the canteen, I told him about Michael's acceptance and I could see his eyes lit up a bit. Then he told me that Walter and Monika had asked him to go over the next weekend as they'd had news from the consulate that they were accepted and would most likely leave for Vancouver by the end of the year, and he'd promised them we'd go. I missed something: waiting for the mailman to bring letters. I told my parents our engagement was over and that there would be no wedding and I saw their eyes light up a bit but it made me feel somehow sad because they knew how much Michael meant to me. Maybe they were just happy that I wouldn't leave Germany, or at least not in the near future.

On the weekend Karl and I went to see Walter and they showed us the papers. That also meant Karl Heinz would be able to follow them in 1956 and they seemed really happy. When he took me home, we talked a lot about Canada. He'd never worked as a carpenter before and neither had Walter, so it would be quite a change in their working lives but maybe after a while they could change back to his old occupation and even open a little car repair shop. There were so many things to prepare and even if Germany was reunited, they could come back with the money they saved over there. There was a lot of dreaming going on, but of course it didn't include me.

That night I looked at my memory wall and it really hit me hard that all the things I'd read about San Francisco: The Golden Gate Bridge, Fisherman's Wharf and the Crooked Street, I'd never be able to see; everything was just a dream. I didn't want to give up and decided I had to talk to Brigitta, that maybe she could help me to go, at least for a year, to where I couldn't hear shooting at border checks at night. Instead of getting better, the situation had got worse with people from the East trying to flee to West Berlin and West Germany. When I saw Karl Heinz, I told him I wanted to talk to Brigitta about some kind of job in Eltham and I noticed he looked a little surprised but he promised we'd do it the next Sunday.

In a way I was glad it was over but sometimes I had days when I felt I'd lost half of myself. By the middle of July there was no reply from Michael but I'd told Janet about the letter I wrote to Michael and, well, eventually there would be an answer. My life went on with working as usual. I tried to avoid talking to Karl Heinz as much as I could but he knew. He just gave me time. After four weeks, when I was ready to go home from the kitchen job on Saturday, he was there with the car and somehow I was glad to talk with him When I got into the car he asked me why I was avoiding him, saying, "We're friends and you could have talked with me. I knew what you'd done," and finally I was able to talk with him, at least with someone, about my decision.

I told him about being afraid to fly over by myself and marrying there without anyone I knew into a completely different environment, and that it would be a little too much to handle. Maybe it had a little to do with Rita and not knowing what happened to her, as well as Daniel sort of disappearing. Karl Heinz didn't say a lot—just that I would get over it as he had done and that things like that make you stronger. He was probably right and at least everything was now in the open. The next month, August, Karl Heinz course would be finished and he was waiting for his friends to get the okay to leave for Canada.

At the beginning of August, there was Michael's reply. My hands were shaking while I opened it and, like mine, his reply wasn't too long. He accepted my decision, it was kind of emotional, but he didn't want me to be unhappy. He also wished me the best for the future and asked me to stay in loose touch, saying that should I need any help, he would always be there for me. He wrote his phone number and address at the bottom of the letter and said he would always let me know what was going on in his life and that he wanted that from me, too. His last sentence was "I feel we will meet again, you will always be 'My little bird.'" My emotions were running high but I could now start anew without feeling like a guilty dog doing something wrong. I knew it would take a while but it would get better with every day.

Karl Heinz had finished his course and I thought it had been quite successful and worth the money, mostly because his writing had improved a lot and the colloquial language itself he would pick up when living there. At the end of August Janet wrote a long letter giving the news from San Francisco and I knew she was going well but every time I read about the Mendez family it still hurt—not as much as it used to, but there was still an empty hole She also told me the same as Michael—to stay in loose touch—and there was the phone number and address which I already had. There was a little bit about Michael, saying he was very busy but otherwise he didn't do anything except spoil his little girl, who was almost five months old already. She said I should let her know when I was ready to look at a picture of her and she would send one in her next letter. She was the sweetest "almost" sister-in-law.

When we visited Mrs. Kinds, Karl Heinz mother, she was very excited because she'd received the first letter from Horst saying he was as happy as can be. His so-called foster parents for a year were quite well-off and he had his own room with his own television and, the best, his own phone, but of course no calls overseas. I could see in Mrs. Kinds' eyes that she was so happy for her son, but with some sadness as well as she couldn't afford to spoil him like that. I had the thought that maybe whoever had selected that environment for him hadn't thought about Horst having to come back home when the fairy tale year had ended and that he might be disappointed and unhappy. I might have been wrong with my thinking; he was still a 19-year-old teenager and thought that was the life he should have. Brigitta and I talked about a job for me in Eltham or surrounding area and she said she'd definitely try to do something.

It was a nice, relaxing afternoon and driving me home Karl Heinz said, "So, have you really made a break with Michael or will he be able to change your mind again?" At first I thought it was none of his business to ask me that, but he was definitely right: Michael was a very convincing person and I guess he could sell a freezer to an Eskimo for his igloo or extend a saving account for another 20 years for a 90-year-old person. Karl Heinz knew that but for me, now, it was really over.

Fall was starting and the leaves on the trees were changing and it looked beautiful even though it was a dying process and I remembered reading in my book that San Francisco had palm tree which never die. I answered Janet's letter and told her that if she found a picture of little Bianca she could send it, and I also asked her if she was getting married that year. Finally, I received a letter from Daniel telling me that Michael had sold his house and what a good realtor he was. He also said he'd leave Fan Francisco and move down the coast to San Diego and start anew. It showed me how our little group was falling more and more apart.

Karl Heinz and I only had time on the weekends to go for walks and we talked and talked. There were actually so many things we had in common but on about half of them we had different opinions, so we needed a lot of time to convince the other one they were wrong and most of the time I lost anyway. We also spent time with Christina and Werner. Their baby was due in January and we enjoyed their big yard with the fruit trees and sometimes barbeques at the weekend, so I was almost back to normal living. Only on some night were my memories far away and dreaming about the past but I still wasn't able to smile about it.

I received a letter from Janet at the beginning of October and I knew it was the picture. I was at home alone, thank God, and I opened the letter and saw Bianca, the most beautiful little girl I ever saw. She almost looked like Michael except for her slightly darker skin from Mexican Juana, and she even smiled like Michael. Yes, I understood why she meant everything to him. I didn't show that picture to anybody and decided that the next time I saw my Grandmother I'd open that little locket Mrs. Bohn had given me and put the picture in there along with all the little presents Michael had given me. I felt good for seeing her and it closed another little hole; she was a lucky little girl.

We promised Walter and Monika we'd help them clean up and sell some of their belongings as they had received word that their departure to Vancouver would be in November and that they would have to be in Bremerhaven by a certain date, which would be told to them. That meant Karl Heinz would leave some time in 1956.

I thanked Janet for the picture and said that Michael was very lucky to have her. That October was already pretty chilly so our long walks on the weekend had already been cut short but we needed time to help Walter anyway as they'd had word that they'd leave from Bremerhaven on November 26th, which meant they had to leave home at least five days before then. They were hardly able to take any belongings as it was a very long trip and they'd been told the trip from Bremerhaven across the Atlantic towards the East Coast of Canada might take six to eight days, depending on the weather. That wasn't all—they then had to take a train across Canada, a distance of about 2,700 miles or 4,400 kilometres and then if they were lucky they'd reach Vancouver in three days. All of that was during wintertime but they were told that was the cheapest ticket to get and they were a family, so they could help each other. It was also possibly to fly, but who could afford that?

On one of the weekends Karl Heinz and I talked about that trip and he mentioned that he had to start saving now for next year because his family also needed every penny and that he therefore wasn't able to eat in the canteen any longer. "Well," I said to him, "how about if I ask my mother to make lunch sandwiches for me for the office, since I don't like that food there anymore, and then we can share the sandwiches?" I knew my mother always made double the food I needed anyway, so I'd have enough to eat. He grinned and said, "Well, don't tell her it's for me too. I'd be ashamed." But after telling my mother that, she was happy to do it for me: if she could, she would feed me like my grandmother in Poland used to stuff her geese. At that time, if you were skinny it meant you were poor, but if you were overweight people would think you were rich because you were able to buy food on the black market. That sandwich deal was perfect and sometimes I took a pot of soup to work with me so that Karl Heinz could have some soup at night. I thought my mother must have wondered about the amount I was eating and not gaining a pound but much later when we talked about it, she admitted that she knew she was feeding the two of us and didn't mind.

Two more months and another year passed by and there was still no sign of me finding a job overseas. The next month, November, was my birthday and I wondered if Michael would remember. I sometimes still had bad days looking at the memory wall and that was the reason I didn't want Karl Heinz to come into our apartment and see the wall, but I knew some day it had to come down.

We did a pretty good job of selling almost all of Walter and Monika's belongings, so they had enough money to pay for the trip and Walter already knew he could start working straight away in Vancouver. Monika told me she'd look for a housecleaning job as well but there was their daughter to consider and to find a school right away wasn't easy so they decided to keep her at home until the next summer. That way she'd be able to learn the language and wouldn't be laughed at in school and for the time being they could stay with their friends until they were settled, which was a big help. About 20th November friends of theirs took them to Bremerhaver passing lots of checkpoints by driving through East Germany but they had immigration papers to show, which helped. Walter told Karl Heinz that as soon as they were settled, he would tell him to come and Walter was an honest man and did what he promised but it was sad seeing another family leaving and we all knew there was a hard time ahead for them.

Two days before my birthday the mailman brought a letter from Janet and when I opened it there was a birthday card and another letter from Michael as well. When I open that as well, there was also a birthday card with a hundred-dollar bill. I couldn't believe it. I was very happy that they hadn't forgotten my birthday but the 100-dollar bill I didn't feel good about. I couldn't tell anyone about it as they wouldn't believe me anyway, so I had to be quiet, but I had to ask Janet to tell Michael to stop it because otherwise how would we get over our break-up. My birthday was on a Saturday and I didn't want a party so when I got off my kitchen job I had lunch with my parents. Mrs. Kinds and Brigitta were busy anyway because Brigitta was leaving for Britain the first week of December and nobody was really in the mood for celebrating. I asked Karl Heinz if he'd like to go to dinner with me in a new Italian restaurant which had just opened a few weeks before and that's what we did. His birthday present to me was a beautiful candle which he told me he'd bought from the Thrift Store. It was a nice birthday.

Brigitta was getting ready for her immigration to Great Britain and I felt sorry for Karl Heinz' mother, who was losing two of her children in one year. Horst would be back next summer but it was Brigitta she was very close to and she didn't know when she'd see her again. There were still Christina and Werner but I had the feeling they weren't getting along too well and if everything went well, Karl Heinz would be gone the next year as well. Whatever came, I would try to make the best of it.

After Brigitta left, Karl Heinz and I were trying to decide on a plan so that everyone would have a nice Christmas. His idea was to take Christina's apartment, which was the largest, and for us all to go there—which meant his mother, my parents and the two of us, so it would be the easiest. My thinking was that as Christina was eight months pregnant, we had to at least ask her, and when we did, she agreed on condition that she didn't do any cooking or decorating. Cleaning up was acceptable, so that was taken care of. When I told my parents about it, they agreed but not whole heartedly; my parents were not party-goers and preferred to stay at home but I think they agreed in order to get to know Karl Heinz.

I then had to fight with my emotions over whether or not to send anything to Janet and Michael for Christmas. Janet I could send a coffee mug with "Berlin" on it, but Michael was harder. Maybe I would just send Bianca something, perhaps a little doll—that would do it—and nothing for Michael, but that wasn't fair either even though he had everything. Maybe a lighter, as I knew he was smoking and I'd seen some with "Berlin" written on them. The other problem was how to get things; I'd have to take the bus to Ku Damm to a tourist shop. I had to take half a day off work and just get it and also get something for Karl Heinz, his mother, and my parents. Now I was happy I had the 100 dollars and the 50 Michael had sent me and if I couldn't find something nice for them, I would give them money, which would be even more useful for them.

I told Karl Heinz about it and he wanted to drive me but I refused and said no as he wasn't supposed to see things. I had the feeling he didn't quite believe me, but he had to. I found a nice store and got exactly what I wanted, including Christmas cards, and had enough money left for the others and a nice briefcase for Karl Heinz; he needed a new one. Over the next two days I had enough time to mail that little package to San Francisco, although my mother actually did it for me. I enjoyed doing all that since I'd always wanted a big family. I still had grandmother and grandfather to get something for but there was still time for that: only that San Francisco package was urgent.

We helped Werner to decorate their apartment for Christmas and it looked really nice with the decorations we used. It was then like a pot-luck meal with everyone bringing something—my mother had her famous potato salad, Mrs. Kinds baked a chicken and we had sausages, vegetables and the famous crumb cake. We had time off from the kitchen over the holidays, which was nice, but before Karl Heinz picked us up, we stopped there and visited grandmother and grandfather. We took them sweets and warm socks and some new blankets. Grandfather was getting old but Grandmother was still in pretty good shape. It was the first time she'd met Karl Heinz and she was friendly but distant to him and asked me in Polish how Michael was doing. I couldn't answer her since Karl Heinz was standing next to me, and I was sure he understood as he'd lived in Poland for two years as well during the war, but he didn't say anything and anyway had no right to get mad as we were just good friends.

We had a nice Christmas Eve and even my parents enjoyed it and they also liked Karl Heinz. Everyone enjoyed my monetary gifts and Karl Heinz loved his new briefcase. I got a little nick-knack from Mrs.

Kinds. She asked me where I got all the money from and I told her I had two jobs and didn't have to give money to my parents for housekeeping and she looked surprised. Karl Heinz was standing next to us and he knew where the money had come from. It was late when we went home but my parents seemed to have enjoyed it and Karl Heinz promised to stop by the next day. Later, I was sitting on my bed and staring at the memory wall. There was no Christmas card from San Francisco this year and I hoped they'd received my little package in time. Little Bianca's first Christmas; she was already eight months old and I wondered if Juana was seeing her sometimes. Yes, that night I really missed Michael and I had to take those Valerian pills.

I was sure I'd still have moments like the one last night but that it would get better with time and, hopefully, one day I'd even smile about them. We had two Christmas holidays ahead of us, so we had time for walks and we checked out relatives, mostly Karl Heinz mother as she hadn't even had a Christmas card from Horst, though Brigitta had arrived safely in London and was already homesick. In the last week of December, we only had four days of work since the kitchen was closed for us and another crew was working until we started again in January 1956. New Year's Eve was a Saturday again and we didn't know what to do with our best friends gone, but Karl Heinz knew some people from work so he wanted to ask them if they'd like to meet in a restaurant just to listen to some music and say "Prost" to the New Year.

When I got home from work on Thursday there was a letter from San Francisco from Janet, more like a Christmas card, and another letter was included from Michael. There was a card showing a lovely Christmas tree surrounded by palm trees and a 100-dollar bill. He wrote in the card that he knew not to send money because Janet had already told him but that he wanted to send me a present for the holidays. He couldn't do that because he was afraid I might get into trouble with my parents because of his behaviour, so he did send the money so that I was able to get something for myself. It made sense but it didn't help my emotions for him and apparently he hadn't received my package yet. Again, I didn't say anything to anyone. My mother, of course, thought the mail was from Janet since Michael's letter was enclosed in

Janet's. I wondered how long that play was going to go on: most likely until he or I would find another love. It somehow bothered me not to talk to anyone about our long-distance affair, but I still felt pretty close to San Francisco.

Karl Heinz found some friends, so we were going to be a little group for the New Year's party. He'd found two couples from work who were also looking to spend New Year's Eve with other people, so that was fine. I knew them too as they worked in our office as well, but in a different department so I hardly ever saw them. So, everything was set for Saturday, New Year's Eve. I told Karl Heinz not to take the car and that we'd get a taxi, otherwise he wouldn't be able to have a drink since, like all over the world, the police were checking everyone. He picked me up with the taxi at home and we drove to the restaurant. The other two couples were already there—a little older than us and I remembered the men from the canteen. The ladies worked somewhere else as our office rules were that you weren't allowed to work there as a married couple. Both couples had met at our office but after they were married, one of them had to leave.

They seemed to be nice and I was surprised they weren't talking about the fastest way to leave Germany. We had a nice, typical German New Year's Eve dinner: Bratwurst and Sauerkraut. The saying is that if you eat a lot of Sauerkraut, you are going to be blessed and wealthy for the New Year but the saying doesn't tell you that you can also get pretty sick from eating too much Sauerkraut. One of the couples brought a Bleigiesser Kit along, with which you can have a lot of fun. Bleigiessen (lead pouring) is a very old tradition used on New Year's Eve in Germany, Austria and Switzerland but you have to have quite a bit of fantasy and imagination. You need little piece of lead metal and hold it in a spoon over a burning candle, letting it slowly melt before dropping it in a pot of cold water and waiting for it to cool off. Whatever shape it looks like then, that will be what happens to you next year. Some people see the funniest or even most dangerous things in it but of course a little beer or wine will help you with that. We saw a huge nail in Karl Heinz piece, which made sense: a carpenter in Vancouver, and I saw a crooked half broken ring in there which didn't make any sense.

I have to admit that I had a very good time and hadn't laughed so much for a long time, and then the clock started the countdown: Prost Neu Jahr, Happy New Year, 1956. Everyone was hugging, crying and kissing each other and I gave Karl Heinz a big hug. He looked at me kind of seriously and said, "Don't I get a kiss for the New Year?" Yes, he deserved a kiss for making me laugh so much that night.

Yes, we were in 1956 and what would that bring us? Maybe a United Germany, maybe a job overseas! I think starting a new year, those thoughts go through everyone's mind. It was late and everyone was tired, so we called a taxi to take us home. Karl Heinz and I were both quiet; maybe that so-called "New Year's Eve kiss" went through our minds but it was just a New Year's kiss between good friends. He said that the next day, January 1st, he wanted to go for a nice walk and that was fine with me. I found myself sitting on the bed and at first I wanted to write a thank-you letter for the Christmas cards, but I decided to wait until I heard whether they'd received my little package. It had been a nice New Year's Eve; different from the last ones, and I slept pretty late. My mother wanted to know how everything had gone so I told her and she was pleased I'd been in good company.

When Karl Heinz showed up, we visited his mother and Christina and wished them a Happy New Year. Our boss was on vacation so Karl Heinz had the car and we could do a little joy riding. He was wondering how Walter and Monika were doing in Vancouver and he was expecting some news on how everything was going. He asked me if I'd heard from Michael and, yes, I lied again, saying, "Just a Christmas card from the Mendez family." I felt I had to do something about this: even though I liked him a lot and he was funny and smart and I could talk to him for hours and even though we both wanted to get ahead in in life and maybe see something of the world, I wasn't ready for a relationship. It was time to get back to work so there was no time for those kinds of thoughts.

The best news was that I'd received a letter from Rita saying they were in Miami but she told me there might be the possibility of a split-up with Jonathan as some things weren't as she'd been told and she'd let me know more. I'd be so happy if she came back as I'd have someone to talk to, but of course that was selfish. I was wondering why she wrote to my home address as if everything had gone well I would have been married and living in San Francisco, but I was sure I would find out.

The first week of January went by fast and it was nice to be working again. Brigitta was getting settled in London but said she'd almost got run over by a car because she wasn't used to cars driving on the left side of the road and had looked in the wrong direction while crossing the street. It took almost two weeks to get confirmation that the package had arrived safely. Janet loved her coffee mug and also told me they were most likely to get married in the summer as both were still trying to finish their education. Like last time, there was a letter from Michael in Janet's letter and a picture of Bianca with the little doll I'd sent her, she looked adorable. He said that the lighter was very nice but he'd stopped smoking so would keep it as a souvenir. Little Bianca really seemed to have changed some of his bad habits.

Karl Heinz told me he'd heard from Walter and Monika who were trying to settle in Vancouver, though it wasn't easy. Walter was working as a carpenter for a company and the owner was a German. He was very strict but generous and that would be the company Karl Heinz would be working for as well. But, Walter wrote, that boss or owner must have been a former or most likely one of the first Nazis (meaning a member of the National Socialist German Workers Party, which was controlling Germany from 1933 to 1945 under Adolf Hitler's rule). During World War 2 when the carpenters came to work in the morning, they were not allowed to say "Good Morning" or "Hi"; they had to say "Heil Hitler" (German greeting). Nobody really knew how he got to Canada, but he only hired German immigrants. I found that very interesting and rumours were going around that he made it out of Germany through Austria. His name was John, which is not a German name at all, and Walter wrote that he was married to an Austrian girl, which was very strange. However, Walter was making good money so he didn't care who he was in reality.

When I answered Michael's letter and thanking him for the cute picture, I was almost ready to tell him about Karl Heinz, but I couldn't, so I had no clue how that so-called long-distance affair would end.

Meanwhile, Karl Heinz was thinking about taking a part-time job because he knew he would need the money if Walter told him to come.

It was quite hard for Karl Heinz to find a part-time job as hardly anything was available in the evening, so he had the idea of maybe delivering newspapers in the morning before work. Well, I had my bike which he could use, but it was wintertime and I didn't think it would be easy but he was looking for a paper route anyway.

I received a letter from Michael who was on his way to Los Angeles for a meeting and he told me all about his job and Bianca and the letter was lovable and sweet as always but there was no question about how we were doing. I knew he meant well but our lives had become so different and I thought we both knew it, but neither of us would let go first. Yes, what we'd had together was very special, but it wasn't meant to be and so I decided that I would let go first. It was a few days before I was ready for it and, also, I wanted to write to Janet first and tell her everything, so January was almost over when I wrote the letter to Janet and two days later, the one to Michael. It wasn't easy as I still cared for him a lot, but I wrote that I would never forget him and he would always have a special place in my heart; that maybe as he'd written before, we would meet again—it might be true, maybe not, but let's stay in loose contact and see how our lives would go. I even cleaned up the memory wall but I kept Bianca's picture with the little doll which I'd sent her. All the memories were now hidden in my heart.

Karl Heinz had found a paper route delivering newspapers between 5 and 7 in the morning. The pay wasn't bad but it was hard work and it was pretty cold in the morning hours. I felt sorry for him but he needed the money for his ticket to Vancouver. So far there was no news from Rita and I hoped she was o.k. Christina and Werner had another little boy, so they were also pretty busy with their lives. I was wondering if Michael had accepted my wish, but Janet would tell me anyway, and slowly I was on my way to becoming a German again. Karl Heinz was really stressed out with both jobs, mostly with the newspaper delivery one, and sometimes when he went home in the evening there was a little too much beer consumed, but his savings account grew and, anyway, he wanted to stop that job in the summer.

After mailing Michael's letter, I thought a lot about who to blame for all that had happened and, of course, I blamed it all on the war. We should have known better: they, the U.S. military, were the winners of that war and we were just the loser, but both sides were just human beings with feelings and that's why things like that happened. Under normal circumstances, Michael and I would never have met; living in different countries and with completely different lifestyles, and somehow that helped me through that separation phase.

It was almost four weeks, at the end of February, when a letter from Janet arrived and, yes, I was a little shaky opening it. The letter was quite long; she understood me completely and wrote that Michael wasn't a bad guy but couldn't control his passion for women and he'd said he still hoped it had gone differently, that he talked about me a lot. She said that she'd seen him on dates a few times but always with a different woman. She wished me all the best and said we must never lose contact. Yes, I cried a lot after that letter but I also felt better. I remembered that saying that the Mendez men loved their families but there was always some sort of affair involved. Janet also wrote that Michael would write to me as well, but he was on his way to New York: that would have been my life and that wouldn't me have made me happy.

We were almost at the middle of March and you could feel that Spring was just around the corner. It was still cold but the days were longer and the sun was already nice and warm. At the beginning of April, we had Easter, the second one since Michael left. I was still waiting for his answer to my letter but perhaps he was still in New York. Things were a little easier for Karl Heinz as it wasn't that cold in the mornings any longer and he wanted to stop that job in June anyway.

Towards the end of March, I received a letter from Michael—warm and understand and he agreed to everything I wanted; only, again, I had to promise to stay in contact since he still felt our paths would cross again. I had mixed emotions: in one way I was relieved it was a clean break but on the other side, now I'd really lost him for good. But it had to end one way or the other so for Easter I thanked Janet and Michael for their understanding, wished them Happy Easter, and was very sure that was the last letter for a long time.

Karl Heinz told me that Brigitta had written saying that at the moment it was pretty hard to find a job for me except maybe in the hospital as a "Girl Friday" doing anything that came along, including deceased people, and that I couldn't handle so I had to wait for another chance. We didn't make a lot of plans for Easter; it was still pretty chilly to do anything outside so we just visited relatives and wished them Happy Easter. Karl Heinz was waiting to hear from his friends in Vancouver so that he could start to make some plans. Horst had written to tell his mother he would be home around June but was planning to go back to Columbus, Ohio, as soon as possible. He loved it there and planned to use the University to study Business Communication, but he didn't mention who would pay for it and Karl Heinz' mother was really worried as she wasn't able to afford it.

So far I hadn't heard anything from Daniel, which was kind of disappointing although it was understandable as after selling his house and most likely moving to San Diego, he'd had lots of other things to deal with. There were still days in between when I wasn't sure if I'd done the right thing since I thought a lot about San Francisco, but time went by fast, Mother's Day was coming up, and the lilac trees were in full bloom; and although the memories were still there, the hurt was no longer as bad.

That Saturday before Mother's Day Sunday, Karl Heinz picked me up from the kitchen job. He had the company car and invited me for dinner in a nearby restaurant. He looked kind of serious and I wondered if something was wrong and then he ordered a glass of wine for me and a beer for him, which was also unusual as we hardly went out for dinner anyway. While we ordered our dinner, he was somehow nervous and then he started to talk, telling me that he'd been thinking for quite a bit now that as I also wanted to leave Berlin, at least for a while, why shouldn't I go along with him, as I wouldn't be alone and we had friends there already. He was thinking of staying in Vancouver for four years to save money and then come back to Berlin. For a minute, I was speechless. I was so involved with Michael that there wasn't much room for anything else and it had never even crossed my mind. I looked at him and said I'd need a little time to think about it but that it wasn't a bad idea and after hearing that, he had three more beers. After that we had to have a few coffees and a little walk so he was able to drive again and, after dropping me off, he gave me a big hug. His old grin was back and he promised to come tomorrow so that we could get our mothers some Mother's Day flowers.

I sat down on my bed in a kind of daze trying to think what to do. I had a few days to think about it but in a way I liked the idea, though I was also scared. For an instant I thought of telling Michael what had happened but then didn't think it was such a good idea. Somehow all my thinking had been centred around Michael for a long time.

On Sunday, Mother's Day, Karl Heinz came over in the morning and we tried to get some lilac flowers. I remembered being young and how I went and stole blooming branches from the cemetery and he laughed and said he'd done the same. We settled on stealing just one little branch, just for old times' sake, and the other flowers we were going to buy. Also, we were not the only ones in the cemetery. We passed the tree where I buried Wolfgang's little presents, but I had to smile about those memories. First, we saw Mrs. Kinds who looked depressed, perhaps about her daughter, whom she really missed, but she also had Horst leaving Berlin again to go to University in the States— at least, that was his dream. Then we saw my grandparents. Grandmother was looking at Karl Heinz but you could see it wasn't the same look she had for Michael, but this time she was quiet. We then saw my mother who was really smiling to see us and I realised she didn't approve of Michael that much but had never said a word.

It was a nice Mother's Day and it wasn't too late so we were able to do a little walking. I thought Karl Heinz would ask me about my decision but he didn't; apparently waiting for me to tell him, and I wasn't quite ready with a complete answer. I thought I knew the answer already but wanted to wait a few more days to tell him and as tomorrow was the start of another working week, we went home. The next day after work I wanted to go to a bookstore nearby and try to find a book about Canada, especially Vancouver, and find out all I could as I'd done with San Francisco so that if I went, I would at least know something.

The next day I went to the little bookstore and found a book about Canada so I bought it and started to read about Vancouver being a West Coast Seaport city in British Columbia Province. It's known for its beautiful park, the Stanley Park, like an oasis in urban Vancouver, about 400 hektar (1 hektar = 2.47 acres) so about 1000 acres big with trails, waterfalls, beautiful greenery and a fantastic view of the Canadian mountains. I also read about the Capilano Suspension Bridge crossing the Capilano River in North Vancouver about 140 metres long and 70 metres above the river. Also, Vancouver has one of the mildest temperatures in Canada averaging from 20 Celsius (70 Fahrenheit) in summer to 0-5 Celsius (about 45 Fahrenheit) in the winter, with hardly any snow in the winter but rain instead. After reading all that, I found it a pretty nice destination and thought I would be able to handle that for four years. So, I decided to have a talk with Karl Heinz the following weekend to tell him I would also immigrate to Vancouver for four years. I felt sad about telling that to my parents, but if I'd married Michael, I wouldn't have come back after four years, so this decision was much better. Also, maybe in four years Germany would be united again, and somehow I felt good about leaving caged-in Berlin for a while.

That week I received a letter from Janet saying that their father had had a stroke and needed a lot of rest. Because he and Gloria, their step-mother, were separated and Michael was really busy with the business and little Bianca (who was who year old already), he'd matured a lot, she wrote, and they'd hired a nurse for their father and there was the nanny for Bianca. She told me that she and Stefano were getting married in July and there was a possibility they might move back into the house—it was big enough and she might start working in their real estate business. When I answered her letter, I didn't say anything about my plan to go to Vancouver; there was still a lot of planning to do.

I was ready to tell Karl Heinz I would also immigrate to Vancouver for four years and I knew he would love that, but I had to find out what kind of papers I would need. When I saw Karl Heinz in the canteen having a coffee, I asked him if he had time next weekend to get a bite to eat so that we could talk and he said he did. In the meantime, I thought about what to get Janet for her wedding. She'd told me it wasn't a big event, just the family and some close friends. I knew they were Catholics, so maybe a nice candle blessed by our priest; well, there was still a little time.

On the Sunday, Karl Heinz and I went to the little restaurant nearby and I told him of my decision and, yes, he was very happy and wanted to write to Walter the next day telling him I was also coming along. Now it was time to talk to my parents but I was quite sure they would accept it. Karl Heinz wanted to be there as well but I told him I'd rather do it alone and they weren't really surprised, they must have somehow expected it. The only thing they asked me was whether we were getting married before leaving, which I denied. Even his family thought we were getting married, but he really was just my best friend. That evening, for the first time, I thought about getting married to someone else; until then it had always been just Michael and no one else. It was a strange feeling so I stopped thinking about it.

We were getting ready for Horst's return home from Columbus, Ohio, as he'd said it would be the beginning of June and Karl Heinz' mother was really excited to be getting her baby back. Then came the day when we went to Tegel Airport to pick him up. He definitely looked different from a year ago when he left and now had a crew cut and even walked differently. And, I had the feeling he wasn't too happy being back in Berlin. Mrs. Kinds was beaming and I told Horst how happy his mother was because he was back, but he looked at me quite seriously and said, "No, my mother is in Columbus, Ohio." I thought I wasn't hearing right and Mrs. Kinds was right behind us so that I wasn't sure if she heard us or not. I was so mad at Horst for saying that, but Horst was too young to understand that and it was the fault of the student exchange agency who put those young people in completely different lifestyles. Of course, to him, everything back home was nothing, everything was backwards and we were all poor and, compared to the U.S., we were. He started doing everything he could to get back to the U.S. but what he didn't know was that his so-called "family" in Columbus had to sign papers agreeing not to help him in any way to get back to the U.S., it was just a program for young German students.

Karl Heinz got word from his friends in Vancouver that everything was going well, they'd found a school for their daughter, Walter's job with that German boss was going very well and, also, Monika had found jobs housecleaning for which she earned one dollar an hour, which was pretty good at that time. She was working mostly for Jewish families. The next thing they were working on was to rent a small house and Walter was looking for a used car which maybe he could fix up, since he was a car mechanic by trade, like Karl Heinz was. So, it looked like Karl Heinz, or now both of us, would be able to go over in a few months and Karl Heinz wrote to them to say that I would also be going along. As Karl Heinz and I were mostly doing things together, we weren't fighting that much anymore and became really good friends and I even started to like him. I still had days when I thought about Michael a lot, but they became less and it didn't hurt that much anymore.

More and more, I became interested in leaving Berlin for a while and living in Vancouver, since it was easier to immigrate to Canada than to the States. June was almost over and it was time to get that candle for Janet's wedding and this time I told Karl Heinz I was sending a little present to Janet as I didn't think it would bother him. I found a beautiful heart-shaped candle in the thrift store and saw the priest to have him bless it. He asked me about Michael and when I told him everything, he said that wasn't the first time he'd heard about those happenings and that we were fortunate we weren't married and that there were no children involved. In a way he was right, talking from the viewpoint of a priest, but he'd most likely never been through a situation such as I had.

I went to the Consulate to get the papers to fill out for immigration into Canada and there were so many questions. Karl Heinz offered to help me as he'd already done it and when I wanted to specify that I wanted just four years, he said I'd most likely not get a residence permit if I set a time limit. That made sense and after filling everything out, I took it back to the Consulate who told me they would get in contact with me. We told Mrs. Kinds our plan and she wasn't a bit surprised, so I wrote a letter to Brigitta in Eltham, telling her that I'd changed my plans and would leave for Vancouver. I was kind of proud of myself and the fact that I didn't need any help from other people, except the little bit of help I had from Karl Heinz, who more or less gave me the idea. There was still no word from Rita and I had the feeling that something had gone wrong.

Then, in the middle of July, a letter arrived from Janet saying that the wedding was over and they were moving into the house, and also that Janet was starting to work with Michael in the real estate business, as their father had retired completely. She wrote that she liked the candle a lot and she also enclosed a wedding picture. She was a beautiful bride and Michael was also there, looking as handsome as ever and with a good-looking lady pretty close to him. To see it better I found a magnifying glass and had a better look; she was also good looking, was wearing a lot of make-up and must have been at least ten years older than Michael. I felt really foolish but also a bit jealous, even though maybe she was just a friend of the family. Everyone looked very sophisticated and I knew I would never have been able to keep up with them, but in my next letter to Janet I knew I'd ask her who that lady was.

Horst was behaving as if he was being treated unfairly and wrote one letter after another to the people he'd lived with for a year, but there was no answer from them so he finally gave up and went to the American Embassy to find out what he had to do to get back to the States. They just gave him papers to fill out like everyone else. When Karl Heinz and I went on our walk, we talked a lot about Vancouver and sometimes we even held hands. I guess both of us were a bit scared but now that we were so far head, there was no going back.

The next month, August, was Karl Heinz' birthday and I already knew what I'd give him as at the thrift store I'd seen a good, almost new-looking backpack and suitcase, both of which he'd need for the trip, though so far we hadn't heard anything from the Consulate.

I was surprised to receive a letter from Michael who told me about the wedding and Bianca and asked me how I was doing, which was almost a first as before he'd only talked about himself. He also wrote that Juana, Bianca's mother, had gone back to Mexico with the settlement she'd received from him and that she'd be able to live a comfortable life there. I thought about it; maybe he realised not everything he planned went the way he wanted, and I had the impression he was lonely. In a way I felt sorry for him but he'd brought everything on himself and although I still felt close to him, I knew there would never be a togetherness again. I still planned to write back, but not straight away and I was glad that slowly my sense of reality was coming back.

Karl Heinz started to plan his birthday and as August was still warm and we could use Werner and Christina's yard for a barbeque, it was quite easy and there wasn't too much to prepare. I gave him the presents from the thrift store and he really liked them. He had word from his friends in Vancouver that they'd found a nice three-bedroom house to rent, so they'd be ready to take in Karl Heinz as soon as he had his papers, but there was no mention of me staying there as well. That worried me a bit, but Michael just said he'd known them for a long time and they'd probably forgotten about it.

It was a nice birthday party. Even Horst was there and he had a girl-friend who was quite nice and who adored Horst because of his year living in the States and all his experiences. I really felt safe and accepted in that family—yes, we had the same background—and on that birthday, our relationship began. It was very emotional for me or, I would say, for both of us, but maybe this time it was meant to be. We didn't tell anyone about it but now we could even make plans to get married before we left for Canada, which would make it a lot easier.

There were evenings when I sat on my bed and even felt guilty because I'd left Michael, but then he was the one who left me and I decided to answer his letter and tell him about Karl Heinz and Canada; he deserved to know the truth. Karl Heinz and I decided to maybe get engaged at Christmas and then get married in 1957, the next year, so that as soon as our papers were ready, we could leave. It was a secure feeling and he told me one day that he'd liked me from the first time he met me, but I was engaged to Michael. After my break-up with him, he started to try and get me interested in him, saying that sometimes he was really mad at me but wouldn't say anything because he'd be the loser in the end.

It took me a while to write to Michael but I just told him I'd met someone else, which was all I could say. Finally, we told our parents what our plans were and both sides happily agreed so the date for our engagement was set for Christmas Eve. It wouldn't be a glamorous event as we now had to save all our money for our tickets to Vancouver.

Since I'd written to Michael, I also wanted to inform Janet and maybe I could even tell her the whole story. I still somehow felt attached to them and I wrote about Karl Heinz and our engagement plans as well as our possible marriage, but I couldn't bring myself to write about Vancouver. I also had to ask her about that sophisticated lady next to Michael in the wedding picture so that perhaps I shouldn't feel guilty about leaving him: maybe he had already left me again.

Mrs. Bohn's daughter showed up one day telling me her mother had passed away, most likely because of loneliness. After she sold her house and moved to a senior housing centre, she became depressed and gave up her will to go on living. She'd given her daughter a very old rosary and a very old Hummel figurine for me as a memory of her. That Hummel figurine, called "brother and sister," was beautiful. A nun by the name of Sister Maria Innocentua Hummel (real name Berta Hummel) was born at the beginning of the 1900s and had a wonderful talent: she loved to draw and her specialty was drawing children. Her drawings came to the attention of Franz Goebel, the head of W. Goebel Porcelain Company and the Goebel Company received permission from the convent to start work from the drawings to create beautiful figurines which became quite famous in Germany and later all over the world, and also became very expensive with age. Mrs. Bohn knew from when I visited her in her house that I always admired the figurines, of which she had quite a few, and now she'd left me one of her oldest ones. I felt so grateful and asked her daughter if she was buried in the cemetery behind the church and she told me where her grave was. I asked Karl Heinz if he would come with me to take some flowers, so we went and put some flowers on her grave. When I saw the grave, I noticed it wasn't really taken care of and I could almost understand her giving up on life if she was treated in life like her grave was now.

Karl Heinz had given up his paper route and was now repairing cars in his free time, which was easier than that paper route. We told our parents about our engagement date on Christmas Eve and they agreed, also joking that we would never forget the day—we might forget the year, but not the day. My father laughed as he quite often forgot their anniversary, which made my mother mad.

Time went by pretty quickly and Fall was approaching when I received a letter from Janet. She wished me well and still wrote that it would have been nice if I were there with them, and told me that the day Michael received my letter about meeting someone else, he got drunk, very drunk. She said the lady next to him in the wedding picture was a divorced high society lady twelve years older than Michael and that she didn't know what was really going on between the two of them but that she came to visit. Her name was Cassandra and nobody really liked her as she was kind of snobbish but Michael must like her, and we both understood. Yes, that was one of the times I looked at the memory wall, but it was empty.

After reading the letter about Michael's new whatever-it-was friendship with Cassandra, I wondered if maybe he needed someone older and more mature than he was as he'd once told me he wasn't happy growing up without his mother and only having nannies and relatives as his father was hardly home because of his business dealings. Whatever it was, I wished him the best.

Karl Heinz received instructions from the Consulate; they were working on his paperwork and if everything was correct he should have his okay within three to four months, so now it was official. It was the beginning of November and getting a little hectic now; first our engagement on Christmas Eve and then we would get married in late spring or early summer. Perhaps my papers would be ready earlier but there was also a name change to take care of so we went to the Consulate and explained our situation. They were very understanding and checked my papers, which would not be ready for examination for quite a while and wrote "urgent" on them. We must have looked like two little schoolchildren, since they smiled a lot while looking at us. They told us to get married next year after Karl Heinz' papers were done and to take in our marriage certificate, then they would take my papers and do the change of name.

Well, we figured out that there would be no big engagement party and no big wedding party as we needed all our money for the tickets and also some spending money for our start in Vancouver. We were going to work as long as possible and Karl Heinz was promised he could start working in Vancouver right away, so everything was pretty much under control. My birthday came up and we told everyone "no presents" but that if they wanted to give us something, what we needed was money for the trip.

I wondered if San Francisco would remember my birthday. I knew it wasn't right to think like that but it's hard to control your thoughts and then two days before my birthday I received quite a thick letter from Janet and I knew there was another letter inside She sent a beautiful birthday card and also the news that she was pregnant and the baby due next summer. I was really happy for her; she was like a sister to me, one I never had, and I guessed she felt the same. The other letter was from Michael and included, yes, a hundred-dollar bill for a present and flowers. In a way I was glad about the money, which I knew I couldn't tell Karl Heinz about as he would have thrown it in the waste basket, but on the other hand I wondered when we would really be disconnected from each other. He asked me how everything was going and if mine was a serious relationship and he also told me about Cassandra, saying she was a good person and very nice to Bianca and that she had two boys from her marriage. He said they were getting along well even though she was older, but he didn't mention how much older and then ended by saying that some days he still missed me a lot.

My birthday came and went and we prepared for Christmas and our engagement; every buying rings we went to the Thrift Store as there was also a pawn shop included and we hoped to find something there.

We were in luck and found two gold plated rings at the Thrift Store. In Germany people wear their engagement band or ring on their left hand and after the wedding ceremony they put the same band on the right hand; men also wear their ring on the right hand after the wedding takes place. The rings were only gold plated but that was fine and at least they weren't too expensive and that was taken care of, so now we only had to make plans for Christmas Eve and our engagement. We talked to our parents and came to the conclusion that we'd do it like a pot-luck meal, where everyone brings something, and that it would happen at Werner and Christina's apartment with only family invited.

That night after we bought the rings I sat down on my bed and felt like writing to Janet and Michael to wish them a Merry Christmas and all the best for the coming year. I told Michael about my engagement and marriage next year but couldn't bring myself to tell him about Canada and after finishing that letter to him I felt for the first time that that episode of my life was over. I was still planning to stay in touch with Janet, though I couldn't say for what reason.

We had a lovely Christmas Eve and engagement; our mothers cried a lot and even my father had teary eyes. Everything was so practical, almost perfect and maybe that's the way it should be to make it right. We also received a congratulations card from Janet and Michael, nothing personal, just best wishes, and I told Karl Heinz I'd heard from Janet that Michael was also getting married, though I made that part up.

Time went by quickly and before you could blink an eye we were in 1957. After going back to work in January we told our boss about our plans and he said that after we were married one of us had to leave the office as the rules were that a married couple weren't allowed to work in the same office. He then added that it didn't apply to us since we were leaving anyway. There wasn't much social life left, just working and waiting for Karl Heinz' papers to come. If everything went well, we were planning to get married in May and then leave right after that and we were planning a small wedding. After church we wanted to go and have dinner with the family and then I was supposed to stay with Karl Heinz at their apartment until we left. Memories came back about the special room at Daniel's house.

Almost everyone in the office was surprised at the news of our engagement: some were for it and some against it because of our plan to leave Berlin. They told us it wasn't that bad anymore; maybe we were all so involved in our own lives that we didn't pay too much attention to what was outside of caged-in Berlin. We'd lived like that for a number of years, hearing shooting on the borders when people tried to cross over to West Berlin, but it had just become a part of daily life.

More stores had opened up and the air traffic in and out of Berlin was much better, as well as trains being easier to use but the problem which remained was that people from the East didn't stop trying to cross over to the West. There were jokes going around that if it continued like that, there'd hardly be any people left in East Berlin and East Germany! Then the rumours popped up again that we, the West Berliners, should build a wall around West Berlin so that no one could climb up the wall without being seen. Maybe then West Berlin would be its own state-in-a-city protected by a cement wall, just like Vatican City, surrounded by Rome/Italy like an independent city-state; it would then be known as West Berlin an independent city-state surrounded by East Germany. But those were just rumours.

We tried to save as much money as we could because we knew we couldn't depend on our parents who'd already had that struggle themselves. Mrs. Kinds was sending money to Brigitta every month and she also had a hard time getting by. We were almost at the end of February when Karl Heinz was contacted by the Consulate who said that in about two weeks his papers would be ready to be collected and that everything was alright. That would be the middle of March, so we then had to get married before May to get the marriage certificate so that my papers could be finished with me registered as Mrs. Kinds. We therefore figured we'd get married in April and take the certificate in and then as soon as we had our papers completed, we could leave, hopefully in June. That would be a disaster for our savings. We talked it over with our parents and agreed to get married at the beginning of April. Like everything else, it would be a small wedding, but that was all we could afford.

After that decision, I was thinking about San Francisco one evening and I wrote to Janet. I hadn't heard from them for a while and I told her the whole story, including about leaving for Canada. It was one of my emotional moments but I felt better after writing the letter.

Things were getting quite confusing and everyone seemed to know something better so we tried, just the two of us, to make some sense and we met at Werner's apartment to talk things through. We knew our money situation was very tight and we really didn't know how long it would be until my papers were ready but once we were married, one of us had to leave the office and no one would hire you for just a few weeks. After hours of discussion, we came to the conclusion that after Karl Heinz had received his papers and we were married, he would leave alone. He was going to write to his friends in Vancouver to say he would most likely be there in May, but without me as although we were married, we didn't have enough money for two tickets. Another fact bothered him: he wouldn't like me to travel by boat by myself as he'd heard from others that those boats were like party boats and he therefore wanted me to fly to Vancouver and that was even more expensive. Since we could not afford to buy two boat tickets we had to go this route. Karl Heinz would be able to start working in Vancouver straight away and if I didn't have to stop working in the office, we'd be able to get the money together faster and although it was a hard decision, there was no other way for us. After telling our relatives our decision they sort-of agreed, especially my mother who would have me at home a few weeks longer.

Our wedding was still planned for the beginning of April. Karl Heinz could collect his papers in the middle of March and then we'd be able to take our wedding certificate over to the Consulate while Karl Heinz was preparing to leave. He was going the same way as Walter and Monica, taking the boat to the East Coast of Canada and then travelling by train across Canada to the West Coast. When he picked up his papers he was told the next boat was leaving at the end of April and to make reservations, so we set our wedding date for the middle of April. There were no problems and Karl Heinz was able to get a place on the boat at the end of April.

Our wedding was simple but very nice with just our relatives there. Everyone understood and that took away a lot of stress. Werner was able to get a van from a friend of his, so that was great and Werner, Karl Heinz, my mother and I drove to Bremerhaven, the centre for immigrants to leave for Canada. It was a bitter-sweet goodbye and after hugging and kissing each other, Karl Heinz turned around and walked toward the boat and, yes, he turned around and waved; he was the first one to do that.

Now the waiting game started. We had taken the marriage certificate to the Consulate but weren't told how long it would take. In a way our idea wasn't too bad as we could save more money and I didn't need to take that strenuous boat ride, instead I could fly, even though it would be my first plane ride. My mother was smiling at having me back home for a little while longer and it felt good being at home. I wondered how long it would take to hear from Karl Heinz, most likely about three weeks, and it was a strange feeling—being married and yet alone again.

One evening I just sat down on my bed and started to write letters to San Francisco, one to Janet and one to Michael. I knew Janet's baby would soon be born, so I asked her how she was doing and those letters became like a diary again. I told her that Karl Heinz had left for Vancouver alone but didn't tell her the real reason—that we hadn't enough money for two tickets. I wrote almost the same to Michael and asked him how he was doing and how Cassandra was. Bianca would soon be two years old. Well, I knew it was wrong but I felt better and both of them were my best friends.

I knew Bianca's birthday was May 9th but I didn't want to write again as I hadn't received a reply yet. Karl Heinz had been gone almost two weeks but it was still a little early for a report. I started to gather things to take along on the plane but there wasn't much to take along and I was really very nervous—my first plane ride and that long distance and all by myself.

Finally, I received a letter from Karl Heinz saying he was in Vancouver and that everything was alright so far. The boat trip was as he had expected—a bunch of wild people, all of them immigrants from Germany to Canada and most likely all of them scared about the future, so it was the last hurrah for them. He was staying with his friends and had already spoken to the German boss who said he could start working as soon as he was settled, so that was good news. He wrote that everything was so different from Germany: the streets were wider and everything was bigger and the mountains beautiful. He told his boss about our situation and he could have as many hours as he wanted to make more money; he was a really fair boss. Of course, the work as a carpenter wasn't easy but he was very sure he'd get used to it very quickly.

I also received a letter from Michael, who now knew the whole story—that I was married and my husband was in Vancouver. As always, he was very nice and charming, asking me if I needed help. I surely did but I refused, of course, and told him Karl Heinz went first to prepare everything before I got there. He also wrote that his relationship with Cassandra was getting serious and he was planning to marry her and also looking for a house to buy in the San Francisco Bay area. Well, with him being one successful realtor, it couldn't be too difficult. So, finally, it looked as if our lives were going in different directions but like most times, at the end of the letter he said he still missed me and the time we had together. I couldn't say if he really meant it or it if was just like a saying. I didn't tell my mother about those letters. I think if I'd told my grandmother she would understand, she was a woman who could understand almost everything, she was amazing.

We reached June and Karl Heinz sent me his first pay check, just keeping a little for himself, and he wrote that it was going very well. He'd lost a few fingernails because he wasn't used to working with a hammer, but he hoped that in three months he'd have the money together and with that and my savings, we'd be able to buy that plane ticket. That was so nice and he'd also met another German couple who had a house and two apartments for rent, so he wanted to rent one so that we'd have our first real home.

It looked as if I'd be able to leave Berlin around September and I was happy but also scared. As I hadn't got a definite date I didn't tell anyone about it except my family and I could see that my father was taking it pretty hard. I just joked that the four years would go by very fast even though I didn't feel that great either. Some evenings I just sat on my bed thinking about the future and what a different direction I was going in from two years ago and I decided to write to Janet and tell her about what was going on in my life; I still felt somehow attached to the Mendez family.

Another month passed by and I received a letter from Janet. She was now waiting every day for her baby to be born and also wrote about

Michael and his plans to marry Cassandra by the end of the year. She said Cassandra seemed to love Michael a lot and Janet believed she would forgive Michael anything, including affairs, so was most likely the right woman for him. Well, I really wished him all the best, even though he still had such a special place in my heart and most likely always would have.

Karl Heinz sent another letter with ticket money and we now had more than half of the money we needed for the ticket so I started to prepare to leave in September. He also wrote that he was going to rent that one-bedroom apartment from his German coworker, starting in September, so that we would have our own place. Just to check it out, I went to a travel agency and asked for information and the price of a one-way ticket from Berlin to Vancouver and they gave me all the information I needed so that I could tell Karl Heinz and the ticket was a little cheaper than we expected, so we were alright. He later told me he'd borrowed some money from his friend so that we'd get the money for the ticket faster.

In the meantime I received a letter from Janet saying she had a healthy little boy and also a letter from Michael asking how I was doing and saying he would most likely marry Cassandra by the end of the year and that he hoped she would be a good mother to Bianca. At the end of the letter, as always, he said he still thought a lot about me and would be there for me if I ever needed help.

Two more letters arrived from Karl Heinz enclosing money for my ticket to Vancouver, which meant I was able to go to the travel agent and make reservations to leave Berlin in September. I already had all my immigration papers ready and the money to buy the ticket, and I asked my mother to go with me to the travel agent's office. We found a one-way ticket from Berlin via Amsterdam to Vancouver for September 7th for a reasonable price, so I still had some money left. My mother and I didn't talk a lot on our way home and I had the feeling that if I said anything then, I would start crying.

I now had to make plans and I had to give notice to my boss that I was leaving so I did that the next day saying that August 31st would be my last day. He more or less expected it but he told me that if or when

I returned after four years, I could start working there again and that made me proud. That evening I sat down on my bed and started to write a letter to Janet and Michael telling them that I would leave on September 7th and would let them know when I had a new address and it then hit me that I would be living on the West Coast as well: in a different country but only about 1,000 miles away, which would be closer than now. I knew I had to forget that thinking right there.

A really hectic time started. I had to say goodbye to people and when I went to the priest I was surprised when he asked me how Michael was doing. I told him the story and he only said, "It is better like that." Maybe he was right. Time went by very fast and by the end of August I had two letters from Janet and Michael wishing me a safe trip and asking me to let them know my new address and phone number; I'd never thought about a phone—maybe we would have a phone and I'd be able to call my parents. Well, my last evening in Berlin arrived; a very strange feeling, but I'd be back in four years. I had to take some Valerian pills to get some sleep.

I said goodbye to my father in the morning and he pretended to go to work early but when he left, I saw he was crying. The taxi came and took us to Berlin Tegel Airport, where I noticed my mother was almost shaking so I told her to go home and that I would wait for the plane: a last hug and kiss and she was gone and there I was again, alone and feeling I was the only person on earth.

I had to pull myself together and look for the gate my plane was supposed to leave from for Amsterdam and a lot of people were doing the same, so I tried to look like a world traveller so nobody would realise it was my first plane trip. I finally found the gate and saw the plane outside and I was ready to run. Quite a few people were standing in line to get their boarding passes and when it was my turn I was relieved that everything was correct. I heard the loudspeaker come on calling for passengers for my flight number and saying the flight was ready for boarding, though I hardly heard the number, just "Amsterdam." I don't clearly remember how I got into the plane but I found my seat at the window and sat down and looked around. The plane wasn't quite full and the passengers all looked pretty relaxed and then the pilot's voice came through the loudspeaker. I didn't understand a word but the propellers on the plane's wings started and the plane slowly taxied towards the runway and I assumed we were ready to start.

Everybody had to sit down, including the three stewardesses, and the plane picked up speed until you could feel it was taking off and I found myself lifting my legs up as I'd done travelling on a train to Poland when it took a turn. I looked out of the window and found we were quite high up already and I could see little villages and little houses and it was actually quite interesting—the only scary thought I had was that if one or even two propellers stopped we'd fall like a rock, but that was a childish thought. Time went by pretty fast and then the pilot came on telling us to sit down and that we'd be landing shortly. I looked out of the window and saw the ground coming closer and closer until the plane touched the ground and levelled off and taxied to the gate.

Well, I thought to myself, that wasn't too bad. I was in Amsterdam, Holland, the first time I'd been in a foreign country except for Poland, but that was just like being in Germany. It was a big airport and I had to wait a while for the next plane to Vancouver so I started to look around. I made sure not to go too far so that I didn't get lost but I saw a sign saying, "Post Office, Letters & Telegrams," and I still had some money left, so I sent a telegram to my parents saying that I was safe in Amsterdam. I also wanted to send a telegram to Karl Heinz but I didn't have his new address. Yes, I wanted to send one to San Francisco, but that would not be right.

Time went by slowly while waiting for the flight to Vancouver and I was getting hungry so wanted to find a little store to get a sandwich and something to drink. I finally found a souvenir shop with a coffee shop attached but there was a small problem in that I didn't have any Dutch Guilder (Holland's currency) to pay for anything. There was supposedly a bank but fairly far away from my gate so I was scared to leave and I couldn't buy anything but the loudspeaker finally came on announcing the departure of the flight to Vancouver.

This time it was a much larger plane which was almost full and it was also an overnight flight so I hoped we'd get something to eat as I was really hungry by then. I now knew how a plane started so I wasn't that scared anymore but it was still amazing for me how a plane, now with a lot more people, could take off and stay in the air. Well, it took many hours and I didn't sleep at all: I was constantly watching the propellers and the faces of the stewardesses in case there was any sign of fright or anxiety to see, but we did get something to eat and drink. It then started to get light outside and the captain came on telling us he'd start our descent into Vancouver in about an hour, so that was it—I'd made it and this would be my home for the next four years. When I looked outside and saw the sun coming up over the Canadian mountains, it was a beautiful sight and I wondered if I would have had a beautiful sight like that landing in San Francisco.

The plane touched down much harder than the first one, but of course it was a larger plane and carrying more people. It taxied to the gate and stopped and everyone tried to get out as fast as possible. Everyone almost ran to get their luggage and I just followed them and collected my little suitcase and went outside, where the first thing I saw was Karl Heinz waving and grinning. Was I ever glad to see him: I was no longer alone. Maybe we both felt the same way. "Welcome to Vancouver," he said, and gave me a single red rose. He told me he had a car, which really surprised me, but he explained that his German boss knew I was coming and had told Karl Heinz to take one of his cars, which was really nice of him. I didn't see a lot of the scenery; everything was so overwhelming, and I only remembered the name of the street we were going to: it was Trutch Street, where our little apartment was.

Our little apartment was really cute and our landlords were very nice; they were also German but had been in Vancouver longer. Karl Heinz' boss had given him three days off to help me get settled and we could even keep the car until we could afford one of our own and that was our first priority—to get a used car—as I intended to get a job right away.

My biggest concern was to let my parents know I'd arrived safely so I asked the landlady about mailing letters and where the nearest post office was. She then showed me that every house had a little mailbox in front of the house where the mailman delivered the mail and showed me that if there was mail to send, there was a little red flag on the mailbox which you had to lift up to let the mailman know there was mail to send out and he then took the mail to the post office to be sent. That solved my problem and right away I mailed a letter to my parents. Of course, we didn't have a phone but it wouldn't make sense anyway because my parents had no phone.

Karl Heinz, my husband now—that sounded strange—drove by his boss's house and we went in to say hello. He didn't say anything; maybe we should have said "Heil Hitler," the German greeting during the war, but he told us to go in. He had a beautiful house and a lovely wife who came from Austria and was at least 20 years younger than him. She told me they'd met in Austria and it must have been when he was smuggled out of Germany after Germany lost the war. He must have been a high-ranking officer of the Nazi Regime and been taken through some back channel into Austria and then to Canada but he never talked about that, which was understandable. His wife also offered me help if I should need it.

Karl Heinz drove me around Vancouver a little and showed me a grocery store around the corner so that I could cook dinner when he came home from work and that was another problem as I'd never had to cook at home where my mother did everything, so I'd have to learn. When the three days were over and he had to go back to work, I wrote to my parents, which I did every single day. They also wrote back every single day: in other words, I was terribly homesick. Yes, I wrote a letter to Janet and Michael as well, letting them know my new address.

It took me a while to prepare a meal and honestly the taste wasn't the best, leaving a burned meat aftertaste. I felt sorry for poor Karl Heinz and I noticed he was never really hungry at dinner so I assumed he must have eaten some place before he came home, for which I couldn't blame him. I was sick and tired of sitting around all day, so I asked my landlady if she knew of any kind of job for me. She said she only knew of cleaning jobs and she'd look around and let me know. I told Karl Heinz about it and he seemed relieved at the idea and also that I would be getting out of the house and not sitting around feeling homesick.

It took about a week before my landlady told me that there was a family not far from where we lived who needed a housecleaner for one

Canadian dollar an hour. They had a baby and her husband was a pilot for Canadian Airlines and she asked if I wanted the job. Of course, I did want the job but I saw another problem: I'd never really cleaned a house before. Anyway, I told my landlady I really would like to take the job and I was supposed to start in the coming week.

She gave me the address and Karl Heinz and I checked it out so that I would know where to go and it was about a thirty-minute walk. There were more jobs available on the other side of town but we'd have to cross the Lions Gate Bridge to get there and although there was bus transportation available, I wasn't ready for that yet. Karl Heinz and I had discussed whether he could ask his German boss if he would allow us to buy the car we were using and make monthly payments on it when I started to work, and he came home from work the next evening to tell me his boss had agreed: we could buy the car for $500 and make monthly payments. It was an old car but Karl Heinz was a car mechanic by trade and was able to repair what had to be fixed, so we were really happy with that deal.

Then the day came to start my job. I was nervous when I got to the house but it looked pretty nice from the outside so I knocked on the door and the lady answered holding the baby. She seemed quite young. She asked me a few questions about where I came from and where I lived but she already knew about me from my landlady. "Go ahead," she said. "All the cleaning stuff is in the kitchen under the sink. I won't be back until early afternoon," and then she left and there I was—not knowing where to start or what to do, but we needed the money. First I had to find the cleaning stuff, which was in the kitchen, and then I looked around. There were three bedrooms and two bathrooms, a kitchen, living room and family room and I almost had a panic attack thinking I could never finish all that in a day.

I sat down in the kitchen and thought about home: how lucky I was having parents who'd done everything for me and how unthankful I was sometimes. Anyway, I had to start so thought I'd do the kitchen first, which took me over two hours to finish, but I wanted to do a good job. I then started on the first bathroom, which was kind of messy so took some time, and I was almost ready to do the master bedroom when

I heard the lady coming back. Well, I hoped I'd done everything right but she came in and said, "You're not finished yet?" I tried to explain that it was my first job but she turned around, gave me five dollars and said, "Well, you can come back after you learn how to clean a house." Yes, she actually threw me out! I felt very embarrassed, especially because of my landlady, but when I got home my landlady saw from my face what had happened. She smiled and said, "That happens to many German girls, don't worry. I think I've found another family, who are Jewish, and I'll let you know." Well, that helped a little. When Karl Heinz came home, he saw what had happened but he was very nice about it, just saying, "Next try will be better."

Well, I hoped I'd do better on my next job with the Jewish couple and I also realised I hadn't had an answer since I told Janet and Michael my new address. Well, they must have been busy but I got my daily letter from my parents and, yes, I was still quite homesick though Karl Heinz did everything he could to make me feel better. My landlady gave me the address of the Jewish couple and we checked it out. It was a little further away but the house was a little smaller. There was a bus stop right in front of the house and I realised I really had to try to use the bus from now on so I told Karl Heinz and he seemed to be relaxed about it. The landlady told me to start as soon as possible and gave me the name of the bus stop so I decided to start the next day. I wished I had some Valerian pills to get some sleep but there was no pharmacy nearby so I hoped that I would see one while travelling on the bus.

The next morning, I left the house and went to the bus station where a few people were already waiting, so I put myself at the end of the line so that I could see what they were doing. The bus came and I followed the lady in front of me and watched what she did and with my five-dollar bill I did the same as she did, got my ticket and my change back and that all seemed to be okay. The bus driver announced the stops, so I only had to wait for the name of the stop where I was supposed to get off and everything went well, so I was somehow proud of myself.

When I arrived at the house, the lady opened the door. She was pregnant but seemed to be really nice and I found out my landlady must have told her about me and my first job experience. She flatly told me, but in a very friendly manner, that she knew I was just starting this so she would pay me 80 cents an hour for what I did. I agreed; what else could I have done? I tried my best and went as fast as I could and I was already a little faster, not trying to clean the toilet with a toothbrush, as the saying goes. I finished the whole house except for one bathroom and bedroom and I worked for five hours. The lady gave me five dollars as well and told me to come back, which was the most important thing. I figured if I could work four or five days a week, I could make about $20 a week, which wasn't too bad at that time. Going back home I did the same thing, watching other people to see what they were doing and it worked quite well.

Arriving home, I found a letter from Janet in the mailbox and one from Michael inside Janet's, thanking me for letting them know my address. Janet told me about her baby boy and how happy she was. Michael told me he would be getting married to Cassandra at the end of the year but still thought a lot about me. Well, I had to admit, so did I about him. At the end of the letter he again said that if I needed help he would always be there but I knew I would never ask him for help.

Because I was in contact with my parents through their daily letters, I knew what was going on in Berlin: there were moments when the Allies and the Russian troops were confronting each other with tanks at border points, ready to start shooting, so instead of getting better things had started to get worse and talk about a wall around West Berlin became more frequent. It was sad we couldn't afford to get a phone because I could call my father at his job, but maybe it was better not to have a phone as I might have called San Francisco in an emotional moment.

I had the job with the pregnant lady but I wanted more jobs in order to get out of the house and stop being so homesick, so I spoke with my landlady again and she said she knew a few people in West Vancouver. For that, I had to use the Lions Gate Bridge to get there but by now I was getting better at using public transport and I was able to talk to people and ask for help instead of playing deaf. I found two more families who needed help with their cleaning or running errands and even babysitting sometimes, all for a dollar an hour, and sometimes I stayed a whole day, which was great. Sometimes when I worked a whole day, they gave me food to take home for dinner.

Karl Heinz' German boss gave him a dollar an hour more and with me working we were able to more quickly pay our debt on the car and also the money he'd borrowed for my ticket. Over the weekend we took long walks in Stanley Park and talked about what we would do after the four years were over and we had enough money saved to buy or rent a small newspaper store selling cigarettes and alcohol: that was Karl Heinz' dream. Time was passing quickly and some weeks I worked five days; I was getting a lot better at the cleaning jobs as I'd learned a few tricks to get things clean faster.

Christmas was approaching and we wanted to get small presents for our parents. Karl Heinz wrote a card and sent some money to his mother and I wrote to our grocery store and asked them to take my parents a gift basket with fruit and chocolate on Christmas Eve and I put twenty dollars in with the letter. From my cleaning jobs I got little presents of some money or chocolates and, yes, I received Christmas mail from San Francisco. Michael told me he was getting married on December 28th and that although he wanted a small wedding she wanted to make a big event out of it because both families were well known in San Francisco: maybe they wanted to make it like a business event. Well, he put $200 in for me to buy something nice for Christmas but I didn't want to use the money so I sent it to my parents to save for us. It was strange, neither of us mentioned our partner as if they didn't exist. For a moment I couldn't believe Michael was getting married, but I was married, too!

I thought about the wedding in San Francisco and also about Bianca and sincerely hoped Cassandra would be a good mother to her. I'd always felt close to that little girl because she was the reason my relationship with Michael had broken up. It definitely wasn't her fault, but she played a big role in our future. It was the beginning of December and Michael's wedding was coming up so I felt I had to congratulate him. Luckily, there were also thrift stores in Vancouver, so I could get something for little Bianco for Christmas and I bought her a little doll with a cute little handbag with a mirror and hairbrush attached. I thought she might like it and hoped she wasn't too young for that. I also got a pretty wedding card for Michael and Cassandra and sent Janet and her family a nice card, in which I asked her to tell me her son's name.

There was a lot of work for me over the holiday season as everyone wanted their house cleaned and help with Christmas decorations. I always liked doing those things, so I was pretty busy, which was good as it took my mind off being homesick, especially at that time of the year. It was the first time in my life without my parents. I received a lot of presents from the people I worked for and also monetary gifts. On Christmas Eve we were invited by the German boss as they still lived the German tradition where Christmas Eve was the most important day and presents were opened on Christmas Eve and not Christmas morning. It was a really nice evening with singing German Christmas songs and with the children opening their presents, except that Christel, the German boss's wife, was very homesick. Even though she'd lived in Vancouver quite a while, she'd left her family back in Austria and I knew exactly how she felt. Christmas Day Karl Heinz and I took a long walk in Stanley Park and all in all, it was a nice Christmas.

I then had a busy week ahead of me taking down the Christmas decorations and decorating for New Year's. I received a letter from my parents saying that my grandfather wasn't feeling well and I thought he was giving up on life; being blind there wasn't much for him to do. I really missed my grandparents, mostly my grandmother with her sparkling eyes and the smile she had when Michael came to see her. We didn't have a plan for New Year's Eve, so we just stayed at home and did what we always did: we talked. Karl Heinz bought a bottle of champagne to say Prost New Year 1958. There was one good thing: we only had a little over three years until we could go back home, hopefully with enough money to get that newspaper store.

Sometimes I wondered if Karl Heinz knew about my loose connection to San Francisco but if there was a letter it was from Janet since Michael put his letter in Janet's letter, but he never mentioned anything about it so I assumed he never saw a letter, but I never found out. Michael was married now, too, and after a few weeks Janet wrote about how it had gone and she even sent me a newspaper story about the wedding as it was a high-profile event. When I saw the wedding picture in the paper, yes, I had teary eyes for a minute. They looked very sophisticated but you could see the age difference; at least I saw it, although maybe it was just my imagination. Janet also wrote that they left on their honeymoon to Mexico since Juana, Bianca's biological mother, had asked Michael if it would be possible to see Bianca in Mexico City for a little while. Michael agreed and Bianca and her nanny and Michael and his new wife flew to Mexico City where they met with Juana, and then the newlyweds went to Acapulco resort area where they spent their honeymoon before picking up Bianca and her nanny on their way back. Janet meant well but I wished at that moment that she hadn't told me. Her son's name was Marcus and I liked that name.

When the holiday was over, Karl Heinz and I went back to normal life. I was now working five days a week, some days full time, and it helped me not to think about things I shouldn't think about. Only on the weekends were we free to explore Vancouver's surroundings. There were beautiful little villages and farms at that time, like Lulu Island, Richmond and Burnaby; real country living and what I liked most were those little stands on the highways where you could buy fresh eggs, vegetables and blueberries. Some farms had signs out saying "Pick your own blueberries" and that was our weekend fun. Karl Heinz and I loved those trips and everything was a lot cheaper than in the city as well as being a lot fresher. If we were lucky we were able to buy Pee Wee eggs, the first ones a chicken laid, and they were small, but the price was good—three dozen for a dollar.

I still wrote a letter to my parents every day and they answered every day even if it was just two or three sentences. Sometimes I wondered how Michael was getting on with being married but I hadn't had a letter from either of them now for over two months. We started to make a few new friends then and some were really nice—all Germans but a few who hadn't been in the country even a year, pretended they'd lost all their German words and just spoke English. Of course, it was broken English and it was really funny listening to them. Life became a little easier as I had some girls to talk to and most of them were about our age. We had Spring and it was beautiful and also a letter came from Janet and Michael asking how I was doing. Janet wrote that the real estate office was growing fast and Michael was hardly home—travelling all over the country—and Janet didn't know if he wanted to do it or had to do it. I remembered: the Mendez men love their families; but those affairs.

During May I started to have back pains and I wasn't feeling that great and a thought came to my mind that those were the same pains I had three years ago, so could it be that I was pregnant. I didn't tell anyone yet but I would be really happy to have a baby as long as it was healthy.

I was almost certain I was pregnant because the signs I had were similar to the last time but I didn't tell anyone, feeling I had to find a doctor first. Someone told me there was a German doctor not very far from us but he wasn't a specialist of any kind—he treated patients with normal illnesses and if he wasn't really sure what kind of illness it was, he sent them to the hospital, the same as the doctor in our little Polish village. I decided to wait another month and then see him and I only hoped it wouldn't be too expensive as I didn't think we had any kind of health insurance. And there was something else bothering me: if we had a baby, I wouldn't be able to go to work as I couldn't take a baby with me to go and clean houses. But nothing was certain yet.

Well, a month went past and I wasn't feeling any better so I talked to my landlady about seeing a doctor. I guessed she knew why I wanted to see the doctor and she gave me the address and told me he was very nice. I didn't tell Karl Heinz anything, waiting until I was sure, and the next day I just took the bus and went to see the doctor. When I got to his practice, the office looked a lot like the one in Berlin and a lot of memories popped up of seeing the doctor back there. I went to the desk and talked to the receptionist, who also spoke German, and had to fill out some papers and pay ten dollars and then I was sent back to the waiting room, which was empty. Before long, I was called in to talk to the doctor. He was a middle-aged man and asked me where I came from and what problems I had so I told him why I was there and he checked me over and confirmed I was three months pregnant. It didn't shock me as I suspected it anyway. I told him about my previous problems and losing the baby but he confirmed that everything looked normal and said the baby should be born in January 1959. "Everything will be fine," he said, and I remembered hearing those words before when everything was not fine. He then told me to return in a month.

So, when Karl Heinz came home from work that night, I was very emotional and told him everything and he was the happiest person I'd ever seen. We decided I would work a few weeks longer and then stop and then we had to decide what to do: maybe I could find some work to do at home. I told my parents and they were happy but also scared and hoped everything would be fine. So far I didn't have a lot of problems, not like the last time, so I was optimistic that this time it would be fine. I stopped working in September and the money we had saved lessened but we never received a bill from the doctor and I didn't remind him either.

I received a letter from Janet and just a short "hi" from Michael saying their father wasn't doing that great and Michael was now the boss of the company. I wrote back but didn't mention anything about our baby. Karl Heinz wanted to take a second job but he was already too tired from the first one, and our landlady found two jobs for me—one just babysitting and one taking care of an elderly lonely lady, like I had with Mrs. Bohn in Berlin, and that really helped us. In the meantime, we were searching for names—Thomas if it was a boy and Isabella if a girl.

As I wasn't working any more, I had time to look around in thrift stores for baby stuff and also a crib and I was lucky and found lots of nice things which were also cheap. I saw the doctor twice more, the last time in November when he mentioned that my body was trying to prepare for birth. That was the same thing the doctor in Berlin had told me, but this time it was already the seventh month so if something should happen now, we had a good chance of having a baby even though it would be premature. He told me that if I started getting cramps, I should go to the hospital right away—that was the Grace Hospital he was working with. I was very careful but the doctor told me a seven-month-old premature baby has a better chance of survival than an eight-month-old premature one.

One day I was very depressed; my parents were far away and I missed everyone and I was scared the baby would be sick, so I just sat down and wrote to Janet. I knew she would understand and I also knew she would tell Michael, but I really didn't care at that moment. My cramps went on for another week and we decided to go to the hospital so Karl Heinz drove me there and dropped me off as at that time no one was allowed to be in the labour room except the patient and the nurse or doctor. They checked me out and, yes, the baby was on its way though it might take a few more hours. Well, the nurse told me what to do and there were three more women in the room. All of them had their babies delivered and I was still struggling.

They must have called a doctor as I felt kind of sedated and I just heard a little squeak and the nurse ran out of the room with something in her arms. Then the doctor came and talked with me, telling me I'd delivered a little boy, premature at seven months and weighing only three pounds, but otherwise healthy, and that he had to be in an incubator but didn't need oxygen as he was able to breathe on his own. The nurse then wheeled me to the incubator room and there he was: our little Thomas. I looked at him and he was beautiful but so small and he had no eyebrows. The doctor looked at me and smiled, telling me they would grow and that his other organs were all healthy but he had to stay in the hospital for six weeks. It was November 9th, so it would be a long time.

Karl Heinz came later and he was so proud of his son. They released me after two days and asked me if it would be possible to bring my milk every day or second day to feed him, since mother's milk would be the best for premature babies and we did that for six weeks until we could take him home. Later I found out that my doctor was actually a dentist.

It was actually a little longer than six weeks but he had good care and at the beginning of January, 1959, Thomas was home. In the meantime, I'd had a letter from Janet and Michael replying to me telling them we had a little Thomas and what had happened, so they congratulated us and Michael sent a separate letter inside Janet's letter. It was a lovely congratulation and a reminder of three years ago. I had the feeling he was still sorry for what he did and that our lives had gone in such different directions and I felt we would never really lose contact for the rest of our lives.

Since our son was now home, we had to think about finding a job for me and I had the idea that if we maybe moved out into the country and tried to find a place where we could have chickens, I could sell the eggs at the roadside as we'd seen before on our trips: I could then stay home and still would earn money. The idea was great but where would we get the money from to buy the chickens and the feed until they started laying? We knew there were quite a few little farms available for rent or lease and also with chicken houses attached and we had the option to ask the German boss who sold us the old car and whom we'd paid back the loan faster than we needed to; maybe he would help us again.

Well, Karl Heinz wanted to ask him the next day and explain our situation. He seemed to like us so we might have a chance and Karl Heinz came home the next evening grinning all over his face and telling me he would help us as long as he would get all his eggs fresh and free, so we should look around and get an idea about how much we would need to start that chicken business. That really was a super offer and the next weekend we started to look for farms with chicken houses attached. Actually, we were looking more for chicken houses with houses to live in. I really got a bit scared about how I would handle all those chickens: we were thinking about 2,000 baby chicks. There would be no roosters, just laying chickens, and we were told Leghorn were the best, that they lay an egg almost every day, which would mean almost 1,500 eggs a day. That thought was overwhelming and they start laying between 16 to 18 weeks old, then lay for about a year straight, after which you can sell them to a Chinese restaurant.

Well, that day we went home and started to count back and forth how much money we would need so that we could tell the German boss what it would cost to start that business. We decided to go again the next day to try and find out what the rent would be for a farm like that. If we could make good money, we would be able to pay back the loan and then maybe after a year of those laying chickens and the selling of them to the Chinese restaurants, we could go back home and Karl Heinz could get his newspaper shop.

Our future looked pretty bright now and we were so fortunate to know the German Boss and his wife Christel because they were so nice and always trying to help us. Maybe it was because we only spoke German with them and mostly lived a traditional German lifestyle and never talked about the past, meaning Nazi Germany and the FUEHRER Adolf Hitler. We actually found something with enough space to keep a lot of chickens—a little blueberry farm of about three acres in the district of Richmond/Lulu Island and it was fenced in and also covered with a tin roof. It only had a little cottage with one bedroom, bath, living room and kitchen and it was quite small but big enough for the three of us. Additionally, it was situated right on the highway, so people could stop and buy fresh eggs.

We found the owner of the place, who was the mail delivery man for that area, and he agreed to let us rent it for a reasonable price because the cottage was so small and also had to be renovated. We only needed it for a year, so it was fine for us. The best thing was that there was a phone connection in the house so once we'd registered, we would have a phone, the first one in my life. I was in heaven and, yes, I knew there would be a time in the future when I wished there was no phone, but I would deal with that then when the day came.

So, everything was set in place and we went to the German Boss and they came with us to look at the place. Well, they had a beautiful house, which couldn't be compared to this, but they understood and since we needed some time to renovate and clean up the chicken area, we decided to start on March 1st. We told our landlord we would be moving out and they understood but as that apartment was furnished, we needed to buy some furniture. It was a good thing the cottage was so small as we didn't have to buy a lot of furniture and the thrift store was good enough.

We cleaned up and renovated the place and it looked pretty decent and we then visited the hatchery and ordered 2,000 Leghorn baby chicks for the first week of March. They were all laying chickens, no roosters, since they were able to tell the gender. We were also told to

get heating lamps to keep them warm and they gave us a lot of good advice as well as a bonus of 20 Rhode Island chickens which are larger than the Leghorn, do not lay an egg every day, and are more like a meat chicken. Our heads were spinning and we weren't sure at that moment that we were able to handle our new business.

Then our big day: we had our phone connected and we were really proud of what we'd already achieved. I told my parents what our plan was and also gave them our phone number, just in case something important came up. I also wrote a letter to San Francisco with our new mailing address, but no phone number. It was a very busy time for us, having our son and seeing him grow and, as the doctor had said, his eyebrows did grow.

We got most things under control and decided to move into our little cottage a few days before our chickies would arrive. There was another good thing in that Karl Heinz' job site was closer to home than before since they were building new houses and other developments outside the inner city, the trend being to move out into the country. Our little Thomas was doing great and was already sleeping through the night; that was the best thing for me—not having to get up every four hours to feed him. We were told by the hatchery that the chickens would probably start laying at the end of July/beginning of August and all in all we were ready for the big business. We had all the heating lamps installed, bought all the feed and had the water pipe running and prayed we'd done everything right.

Then one day our phone rang; I was so proud of the sound of the ringing! It was the hatchery calling, asking us if everything was ready for the little girls and saying they would come and deliver them—not all at once but in three instalments, which would be easier for all of us. We agreed and two days later the first batch arrived, perhaps around 700. Were they ever cute and the delivery men helped us to set them up. We set the temperature of the heating lamps right and there was nothing else to do for the moment except just watch the water flow and be sure they had enough food, and they said they'd be back with the second batch in two days. I stood there and watched those little fur balls and thought about Poland when my grandmother had her little ones,

407

but they had their mother hen whereas these little ones had only themselves. Finally, we went to bed exhausted.

The next morning Karl Heinz and I went to check on them and found some dead—they'd either been trampled to death or the heating lamps were too hot. I had got used to death since I saw a lot of that during the war. Well, I checked the water, cleaned the pipes and put new pellets into the feed container and that was all I could do except wait for the next sets to arrive. It was harder than I expected, but there was no way back. I looked at the phone and yes, I wanted to call, but I didn't. The next night was better, there were just two dead and when the delivery men came with the second set, I told them what had happened and they just said, "That happens, you will lose around five to eight percent of them until they're strong enough, there is nothing you can do about it."

The next morning, we found some more and two days later the last set arrived. There were always some dead ones and we must have lost around 140 altogether, but we were told that would stop after they started laying. Well, that would be another four months at least, but we were getting used to it by now so we just kept feeding them, gave them clean water, and waited for the first eggs. It was fun seeing them grow but another problem came up: they started to peck at each other. We asked for help and were told we would have to de-beak them.

Debeaking was a word I'd never heard before and the only thing it could mean was the cutting off of the beak, but how could they eat? Well, since we now had a phone, we called the hatchery for help and they sent someone over who explained that chickens are cannibals and attracted to blood, so whenever there is an injured animal—a chicken, bird, or any other kind of animal, they will go and peck it until it starts bleeding, when they then might kill it. Well, what could we do. He looked at us and said there was one other possibility: we could buy a red paste and smear it on maybe 50% of our chickens, so they might go for it and start pecking that chicken but the terrible taste would make them let go. "But," he said, "it's not really safe," and pointed out that I'd have to treat about 1,000 chickens with that paste and in the meantime the others would start pecking on the 50% of the chickens without the red paste. I couldn't handle that so we had to use the debeaking procedure.

He explained how it would be done, saying we had to use a machine, which they would provide for us. That machine removed part of the upper beak so that the lower beak is somewhat longer than the upper beak so that they can no longer peck other animals. The procedure should be done before they start laying, and also should be done at night as the chickens don't move at night and it's easier to catch them than during the day. Well, we had no choice. The helper told us he'd bring someone with him and we should do it on the weekend and that we might need two nights to get it done.

We agreed on the coming weekend and as soon as it was getting dark and the chickens settled down to sleep, we started. Karl Heinz and I caught a chicken, brought it to the helpers, who de-beaked them and brought them back. Everything went quickly and we finished it all in one night, though I was so tired I could hardly walk. Even the helpers were surprised, the main thing being that we didn't lose even one chicken and they were all in super shape the next morning. We wanted to pay the helpers but they just said no—all they wanted was fresh eggs when they needed them. We found out later that they were also immigrants from Germany but had been in the country longer than us. When we fed the chickens, it looked so funny watching them eat; they didn't peck at the food but kind of shuffled it into their mouths because of the shorter beaks, but that was a problem solved.

In the meantime, I received a letter from Janet asking how we were doing as it was almost three months since we'd been in touch. I was so happy to hear from her, so I just told her about our chicken farm; why should I lie. We now had all the nests prepared with hay and were waiting almost every day for our first eggs so we could start selling, but I realised I couldn't do it all by myself and that most likely we would need some help.

I didn't want to disappoint Karl Heinz but I wasn't sure how I would be able to do all that work when the chickens started laying. He was so proud of what we had achieved. I then had the idea that we had to sell some of them and I figured we would get a good price for them as they were ready to lay and whoever bought them wouldn't have all the initial work with them, like the heating lamps and the debeaking process. Well, it would be worth a try and better than hiring a helper but I thought I would ask the mailman, our landlord, first. The next time I saw him, I talked to him since he was really surprised how nicely we'd renovated that property. When I told him about my concerns, he started to laugh and said, "I was really wondering how you would handle all that." He asked me how many we were thinking of selling and I told him I'd have to talk to my husband first but I was thinking about 800, so that we'd have 1,000 left. He didn't look surprised and told me he'd look around and let me know.

That evening when Karl Heinz came home, I told him we needed to talk so we sat down and I told him everything and to my surprise he didn't look disappointed or angry and just said he was thinking the same thing. I was really relieved, and if we could sell them for a good price, we could pay the German boss back some money straight away. A few days later the mailman came back and said two parties were interested, one was his brother, and each of the parties wanted 400 and even the price they offered wasn't bad. I was so happy and was pretty sure I could handle the rest with perhaps one helper. The buyers came and picked them up and I was kind of sad seeing them go since I'd more or less raised them, but it was better for all of us. I kept my Rhode Island Rocks: all 20 had survived and I loved them. They were larger than the Leghorns and it was so funny watching them run—they could run pretty fast and it looked as if they were jumping from one leg to the other leg and then really taking off.

Janet wrote back and said she liked the idea of the chickens and told me what was going on; that their father was getting worse and they might have to take him to a seniors' facility as Gloria, his wife, didn't really care how he was. It was sad to hear that. She also wrote that Michael was in New York for a week for a convention but she had the feeling he was back to his womanizing ways since there was always some convention under way. Well, I thought, would he have done that with me as well?

Then the day arrived; the day of the first eggs. I found quite a few in the nests and on the ground and I didn't know what to do first so I ran and got the egg cartons and put the eggs in, which took me quite a while. I ran to the little stand on the highway and put our sign up—"FRESH EGGS FOR SALE. 3 Dozen Pee Wee for $1." I was a nervous wreck but within a few hours the cartons were sold and I had to change the sign and put up "SOLD OUT." But then it hit me that they were not really clean; they had to be cleaned and then put into the cartons. When Karl Heinz came home and saw the mess he said he'd stay home for a week and help me get organised and look for a helper and said his German boss would understand.

We tried to get everything organised within the week Karl Heinz was home. Our landlord found a German couple not far away from us—he had a painting business and his wife stayed at home because they had a little boy as well and she was sometimes bored and agreed to come and help me for half a day. That was great; she was my age and she came from Munich; her name was Gerrit. So, we paid her $1 an hour plus fresh eggs. She didn't really need the money because her husband's business was doing very well but she said it was a little pocket money for her and we did great; the chickens were doing well and there were lots of eggs to sell.

There was one funny thing—some people demanded to have their eggs the way they were laid, meaning not washed. For them that was really fresh and it was better for us as it was less work, so we sold two kinds of eggs—clean ones and not-so-clean ones. As the eggs became larger, we stopped that three dozen for $1 deal and sold the large eggs for .80 cents a dozen. Our biggest hit was the brown eggs, but those chickens didn't lay every day so we had them on order for $1.50 a dozen. The only thing was that we never had a free day and the weekends were the busiest days, so we closed on Mondays. We also had a hospital for sick chickens and those that never laid an egg we also kept separate. One of my favourite chickens was a Rhode Island one which I called Quasimodo from the novel *The Hunchback of Notre Dame*, since it had a completely crooked neck which made it look like a hunchback. It never laid an egg, of course, but was so friendly that whenever it saw me it came running up to me and I had to pet it. Even though it was hard work, it was fun as well once we'd got used to it and Gerrit and I became good friends.

Our little Thomas became a really cute little guy and had the longest eyelashes and the nicest looking eyebrows and by the end of the year he would already be a year old. If everything went well we might be able to go back home the next year as the chickens would have been laying a year by then and would have to be sold.

The letters from Janet and Michael became less; of course, we were all busy, but there were still times I thought about him and how his life was going. In Janet's last letter, there was a separate letter from Michael and he wrote a little bit about himself. He was proud of what he'd achieved in his job and a proud father to Bianca, who he adored, but his last sentence was "I miss you sometimes, little bird." I was almost ready to smile about those words, even with teary eyes. I wondered whatever happened to Daniel or Rita and Jonathan but there was no way to find out. Maybe when we got back home to Germany after four years I would have a chance to find out, at least about Rita. I missed my parents terribly and there was no longer a letter every day but at least three a week.

But Karl Heinz always found a way to cheer me up if I got homesick. One Monday evening, he told me we were going to see a movie and when I asked him what about the baby, he said we'll take him along. I thought he was joking but we went to an open-air theatre where you could drive in with your car and sit in the car to watch the movie on a big screen. We took little Thomas and his bedding and put him on the back seat and off we went; it was really nice and a lot of fun. After that first time we went whenever we could because we could take the baby with us.

Karl Heinz mother wrote that Horst, Karl Heinz' brother, who had been in Columbus, Ohio, as an exchange student, had made it back to the States, most likely with a little help from his foster parents, and he was finishing his high school year there and wanted to join the Army because he'd been told he could be transferred either to Japan or to Germany as an American soldier there. That was quite interesting, he'd become an American citizen. I thought about how the whole family had fallen apart with only Werner and Christina, Karl Heinz oldest sister, staying back in Berlin.

Our egg business did pretty well and we were able to pay back a lot of money to the German boss as well as being able to save and we still had until next summer to go. We also started with the blueberry picking. The area wasn't too big but people came and picked blueberries. Of course, they ate more than they picked to take home but there was no work for us involved and still a little money in it. I wished my grandmother could be there with us; she would have loved our little farm.

One day I got a letter from Janet and Michael, telling me their father had passed away. They were both very emotional and I felt very sorry for them and I sat down and wrote both of them a long letter. I really wished I could be with them and told them so. It took a while to get a return letter because there was a lot of paperwork to do but Janet and her family and Michael and his family were able to keep the house in which they grew up and which they loved, and also the real estate business. Somehow I wished I could be with Michael and help him but it would make no sense as we now lived different lives.

I sometimes wondered if we would leave Canada after four years and go back to Germany. My parents wrote that there was no sign that Berlin would ever be one again and the talk about a wall around West Berlin was heard more often. Too many people from East Germany and East Berlin were trying to get over to West Berlin. I thought back and forth about whether there would be a possibility of getting my parents out of West Berlin and over to Canada. I knew my mother would most likely do it but I wasn't sure about my father, both because he was older and because he didn't speak the language. And we were not really settled there, either.

Pretty soon the year 1959 would be over and little Thomas would be a year old. Then, the next summer-to-fall, our egg business would be finished since the chickens would stop laying after one year. The four years wouldn't be over either and starting a new batch with baby chicks was something neither one of us was ready to do, so we had to think of something else. I wouldn't be able to go to work with the baby and also we only had one car and I had no driver's license. We still had time to think about it before the next year but we didn't know how much money we would have been able to save to go back home. One thing that really bothered me was that my family hadn't seen their grandchild, but there was nothing we could do at that moment, so we kept on selling eggs and saving money.

Just before the end of the year, Karl Heinz came home one day and told me about a coworker of his who was trying to find out about the Hawaiian Islands, which had just become the 50th state of the U.S.A. in August that year. They were situated in the Northern Pacific Ocean, an Island chain of eight major islands and some smaller ones and the distance from Vancouver to the islands, Karl Heinz told me, was around 2,700 miles or 4,300 km. The main island was Oahu with the capital city of Honolulu. I looked at him and didn't know why he was telling me all that and then he said that his coworker had found out that those islands were starting to boom because they now belonged to the U.S.A. He said that they were looking for all kinds of workers, most of all carpenters to build hotels for tourists and apartment buildings and that if you got a job offer from a company you would be able to work for a certain amount of time while applying for a U.S. Visa and later on for citizenship if you wanted to.

He got really excited about that and said we could go for a year, then we'd have the four years and more money and I wouldn't have to go to work or do that hard chicken business again. It sounded like a good idea but we had to find out more about it and most likely Karl Heinz would have to fly over to the islands to get that job offer. His coworker was planning on flying over at the beginning of the next year to find out more and in the meantime I tried to get a book to find out more as well, as I'd done with San Francisco and Vancouver. I had to smile as now I'd see more of the world than Michael; I didn't think he was ever in the Hawaiian Islands, since they only recently became U.S. territory. Yes, it was childish to think like that because I didn't even know if we were able to do it so whenever I had contact with Janet and Michael again, I decided I wouldn't say anything. It felt good to at least have a plan for after the chicken episode.

The old year passed and we were waiting for the coworker to fly over and check things out so that we would know more. We exchanged lovely Christmas and New Year's wishes with San Francisco and Michael seemed to feel better about his father's death, but strangely he never talked about his wife, only about Bianca, and at the end of each letter there was always a lovely phrase. Sometimes I wondered if we would ever see each other again.

I remembered hearing about Hawaii while still in Germany but we hardly knew where it was, just one island in the Pacific Ocean but so far away, halfway around the globe: a tropical island with palm trees and beautiful beaches, always with nice and warm weather, but it wasn't really of any interest to us since we knew we would never get there. Now we might even live there for a little while, it was hard to believe that and I stopped thinking about it because it might not even happen.

I received a letter from Michael, who was on his way to Munich, Germany, for some kind of convention and he had thought of having a stopover in Berlin, but then he wrote that after thinking it over, there was really nothing left for him—no friends, nothing, just memories, so he decided against it. I had the feeling he wasn't really happy with his life.

It was around March of 1960 that Karl Heinz came home from work telling me that his coworker, also named Horst, had told him he was ready to book a charter flight from Vancouver via San Francisco to Honolulu for US$129.00 for the round trip. Of course, no jet flight, just a propeller one, so maybe an 11-hour flight, but he wanted to find out if what people were saying was really true. As he was single, he could do it and he would then tell us what he found out. For the first time, I mentioned it to my parents but they already knew about the four-year plan so they weren't really disappointed. Karl Heinz was really excited and could hardly wait for Horst's return in two weeks to hear what he would say.

Finally, the two weeks were over and Horst was back and told Karl Heinz he'd come over to our cottage and tell us what he found out. He came the next evening, all happy, and showed us his job offer as a carpenter for a building company in Honolulu, starting as soon as possible. He said he would get $13.00 an hour, which was a lot of money, but he worked as a foreman as his trade was carpentry, which he'd learned in school in Germany. He said he would leave Vancouver as soon as he could clear everything and told Karl Heinz that as soon as he was settled in Honolulu, he would tell Karl Heinz to come over and would see that he got a good job offer. Well, I'd heard that before regarding Berlin to Vancouver. He told us a little about the city and the beautiful beaches, especially one he liked a lot called Waikiki Beach, and the beautiful Hawaiian girls. And one word, he said, which we had to know, was "Aloha," the greeting word in the Islands. "'Aloha' has a lot of meanings," he said. "You say it when you greet someone, or say farewell, and it also means love and peace." After telling us all that my head was spinning but Karl Heinz eyes were sparkling and when Horst left, they both said "Aloha."

I still had to remind my husband that we couldn't leave before the chickens had finished laying and we'd sold them, which would be in the Fall. He understood, at least he told me so. That would still be another six months. I told Gerrit about it and she laughed and said, "You're moving again. And where will you go after Honolulu?" I said, "HOME!"

Whenever I had a little time between washing and selling eggs, petting Quasimodo and running after my son, I tried to read more about the Hawaiian Islands. It was actually very interesting; on one island, called the Big Island of Hawaii, there were two volcanoes, Mauna Loa and Mauna Kea, supposedly the tallest volcanic mountains on earth. I remembered from my school days that Mount Etna in Italy was an active volcano but that was actually all I knew about active volcanos. Well, if it should happen that we really went there, it would be a very interesting experience and as well as I knew my husband, he would do everything in his power to make it happen. I felt a little proud as I realised when I was with people that mostly I was the only one who had any experience of travelling and I thought about when I returned to Germany and I'd be able to tell about everything I'd experienced, but there were still six months of hard work ahead of me.

Karl Heinz told me his coworker was almost ready to leave Vancouver to fly to Honolulu and although he didn't say more, I could see on his face that he was thinking that after a while he would have to fly to Honolulu as well in order to get that job offer. It was a good thing I had Gerrit, otherwise I'd be all by myself with the chickens, the blueberry picking people and my son, who was constantly trying to crawl into the chicken house to play with the chickens. I told my husband for at least two weeks that we had to buy a playpen before he left for Honolulu, so I would be able to contain my son there, but I could tell his mind was already halfway over the Pacific Ocean. I could understand that, since he wanted the best for us so that we could have a better life later. Horst, the coworker, had already left and we were waiting to hear what happened with his job and when Karl Heinz would be able to go. In the meantime, we sold eggs and tried to save money.

It took a few weeks until we heard from him. He was happy-go-lucky and wrote that everything was almost perfect and he'd found an apartment near the Ala Moana Shopping Centre. We didn't know where that was, but he had an apartment and when Karl Heinz was there, he would be able to stay with him and he could start with him at the same company. That was a big help as he wouldn't need a hotel. So, we started to search for charter flights and found one on the same route Horst had used. It was a little more expensive, but not much, and two weeks later he left and we hoped for the best. I felt alone again but after a while you get used to it. There was no family near me in this big Canada, just myself and little Thomas, who really didn't like his pay pen and tried to get out of it whatever way he could. The first night I was alone, I sat down and wrote to Janet and I told her everything—all my hopes and my fears—and I knew she understood.

After writing to Janet I felt a little better but being alone in the cottage for the first time that night, I was scared and wished we had a dog. I hardly slept and also thought about the stop-over in San Francisco which Karl Heinz had to do Next morning when Gerrit showed up, she told me that she and her husband had been thinking about me being alone, and she said if I wanted her to, she would stay with me overnight until Karl Heinz returned. That was the best offer I'd had in the longest time and everything seemed to be easier; Gerrit was such a big help. A week went by and there was a telegram from Karl Heinz telling me how great everything was there and that he would be home in about ten days with a good job offer. That was all fine, but we still had to finish our chicken business before we could leave and that would be in October at the earliest.

I talked to Gerrit about it and she had the idea of trying to sell some laying chickens. They were still good layers and most likely we would get a little more money for them than selling them to the Chinese restaurant. Well, we tried it and it was slow but we did sell some of the Leghorns. Gerrit promised me she would take the Rhode Islands since they would lay for much longer and I was happy because Quasimodo would have another home.

Karl Heinz came back all excited and almost ready to leave and also with a nice suntan, so it was a "go" then and the idea of already selling chickens he thought was great. So, we set our goal for October and with that we had some time to organise. We had our old car to sell so we had money saved and with the sale of the chickens, we weren't too badly off. Everything went quite well and we were selling more chickens too; I think we were the only ones who were selling laying chickens.

Janet wrote back and wished us good luck with our new adventure and also told me things didn't look too great for Michael's marriage but Cassandra was holding on to him and letting him do whatever he wanted. In a way I knew that would come, but not that soon. Still there was a special place in my heart for him.

In the meantime, Horst kept asking when we would come because he'd then start looking for an apartment for us. I knew Karl Heinz was desperate to leave so we started to make plans to shut down our chicken adventure at the end of September and then would be able to go at the beginning of October. Karl Heinz told his German boss about it and he understood and wished us all the best. We got in touch with Chinese restaurants and I felt sorry for the chickens but I was the one who wanted to do that so I had to keep quiet. We also started to look for one-way charter flights since we wouldn't come back to Vancouver and sometimes I felt like a zombie, with the start of another beginning in my life. The day the Chinese were coming to pick up the chickens I stayed at Gerrit's house; I couldn't handle seeing them being taken away.

We found a pretty good charter flight and booked it and wrote to Horst to get us an apartment for the end of October, and at last the day came when Gerrit took us to the airport and kept the car. Before we left the house, I had to pet Quasimodo one last time and Gerrit said, "Don't worry, he'll die of old age." I had written to Michael a few days earlier telling him our plans and that I would write as soon as I had a new address in Honolulu but I didn't tell Janet and Michael about our stop-over in San Francisco.

While the pilot of preparing to land in San Francisco, I looked out of the window and saw all those landmarks which I'd looked up in Berlin when I was supposed to marry Michael and live there. They looked exactly as they had in the book. I didn't know if Karl Heinz still remembered that but he didn't say anything and I guessed his mind was already in Honolulu. Little Thomas was cranky and I started to have a toothache: that was all we needed with a long flight ahead of us but there was a little newsstand with newspapers and some over-the-counter drugs, so we got something for Thomas to make him sleep and the lady gave me some pills to take away the tooth pain until I could see a dentist. You could see she felt sorry for us.

Well, we started to board and the flight was full, with the flight crew, pilot, copilot and engineer sitting behind screens; it sure looked scary and all the time it was just water underneath the plane but everyone looked happy and relaxed and we were greeted with "ALOHA!" I thought the flight would never end; it was an overnight flight and almost everyone was sleeping but I looked through the window and admired the beautiful sky with a lot of bright shining stars. Well, I was on my way to a tropical island. The sun started to come up and it looked so beautiful, as if the sun was jumping up out of the ocean. For breakfast everyone received an apple and a banana and then the pilot came on saying, "Good morning" and "Aloha," of course, and telling us that we would shortly be landing in beautiful Honolulu where it would be a gorgeous day with a temperature around 84 degrees Fahrenheit (28 Celsius). Everyone looked so happy as if there were no problems in the world and Karl Heinz looked at me looking so happy and said, "Maybe we've found Paradise."

Horst was there to pick us up and take us to our apartment and he was living right across from us. We then found out what Ala Moana meant: it was the largest shopping area in Honolulu, the Ala Moana Shopping Centre, and the best thing was that it was within walking distance of our apartment. Our apartment was fully furnished so the only thing we needed was food. Everything we saw was amazing, including the huge palm trees, and the air smelled like a flower garden. Also, within walking distance was the Ala Moana beach park and right there was the beach. Horst told Karl Heinz he could start any day but should take a rest for a few days and get used to the warm weather. We then went to the Ala Moana Shopping Centre and got food, went to a small diner and had freshly made sandwiches and then went back to the apartment. Thomas got some more calming-down medicine and Karl Heinz and I had a glass of beer, which you shouldn't have in a warm climate if you're not used to it, but we had a good night's rest.

Since Horst was his boss in a way, Karl Heinz asked him if he could take three days to get organised and help me too before starting work. Horst totally agreed and even offered Karl Heinz his car to use during the day so we could get to know a little more about the island, and we gladly accepted the offer and went sightseeing. We talked to the mailman and got our new address but we didn't have a phone connection, which was fine as we hardly used a phone anyway. Our apartment building had ten one-bedroom units, five downstairs and five upstairs and ours was upstairs. We were the only HAOLE people living in the building, Haole meaning not Hawaiian Native. Haoles were mostly white people, which made sense because now it was the 50th state of the U.S., it was mostly white people immigrating to Hawaii from the U.S. Mainland and Canada.

We had mostly mixed races like Hawaiian/Japanese, Hawaiian/Chinese, Hawaiian/ Samoan living in the apartment building. If you saw a Hawaiian person with red hair, that was a pure Hawaiian but there weren't that many around anymore. There were a lot of new customs to learn, one being that if you were visiting friends, you had to take your shoes off before entering the house or apartment. As people mostly wore slippers, it was fun finding your slippers again and someone might well have taken yours. Another rule I had to learn was never to leave anything edible, including leftovers or dirty dishes, outside, as within minutes there would be dozens of cockroaches crawling around. I found them the ugliest insects ever. They don't bite, they just look ugly and some of them can even fly and they grow up to three inches (7 cm) long.

So, after three days of rest, Karl Heinz went to work and I knew it would be hard because they were working in the sun. For the moment, we didn't need a car as Horst took him to work and brought him back and I could walk and there was also bus transportation. I wrote a letter to my parents and to Janet and Michael giving my new address. During the day little Thomas and I went to the beach. It was hard to believe it was almost Christmas; we went swimming and I had to decorate the Christmas tree whilst sweating. That was the first time I missed the snow at Christmas time.

More German immigrants arrived from Canada, just as we had, because the economy was booming and there were so many jobs opening up, and some of the ladies started to work in restaurants as waitresses. I thought it over and decided to talk to Karl Heinz about it as I, too, wanted to start working the following year. If I could find a job as a waitress at night, so Karl Heinz was home with Thomas, that would be perfect. I told Karl Heinz and he agreed because his job was hard, working in the sun and having sun-burn most of the time. So, we agreed—next year I would look for a job.

My parents wrote to say that my grandfather was in hospital because he'd fallen and broken his left leg. That was bad news as if something should happen, my grandmother would have to go into another senior home and most likely would have to share a room with someone else. It was another reason for me to go to work so we could save more money and maybe be able to leave sooner. If we were there in Berlin again, we could take a larger apartment and I could have grandmother to live with us because her pension would come to us and I could take care of her. It was a nice thought and I really hoped it would work.

I wrote Christmas cards to Janet and Michael. I really missed them both, but just as friends, and I asked Janet if I could have a picture of her little boy and Bianca. Christmas Eve arrived and we were sitting on the beach watching the sun go down; it didn't feel like Christmas at all with no Christmas spirit and almost 30 degrees Fahrenheit. As Honolulu was a tourist attraction, everything was open and the palm trees were decorated with Christmas ornaments, but it still wasn't Christmas for me. I had the feeling Karl Heinz felt the same, but he was quiet too.

Horst was dating a beautiful Hawaiian girl called Lani and we decided to celebrate New Year's together but wondered what to do with Thomas. Horst knew one of Lani's relatives was operating a childcare business, of course only during the week, not on holidays, but decided to ask if she would watch Thomas just for that night. There was another week of work for Karl Heinz before New Year and I received a letter from Janet and Michael, also wishing us a Happy New Year. In Janet's letter I found a picture of Marcus and Bianca and she was beautiful. Michael, as always, was charming—well, that was his trademark—and a $100 bill was enclosed with a note to say it was for little Thomas, to buy him a huge teddy. I had given up arguing about that with him but I decided I would tell Karl Heinz about it.

Lani told Horst to let us know that her relative would watch Thomas as she also had other little children to take care of as well. I didn't feel that good about leaving Thomas with others as it was the first time we'd done that, but I liked the idea of going to that nightclub. We had a nice dinner and watched Hula dances and waited for the year to end. (Hula is a Polynesian dance developed in the Islands by the Polynesians who originally settled there.) We didn't care for fireworks so left right after everyone said Happy New Year and took a taxi to pick up our son and go home.

Thomas was fast asleep so the two of us had a glass of wine and I told Karl Heinz about the letter from San Francisco and the money from Michael for Thomas. He smiled and said, "I guessed you were still in loose contact with them, but that is the past and I sometimes think back about my deceased girlfriend, too." I really thanking him for saying that.

I was relieved to have told Karl Heinz about San Francisco and went and bought Thomas a huge teddy. At the Ala Moana Shopping Center, I also saw a shop which took photographs and since I had quite a bit of money left over, I thought it would be a good idea to have a picture taken and send it to them, so that's what I did. It came out really nice: the three of us with Teddy in the middle and Thomas and I on the sides. Since there was also a post office, I mailed it straight away and wondered what comments I would get from them.

I asked Horst if it would be possible to talk to Lani to see whether she might know of any restaurants in town who would hire a waitress who could only work in the evenings. I was nervous since I'd never worked as a waitress, but it was worth a try and as Lani had been born and raised in Honolulu, she knew a lot of people. One evening she came over to our apartment and we discussed it. She told me she knew of a little diner at Kalakaua Avenue, which was the main street in downtown Waikiki where a lot of local people and also tourists go in the evening for a snack and a drink. It was parallel to Waikiki Beach and she said it would be great because I'd never worked as a waitress before and there wasn't a big menu, but only small dishes. She knew the owner—a Japanese man—who she said was very nice and if I wanted, she would come with me.

Well, a few days later we went there and talked to him. It was a small restaurant but nicely decorated and with Japanese and Hawaiian music playing in the background. The owner, whose name I could never properly pronounce, told us that, yes, he would hire me because he'd heard a lot about Germany and World War 2. He would pay the minimum hourly wage but he mentioned that the tips I'd get were very good. The restaurant opened from 5 P.M. to 10 P.M. so I would work five hours a day from Tuesday to Saturday and I was in heaven; I had a job again. I asked Lani on our way home how many other waitresses were working there and she told me there were three other Japanese girls and I would be the only Haole. I didn't know if that was a good or bad thing but I usually got along with everyone, so why not with Japanese girls. When I told Karl Heinz about my new job, he laughed but wished me all the best. I wondered why they were kind of surprised I was working in a Japanese restaurant. There were a few days left before I could start and I hoped that if I was really friendly to the guests, I would make good money with tips.

I had only two days before the start of my new job when Lani stopped by and brought me two menus from the restaurant. One was written in English and Japanese with only Hawaiian and Japanese specials, the other one was for American food only. She told me to look at them so I would have some idea of what they were serving and told me to concentrate on the local specials, which was really nice of her and she was definitely right on that because when I looked at the local menu I had no idea what it meant. She was smiling and said, "I'll just tell you a little about it and the rest you'll learn later."

Sashimi was the first one on the menu and she said it was a Japanese delicacy of raw fish sliced into thin pieces, dipped into soy sauce and eaten with chopsticks, which are eating utensils consisting of equal length sticks and mostly used in East Asia.

Poke was the second on the list and is a traditional Hawaiian healthy raw fish food made from Ahi or Salmon, mixed with soy sauce, sesame oil, onions and sesame seeds, created for adventurous eaters.

Laulau was the third on the list: pork, chicken or fish wrapped in Taro leaves. Taro is a plant with large green leaves and they're available all year round. Those leaves can't be eaten raw, but they are an excellent source of vitamins such as iron, zinc, vitamin B and C, potassium and copper, so you wrap your chicken, pork or fish into the taro leaves and steam them for three or four hours, then they're ready to eat.

Saki is the drink to have with all of that—an alcoholic beverage made by fermenting rice. Lani looked at me and said, "Now you know a little about the special local food that they serve there and the other menu is easy—it's just sandwiches, soups and salads." Well, it was so helpful and at least she'd told me the basics about the local food. When the Tuesday evening came, my first working day, I was quite nervous but Mr. Anotokai (I finally remembered his name), the boss, introduced me to the waitresses and the kitchen staff and then I was on my own. There were maybe 15 tables and by 6 P.M. the first guests had arrived.

I let the other waitresses go first and just watched them—they were mostly serving tourists and they ate the American food—but then two local couples came in and as the others were busy I had to go. I tried my best and they ordered Sashimi with breadsticks and Saki. I felt like fainting and they must have known I was very new but they were nice and almost helped me with the ordering. Everything seemed to be okay except that I forgot the chopsticks but they reminded me and I took back the knives and forks and gave them the chopsticks. They gave me a ten-dollar tip and I felt great. I had two more guests after them but they ordered from the American menu. The Japanese waitresses were a lot busier than I was but it was fine: it was my first day and I had 15 dollars in tips. When it was almost time to go I was told to clean the tables but that was the easiest part of my work and I got home around 11 o'clock. Karl Heinz was still waiting for me and asked me how it was and I told him, but was so tired I fell asleep in the chair.

The next day I felt better and I was sure that in a few days I'd be able to handle it well. It was a lot better the next day but I had more tourists than local guests and that was easier. The Japanese waitresses tried to get more of the local guests and I assumed they gave better tips. When the first week was over I really enjoyed staying at home in the evening but I'd made forty dollars in tips and I was proud of myself.

On Sunday we rented a jeep for a day and went sightseeing. Horst had told us to drive up to the Pali Lookout which offered breathtaking views of the windward side of Oahu and we did that. It was really true, so we decided to do something like that every Sunday as that was the only day we could spend together. Karl Heinz mentioned that on one of the coming Sundays he wanted to go to Pearl Harbour and have a look around to see if he could find an old jeep to buy so that we could do little tours like that, because we were very sure that after we went back to Berlin we'd never make it back there again.

Karl Heinz told me Horst and Lani had split up but said it had happened before—Horst being a suborn German from Hamburg and Lani being a temperamental Island Girl, they argued a lot, but it didn't take too long to make up again. I really hoped so since she was the one I could go to and ask for help.

The second week went quite well and one of the first two couples who were my first guests, came back again and one of the Japanese waitresses dashed over to greet them and wanted to take their order. I didn't understand what they talked about but I did understand the one word "Haole" and the waitress turned around and looked at me, saying, "It's for you." I was surprised they were asking for me, so I asked them what they wanted and this time they asked for Laulau and breadsticks again and Saki, and this time I didn't forget the chopsticks, which they smilingly noticed. The lady asked me where in Germany I came from, since I had a German accent and when I told them I was from Berlin, she told me one of her friend's son was stationed in Germany after the war, in the Air Base Ramstein. He loved it over there, especially the German beer, and he even married a German girl, but they now lived on Maui, a neighbouring island. He came from Texas but now that Hawaii belonged to the U.S., he and his wife came to Maui. That brought back memories but I didn't mention anything about San Francisco. They gave me another tip again and I noticed that one of the Japanese waitresses saw it. After cleaning the tables I could go home and I told Karl Heinz about it but I didn't pay too much attention to it.

At the end of the week I received a letter from Michael thanking me for the teddy picture. He wrote, "Your son looks so cute and I am so sorry." Yes, he still had a special place in my heart. Karl Heinz found an old cheap jeep which needed some repairs but since he was a car mechanic, he could fix it himself. The second week was over and I really felt more secure at work, except for feeling a bit insecure with the waitresses.

I was happy, however, since the money I earned helped quite a bit and sometimes we had leftovers in the kitchen which we were able to take home and that helped, too. It was then three weeks I'd been working there and I'd started to like it. Spring had almost arrived, not that it made any difference in the weather except perhaps being a little warmer than in the winter, but really only a little. Horst and Lani were back together again, so thank God I had my adviser back, and Karl Heinz was fixing up our jeep so that we could go on our Sunday sight-seeing trips.

Then, on Sunday morning, we heard our doorbell ring and thought it was Horst and Lani coming to pick us up for a swim but it was Mr. Anataiko, my boss. We were surprised but we asked him in. I noticed he was kind of nervous and he gave me a check, telling me he was sorry because I was doing nicely serving the guests, but his Japanese waitresses were complaining that I was serving local guests, since I was a Haole, and they had threatened to quit if he didn't let me go. He then apologised and left. I was shocked because I realised I'd lost my job, but I wasn't going to give up.

We went over to Horst and Lani and she was upset but admitted having her doubts the first time she saw the Japanese waitresses. "But, that's not the Aloha spirit," she said, "we'll find you another job." Then she told me something which at first I didn't understand but later I did. She said, "Whenever someone calls you 'Haole,' tell them yes, you're Haole, but not a Mainland Haole—a German Haole." That is all she said, nothing else, except to give me hope saying that we'd find a restaurant which had all different races working there.

I had to have another job as we needed the money now we'd bought the jeep and also to save to go back to Germany. I still had the 200 dollars with my parents, the money Michael had sent me, but that wouldn't go very far either. It looked as if we'd have to wait until next year to go back home, which would be another full year, but we'd said four years anyway. Lani thought of a more tourist-like restaurant in downtown Honolulu called The Vikings, which served continental food and Hawaiian food but when we went there and applied for a job as a waitress, he said he was sorry—only a dishwasher's job was open, so I took it. I also had to wait until the other dishwasher was gone before I could start so it wasn't what I expected, but I had no choice.

Behind our apartment there was a place with toys and swings for children to play and also some chairs for parents to sit and watch their children. One day I found a chair and sat down to watch Thomas; there were other little children playing and he was so happy with the other little ones and told me, "Mama, Tinner," that meant "Kinder" in German, "Children" in English. Since we only spoke German at home between ourselves, his first language was German. Suddenly a local lady approached me trying to push me off the chair, yelling. "Get off, Haole, that is my chair." I really didn't know what to do, but Lani's words came into my mind: "Tell them you are not a Mainland Haole, you are a German Haole," and as soon as I said that she changed and became friendly, telling me, "That's fine, I'll look for another chair." Was it really living in Paradise?

I tried not to pay too much attention to the Mainland German Haole situation and was only hoping the dishwashing job would be easier. I finally got called in for the coming week and the evening shift from 5 P.M. to 10 P.M. Tuesday to Saturday: the same hours and the same days. I just saw one small problem—that since I wasn't a waitress I wouldn't be getting any tips, but when I talked to Lani about it, she told me that restaurants like that usually put all the tips into one pot and then divide them up between the waitresses and the kitchen staff and that sounded pretty good to me.

We still had the Sunday left and as it was a nice day, we went to the zoo. It wasn't really a big one but they had a little animal petting area and little Thomas loved the animals. There were also two elephants which caught Thomas' attention. He looked at their big feet and at his own little feet and because he was wearing slippers, he must have wondered why they weren't wearing them as well. We never did find out what his thoughts were but he took off his own slippers and threw them over the fence, saying, "Hi, Hutsafant," and then stood there for a while, perhaps wondering why they didn't put them on. He did it twice more, so in the end we had to take his slippers off before we went inside.

Well, on Tuesday morning I wrote a letter to Janet telling her about my new job; I knew it wasn't a big deal being a dish washer, but there wasn't much to choose from and I knew she would understand. Karl Heinz came home from work and I got ready to leave. I wasn't that nervous as I couldn't do a lot wrong except break dishes. When I went to the manager, he took me to the kitchen, which was quite hot and with plenty of dirty dishes. Another local man was responsible for washing the pots and pans since they were quite heavy, and I had to do the plates and cutlery: it was all dishwashing by hand in those days. Thank God the restaurant was slow on Tuesday, so it wasn't really hectic. He told me he'd been working there for almost six months and it really wasn't very easy work but usually the tips weren't bad if the restaurant had lots of customers. He told me that sometimes, perhaps once a month or even more, a famous movie star called Ava Gardner came in with her friends and that they tipped a lot of money. He also gave me some good advice—that since the water was hot and the dishwashing soap hurt your skin, it was a good idea to use gloves and buy some ointment to massage into my hands. He was a nice man and I didn't have to tell him I was a German Haole.

I was tired when I got home and wanted to tell Karl Heinz what had happened but he was already asleep with two bottles of beer next to him. I was somehow disappointed; I knew his job was hard too, but so was mine going to be. I didn't want to make a big deal out of it as it hadn't happened before, but I was worried about Thomas who was very careless and could hurt himself if there was no one around to watch him. It took me a while to fall asleep that night: a lot of memories popped up which should have already been forgotten.

The next morning, I didn't say anything and neither did he except "How was your first night?" Well, I said I wanted to tell him but he was already asleep and he just said that he was really tired the day before. We didn't mention the beer. I could understand that he was working very hard and we just had to make it through this one year and by then we should have enough money to go back home. We'd still be caged in there and not able to go to too many places but here we could go to a lot of places but were too tired to go.

My work week went by pretty fast. I bought gloves but found I had a problem working with them and broke a few plates, but my coworker, Randy, hid them to keep me out of trouble. He had a wife and two small children so his wife worked during the day and he worked at night, just the opposite of us. It was hard for them, too, but they were planning that in about a year they would leave Honolulu and move to a neighbouring island, Maui, where their families lived. Sometimes it helped me to understand that it wasn't only us who were struggling and getting mad at each other sometimes.

We had the Sundays for ourselves, when we either went to the beach or drove around the island into the countryside. We came to the decision that we would stay until Spring of 1961 and Horst and Karl Heinz quit their jobs and became partners, opening their own construction company. This way was a bit easier for them and whenever there was really hard work like carrying big pieces of lumber, they could hire helpers. I was still working as a dishwasher but was promoted to "salad girl" and whenever Ava Gardner came for dinner, I served her the side order of salad just to look at her; she was really beautiful. There were evenings when I came home and found Karl Heinz snoring in front of a few beer bottles, but I didn't say anything.

Michael still wrote to me. Not as much as before but it meant we knew what was going on in each other's lives. Bianca was already going to Kindergarten and Michael spoiled her like crazy. If he stayed married to Cassandra, there most likely wouldn't be any more children. Even with letters, we still had a special bond and he kept writing that we would see each other again, even though he knew we were going back to Germany the next year. My parents could hardly wait to see us and their first grandson and I felt the same. Lani told me that she and Horst were planning to get married the next year and wanted us to be witnesses at the marriage, which would be great as we could do that and then after the wedding we could go back home.

The year went by quickly and my parents had written to say that my grandfather wasn't doing too well and that we should be prepared for the worst; I so much wished to be there with them. Lately, I'd been kind of depressed; maybe it was too much work and also because I had no rest during the day since little Thomas wasn't one of the quietest children.

Lani stopped by one day and told me her wedding would most likely be earlier and she was thinking before Christmas. I had the feeling she was pushing a little but Horst was a really good, honest, guy who was always working and trying to help others and he adored her. Horst's hobby was sailing. He grew up in the Northern part of Germany in Hamburg on the North Sea and his dream was to have his own sailboat one day. Lani had grown up in the countryside of Oahu on a farm and she loved horseback riding and hoped to one day have her own horse. When she told me that, it reminded me of my situation years ago with Michael—growing up in different lifestyles and also in different cultures. I just said, "You sure have different hobbies," and she started to laugh and said, "If Horst has his sailboat and I have my horse, then I'll take my horse on the sailboat and we'll go sailing, so we both have our hobbies in one place." She was really funny sometimes and so full of life.

Horst sometimes complained to us that whenever they were to meet at a certain time, she was never on time and when she arrived an hour or so late and Horst was angry, she just laughed and said, "I'm here now; be happy I'm here." They decided to get married in December and Horst had an unusual idea: he wanted to rent a sailing boat for the four of us, get a Minister, and sail out on the ocean about a mile or so off Waikiki Beach to get married at sunset. I thought it was more her idea than his as I didn't think he could be that romantic but I liked the idea a lot and told Lani that it should be fine as long as she didn't take her horse along. Usually the weather in December is nice since the hurricane season goes from June to November. After the marriage ceremony on the ocean we were all to go to Lani's ranch in the country and have a luau (a Hawaiian celebration), and she would tell us more later, so we were really looking forward to that marriage event.

Janet wrote me a letter telling me the latest news—that they were thinking of having another baby. The Real estate company kept on growing and they'd hired more salesmen, so she was only now working half a day and Michael, now the boss, wasn't in the office a lot—always away on conventions and if it was only a short trip he even took Bianca along.

I also received a letter from home saying my grandfather had passed away. It was expected but it was hard and I felt so sorry for my grandmother, wondering if she would have to go to another care center and be with a strange person. I so much wished I could go over but it was not possible. Because he'd known him well, I sat down and wrote a letter to Michael telling him about it. Karl Heinz gave me money to send home for a wreath for his funeral.

I told Karl Heinz that my parents thanked us for the money we sent for a wreath for my grandfather's funeral. Karl Heinz also liked them a lot, especially my grandmother, but he asked me if I'd told Michael as well because he knew we'd spent time with my grandparents and I told him that I had because my grandmother really liked Michael, too. He said that was good, which surprised me, but it made me happy to hear that he felt like that. In the meantime, Michael sent me his condolences for the death of my grandfather and wrote that he would always remember my grandmother's sparkling eyes; surprisingly, he had not forgotten that. Sometimes I wondered if he really meant things, but it was the same with me; I still remembered almost everything as well.

We'd also received a letter from Karl Heinz' mother telling us that Brigitta was going to get married in Eltham and that if she could get a visa, she might fly over to London for the wedding. The only thing that bothered Karl Heinz was that Brigitta's husband-to-be was eight years younger than Brigitta, but I told him it was her life and he seemed to accept it.

Horst and Karl Heinz' construction company picked up too and they got a contract to build a small apartment building—only one floor with six units and pretty close to the beach. Because Horst went to school in Germany, he knew what to do about building codes and permits, which was a big help, and he'd also worked as a foreman carpenter in Vancouver for over two years. The only problem I saw was the length of time it would take to finish, because I really wanted to see my parents and grandmother.

When they started to do the paperwork for the apartment building, it was already Fall and one evening I started to talk about our plan to go back home the next year. I could see on Karl Heinz' face that he was a little nervous and I knew what he was thinking. He told me that he'd thought about that as well and had wanted to talk to me about it. His idea was that if they hadn't finished the project by Spring next year, which I knew they couldn't, then he would let me and Thomas fly home to my parents for a few weeks' visit and then come back. After the project was finished we could then go back home together. I told him it wasn't a bad idea and thanked him, since he really wanted to make that money for our future and his little newspaper shop.

He also told me I could stop working by the end of the year and that was the best news: I could then be home in the evenings and he could rest, because his job wasn't the easiest, either. I felt great—there was a lot to look forward to with Horst and Lani's wedding coming up and a likely trip to see my family the next year. When Lani and I were talking about the wedding, I asked her what to wear as their marriage witness and she said, "You have to wear a Mumu." I had no idea what a Mumu was and she laughed and said, "We'll go and get one for you— a Mumu is a loose, long, flowery printed dress which a lot of Hawaiian ladies wear for special occasions like weddings or anniversaries and they have some really nice ones." I was then really looking forward to going and buying one.

Our lives were really busy with the start of the apartment building and the upcoming wedding and, next year, my "maybe" trip back home, and Horst and Lani set their wedding day for the middle of December.

My parents wrote that more and more tension was growing between East and West Berlin and the talk about building a wall around West Berlin was also increasing. But people in caged in West Berlin were used to being isolated and my father wrote that they didn't pay too much attention to the rumours and even then, new businesses were popping up as the East had to do something to keep their people from immigrating to the West Side. It was hard to believe a wall would be built through a city but maybe it was just a rumour.

I did write to Janet and Michael about our friends getting married and told them it would be a typical Hawaiian wedding, so Michael wrote back and asked if they could have a picture. I promised they could; the letters with Michael were becoming like ones between good friends and it was easier that way. Lani picked me up one day to buy a Mumu for the wedding. She had hers specially made but we found a very pretty one for me and when I looked in the mirror I found myself actually quite good looking. Then Lani said that we also needed flower Leis (flower garlands) to hang around our necks, usually made from the flowers of the Plumeria tree. We were then set for the wedding. Horst arranged the Minister and rented the sailboat and although I'd had a few highlights in my life already, this event was one of them.

It was December 10th, 1960, a beautiful day, and our flower leis were delivered fresh in the afternoon. Horst then came with a limousine to pick us up, then we picked up the Minister and, at last, Lani. She looked stunning in her white Mumu. We then drove to the harbour where the captain of the sailboat awaited us to take us sailing into the Hawaiian sunset. It was the most romantic wedding I'd ever seen. Yes, my thoughts were in San Francisco a few times, but very briefly, like memories, and that was all.

Afterwards, Lani's family and friends had prepared a luau (a traditional Hawaiian party) for them on their farm in the country. They had a Hawaiian specialty called Kalua Pig, which is a pig cooked in an underground oven filled with hot stones. The pig is wrapped in wire so it will not fall apart and cooked for about nine or ten hours. It's then served with raw fish, rice and other Hawaiian specialties and tastes delicious. Plus, of course, a lot of beer. There was a small band singing the famous Hawaiian Wedding song while Lani danced the Hula and I believe most people there had tears in their eyes. Karl Heinz was holding my hand and saying, "Let's marry again like that." Everything was so different from weddings in Germany—maybe it had a lot to do with the scenery but I felt as if I was watching a movie. Little Thomas had been there since before, and while we were at, the wedding ceremony, so we stayed on with them overnight and the next day Horst and Lani flew to Maui for their honeymoon.

The newlyweds only stayed a week on Maui for their honeymoon because Horst had to be back for the start of the apartment building but they both enjoyed Maui, which was still very laid back, unlike Honolulu. Lani called it a tropical paradise and looked at us laughing as she said, "And not too many Haoles." "Well," Karl Heinz said, "you are married to a Haole now, but he's a German Haole." It had now become a joke. I was glad that some of Lani's friends had taken pictures of the celebration and also that the Minister took some on the sailboat of the four of us with a beautiful background of palm trees in the far distance and the sunset. They came out really nicely.

As Christmas was approaching, I bought Bianca a cute little Hula girl and a small T-shirt for Janet's little Marcus and sent the nicest picture I had. I gave notice to my workplace that I would be quitting my job by the end of the year and found that my coworker, Randy, the other dishwasher, was also leaving. He and his family were leaving for Maui because of that stressful life in Honolulu. I wished him all the best; he really was a nice man and had helped me a lot in the beginning.

Well, I still wasn't really in the Christmas spirit and I hoped so much that next Christmas we could play in the snow. Before long, I received a little package from San Francisco: Janet sent a cute little T-shirt for Thomas with his name written on top and I was quite relieved that it wasn't "San Francisco" written on it. Michael wrote a romantic letter again thanking me for the picture but there wasn't a comment really—just one sentence: "I cannot tell you how I felt when I saw you." There was a hundred dollars in it again; I guess that was his way of handling it since he didn't know what to send. I told Karl Heinz what I got from them—both the little shirt for our son and the $100 and he just grinned and said, then we can go out for dinner with the $100 but I knew his mind was sidetracked with the apartment building, so he just joked it off. I also thought about Michael's comment about the picture and I realised we would most likely never lose contact unless I stopped it and I wasn't ready for that. We were just writing letters and I would never try to face him and I also told that to Karl Heinz and he was okay with it, saying it would stop by itself later anyway.

We had a really quiet Christmas. Horst and Lani were on the farm and we went to the beach on Christmas Day. Thomas was playing in the sand and I told him, in German, not to go into the water by himself. He looked at me and said, "Mama, no wasser" (German for "water"). We realised he had a problem handling two languages but we wanted him to be bilingual. It would stop anyway next year when we were living in Germany again, so we continued speaking German but we noticed that he hardly talked at all.

At the end of the year I stopped my dishwasher/salad girl job and it felt great being at home. We also had a quiet New Year and were looking forward to 1961 to start anew in Germany AGAIN. I went to the beach sunbathing almost every day and had the idea that if I had a nice dark suntan when I got to Berlin in the Spring, people would look at me thinking I must come from some tropical island. Karl Heinz asked me to stay as long as the hardest work at the apartment was still to be done, at least until the roof was up and they didn't need to work in the sun all day, and of course I agreed so that when he came home at night he could rest and didn't have to watch Thomas or cook dinner. I was home anyway and did that but he was really overworked and so was Horst. Lani told me they hardly even talked when he got home and that he sometimes fell asleep at 7 P.M. We figured I could leave around May, which was fine with me as the change of weather wouldn't be so bad and May is a beautiful month when all the trees start to bloom.

Because I was worried about him not talking, I took Thomas to the children's playgroup with friends of Lani's so that he could be with other children and the English language. I did that three days a week, just for half a day, which left me time for other things. I couldn't go to the beach every day or I would have no skin left, so people in Germany wouldn't be able to see my suntan and think I came from a tropical is-land—that was the end of that childish idea. Instead, I tried to help as much as I could and went to the apartment building site and helped there, cleaning up after them and generally helping. Sometimes special lumber had to be treated for termites, so they gave me a large brush which I had to dip into a bad-smelling liquid and brush on some lumber pieces. They called me "carpenter assistant" but they didn't pay me; they called it family volunteering. However, I was invited for dinner and it was really fun doing all that—like climbing up the ladder of suc-cess from dishwasher to salad girl and now to carpenter helper. It was also very good for Thomas. It was more or less a pidgin talk between the German and English language, but at least he started to talk.

I received bad news from Michael, who wrote to tell me that he'd found out Daniel had passed away in San Diego after apparently suf-fering a heart attack. Michael thought he was also suffering from de-pression and loneliness and you could feel from Michael's writing that it had hit him hard. It also made me feel sad since we'd had quite a few good times together. Maybe if Elena hadn't left him, it wouldn't have happened and I believed Michael felt the same way because he was a big part of that problem. I wrote back to Michael and tried to tell him it wasn't only his fault alone and that Elena was part of that affair, too.

I wrote to my parents to say Thomas and I would be coming in May for sure and that so far it wasn't really clear what would happen but we'd discuss that when I was there. I was very happy to be going to see my parents and Berlin again but sometimes I had times when I didn't know what would happen to our future after that apartment building was finished and wondered whether Karl Heinz would be happy with that newspaper store or whether he'd like to continue building. I overheard Horst and Karl Heinz talking and saying that there were quite a few building projects coming up on Maui, which made me wonder if that meant they wanted to go over there. I didn't ask and they didn't say anything.

It amazed me how quickly those four years passed. Brigitta got married in Eltham and my mother-in-law went over for the wedding. I really gave her credit for doing that; she was a strong woman and I think she became like that because of what she went through trying to survive during and after the war and being alone with four children. I received a letter back from Michael and I was right—he felt guilty about what had happened between Elena and him and he also wrote that he felt guilty about quite a few things; I knew what he meant.

The job at the apartment building went very well and the roof was almost up, so I could start making plans for our trip and Karl Heinz and I went to a travel agency to make our reservation for the flight for Thomas and me. We just reserved a one-way ticket because it was up in the air and we didn't know when or if I would come back to the islands or if Karl Heinz would come back to Berlin, which he promised me he would do. It was really exciting and we were searching for the best route to take. There was a stop in California and I knew what Karl Heinz was thinking so I told the travel agent that I didn't care where I stopped in California, but not to book a stop-over in San Francisco. I thought I heard a stone dropping on the ground; it must have fallen from Karl Heinz' heart.

Well, the travel agency found a pretty good flight from Honolulu to Berlin, one way, leaving on May 17th with stopovers in Los Angeles, then New York, then Frankfurt, Germany, and then on to Berlin. If there were no delays we'd arrive in Berlin on 19th May. The worst part was the 12 hours' time difference between Hawaii and Berlin which would most likely kill us as it is halfway around the globe so that you'd be dead tired during the day and wide awake at night—that so-called jetlag which I'd been told took your body four or five days to adjust to. Poor little Thomas would be completely confused so I had to go to the pharmacy to get those pills or drops I'd used before.

We picked up the tickets with the dates and times so that I could write to my parents to let them know in case they wanted to pick us up at Berlin Tegel airport, though if they had no time I said not to worry as I could always take a taxi. I knew my parents; they felt insecure in strange places, even though they'd been to Airport Tegel before. I also wrote to Janet and Michael saying I was flying to Berlin, either on vacation or to stay, I didn't know which myself.

The day of our departure arrived and in the evening Karl Heinz took us to Honolulu International Airport. Thomas had had his so-called "numbing drops" and he was already getting tired. We had our first overnight flight ahead of us—we called it the red-eye flight—on to Los Angeles. Karl Heinz and I said goodbye, and Aloha, and it was emotional since we really weren't aware of what would happen. But I turned around and waved to him, because I was so used to the situation when the leaving person didn't turn around and then mostly I never saw that person again.

The flight to Los Angeles was quiet with no turbulence and I even slept a little. We then had to wait awhile for the flight to New York and then the second overnight flight to Frankfurt was ready to depart. Thomas was pretty good because he was "doped" but the pharmacist said that if you only did it once in a great while, it was fine—better than having him crying and restless for the whole time. After the second red-eye flight, we landed in Frankfurt, Germany. I noticed people running and hustling around and it was raining heavily and also chilly. Somehow they were different from the Haoles in Honolulu, but I pushed the thought away; I was HOME.

We boarded the flight to Berlin Tegel and after a little while the plane dropped altitude, not a lot, but it was very notable. I looked around but none of the passengers paid any attention and I then looked out of the window and saw a plane quite close flying at the same altitude as us; it looked as if it was guiding us into West Berlin. I asked one of the stewardesses what that meant and she realised it was new to me—maybe she noticed my healing sunburn—and she explained to me what it was. We were in one of the West Berlin Air Corridors and Control Zones which the plane had to use. There were three controlled airways for the civil and military air traffic of the Western Allies between West Berlin and West Germany, passing over East Germany. I told her I'd seen another plane close to ours, it must have been a sowjet plane, and she nodded, saying they were so used to that that they didn't look at it anymore. Shortly before landing at Berlin Tegel Airport, the other plane turned around and flew away.

Well, I was back home in Berlin, the town I wanted so desperately to leave and now I was so happy to be back. I got my luggage and looked for my parents but they weren't there so I called a taxi and drove home. It really was a bittersweet feeling; a lot of new buildings had popped up while I was gone, but the area where we lived was still the same, nothing had changed. When we reached our apartment complex, my parents were just coming out of the door to pick us up when they saw us coming. There was a lot of crying and hugging and I became second place, little Thomas was first; it was beautiful. When we got into the apartment, my mother said, "Look over there at what came for you," and it was a telegram from Karl Heinz asking me if everything was alright and telling me he missed me already. That was unusual for him: he didn't show his emotions very often. On the other side of the table was a huge bunch of Lilacs and I knew where they'd come from and who knew I loved them and there was a little card attached saying, "Welcome Home. Michael." I didn't know how he did that.

I was overwhelmed by being at home and also very tired after that long trip and when it was only noon my mother was already in the kitchen cooking all my favourite things. Thomas was confused—everyone was speaking German and he didn't say anything again. The only thing I told him was that this was his Oma and Opa. I just crawled through the day and decided to start afresh the next day, sending Karl Heinz a telegram and writing a letter to Michael thanking him for the flowers. I was really surprised he still remembered all that and saying that we would have a loose contact forever, but that wasn't important at that moment. I had a lot of other things on my mind and being in Berlin brought back a lot of memories, especially looking at the lilac flowers.

Thomas and I slept like rocks that night and the next day my father went back to work so it was just my mother and myself at home and we could talk. My parents had bought a lot of toys for Thomas to play with, so he was occupied. My mother told me that the German Democratic Republic (East Germany) really was starting to build a wall pretty soon; they had to do it because more than 2.5 million people had escaped from East Germany, including East Berlin to West Berlin and West Germany, because the life was so much better in the West. As East Germany, including East Berlin, had only 17 million people, they hoped that the wall would stop people from leaving the East—in other words, not only we West Berliners were caged in, now the Eastern side was as well, but West Berlin was actually booming and had become a tourist attraction. Even with all that wall building ahead, people from West Berlin were looking into the future.

I sent the telegram to Karl Heinz and it took us about three days to get organised again before we went and visited grandmother. She really had lost the sparkle in her eyes but she cried seeing Thomas and still had the rosary in her hand which Michael had given her. She was still in the same senior center where they were when my grandfather was still alive.

Finally, I had some time to write a letter to Michael telling him how some places had changed. I got emotional and told him Complex Wannsee and Complex Gatow weren't there anymore and some places were not "our" Berlin anymore, and I thanking him for the flowers.

I then went to see my mother-in-law who had found a job in a medical lab and was making good money She told me about Brigitta's wedding and how much she liked Eltham, and we laughed after she told me how she enjoyed being there; not talking the language but getting along talking with hands and feet. I started to get colds, it sure was a change, weather-wise. I also received a letter from Karl Heinz letting me know that there was a lot more work at the apartment, that they were now working inside putting in cabinets and bathrooms and kitchens, so he couldn't give me any timeframe as to when the job would be finished.

My father came home one day and said he'd heard the building of the wall would most likely start in August and would most likely be a concrete wall about 12 feet high and 28 miles long with a few guard towers and thousands of explosive devices like landmines. I could hardly believe that and asked my father who had ordered the construction of the Berlin Wall and he answered that as far as he knew, it was Nikita Khrushchev, the President and leader of the Soviet Union at that time. There were only a few weeks left before the start of the wall construction but I still hoped it was more just a rumour than reality.

I'd been back in Berlin almost six weeks and if I hadn't known I was living in a cage, I wouldn't have noticed and even the thought of a wall being built didn't scare the West Berliners. I was waiting for an answer from Karl Heinz as to how his project was going and when he would be back in Berlin, because I was torn between never going back to the islands and staying in Berlin and starting anew again.

I visited my old workplace, the Workmen's Compensation Board office, and said hello to my boss who smiled and said, "I knew you were coming back and you have a job here any time," which made me feel really safe. Janet and Michael wrote asking me about the situation because they'd heard something was going on in West Berlin—if they knew about it over there, then there must be some truth in it. I wrote to Michael telling a little of what I knew and saying maybe I would stay. Yes, being back in that area where we'd met, I missed him even though I knew it was just a dream. I talked to my parents about making a decision but they didn't try to influence me either way.

There were a few children in our apartment complex and Thomas very slowly started to get in touch with them and almost every day I heard another German word. I received a letter from Karl Heinz telling me we should return to Honolulu since although his project would soon be finished, they had another offer to build an apartment on Maui, which might take another year or so as it was larger than the one they were just finishing. I almost knew it would come out like that. It took me a day or two to think it over and then I made the decision that I was not going back, either to Honolulu or to Maui and I told my parents what my plans were—even that if we were lucky we could take my grandmother out of the Senior Center and she could live with us. I then wrote a letter to Karl Heinz telling him we were not going back to the Islands, that the four years he'd promised were over and people were living quite well in Berlin, too, and we had enough money to start a small business; that we were waiting there for him to come back.

Deep down I knew it wasn't really fair to him, because if I'd married Michael, I wouldn't be here either, but I had a reason: with Michael I would have a home in San Francisco, now we were jumping from country to country or from island to island, and Thomas wasn't really handling two languages, so I hoped Karl Heinz would see that too. I had a really bad time being homesick in Canada and I was afraid it would happen again if I went back now. It took longer than usual to get an answer from him and I was very nervous when I opened it, but he wrote that I was right and that he would be back in December at the latest; that we could look for a small business and have my grandmother living with us, which would help, and that he missed me. I was very relieved. I had my family back and we could help each other and when I told my parents that Karl Heinz was coming back, my parents had teary eyes.

I also told Janet and Michael that we would be staying in Germany and not going back to the Islands. Michael wrote back pretty fast; he claimed to understand me but I wasn't sure and for the first time he wrote about his marriage, saying that if it wasn't for Bianca, he would have left already. He said Cassandra was a very good mother, or call her stepmother, and Bianca loved her even though she knew she wasn't her biological mother. He said he and Cassandra were good friends—I'd had that feeling a long time already, but there were always the conventions.

We were approaching August and it looked like the construction of the wall was imminent and then it happened: on August 13th, 1961, the construction of the Berlin Wall started. Now West Berlin really started to be caged in and barbed wire was installed together with fences built out of concrete. The very saddest thing I saw was that some streets were divided by East and West Berlin, so some families were living on the right side of the street and some members of the same family were living across the street on the left side and they were not able to visit each other—they could only wave to each other out of their windows.

I received a telegram from Karl Heinz asking how we were doing and I sent one back saying that nothing had really happened, only we were now really caged in with barbed wire and concrete walls to stop anyone crossing the borders or getting arrested or shot at.

Well, I started to have doubts about whether my decision to go back was right but I couldn't leave my family there and just take off again. Maybe it wouldn't be that bad and after a while they'd take the wall back down again. Somehow it worked and hardly anyone from East Berlin or East Germany tried to cross the borders. At that time Checkpoint Charlie was constructed for Allied diplomats, military personnel and foreigners to cross the border to East Berlin. It was located in Friedrichstrasse, a historic street in the center of Berlin and no East or West Berlin people could pass that point. It was controlled by the Allies on the west side and by East German military on the East and was also later used occasionally for prisoner swaps and for showdowns between the United States and Russia. A few things were different from before: using the autobahn from West Berlin to West Germany, you had to drive through East Germany but you were not allowed to leave the Autobahn while driving through East Germany and you had to stick to the speed limit; if you were caught out by police you were punished by a very high fine. Otherwise, life was like before.

Karl Heinz was coming home in December so I had a few weeks left and I told my parents I was thinking I might go back to my old job and see if I could work there for three months since my boss had told me I could come back at any time. I had to find out if I could work for only a few months and if my mother would watch Thomas during the day, which she said she was happy to do. I then talked to my former boss about it and he let me go back even for a short time, so I started again. A lot of the people there were new as some of the old ones I'd worked with had retired or left to go to West Germany because of the political situation in West Berlin, which meant I didn't have to answer too many questions.

I wrote to Karl Heinz to tell him what I was doing until he got back and he liked the idea, writing back that every cent helps. I also got letters from San Francisco asking how we were doing and asking if I needed help. I also received one of those "mea culpa" letters from Michael but I wrote back to say he should stop feeling that way, that for whatever reason it was just not meant to be; but that wasn't really what I thought sometimes.

I really liked working again but I noticed I must have changed a bit since there were situations which I handled differently now, though most likely I would have done them the same way as my coworkers before I left. Time went by quickly and Karl Heinz wrote that he would be back at the beginning of December. I really felt good knowing my whole family would be together for Christmas and we would bring my grandmother over for Christmas Eve. There would be a lot of talk between Karl Heinz and me over what our plans for the future would be but one thing I knew for sure was that somehow I had to get a driver's license; something I'd wanted to do for quite a while already.

Karl Heinz arrived at the beginning of December and we decided that after Christmas we'd have to stay in my parents' apartment. It would be a little crowded but Karl Heinz' mother's apartment was even smaller. Then, in January, we'd know what business we'd do and could look for a larger apartment and eventually get my grandmother to us.

We had a nice, quiet, Christmas: my grandmother was there as well and my mother-in-law stopped by so we were really a family again and even Karl Heinz liked it. And so, the old year passed and we had to look at what we wanted to do. Michael wished me Merry Christmas and asked me to give my grandmother a hug from him. I had the feeling he really missed having a big family since he'd never really had one growing up. He and his family, Cassandra and Bianca, flew to Mexico so Bianca was able to be with her biological mother, Juana, and I really gave him credit for doing that; whatever he did with his affairs, he was there for his little family.

In January, we went to a little newspaper store in which Karl Heinz was interested, but it was no longer available, so we used our savings to buy a used but very good condition, Volkswagen, called a Beetle. Volkswagen was a major German automobile manufacturer with its head-quarters in Wolfsburg and was founded by the German government in 1937 as a low-priced "People's Car." As Karl Heinz still had a connection with his former working place where he'd worked as a car mechanic, we had a great deal. We were so proud and there was my wish again—I had to have that driver's license.

When we picked up the car there were still two of Karl Heinz' previous coworkers from his apprentice days there and we told them our story about looking for a small business. One of them told Karl Heinz he knew of a small service station with a tiny repair place attached where they also sold tires and other automobile equipment. The only problem was that it was close to the West Berlin/East Germany border, but the area was very pretty with lots of greenery and trees and also a fish pond, so we thanked them and drove off to have a look at it.

The direction we went looked familiar to me and I realised we were going in the direction of Complex Wannsee, which was one of Michael's and my favourite places. The service station was pretty close to Complex Wannsee, but I had to get used to that since it was my past and now we were looking for our future. We found the service station, which looked nice and clean and as we needed gasoline for our car anyway, we drove in and waited for someone who would fill up our car. At that time, you weren't allowed to do it yourself.

An elderly man came out and filled up our car, cleaned our windows and checked the oil and the air in the tires. It was really good service but it was all about getting a tip. Karl Heinz asked him if he was the owner and he said, no, the owner was the service company and he was just leasing it. He said he wanted to quit because his health was failing and Karl Heinz asked him for the address of the company so we could go and talk to them about leasing the place. He grinned at me, saying that now I'd have to learn all about servicing a car and that if he was busy with other things I'd have to fill up cars. I looked at him and asked, "What about Grandmother if I have to work here all day?" He said, "Just to help me get started, then we can hire a full-time car mechanic."

That was actually not what I expected, but just to help get started, it was fine. I had ideas, of course: only in the summer time, we could get some tables outside and serve coffee or sodas and snacks; I always liked decorating. We went home and told my parents about it and they thought it was a good idea, because my mother could take care of Thomas and my father said my grandmother would still be okay because they visited her often; that as soon as the business was running, I could stay home and then we could take in my grandmother. But, of course, we had to talk to the company first to see how much money we would need for the lease.

Now that we had our little Volkswagen, it was easier to get around and as we had the address for the headquarters of the service company, we went there to find out more about leasing that place. We only hoped the cost wouldn't be too high as we needed some money left for decorating. We told the girl behind the desk what we wanted and asked to talk to the manager for more details and she knew right away which service company it was. I didn't know if that was a good sign or a bad one but the boss or manager asked us in and was very friendly when he knew what we wanted to talk about.

There was a deposit to make and a monthly lease plus a certain percentage of the profit we made. Well, the lease was fine but we would have struggled with the deposit, which he understood, and he offered to take out a certain amount every month for the deposit, until the deposit was paid in full. We agreed to it but he told us, "You know, the location is not the best because of the Glienicker Bruecke (Glienocker Bridge)." We knew the bridge and the story about it, it is the bridge over the River Havel connecting the district of Wannsee (West Berlin) with Potsdam, the capital of the State of Brandenburg (East Germany). After the war, the bridge was used several times as an exchange place for captured agents and Western spies and it was closed for civilians. A movie was even filmed about that bridge, called the *Bridge of Spies*, filmed by Steven Spielberg.

The boss smiled and told us he would draw up the lease papers to sign and patted our shoulders and said, "That is what that station needs, young and energetic people." While we were leaving, he told us that sometimes Russian Officers came over from Potsdam because they were allowed to use the bridge with their vehicles to have their cars filled up and also to have some repairs made, and that that was good money because the station was the first one as you entered West Berlin and was close to the bridge. We were really excited about it and were ready to do our best to make it a showcase. Even my father liked it and told us he would come and help us over the weekend. We went back and signed the papers and could start on April 1st.

In the meantime, Horst wrote to Karl Heinz saying the offer to build that apartment on Maui had fallen through. I had to laugh, telling Karl Heinz that I knew it would, but Horst wrote that he and Lani would move to Maui anyway as it was still laid back and prices were a lot cheaper than in Honolulu, and he would tell Karl Heinz as soon as something new came up, so that he could return. If I had known what was in that letter, I most likely would have hidden it.

Slowly, we started to prepare for the opening, buying a few tables to set up, since we were entering the summer months and would have treats, coffee, and maybe ice cream. It was exciting. I wrote news about everything to San Francisco and actually forgot if I told them about the car in the excitement, so I did it again. I got a little package back from Michael pretty fast and when I opened it, I had to laugh: there was a little toy Mercedes Benz in there with a little sticker attached, "Is that going to be your next car?" That was Michael—always funny; that's what I liked about him. He was on his way to a convention AGAIN.

We were getting really busy and there wasn't too much time left until April 1st. We wanted to make it really special and get signs made, saying "Under New Management." "First Day 10 Percent Off if you fill your car," things like that. It wasn't the German way but we'd seen it in Canada and Hawaii and liked it and it really was fun doing it—also not really that expensive and my father helped us over the weekends. Being busy like that, we didn't pay too much attention to the erection of the wall and we had to laugh about starting our new adventure on April 1st, April Fool's Day, the only day in the year when people liked to play tricks; may be it would bring us luck. Karl Heinz showed me how to clean the car windows and also use the pump to fill up cars. He also tried to show me how to measure the air in the tires and check the oil, which wasn't too hard to learn. Only that measurement, I never really learned.

The first day was actually very good and we had a lot of people coming to check us out and buy some gas. They didn't fill up their cars but that wasn't too bad as we saved the 10 percent. As it was a Sunday, my father was able to come with us to help. We decided to try to open from 8 A.M. to 5 P.M. on Sundays only, and the rest of the days were to be from 7 A.M. to 7 P.M. We knew we couldn't do it for a long time, just the two of us, and we had to hire another helper who would come at noon so that I could leave, but for the first four weeks we tried to do it by ourselves. My father was responsible for the coffee and some treats and I guessed he was pretty proud of us as he did everything with a smile. I was also sitting in the little office and was collecting the money and after closing up that first day we realised we wouldn't make it alone and needed a helper. Karl Heinz found a young car mechanic he knew from way back when he was still in school; he was very nice and a good worker, so at least I could leave to go home at noon. It wasn't an easy job but we made a pretty good profit.

I then saw my chance to get my drivers' license and when I talked to Karl Heinz about it he just grinned and said, "I was waiting for that." He promised to talk to a driving school so that I could take driving lessons. We were also looking for a larger apartment so that if everything ran smoothly, I would be able to stay home and we could take my grandmother with us. What was also really great was that now everyone was speaking German, Thomas started to talk.

I felt like telling Michael and Janet how everything was going and I told Michael I was going to get my driver's license because he'd known for the longest time that that was my wish. Some days I felt I could talk with him for hours and that letter belonged to one of those days. Karl Heinz found a driving school and I started my driving lessons with a driving instructor. It was a good thing those cars had two brakes and two steering wheels, so that the instructor was able to intervene right away if the student did something wrong. He had to do it a few times with me driving but he was always calm and friendly; maybe he took some numbing drops before getting in the car.

I had to take 18 hours of driving and then he felt I was ready to take the test. Before I got to the office to fill out the papers, I took two Valerian pills. We were about 12 mostly young people there to take the written test and I sat there so calm that I couldn't remember a lot of questions. Anyway, I failed the written test and wasn't allowed to take the driving test. I was so embarrassed but the instructor just laughed and said, "You weren't the only one." I had to take five more driving lessons and do the test again and that time I didn't take the Valerian pills and I passed. I was so proud but I didn't tell people I'd failed the first try.

Michael wrote back saying he was so happy for me and that he still missed me, but I knew that already. My mother-in-law told us Brigitta was pregnant and the baby would be due the next May and wanted to know if we might go along to visit her in Eltham.

Seeing Brigitta the next year wasn't a bad idea but we had just started our business and even though we were doing quite well, there were so many other things to take care of. Surprisingly, the building of the wall didn't affect us too much—maybe because we had the feeling we were used to it as we'd always been caged in; it really had already been like that for a long time.

We met another young couple who lived across from our service station, Helga and Thomas, who owned a towing truck business and also had a son, Werner, the same age as our Thomas, so those two became playmates. Thomas had a contract with the county of West Berlin to pick up accident damaged cars or ones which were too old to be repaired and as Karl Heinz was able to repair some of them, we found one, another Volkswagen, which was still able to be repaired if you knew how to do it and as Karl Heinz knew how, he fixed it and painted it and it looked really good and became MY car. I was so proud that I had to tell Janet and Michael. Those two became my diaries again.

We also found a larger apartment but there was a waiting period of six months, which was fine with us. Some days I felt I could show Michael what we'd achieved: we had two cars now, not the newest, at least not mine, but I could drive and I found out I loved to drive. I worked only half a day and did the book-keeping at home. Michael wrote back and was amazed at what we'd done. He asked me many questions and I was surprised what he remembered about our being together, sometimes remembering things I had already forgotten. There was still that bond between us but my marriage was fine, though I wasn't so sure about his.

One day a huge car came into our service station and we knew right away who it was, that it must be the Soviet Officer from Potsdam trying to fill up his car as the manager from the leasing company had told us. The driver jumped out and was trying to clean the windows, but Karl Heinz was faster to do it. When the officer came out to pay, he gave a big tip to Karl Heinz and said, "Coca-Cola," those were the only words spoken because of the language problems. He wanted to pay for the drinks, too, but we said, "nyet" (no). I knew a few words of Russian because I'd learned Russian in school for six months before I gave it up; it's a very hard language to learn, or at least it was for me. The officer said, "Danke" (Thank you)—he most likely knew more German words than we did Russian ones, and we were very sure they would come back.

We reached the end of the year and were looking for Christmas decorations because we wanted it to look very nice and we were right—that officer came back and brought us two more customers, also officers from Potsdam, and all of them wanted Coca-Cola, all for free, but it was worth it for what they bought from us. Shortly before Christmas the first officer who came need some oil to be changed in his car and while he was waiting, his driver came over to me with a little bag. He opened it and in it were coffee beans. He said, "Kofe" (Coffee) and his face looked so happy that he could give me a Christmas present. He must have thought we couldn't buy coffee in West Berlin. I could have given him a hug for that but I didn't know if the officer knew about it, so I didn't, but I never forgot his happy face and his sparkling eyes even though we never ground the beans.

We had a nice Christmas and received lovely letters from San Francisco. Michael even sent greetings to Karl Heinz and it made me happy that both of them realised it was the past and accepted it. That New Year, 1963, was approaching but nothing changed with the wall and people still tried to cross the border—they tried climbing over it or even dug tunnels, but not as many as before. We realised that the people from the Eastern side became different; it looked as if they were accepting two Germanies. Since we were allowed to leave West Berlin, even we had to stay on the autobahn and weren't able to leave it—also, flying at a lower altitude, we were getting used to it.

If everything went well, we might be able to fly to Eltham to see Brigitta and help her when the baby arrived. Also, we might be able to put our Thomas into kindergarten, so the future looked great and if we could get the larger apartment, we could have my grandmother with us. Sometimes I wondered if Karl Heinz was happy or if he would rather be in Hawaii building houses, but he didn't mention anything. We had word from Horst and Lani that they had moved to Maui and that it was a lot nicer than Honolulu and that although construction was picking up slowly, there was still a lot more Aloha spirit than in Honolulu. I watched Karl Heinz while he was reading the letter and I thought his eyes were distant.

Janet wrote that she was pregnant again and was hoping for a little girl but also said she was worried about Michael, who was living the high life. She said he still did everything for Bianca, who would be almost ten years old already, and that Cassandra sometimes had too much to drink.

We discussed the London flight with Karl Heinz' mother and she convinced us to go with her. My mother would take care of Thomas and our two helpers could handle the work for a few days. I really wanted to go. I'd heard London was a very interesting city and I started to read about England. I knew about their famous fish and chips and their afternoon tea, but there were also other famous dishes like Beef Wellington and Shepherd's Pie, for people who liked lamb, which I did although I very seldom got to eat it. "Well," I told Karl Heinz, "okay, we can go. I know what to order." Karl Heinz warned me that we'd have to watch out as vehicles drove on the left side of the road, but we didn't expect to drive there anyway. I was really looking forward to going and I was smiling, since I most likely would then have seen and travelled more than Michael—and I was the one who'd admired him because he'd already travelled from the United States to Europe.

Once in a while we heard from Horst, Karl Heinz' brother, who was back in Columbus, Ohio, and who had become an American citizen, of which he was very proud. Sometimes I wondered whatever had happened to Rita and Jonathan; they simply disappeared.

Everything went smoothly with the service station and the officers from Potsdam came on a regular basis, which really helped as we were also able to do little repairs on their limousines, so we decided to do the visit to Brigitta in England. The months passed and it was already summer and my mother-in-law went to the travel agent to make the booking for us to go away for a week in June. I wrote to Janet and Michael about our trip to London and how excited I was and Janet wrote back saying she'd lost the baby and was very sad; I could really understand her feelings. Michael was joking and calling me a world traveller but he seemed in a good mood. The sentence at the bottom hardly ever failed—"There are days I really miss you"—so I joked back that he would stop missing me when I was old with grey hair and lots of wrinkles on my face.

We got everything ready for the flight and called a taxi to take us to Tegel airport for the flight to London's Heathrow Airport. It was a full flight again and we had pretty bad turbulence so we hardly noticed the lower altitude the pilot had to fly and there was also no other plane guiding us. It was amazing how big that airport was and the stewardess told us it had started operation in 1946, right after the end of the war.

Brigitta's husband, Kenny, picked us up. I had to admit he looked really young compared to Brigitta and I also had problems understanding him since he spoke Cockney English which is a dialect of the English language, mostly spoken by working class Londoners from London's East side. It was about 25 miles to Eltham and it felt scary driving on the left side of the road; as much as I loved driving, I would have been too scared to drive there. Brigitta was so happy to see us and to finally show us her little baby boy, Andrew, and we had the famous English Fish and Chips supper, which they had bought before. It was very delicious and after dinner Karl Heinz looked at me grinning and told me, "Now she has two sons." He didn't agree with her marrying a much younger man.

We made plans to see some of the tourist attractions and they suggested a visit to Madame Tussauds Wax Museum, which was opened in 1835 and by then was almost 130 years old. It sounded very interesting so we decided to go and when we got there it was amazing to see the life-sized figures of the Royal Family, Presidents, and celebrities from the movie industry and sport; they all looked so real. My head was spinning from all that excitement so we took a day of rest and just stayed home and then the next day we went to see Big Ben, the great clock at the end of the Westminster Palace, which had been completed in 1859 and was 96 meters or 315 feet high. Kenny was working as a tour guide so knew a lot about the history, and he told us all about it. We only had three days left and we decided to go out for supper one evening and that that would be enough for the first visit because we were sure we'd go back again since we could stay with Brigitta and didn't need a hotel. Going back to caged in Berlin we found quite a change between Berlin and London, since there was no sign of a war in London.

It was nice to be back home again but I'd found out I enjoyed travelling. We got word our larger apartment was almost ready for us to move in, which meant we could have grandmother with us and also that I wouldn't have to go and work at the service station, which in a way I would miss as we met some quite interesting people. There was an opera singer who came quite regularly and he always sang a song for us, and of course the officers from Potsdam, though none ever brought me coffee beans again. I asked my mother if she would be able to come perhaps two or three times a week in the morning to watch my grandmother since Thomas was going to kindergarten till noon and I would come home at noon, which mean I could be at the service station and be the cashier, and that was agreed on.

The apartment was really nice and big and had three bedrooms so my grandmother had her own room, Thomas had his, and we had ours and we even had a little balcony. It worked out pretty well and the day we took my grandmother "HOME," she had her sparkling eyes again. My mother did a great job watching my grandmother until I got home. We also had a phone connection in that apartment and one day my father visited us and had to make a phone call to West Germany. After dialling the number and when someone answered, my father started to scream into that phone. When I asked him why he was talking so loudly, he just looked at me and said, "Well, it was so far away, I just wanted to make sure that person understood me." I never forgot that proud face about the long-distance call since if he used the phone, he only called West Berlin.

One afternoon, when I hadn't heard from them for a while, I wrote a letter to Michael telling him we had my grandmother staying with us and I got a letter back really soon saying he found it so great that we had my grandmother with us. He said he had problems with his wife, who was suffering from depression and was under a doctor's care; it sounded as if he was a bit worried. Sometimes I watched my grandmother and she was just staring into the air, which worried me a bit and my mother spoke to our doctor, asking if he could come over and check her out. When he came he said she might have had a little stroke and he could see some signs of dementia but there was nothing really that could be done, so he just gave us some pills to make her feel good. I felt sad but at least she was with us and not with strange people.

I still enjoyed the hours at the service station and we became kind of friends with the family that owned the towing truck company and sometimes invited each other for dinner at home, so it was like a competition between her and me as to who was the better cook. My parents came over to watch my grandmother and Thomas when we went to their house for dinner and I guess she was a better cook that I was; she was very ambitious and very pretty.

So, the days went by and we were preparing for the end of 1963. My grandmother had changed a little bit and I was scared to leave her alone even for a few minutes so after getting her and Thomas to bed I was just sitting and waiting for Karl Heinz to come home. Some evenings it was a bit late and there was the smell of alcohol on him and although I didn't say anything, I was worried he might have an accident.

Nothing really changed with the wall and I sometimes wondered if it would stay like that for the rest of our lives. My father mentioned that he might retire the following year since there was no chance of getting our property in East Germany back and no chance of building his dream house there. I didn't know why he told us this but had the terrible feeling he might leave Berlin and move to Southern Germany, since he loved the mountains and loved to walk in the woods for hours. I didn't say anything and just waited to see what would happen to my grandmother and if he would really retire, because he still had two years to work if he wanted to.

I mentioned it to Karl Heinz but I had the feeling he wasn't really listening to what I had to say. I was also worried about him coming home late and I asked him one day why it was. He just replied, "Oh, Helga and Thomas come over and we have some beer together." I didn't really like it but he worked hard all day, so he was just relaxing, which was fine, though that drinking and driving scared me.

I started to get ready to send Christmas cards, including to San Francisco, but I decided just to send cards and no presents as I couldn't think of anything special for them. I just used Michael as my diary again and told him some of my news, including about my grandmother being ill and my parents maybe leaving Berlin for Southern Germany, but I didn't really have the Christmas spirit that year. I received nice Christmas cards from Janet and Michael and he asked me if everything was alright as he felt my letter was emotional.

It was sad to see how my grandmother was changing; she was sleeping a lot but she wasn't in any pain. We closed the service station for the Christmas days so we were planning a quiet family Christmas with my mother coming over to cook our Christmas dinner, and my mother-in-law also wanted to come. One evening before Christmas Eve, I was waiting again for Karl Heinz and it was already getting late so I called the service station but there was no answer. It really worried me so I called Helga and Thomas' house and when Thomas answered I told him that I'd called the service station. He couldn't understand and just said that Helga was over there, that she went there quite often, but he wanted to check. An hour later Karl Heinz came home but we didn't talk about it as I didn't feel like arguing, even though it reminded me a lot of Michael and Elena. I tried to make it a nice Christmas for my family and nobody noticed the tension between Karl Heinz and me.

We started the New Year quietly and I hoped everything would be fine. Horst and Lani wrote that they loved Maui and that Horst was trying to get new jobs lined up and would then call on Karl Heinz. For the first time I thought about the Islands again: if my parents moved to West Germany and my grandmother passed away, I would actually have no one left in Berlin and, yes, Helga would still be having beer at the service station. It was a very short thought and I was surprised at myself: how could I leave Berlin again? But it was just a dream.

My grandmother took a turn for the worse and slowly she became bedridden. One morning when I went to her room, she wasn't in her bed and I almost panicked as I knew she wasn't able to leave the apartment by herself. I called Karl Heinz and we found her sleeping under the bed. When I called the doctor and told him what had happened, he said, "Yes, it's going to be hard, but her heart is still strong." She'd been there for me and now I had to be there for her. I now had a good reason to stop those cooking competitions with Helga. We never talked about that evening and I never asked.

My father came up with the idea that in the summer time he wanted to take some vacation, maybe for three weeks, and do a bus tour looking for bed-and-breakfasts in one of those little villages in Southern Germany to check out if they would like it there. He was thinking of the Berchtesgaden area where there were a lot of very pretty little alpine villages. He said he'd seen pictures, just like I had when I moved. The area was located at the southern edge of Germany, also close to the border with Austria. Looking at him, I realised he was quite serious about it. That was the first time I actually noticed the effects of the wall because my father was now ready to leave Berlin. Although he would have loved to build his dream house, he'd lost everything he'd worked for all his life: a nice retirement and his own house. I hated the war.

I wasn't able to go to the service station as often as I wanted but sometimes my mother came over and stayed with my grandmother so that I could go there for a few hours. Then we reached the spring and the first Lilies of the Valley were popping out of the ground and pretty soon the lilac trees started to bloom, and a lot of memories came back again.

Grandmother wasn't doing well at all and didn't recognise me anymore, calling me "Schwester" (Nurse). I had to feed her but she hardly ate and kept on telling me her husband was visiting her almost every night. She was so skinny; her weight wasn't more than 60 pounds. One morning I noticed black spots on her body and when I called the doctor, he said those spots come out shortly before you pass away, in other words: she was dying. He said she now needed special care and he would send her to the hospital right away. I said I didn't want her to go to the hospital so the doctor said, "Then I have to send you to the hospital," but I didn't know why he said that. When the ambulance came to pick her up, I had to take my car as they wouldn't let me sit in the ambulance with her and at the hospital the nurses were not very friendly and told me, "You are just bringing her here to die." The only thing I could tell them was that the doctor arranged that, not me, and that night she passed away.

Even though I was very sad, in a way I was happy to have been able to take care of her until the last hours of her life. While she was still partly healthy, I asked her why she liked me so much, why we had such a strong bond but she only smiled with sparkling eyes, "It was the love of my life." Since she didn't say more, I didn't know what she meant, I just guessed it but I never told anyone about that.

With my grandmother gone, I had to look for a full-time job or go back to the service station so had to talk that over with Karl Heinz. I wrote to Michael about my grandmother's passing and he wrote right back, giving me his phone number and saying I could call him any time I wanted or needed help. It was nice of him but there would be no sense in doing it; it would create problems.

Karl Heinz and I talked about it and decided the best way would be for me to go back to my old job full time and then go to the service station to help out on the weekends. I realised it was our seventh year of marriage and a saying in Germany says the seventh is the most critical year for a marriage. One evening my parents came over and wanted to tell us their plans but first my father gave me some money my grandmother had saved and which he felt I should have, since I'd taken care of her until she died. They were planning to take the tour to Southern

Germany for three weeks and asked us if maybe we could go along for a few days. That sounded great as Thomas would be on summer vacation from school and we could take him along and I had the money from my grandmother to pay for it. And we were a family again. I talked it over with Karl Heinz and he agreed and my parents were really happy that we could make it for a few days. We planned it for July and my parents found a little village and made reservations for them for three weeks and us for a week.

They left about a week before us and when we left West Berlin to enter East Germany's Autobahn, it was kind of scary for me. The checkpoint was full of people and the control by the East German police was pretty strong. Even though we were all Germans, we had the feeling we were entering a different country with people who spoke the same language but were different. When we entered the Autobahn we didn't look left or right and kept to the speed limit as there were a lot of police on the roadside watching the traffic, and after a few hours of slow driving we reached the border where we left East Germany and entered West Germany. We were very relieved that we were now on our way to Munich.

I remembered being in Munich years ago with the children from our church who we took to that farm for a vacation. When we passed Munich and as it was a clear day, we could see the Bavarian Alps in the far distance and they looked beautiful. We then had to drive another hour to reach the village where my parents were staying right in the middle of the Bavarian Alps pretty close to the famous Berchtesgaden, sometimes called the romantic corner of Germany. It had become really famous during the war as Hitler's Eagles Nest, standing on the top of the Kehlstein above the Obersalzberg, when it was only used by Hitler and his Nazi Party.

It was a beautiful area in the winter and also in the summer and the specialty of the Bavarian houses was that they were mostly older by that time but decorated in the summer with flowers hanging from windows around the house. My father had picked a nice place and we had a wonderful week with my parents and took tours almost every day. My father really liked the area and I had the feeling they would eventually move there.

Well, the week was soon over and we were heading back to caged in Berlin. Now you could definitely see the difference between West Germany and caged in Berlin. I had the feeling Karl Heinz wasn't really happy with our service station and most likely was waiting for Horst to tell us to go back to the Islands. I wrote to Janet and Michael about our trip, since I'd bought some souvenirs, like postcards and magnets with "I love Bavaria" on them, and then I tried to get a job back with my old company. Somehow that trip changed my feelings for Berlin and my love for Berlin was not as it had been.

I went back to talk to my boss from the compensation company and he was sad to say that at that moment there was nothing really open and that I should check back with him in a few months. I was a bit disappointed but I had the service station to go back to even though, of course, it was only half a day. I found myself thinking more and more about the Islands: maybe it hadn't been so bad but with me being so homesick, I'd seen everything black even though we had a good time over there. I didn't say anything to Karl Heinz about it, deciding to wait to see what Horst would come up with. If everything went well with new jobs on Maui, we would earn money and could come on vacation back to Berlin or to Bavaria where my parents would most likely live and also my parents could come over and visit us. My brain started to think the opposite way now and it felt strange.

One evening my parents came over and gave me a letter, which was addressed to them, but the sender was Rita who was writing not from the States but from West Germany. I was really happy to hear from her. She asked my parents for my address, since she didn't know where I really was—in the States or in Berlin—and I wrote back right away giving her my address and our phone number. It took a little while until the phone rang and then we were on the phone and we cried hearing each other's voices. We took a long time talking but there was so much more to say that we made plans for her to fly over to Berlin and I said she could stay with us. She only asked if it was safe to come to Berlin and I could tell her that we lived like the people in West Germany, except we had a wall build around us, like an enclave. When I told Karl Heinz about it, I thought he really didn't like the idea too much and I said, "Remember, it's the past." She set a date and I told her I would pick her up from the airport as I had my car, which was getting kind of old as well. I was stopped by a police officer once because my exhaust pipe was kind of loud and he told me not to drive by the cemetery, otherwise I would wake up the dead.

It was so nice to see Rita and she looked nice but I could see she wasn't really happy. At home, she stayed in my grandmother's room and she told me her grandmother had passed away as well. She told me how Jonathan changed being back in the States, that he couldn't find a steady job and they moved from town to town in Florida and that his relatives didn't care for her at all—yes, they thought of her as a German Frae-ulein. He met his old friends again and he was hardly home at night, mostly out drinking with them in bars. She stood by him as long as she could until she couldn't handle it anymore, and then she left him. Who would have thought Jonathan, who was always so nice and helpful, would turn out that way.

I asked Rita if she would like to move back to Berlin but she was happy in West Germany, where right now she was living with relatives but was looking for her own apartment and a job. She said maybe I should go to West Germany as well as there was no future in West Berlin and maybe the wall be would there for years or even forever. We also talked about the past and Michael and she said, "Maybe you shouldn't have been so harsh, you would have a good life in San Francisco," and I had no answer for that. After three weeks, she left and I really missed her.

My mother-in-law told us Horst would come and visit in the Fall and we were all looking forward to that. He looked great when we picked him up at the airport but I guessed he was happy to be back in Berlin. He told us he'd most likely get married the next year to Jennifer and he showed us a picture of her: she looked great and also came from Columbus, Ohio. Her parents were sort of well off and he had started to go to the University to study Business and Communication. He asked us what we wanted to do besides the service station and I could see Karl Heinz was kind of embarrassed: maybe he didn't like being a car mechanic anymore. Horst said he should go back to the States, that there were a lot of opportunities and if he needed a sponsor, he could count on Horst. I looked at him since he acted high-nosed and he saw that and said, "Yes, I made it." I thought Karl Heinz was hurt; he was his little brother and he'd achieved so much already, and it was partly my fault too, since I was so stubborn about coming back to Berlin. Maybe I should have been more understanding about going back to the Islands but I couldn't imagine living in the Islands for the rest of my life and so far there was no news from Horst about new jobs on Maui.

Well, we passed the year and my father decided that since there was no sign of taking the wall down and reuniting East and West, he would most likely leave in 1967, which meant he would still work two more years to receive his full pension, One evening, Karl Heinz and I were talking and I asked him what we would do if Horst asked for him on Maui. He didn't say a word but I told him that as soon as my parents were leaving for Bavaria, we could go too, and I never saw him look happier than at that moment. It felt good: we had a plan again for our future and when we told my parents about that, they somehow felt good too. My father told us they were planning to go there again this summer to have a look around and asked if we could go as well, and I agreed since I liked that little corner of the world. I told Janet and Michael about our plans of going back to the States and they thought it was a great idea and his letters were still the same as ten years ago. And he was right, we'd never lose our bond, even thought he was now in his mid-30s.

We looked forward to our mini vacation in Bavaria in July and even our Thomas was glad we were going, even though it took almost eight hours to drive there. We noticed that the control by the East German police was even stronger than the last year and we had to get out of the car while everything was searched, but we still had the same happy feeling being in West Germany after crossing the border.

We stayed in the same bed-and-breakfast place as the year before and they also had a son just a little older than Thomas. They told us that this time we definitely had to go and visit Salzburg in Austria, which was the birthplace of Wolfgang Amadeus Mozart, the most famous musical composer of all time. You could even visit the place where he was born in 1750, located in the famous shopping street Getreidegasse. That sounded so interesting that we decided to take a bus tour while my parents stayed back and just took walks in the woods and little forests.

We booked a tour bus to Salzburg and were amazed by the beauty of the city. Our tour guide was very knowledgeable about the history of Salzburg and we even visited Mozart's birth house. I noticed the furniture that was still in there—of course it was very old and you weren't allowed to touch, but things were so small and even the beds were kind of short, so people must have been short as well. The guide told us that Salzburg is divided into two—the old Salzburg and the new Salzburg, divided by the River Salzach. It's an amazing city as Austria is famous for castles. We were taken to a restaurant for lunch and, actually, in Austria and Germany as well, lunch is the main meal of the day and in the evening you only eat sandwiches. We had a delicious Wiener Schnitzel, which is a thin, breaded, deep fried piece of veal. The tour guide said, "Gruess Gott," meaning "May God greet you," and expected a tip, and he was really worth a good tip as he did such a good job. We all had an Austrian white dry wine and we really enjoyed the day. The tour took almost a whole day and we were tired when we got back.

That week went by too fast and then we had to drive back to Berlin, where there was a letter from Horst telling Karl Heinz they would go back to Honolulu for a year or so, since he had an offer to build two single houses. After that he said they would go back to Maui and since there would most likely be a good opportunity for them to build an office building, he most likely would want Karl Heinz back in 1967. I could see how happy Karl Heinz was and for the first time, I was looking forward to that, too.

The year 1965 was coming to an end and we talked everything over with my parents. My father was planning to leave in 1967 and since they'd become good friends with the bed-and-breakfast couple, they told them that they would look for a nice apartment for my parents when they were ready to move there. Even I was happy for my parents. It was sad that we would be so far apart but they would be happier in a free area where they could walk and weren't caged in.

Our plan then was to cancel the lease of the service station the following year but we had to check with Horst how everything was going on Maui and how long it might take. He wrote back very quickly saying he would be ready to start in 1967 or 1968 as he was starting his own company but everything worked slower in the Islands, at least at that time. That was perfect as it even meant we were able to help my parents to move.

At the beginning of 1966 we went to the service station officer and spoke to the same manager who did all the paperwork for us when we started. He understood and accepted our cancellation but told us it might take a while since they'd have to find someone else to take over, but we still had time. He laughed and said, "I would leave in a minute if I had the chance to work in the Islands," and Karl Heinz was happier than before which made everything easier.

I wrote to San Francisco about our plan and they liked it a lot. Michael wrote to me that he had problems with Juana because she wanted to come back to the U.S., most likely to be closer to Bianca even though she'd signed all her rights over to Michael. He sounded frustrated and a bit scared and in a way I felt sorry for him but there was nothing I could do to help him.

I worked at the service station full time now and Thomas went to my parents after school, which worked out fine, and after about seven months the service station manager showed up one day with a young couple who were interested in leasing the service station. It was a little earlier than we expected but we would have to think of something else. In the fall of that year, the deal was finished and we left the station and—one good thing—we got our deposit back, which was a nice help, but we still had to work until next year. One of Karl Heinz' friends told him there was a small company which was selling car tires from West Berlin to Great Britain and that the owner was looking for a salesman who could speak English, so he went and talked to the owner. Karl Heinz was a good salesman; I thought he could sell freezers to Eskimos. He had to do the ordering and the boss told him he might have to fly to London on special orders. That was something for my husband and would hold us over until Horst was ready on Maui but I also had to find a job and there were still no openings at my old job.

However, my old boss told me he had heard that the West Berlin Court House was looking for secretaries and that I should try there. I wasn't so sure I'd be good enough to do that kind of a job but I wanted to try. When I got there, I was scared and everyone was rushing around in a very impersonal atmosphere, but I was called into a room to do a test and then a not-so-friendly looking employee asked a few questions about what I'd done so far. Because I was able to write shorthand and also spoke English, that helped me to get the job and that unfriendly looking employee became somewhat friendlier after learning that I'd lived in the Islands for a while. The pay was pretty good and there was a trial period of three months, which would take me to the end of 1966, which looked perfect.

Karl Heinz liked his job and he was only waiting for a special order for tires, so he could fly to London. My job was kind of interesting as well as sometimes I had the opportunity to sit in the courtroom taking notes while the judge was listening to the lawyers and their clients, but that wasn't very often and mostly there was just office work. The three-month trial period passed, so I could have worked there until retirement, but I didn't tell any of them what my intentions were.

Christmas was coming but we didn't have any plans and for my parents and us this would be the last Christmas together for a long time. With my full-time job, I sent Christmas cards a little late to San Francisco but theirs came right on time. They were doing fine except that Michael had a hard time with Juana and he wrote that he would most likely have to go to court as he had the feeling she came to get more money. Cassandra was still under doctors' care and he still had to go to conventions.

My parents were ready to leave in the summer but the way things looked we wouldn't be able to go with them to Bavaria because of our jobs. The bed-and-breakfast people were starting to look for a nice apartment in that little village and my parents started to get ready to move. It was a sad time for us as everything became so final, but Karl Heinz got to fly to London because of a special order. He contacted his brother Horst in Columbus and told him about it and also that we might need him as a sponsor since we were going back to the Islands.

I could see how good he felt telling Horst that; it must have bothered him a lot.

He received a letter from Horst saying he might be ready with his company and the offer for the office building by Fall and he would then send Karl Heinz a job offer, which he would need for the immigration office to get a visa for us and also a sponsor, who had to be an American citizen. We started a busy time and there was another problem in that Thomas now only spoke German and we hoped he would adjust and not stop talking at all like last time, but he was older now and could understand what our plan was. There were some nights I had to take those Valerian pills because I knew this time I wouldn't be coming back in four years and maybe I would never come back to Berlin as my parents wouldn't be there either. Yes, I prayed often, mostly to my grandmother who I missed a lot; she was an amazing woman.

My father retired in Spring of 1967 and was preparing to leave in the summer. He went to see a lawyer to make his last Will, just in case the wall came down one day and there was a united Germany again, in which case I would inherit the property we had in East Germany, and the lawyer gave me a copy, saying, "Miracles do happen."

The months went by quickly and the summer was there and my parents' furniture was all packed up and ready to go to a nice apartment which the bed-and-breakfast people had found for them, just a few houses away from them. Thomas and I took them to the bus as Karl Heinz was in London, and it was one of the hardest days of my life. I promised them I'd go and visit them as soon as possible and, like always, they didn't turn around—just boarded the bus and off they went leaving me feeling alone in the world again. I hated saying farewell to anyone, it might have been a flashback from the war after saying goodbye to people and never seeing them come back. But I still had my son to take care of.

If I'd been able to call San Francisco, I would have done it that day but it wasn't possible from our phone as if you wanted to call the U.S., you had to go to the post office and sign in with the number you wanted to call and then wait until a line was available for you, and sometimes you waited for a long time. I'd never tried it but had been told by people who had. But I did sit down and write a letter to them, just like talking, and I felt better.

It was bad for Thomas as well as he had to use that after-school programme and then either Karl Heinz or I picked him up after work. The next day my father called and told me everything had gone well and the furniture was coming a day later and that they could then move into their apartment. We were now waiting for a letter from Horst about the job offer so we could go to the Embassy and apply for a Working Visa and then contact his brother to be our Sponsor. Meanwhile, Michael wrote back a lovely letter saying there was a reason for everything and even if it didn't make sense at all, it was nice to read. I got letters from my parents and sometimes a phone call and they were happy there, which in turn made me happy. My plan was still to take them over one day, maybe just for a long vacation. Then, in October, Horst's letter with the job offer came and in a way I was happy to leave, since there was really nobody left there anymore.

After receiving the job offer and a lawyer-signed sponsor from Horst and his fiancée and her parents, we went to the Consulate to apply for the visa. We were very thankful to Horst's future in-laws for their help. We were told it might not take too long to get the papers together and that they would contact us. We tried to find a student to teach Thomas the basics of the English language, but it wasn't easy, and just to be really sure that everything would work out with the visas, we didn't yet ask for a termination of our jobs. It was close to Christmas and we didn't believe we would leave in 1967 but there was nothing we could do except wait, and Christmas and New Year wasn't one of the happiest. I spoke to my parents who seemed to really like their move to Bavaria. My father loved his daily walks but the sad news was that he was diagnosed as being diabetic, so they had to change his lifestyle and watch their diet.

I received a nice Christmas card from San Francisco and a picture of Michael and Bianca. She was a beauty and actually both of them looked just great. Maybe one day I would meet Bianca, since Michael always told me we would see each other again.

Anyway, we made it through the holidays and at the end of January

1968 we received a letter from the Consulate arranging an interview. We were asked if we needed an interpreter but we told them we'd lived in the Islands before for a little while. I noticed that whenever we mentioned the Islands a smile came up on their faces; maybe they were touched by the Aloha spirit. It was a very short interview and everything was in order and we got our visa put into our passports.

I was happy and sad at the same time as now we had to make f travel arrangements, but first we had to cancel our jobs. They weren't that enthused about us leaving at such short notice but, even though we were wrong, they accepted it after we told them where we were going, and they smiled again—it must have been the Aloha spirit.

We found a one-way flight from Berlin Tegel via London to John F. Kennedy Airport in New York but we had to stay overnight in New York and then fly the next day via Los Angeles to Honolulu, after which a 45-minute flight would take us to Maui. It took almost all our savings but Karl Heinz could start working right away and I was going to Look for a job right away as well. So, it was farewell to Berlin again and an emotional time again taking off from Tegel Airport, when I looked out of our window and saw the wall and wondered if I ever came back to Berlin again, whether I would still see the wall or not.

When we were approaching landing at New York airport, I showed Thomas the Statue of Liberty and also all the high-rises, which we hadn't had in Berlin at that time. He was fascinated but his English still wasn't good enough to understand and read everything. After clearing customs, we took a taxi to our hotel and while we were waiting, Thomas told me he couldn't believe how big the cars were here compared to our little Volkswagen Beetle. We went into a little diner next to the hotel and he had his first hamburger. He was too small to remember the time when we went back to Berlin from Honolulu. Being back in the States again felt strange, maybe Karl Heinz and I were both overwhelmed and also somehow scared.

The next morning, we boarded the flight to Honolulu with a stopover in Los Angeles. Thomas couldn't believe how warm it was because we'd left Berlin in the wintertime. It was already getting dark when we left Honolulu for Maui and I was looking forward to seeing Maui because everyone was so excited about it. When the plane was getting ready to land and I looked out of the window, I saw houses but only about eight or nine were lit up and the rest were dark, and then the pilot came on saying "Aloha" and "Welcome to Maui's Kahului Airport."

The airport was pretty small and it was built around a huge palm tree. It sure looked quite tropical but in a way beautiful. Horst and Lani picked us up and we were able to stay a few days in their apartment until we could find a cottage. It was really laid back and not at all like buzzing

Honolulu. Horst told us not to stay in Wailuku, which is the capital of Maui, but instead to move up-country, as they called it, as it was cheaper and was mostly farmland located at the bottom of Haleakala. Haleakala, a dormant volcano, is an active volcano which is not erupting. There was also a catholic school for Thomas there, so that was what we did and we found a little furnished two-bedroom cottage for a reasonable price, with the post office and little local food stores all within walking distance.

We then had to look for a car, since Karl Heinz had to drive to work in Wailuku, which was about a 30-minute drive, and that meant I had to walk around that little cowboy town. Horst saw that Thomas had to go to school and there was no school bus service at that time, so he offered to lend Karl Heinz the money for a used car and said he could pay it back later. We were a little disappointed as we'd believed Karl Heinz would be his partner, but he was just a carpenter.

As soon as I could, I wrote a letter to my parents and, of course, to San Francisco, giving my new address and saying we were fine. Karl Heinz found a used car, so at least I could get around: I had to go and register Thomas for school and was also thinking of looking for a job for myself. We had very nice neighbours, an elderly couple, and the lady told me it was hard to find a job there. She said there were some Haoles living there; there was that word again, so I reacted quickly and told her I was a German Haole, to which she smiled and said, "I thought so," though I never found out why she thought so. Anyway, she said they were always looking for cleaning girls and that a little further up there was an expensive boarding school where rich people sent their children and that they were also looking for kitchen helpers and cleaners. Well, it would be a start.

Just like last time, I was pretty homesick again and I really didn't know if I was homesick because of Berlin or my parents, or both, but I found myself watching planes taking off from Kahului airport. It was time to register Thomas for the school, which was run by nuns, though there were a few local teachers as well. The first day I took him to school, he had a Japanese lady as his teacher and he stood there not really understanding what was going on. They set him back a year and said when he caught up, they would put him back into the class he belonged in. When I left the school and went home, I sat there for a while crying; I felt so sorry for him and he looked so alone. When Karl Heinz came home, he asked how his day had been but I didn't know, since he hadn't said anything.

Karl Heinz and I had a long talk that night and I told him I would go to the expensive boarding school and try to find out if there were any openings for me. It looked as if the school had an after-school programme, which might be good for Thomas as he could play with other children until we picked him up. When I collected him from school the next day, he was very quiet and just asked me, "What is a Haole?" I tried to explain to him that it means someone coming from another country, like we came from Germany, and he kind of smiled and said, "I thought it was something bad." It somehow helped him to know what it meant.

I went to that boarding school and talked to the Director and asked if there were any job openings and he explained to me that at the moment there were no kitchen jobs available but that if I wanted, I could have a job as a house cleaner for some of the teachers as there were four little cottages where the teachers were staying. I accepted, of course, and the Director promised me that as soon as there was an opening in the kitchen, I would get it. I used San Francisco as a diary again but didn't tell them where I was working; I just wrote about the beauty of Maui, and I did the same thing with my parents.

I checked with the teachers how Thomas was doing and they were very amazed at how well he was talking English. It seemed they had somehow forgotten mathematics as he was very bad with numbers but when I told them that, one of the nuns said they were concentrating on English first, and she was right. My cleaning job wasn't bad since I had experience from Vancouver so knew the tricks of the trade pretty well and because I was working, my homesickness was getting better. Then, one day, Thomas came home from school saying he wasn't talking German anymore, just English, and after telling me that, I knew he was okay. Karl Heinz told him he could speak whatever he wanted outside but that at home we would speak only German and he didn't speak to us for two days until he needed some money and we weren't answering him, when he gave up and spoke German with us again.

I got a letter from Michael from London—he was there on vacation with Bianca and a business associate and I was very sure it wasn't a male associate, and he said he loved London. His famous last words at the bottom of the letter were "I do miss you sometimes." It was over fifteen years since we met and we were still in contact and I sometimes wondered if he was still the same or had changed.

That year went by quickly. My parents were fine and my father loved where they were. There was no sign of taking down the Berlin Wall; it was now seven years since it had been erected. Thomas found new friends and seemed to be happy, which I was so thankful for.

Christmas and the New Year were quiet. Horst and Lani had so many relatives on the island that they were busy and there really weren't any other friends—and we were still missing the Christmas spirit as we celebrated in warm temperatures under palm trees. Even though I wasn't able to swim and was scared of the ocean, we decided to go to the beach as Thomas loved to play in the sand and around that time there were already tourists with children, so he was kept busy. Maui was already an insider tip because it wasn't crowded like Honolulu and had the most wonderful beaches. I thought of my parents and how nice it would be to bring them over and how much they would enjoy that, but at the moment it wasn't possible. It was the first Christmas I didn't hear from San Francisco. I wouldn't say I was sad but something was missing and I wondered if there was a reason for it.

So we started the new year and when I got to work in January, the director told me there was a job opening in the kitchen because one of the girls was pregnant and was going to take a year off, and he asked if I was interested. That was great and I most happily took the job. The best thing was that we could take the leftover food home and there was always leftover food since the cooks always cooked more than the students could eat because everyone wanted to take food home. It was a nice crowd; they were all friendly and helpful, of course I was that German Haole, I was okay.

Whenever I went to our local Japanese bank to deposit Karl Heinz' paycheck into our account, the bank Manager waved at me and was very friendly and one day he asked me to go over into his office. I wondered what he wanted and he said, "You are German, right? What kind of a job is your husband doing?" I told him he was a carpenter and that I worked in the kitchen at the boarding school. Then he said, "You know, my wife is German, too. I met her when I was stationed in West Germany after the war." Then he continued, asking me if we would be interested in having our own house. I was so amazed and said, "Of course, but we don't have enough money," and he just said, "Next time, bring your husband too, maybe we can help you." I was really happy and told Karl Heinz about it. He couldn't believe it but he could do most of the work himself and I could help him.

Karl Heinz and I talked it over and I made an appointment with the bank manager. He was very helpful but we had no down payment, so he told us if we could just put down what we had saved so far, he would accept that and give us a loan to buy the property and later a mortgage to build the house. We couldn't believe it; it was like a miracle for us. I told the director what had happened and he could understand, so I quit in the summer. When I told my parents about it, they really loved the idea and were so proud of us.

Michael and Janet had written a letter to say they were really sorry but Michael's wife had tried to commit suicide and it was a hard time for all of them. Michael's letter was sad and mad at the same time but she survived and nobody really knew what to do. Michael was scared to file for divorce because of her condition but it was mostly his fault anyway, so I just wrote back that it was his decision what to do. I also wrote to Michael about the house building and he said he felt so bad about Cassandra and would change his behaviour.

We found a nice little lot big enough to build a middle-sized house on and we tried to do as much as we could ourselves but it was hard on Karl Heinz and Horst told him he should stop working for him until the house was finished and then he could go back. We had the mortgage so we could live on it too as we didn't hire any labourers except where we had to, like plumbers and electricians, and that was a great saving. The house was almost up when I realised I wasn't feeling that great but I blamed it on the hard work I'd been doing.

I didn't tell Karl Heinz about it but it worried me a bit. I knew I had no health insurance through my kitchen work and I wasn't sure whether Karl Heinz had health insurance; we'd never been to see a doctor while we were on Maui, so it had never bothered me.

I was working quite hard: I was treating lumber for the house with some liquid against termites and for that I had to carry the lumber around and it was kind of heavy. Sometimes my whole body was aching but it really was fun seeing the walls go up and knowing it was our house. Sometimes we hired one or two helpers over the weekends to give us a push forward and even our banker came up one weekend to look at the house and take pictures and he was amazed at how far along we already were, although he did tell me I shouldn't work so hard as I didn't look quite well.

We hoped that by Fall we could be ready to move in, as providing we had electricity and water, we could finish things like painting and wallpaper-hanging while already living in the house, as well as finishing some of the work and laying tiles or linoleum. I was so proud of my first house and hoped maybe my parents could come over on a long vacation. I felt better for a little while but then I started to vomit and my abdomen started to hurt but I knew I wasn't pregnant as my monthly cycle was normal.

I told Karl Heinz what was happening and also asked about the insurance, and he was very sure that Horst had paid the basics for us and wouldn't have cancelled it as he would be going back after the house was finished. Well, there was a German doctor in Wailuku so I made an appointment and he checked me out and when I told him the symptoms, he told me I wasn't pregnant. He then went out of the room and was talking to his nurse and I overheard the word "cancer." When he came back in again he said he would have to make some tests and that I should make an appointment in two weeks; I was kind of nervous about that word "cancer."

When I got home, I told Karl Heinz what the doctor had said and he, too, was afraid, and over the next few days my abdomen pain got worse and I had problems walking straight. One morning I woke up with very bad pain and I was also bleeding but Karl Heinz had already taken Thomas to school and gone straight to the house. I felt like fainting and wasn't able to drive so I more or less crawled to our neighbours and they said I looked as white as a sheet. The lady said she'd take me to the hospital right away and tell my husband later.

She took me to the emergency room and then after checking me over, the emergency doctor told me I most likely had an ectopic pregnancy, which means the foetus develops outside the uterus, usually in the fallopian tube. In my case, it was on the right side but the tube had already burst and most likely I was in the third month of pregnancy. Because I'd lost a lot of blood and some was in the abdomen, he said they would have to operate right away so my neighbour said she would tell Karl Heinz what was happening. I was hardly aware of anything except that the doctor said, "We cannot operate right away, she needs a blood transfusion first."

I didn't remember much about that day only that in the evening Karl Heinz was by my bed; he was very worried and told me after talking to the doctor that they would operate later after I had enough blood again. He then left and I must have fallen asleep and when I woke up, a priest was standing by my bed and praying. I only remember thinking one thing—that I was being punished for something and now I had to die. The nurse then came in and wheeled me into the operating room and there was that huge light above my head; someone gave me a shot and that was the last thing I remembered. When I woke up, I guess a few hours later, the doctor and a nurse were standing by my bed and he said, "Welcome back. It wasn't easy, but you'll be fine." So, I realised, I didn't die.

I really didn't remember what had happened over the last few hours but the doctor sat down and tried to explain about ectopic pregnancy and the statistics which show that one in 100 women will have one because the tubes are blocked for whatever reason. He also said that they had almost lost me, which sounded really scary, but he assured me that I would be fine and would just have to take iron pills because I'd lost a lot of blood. I asked the doctor if it could happen on the other side as well and he answered that he'd never heard of that and didn't think it would happen. He said I had to stay in the hospital for a week and not do any heavy work for a while, which wasn't such good news since I had to finish a lot of work inside the house.

Karl Heinz came in the afternoon, looking tired and stressed out and his eyes were kind of reddish. "All that matters," he said, "is that you are alive." We were in the house and the hardest work had been done so now we could go slowly and he decided to go back to work and do the inside work on our house in the evening and over the weekends. After a week I was allowed home. I felt fine, just tired, but I came home to our own house. The girls who worked in the kitchen with me came over almost every second day and brought food; that was the ALOHA spirit. I intended to go back to the kitchen in three months, shortly before Christmas, and when I talked with my doctor, he said that would be alright.

I wrote a letter to my parents and told them what had happened but not really how serious it was, and of course, I wrote a letter to Janet and Michael. It was an emotional letter to Michael because we'd been through something like that together years before. Otherwise, I really enjoyed being a so-called housewife, doing the cooking and taking care of the house. We were a real little family and I thought Karl Heinz liked it too. We started to make plans, not for this year's Christmas, but for 1970 to 1971 when if the house was ready and we had money left over from the mortgage, maybe we could afford to fly over to Bavaria to spend Christmas there. I'd heard about a club called the German Club, which had contacts with Charter Flights to Germany which were pretty affordable, so that would be nice.

I received a letter back from Michael and the way he reacted to what I'd told him, I felt there was still a kind of bond between us. He told me about Cassandra and him, saying they were trying to save their marriage and seeing Therapists and he seemed to have matured more since her suicide attempt. I kept that letter. It was special and I read it more than once.

At the end of November, I went back to the kitchen job. I was really looking forward to it, since I wasn't used to just staying at home and also we had our leftover food again, which helped a lot. That year Horst and Lani had a big Christmas party and we were invited; it was a typical Hawaiian thing at the beach with Hawaiian songs and food. I noticed that Horst and Lani were different to how they'd been in Honolulu; they hardly talked to each other and Lani had a little too much to drink and was flirting and dancing. Later, Karl Heinz told me that Horst had mentioned to him that there were some problems because of her drinking, which was too bad as I'd thought they were the perfect couple.

I knew my kitchen job would finish in the summer, since the girl who took a year off because of her pregnancy would return, and I was wondering where my next job would be.

We were at the beginning of 1970 and sure hoped for a better year than the last one but we were doing quite well with the inside work of our house. The living room was done; we just had to lay the carpet and I was really proud of our OWN house, even though Karl Heinz used to joke that it still belonged mostly to the bank, but I knew he was proud too. Thomas caught up pretty well in school and was put back into the class in which he belonged, and I was still hoping we could make it to Bavaria to see my parents at Christmas. The school director told me that when the other lady came back in the summer, I could still go and clean the cottages if I wanted to and I thought if there was nothing else, I could do that as it wasn't hard work and I liked the teachers; they all came from England and I loved their dialect.

So far everything was going well but I sometimes noticed I had backpain and some cramps, though I didn't pay too much attention to it since the doctor had said everything was fine and an ectopic pregnancy doesn't happen twice, and also my menstrual cycle was in order.

I didn't tell Karl Heinz anything and even though I was sure it wasn't anything serious, I was a bit worried because the symptoms were almost the same as the last time. I decided to wait a bit longer and that if I did see a doctor again, I would go to the one who did my operation and not the German one who started treating me as if I had cancer.

But it didn't get better; I would say it was getting worse, and I then had to tell Karl Heinz. He couldn't believe it after what the doctor had told him, too. Surely it couldn't happen again. Well, it was the beginning of March and finally I decided to see the doctor again as I knew something wasn't right. This time we went straight to the hospital and asked for that doctor and luckily, he was on duty and not very busy but when he saw us coming his face got quite serious. He asked us into his office and I had to tell him what was happening and after listening for a while, he told us to come back to his private practice in a few days for a check-up, but he looked worried.

I had to admit, I wasn't feeling that great either, but I was still hoping it wasn't what I thought it could be, because if it was, then I wouldn't be able to have any more children at all and I was still hoping we would have another one. A few days later, his nurse called me and we made an appointment for the next day and, yes, I was very scared about what we would find out. After a few tests he said, "I have to put you into hospital for more tests and then we'll know more," and that's all he said, but by now I was almost sure I had another tubal pregnancy and the next day Karl Heinz took me to the hospital. I felt so empty and couldn't concentrate on anything.

The next day I was put under sedation and they started with some kind of test and in the afternoon the doctor came and sat down by my bed. I saw that he had a hard time telling me that I had another tubal pregnancy on the left side and that there was no choice but to operate before it burst like the last time. I felt empty inside and couldn't even cry. He saw that and told me, "Think about it. You have a son, who needs you, and there is always the option of an adoption." I felt there must be a reason why I was being punished like that. Maybe I shouldn't have met Michael, I didn't know. Karl Heinz came that evening. It was an emotional one but he also mentioned adoption. The operation was set for the next day because they didn't want to wait any longer as I was around nine weeks pregnant and there was the risk it might burst.

Like the last time, they put me under sedation and when I woke up, the doctor was there and told me that everything had gone well and I would be fine and only had to be in the hospital for four days. He said, "And after you've recovered, we'll talk about adoption if you're interested." Karl Heinz came that night and we were both completely stressed out and after telling him what the doctor had said about adoption, Karl Heinz said, "You have to recover first before we talk about that."

I left the hospital after four days, physically okay but mentally a mess, and we decided I would stay home for a while to recover, which the director of the school understood. We decided to stay in touch as I liked that kitchen job and had made a few nice friends. I wrote to my parents about what had happened and also told Michael. My mother was very sad and I remembered that she'd mentioned something to me years ago after I lost the first baby, saying she knew how I felt, though that was all that was said, so something must have happened to her as well. Every day I thought about adoption. I knew it wasn't easy if you had to go through an agency, that you had to have a certain amount of money, take on a lawyer and go to court to have everything legalised. Michael wrote back and his letter was so lovely. I'd told him about a possible adoption and he asked if I needed money but I wrote back that we were doing fine. I kept that letter, too.

It was the beginning of May when our phone rang and it was my doctor asking me how I was doing. I told him I was getting better and for a moment there was silence before he said, "I have a little girl who is looking for a big brother." I thought I wasn't hearing right. He said she was born a little premature but not by much, and had to stay in the hospital for a few days. I could hardly say a word but managed, "Yes, she will be my daughter. When can we see her?" The doctor said, "Talk it over with your husband and we'll talk tomorrow."

When Karl Heinz came home I was laughing and told him, "Today you became the father of a little girl." He looked at me kind of amazed and then I told him about the doctor's call. "Let's sit down," he said, "I have to tell you something. First, I think it is too soon and that you're not yet strong enough for a newborn. Secondly, I was thinking: how about selling this house? Real estate prices went up sharply and we can pay back the loan and the mortgage and still have money left over for another lot without borrowing money. We could use our own money and would only need money for the mortgage." I was silent for a moment but then I thought the idea wasn't too bad and, of course, I was thinking about the adoption. I looked at Karl Heinz and said, "If we try to sell the house, then we go ahead with the adoption." I couldn't see what his real thoughts were but he grinned and said, "Yes, maybe the doctor's idea wasn't bad." Yes, Karl Heinz was a very good salesman.

When the doctor called the next day, I said, "Yes, it is a go," and asked what we had to do. He said his lawyer would handle everything but that we would need to pay the lawyer, the court, and the hospital bill for the little girl and her biological mother. I didn't ask him how much it would be and just hoped the savings we had would be enough. When Karl Heinz came home that night, I told him what had happened and also told him to wait a little longer with the sale of the house until the adoption was legalised and the little girl was home. He agreed to that and then we were just waiting for the doctor to call.

The doctor called the next day and told me we had an appointment with the lawyer the following day to sign the papers to get the adoption rolling and that it would take about a week before we could take her home. I couldn't believe how lucky we were and asked the doctor about the money we'd need. He said that when we picked her up from the hospital we would have to pay the hospital and the doctor's bills but that the lawyer and the court bills would come later; the court hearing would be in about four weeks and then we'd get that bill. He mentioned the approximate amount for the hospital and we had that, but we would have some problems with the rest of the money, although I knew we would make it.

I called the doctor back and asked him when we could see her and there were a few seconds of silence before he said that children who are being adopted are in a special department of the hospital for security reasons. I found that a bit strange but I was so set on that little girl that

I brushed it off. The next day we went to sign the papers at the lawyer's office and passed by the hospital and I looked over and thought, *Somewhere in there is my daughter.* I had no idea what she looked like but it didn't bother me, she could even have been really ugly and it wouldn't have bothered me.

We signed the papers and paid the hospital bill to the lawyer and the lawyer told us he would give us a call to let us know when to pick her up and that we should buy some baby clothes and a little pram to put her into. The lawyer then said that for security reasons, we should pick her up there in his office, which sounded a bit strange, but maybe it was a different process there on Maui. We then sat down and looked for a little girl's name. There were so many options but we decided on Angela since she was like a little angel to us, and I then went and bought the prettiest little clothes for her and a really cute little pram. We also went to a real estate agent and put our house up for sale. We never even put carpet in the living room, I'd just painted it over, and it really hurt a bit to be selling our house so fast, but it was for a good reason.

After about a week, the lawyer's office called and told us we could pick up our little girl the next day. I was overwhelmed and nervous as well and Karl Heinz couldn't come with me because he had to work, so I decided to take Thomas with me to see his little sister for the first time. When we got there with the clothes and the pram, we saw her and she was beautiful, with big brown eyes. She was still wearing her hospital gown and I had tears rolling down my face. The name we gave her was perfect for her: Angela. After we'd dressed her and put her in her new pram, the lawyer took some pictures and although Thomas seemed a little confused, he, too, looked happy. I thanked the lawyer and he told me he would let me know about the court hearing and would give me the pictures then. At home, Karl Heinz was already waiting for us and when he saw her, I think he had tears in his eyes. That day was very special for us and although I would have less sleep than before, I loved it.

It sure was a change of lifestyle, but it was a beautiful change. I wrote to my parents about how happy we were and also to San Francisco. Michael was really happy for me and he wrote a sentence, "U felt sad." He wrote that he would have liked to have more children too, but that most likely it wouldn't happen. Bianca was a full-blown teenager already and more interested in young men than in her father; I thought he sounded a bit jealous.

Sometimes I thought about caged-in Berlin where people were still living behind the wall and nothing had really changed. It was now already ten years since the wall was erected and now hardly anyone even thought about it. I had my little family and I was happy and Maui became more my second homeland, though Berlin would always be first because there were so many memories, both good and bad ones.

After a month we had the court hearing. The judge was very nice and friendly and when he asked me when we got married, I couldn't remember. I was so nervous and scared the judge would deny the adoption, but he started to laugh and I did then remember when we got married. Horst knew we were selling our house, so with his help we paid our bill and everything was over. Even so, whenever we went shopping and had Angela with us in her little stroller, I tried to hide her because I was afraid someone would recognise her and take her away: we were living on an island with a small population and a lot of people were related or were friends and might know about the adoption.

The pictures the lawyer had taken of Angela were so pretty that I sent one to my parents—her GRANDPARENTS—and also one to Janet and Michael. My parents loved that picture and you could read between the lines how much they wanted to see her. Michael wrote back that she was going to be a beauty and some more compliments; yes, charming Michael. Then it was Fall already and Angela started to crawl; she was a handful.

Karl Heinz and I talked it over and decided that after we sold the house, we would buy another lot and build a slightly larger house on it and eventually start our own building company, as Maui had started to boom. I found out I'd started to like house painting and wallpaper hanging and decorating a house. We received two offers for our house shortly before Christmas but, talking it over, we decided we didn't want to fly to Bavaria during the wintertime as it would be too cold for the children. However, we accepted the offer: it was a pretty good price we got for it and we paid back the bank loan and the mortgage and the banker was very happy and told us that any time we were ready to build the next house, just to go on in.

Now we had to look for a rental house as our plan was to fly to Bavaria in the spring to visit my parents. I couldn't believe it, everything was so perfect, and we found a nice rental house and then joined the German Club because of the affordable charter flights to Germany.

It was the first Christmas for our little family and we had a lot of fun playing with the children; I loved watching their sparkling eyes. The rental house we were in was quite nice but I somehow missed having my OWN house, though I knew we'd have another nice OWN house.

I wrote Christmas cards to san Francisco and told them we'd sold our house and would most likely see my parents in Bavaria in the spring. Janet really liked the idea and told me they were thinking about adoption, too, and she also wrote that Michael wasn't happy in his marriage and she had the feeling that he'd found someone else and it looked serious. I knew something like that would happen and in a way I felt maybe what had happened between us with our breakup had saved me a lot of stress and sadness, because I was quite sure he would have treated me the same way as he did Cassandra.

Through the German Club, we found an affordable charter flight to Munich and would then have to either rent a car or take the train to that little village. We had put money in the bank to buy a lot after we returned from Germany, so thought maybe we could afford to rent a car instead of using the train. We booked the flight for April for three weeks: that was all we could afford, but we'd be able to spend Easter together since Easter was in the middle of April.

Everybody was excited and Angela took her first steps and started to walk while we were on the plane. It was a long flight and we were happy when we landed in Munich. For the first time we used our "Green Card" at customs—the Green Card meant we were permanent residents of the United States and we'd applied for that card when we went back to Maui, so it had taken us over a year to get it.

We rented a VW Beetle again and I noticed that Thomas wasn't so happy about it, but it was big enough for us. When we arrived in that little village, I had the feeling the whole neighbourhood was waiting for us. I was so happy to see my parents; they looked great and my father had lost some weight because he'd had to because of his diabetes. Of course, the centre of attention was Angela and now she realised she could walk, she was all over everywhere. Even though we were very tired and also had the twelve-hour time difference, we had a hard time falling asleep.

It was nice to be back in Germany. My father was crazy about his granddaughter and tried to carry her all around. I noticed she wasn't really eating well, which worried me a bit, but when I talked to my mother about it, she only laughed and said, "Don't worry. Your father is always giving her treats, like cookies and chocolate, no wonder she's never hungry at dinner time." We had a nice Easter and the weather was perfect for egg hunting; we had a great time. Time went by quickly and my parents told us they had saved some money and were thinking of maybe coming to visit us. I couldn't believe that—my parents and flying—but it was a very good idea and they wanted to come at the end of summer, which also meant they could watch the children and Karl Heinz and I could start the next house. We talked it over and it was agreed that they would apply for a visa right after we left. I couldn't believe how brave they were taking that long flight, but I was very happy.

Saying goodbye that time wasn't that bad, since we knew we'd see each other again pretty soon. It was sad that we had to leave when the trees were starting to bloom and people were starting to decorate their houses, but I was sure we'd be back again. In a way I felt sad not seeing Berlin again, but there was really no reason that time, especially as my mother-in-law was constantly travelling between Eltham and Berlin as there was always something going wrong with Brigitta—though she mostly needed money and my mother-in-law always helped with whatever Brigitta always needed.

Well, we were glad when we landed back at Kahului Airport after the long flight and I felt as if I was home. It took a few days to get organised again and then we started to look for another lot and we found a few nice ones, but prices were really going up fast. We took one of the less expensive ones since somehow I knew it wouldn't be our last OWN home.

My parents wrote that they'd applied for their Visa and that it might take a few months, so they hoped to be on Maui around the end of September or beginning of October. Meanwhile, West Germany's economy was picking up nicely and people started to travel again, and that included West Berlin as well. Only East Germany and East Berlin weren't doing that great and they were getting frustrated but there was still no sign of reuniting since there were in fact really two separate Germanys.

Karl Heinz and I talked about opening a construction company, for which you needed to have a contractor licence. You could build a house as owner/builder but for buying and selling real estate, you had to have a licence and that meant Karl Heinz would have to take a course and pay a licence fee, which would "make him legal," as they used to say. Since we had the property already, we went to our banker and discussed our situation and he gave us a mortgage to build the next house and said he thought the idea of Karl Heinz taking that course was a good one.

Michael wrote a letter asking me how Germany had been and what our plans were. I told him what we wanted to do and in his return letter he said that was great—we could erect the houses and his company would sell them for us. I had to smile about that—he was still the old Michael but he sounded happier ... but there was still a lovely sentence at the bottom of the letter.

Angela became the cutest little toddler and I was so proud when people turned around and looked at her and smiled and I showed her how to wave at them. Karl Heinz applied for that contractor's licence and had to fill out a lot of papers and the fee wasn't cheap either, but we had to do it. It wasn't easy for him and I couldn't help him; I was not a carpenter but while he was doing that, I did the paperwork for the county, like getting permits for all kinds of things, water meters, grading permits, electricity poles: there was always something to pay for. After making all the payments to the Contractor Licence Board, he was able to start the course: he could study at home and when he felt he was ready, he could go and take the test. It took him a while and he was pretty stressed out but eventually he felt he was ready to do the test and the day he went to the Board to do it, we were pretty nervous. I had to pray and I prayed to my grandmother; she would understand. In the afternoon, he came home smiling and holding a bottle of champagne; I knew he'd made it.

He told me he'd barely made it as it was quite tough, but we were legal now. I got a letter from my parents saying everything was fine with the Visa and they'd be here by the beginning of October and would stay six months, so I was looking forward to a wonderful Christmas season. I wrote telling them not to bring too many warm clothes because even though they knew Christmas would be warm, I didn't know if they believed me; most likely not.

I was so worried about my parents on such a long flight, starting in Munich and going via Philadelphia to Los Angeles and then on to Honolulu and Maui. One evening I told Karl Heinz about my worries and asked him for a favour: if he would fly to Los Angeles and meet them there, maybe stay a night in Los Angeles and then fly with them to Maui. I knew he loved flying and thought he might do it and when he agreed, I wrote to my parents telling them what we were planning to do. I got a big thank-you letter back, I guess they were relieved, too.

We started with the preparation work on the lot so that when my parents arrived we could start building. Time went by quickly and it was time for Karl Heinz to leave for Los Angeles to meet my parents. Everything went fine and he picked them up and they stayed in a hotel overnight and then flew to Maui. That evening I sat down and told Janet and Michael my parents were coming; I just had to tell them, they were my closest friends even though we never talked or saw each other. There were many times I wanted to dial his number but couldn't: maybe I was afraid he had changed and then I would have lost my dream about him.

The next day, I went with the children to pick them up from the airport and my heart jumped for joy when I saw them. I looked at my father and got scared, though, because he was as red as a tomato and sweating and looked as if he was running a high fever. I asked Karl Heinz if he was okay and he grinned and said, "If I was wearing long sleeved underwear and long pants and a pullover under a coat, I would look like him too." So, I knew he hadn't believed me when I said it was warm here even in the winter. I was relieved and asked my mother if she could convince him to take those warm clothes off, but he realised it was really warm and changed his clothes by himself.

Everything was different for them but they started to like it; at least my mother did. My father enjoyed working on the property, he carried the lumber around and we both treated the lumber with that termite stuff and it was fun working with him. One Sunday, we decided to go to the beach. My parents had never seen an ocean and the idea of swimming in the winter was completely impossible, so I enjoyed watching them. They were like little children playing in the water and I even caught my father looking at pretty girls in their bathing suits.

There was only one thing I didn't like: my father sometimes had red eyes and when I told my mother about it, she just mentioned that it might have something to do with his diabetes. Some evenings he had a few shots of vodka and as far as I knew, being a diabetic, you're not supposed to drink alcohol, but I didn't say anything and didn't want to spoil his fun.

Christmas was approaching and I decided to make it really special. We bought a beautiful tree and decorated it nicely and also put little lights up all around the house. Angela would enjoy this Christmas more; the last one she was too small to remember.

I received a Christmas letter from Michael with a picture of him and a very pretty lady, I guessed at least 15 years younger than him, telling me he had filed for divorce from Cassandra and that Aimi, the girl next to him, would be his wife. He went from one extreme to the next—an older woman to a much younger woman. I showed the picture to my mother and while looking at me, she said, "I knew you would never really get over him." I guess she was right. On Christmas Eve, we went to church and the priest greeted my parents in broken German; my parents felt so special and so proud.

We had a lovely Christmas with my mother cooking German food, and we also had a nice New Year's Eve trying that lead dropping to SEE into the future, but we couldn't find lead metal to buy so we tried it with candle wax—it wasn't the real thing so whatever we could make out was fake. Then we were in 1972 already and we were doing really well with the construction of the house. This time Karl Heinz hired two carpenter helpers because my father and I couldn't handle those heavy lumber pieces. Because we were now legal, we had to do a payroll but since I'd done bookkeeping in Germany it wasn't that hard and was quite easy for me to figure out and what I didn't know, I asked our banker about and he helped me.

The house was up and ready for the outside to be painted and as I really loved painting, I told Karl Heinz I was going to do it. He wasn't sure if I would be able to but agreed and we bought the paint and rollers and brushes and I started. I really enjoyed it and people walking by couldn't believe seeing me on top of a ladder and painting. The talk of the town was the "German lady," the painter, and now my nickname was German Lady and not German Haole any more. I eventually spoke to Karl Heinz because doing the bookkeeping and painting the house was a bit too much. As I'd rather paint than do the bookkeeping, I spoke to my banker friend and he brought us a bookkeeper who would do it for us as it wasn't a lot of work with only two employees.

My father started with the yardwork and he really enjoyed that, but his red eyes worried me. I told my mother he should see a doctor as he'd also begun being tired, but she said he'd never go and see a doctor because he couldn't speak English. Even though I offered to go with him, he still wouldn't go. They were leaving in April and it was March already, so my mother promised me he would go to the doctor as soon as they were back in Bavaria.

The house was painted outside and I was kind of proud and I then wanted to start on the inside, which was a little trickier than the outside. I really wanted to buy a camera now so that we could take pictures and, yes, it had something to do with San Francisco: I wanted to show off what I could do—I could paint houses.

The sad day came when my parents had to leave and I took them to the airport. They were planning to do the same trip again the next year: they would come in the Fall and stay six months over the winter months. They walked out to the plane—at that time there was no walk-way onto the plane, but the plane was parked on the tarmac and you had to climb up the stairs to get on board. I watched them go up the stairs and on top, before entering the plane, my father turned around and waved at us. I wasn't used to that; no one who left ever turned around. He then went into the plane and they took off and there I was, again, feeling all alone in the world.

I so hoped everything would go well because I was worried about my father and I gave them our phone number so that they could give us a call. I knew the bed-and-breakfast people had a phone and maybe there would be a chance to call us so that we knew everything was fine; if not, then they could call from the post office. After three days I got a call in the middle of the night from the post office and I spoke with my mother, who said they were fine but very tired. My mother said they would call from a private phone but would first have to register and wait until a line was available.

Our house felt empty and I was only helping with the inside painting when Angela was sleeping. I thought a lot about Michael's future wife, Aimi, these days: since she was young, they could have children and Bianca was almost ready for University. I thought Michael would like that and he was young enough to become a father—he was only a little over 40. I had to stop those thoughts; he had his life and I had mine.

I received a letter from my parents to say my father wasn't feeling well and the doctor had ordered him to the hospital to check him out and he would have to have insulin injections because his blood sugar was too high. Now my mother found out why his eyes were so red—he'd run low on his medication, so first he halved his pills and then they were gone too and he was out of medication for days. When he got back to Germany, he ate all the food he didn't get on Maui, along with some beer. So, she wrote, she would let us know. I was still worried but knew that being in the hospital he was under good care.

About a week later, we received a call in the middle of the night and I knew immediately that something was terribly wrong. When I answered the phone, my mother was crying and saying that my father had passed away; she was calling from the bed-and-breakfast people's phone.

I told her not to do anything and that I would go right away and try to get a flight out the next day; that I would call when I landed in Munich. I was numb but the next morning I went to the travel agency in town to try to get a flight out that day. It was May 14th, 1972. There was one available which was very expensive since it was such short notice, but I had to take it.

When I was in town, I sent a telegram to San Francisco telling them what had happened and that I was leaving for Munich that night and I gave them my parents' address and the bed-and-breakfast people's phone number. I then went home and packed a few things. Karl Heinz wasn't able to come with me because of work and the children. I wished I had a few Valerian pills, but they weren't available on Maui.

I got on the plane like a Zombie and only hoped Karl Heinz would be able to handle everything at home with the job and the children as I didn't expect to be back within three weeks. I guess I was sitting in first or business class, because the stewardess came and offered wine and although I really didn't care much for wine, I took a glass and was pondering what to do with my mother. I wasn't going to put her into a seniors' home, since I remembered my grandmother being alone in one after my grandfather had passed away. She had nobody in Bavaria and I couldn't send her back to Berlin either, since her family lived in East Berlin or East Germany and she couldn't visit them either. At that time the husband was the man of the house and she had been quite dependent on him, especially financially as he took care of everything which had to be paid. Women at that time were just housewives. There were exceptions, of course, but the majority of German women didn't own a car and she had no driver's licence. All those thoughts ran through my mind and so far I could see only one option: that my mother had to live with us.

I knew I did the wrong thing by telling Michael what happened and giving him the phone number but when I received the news about my father's death, Michael came into my mind as he belonged to my family at that time and had to be told what had happened. With all those thoughts, time went by quickly and a few glasses of wine helped me to fall asleep.

We had a stopover in Philadelphia and while waiting for the next plane to Munich, I remembered that a cousin of mine was living there; she'd married an American soldier and after her father passed away, she had taken her mother over there to Philadelphia. I would have to get in touch with her and find out what to do, but I knew now that my mother would come to us. I knew I had to convince Karl Heinz but I was very sure he would agree since it would mean I was able to work in the construction company while my mother took care of the house and children.

I was feeling more relaxed and after landing in Munich, the bed-and-breakfast people were there to pick me up. They told me they had had a call from America, that a "Michael" had called asking for me. They had a hard time understanding him since he couldn't speak German, but they were able to talk a few words of English and he left a number for me to call him. I explained that he was a good friend of mine and that I would call him the next day. The lady then said my mother was pretty depressed and was having a hard time coping with things.

When my mother saw me, she cried: she looked so tired and exhausted and I told her I would stay as long as she needed me, that we would talk about it after the funeral. I explained the situation to the breakfast people and asked if I could use their phone the next evening to call America and the lady was very friendly and said it was now a lot easier to call overseas and that sometimes the wait was only for an hour.

My mother felt better and we started to talk about the funeral and making all the preparations; even though I was so tired, I had to help her. I told my mother we had to go to the post office first thing in the morning to send Karl Heinz a telegram to say I'd arrived. He had the phone number for the breakfast people and maybe he could try to call. I had to talk to them the next day to ask if I could use their phone while I was there and I also needed to ask them for their names.

My mother made some soup and I ate some but almost fell asleep at the table, so we went to bed and I slept in my father's bed next to my mother, like a child, holding hands.

I must have slept as if I was in a coma and the next morning my mother had breakfast ready and then we had to start with our preparations. While we had breakfast, I told her our plan, and I already included Karl Heinz, and I saw her smiling while tears ran down her face. I didn't even have to ask her if she would do it; I could see on her face that she was happy and she said, "Oh, like Maria—she went to America after her husband died." I knew she meant my cousin in Philadelphia and I just said, "Yes, like her."

The first thing we did was to go to the post office and send a telegram to Karl Heinz telling him I'd arrived safely and I also told him my decision about my mother and asked him to think about it as she couldn't be left by herself. Then we had to go to the mortuary to get a coffin; it was a very hard thing to do and that was enough for the first day, so in the afternoon we went over to see the bed-and-breakfast people and started to tell them about our plan.

Their names were Irma and Klaus and I asked them for their help with my mother, telling them that we would, of course, pay them for their help, but they declined. The plan was that my mother would keep her apartment for the time being so that when we came to Bavaria, we would have a place to stay and also still have time to think about what to do. I also told them I would come back in the evening and try to call my friends in America, telling them that that they lived in San Francisco and explaining that there was a nine-hour time difference, so they were nine hours behind us. They were very nice people.

After that we went home to take a rest and my mother asked me if I was calling Michael. I just nodded and she didn't make any remarks, just patted my hand. The next day we were planning to see the priest and would find out what time was available for the funeral. In the afternoon I made a list of what had to be done after I flew back to Maui and what I had to discuss with Irma and Klaus.

Well, when it was almost 6 in the evening, meaning 9 in the morning in San Francisco, my mother came into the room and in her hand she had two Valerian pills. She knew how I felt. I checked the phone numbers and found they were different but noticed the one he gave to Irma was the office number. I felt relaxed after taking the pills and went over to them. They were already waiting for me and told me to dial a number and that the operator would then tell me what to do, and with that they left the room. I dialled the number and the operator came on telling me they would call as soon as a line was available. Irma came in to check on me with a cup of tea and we started to talk while I was waiting.

I don't remember how long we waited until the phone rang but then Irma left and I picked up the phone to hear the operator telling me that she was connecting me now. The phone rang and a voice came on, "Mendez Realty," then silence. I kind of whispered, "Hi." I knew it was Michael. "Hi, my little bird." We were both very emotional: it was almost 20 years since we'd actually talked. He told me how hard it was when his father died but that time would heal. We talked a bit about the past and how he still felt about me but neither of us talked about their partner. He still insisted that we would see each other again. We had to stop because it was most likely getting pretty expensive and instead of writing romantic things at the bottom of a letter, he spoke them now. He said he would try to call again in about a week to find out when the funeral would be.

I wasn't sad or mad or anything, it was just like being 20 years younger. I realised that bond was still there and it wasn't a dream, that Michael was still the same. I also realised that that phone call would most likely be the first and last one. I asked Irma about the cost of the call and she didn't know yet but she saw I was kind of different and when I got home my other just looked at me and knew how I felt. I went straight to bed; there were a lot of things to do the next day and most likely I would hear from Karl Heinz. Oh, I missed my little family!

I didn't hear anything from Karl Heinz the next day; he must have been very busy, but most likely I'd hear the next day. I thought a lot about Michaels phone call and it brought back memories: even after so many years, that special place for him was still there.

We saw the priest that day because we had to buy a plot and talk about the funeral date. We came up with May 24th and decided a Wednesday was fine since it would be a very small funeral. The church was beautiful and the graveyard was between trees from where you could even see the Alps. I knew my father would have liked the place and the one thing which made me feel glad was that he'd had such a wonderful time with us on Maui. We wrote to our relatives in East Germany and

East Berlin about my father's passing and the time of the funeral but there was no opportunity for them to come to the funeral.

When we got home from the church, Irma called us in. She had dinner ready for us so that we didn't have to cook and she mentioned that there had been two calls come though that day but that there was apparently no one on the line, just a very bad connection. I was very sure it was Karl Heinz; we'd experienced that situation even calling between the islands and I decided to wait a day or two and then try to call him if I hadn't heard anything. We talked over the plan and whether they would help her with extending her visa and making reservations for her flight to Maui. They were so helpful and my mother started to relax, since she knew she wouldn't be alone, and the only thing they wanted was to be able to stay with us if they should ever come to the Islands on vacation.

As I'd promised Michael I'd let him know what day the funeral would be, I sent him a telegram. The way it looked now; I would be able to leave by the end of May. We had most things under control and even started to make little plans about how we would work out a schedule so that I could work almost full time. It took two more days before I heard from Karl Heinz by telegram, telling me he was having a hard time connecting to Bavaria by phone and that I should call him, so the next evening I talked to Irma about calling my husband.

There were twelve hours difference in time so we started to call at around 6 at night and the operator told us the same story, "Wait till a line is available." It took a bit longer than to San Francisco but eventually he was on the phone with a bad connection saying that everything was fine there and asking if my mother was alright. I told him my father's funeral would be on the 24th and also that I would be home by the end of May. He never really showed emotion but he said, "We all miss you very much." I told him I'd keep him posted, either by phone or telegram.

A few days before the funeral, I received a telegram from Michael, telling me to get a wreath from Janet and Michael for the funeral. He wasn't able to send the money that fast but a letter with the money in it was coming and he would call me on the 23rd, in the evening, one day before the funeral, and that I should wait for the call. I asked my mother what to do and she just said, "You're not doing anything wrong, you're just talking, but leave it at talking," and I felt better after that.

We went to the florist and ordered the wreath with, written on a loop, "Rest in Peace, Janet and Michael." I started to look around and found there was a travel agency in that little village so I went in there to find out about a cheap one-way ticket to Maui. They looked at me as if I wasn't quite all there; they'd never heard about the Islands. I explained the route I was trying to fly and they slowly caught on, since they'd heard about Honolulu, but I wasn't sure if it would work with them and thought I might even have to drive to Munich.

The day before the funeral, I went over to Irma's to wait for Michael's call and finally, the phone rang and I picked it up and it was him. It was a bad connection but I told him I'd got the wreath and that we'd take some pictures and mail them to him. He wished me strength, telling me he would be with me in his thoughts and that we'd talk after the funeral and before I left Bavaria. I really didn't believe what he said but maybe he really meant it, and if he didn't it still made me happy.

The night before the funeral I had a bad dream, like a panic attack; I dreamed that they couldn't put my father in that coffin because he wouldn't then be able to breathe any more. I woke up shaking and sweating and my mother wanted to get a doctor but I remembered having those panic attacks way back in Berlin when Michael was still there, though this one was scary. My mother gave me some pills which she'd got from the doctor after my father passed away and they really helped, but it took a while to calm down and I wished the funeral was over and I could fly home and already have my mother with us. I also had to stop those calls with Michael, but they would end automatically when I got back home.

The next day, Irma and Klaus drove us to the church. There were hardly any people, just the four of us and those people who go to every funeral there is. I thought my mother was stronger than I but when they let the coffin down into the ground, I thought she was going to faint. Then it was over and final and the camera man took some pictures; there were only three wreaths—Irma and Klaus, Janet and Michael and my mother and me.

When we were home in the afternoon, I got a telegram from Karl Heinz asking me to call him the day after the funeral because he had problems connecting. And—there was still that evening to wait for Michael's call. I didn't know what to do but my mother told me that as I'd promised him, I had to go. I thought, *She still likes him, she always liked him and he liked her, too.* I hadn't waited too long when the phone rang and he was there asking me how I was feeling. I told him about the panic attack and he said, "Yes, I do remember them," and he talked to me like a therapist. He also told me about Aimi and said they would most likely get married the next year, that she was a nice girl and very down-to-earth. One question he asked: "Are you happy?" I replied, "Yes, I am," but he didn't answer. We had to end the call for both our sakes and I just told him that I'd let him know when I was leaving Bavaria. He still ended the call with a lot of heart. When I got home, my mother asked me how it had gone so I told her and then she said, "I know how you feel." There must have been something in the family that I hadn't been told about and which I never did find out.

The next day, we went to the travel agency and they proudly told us they had found a flight. They must have worked day and night on that and it was arranged that on Thursday, June 1st, I would leave Munich in the morning and travel via New York and a stopover in Los Angeles, on to Honolulu before the last flight to Maui. It was much cheaper than coming over and I was glad not to have had to drive to Munich. I told them that my mother would be coming in to get a one-way ticket to Maui as well and they gave me their address so that I could get in touch with them when mother was ready to fly.

That evening, I tried to call Karl Heinz and it took quite a while and again was a bad connection, but I told him when I would be home and how the funeral was and I could hear in his voice that he sounded happy. We had a few days left to rest and during that time we had to find out what my mother would have to do to get her visa extended.

My mother and I discussed what to take along: she didn't need much, just a few clothes and then whatever else she needed, we could buy on Maui. I contacted the Consulate in Munich and explained our situation and it was easier than I expected and we didn't have to drive to Munich. Because she already had a visa all she had to do was to send in her passport with an application for an extension and a fee, and with that she was alright. We could do that while I was there and they didn't tell me how long it would take but that didn't matter as long as we had everything under control.

The letter from Michael with the money for the wreath arrived. I knew he would do it, and I sent him the picture of the wreath. Janet also sent a letter saying how sorry she felt about my father and very briefly mentioned that she didn't really like Aimi and thought she was just after the money. But, if Michael was happy with her, it was his life. I would feel sorry for him if it was true but just maybe he would realise then what he was doing with his relationships and how he was hurting the people who really loved him.

I'd promised to say goodbye to Michael before leaving Bavaria so on the last day before Irma and Klaus were to drive me to Munich Airport, I tried to call him. It took a while to get a line but then he was on the phone and told me he'd been waiting for my call. I thanked him for the money and told him the pictures were on their way but it started to get emotional again and we had to stop. He mentioned again that we would meet again one day; maybe it was just a phrase and the only thing I said was "Yes, maybe in heaven, but I'm not sure they'll let you in." He said, "Just tell me you got home safely," and that was the end of that call, most likely for quite a while.

I didn't sleep well that night worrying about my mother because even though I knew she was in good hands with Irma, she still had to fly that long way by herself. After I was dropped off at Munich Airport, I had a little time to think. I had to get in touch with my cousin in Philadelphia to find out how she was getting on, since she'd brought her mother over after her father passed away and it was the same situation that I was in. I had to talk it over with Karl Heinz but as my mother had given me all their savings, maybe we could fly to Philadelphia and pick my mother up there—that way she would only have to fly by herself non-stop from Munich to Philadelphia. I thought it was possible and that way we could visit my cousin and my mother would be able to see her sister-in-law, Maria. It was a long flight but I was glad to have it all almost figured out.

Finally, we landed in Kahului and there they were waiting for me—my little family—and I was so glad to be home again. I was too tired to talk about everything and the only thing Karl Heinz told me was that the house we were building was almost sold once it was finished up. That meant we had to stay in the rental house and start building another one for us, but the profit was very good and I knew the rental house was big enough for all of us, so I really didn't care as long as we were together with my mother. I fell asleep on the table and that was all I remembered until the next day.

I felt a lot better the next day and Karl Heinz and I were able to talk everything over. I somehow remembered Karl Heinz telling me about the offer on the house we were just building, which all the time I had thought was for us. But Karl Heinz, being a good salesman, convinced me that we should take that offer and sell the house and that the next one would be for us. "If not the next one, then the one after the next one, for sure," I told him, and he had a good laugh at that. As he agreed my mother could live with us, I didn't say anything but I realised it might take a while until we had our OWN house.

I got in touch with my cousin in Philadelphia and told her our situation and the plan we had to pick my mother up in Philadelphia and maybe stay a few days so our mothers could have a good time. She was really excited about it and said just to let her know when we would be there.

I received a letter from Michael; he was worried about whether I got home safely—while making all those plans, I'd forgotten to let him know. He thanked me for the phone calls in Bavaria and said he missed them. I had days when I thought about our so-called "loose" connection and why we did that; there must have been some kind of bond even though he knew I would never leave Karl Heinz and he would never give up his affairs.

I wrote to Irma saying that mother would only fly to Philadelphia and that we would pick her up there and then I tried to work on the inside painting of the house as much as I could, but it was hard with the two children. Thomas wasn't too bad: he was a teenager already and liked to be on his own of course or with his friends, but Angela was too little and she had to be watched all the time.

Almost three months passed before my mother wrote to say that she had received all her papers back from the Consulate and was ready to come. She sounded so excited and wrote that Irma would take her to the travel agency to get her ticket. I had told her before that she needed only to fly to Philadelphia and had to write back quickly to tell her she didn't have to buy the ticket the same day but should wait about three weeks because we had to make our reservations as well.

I was so busy telling everybody what to do and what not to do that I hardly had time to finish the painting, but finally we had everything together and I was able to tell my cousin that we would arrive a day ahead of my mother and would most likely stay for four days. We took the offer for the house and everything was in Escrow with just little touch ups to be done which would be a lot easier with my mother there.

The flight to Philadelphia was alright and my cousin picked us up. They had a nice big house and already had three sons and Aunt Maria looked so happy. I couldn't wait to pick up my mother the next day. Her plane from Munich was arriving in the afternoon so my cousin took Karl Heinz and me to the airport and when I saw her coming through customs, she saw us as well and she cried. I knew then that she would be with us for the rest of our lives, like I had been with my grand-mother. We had four wonderful days and the two mothers enjoyed it; talking about old times and looking at pictures, and they promised that next time they would visit us on Maui.

We had four wonderful days together and now we had to start work-ing. We had three bedrooms and a very little guestroom which looked more like an overbuilt walk-in closet attached to our bedroom, so we put Angela in there and everyone had their own bedroom. We finished the house and made a really good profit, so Karl Heinz started to look for the next property to build the next house. It was so much easier for me: my mother cooked and when we came home everything was ready.

Michael and I kept in very loose contact but we always knew what was going on in each other's lives. It had now become more or less routine and, being honest, I would have missed it. My mother was trying to help us by answering the phone during the day but it was hard for her so we taught her to just pick up the phone and say, "Nobody home, call after 3." We really were the talk of the town; my mother being the operator and I was the painter.

The Christmas season started and it was a lovely time. Even though my father wasn't there anymore, we still had my mother and she baked German cookies and Christmas Stollen. As we'd started the next house, we took some of those sweets along to the house and when people stopped and looked, they ate some and loved it.

We then had to think about my mother's visa, which would expire in May the next year. Our banker friend told us about another German couple with their mother who had applied for the green card for their mother. If that would work, we wouldn't have to leave the U.S. every six months and then come back in again for another five months, so we decided to start that process at the beginning of 1973. We were also thinking of applying for American citizenship the next year.

That Christmas, I decided to send some Christmas cookies to Janet and Michael as they always sent me something. I told my mother about it and there were no remarks, so I got two bags and sent them off. Just shortly before Christmas Eve I got Christmas cards from them but there was no mention of the cookies—but they couldn't, since they most likely hadn't arrived there. That's what I wanted.

We had a lovely Christmas and Horst and Lani stopped over; Horst enjoyed the German treats. They were thinking about adoption because Lani wanted a child so badly, which I could really understand, and there was a possibility of adopting a little Japanese girl, which they were working on.

When the holidays were over, I got a letter from San Francisco and a big thank-you for the cookies and a lot of romantic words as well. Maybe that was it, I liked the romantic words.

We were getting really busy and had to hire another carpenter and I couldn't keep up with the painting anymore. One night we started to talk about the house building and had the idea of building a model house, nicely decorated so that people could look at it and maybe picture themselves living in it. We decided to try something different: there was a nice furniture store in town so we talked to the manager and told him our plan. We wanted to lease the furniture for the whole model house from them and furnish the whole house. If I found the time, I would wallpaper the model as well so that it looked really nice and even a little elegant. People without a lot of imagination really were excited. But when people bought a house off the model, all the furniture came out and it would look quite different, so the furniture store would give the buyer 30 percent off the furniture they bought from them. The dream of the OWN house went further and further away, but I knew one day I would have one.

In the meantime, I contacted the Consulate in Honolulu about the green card for my mother. The employee was very friendly but he told me we would have to go to Honolulu since they had to take a picture of my mother and we had to sign the papers in front of a lawyer. I therefore took my mother and we flew to Honolulu, had the picture taken, and I signed the papers to say that Karl Heinz and I were completely responsible for my mother. Karl Heinz had to sign as well, so he would also have to go to Honolulu. The employee also advised us to file for citizenship, saying it would be better if we were doing business in the State. When we left, he said, "Auf Wiedersehen" (Goodbye) and said he knew a little German because he was stationed in Berlin in Germany after the war. I really had to smile. "Yes," he said, "I had a really good time in Berlin." I didn't say anything but thought, *I bet you did.*

I was glad we had that problem with my mother's card behind us and we also applied for citizenship. As we were getting busy and the idea with the furniture was really great, we decided not to fly to Bavaria that year; that we would wait until the next year but maybe have a weekend trip to Honolulu to show my mother a little bit of that island. Also, we were looking for a lot for us—not for a model house but something different that might take a while to build but which we could do when time was available to work on OUR house.

I received a letter from Michael asking me how we were doing, since he knew my mother was with us, so I told him everything and he was really impressed. He just wrote, "Lucky Karl Heinz," and said that Aimi and he would be getting married in the summer and that she wanted to go to Europe on their honeymoon. I wrote back, "Lucky Aimi," but I couldn't complain. We were doing really well and who would have thought that the caged-in girl from Berlin would be able to travel and one day would have her OWN house. Miracles do happen!

We had our lives pretty much under control but sometimes I had the feeling my mother was a bit homesick and I could understand that very well. I thought about the German Club and wanted to find out if there were any elderly ladies there that she could maybe meet for a little coffee gossip once or twice a month, and I found one in the same situation as ours. She was living with her daughter after her husband had passed away. I called the daughter and told her my plan and she had the same thought about doing that for her mother, so we set up a date for me to pick her up and take her to our house. When I told my mother about it, I could see she was pleased and looking forward to it.

When the day came for the meeting, I noticed my mother took out a nice dress, curled her hair and even put on a little lipstick and perfume, and I had to smile. After picking up the other lady, I realised she must have been about my mother's age and was also a little dressed up and when I got her home they looked at each other and started bragging about everything. It was so funny, I really had to laugh about it. After a while they calmed down and must have realised they were behaving like teenagers and they later became really good friends and went shopping or had lunch together. There was just one thing my mother couldn't stand, she told me, and that was that she always used English words in their conversation and she knew better because she spoke perfect German.

We found a nice property for our house and made a down payment and whenever there was time, we started to clear it. It was located on a little hill and had a terrific view over the valley and the ocean and there were times I just went there and sat down and watched the view and thought about the past and also the future. Thomas would be starting high school that year but so far we hadn't seen any signs of what he would do when he had finished. Angela would start kindergarten and was getting prettier every day. Since I had a camera, I took pictures of our property and sent them to San Francisco; I don't know why I did it—maybe to show that I wasn't that poor girl anymore.

As we were so busy, we thought it would be a great idea to fly to Honolulu during the Christmas season when everything was so nicely decorated. The Fall season started and I received a picture from Michael of him with his wife Aimi. He wrote that it was a small wedding and then they were going on their honeymoon to England and Italy. He didn't mention Germany and also never made a remark about the picture of the property. I kept it to myself and didn't even tell my mother, but I slowly decided to stop writing to them anymore.

We were a little slow in October and just in-between selling a house and getting all the permits for the next one, so we took the opportunity and decided to fly to Honolulu for a long weekend. Thomas wasn't interested in coming; he wanted to stay with his friends, and that was fine with us. We decided to look around the Ala Moana Shopping Centre and Pearl Harbor on the Saturday and fly home on Sunday—that would be enough for my mother and Angela. Karl Heinz wanted to stay at the Sheraton Waikiki Beach Hotel where you could just walk out of the hotel right into the ocean. Since we were "Kamaaina," meaning people who are residents of Hawaii regardless of their racial backgrounds, we always got nice discounts on the rooms. I thought my mother would enjoy that.

I got a postcard from Michael from Rome but I pretended not to care since I was going to Honolulu and going to stay in a nice hotel at Waikiki Beach. I showed my mother the card and she looked at me and said, "You are childish," and she was right but I'd been thinking like that after the calls we had in Bavaria.

Well, we flew over on the Friday night and the hotel was gorgeous but while driving through downtown Honolulu, I realised how much everything had changed since I left almost ten years ago; no wonder Horst and Lani had moved to Maui. There were a lot of high-rises, condominiums and apartment building and it really took away the feeling of being in a tropical place. We had a little 1 bedroom suite facing the ocean so Karl Heinz slept in the living room and my mother, Angela and I slept in the little bedroom.

The next morning, we had breakfast in the hotel restaurant outside directly by the beach, after which we wanted to go and look at the Waikiki marketplace—quite interesting with little shops with antiquities but pretty pricey and I just bought my mother a little bracelet. Looking at her and her sneaky smile, I knew what she was thinking: "Now I have something to brag about when I go to lunch with my girlfriend." I had my camera with me so I took a picture of my mother and Angela in front of a treehouse and, yes, that picture would probably end up in San Francisco.

We had a little lunch in one of the local restaurants and next to the marketplace was the Honolulu Zoo. That was something for Angela, so instead of going to Pearl Harbor, we went to the zoo, and she had so much fun riding on a pony and playing with little goats, that we stayed there the whole afternoon, after which we were all tired and went back to the hotel. In a little sandwich store, we ordered a sandwich and Angela wanted soup but after our food came and Angela started to drink her soup, she fell asleep with her face dropping into the soup bowl. That was the end of the day.

My mother and Angela went to the room to sleep and Karl Heinz and I went into the bar for a drink. We had had a lovely day and Karl Heinz looked very relaxed and also proud of what we had achieved, but we had worked hard for it. The day our plan was to go to Pearl Harbor, but we changed it after breakfast and just sat on the beach. It was more relaxing than visiting Pearl Harbor and we could do that the next time we visited Honolulu. Since we had to leave the hotel at noon, there was still a little time left and we went playing in the ocean before flying back home in the afternoon, when we decide to do that more often.

I looked at the postcard from Rome again and tried to stick to my promise to go slow with our contact and I didn't send the picture of my mother with Angela; I was so busy with other things that I didn't need to have to pay that extra attention. Horst and Lani were able to adopt that little Japanese girl and Horst was the proudest father you ever saw, and we started to work on our house. Karl Heinz had big plans—he wanted a two-story house with a sauna and a swimming pool and it all sounded like a fairy tale, but we were working on it.

That year, 1973-1974, we were going to stay at home but the next summer we intended to go back to Bavaria and sell my mother's apartment, since she wouldn't go back there anymore. We also had a court hearing for the American citizenship, since we'd filled out all the papers. We had to learn American history and the names of the presidents; it was quite a lot to learn and we were told the hearing would be sometime in the spring of 1974. There was a lot going on in our lives.

Because I hadn't answered Michael's postcard, after returning to San Francisco he sent a little box asking if we were alright. In the little box was a beautiful cross from the Vatican and he wrote that it had been blessed by the Pope. Well, I didn't think the Pope had specially blessed that cross but it meant a lot to me that it came from the Vatican. I showed it to my mother and there were no remarks again but I felt I had to at least thank him and while I was writing the letter to him, I put in the picture of my mother with Angela.

We worked a lot on our house but this time I made sure Karl Heinz wouldn't sell it when it was three quarters finished. We were getting ready for Christmas but for whatever reason, I wasn't in the Christmas spirit at all. I thought I was kind of not feeling well. Janet and Michael sent Christmas cards and Michael said he liked the picture a lot but also felt I wasn't quite alright; maybe he noticed it from my last letter and I had the feeling he knew me better than I knew myself. He just wrote that he was wrong to send me the wedding picture. I was really embarrassed, so in my Christmas card to him I tried to defend myself by telling him that wasn't so and I was really happy for him that he'd found Aimi. I didn't think he'd believe me.

Even Karl Heinz noticed that I was a little different and I asked my mother if she thought so, too. She admitted it but said it was most likely I was in menopause and my emotions and hormones were running wild. She told me she'd been really sick sometimes but that there was medication which helped and I should see a doctor. She was most probably right and knowing that already made me feel better. I tried to control it but made a doctor's appointment for the next January. We had a wonderful Christmas again with German cooked food and a peaceful New

Year with no fireworks; I couldn't handle them—it must have been left over from the war and it stuck with me all my life.

I had set up a doctor's appointment for January to find out if there was anything wrong with me and my mother was right—I'd started the change of life and the doctor gave me some pills and said I would be fine, so at least that was alright. We were also notified about the citizenship hearing in February, so the year started out quite hectic again.

After discussing the lease on my mother's apartment in Bavaria, we had the idea of keeping it for another year. I had the feeling my mother wasn't ready to let go of the apartment and her belongings there and, also, if we visited Bavaria that year, we would have a place to stay and enjoy our vacation without having to start packing and moving around; I was tired of constantly moving. My mother really liked the idea and Karl Heinz told us the four of us could fly over as soon as the children's summer vacations started and stay over for the summer. I was really looking forward to that even though Karl Heinz would only come for three weeks because he couldn't leave our business alone, and he promised to have our house ready by the time we came back from Bavaria.

In February we flew over to Honolulu to the Court House and became American citizens. The judge asked us a few questions and there was one question I had a problem answering. It was "In the case of a war between Germany and the U.S., would you fight against your homeland?" It took a few seconds to answer but of course I had to say that, yes, I would fight against my homeland. I felt I had betrayed my homeland even though I had no other choice. I didn't talk to Karl Heinz about it but I'm sure he felt the same way.

We met the owner of a travel agency who wanted to buy a house and we became sort of friends and after a few meetings we signed the contract, so we then had to hire another carpenter. I was busy running around getting all the permits together and the owner of the travel agency, whose name was Charly, talked to Karl Heinz about an employee of the County of Maui who was a Samoan lady and somehow involved in politics in American Samoa and who would be very interested in doing some building in Pago Pago, the capital of American Samoa. Karl Heinz told me about it and said he was very interested in it and so was Charly so those three—Karl Heinz, Charly and the Samoan lady, made plans to fly over to Pago Pago to check it out. Since Charly owned the travel agency, the flight to Pago Pago was free for Karl Heinz.

I would have liked to go as well but could not leave everything alone, especially at such short notice, and Karl Heinz promised me that I could go with them the next time. Their flight would be about six hours, which wasn't too bad, and they were planning to stay for four days, with the possibility of having a stopover in Apia, the capital of Western Samoa. They found a flight which would leave in about ten days since the lady, whose name was Linda, had to ask for leave. The only hope I had was not to have to move to Samoa in the next two months. I knew Karl Heinz felt a bit guilty but as long as we could stay on Maui, I didn't mind.

I remembered I hadn't told Michael that we'd become citizens and, yes, I wrote about our American Samoa adventure. I must have felt very special writing to Michael about those things, why else would I write them.

After mailing the letter, I felt stupid but it was already too late. Karl Heinz was getting ready for the Samoan trip and I could see he was excited since Linda had told them she had good connections to a bank in Pago Pago, just in case they did want to start building there. My mother overheard a conversation about it and said to me later, "I hope you are able to handle all that."

Thomas was a full-blown teenager now, wanting to go and play golf with his friends and, of course, to get his driver's licence. Because there was no driving school on Maui, I was the one who had to teach him and that wasn't an easy job so I waited until Karl Heinz left. In the meantime, Michael sent a letter saying he might call me so that I could tell him all about what had happened. In a way I knew that would happen but this time it was all my fault and I could not blame anybody for it.

Karl Heinz then left with a lot of instructions about what I had to do over the four or maybe six days he was gone, so Thomas had to wait for his first driving lesson until Karl Heinz was back. Karl Heinz called telling me it was still kind of laid back but there were a lot of opportunities and they had a meeting with a banker in Pago Pago.

One evening the phone rang and I knew it was Michael. It was easier than talking the first time in Bavaria, more like talking to an old friend, which he actually was. He told me about his honeymoon and said he felt the age difference between his wife and him; she had so much more energy than him and could run around all day. I kept my mouth shut but we had to laugh about it. He didn't tell me how old she really was. It was a nice conversation, not an emotional one, just the lovely words at the end of the conversation made it special.

Karl Heinz returned after five days and was pretty excited but said there were many things to talk about. I told him Michael called the house and that he had married again and Karl Heinz just laughed, asking me how much older or young the wife was.

Since we were planning the trip to Bavaria, which I was really looking forward to, Karl Heinz told me there was a possibility he would have to fly over to Samoa again but for me to go along and also Charly's wife, Grace, as well. In a way I was excited to go but also a bit worried whether my mother would be able to handle things, but Thomas promised to help her and it was just for a few days and if she really needed help, Horst and Lani would be there. Also, the tickets were all expenses for Charly, so it was okay with us.

The flight to Pago Pago was fine; it was only six hours and after driving our rental car to the hotel, we had dinner. I liked the hotel—it was simple but cosy—and we decided that the next morning we'd do a little sightseeing because the meeting with the banker wasn't until the afternoon. It was a lush, tropical island with a lot of forests and waterfalls and you could rent a sailing boat and visit the little surrounding islands, but we had no time for that because of the afternoon meeting.

Grace and I decided not to join the meeting, that we'd rather sit at the pool and enjoy the scenery and after about two hours, the meeting was over and they came and joined us. I had the feeling the excitement about the "opportunity" was a little less but I would talk to Karl Heinz in the evening. We were told there was another meeting the next day but as I was really enjoying the relaxation, I told Karl Heinz I wouldn't join the meeting and that most likely Grace wouldn't, either. The meeting was set for the next day at noon and I was right—Grace didn't join in either, so we had a nice time at the pool and started a little conversation. She told me she wasn't really interested in that so-called opportunity because, she said, Charly was known for making fast decisions—sometimes too fast and that had caused them problems already. I knew exactly what she meant because in a way Karl Heinz was the same.

After they came back from the meeting they told us there was a lot to think about. The Samoan people do not live in houses built out of timber, they have houses called a Fale which are usually round and built with a tin roof and palm tree leaves on the sides, with pebbled floors, and I didn't think our group expected that. We visited a fale later on and it was beautiful but not the way they wanted those houses built. I couldn't understand Linda as, having grown up in Samoa, she knew how the houses were. Maybe she just wanted to get two free trips to see her relatives.

Since we were there already and it was only a 30-minute flight from Pago Pago, we decided to have a side trip to Apia in Western Samoa. Apia was a very small but cute airport and we were told we should definitely stay at the Aggie Grey Hotel, the famous and most historic hotel in Apia. It opened in 1933 and became a very popular gathering place for American servicemen stationed in Samoa during World War 2. On our way to the hotel we saw people walking barefoot in the streets and that's what I understood by "tropical island" and I fell in love with this island. It might have had something to do with Complex Wannsee in Berlin and the American servicemen stationed in Berlin after World War 2. We had two beautiful days at the Aggie Grey Hotel before leaving again for Pago Pago and on to Maui. Grace and I were very thankful the opportunity didn't work out.

I was glad to be home again and see my mother and the children and my mother had done a great job keeping everything in order. She asked me how it went and whether we had to start packing again to move to Samoa but I assured her that wasn't going to happen and she was very relieved to hear it. We started to build the house for Charly and Grace and also continued on our own house.

It was almost summer and we were preparing for our trip to Bavaria and it looked as if Karl Heinz would be able to finish our house so that we might be able to move in after we returned from our summer vacation. Thomas was begging me to give him some driving lessons so that he could have his driver's licence when we were in Bavaria and I knew he was thinking of renting a car and driving around. What he didn't know was that in Germany you have to be 18 to drive or even get a licence for that matter, but I wasn't going to tell him that since he wouldn't have believed me anyway; though he did get his licence for Hawaii.

We could hardly wait to leave and I wrote to Janet and Michael giving my plans for Bavaria. Karl Heinz would be able to come for three weeks, that was all we could afford. We contacted the bed-and-breakfast people, Irma and Werner, and asked if they could pick us up at Munich airport. They promised and then there was the problem of the car—to rent one for the summer would be too expensive, but I would discuss that with Irma. Michael had written back to say he would call me in Bavaria, that he missed the phone calls: that was charming Michael alright.

After that long and tiring flight, we arrived in Munich and they picked us up. I asked Irma right away about the car situation and she had a very good idea: one of her relatives owned a car which he wanted to sell, but he would rent us that car for the time we were there for a good price and then sell it afterwards. Thomas thought he could also use it but Irma told him he was only 18 and couldn't drive: I have never seen a longer face than Thomas had at that moment. It wasn't the best-looking car but for our purposes, it was perfect.

I could see my mother was enjoying herself and she told me it was great to sleep in her own bed. I sent Karl Heinz a telegram saying we had arrived safely and also that we had got that car pretty cheaply. Irma asked me if I was expecting those phone calls from San Francisco again and I nodded: she said just to let them know what time and day they would call so that they could wait for the call. It was really nice to be back in Germany again and the only thing I missed was seeing Berlin again. We could have driven or even flown to Berlin as we were now American citizens, but there was no place to stay and our relatives were all on the Eastern side, so there was no sense.

Of course, we could have visited my mother-in-law but she was in and out of Berlin visiting Brigitta in Eltham because she had three children now and needed help with everything. I don't think she would have really been too happy housing all four of us and I don't think my mother would have come anyway, but in any event we were happy where we were. Thomas was riding a bike to the public swimming pool, something he wasn't used to because on Maui hardly anyone rode a bike, there were only cars and some people walking.

We also took Angela to the public pool since there was a kiddie pool where children could play if they weren't able to swim. She really loved it so I told my mother that when we got back to Maui we could build a pool in our house and she had to learn how to swim. Another good thing was that they had a lifeguard there in the mornings until noon to watch the kiddie pool and we could relax knowing nothing would happen, since it wasn't deep anyway. As it was a little village with lots of tourists with children, it was perfect. I had the mornings to myself. Michael wrote to tell me what day and time he would call so that I could wait at Irma's.

My mother and I had to see the bank which took care of her accounts for things like paying the lease for the apartment, the electricity bill and any other bills which needed to be paid, and when we got to the bank the manager saw us and came out of his office to greet us. My mother was so nervous talking to the manager that she was almost shaking; what an honour. In a lot of things, she was very old fashioned but in some ways her thinking was ahead of her time. He asked us a lot of questions about Hawaii because at that time Hawaii was still a dream for many people. We told him we would extend the lease of mother's apartment for another year and he was happy to do that. He asked me when or if my husband would also come or if he was too busy and I told him he would most likely come for three weeks in August, and I had to promise him that we'd stop by as he wanted to meet him. My first thought was that he wanted to come to Hawaii or that it was another "opportunity" like Samoa, perhaps to start building in Bavaria, but I kept quiet and didn't tell anyone about my evil thoughts.

Then it was the day when Michael had told me he'd call and I went over to Irma's to wait. It didn't take too long before the phone rang and it was him. It was nice to hear his voice again and we talked about our newest happenings. We even talked about the time in Berlin and I realised there really was a bond between us and I didn't fight it anymore. He just realised I was happy again in Germany and he told me about his wife, that he sometimes had a hard time keeping up with her, but it looked like he liked her a lot. At the end of our conversation, he had the same lovely words and sometimes I even believed him. He told me he would call every week, same day, same time.

My mother and I had a great time. We drove to Saltzburg where they had a great farmer's market with the freshest fruit and vegetables and a lot of Austrian specialties, like Wiener Schnitzel, Apple strudel and much more. Otherwise, we toured the surrounding areas of little villages like Berchtesgaden, which was almost a day trip because the car wasn't the fastest.

Karl Heinz told me they were doing really well with the construction of our house and that it would be ready to at least move into when we came back and that we would finish the rest of the inside then and he wasn't taking any offers for the house. That meant he missed us. And he would be with us in August for three weeks.

It was a really nice vacation and I took walks to a little chapel about two hours uphill walk away in the wonderful mountain region of the Bavarian Alps. I knew my father used to walk those hills, too, so there were a lot of memories involved and I loved those mountain regions; it was all so peaceful with hardly any cars or people around and on top of that hill was a nice restaurant and monastery where you could have a good lunch or dinner. I did that quite often and sometimes I bought a bottle of Kraeuterlikoer (a special herbal and spice liqueur, used to treat indigestion). It was brewed by the monks and they must have liked it a lot as whenever you saw a monk, he was always happy and smiling. My mother usually took a small glass as well since it was good for your intestines.

I had another call from Michael talking about nothing and a lot. Bianca was finally going to University in New York to become a lawyer in the Fall. I thought Michael would be heartbroken but he actually wasn't; he just said she was sometimes a troublemaker and I couldn't help but say, "She must have her father's genes," and he only said, "You are right." They were planning a trip to Tokyo as his wife loved Asia, so we would get in contact again when both of us were back at home. It was different saying goodbye this time, we just could not stop talking.

We were looking forward to Karl Heinz arriving and to getting all the news from Maui. We picked him up from Munich airport and got onto the Autobahn, where we had to stay at the very right side, where only the slowest vehicles had to drive. Even the biggest and largest were overtaking us, which was kind of embarrassing for Karl Heinz and I had to laugh since sometimes even a bike could overtake us, but we made it safely to the village. He was glad to be home with us again and told us we'd be able to move into our house when we went back, that it wouldn't be completely finished but would be in a few weeks and that they'd even started to dig the hole for the pool, which Angela enjoyed hearing. She really loved her father.

I told him about the bank manager and that he wanted to meet him and after he got over his jetlag, we made an appointment and went to meet him. He was really friendly and I could feel he was a very good businessman and he invited us, the whole family, to his house to meet his family and for coffee and cake. Well, Karl Heinz was excited and ready to talk "business" again. I didn't say anything; maybe I was wrong and he really was just a friendly man.

When we went, my mother did not come, she was too shy. They had a beautiful house and his wife, Inge, was as friendly as him—Hans was his name and they had two teenage children, a son and a daughter. Both of them were hunters and they had lots of trophies like animal heads, hanging on the walls, which I didn't exactly enjoy looking at, but it was a nice afternoon and we talked a lot about Hawaii. They were very interested in it and asked us for another meeting over dinner; apparently she was a very good cook. The only time we needed to have to ourselves was two days to visit Vienna, the capital of Austria, which was about a four hour drive on the Autobahn, though we didn't know whether with our car it might take a whole day.

We had the second meeting with Hans and Inge and a wonderful dinner of wild deer ragout with dumplings and red cabbage and I felt very sure the meat came from one of the beasts belonging to one of the heads hanging on the wall, but I had to admit it was delicious. As I had already thought, their plan was to visit the islands, maybe in a few years, but he also had other plans on his mind and asked us whether, when my mother got older, she would have problems on Maui because she had no health insurance. Also, he said that maybe Thomas would do his studying there in Germany, maybe in Munich, and that then a little house would be nice for him, and even for us if we came on vacation as we'd have a nice place to stay and that maybe even Angela might go to school there.

He said it didn't have to be now because Thomas still had to finish high school on Maui first, but he would be finished in 1977, so when we came next year we could start looking for property and that as Inge was in Realty, she could help us. Actually, it was not really a bad idea but we really needed to think about it as it came rather suddenly. I had noticed that Thomas liked it there and my father was buried there as well, but you could feel that living in West Germany was quite different from living in West Berlin. West Germany really was booming, whilst caged in Berlin was behind but still a lot better than East Berlin and East Germany. Even with the wall, people from the East still tried to flee to the West through tunnels and tried to crawl over the wall, even though that wall had been erected 13 years before. We told them we would think about it and let them know.

We still wanted to visit Vienna but decided to leave the children with Irma. The same thing happened on the autobahn—big and long trucks and trailers overtook us, some looking pityingly at us as though we were refugees from the East trying to reach Austria to start a better life, but we made it to Vienna even though we knew we couldn't stay too long before we had to go back again. But: just seeing Vienna was amazing: seeing the cruise ships on the Danube river and knowing Vienna was an intellectual city which housed residents like Mozart, Beethoven and Sigmund Freud. It's also known for its architecture and palaces and the famous Palace Schoenbrunn as well as, as the saying goes, for the charm of the people.

To really enjoy all that takes quite a while: time which we didn't have, but we did have enough time to have a delicious lunch and—of course—we had Vienna Schnitzel. Next time we visited, we knew we would have to plan more time. The driving time back wasn't too bad, or perhaps we were getting used to the speed, but it was a very nice excursion. When we returned, Angela was already sleeping on Irma's couch and Thomas was driving around on his bike with his friends, both male and female. I really enjoyed that day and I realised I was still a lot European and not a Hawaiian lady. I told Karl Heinz that and he answered, "But remember, it is summer now. Think about the long, snowy, cold winter." Yes, he was right, but a sunny, snowy, cold winter day was not bad either.

All in all, we had a wonderful vacation thanks to all the new friends we had made. The idea of a house in that little village wasn't bad but we had to see if we could afford it all: if our construction company kept on going as it was, we might be able to. Sometimes, our situation scared me. We were not used to living like that and somehow we'd always had to struggle, both during the war and after the war and it was only after meeting Michael that my family and I had a better life. Then, getting married and immigrating to Canada was a struggle as well. Just getting back to Maui, we started to live a better life but the main thing was that we were always healthy and could work. There was a saying in Germany that "the higher you go, the deeper you fall," and that saying always stuck in my head. Anyway, our time was up and we had to leave and go back home. I was not so sure if my mother was looking forward again; I thought she'd miss Germany but being with us was her only joy. She bought a German beer stein for her girlfriend in Maui and even admitted that she wanted to brag with that but would give it to her as a gift.

We arrived on Maui and had that lovely smell of tropical flowers in the air; we really were blessed that we had the best of both sides of the world: the tropical climate on one side and the fresh mountain air on the other. Charly and Grace picked us up and took us to our new house, which looked beautiful. It still needed to be finished, so we had to stay a little longer in the rented one, but not more than three or four weeks.

There were a few days rest and then school began: Angela went to kindergarten and Thomas to high school and both went to the same school so I really started to get going to finish our house. It was really fun painting, wallpaper hanging and cleaning around the house and gluing on tiles in some areas and so hoping that there was nobody who would come with a ridiculous offer. If Karl Heinz tried to sell, I told him I would get a divorce and I think he realised I meant it. Everything was done except that the pool wasn't ready, but we started to slowly move in. My mother and the children were upstairs and Karl Heinz and I lived downstairs and we even had a fireplace built for the Christmas season and used it even if we were sweating.

We started to feel comfortable in the house and the swimming pool was ready as well as the sauna, so we had our OWN house again. Charly showed up quite a bit and he and Karl Heinz were talking and talking on the veranda and I hoped there wasn't another "opportunity" coming up as Karl Heinz didn't talk about what they were discussing.

I mailed a letter to Michael telling him we were back and I asked him how Tokyo was but it was quite a while until I heard back from him that he and Aimi were back in an Francisco and that he had broken his right ankle while using an exercise machine in an exercise club. Reading that letter, I had to laugh: I saw him showing off in front of other, most likely younger, people.

I thought about Michael and that maybe he wasn't accepting getting older and in a way I felt sorry for him. Karl Heinz finally told me about the discussions he'd had with Charly—there was a property for sale in Kihei, which was mostly beach property on the south west shores of Maui, known to be one of the driest and hottest parts of Maui and so far it was mostly undeveloped and at that time quite affordable. I immediately had thoughts of selling the new house and starting all over but this time Karl Heinz got serious and said, "No, we're talking about an apartment building," and I felt a lot better.

Charly, being a local, had a lot of connections to the county officials and he also organised various kinds of local events. He had heard that some mainland hotel chains were interested in investing in Kihei's "Gold Coast," as it was also called. It was also commercial zoned and the property was one block off the beach. They were thinking about an apartment block of 16 one-bedroom units. I had a few sleepless nights about that but maybe they were right and it would bring us in a good monthly income, so they went and talked to the banker and since we had a good record and Charly had the travel agency, they somehow put a deal together. I couldn't say too much because I didn't know the rules and regulations or building codes for that matter.

My mother didn't say much, only, "I hope you are not painting that whole building." I'd never thought of that, but that was impossible. That year was almost over and we decided to start the following year, since we had the okay from the bank for the loan and also the owner of the property knew about us.

Karl Heinz received a letter from his oldest sister, Christina, from Berlin, saying that Brigitta had been diagnosed with lung cancer and that his mother was devastated. She had three children, of which two were still young and so my mother-in-law stayed in Eltham and tried to help with whatever she could. There was nothing we could do except for Karl Heinz to send some money to his mother to help with the expenses but it overshadowed the Christmas spirit a bit.

Karl Heinz was worried as well because she wasn't even fifty years old, but we knew she was a chain smoker and had started at a young age and by then everybody knew smoking wasn't good for your health. We had a nice and peaceful Christmas and New Year and hoped that it wasn't too late for Brigitta.

I received very pretty holiday cards from Janet and Michael. Janet and Stefani were looking to adopt as well and Michael sent a Christmas card shaped as a heart; he always had the most unusual ideas. He told me his ankle was getting better and that they were planning the next trip to Singapore, since Aimi was Asia-crazy. Almost every time he wrote letters I wanted to stop answering him, but I couldn't.

Charly's house was almost finished and then they got notice from the owner of the apartment property that because it had taken so long, unless we were willing to pay a higher price, he was cancelling the pending sale because he was losing money and had received a higher offer. Of course, he was just telling us a story, so we decided to pull back as well. In a way I was relieved—that whole apartment deal was a bit too high for me and I was scared.

But they didn't stop: they started to look for another piece of property because Kihei had really started to develop quickly and after a few weeks they found another property, almost like the other one but cheaper because the owner lived on the mainland and apparently wasn't aware of the rising prices on Maui. They made an offer and the owner accepted but the paperwork took longer since he didn't live in the islands.

We got a call from Christina saying that Brigitta had passed away but my mother-in-law was in Eltham and even though we accepted it, we were shocked. Karl Heinz said he wasn't flying to England—that he couldn't because he was in the middle of negotiations with the apartment building. Horst, his younger brother in Columbus, Ohio and Jennifer, his bride, were in the middle of their studies, so my mother-in-law had to handle everything. The hardest part was the three children and the more than fifteen years younger husband but my mother-in-law was a strong woman and had handled her four children during and after the war all by herself because her husband was in action and never came back.

We then had to also sit down with my mother and have a talk about the plans for that summer. We had to tell Hans and Inge in that little village to extend my mother's lease on the apartment until 1976, because we didn't think we could go to Bavaria in the summer and it would most likely be in the winter. I looked at my mother and she didn't look too happy.

I felt sad for Brigitta's husband, who was now alone with the children, and I remembered my mother-in-law telling me one of the little boys had been born disabled. The reason was a drug called Thalidomide, also known by the brand name Contergan, which was prescribed by doctors to pregnant women to help with better sleep and to prevent nausea feelings during the first three months, a so-called sedative. Those babies were born with mild to severe deformities as a result of a German pharmaceutical company coverup which started at the end of 1958. It continued until the German press discovered that the drug producer Chemie Gruenenthal was behind it and put them under pressure to withdraw all the products that contained Thalidomide.

I remembered seeing pictures of deformed babies, some born without arms and legs, and it was a big scandal. Brigitta's little boy, Brian, was one of them, and he was born with a very short left arm so Brigitta must have taken that medication as well. One night I had a hard time sleeping and I had the idea of adopting that little boy into our family. As they were close in age, it would be great for Angela because Thomas was older and his interests were quite different from Angela's. I was very excited about the idea and the next day, when I told Karl Heinz about it, he liked it too, so we then had to get in contact with Brigitta's husband and we also had to inform Karl Heinz mother about it and needed the address in Eltham. Karl Heinz mother sounded very depressed in her letter to us, as though she had given up the will to live, but we got the address and contacted Brigitta's husband. It took a while before he wrote back a kind-of friendly but short letter saying, "Thank you, but I am keeping my son." Well, I was sad, but of course I could understand him, and that letter was almost the last contact we had with them.

It was in the middle of summer and we received mail from Hans and Inge saying they'd extended the lease for my mother's apartment for another year and also told us that the offer to build a house in the little village was still open, but we had so much going on at that time that that was the least of the worries on our minds. Charly's house was finished and we were working on all of the permits for the apartment, which turned out to be a bit larger than the first one so we were able to put a nice yard around the building. We then had a phone call, again in the middle of the night, and it was Christina calling from Berlin, which didn't sound good. I gave Karl Heinz the phone and I could see on his face that there was no good news alright. He said his mother was in the hospital with something wrong with her intestines and I knew he wanted to fly to Berlin to see her so I said, "Of course, you fly over," remembering that I had left just a few hours after my father had passed away.

The next morning, we called Grace and Charly to get a flight to Berlin, explaining that Karl Heinz' mother was in hospital and that we didn't know how long he would stay, and they found one and he flew out of Maui the same night. I was so glad my mother was there otherwise I'd have had that feeling again of being all alone. I knew I shouldn't do it but I did it anyway and the next day I tried to call Mendez Realty, not even caring if Aimi answered the phone or knowing if they were back from Singapore or hadn't yet left. The phone rang and Michael was on the line and, after hearing my voice, he just asked, "Are you okay?" so I told him everything and I knew that, as always, he'd find the right words to calm me down. It was nice to talk to him and I had to promise to let him know what happened. There was a moment of silence when neither of us said anything, and then we just hung up.

One good thing was that Christina had a phone connection now so Karl Heinz and I could stay in contact, but even so it was quite expensive—more expensive calling from Europe to Hawaii than from Hawaii to Germany—but at least it was faster than letters and telegrams. After two days Karl Heinz called me and told me his mother had had a blockage removed by operation and seemed to be okay. The doctor told him she was so happy that he was going to take her with him to Hawaii and that she kept telling everyone that she was going to go to Hawaii to live with him. At that moment he knew something wasn't quite right and when he saw her in the room, she didn't really recognise him and it took quite a while until she remembered who he was.

After telling me that, we knew she couldn't live alone anymore and Karl Heinz was assured by the doctor that we had to look for a senior's home for her. Karl Heinz found a nice one and when she was released from the hospital after about three weeks, she would go there. We never could understand why she had problems with her mind after the operation but someone later told us that maybe during the operation she hadn't had enough oxygen to feed the brain cells, though we never really found out. Karl Heinz tried to organise as much as he could, but Christina then had to clean out the apartment, which was a job in itself, I knew how stressful moving can be.

Well, he was home after two weeks but he was exhausted and there wasn't much rest because we started on the apartment building, grading the property and staking it all out. Christina kept us posted and said her mother got out of the hospital and into the senior's centre. It was a small one with just eight seniors living in there. Her pension was pretty good and we were going to help with the payments if need be.

For the first time, it hit me: what would happen to my mother if I should get sick and have to go to the hospital, then the idea of that little house in the alpine village wouldn't be too bad after all. But we had to finish that apartment first, then sit down and make a plan to either sell it for profit or keep it for income. But you can make as many plans as you want; they mostly turn out quite different.

Then there was that night call again with Christina telling us mother had passed away peacefully in her sleep and that Karl Heinz should go over since he had the power of attorney to all of her bank accounts and pension plans. We knew it was the best thing for her so we just had to deal with it and Karl Heinz flew out again the next day to take care of all the legal matters.

Yes, I called San Francisco again and told Michael all of it and we had a long talk. He told me his plans and I told him my plans but both of us knew there was no future for us, we both of us more or less accepted that but we had so much in common that it was nice to share ideas and dreams.

Karl Heinz finished up everything in Berlin and returned looking tired and stressed out. He gave me a letter from his mother addressed to me, which he hadn't opened. It wasn't a long one and she just wrote, "If you read this letter, I won't be here anymore but I know you will take care of my grave and maybe once in a while you will put flowers there." It really shook me up, and how could I take care of her grave being there in Hawaii? I got in touch with Christina and asked her if she could take care of the grave and said that next time I went to Berlin I would make arrangements for a florist to do that for me. It was almost the end of 1975 and she was in her mid-70s when she died.

Life went on. We got busy with the erection of the apartment and weren't able to fly over to Bavaria during the Christmas holidays. Thomas also had to work with us so that he had pocket money because he wanted to buy a car. It really was a lot of work as there were eight units downstairs and eight units upstairs and it was like a family business with my mother sewing the curtains for the windows (as everyone still had sewing machines at the time), and a girlfriend of mine and I carrying the bathtubs into each unit. The downstairs were easy but the upstairs ones were another thing and our two carpenters and Karl Heinz built us a ramp so that we could carry them up; we lived dangerously in those days.

And, of course, there was the painting. I never thought I would be able to do it, but I did. The inside painting of the units wasn't too bad but, like the bathtubs, the outside of the building became the problem. Starting to paint the upper units we had to use tricks and although we had a long ladder, which was fine, I was always afraid of heights so they put a rope around my waist attaching me to the inner roof. I was doing alright until one day when I was almost done with the painting of the whole building, inside and out, and I thought I saw white elephants running on the roof. I jumped off the ladder, threw the paintbrush and the bucket of paint into the bushes, jumped in the car and drove off. I had maybe twenty feet left to paint. That was the painting for me for quite a while but we finished the apartment building, even if I didn't paint the last twenty feet.

We rented it out pretty quickly and we still had money left over from the construction loan from the bank, and our plan was to go to Bavaria the next year in the summer to stop my mother's lease agreement and because Karl Heinz was thinking of buying a nice car.

Michael and I exchanged a few letters and I told him about my adventures with the apartment but he really didn't like it because of the danger involved. I missed talking to him but we were both either too busy or—better—had no chance to do it.

We still couldn't make up our minds what to do with the apartment, whether to sell it or keep it. It was a lot of work collecting the rent every month and not every renter had the money on time, so we had to go a few times. Then we received a letter from Hans and Inge, the hunter from Bavaria, asking us if we were going to Bavaria in the summer and saying that there were some nice properties available. They also wanted to come to Maui in the Fall to visit us, so there was our plan already for 1976.

We hoped and prayed 1976 would be a better year—not that we were complaining financially, but we'd lost people we loved. Our model house was still in existence and we had people looking and some were quite interested, but since we finished the apartment we hadn't been pushing too much to build another house or houses and were concentrating on our trip to Bavaria and figuring out what to do with the apartment building and Karl Heinz was pushing for a new car. We also knew we had to make a decision quickly if we were going to start building some kind of house in the little village.

I knew Karl Heinz wanted a car very badly, so we flew to Honolulu to a car dealer who was a friend of Charly and who specialised in Mercedes Benz cars. Well—that much I knew about cars—that Mercedes Benz was a German automobile company and known for luxury vehicles and its headquarters were in Stuttgart, Germany. A thought crossed my mind—after I'd got my driver's license and bought that old car and told Michael about it, he sent me a toy car key with a cute little Mercedes attached and it was really funny that maybe now we really would own one.

When we got to the showroom, I think we must have looked a bit undecided and of course, a good salesman sees that, so he showed us a lower priced Mercedes first and then took us to the better one, a Mercedes 450 SEL, the top of the line. I could see Karl Heinz' eyes almost popping out and I had to admit, it was a great looking car—silver grey with a black interior. Not only Karl Heinz' eyes were popping out but the salesman's eyes were as well as he most likely thought about the commission he would make. He told us to test drive it and, of course, we bought it. The salesman told us a new car the same would be ready for delivery in July and that it would come from Stuttgart to Honolulu so we could pick it up there. As we were going to be in Germany in the summer anyway, we told him we'd pick it up in Stuttgart ourselves and he thought that was a great idea as we'd save money on the shipping. For the price we paid for the car, the shipping wouldn't make a lot of difference because we had to pay to ship it from Germany anyway, but then after driving it through the summer.

We decided that after we came back from Bavaria we'd put the apartment building up for sale since we still had the construction company to build houses. When I told my mother that, she didn't say a lot but I could see she didn't like it much. I had to write to Michael to tell him that and the response was like "Now you have a better car than I have."

We started to prepare for our summer trip but decided to have a family meeting to discuss our plans and we told them our plan was to sell the apartment when we returned and that there was a possibility we might build a house in the little village. Well, Angela was too small to decide anything but we knew she liked it there too, and Thomas, coming from Hawaii, was the king of the town, so he suggested that after finishing high school the next year he would go over to Bavaria and join the Goethe Institute, which is a global institute founded by the Government of Germany for foreigners to study the German language. They actually had students from all over the world attending and that would be for one year and would be in Munich. We were surprised to hear that but it wasn't a bad idea because if we decided to build a house, he could keep a watch over the progress. My mother agreed to everything, just to be with us.

We knew we had to pick up the car in Stuttgart in July so we had to make our plans around that time and when we told Charly and Grace about it, they said they had a special going on through June to July—30% off if you fly for a week to the Bahamas, which somehow sounded exciting since it was almost on our way to Germany. Well, we told our family about it and all agreed, so we told Charly we'd do it and asked him to make reservations for us in July. We still had to find out from the dealer the date of the car pick-up in Stuttgart. Before we left Maui, I wrote a letter to Michael to let him know where we were going and saying that I would contact him as soon as I was back from Bavaria. It was like a must for both of us to let the other know where we could be found.

Horst and Lani took care of our house and apartment while we were gone and our flight went from Honolulu to Miami, Florida, and then another hour on to Nassau, the capital of the Bahamas. We stayed on Paradise Island, which is only accessible through Nassau Harbour bridges, and I really enjoyed that island, which is known for its beautiful beaches, coral reefs, diving and snorkelling and also the pink coloured

British Colonial buildings like the Government House. That week went by so fast and then the next excitement was waiting: the car pick-up.

We left Nassau for Germany and I remembered from school that we had to fly over the Bermuda Triangle, also known as the Devil's Triangle, in the Atlantic Ocean, where aircraft and ships had disappeared under mysterious circumstances. I had to admit that my nerves were a bit jittery and after we took off from Nassau, I told my mother the story, which I shouldn't have done because she then had one drink too many, and I never saw my mother drinking, but we did make it safely across the Bermuda Triangle.

Landing in Stuttgart, we rented a car and the five of us looked kind of unique with our Bahama straw hats and coloured clothing, not at all like Germans about to pick up a highly priced Mercedes Benz.

After driving into the parking lot and almost falling out of the car with our luggage, one of the employees took us into the waiting room where papers were checked before the car was brought out to you. There were a few people already waiting and I noticed their faces as they looked at us, obviously thinking those people must have the wrong address, they can't be here to pick up a Mercedes. We signed in and sat down and two more parties came in after us, also looking at us in disbelief. We were then called to the desk and the employee looking at the papers looked at us at least twice before he asked for our passport, sales contract and everything we had to prove that we were legal. It was really funny; we must have looked overtired and a bit run down after the long trip from Nassau. Well, he must have believed us as he even smiled and then said, "Your car is outside. Congratulations." Yes, everything was the same—it was the same model and colour and interior as the one we test drove in Honolulu.

After reaching the autobahn, we didn't have to drive on the far right-hand lane and were able to stay on the left side most of the time. That car sure made us laugh a lot. When we reached my mother's apartment, Hans and Inge were already waiting for us but we were too tired to do anything that day, so we told them we'd get together the next day.

Hans and Inge invited us for dinner a few days later and I really wasn't that happy to go, thinking about those animal heads hanging on the walls but I had no choice. After telling them our plans for selling the apartment, Hans suggested we look for some property while we were there. We also extended the lease on my mother's apartment for another year, until 1977, so that if Thomas went to the Goethe Institute, he would have a place to stay and my mother didn't mind since it meant she still had her own place.

We then actually found a nice lot in the middle of the little village with a terrific view of the Bavarian Alps and it was priced down because the owner was in financial difficulties, so we bought it and talked with Hans about building a nice little house on it. He knew a construction company in the next village and we got in touch with them and decided Karl Heinz would make a house plan and they would start work in the Fall, though of course they had to stop during the winter months. Hans promised he would oversee the construction a little and of course he made a little commission on everything and we weren't the only ones for whom he was overseeing building processes. They had wanted to come and visit us that year but had to change their plans to the next year.

Everything was set, so we left at the beginning of September, drove to Munich and left the car with a forwarder to ship to Hawaii. We were told it might take six to eight weeks to get there and it would be shipped direct to Kahului Harbour on Maui. I was really glad to get into the plane and head back home and the only real vacation we had was one week on Paradise Island in the Bahamas.

I could see my mother was also glad to be home again and we started on the house plan for Bavaria and also concentrated on pushing the construction company again. Most importantly, we had to put the apartment up for sale. The first chance I had, the letter to San Francisco had to go out and I told him about the house we would build in Bavaria and the Bahamas. I actually had no one else to talk to about them and he was an outsider, so saw everything differently from the way I saw things and I was a bit scared of all those developments. In the meantime, we had two offers on the apartment, which were pretty good, and the car arrived in Kahului without any damage and Karl Heinz was happy.

I finally received a letter from Michael explaining that they had been in Singapore and received my letter after his return and that his wife had really enjoyed the city. He wrote that maybe we were going too fast trying to get rich, since he knew my nervous system wasn't the best, and also mentioned that I should check my post office box. I did and there was a package with two single records sung by Elvis Presley, the most famous American singer at that time, also known as "The King of Rock 'n' Roll." I knew he loved his songs and he'd also liked being stationed in Germany from 1958 to 1960. The two records he sent me were "It's Now or Never" and "Spanish Eyes" but as we didn't have a record player, I had to hide them with my other memory items. Only my mother knew about it and for some reason which I never found out, she just looked at them and smiled.

We sold the apartment and made a pretty good profit and then Karl Heinz started to work on the plan for the Bavaria house. Our construction company was picking up, too, and Karl Heinz met a couple from Hong Kong who were having a vacation on Maui. They were originally from Great Britain but had moved to Hong Kong when they were very young. They also had two little girls almost Angela's age and were interested in having a house built in Kihei because they really enjoyed Maui and were planning to visit more often, so having a house would be nicer than staying in a condominium or apartment. It was all set and they bought a lot and Karl Heinz got the contract signed before they left for Hong Kong. The best thing was that they invited us to visit them in Hong Kong and we could even stay with them. For some reason, I'd always been interested in visiting Hong Kong.

While we were doing the house plan for Bavaria, it somehow became a little larger than we had first planned but we sent it over to Hans and Inge, who were taking care of the planning, even though the construction had to wait because of the approaching winter months. That was fine with me as it meant we had a little breathing room.

I finally had a chance to buy a record player because I really wanted to listen to those records. Knowing Michael, I took some handkerchiefs with me, just in case, and I knew I would cry. They were beautiful and I sat there thinking about Berlin, the city I really loved and which I somehow felt guilty about just leaving, and also about the wonderful time Michael and I spent there. Somehow I knew I would go back to Berlin. Maybe not to live, but to spend time there again, and that one day the wall had to come down and Germany would be reunited.

Since it was the Christmas season and I enjoyed those two records so much, I thought about sending Michael a Christmas record of authentic Hawaiian music. I was thinking of a famous Hawaiian singer, Don Ho, and his most famous song "Tiny Bubbles," which was the kind of music we both liked, even though it wasn't really a Christmas song. Maybe it was a bit too romantic, but it was Christmas and just a record.

I started to worry a bit about my mother as I could see she was becoming a little slower in everything she did. Of course, she was getting older, but the idea of the house in Bavaria wasn't a bad one because Thomas would be there and if she got really sick, she couldn't stay on Maui because there was no health insurance for her. I wouldn't leave her alone; I would go to Germany with her and would also take Angela with me, who could even go to school there if need be. I always had to have a plan B that made me feel secure.

I bought the record and sent it to San Francisco, together with some Hawaiian chocolates and famous Kona Coffee and we had a nice and relaxed Christmas. Karl Heinz was so happy with his car and the way things were going with us. We really had come a long way.

Another year had passed so we were now in 1977 and were making plans for that year. Karl Heinz started on the house for our new friends from Hong Kong, Janet and Peter, and had the "GREAT" idea of visiting them in the spring, which was alright with them. Since we had to fly to Bavaria in the summer and Thomas was leaving for Munich after his graduation from high school, we didn't know what the future would bring so decided to take that "side trip" to Hong Kong. I couldn't take my mother with me as it would be too much for her but Charly and Grace told us they would take care of my mother and even wanted to move in and stay with her for those two weeks, so we were gone. That is the ALOHA spirit and I was really excited about the trip and so was Karl Heinz.

I wrote to Michael about our plan and he wrote back saying that he and Aimi were also planning to visit Hong Kong, so we were making sure we weren't there at the same time. Both letters made us laugh about meeting in Hong Kong at the same time but was it really funny? We didn't talk about it.

We chose March because Janet and Peter told us that because of the weather situation the best time to visit would be March or April when the temperature was around 20 Celsius/70 Fahrenheit and with lower humidity. As I usually did whenever I visited a place I hadn't been to before, I tried to find out what to expect. I remembered that in school one of my favourite subjects was Geography and I was very interested in Asia, though of course I never thought that one day I'd be able to see it. I looked into my smart little book but there wasn't a lot to find out, only that Hong Kong was a British Colony which had been occupied by Japan from 1941 to 1945 during World War 2 and that it was a bustling city and a shopping paradise. Well, at least I knew a little.

There was also a time difference between Honolulu and Hong Kong of eighteen hours, which meant Hong Kong was eighteen hours ahead of us, so there would be a lot of mix-up with day and night, the same as flying to Germany with the twelve hours' time difference, but we were looking forward to it and at last the day arrived for us to leave Honolulu for Hong Kong.

After long hours of flying we finally started to descend into Hong Kong International Airport and while I was looking out of the window I got really scared. There were houses left and right of us and I thought the pilot was crashing into a street but as we got lower I saw it was the runway and not a street; it was the most scary airport I ever saw but all the other passengers, mostly Chinese people, were either sleeping or looking relaxed and of course, they knew the airport. We have been told that only pilots with special training were allowed to land in Hong Kong.

As we were four people with luggage, the easiest thing was to take a taxi and we arrived at the flat (which is a family suite in a building with more of those suites) and when the door opened, Janet greeted us and let us in and there came their maid, bringing us a drink. I was so amazed—it was the first family I knew which had a maid. I couldn't believe we were really in Asia and I had a new drink as well—a gin and tonic—but we were so tired I couldn't even remember going to bed.

The next morning the maid was there with coffee but Thomas and Angela were still sleeping and we decided not to do anything that first day. As we were only staying two weeks, we thought we wouldn't do a lot—maybe just do a little shopping and see one or two tourist attractions. We were told we should definitely see the Peak Tram and also have a look at the Hong Kong Harbour, and that would be enough for the first time since we were sure it wouldn't be the last time we'd be in Hong Kong. Everything was so new to me that I didn't need to see any other tourist attractions.

One day, we went shopping and it was overwhelming what you could buy or, better, not buy—jewellery, clothing, mostly brand names—there was everything you could think of—but I felt caged in and almost had a panic attack. Karl Heinz knew my fear of being in a crowd with lots of people. I never really was a jewellery person but I managed to buy a little bracelet. I hardly wore rings but I loved earrings. I noticed a lot of high-priced cars driving around, such as Rolls Royces, but that made sense as it was an English company which built them. As far as I knew, they were made mostly by hand.

One evening Janet and Peter took us out for dinner in a fancy restaurant and when I looked at the menu I had no idea what to order. There were about six Chinese waiters standing behind us waiting for us to order so I just watched the others and ordered what they did and we had a delicious fish dinner. If you wanted a soup, you could have the soup cold or hot, it was amazing and I enjoyed it a lot.

We decided to return the next year because this time we could only stay two weeks because of Thomas' graduation and we also had to fly to Bavaria because of the house building and because my mother was waiting for us. We had nice evenings together playing games and talking; it was so different from being at home on Maui. One sightseeing trip we did was the Victoria Peak, which is the highest hill on Hong Kong Island. You can reach the top by bus, which would take about an hour, or by tram, for which you only need ten minutes, so we decided to take the tram to the top and admired the panoramic view of Hong Kong Island, which was

breathtaking. The two weeks went by much too fast but we had no choice and had to leave, but we knew we would see each other soon anyway because their house in Kihei would be finished. We had a very hectic year ahead of us but that was the way our life was at that time. Leaving Hong Kong Airport, I was prepared now for the pilot doing the right thing and taking off between houses.

In a way I was happy to be home again and with my mother and everything was in order because Grace had stayed with her. After not seeing her for two weeks, I noticed she looked kind of frail and told her we should see a doctor to check her out, but she just smiled and said she was feeling fine. I didn't want the same thing to happen to her as had happened to my father when he didn't want to go to the doctor to get his diabetes medication because he couldn't speak English, but I could not force her to go and it worried me.

Janet and Peter's house came along nicely and we thought they'd most likely come to Maui in the Fall. As promised, I wrote to Michael about Hong Kong, since they were planning to fly there too, and writing back he said he was looking forward to that too. There was no mention of Aimi and he sounded a bit down but at the end of the letter there were those lovely words again; he never missed that. If we found another chance to talk on the phone, I would ask him if he was alright. Then I remembered: maybe he was depressed since his 50th birthday was coming up in two years.

We received word from Hans and Inge that they were starting on the house, so it was almost time to prepare for our trip to Bavaria and there were a lot of decisions to make. Thomas' graduation was coming up soon and we registered him at the Goethe Institute in Munich for a year and also extended the lease on my mother's apartment for another year so he had a place to stay. Our plan was that my mother, the children and I would leave after Thomas' graduation, while Karl Heinz had only three weeks available to come to Bavaria because there was too much unfinished work, so we left shortly after Thomas finished high school.

Because of the long flight, we decided to stay maybe two days in New York to rest because I was worried about my mother's health. The children were trying to convince us to stay at the Waldorf Astoria Hotel in New York and as we could get a discount through Charly and Grace and her travel agency, we told Thomas it would be his graduation gift. At that time, it was a world-famous hotel and many films were made there, and from 1931 until 1963, it was the world's tallest hotel until it was surpassed by Moscow's Hotel Ukraina by 23 feet.

It was an amazing hotel and very luxurious but mostly antique and there wasn't really much to do since New York was pretty hot at that time. We had a nice dinner at an Italian restaurant on Park Avenue and then went back because we were tired and the next day we just went window shopping. Everything was very expensive, so we didn't buy anything but I did send Michael a postcard and told him I would call him when I was there.

We made it safely to the apartment and my mother was really glad to be sleeping in her own bed again. The next day we checked out the house building but there wasn't much to see and in a way I was glad, since we still had my mother's apartment. We said hello to Irma and I asked her if I could use her phone later to call Karl Heinz and tell him we made it and it was actually nice to be there: a little chilly compared to Maui, but crisp and clear air. We went and visited my father's grave; it was always hard to believe he was gone. We also stopped at Hans and Inge's and I told them to wait for a meeting about the house until Karl Heinz arrived in about four weeks. I just wanted some distance from meetings and talk about house building.

Thomas had found some friends already and he had a great time and Angela also found a little friend with whom she was constantly doing something and she learned how to ride a bike—it made me happy to see them enjoying themselves. I called Karl Heinz that night and told him we were all okay and he said he hoped to arrive in four weeks. I told Irma I would go again the next day to call San Francisco and she said she was glad we were there again.

I went over to Irma's for the call to Michael and the connection was better now with no need to wait for hours. He was on the phone after the second ring and it was nice to hear his voice again. We talked for quite a while and he told me he'd been contacted by Rita—the Rita who was with Jonathan and with whom we were friends way back in Berlin—and that she'd asked for my address. A lot of memories came back but at least we could talk about it. He didn't mention Aimi at all and I didn't ask and I had to promise him I'd call him the following week on the same day and at the same time. I told my mother about the call and she said, "You look much

better." Even I knew it was wrong but it helped me to get over my thoughts and emotions.

I enjoyed my walks up to the little chapel. I had the feeling my mother was not telling me the truth, but she didn't want to see a doctor. My life was changing; Thomas was not coming home with us anymore and my little nest was getting empty. Well, Karl Heinz called after two weeks saying he was preparing for his trip and It felt really good, since we had to talk with Hans and Inge and had to take Thomas to Munich. My weekly talks with Michael helped me a lot; he said he was my emotional therapist.

Hans and Inge lent me their car so that I could pick up Karl Heinz in Munich and I was really looking forward to that. I was prepared to have a relaxed vacation together but that was nothing for Karl Heinz, he was always on the go. Our house already started to look like a house and was going to be a nice looking one and one evening when Karl Heinz and I were going for a walk, we passed our house and heard people walking behind us saying that some crazy Americans were building that house. They said, "The property belonged to our mayor, why did he sell it to Americans? Our land should stay in Bavarian hands." First we had to laugh but then we thought, maybe they were right. We were Germans but of course they didn't know that.

The construction company told us the house would be completely finished the next spring, which meant that Thomas would most likely not be able to stay in there over the winter months and we could not come back again over the Christmas holidays. We had an offer for Thomas to stay either with Irma, since they had a bed-and-breakfast place anyway, or with Hans and Inge, so it was up to him. He had to start in August, so we had to take him to Munich to the Goethe Institute, where they also had little apartments to rent to students. They were very expensive so we just rented one for a month and then he could travel by train to our little village, which was just one hour away. I had a hard time dropping him off in Munich and really suffered that empty nest syndrome. It was a good thing I still had my mother and Angela.

When we were ready to fly back home, Thomas came to Munich airport to say goodbye. So far he liked it but he called me over telling me he'd lost his wallet with the money that he had. I felt so sorry for him and gave him way too much. Hans had opened a bank account for him so that we could transfer money to him from Maui.

We arrived home safely but it was different: one was missing. Karl Heinz mentioned that he hadn't wanted to say anything before but that Thomas could have stayed in my mother's place, which would have been a lot cheaper. I thought the same thing but I knew my mother wouldn't have liked it and would have been afraid Thomas wouldn't have taken good care of her belongings, and she might have been right.

Well, I missed Thomas everywhere but what was worse—my mother changed. She was no longer that nice, lovely person she'd been all her life and she became grumpy and sometimes rude and kept on telling us she'd rather be home and in her apartment. I knew something was wrong but I could not get her to see a doctor and told Karl Heinz we had to find a solution about what to do.

Janet and Peter's house was finished, so they could come anytime and have a vacation and stay in their house, and there were more jobs in the making. We thought we had everything under control but somehow it was chaotic. Thomas also wrote and called us saying he wanted to quit after six months because he knew more German than the other students and it was boring for him. He was staying with Hans and Inge but had found a friend in a larger nearby city whose parents owned and operated a brewery and he'd rather work there and make money. As we paid the tuition monthly, that might be alright, in which case he would be finished in February of next year.

So—Karl Heinz and I made another plan. Since the house in Bavaria would be ready in the spring, my mother, Angela and I would go over there for a little while and find out what was wrong with my mother and Thomas could stay in our house and Angela could go to school there. I could give up my mother's apartment and then see what would happen. We were thinking of being there for about a year; Karl Heinz would come over as much as he could since there was no chance of giving up our business on Maui. It was by no means the best scenario but we had no other choice.

We were planning on going over in the spring of 1978 and Karl Heinz would come with us and help us get settled before leaving again. We told Thomas he could leave the Goethe Institute and start working at the brewery, since it looked as if that was all planned already anyway. I told Karl Heinz we had a year to decide what to do: if the worst came to the worst, we could sell the house in Bavaria—but there was my mother to think of, though we had that year. When I told my mother about it and told her that if we went back the next year she could have a nice room in the house and her own bed again, she just looked at me and said, "You can live in the house, I'll stay in the apartment." It was then I knew something was seriously wrong with her.

We had a very quiet Christmas. I just sent Christmas letters to Janet and Michael but didn't say anything about our plans. I really wished I could talk to Michael; he always seemed to bring me back on the right track. Somehow Karl Heinz felt bad and he told me I could take the Mercedes to Bavaria as we still had the van at home, which he could drive until our life became "normal" again.

I got a letter back from Michael telling me he and Aimi had separated but were trying to work out their problems and I thought to myself that he might go on those business meetings again. He also mentioned that Bianca would be getting married to a famous lawyer in San Francisco.

I couldn't believe how fast time went by. Sometimes I thought about our property in East Germany and whether I would ever get it back: I still had all the papers from the lawyer from when my father signed the property over to me after their death. Karl Heinz was feeling really bad and came home one day saying, "What do you think about going on a cruise to Europe? We can even take the Mercedes with us on the ship." I looked at him and thought he was joking but he said he'd been in Charly's office that day and saw a cruise offer from Honolulu to Southampton, Great Britain, and he wanted me to look at it.

I really wasn't so sure if it would be a good idea, especially with how my mother was now, though lately she'd been a bit better. Either she was afraid to go back or happy to go back, but I would never leave her alone in the apartment. Karl Heinz and I went to Charly's office to look at the cruise ship offer and they had a brochure to look at but since it was such a big thing, I asked if I could take one home and look through it. On the front page there was a huge ship, the SS *Oriana*, which would take about four weeks to go from Honolulu to Southampton and we would have to go through the Panama Canal. That was a bit too much at the moment, so I put the whole brochure aside and had to take a deep breath but Karl Heinz started to laugh and thought that was the trip of a lifetime. He was right on that but we had to take my mother and Angela with us and I really had to think about that, but we had to make a decision quickly as it was the beginning of the year and our plan was to be there in the summer.

I looked it over again. It was a huge ship which could take up to 2,000 passengers and had a lot of entertainment on board including movie theatres as well as playgroups for children, so maybe it wouldn't be such a bad idea as we could relax. I found out we had stop-overs as well and went from Honolulu to Vancouver, Canada, which make me smile remembering our chicken farm and my chicken hospital and Quasimodo with its crooked neck. Then the ship went back through San Francisco, and I wondered if Karl Heinz would make any remarks, before going south to Panama City/Balboa to cross through the Panama Canal. I could only read a little each day, it was too overwhelming.

Well, Charly's travel agency did really well, mostly from groups who travelled together, and we always got a big discount so we decided to go. We'd planned to be in Bavaria around may, which meant leaving in April but when we spoke to Charly about it, he said the Oriana only sailed in May, so we had to make reservations for May and would not get to Bavaria until June; there was no other choice. Just in case my mother got sick, I asked Charly if there was a doctor on board and he said there was even a little hospital there. I wondered what they would do if someone died and hoped they would not do what I thought.

Slowly, I was getting prepared for that adventure and I hoped I wouldn't get seasick. I wrote a letter to Michael telling him about our trip and that we would be passing through San Francisco under the Golden Gate Bridge and his answer was "Tell me what time you'll pass under the bridge; I will be on it waving at you." I was glad he had his sense of humour back. I had days when I got scared thinking about our future. There was a saying that if you pull your roots up once, you're never really at home anymore, and that is how I sometimes felt.

Once we knew we were definitely leaving, I didn't bother reading any more about the route of the ship as I'd have enough time on the ship to do that. Since no one would be in the house for four weeks, we asked Grace and Charly to just check maybe twice a week and we also asked our neighbours to watch the house. We covered the pool and hoped everything would be alright when Karl Heinz returned. I wasn't feeling that great about the uncertain future we had at that moment but kept quiet and hoped that I'd be fine after resting on the ship.

We told Thomas and Hans our most likely arrival date but we had our car, so we could drive to our little village, most likely from Calais in France. The house was ready to move into, so we just needed a few pieces of furniture, like beds, and we would also take my mother's furniture from her apartment into her room at the house; everything else we would arrange while Karl Heinz was still there. We told Thomas to apply for a phone connection to the house and my mother seemed alright so far, though we hadn't told her about the apartment.

Well, the day came to fly to Honolulu and board the ship. It was unbelievably large and had quite a lot of people on board. We had two cabins, one for my mother and Angela and one for us—not very big but they were connected, which was very good. We tried to get settled as best we could while nice Hawaiian music was playing in the background and it was almost sunset when we left the harbour for the ocean. I stood on deck and watched the Honolulu skyline get smaller and smaller; it was a feeling I never forgot.

We had a most delicious buffet-style dinner with some wine to make us sleepy but I hardly slept that first night. It was, again, quite a change in my life and even Karl Heinz was quiet, so I knew he felt the same. The next day they showed us how to put on the life vests in case of an emergency and my mother was shaking until she understood what they meant—just in case of an emergency but they had to show us even though it would never happen. I didn't know if she believed it or not, but she seemed calmer.

The captain told us it might take up to five days to reach Vancouver and we would then have a two day stop-over and he assured us the weather was fine and the ocean was calm. There was a lot to do on the ship, which had an exercise room, little shops, and even beauty parlours; it was amazing and even my mother liked it. Angela went to the play-groups and we even went to see a movie and in the evenings there was a lot of entertainment.

Finally, we reached Vancouver, which had surely changed after we left and now had high rise buildings and hotels, but we didn't leave the ship. Karl Heinz went on a city tour but I couldn't leave my mother and Angela alone, though sitting by the pool was nice, too, without any stress or pressure. The two days went by quickly and we left for San Francisco. There was no stop-over there and the next stop was Panama City but I went outside on deck while we were passing the bridge and tried not to get emotional and there were no remarks from Karl Heinz, either.

Then we were on our way to Panama City, where we had a one-night stopover. We were thinking of doing a short city tour, just Karl Heinz and myself, but after listening to the captain's advice that if we did that it would be at our own risk, we decided not to go. The next morning, we started to enter the Panama Canal, which is an artificial waterway in Panama, about 80 km or 50 miles long, and connects the Pacific and Atlantic Oceans. Panama was used to build the canal because it was the narrowest landmass between the two oceans.

It was very interesting and I realised then that Karl Heinz was right—it was the trip of a lifetime. The captain came on telling us it would take a whole day of eight to ten hours to pass through the canal and reach the Atlantic Ocean, heading towards the Bahamas and Nassau, where we would have a one day stop. Sailing through the Panama Canal was really something else and it was so hot and humid that you almost had to stay inside the ship. I was surprised that there were little islands with beautiful flowers and trees; I'd never thought it would look like that and it was really very tropical.

We reached the Atlantic Ocean after almost nine hours and could immediately see the difference between those two oceans. The Atlantic didn't look as calm as the Pacific and was also colder. We reached Nassau in the Bahamas and docked for one night before leaving for Fort Lauderdale in Florida, which was a short trip away and where we also stayed one night. Slowly, I was looking forward to the end of the trip and feeling steady on my feet again, but at least none of us got seasick, and then the last leg of our trip started with the crossing of the Atlantic Ocean towards Southampton. People were talking and wondering how they would survive after leaving the ship and being so spoiled and then we arrived in Southampton and the life of luxury was over.

We had to wait a while to get our car and to start driving to Dover, where the ferries left for Calais, and that wasn't that easy because of having to drive on the left side of the road. We managed to leave the harbour and find the right direction to Dover, but then we got stuck on a roundabout which it took us a while to exit and all the relaxation we'd had on the ship was gone. We'd been told it took only about three hours to drive. Maybe for them, but not for us and we only hoped we didn't get stuck on too many roundabouts. We got there in the middle of the night and had to wait until the morning for the ferry to Calais, which meant we had to sleep in the car and my poor mother was slightly confused.

We were so glad when that night was over and that the ferry to Calais would soon start and we were told that it was only 50 miles (80 km), so we should make it in under two hours. There weren't too many passengers on the ferry and it wasn't too bumpy, either, but I could see that my mother and Angela were very tired and we told them they could sleep in the car while driving from Calais to Bavaria through Munich.

The Captain told us that when the weather was clear you could even see the white cliffs of Dover from Calais, but it was a cloudy day so most likely we wouldn't be able to and I didn't really care much: I just wanted to go and be in a "house" again. I was a little worried about my mother but she slept a lot on the ship and as soon as we reached the village she'd be seeing a doctor.

We reached Calais and found we had another long way to go—about 1,000 km drive to Bavaria, so at least another nine hours' drive, though it was mostly on the Autobahn and our car was really meant for that. First, we needed some coffee and breakfast and we had a typical French breakfast of baguette with jam and pastries and it was delicious.

Karl Heinz and I then decided to share the driving and change every three hours so that we wouldn't get too tired. We turned on a little music and hoped my mother and Angela would fall asleep but it didn't quite work out that way as they were wide awake and, instead, I fell asleep. Karl Heinz did his three hours and then it was my turn and I was fine for about two hours before I started feeling sleepy and we had to stop and get some fresh air. We were driving through Luxembourg so stopped at a nice old-fashioned looking restaurant for lunch but as we didn't know what to order, we asked the waiter for a specialty. He recommended a specialty of smoked pork neck with beans and sauerkraut and calves liver dumplings and although we didn't know it, we ordered it anyway and liked it very much—it was different but delicious. My mother and Angela ordered chicken and fried noodles and a large portion of ice cream.

I still had an hour to drive but noticed I was kind of tired and while driving I must have closed my eyes for a second and must have slept for a second. It really scared me and from then on we changed drivers every hour until we reached the little village. We were very happy to be there.

I felt bad because we'd cancelled the lease on my mother's apartment without telling her and we thought it would be best to check out the house before looking at the apartment. The house looked really nice and when we went in we were so surprised to find all the basics were in there and we recognised my mother's room because all her furniture, including her bed, were there. Someone must have been quite busy. Then Thomas came in with his new friend, Peter, who also worked in the brewery, and with Hans and Inge; they'd done a great job and at least we could sleep in the house and then do the rest ourselves. Even my mother liked it; she was just happy to be in her own bed. What they'd done for us was such a big help and when we went to check the apartment out, my mother didn't even want to come and look at it, which I could completely understand.

As Thomas was also moving into the house, there was the question of how he would get to work and I remembered that Irma had got us that old car before; maybe those people had another one, maybe a little newer, and we did get one which wasn't that bad. Thomas wasn't jumping up and down but he had a car to show off together with his Hawaiian driver's license and slowly we got a lot under control. We were just waiting for the phone to be installed.

I went to register at the school with Angela and had the feeling most people thought like the ones who'd been behind us before and were talking about the Crazy Americans. I wanted to make an appointment with the doctor for my mother but she said that we could do that after Karl Heinz had gone. I was so frustrated with her but I couldn't drag her there. Finally, we got the phone connected, just in time before Karl Heinz left.

Somehow I did not understand why we did all that or spent all that money, but our plan was for my mother and Thomas to live there and that if we went on vacation, we would also have a place to stay. Thomas told us his boss, the owner of the brewery, and his wife wanted to invite us for dinner but we didn't have any time left. We thought Karl Heinz would be back before Christmas but he had to leave by the end of July because there was a lot of work to do on Maui and we needed those jobs. We had a year to decide what we would do.

I had to call Michael to tell him we'd made it safely to Bavaria and that we now had a phone and give him the number, but when I called, a lady's voice came on and when I asked for Mr. Mendez, she said he was in a meeting and couldn't be disturbed. I gave her our number and asked her to call when he was free.

I saw the doctor to make an appointment for my mother but he was over booked and the first one he could give me was five weeks later because it wasn't an emergency. Karl Heinz called and told me he'd got back safely but the house felt so empty and he missed us a lot. I was wondering why Michael hadn't called back; maybe he was really busy, but four days later the phone rang quite late in the evening and it was Michael. He heard my voice and knew he had the right number: he'd been looking through his mail and found the number and recognised that it was a German number. I told him that I'd called and left that number with a lady and he was quiet for a few seconds before saying that it was Aimi but that she hadn't said anything—just put that number with his mail. We talked for quite a while and I felt I could handle everything, so we would talk again in a few days.

Karl Heinz told me that everything was alright, just a lot of work but we needed that because we had no idea what would happen until next year. Next month Angela would start school and I wasn't sure if she needed tutorial sessions in German writing. She could speak perfect German but I wondered if she needed help with reading and writing.

We also went to the doctor's appointment and since he was the only doctor in that little village, he was like a medicine man and did everything. He did some tests but the tests had to be sent to a lab to be checked and that would take a bit of time—his excuse was that it was not an emergency—but at least she was starting to be checked out.

My weekly therapy sessions with Michael helped me and we talked about everything and nothing, but both of us were avoiding talking about our marital status. He still insisted we would see each other again: it was a dream, but dreams can be so nice too.

One evening, Thomas came home and told us that the brewery boss, Herr Keiser, had invited us for dinner at his house on the coming Saturday. It was the Keiser brewery in that small city. My mother wanted to stay home and Angela had a little cold and wanted to stay at home as well, so just Thomas and I went. It was a huge building with the brewery downstairs and the whole upstairs was their apartment. They even had an elevator in the building.

Well, we got there, of course using the elevator because Thomas insisted, and the door opened and there she was—a maid again, the second one I'd seen. The first was at Janet and Peter's place in Hong Kong and this one here, also with a plate, but different drinks as this one had glasses of beer. Then, Mr. and Mrs. Keiser came and greeted us. Mrs. Keiser was a very bustling, extravagant lady. Her name was Alexandra and Mr. Keiser was Karl. I had the feeling I was in a very wrong place but actually they were quite nice and down to earth.

The dinner was outstanding with two kinds of soup, then either fish or meat and mixed vegetables with fried potatoes and dumplings, with ice cream and cake for dessert. And, of course, beer. It was quite an interesting evening and Karl asked if we had a brewery on Maui. I thought, *Not again*, with starting a brewery on Maui. No one in our family knew how to brew beer but Karl Heinz and Karl would be the perfect fit for a new venture. I promised them that we would get together as soon as Karl Heinz returned and I could see on Karl's face how excited he was and I was very sure he wanted to get started with a brewery on Maui.

Angela started school. She was afraid and I remembered taking Thomas to school when we came back to Maui so I talked to the teacher and asked him to let me know if we needed any help. He was an elderly teacher and seemed to be really nice and so were the students. The word HAWAII must have been magic to people. After a few days of school, the teacher told me it would help if she could have some lessons, mostly in writing, and he gave me the address of a retired teacher.

We also had word from the doctor that the test results had come back and that more tests were needed, which had to be done in the hospital. I told my mother about it and wanted to make an appointment but she brushed it off saying that, right now, she was feeling fine and wanted to wait a little longer.

I wasn't in contact with Michael for almost three weeks. There was so much to do and I sometimes felt sorry for myself and didn't want to talk about my problems, but then he called and asked how I was. I told him about the brewery people and about my mother and he gave me some good advice and I tried to stop feeling guilty about our connection. We were just friends and would most likely stay in contact for the rest of our lives.

Karl Heinz told me he was planning to come over in the middle of December and see how things were developing, and then he said he had something to tell me and I knew right away what it was—that he wanted to sell our house, and, yes, I was right. At that moment I really didn't care how good the offer was and I just told him we'd talk when he came at Christmas. Since it was the beginning of Fall, I was able to enjoy the season with the leaves turning all kinds of yellow while nature prepared for the winter months. Some people called it the season of death because all the flowers were dying.

One morning, my mother told me something which really scared me. She said she'd woken up in the middle of the night and heard a knock at the window and that when she got up she saw a person walking away from the house. She said that person looked exactly like Papa (my father). For a moment I couldn't say a word but then I said, "You were most likely dreaming," and she then just said, "Maybe." It shook me up and I called Karl Heinz who told me to get someone to install some bars on the window. I didn't tell anyone else about it, but it bothered me.

Until then, my mother had seemed fine but I did remember my grandmother telling me shortly before she died that her husband sometimes visited her at night and, even though I really didn't believe in that kind of happening, there was a similarity. I decided not to push her into going to the hospital for more tests and that if that was the way she wanted it, I would accept it. Angela was doing quite well and her teacher really liked her, which helped a lot.

One night, I got a call from Rita. She was in Berlin and Michael had given her our phone number. It was so nice to talk about the old days and the times we'd had with Michael and Jonathan and the parties at Daniel's. Yes—it was in the past—but, like me, she was still in very loose contact with Jonathan and that time after the war had been special for everyone—though more for us who were looking for safety and freedom, which we never really found in caged-in Berlin. She told me a little about Berlin, where it was now normal life for the West Berliner almost seventeen years after the wall had been built. I still felt I had one leg in Berlin because of my property in East Germany which I was still hoping to get back one day. After that phone call I took the two records Michael had sent me and listened to them but they didn't make me feel better. I wanted to call Michael but I decided not to; it would have been too emotional.

Karl Heinz told me he was looking forward to being with us for Christmas and that I should start thinking about the new house he would build for us next year, since by then we would know how things were developing. As it was already September, there were only three months before he would arrive.

One morning, my mother woke me up. She looked pale and could hardly stand up and said she felt ill. As Thomas was still at home, he had to take Angela to school and call the brewery to say he wasn't able to go in to work because I had to take care of my mother. There was nothing I could do for her except call an ambulance to get her to the hospital and then wait for a doctor or nurse to come and tell me what was wrong. Finally, a nurse came and told me to come back later when they would know more.

Driving home, I had a hard time concentrating as I somehow felt it wasn't going to be alright. I called Karl Heinz even though it was the middle of the night in Hawaii, but I didn't care and he was on the phone pretty quickly. I told him what had happened and he just said, "Call me when you know more and I'll come over right away."

When I got to the hospital that night, I spoke with the doctor and he told me my mother had colon cancer, that she'd had it for quite a while and that her heart was weak. He said she was sleeping then but that I could come back the next day. When I got home, Thomas told me that Alexandra from the brewery had called and told Thomas to tell me that if I needed any help, I should call her. I hardly slept that night but I decided not to call Michael until I knew how long it would be.

The next day when I got to the hospital and saw my mother, she looked a bit better and even smiled. I didn't know if the doctor had told her what was wrong and she herself didn't say too much, she just complained about some stomach pain but said not to worry and I didn't stay too long because she was tired and fell asleep again. I went to find the doctor to talk to him about my mother but he was pretty busy so I had to wait a while. The first thing he asked me was why she hadn't gone to a doctor sooner and that there was nothing they could now do for her except keep her under painkillers and that because her heart was weak, it wouldn't take too long: maybe a week.

I felt as if someone had pulled the ground out from under my feet; I had known it was serious, but not that urgent, and I don't even remember how I got home. I knew I had to call Karl Heinz and tell him to be prepared to come soon. I went to the hospital again that night but she was sleeping and when I got home, I called Karl Heinz and told him to make reservations to come, at least within a week.

I also called Michael, and since I had his home phone number, I called that and hoped Aimi would not answer, but it was early in the morning in San Francisco and he answered the phone. He knew right away and asked if it was my mother. Well, I cried a lot and he just listened, only asking if Karl Heinz was coming. That crying helped and I promised to keep him posted.

I went to the hospital for the next three days and my mother slept a lot but we were still able to talk a little and when I got there on the fourth day, she was awake and even a little peppy, which I thought was a good sign until I spoke with the nurse. The nurse told me I should be prepared for the worst since shortly before a person passes away, the body takes all the energy that is left to fight the dying process. At least I heard that and that she might not make it through the night but then it took all my energy and nerves put together to go back into the room to try to say goodbye to my mother. I didn't know if she knew what was going on but when I turned around and started to leave, she just said, "Can't you stay a little longer?" I could hardly talk and just said I would return tomorrow.

Outside, the nurse asked me if I would come if the end was near and I said yes, and that she should call me, that I would wait. I walked out like a zombie and found Thomas and Angela were sleeping so I sat in the kitchen and waited for the call from the hospital. It was at around 11 at night when the phone rang and the nurse asked me if I would come, that it wouldn't be too long. I asked the nurse if my mother would still recognise me and when she said no, I told her I wouldn't go, just asking her to call me when it was over.

I couldn't cry, I couldn't do anything, and I just sat there and waited for my mother to say goodbye to me. I didn't know how, just a sign, and I waited all night until six in the morning when the hospital called and said it was over and that I should go and pick up her belongings. There was no sign. I wasn't able to drive and Thomas had to watch Angela and I then remembered Alexandra from the brewery offering to help me if needed. First, I called Karl Heinz and told him and he promised to come as soon as possible, then I told Michael and then Alexandra and I went to the hospital. I also had to go to the funeral house to pick out a coffin and I actually had trouble believing it was happening. For me it was just a bad dream.

We got to the hospital to fetch my mother's belongings and the nurse said if I wanted to see my mother again, she could take me to her. I declined: I'd seen many dead people during and after the war and I wanted to remember her alive the way she was on the last day I saw her. It was the same with my father—I remembered him standing on the steps of the plane, smiling at us and waving. One thing that made me kind of happy was that I was able to put my mother to rest next to my father; I couldn't even imagine what it would have been like if something had happened on the ship. I slowly realised she must have known she was ill and wanted to go home.

We also had to go to the funeral house to choose a coffin and that was one of the hardest things I had to do in life, and also to tell them it might be up to fourteen days before the funeral, since we were going to wait for my husband to arrive from overseas. Those were the most important things I had to do at the time; other arrangements I could do from home over the phone. When I knew when Karl Heinz would arrive I could see the priest and arrange the funeral. Even though I was very, very sad, perhaps for her it was best as after my father passed she was never really at home anymore and I knew that feeling—that's why she was so happy to sleep in her own bed. She was 75 years old when she died. I talked with Karl Heinz and he had a flight and would arrive in ten days, so I could make the funeral arrangements with the church.

I was prepared for long discussions with Karl Heinz about our future as we couldn't go on living like that, it would break our family apart and Angela had to go to school and not be moved from one country to the next. I hated the idea of living in caged-in Berlin but we considered it our home and didn't move from one house to the next.

Michael and I talked a few times and more or less talked about our lives. He felt he'd done a lot of things wrong in his life and so did I, but it was too late to change anything and we had that strong bond between us, which was enough. He also asked me, if I had a chance, to put some flowers on my mother's grave for him. I knew those two liked each other and I knew that Michael maybe saw a mother in her, which he never really had, but why my mother liked him I never did find out.

I picked Karl Heinz up from Munich airport and was glad he was back. He said he could only stay for two weeks and I didn't want to start a discussion before the funeral. When the day of the funeral came, there were not too many people, just Hans and Inge, Irma and her husband, and Karl and Alexandra from the brewery, along with those people who go to every funeral. I was fine until they let the coffin into the ground, when I had the same feeling as I'd had with my father—that they couldn't do that, they wouldn't be able to breathe.

Karl Heinz and Karl from the brewery met and they got along just great and we were invited for dinner over the next few days to talk about the brewery on Maui. That was all I needed at that moment, but I didn't say anything and just knew I had to make sure to have that discussion with Karl Heinz before the dinner party.

It was time to talk to the children about our future and what we would do next as we couldn't afford to keep the house just for Thomas and if all of us were going to live there again, then we would have to give up Maui. Angela told us she would rather give up Bavaria and go back to Maui because it was warmer there and she could go to the beach. Thomas wasn't sure as he had a girlfriend but Karl Heinz and I more or less knew what we wanted as we were now American citizens and if we stayed in Bavaria, we had no jobs and living there wasn't cheap either. Our business was on Maui and we couldn't start anew here, so we could either rent out the house or sell it.

Our immediate plan was for Karl Heinz to go back in fourteen days anyway but I had to stay back, we couldn't all run away together. Karl Heinz would then come back for Christmas and we would most likely then put the house up for sale with the help of Hans and Inge, who were also real estate agents. The house on Maui was Karl Heinz' responsibility. I just wanted some rest and, if and when I went back to Maui, a place to sleep and not a tent on the beach.

We had that dinner meeting with Karl and Alexandra at their huge apartment with the maid above the brewery and Karl Heinz was so impressed, just as I had been when I first visited them. Alexandra was a really nice person and we had to laugh about the two go-getters, Karl and Karl Heinz, who were already planning the brewery. Karl said he had a brew master who started the brewing process for his beer and who was also overseeing a brewery in China, so he could also oversee our brewery. I thought it was a little fast even for Karl Heinz because he told him we would have to look for commercial property first, which would be a lengthy and costly process, but Karl just brushed that off and said, "I will invest in it too and I know some investors who would gladly join in."

Finally, they calmed down and the decision was made to start looking for commercial property on Maui. Alexandra started to laugh and said, "There is a German song, 'There is no beer on Hawaii,'" and, yes, I remembered that song. It was by a German musician whose name was Paul Kuhn, recorded and sung for the first time in 1963. Then Karl said, "In a year or two, that song won't be true anymore," and all in all, it was a nice evening, but perhaps with a little too much beer, so we got a taxi to take us home.

The next two weeks went by quickly and Karl Heinz had to leave until Christmas. It was already getting pretty cold and that made my decision to go back to Maui more certain. I bought a small wreath for my mother like Michael had asked me to, and took a picture and sent it to him, so he called me again. He knew Karl Heinz was back in the islands and we had another long talk. We talked about Complex Wannsee and Gatow and our special room at Daniel's house and we both knew what we wanted to say but we didn't as we would have broken up two families, and so we stayed where we were. I went through a lonely time. Thomas was hardly at home because of his girlfriend so I had to keep myself busy and while cleaning out my mother's room I found that locket she'd taken from my grandmother when she passed away. There was the rosary Michael had given my grandmother for Christmas; I remembered that she hardly let go of it.

It was a good thing I had Angela at home, otherwise I would most likely have started talking to myself. It was just before Christmas and everyone was busy, and even though I was invited out I didn't like to be away in the evenings because Angela had to go to school the next morning and Thomas came home late, if at all. Yes, I missed my mother in all places. I only bought a medium sized Christmas tree, since I had no idea when we would be leaving again.

I bought Janet and Michael a Bavarian Christmas Angel; it was like a music box which you could turn on and it would sing Silent Night, Holy Night, and it was so pretty. Janet and Michael sent me quite a nice handbag with a fitting scarf, which amazed Alexandra when she saw it. I thought it over and asked myself where in Hawaii I would ever wear a scarf, so I gave it to her but kept the handbag.

Karl Heinz arrived four days before Christmas, so our family was at least together for the holidays and we spent Christmas Eve together just as a family. I would have loved to go to Midnight Mass at church but it was so cold and also snowing, so we stayed at home. Karl Heinz told me about the very good offer we had on our Maui house from a pilot flying for a big U.S. airline. He flew mostly on overseas routes, so wanted to buy it as an investment and we could stay in the house until our new house was ready, but of course we would have to pay rent. Well, then, that wasn't too bad.

After Christmas, we had an invitation for dinner with our friends and a big New Year's party was planned at the brewery. Everyone had been invited—Hans and Inge and Irma and her husband, and Karl invited a few investors for the brewery. For the first time, I met Thomas' girlfriend who was a really nice girl and they told me that she would follow Thomas after he got settled in Hawaii again. Yes, I'd heard that story before!

Our plan was to get everything in order after the holidays and that Hans and Inge would take care of the house until we returned in the summer. If they had a chance to sell it, then they could and for quite a high commission, but it would be better to wait until summer. So, it was 1979 already and in January we packed up all our stuff including the car, which had to be shipped as well, and left Bavaria.

After that long many-hours flight, which we'd almost got used to, we were sort of glad to be in a warm climate again and in our house, which soon would not be our house again, but all our furniture was still there so it still felt like ours. We started our model home up again and were selling those packages from the model house and Thomas wanted to work with us building the houses and learning more about carpentry, which was fine. We wanted to put Angela into that International School where I used to work as a cleaning girl for the teachers before later being promoted to kitchen helper. While I was working there, my dream was that whenever I had a daughter, she'd have to attend that school, so when I went to register her, I was so proud. I'd made it; my daughter was attending that school and I wasn't a kitchen helper anymore; I was the mother of a student.

I missed my mother a lot and realised what a big help she'd been to us all those years. Now I couldn't paint the houses anymore, but I decorated them and sometimes hung wallpaper. Karl Heinz was looking for another property for our next house, which should be our dream house and never be sold. In the meantime, he spoke with Charly about the brewery and Charly thought it was too early for a brewery and that we would be too small; that the big breweries on the mainland would kill us, but he promised Karl Heinz that he'd listen around and let him know.

From the profit of the sale of our house, we bought quite a big, nice property close to the school where Angela would start in the Fall. I missed talking to Michael but we wrote letters, so we knew what was happening in each other's lives. Since we were flying to Germany in the summer anyway, we didn't do anything about our new house. Hans and Inge called us to say they had parties interested in buying our house in Bavaria but wanted to wait until we got there.

Meanwhile, Charly had a meeting with Karl Heinz about what he'd found out about the brewery idea from his so-called "business friends." It would be very costly and there would be a lot of permits to be obtained and rules to be kept as it would be a commercial property. A liquor license had to be applied for and a new water pipeline connected—it sounded scary. Charly told Karl Heinz he would not invest in the brewery but he would help him with whatever he could. He said that with a grin on his face, which meant he wanted to be paid too, as well as his "business partners."

We decided not to look for any property for the brewery before we talked to Karl in the summer; I think we were both scared too about where all the money would come from. We started to make plans for the summer to sell the house in Bavaria, since we needed that profit to build the "dream house" in Maui; it was getting complicated. Thomas was not coming with us as he'd found a girlfriend in Maui in the meantime and had broken up with the Bavarian one; that happening was familiar, too. Finally, we had our plan together— that Angela and I would fly first and then Karl Heinz would follow later because he was too busy there.

Angela and I were getting ready for the flight to Bavaria but because of the length of the flight, we agreed to have a one-night stop-over in Chicago to break the travelling time in half. We were ready to fly and felt a lot better because of the overnight stop. Leaving Los Angeles, we passed Lake Michigan, which is the second largest lake in North America and only about ten miles away from Chicago airport.

Yes, it was so nice having that hotel room and we had a lovely dinner and still had until the next afternoon before the next flight to Frankfurt, Germany, and on to Munich. We even broke the time difference of twelve hours in half, so we decided we'd always stay on the East Coast for one night. I wanted to call Michael from the hotel but decided I'd rather wait until we were in Bavaria.

We had a rental car waiting in Munich for the one-hour Autobahn drive to our little village. It was a clear summer day and we could see the

Bavarian Alps in the distance—a view I loved—and we could also smell Bavaria because of their cows in the pasture, and there were many cows.

Finally, we were home. It may not be home for long anymore, but for now it was great and we found food in the refrigerator and freshly cut flowers on the table: it was like having the ALOHA spirit in Bavaria. Hans and Inge and Irma stopped by and said, "Gruess di"—greetings, like a very friendly greeting—and we promised to stop by the next day because we were quite tired. I still called Karl Heinz and let him know we'd made it but I was too tired to call Michael, so that had to wait until the next day.

We were well rested after that first night and that break on the East Coast had really helped a lot. I was glad that we had the small rental car as I didn't want to have to ask anyone if I could borrow one. We went to the cemetery and took flowers but the grave looked kind of neglected, which it had to be as no one had taken care of it. I spoke with the caretaker and he said they had a service for people who didn't live in that village and who weren't able to care for a grave, so I took that service.

On our way back I dropped Angela off at the pool: the weather was beautiful and a few of her former classmates were there and there were lifeguards all over, so she was fine, and I then stopped at Hans and Inge's place to find out about the possible buyers for our house. They came from Munich and were pretty well off and loved that little village, which I could understand since it had happened to me, too, but I wanted to wait until Karl Heinz arrived.

That evening I wanted to call Michael but before I did, he called and wanted to know how everything went. He seemed to be happy. Bianca was pregnant and he would be a grandfather—and not even fifty years old. He also told me he would fly to Berlin on business but he didn't know when and didn't tell me what business, so I didn't ask. I knew he was waiting for a comment but I didn't reply. He said he would meet Rita in Berlin; maybe it was one of his business trips again, and no word about Aimi. It was still nice to talk to him but I was a bit jealous; they would be having a good time in Berlin and I would be here, sitting and trying to get the house in shape for the new owner.

Karl Heinz called and told me he wanted to make reservations to arrive in about ten days so that we could wrap everything up and be out by August. Alexandra then came by to say hello and we started to talk and I was surprised how open she was, telling me that we had to watch our husbands as she knew Karl would go overboard and she noticed Karl Heinz was the same way. Maybe that whole brewery idea was a bit too much for us and now I was glad to have someone with whom to share my worries.

Two days after Michael's call, he phoned again, which surprised me. He asked me how I felt after he said he was flying to Berlin and then he started to laugh and said, "Remember, I did that to you when we first met, because I liked your reaction." Now I realised what he was doing—just trying to make me jealous—and we both had to laugh. "I am not flying to Berlin," he said, "I'm flying to Frankfurt to meet an old friend of mine from the military time." He knew me so well that he'd noticed my jealous reaction, but I laughed a lot about that.

It looked to me as if Michael was still the same with the little games he liked to play—but he then always told you the truth after you were upset; it was never boring with him.

Karl Heinz arrived and while we were waiting for the buyer from Munich, we had another dinner with Karl and Alexandra, during which Karl Heinz told them it wasn't that easy to find a commercial property and comply with all the rules and regulations, especially when alcohol was involved. Karl said he and Alexandra would come over to Hawaii and have a look—maybe in the fall of this year or the spring of 1980. Since we wouldn't have a house or apartment in that little village anymore, we didn't plan to come to Bavaria over the holidays anyway, so it would be better if they came in the spring of 1980. Hans and Inge were also planning to visit—maybe by then we would be ready with our "Dream House."

We tried to convince bouncing Karl to go slowly on that project, since it really was such a big thing. So far we had everything under control and the buyer from Munich was satisfied with everything and let us finish without stress. Even though we'd only lived there a short time, it was still special for me because my mother had passed away there and

I really started to hope, since there was nothing there to keep us coming very year, that maybe we would find a way we could travel to Berlin again one year.

We left Bavaria at the end of August and another episode of my life ended. I'd left Europe again, this time being very sure I wouldn't live there anymore, but still hoping Germany would one day be reunited so that Berlin would be just one city and not divided into two, and that I would get my property back. I felt very melancholic taking off from Munich airport and flying over the Bavarian Alps, but I still had my family and Michael to talk with about the past.

Somehow, it felt good being back on Maui even though there was so much work to do—working from the model house, trying to start on our dream house and also looking for commercial property. The day when I took Angela to that school, I felt quite important not entering by the kitchen door in the back but instead walking in through the front door of the school. One thought I had was that I wasn't dressed up like the other ladies, who were all wearing designer outfits. It was too bad that our Mercedes was still somewhere on the ocean or I could have driven it and would have felt better, but maybe then they would have thought I was just the nanny.

We told our landlord that it might take a little while for us to vacate the house but he was fine with that, as he wouldn't be home that much anyway.

I received a letter from Michael saying he was back home from Frankfurt and was impressed by the progress he'd seen in West Germany. Of course, it was almost thirty years since he was shipped to Germany from the U.S., and he wondered how Berlin must look now and said he really wanted to visit it but would only go if I would be with him. Of course, that would never happen, so I ignored it. After reading that letter, I thought back, wondering where all the time had gone and what would it have been like if I had married him. He would be fifty years old next year—instead of worrying about moving from one house to the next, I most likely would have been worrying about his "business" trips, but I had to smile about it.

Charly was on a tour to Las Vegas with a group. The tour was monthly for four days and was always booked out and Charly always came back smiling. When he told Karl Heinz about it, he said he'd mentioned to some friends about the brewery and they were excited at the idea of being able to invest. So, we had investors already but no property. These developments worried me a bit as we'd never had any investors in what we'd done, just a mortgage which we'd paid off the minute we sold the house. When I told Karl Heinz about it, he just laughed, gave me a hug, and said I had to stop thinking so small and start thinking bigger now. I wished I could talk to Alexandra about it but they were coming next spring so maybe we could find a way to get more organised.

Christmas was around the corner and I was actually glad to stay at home and sleep in my own bed, like my mother used to say. It was just our family and Thomas brought his girlfriend along—a pretty little local girl who Thomas tried to teach the German language and customs, and we had a lot of fun. It was a really nice Christmas and we ate German food, mostly cooked by Karl Heinz and Thomas, and I really missed my mother. I just sent a Christmas card to Janet and Michael. I was honestly too busy to get a present for them, but Michael sent me a monetary gift to buy my favourite perfume; he knew what brand it was.

And so, we entered 1980 and I knew it would be as hectic as all the others since we then had to concentrate on the commercial property and starting our dream house.

Charly invited us to his big New Year's party, which was actually very smart as his friends were invited too and they had a lot of influence over rules and regulations. They didn't really talk business but they were getting to know each other and Karl Heinz told them that a brewery owner from Germany would be coming over in the spring—an idea they liked because it would be good for Maui and would put that Island more into the spotlight. It was more like an introduction than a New Year's party.

Anyway, we were in 1980 and hoping for a good year. Karl told us they would be coming over in March but we still hadn't finished our dream house and they couldn't stay in our rental house now so we looked for a condominium by the ocean on Maui's goldcoast Kihei. In the meantime, our Mercedes arrived without any dents or bumps, so the year started out quite well. Angela liked the school; they had a pool on campus and a tennis court and if everything went well she could make her high school graduation there.

Even though I had a good and exciting life, I still had days when I felt very lonely and I realised something was missing, though I really didn't know what. Michael and I exchanged a few letters and he told me he and Aimi were getting a divorce. H said maybe the age difference was too great but I didn't quite believe him—most likely there was someone else with whom he was involved and, also, he was not looking forward to his 50th birthday. He also wrote that if we met again we'd have a lot of memories: I didn't know why he was so sure we would meet again, it might have been a dream he had or still some guilt about what had happened, now 25 years ago.

Karl and Alexandra arrived pretty tired, so we dropped them off at the condominium in Kihei and they loved it—they could walk right into the ocean within just a few feet. They rented a car for the three weeks they were staying on Maui, which was good as it meant they could explore Maui a little on their own, if needed. We let them rest a little and then planned three outings—Lahaina Frontstreet, Haleakala Mountain, and Hana. After that they would meet Charly and we would start the search for commercial property. I was so happy Alexandra was there; even though she looked like an extravagant lady, she was very much down to earth and we got along very well.

The first week of Karl and Alexandra's visit was almost gone and they were enjoying their condominium so much, it looked as if they wouldn't leave at all but they had to see those three places, they were worth seeing. Karl kept on pushing about finding property because that would be his reason for visiting Maui again, it was really funny. We finally pushed for our first outing, which always took a whole day, and that was the trip to Hana.

It was a dangerous road about 70 miles long which was always being worked on because it was crooked and slippery, often just a narrow one lane road high above the ocean with no rails and you could count on four to five hours for the trip to Hana. When you arrived, you could buy T-shirts with the slogan "I survived the road to Hana."

Hana is located on the Eastern end of the island and had a population of a little over 1,200 people at that time. It is one of the most isolated communities in the State but the vegetation in Hana was breathtaking and the drive there was like driving on another island in the South Pacific. On arrival, they had everything—a tiny school, a church, and a very tropical and pricey hotel complex as well—that was where you could find a tiny cottage next to a mansion which belonged to a Hollywood celebrity.

Karl and Alexandra enjoyed it; Alexandra more than Karl as he was constantly looking around, maybe looking for property—but Hana would definitely not be the place to start a brewery. We had lunch at the hotel, which had only Hawaiian ladies as waitresses, all wearing Hawaiian uniforms—the Hawaiian Muumuu dresses—and full of Hawaiian Aloha.

I took some pictures of them and had a brilliant idea—that we would drive to the end of the highway, where it was closed off because of bad road conditions. There was a beautiful little chapel there and a small graveyard which looked very old but was well kept. I went into the chapel to light a candle and there was a guestbook with names and locations from all over the world, so I wrote my name in it, giving my address not as Maui but just West Berlin, Germany, so my hometown would forever be in that guestbook.

Next to the cemetery, we saw a house built high up on a cliff, overlooking Hana Bay and next to the house was a cottage, mostly built out of glass with a couple of monkeys, and at the entrance gate door there was a huge sign: "If there is a heaven, it's here, it's here!" We went back to the graveyard because I'd been told by Charly that Charles Lindbergh was buried there and we found the grave. That little chapel and graveyard was famous because of Charles Lindbergh who had made the first solo nonstop transatlantic airplane flight in 1927 from New York to Paris. He died in 1974 at the age of 72 years.

I stood at the grave overlooking Hana Bay and wondered to myself what kind of a man he must have been, living an extraordinary life and most likely experiencing great joy for some of his achievements and now he was there, buried away from all glamour, and I wondered why he was buried there in the middle of the Pacific Ocean in little Kipa-hulu/Hana. We had to leave for our return to the city, but everyone was a little quieter as we left.

On our way home, we discussed our trip and everyone was moved by what they'd seen. Hana was so different from the rest of Maui; it was as if Hana was a different island. As Karl and Alexandra didn't have many days left, we thought it might be best if the two men spent more time with Charly and that just Alexandra and I would visit Lahaina Frontstreet, then we could all do Haleakala mountain together.

So, Alexandra and I were really looking forward to our shopping trip to Lahaina. We started quite early in the morning because Lahaina was known to get very hot during the day. The highway to Lahaina was built right next to the ocean and it took us a little over an hour to get there so we were getting hungry and went to get a late breakfast. There was some room at the Courthouse Square under the famous banyan tree, which had been planted in 1873 and had now grown to almost two thirds of an acre, and there was a little museum where you could get all the information about the history of the Banyan tree.

After breakfast, we went on to Frontstreet, which had lots of art-work and some very cute little boutique shops. I bought a T-shirt for Janet and one for Michael: he got a black one with "Lahaina, Maui" written on it as he liked black T-shirts. I hoped he didn't feel too old and hadn't gained too much weight to wear it. Alexandra bought some fashion jewellery and when she saw my two shirts, she asked who those lucky people were. I just told her they were friends from after the war, at least he was, and she looked at me with a tear in her eye and said, "And you still like him; I know that feeling." We stopped that conversation right there.

It was then getting very hot and humid so we had a big bowl of ice cream and started home and when I dropped her off at her con-dominium, Karl Heinz and Charly were still discussing two of the properties they'd found. As soon as they knew what they wanted, Charly could then start talking to his friends about what had to be done and you could tell how excited they were by the number of beer bottles on the ground. Our next outing to Haleakala Mountain was planned for the coming weekend and then, in a week after that, they had to leave.

We started to prepare for our coming weekend trip up the mountain. Karl Heinz and Karl were busy trying to decide which property to choose—they were both almost the same size and price but one was a bit out of the centre of the town in an industrial, newly developed, subdivision, and the other one was almost in the centre of town. They figured out that the one in the industrial area would be better, with more parking available and not so much traffic.

We decided that after our mountain outing we would all have a meeting and make a plan about the best way to start. Charly had told us right from the beginning that he was not going to invest but would be an adviser and a kind of coach between the responsible parties for the rules and regulations and that for that he would like a salary. I could almost understand that because without him we'd have a difficult time getting all those permits.

I still had some time left to get my package off to San Francisco, along with the picture I'd taken in the restaurant in Hana with the pretty Hawaiian girls, so I put it in with Michael's T-shirt, meant for his 50th birthday.

We made an early start on the Haleakala trip as it takes up to three hours to get to the top and the road is winding all the way to the East Maui Volcano, the other name for Haleakala. If you get a cloudy day like we did, you drive through and can't see anything until you're above the clouds. The tallest peak of the mountain is 10,025 feet and the last eruption was between 1480 and 1600 and I heard Karl start to kind of laugh, saying, "Then we are safe today," but I thought he was a little scared.

Slowly, we started to reach the summit and suddenly the clouds started to clear and we saw the crater and were able to look down and see the beaches and little toy houses; it was amazing. But—you could tell the air was thinner and you had to breathe more deeply and we saw that Karl wasn't feeling comfortable and it was also very windy, so we didn't walk around. Even so, being up there you felt like a little ant and it was overwhelming. On our way down, Karl admitted that he wasn't feeling great but said that he'd enjoyed it very much, and that was the last outing we had. We then had to decide at the next meeting which property we would take.

We had the meeting and all of us agreed to get the property in the industrial area, so Charly and Karl Heinz went to the real estate company and told them we were interested in buying that property—of course, he was a friend of Charly, as well. I was glad I didn't have to go with them and still had a few days with Alexandra to relax at the beach.

They made an offer and it was accepted so when Karl and Alexandra left, they knew it might take a while for the first beer to be drunk, but it was the start. There was the possibility that either they or us would have to fly over to Bavaria if Karl found investors and papers had to be signed. It was all up in the air about how long it would take to get all the permits but we knew that we were staying on Maui during the summer and not going to Bavaria or any other place.

We hit the first so-called problem as there were some huge palm trees to be removed from the lot. Of course, we needed a permit for that but couldn't find any landscaping company able to do it. It took a while to find a way to solve the problem but in the end Charly got the permit to remove them and how we did it was unusual: they hired a small helicopter, which was able to lift trees up and out without much damage to the ground or the surrounding area. It was quite an expensive event and even the media took pictures. Sometimes I got quite afraid thinking it was a bit too big for us, and that was just the beginning.

Karl called to let us know that they would most likely be back in the next spring and that he had spoken with the German brewmaster, who was willing to do the brew start for our brewery. At least there wasn't too much pressure, as we had to wait a while for every permit.

Michael wrote a thank-you letter and I could see he was still much the same as 25 years ago; it was a very sweet letter. Sometimes I wondered if we really would see each other again.

While we were waiting between getting one permit and the next, Charly told us he had put together a ten-day tour to Manila in the Philippines and that we would only have to pay half price. Karl Heinz was all for it and I thought he needed a break, too. Charly said it would be in November as that was the best time with hardly any rain and he knew that because he'd grown up there. As we weren't going anywhere that Christmas season, and since it was a good deal, we agreed to go with them, but Thomas wanted to stay back so it was just Karl Heinz, Angela and me.

Charly changed the trip to Manila to a week instead of ten days, which was even better because it was so close to the holidays. Our dream house was coming along quite well and I could see it would be a dream house if everything was finished but we didn't plan a pool— instead just a big jacuzzi and a sauna, because a pool is a lot of work and if you go travelling you always have to have someone to take care of it.

Thomas took us to the airport quite late at night as our flight to Manila left in the middle of the night. I didn't know much about the Philippines, except that it was a ten-hour flight with a stop-over in Guam, so I looked it up in my smart little book. The Philippines is a country in South East Asia in the Western Pacific Ocean and consists of about 7,600 islands and Manila, the Capital, is located on the island of Luzon. That was all my smart little book told me and was actually all I needed to know since Charly was with us and would be our tour guide.

We boarded the plane and our seats were in the front almost behind the cockpit, and the plane only half full including our small group of only twelve people. I noticed the pilot taxied out to the reef runway, the farthest runway from the airport building, and he was driving quickly. It was a DC10, a wide-body plane designed mostly for long range flights. We reached the end of the runway and he started to take off and was a bit off the ground when all of a sudden the lights went out, the cockpit door opened and we heard the captain yelling, "May-day, mayday," and then a terrible impact with the runway: he just let the plane fall down and by doing that he cut all the tires and was just skidding along. I looked out of the window and saw nothing but what looked like smoke, though in fact it was dust, and he tried to pull to the left side because we were just about running into the ocean.

Finally, the plane stopped. Some people cried but there were no broken legs or arms or really serious injuries. The slides were not working but there were enough ambulances to get us out over the stairs. Angela and I were numb and wanted to go home but we were told another plane was coming from Los Angeles and that they would serve breakfast and then start over again. I really had no desire to carry on but I couldn't leave by myself. It took about five hours for the next plane to arrive and we tried again and it went well to Guam. I sat next to an off-duty pilot and he told me we were lucky that the plane hadn't been fully booked, otherwise we would have landed in the ocean.

We made it safely to Guam for refuelling and I looked out and saw a few mechanics on the wings trying to repair something; I was a nervous wreck. Then, we made it to Manila after all but there was no luggage. We waited for a while and then we sent Charly to the airport manager who looked at us kind of strangely and said, "Your luggage is in the other luggage department." Well, we went there and opened the door and looked at a big pile of damaged, half-torn-up suitcases, and were told that as we had no change of clothes even if it was only for a week, we would be given US$50 to buy some new clothes. That wasn't that bad and we would have had our own money to buy clothes but the problem was that the clothing sizes in the Philippines was different from the ones in the States and there was hardly anything available in our size. We finally found a store which must have been for American tourists and which had some clothes our sort of size.

We finally reached the hotel and almost collapsed—at least, that's how I felt. We had almost everything we needed for the week and were able to squeeze into the clothes we'd bought and decided to just relax by the pool. Charly, Karl Heinz and the rest of the group took a city tour but I stayed back and watched the jeepneys or jeeps, which are small buses and the most popular public transportation—usually over-filled and with people hanging off the outside. Manila is a colourful city, or at least it was at that time, but nobody actually really did a lot and I guess we all needed our energy for the return flight. Charly felt a bit sorry but I enjoyed that week. We went to a music/talent show one night which was amazing with a lot of talented performers and I noticed the most beautiful girls were a mixture between the Spanish and Filipino race. I didn't sleep that well the night before our departure, but everything went well this time and we arrived home safely.

Thomas told us our almost full plane crash was even on the news and in the meantime they'd found out that the plane already had a few damaged tires and that was most likely the reason the Captain had aborted the full take-off and blown up the rest. Not too much happened that week and it looked as though we wouldn't do anything with the brewery work until next year, so we could concentrate on finishing the dream house and another house.

After checking my mailbox, I found a letter from Michael. He'd seen the plane accident on the news and was worried we were on that plane, since he knew we were on our way to Manila. It was almost Christmas and it would be the last Christmas in that house, which I really loved, but I truly hoped our dream house would be our home for a bit longer. I only sent a Christmas card to San Francisco that year, telling them they should do the same as we didn't need big presents for Christmas—we just needed warm greetings. Karl Heinz came home with "flu" and we all caught it, so it was a very quiet Christmas spent mostly feeling sick and tired but we somehow made it into 1981.

I was really looking forward to moving into our dream house and if everything went well, we would be able to move in spring, or March, since Hawaii does not really have seasons—there is winter and summer where you feel the difference in temperature, but not spring or fall. You can actually ski on the slopes of Haleakala and two hours later be sun-bathing or swimming in the ocean, but only in the winter months.

We had almost all the permits together for the brewery and when we told that to Karl in Bavaria, he said he had two investors and we would have to go to Bavaria and see a lawyer to sign the relevant papers. We could stay at Irma's bed-and-breakfast, which would be nice. So, we tried to finish as much as we could of the dream house and then, after coming back from Bavaria, we could finish everything up. Thomas would stay back and take care of whatever was left to do as we were just in between—the houses were almost finished and the brewery wasn't quite ready to start.

Michael wrote about his 50th birthday and joked about it, but I could feel that he didn't accept his age. He also had a younger girlfriend again and he'd become a grandfather as Bianca had a little girl. I felt sorry for him, thinking that he would never settle down, but on the other hand I was the same, never staying in a place too long. It might have been because of being caged in in Berlin for a long time, giving the feeling that after a certain time you have to move on before they cage you in again.

We had a lot of help with moving into our dream house. It was maybe three quarters finished, but that was fine as we could finish it up slowly. We were planning to leave for Bavaria right after Angela finished her school year.

One evening, Karl Heinz came home with a bottle of wine and we were sitting on the floor of our living room-to-be and he asked me if I would like to visit Berlin for a few days after we'd finished our business with the investors in Munich. I thought I wasn't hearing right but he had already spoken with his sister, Christina, who said we could stay with them since there was enough space and they had that nice big yard. Yes, of course I wanted to. He had to go and look for a brew house which was for sale somewhere in the Black Forest area. I couldn't wait to leave.

Charly was also working with two investors but we wanted to wrap that up in the fall after our return from Bavaria, so when Angela finished her school year, we were ready to leave. We stayed one night in Chicago as it was so much easier to break the trip in half and then fly the next day non-stop Chicago to Munich. We rented a car again so no one needed to pick us up and Irma was already waiting for us.

Usually, people from Bavaria and people from Northern Germany, including Berlin, sometimes had issues, but it was different with us; we were German/Americans and not "Preussen" like the Northern Germans. It reminded me a lot of Hawaii with Mainland Haolis and German Haolis. I felt really good seeing all of them. I was also happy to see my parents' grave again and that landscape company had done a perfect job and everything was nicely decorated.

Karl called a meeting for the following week with a lawyer in Munich and the investors, so that papers could be signed. It was a very fancy lawyer's office and the two investors acted pretty high-nosed but we later found out that they were very much down to earth. They seemed to be more scared than I was about that brewery deal.

When we went back home to Irma and Karl's, they were talking about the brew house for sale in the Black Forest and Karl mentioned that he wanted to go along, which was understandable since he was the expert, and that was my chance to stay behind in the little village. They wanted to go for two days in order to not make it too stressful. There was also a meeting planned with Mr. Kranz, the German brew master. I promised Alexandra I'd stay overnight in their apartment so we could have a nice ladies' night, and one night I stayed with Irma, because I wanted to call San Francisco. Angela stayed with her former friend and classmate, so everyone did what they wanted to do.

When I called Michael that night, it was early morning in San Francisco and a lady answered the phone. I asked for Mr. Mendez and she replied, "One minute," and I heard her calling, "Baby, someone wants to talk to you," and after hearing that, I hung up. What had I expected? I knew he had a new girlfriend and why did I call in the first place; I was really mad with myself. Five minutes later he called back and asked me why I'd hung up, or was the connection bad, and I didn't answer since he knew why I'd done it and that made me even more mad. The next evening with Alexandra was so nice and we had a great time. I knew she wanted to know about the T-shirt deal and who those people were, but I wasn't ready to talk about that.

Next day, Karl and Karl Heinz came back but that brew house was too expensive and not in a good shape. We still had the meeting with Mr. Kranz, the brew master, to attend before we could leave for Berlin and that was planned for the next week. He was an elderly man, very knowledgeable about brewing beer, but very strict in his ways and whatever he decided to do, that was what had to be done. That was all we could talk about, since nothing was actually ready for him, but he agreed to do it for us so everything there was done and we were ready to leave for Berlin the next day.

We said goodbye to everyone and Karl said to let him know when the building would be ready, because he was looking for a brew house and that Karl Heinz should do the same over in the States. He'd heard that England might be a possible place to get a good one and he said he would then be able to come and help us.

Finally, we were on our way to Berlin—in a way excited and in another way, scared. At first, we wanted to use the autobahn, driving through East Germany into West Berlin, but when we thought about it, being American citizens with American passports and with our birthplace being Berlin, we weren't sure if it was a good idea, so we decided to fly from Munich into Berlin. We dropped the car off at Munich airport and flew into Berlin Tegel and if the plane dropped altitude to fly in that corridor, I didn't notice: I was too excited. Looking out of the window, you could see the wall.

We rented another car and drove to Christina and Werner. Their two sons were already all grown up and out of the house, yes it was already over ten years. It was a bittersweet feeling and a lot of memories came up, thinking about my grandmother, my parents, and even Michael. Michael's memories went back to 25 years ago but they were still there. We had a nice time together but Berlin had changed a lot even with the wall built, and that looked like a part of daily life and fully accepted. Even though I loved Berlin, I realised I might not be able to live there permanently anymore. I took a few pictures to maybe send to Michael, but I hadn't heard from him since our last talk. Of course, he could not get in touch with me. I still felt embarrassed about the way I behaved on the phone.

We made it home safely and summer was over so Angela went back to school and we started finishing our dream house. I found two letters in my post box from Michael, asking me how Berlin was and telling me he felt sorry about the phone event, but he already knew my reaction the minute he heard what his girlfriend said—in other words he laughed about the "bad connection." He was right and I wrote back saying I'd acted childishly, and I put the Berlin pictures in the letter.

We met Charly and told him about the investors in Bavaria and the search for the brew house and he said he'd been told to wait a little while, that in the near future there would be a change in management officials and we could save a lot of money that way. The bad news was that it might take up to two years but Charly's investors were willing to wait. Well, if that was the only way, we would have to do it. I had to admit that I was a bit relieved and, deep down, Karl Heinz was too. Charly wanted to put it on the side burner because he had another deal to offer where he wanted to be a full-time partner; he'd found property on which to build an office building. Karl Heinz told Karl about the brewery delay and he accepted it since the investors in Bavaria had not paid their share yet, they had just pledged to do it, so that was fine.

We had a meeting with Charly about the property for the office building. There was a perfect location in the centre of the city, which was very cheap since we were told it used to be a burial ground for Hawaiian people years ago and was so-called "holy." In other words, it should not be touched for commercial use, but offices were desperately needed. I guess even Charly was a bit afraid but with Karl Heinz in it as an "outsider," it would be okay. We picked the property up for a very reasonable amount but we needed an architect that time to get all the permits quite quickly, compared with the paperwork for the brewery. It still took us until the beginning of the next year, 1982, until everything was documented and approved, so we could then start clearing the lot.

We had a quiet Christmas again, since we were having a stressful life at that time. I sent a "Melekaliki Maka" (Merry Christmas) card to Michael with some Hawaiian chocolates and Michael sent a picture of Bianca's baby, but nothing was said about his girlfriend—not even her name or picture—but I didn't ask. Everything he wrote and explained was so full of life—maybe he'd found the right one this time.

Finally, they were ready to start the building and the lot was graded, even though the bulldozing machine broke down twice—once hitting an electric pole because the brakes were failing, and power had to be restored. The lumber was delivered but some was missing—actually, there was always something wrong. One of the workers told Karl Heinz that every morning around 8 o'clock, they saw a huge black dog on top of the property, just standing there and staring at them for a few minutes before turning around and leaving.

Then, while a worker was digging a ditch, he found the remains of bones—of course, it used to be a cemetery. We told Charly about it and he said he had to find out if the bones were animal or human and it turned out they were human so they had to be reburied. Because there was always something missing or breaking almost every day, Charly said we had to bless the project and that it had to be a Hawaiian priest, so we found a Hawaiian priest who came and blessed the project and said we should have done that right from the beginning.

After the blessing, everything was fine and the black dog never showed up again. You can believe it or not, but if you see something with your own eyes, you tend to believe it. The true Hawaiian people believe in different Gods—a God for fire, one for water, and many more, and maybe one of those Gods was not satisfied with how we treated the Hawaiian graveyard until a priest blessed it. Maybe there was also a God of animals, like the black dog. Anyway, we did the right thing and everything went smoothly after that.

Because of the building of the office block and the renting out of the offices, we intended to stay at home during the summer. There were ten units, five downstairs and five upstairs, and it really was a pretty building. Everything went faster than we expected so that it was ready to be rented out at the end of the summer and we were lucky enough to rent it out pretty quickly. Charly told us that he'd had word that we'd most likely be able to start on the brewery next fall, in 1983, but that was just a "maybe."

Charly came over one day and told us he was waiting to tell us after the completion of the building, but he had a group together to fly to Fiji Island for a week and he wanted us to go as well. I guess he must have made a pretty good profit on those groups. He told us it was just a little over a six-hour flight from Honolulu to Nadi International Airport and compared to most other flights we'd had, that was actually a short trip. I checked my smart little book and found out that Fiji is a country of about 300 little islands in the South Pacific, that the capital is Suva and that it became independent from the British Commonwealth in 1970.

Charly told us it was a beautiful island with the best beaches ever and the timing in August was good, too, as it wasn't too hot compared to Hawaii, but a bit humid. Thomas stayed back so that he could take care of things but it was only for a week, so it was just the three of us and a small group. Charly had reserved a small condominium right at the ocean and it was truly a beautiful beach. I wanted to write a letter to San Francisco before we left but had no time, so I sent a postcard from there.

We enjoyed the beach but just one incident scared me a lot. I was lying on the beach and looked up to see a snake crawling in the sand. As I didn't know if it was poisonous or not, it scared me half to death. I told Charly about it and he told me that some snakes were very poisonous, some not at all, but since I had no idea what kind of snake it was, from then on I was very careful. There were also poisonous spiders and centipedes and although centipedes are not really poisonous, if they bite you it really hurts. After hearing all that, I was looking forward to going back home but, really, it was a beautiful island.

Going home was nice and we decided that was the trip for the year and that we would stay at home for the holidays because 1983 was going to be very hectic if we were able to start on the brewery. For me, then, relaxing was more being at home than going on some short or long trip: only going to Berlin would be different.

I enjoyed the holiday season a lot and had a picture made of Angela and myself to send to San Francisco, while asking Michael for a picture of him and his girlfriend. Michael sent a letter with a picture of him and Bianca and although I'd expected another picture, that was all he sent. Bianca looked a lot like her father, and Michael hadn't changed that much; of course, he was older and had partly grey hair but was still quite good looking, like the spoiled kid from San Francisco, as we called him way back.

Our Christmas was lovely—just our family and Thomas' girlfriend. I realised that Angela would start her teenage years the next year and she had become a little beauty. Karl Heinz started to relax as well because the office building had started to be a very profitable business and was much better than the apartment building because people were just working and not living there.

Karl and Alexandra called wishing us a great New Year and, hopefully, the start of the brewery. Karl suggested to Karl Heinz that he might think about sending Thomas to a brewery school, so he could at least learn the basics as Mr. Kranz would not be with us all the time. He was talking about the Doemens school in Bavaria, not too far from the little village. We thought it over and talked with Thomas about it and he, of course, liked the idea as, coming from Hawaii, he would be the star again. They offered six-month courses and we called Karl saying we would do it and so would go over with Thomas in the summer and he could do the six month course. Charly found out that we would most likely be able to start the brewery around the fall, and it wasn't a "maybe" anymore, so everything seemed to fall into place.

We were preparing for the summer as we had everything under control on Maui, and one day after she'd found out we were flying to Bavaria for the summer, Angela came home saying she had a girlfriend in school who came from India. Her friend had told her so much about the country that she would like to see it and as we would already be in Germany, maybe we could make a stop-over in India. The flight was only 8 hours from Munich to Bombay (in 1995 the name Bombay changed to Mumbai) and I told her I'd have to talk to Karl Heinz about it. He thought maybe it wasn't such a bad idea, since India seemed to be an interesting country and we could make reservations through Charly and would get a good price. I thought maybe they were right and that since we were going to Germany anyway, we should try it.

Charly made all our reservations for the summer trip, even the one from Munich to Bombay, and it was very reasonable, mostly because of the discount he gave us because of being a partner in the office building. We left in June and expected to be back at the latest by the end of July or beginning of August. Thomas would be back in six months, in December, and would come home by himself.

I didn't write a letter to Michael and Janet but had told them earlier about our plans, though I didn't mention India. I still felt embarrassed about my behaviour when I hung up the phone; maybe that was the reason he did not send a picture of her. Maybe, slowly, our so-called bond would stop.

It was nice to be back in the little village and staying with Irma and Werner and we had a few days of rest before taking Thomas to the

Doemens Brewery School. It was about an hour's drive away to Lake Chiemsee, a beautiful area of lake surrounded by the Bavarian Alps in the far

distance. Not too many students were there but a lot of people from all over the world and I could see Thomas liked it; his eyes were sparkling. He could stay overnight in little cabins if he wanted, and also go home if he wanted. We told him we would stop by on our way back from India.

We had a few dinners with Karl and Alexandra and talked about the start of the brewery, hoping we would be able to start in the fall of 1983. Of course, they wanted to come for the opening and it looked as if it would be a big event. The day to leave for Bombay arrived and we started from Munich to Bombay International airport and arrived in the middle of the night.

I should have checked the Indian currency, the rupee, but I didn't, and to get to the hotel we had to take a taxi. There were a few young men waiting to take luggage to the taxis, young men who couldn't be older than 13 or 14 years. We had to walk a bit to the taxi stand and since they were carrying our luggage, I gave the two young men a tip. they looked at the tip, kind of laughed, threw our luggage on the ground and ran as fast as they could. I couldn't find out what went wrong—I either gave them too much or not enough money. Anyway, we got the luggage and went to the taxi and the hotel. Our driver had to make some turns because a few cows were lying in the street and sleeping and the cow in India is protected and cannot be harmed, but we finally made it to the hotel, which was pretty nice and we'd most likely be able to see the ocean in the morning.

Everything was different but very interesting. We didn't do a lot of sightseeing. Angela and I tried to walk around the block, but police came and ordered us back to the hotel so we mostly stayed in the hotel and in the pool area. If we went out on the balcony, there were women holding up their babies and begging for food for the babies, but looking at the babies, they all seemed well nourished, and so were their mothers. So far it was one of my most interesting trips and I was looking forward to seeing New Delhi, but I had to make sure of the value of the rupee.

We took off from Bombay on the almost fully booked two-hour flight to New Delhi and after levelling off we received a snack of nuts and raisins. We were lucky—Angela and myself both had a window seat and were able to see the country and could see out when the captain came on and told us we were flying over the River Ganges, which is a trans-boundary river which flows through India and Bangladesh. One of my favourite classes in school was geography and I remember we talked about India and the River Ganges, but of course I never thought I would ever see it. The river was about 1,600 miles long and I got the feeling the captain was somehow proud to be living in a country with a natural wonder like that.

We landed safely in New Delhi and took a taxi to our hotel. I'd previously checked the value of the currency. The hotel was different from the one in Bombay but also comfortable and I was surprised that a lot of German tourists were there as well. I didn't know how they'd got there but pretended not to understand them. We saw a sign on the front desk saying "Tour Guides Available" and instead of going sightseeing on our own, we thought that was a great idea and booked one for the next day for a whole day tour.

The next morning the tour guide arrived and it was a very pretty lady and a quite comfortable car with a driver. She introduced herself as Shumita and said she had been educated in Oxford, England, and was going to show us the tourist attractions of New Delhi. First, we went to a marketplace where we could buy souvenirs, clothes and jewellery but we weren't really interested in that and just wanted to look. Trying to leave the car wasn't that easy as we were approached by two men begging for money and as I looked at them more closely, I saw blood coming out of their mouths and they hardly had any teeth. I somehow found we'd seen enough and went back to the car and Shumita must have been watching me and came and explained that they had an illness called Scorbutus, caused by a lack of enough fruit and vegetables in the diet making your vitamin C level too low.

After that, she wanted us to see the Mahatma Gandhi museum but I wasn't feeling that great and neither was Angela, so she decided to take us for a walk in a beautiful park where most of the bushes were cut

to look like animals. It looked amazing and after that we had lunch—
an Indian dish called butter chicken which she ordered for us and which
was delicious. We got along very well with Shumita and she was very
smart, too, but Karl Heinz was also feeling tired, so we called it off for
the day and asked her if she could come the next day so that we could
do more, and she happily agreed.

We were quite tired that first day but were looking forward to
seeing the Mahatma Gandhi museum the next day and Shumita showed
up about ten o'clock. Our first stop was to be the museum and Shumita
started by telling us about Gandhi, saying he was a lawyer born in October 1869 and assassinated in January 1948. He successfully led India
to their independence from British rule and, listening to Shumita, she
sounded as proud about her country as did the captain in the plane.

When we arrived at the museum, she told us it was first opened in
Bombay shortly after Gandhi was assassinated and was relocated several
times before being moved to New Delhi in 1961. Everything was very
interesting for us, but most likely Angela had a different opinion about
it; maybe her girlfriend in school had told her different stories; but in
a way I liked that trip and I learned a lot from it. "Our National Gandhi
Museum" was what Shumita called it, saying it had a rich collection of
books, documents and journals and also pictures about Gandhi's life
and work, and we spent quite a while in there.

After that visit, we went for lunch and she told us her father was a
Doctor of Medicine and that she and her parents lived in a gated com-
pound. She said she had told them about us and being German and living through World War 2, and then she said her parents had told her
to ask if we would like to go for dinner that night. I could not believe
it, but we would love to go there and thanked her for the invitation
saying we would be honoured to go. We had another walk through the
park and then she took us home and arranged to pick us up at around
six in the evening.

Now came the problem: what we were going to take with us. I
thought about a bottle of wine but wasn't sure if Hindus are allowed to
drink alcohol so I finally went down to the front desk and just told a
lady working there what my problem was. She started to laugh and said,

"Why don't you buy two bottles." Well, I was really glad—I'd solved my problem and there was a little convenience store in the hotel, where I bought two bottles of wine.

Shumita picked us up and then laughed when she saw the wine, saying, "My parents love a glass of wine." We drove to the complex, which was surrounded by quite a lot of floodlights, and Shumita had to open a gate to drive in. The houses in the complex looked like small townhouses and when we got to their house and Shumita opened the door, her parents were waiting. They were quite good looking and somehow still young in their behaviour. Dinner was almost ready and was another Indian chicken dish and we had a glass of wine. We talked a lot about our lives; they were quite interested in World War 2 and it was almost midnight when we left after exchanging addresses. It was such an interesting evening. We still had three days left but didn't do too much, just walked around a little and enjoyed the pool.

Our stay in India came to an end and we had really enjoyed the experience but, in a way, were glad to be flying back to see how Thomas was doing in the brewery school. After landing in Munich again, we got a car and stopped by at the Doemens School and tried to find Thomas. Well, it was late afternoon and we thought maybe he was having dinner, but we found him at the golf course playing golf and having a lot of fun. When he saw us, he came over and told us he really liked the school; we could see that! We told him a bit about India but he didn't seem too interested and also said he wasn't going with us that day back to the village. I asked him if he'd been back and he said, no, that he'd stayed with friends in the cabins, but he promised he'd come and see us while we were still there.

When we got back to Irma's it felt like being at home and Karl Heinz had a few beers with Werner but I just wanted to go to bed. Irma came into my room and told me sort-of secretly that she'd had a phone call from San Francisco from Michael. She smiled and said he'd spoken in broken German and wanted to know if I was there, so she told him I was in India. She said he just laughed and told her I should contact him. Of course, Irma was the only person in Germany whose number he knew. In a way, I hoped he would try to contact me, but only on

Maui, not here. But that was Michael—he always did something you'd never expected.

We had a few more dinners with Karl and Alexandra and they promised to come over for the opening. There was still that problem with the brew house but Karl was already in contact with England as Mr. Kranz had told him about a brew house which should be in good condition. Thomas came over to stay with us for a few days and he begged us to wait for him for the opening because he wanted to be there, too. That would be in the spring of 1984, which meant the building would be finished and Mr. Kranz would have to come and start with the testing of the beer, so it would not be that easy. We were then ready to leave, said goodbye to Thomas, and went back to Maui.

So, we were finally home and everything was fine: our house and the office building, and Charly as well. As soon as Charly knew we were back, he called the next morning and asked Karl Heinz for a meeting because he had good news. That could only mean that we would soon get the okay for the brewery.

Karl Heinz and Charly had their meeting and he told me that all the permits had been approved except for one—a larger water pipe had to be installed and we had to pay for it. Now we had to tell Karl how everything went and he and his investors had to pay their share. Everything went fine except that for some reason he didn't explain, Karl told us he would only pay half of his investment, but that was fine: Charly had done a good job raising money with his friends.

In the meantime, they got in touch with the brewhouse in England and Karl intended to fly there to have a look but wanted Karl Heinz to go as well, which meant Karl Heinz had to pack his suitcase again pretty soon. Before he left, all the material was ordered so that they could start building as soon as he returned.

After Karl Heinz left for London, Grace, Charly's wife, called me and asked me if she could come over and if we could have some lunch together. Well, I was a bit surprised but, of course, I agreed. When she came over, she told me she was kind of scared and was afraid that the business with the brewery was, she felt, a bit too big for us to handle. I had the same feeling but hadn't talked to Karl Heinz about it.

One evening, I decided to call Michael but when he took the call I didn't know what to say. He then asked me where I was and if I was on my way to the moon and that broke the silence. I told him about India and the brewery and after listening to all of that he only said, "If you ever need help, I will always be there for you.." Much later, I knew what he meant, but not at that moment. It was a lovely conversation and I laughed a lot.

Karl Heinz called me and said that Karl thought that for the price—he didn't say how much—the brew house was in good condition, so they bought it. With the preparation for it to be shipped and the shipping time, it wouldn't be in Maui until the next year, which was fine because the building had to be finished as well.

One good thing was that we stayed home over the holidays, since Thomas was coming back from the brewery school and we would all be together again. The property was ready to start building but this time we remembered to call the Hawaiian priest to bless the property. Most of the material had been delivered, so we hoped to get started in January of 1984. Slowly, the talk went around that the first brewery was going to be built on the island of Maui. We told Karl to talk to Mr. Kranz, the brew master, to tell him to prepare to come to Maui to start the testing.

I thought Charly had something to do with the spread of the news, but it would have come out anyway. We told Karl to come with his investors when the building was finished and the brew house had arrived, so they could see the first beer being brewed. There was so much to do: where to buy bottles from, the labels had to be designed, the distributor had to be found, the name of the beer had to be decided, etc.; it was a huge undertaking but it was also interesting and the work on the building went quite quickly, so we hoped we'd be ready to start producing the beer in the summer. Some evenings, I was so tired that I was too tired to eat—I'd known it would be a lot of work but I hadn't expected that much.

Angela's birthday was coming up, she was 14 already and I couldn't believe how quickly the time had gone by. With all that hectic activity, I forgot my age and didn't get any depression about being fifty years old.

The building was almost complete when the brew house was on the barge from Los Angeles to Honolulu, so we told Karl and his friends and also Mr. Kranz, to get ready to come. Two weeks later they arrived and one week later, the brew house came in as well. Mr. Kranz really knew his business and he developed a taste in the beer which was somewhat close to European beer. We could only hope the local community would like it, since it was a little heavier than American beer.

I took some pictures and sent them to San Francisco; I wasn't sure whether to be proud or scared. Michael wrote back and congratulated us but told me, "Watch out, don't become an alcoholic now." The opening was a success, most businessmen and bank managers were there and even the reporter from the local newspaper, and production started in late summer. Well, we'd got that far, we would make it now.

I was hired as a part-time bookkeeper and was also a "Girl Friday," doing what others weren't willing to do or for which no one was available, but that was fine with me. My salary was pretty good and we had tours of the brewery for tourists so we met quite interesting people. So far beer sales were quite good and we even sold our beer to stores in Honolulu but there were some problems with the local community. Whenever there were parties or other events, we donated the beer, but at one event I saw a person emptying bottles of our beer behind bushes so that they could bring American beer out.

Time went by quickly and we were again in the Christmas season and Karl Heinz was busy with meetings or flying to Honolulu to talk to distributors. There were evenings when I sat down and was listening to the two records Michael had sent me—"It's Now or Never" and "Spanish Eyes," just to get my thoughts into another direction, and for a while I lived in the past dreaming about Berlin and the people I loved.

We had a big Christmas party at the brewery with lots of people but, for me, it wasn't really Christmas, it was too hectic and commercial, but it had to be done like that, Karl Heinz told me, if you are in business, and I guess he was right. I just sent a Christmas card again to San Francisco and wished them all the best. Michael sent a little package with a lovely card and a beer bottle opener: he always knew how to get me to laugh. We were then already in 1985 and more and more restaurants and stores were ordering our beer, which made everyone happy.

One day we were contacted by a huge distribution company in Tokyo who wanted to order a container of our beer. That was really good news but they wanted it as cheap as possible, so Karl Heinz had to have a meeting with Charly and his group and he had to contact Karl and his group about what to do. If we wanted to sell it to them at the price they offered, there was not a penny profit in it for our company but the Japanese promised that only this order would need to be cheap, like a test, and that they intended to order a lot more after that, so we agreed to the cheap price.

It even made the news in the local newspaper—that Maui beer would be sold in Japan—and Charly was even talking about maybe later having to expand, that if Japan should order more than other countries would follow. Karl called and told us he was thinking about bringing a German television crew over for a broadcast about the brewery and us: everyone was now going wild. Charly told us he would put another tour again for the summer, maybe to Tokyo and we could find more distributors.

The container arrived safely in Japan and we were waiting for their response. It took a while before they answered, telling us it might take a little longer to order the next one but that they were even planning to put the beer in stores at Tokyo International Airport. Maui was doing fine with ordering, and so was Honolulu.

Charly was putting a 14-day tour together for the summer. He called it "A Dream Asia Tour" with four days in Tokyo and ten days in Singapore. It sounded fine but it was one of the longer flights again: Honolulu to Tokyo was an 8-hour flight. As much as I liked to travel, sometimes I felt tired and I felt Grace, Charly's wife, was lucky as she could stay home from long flights because she'd been there before and someone had to run the office. But, we couldn't say no to Charly, since he'd helped us a lot and I guess he really thought he was doing us a favour and in a way he was because they were really inexpensive trips for us.

Well, our group was a small one again, which was nice, since we knew each other already. We left Honolulu for the eight-hour flight to Narita Tokyo International Airport and after landing there and getting our luggage, we passed a convenience store and there it was: a bottle of

Maui beer for sale for ten dollars. No wonder they were not able to sell it fast enough with that price on it.

The distance from the airport to the centre of Tokyo is about forty miles, so we took a taxi to the hotel. Charly was very good at organising and our hotel was nice—a little on the old side, but charming. I noticed that everything seemed little and even the doors weren't as high as our doors but, looking around, I saw that Japanese people are not very tall, so it was just perfect for them. Karl Heinz and Charly called the distributor and a meeting was set for the next day.

That night we had dinner at the hotel: a typical Japanese dish which looked delicious, though I didn't ask what it was because I was looking for my utensils and there weren't any. I didn't think we had to eat with our fingers and when Charly saw me looking somewhat helpless, he said, "See, next to your plate are chopsticks, Japanese people eat with those." I looked at the equal length sticks and yes, I remembered them, but had never used them. However, I had no choice so tried it and it was a mess—I had rice and vegetables all over my dress and I think there was more food on the floor and on my clothing than there was in my stomach. No wonder I was still hungry when I went to bed. The meeting with the distributor was the next day and I thought maybe I could find a knife and fork in the kitchen and could take them with me, just in case. Anyway, I had a good night's sleep.

The next day, we had lunch with the distributors and I so hoped I wouldn't have to eat with chopsticks again. The only way out would be to complain about a stomach-ache and then I could drink soup with a spoon. I was right—the restaurant we went to was famous for Japanese specialties and of course there were the chopsticks again. I told Charly I wasn't feeling well and just wanted some soup so they ordered healthy Miso soup and I got a spoon. It was a different shape from what I was used to, but I could manage and actually the soup was very delicious. They then talked about ordering more containers of beer but we could feel they didn't really know what to say, so we told them to let us know whenever they were ready. We never heard from them again.

We only had one day left for a little sightseeing and Charly suggested having lunch at McDonald's. We didn't understand why

McDonald's and he explained that it was a special McDonald's, the first one to open in Tokyo in 1971 and that over the years McDonald's had opened more than 3,000 restaurants nationwide. Even though all the restaurants looked alike, it was quite interesting that this was the first one in Tokyo. As everyone was tired, we decided to leave the sightseeing since we had the almost seven-hour flight to Singapore ahead of us the next morning.

Charly had booked a nice hotel for us—a little newer than the one in Tokyo. The first thing I noticed in Singapore was that it was a very clean city and you couldn't see even one little piece of paper in the streets. Charly explained that Singapore is an island City State in Southeast Asia, and it was really beautiful. The first day, we had breakfast at the pool and I had the best tasting orange juice ever and, after the long flights, we decided to take it easy and relax.

We then took a tour through China Town and admired the little giftshops where one could buy souvenirs and art, and it was lovely. We wanted to stroll along but it was so hot and humid that you felt uncomfortable. We also visited the Botanical Gardens, but there was the problem again—we couldn't be outside for too long as it was just too hot.

Charly said that one thing we had to do was have dinner at the Troika, a Russian restaurant, which was famous and had opened in 1943. Well, we went there for dinner and the restaurant itself was kind of dark with candles burning; different but lovely. We were told to try the special, Borscht, a sour tasting beef soup which originated in Russia, Poland and the Ukraine. It had an interesting, very different, taste, and could be eaten hot or cold and with meat or fish. Since it was a big bowl, we didn't need anything else. We still had a few days left but stayed mostly by the hotel pool and enjoyed the freshly squeezed orange juice. All in all, it was a nice vacation and we were ready to get back to work.

Karl Heinz worried about the brewery a bit but everything was fine and we were only away for fourteen days. It was nice to be back home again and the one who liked it most was Angela: she had missed her friends. I could understand that but our thinking was to show her as much as we could so that later in life she would have a lot of memories to look back on.

Karl Heinz checked his post box and was pretty sad as there was a letter from Shumita's parents saying that Shumita had passed away because of a liver disease. Maybe it had something to do with the Skorbutus: as she had told us, people don't have enough vitamins in their diet. I could not believe the news; she was so pretty and so young, but now I understood why she had never answered my letters.

When I checked my post box, I found a letter from Michael just wanting to know what part of the planet I was on; it was hard to believe that our bond was still so strong after so many years. I had had times in my life when I had problems but after talking with Michael, I always felt better and I sometimes jokingly told him he'd missed his vocation—he should have become a psychiatrist. The answer usually was "I can be different too," and that I remembered.

Karl called us from Bavaria to let us know that most likely a TV crew from Southern Germany would come over around Christmas time and would make a documentary about the brewery and some of our life in general, especially about coming out of World War 2 and not having given up. The show would be shown on German television as well, so Karl and Alexandra had decided to come along, which would be great. I was really looking forward to seeing Alexandra again.

They asked us if it would be possible to get one of those condominiums in Kihei again and Charly did his best to find one even though Christmas was always high season and Maui was very booked up. For the TV crew of three reporters, we thought we'd put them into one of the nice hotels, but they were so sick and tired of staying in first class hotels, they said that if they could, they would have stayed in a tent. We found a bed-and-breakfast for them more or less located in a jungle: I don't think they even had county water but they had a water catchment tank and caught the rainwater and they were happy. They stayed for about ten days and filmed and filmed, even filming our dreamhouse and the beer bottles and the brewery and the brewhouse, and when they left, they told us we would be notified when the documentary would be shown in Germany.

Karl and Karl Heinz were sparkling; those two had a lot in common and it was a lovely Christmas season with Alexandra and I also becoming good friends. The New Year's party was planned to be held in the brewery with free beer and snacks and a lot of people showed up. Alexandra and I had a lot to do and it was fun, but I was glad when I heard the clock strike midnight and we reached 1986.

I wondered what would happen that year. Angela was then a full-blown teenager and very pretty and we were constantly chasing her male admirers off the property. Thomas was still enjoying "Hotel Mom" and Karl Heinz was mostly in meetings but I didn't complain—my family was still together and those thoughts were always in my mind on the first of January each year.

I fell back into the past sometimes for a little while—yes, Berlin and Michael—and how my life had changed. I was still hoping one day to get my property in East Germany back but the wall was still up and there was no sign of it being removed even though there was a lot of unrest at the border and a lot in East Berlin, as well as those in surrounding East Germany being killed trying to make it over the wall into the West. I always had the feeling I would get my property back but that it might take a long time.

Karl and Alexandra went back home and the beer sales went up nicely as we were also then selling to stores and restaurants. We did tours and had also opened up a little store within the brewery selling T-shirts with the beer logo, as well as caps, bath towels and shopping bags and that went pretty well, too. Also, the office building was completely rented out.

On one of the tours there was a couple from Jakarta, Indonesia. They were so polite and friendly and he was a beer drinker and they were on their way to San Francisco, which made them even more interesting to me. We had a nice time together with Abyan and his wife Adinda; he was a doctor of some kind—he didn't specify—and he was going to a convention in San Francisco but promised that on their way back they'd have another stopover on Maui since they both liked it.

Karl called us to say that Mr. Kranz, the brew master, would be on Maui on his way to Beijing, China, where he was also supporting a brewery in Wuhan, and that he would be checking on our production and the beer on his way, so we made sure everything was clean and in order because we knew how strict he was. When he arrived, he had his wife with him and he left her on Maui while he was gone. She was also very strict and there was hardly anybody who could do things the way she wanted them done, but we needed her husband so we were over-friendly.

It was quite a while since Michael and I had been in touch so, one morning, I called his office and he answered the phone and said he was really busy. I replied, "Yes, too many conventions," and he really started to laugh, telling me I hadn't changed and that he was almost too old for those conventions. We had a lovely talk and, yes, he hadn't changed much either.

Mr. Kranz seemed to be satisfied with our performance but said we needed to do more advertising, maybe even trying to sell beer to the mainland. Well, it was easier said than done and we thought we were doing fine, and then he left for Wuhan to correct the people there. As there was a lot to do that year, we decided to stay home and not have any trips, short or long.

One of our customers told us that sometimes there was no Maui Beer available in the stores and we couldn't understand that because we were selling the same amount and we were slowly getting more and larger orders. We finally found out what was happening and that one of the salesmen for another beer company was delivering his beer and then pushing our beer way back on the shelf and putting his beer in front, so that ours could not be seen. Karl Heinz went and talked to Charly about it and as Charly knew and could do anything, he found out who the salesman was and said we had to give him a "Gift" to stop it, but sometimes it still happened.

The German TV crew sent us a video of what they had filmed and said they would let us know when it would be broadcast so that we could tell Christina, Karl Heinz' sister in Berlin, the day and time to watch it.

Also, the couple from Indonesia returned from san Francisco and we spent a few days together. Before leaving, he gave us their address and invited us to Jakarta but we didn't say anything to Charly about it, otherwise he would have put a tour together straight away.

Mr. Krantz returned from Wuhan, still mad about the workers in the brewery, saying there was no order in it and grumbling just like his wife. When they left he told me he or they would be back the next year to check our brewery and Wuhan again and that if I wanted to go along I could—and maybe take Angela along as it was very interesting. I didn't know what to say except that I would let him know.

Karl Heinz had to fly to Honolulu for a day so I had time to call Michael. I wanted to tell him about China and I called his office again and he answered. It seemed to me from his voice that he was happy to hear me, but it might have just been my imagination and when I told him about China, he definitely told me to go. He told me that Janet and her husband were vacationing in Europe and might stop in Berlin if they were not too afraid of the riots and unrest and then, giving me nice compliments, we hung up. I wondered how that whole situation would end and wondered if it would last until one of us died.

Some days, I missed my mother so much. She would understand me, since when I remembered my grandmother's smile when she saw Michael, I had the feeling my family had a secret I didn't know. But, they had now all already passed and there was no chance to find out.

I was thinking a lot about China the next year and when I asked Karl Heinz what to do, he told me to just go if I wanted to. Actually, our plan was to have a trip to Jakarta the next year because those two kept on asking when we would go, but as our brew master had offered it to us and Angela's 17th birthday was the next year, we could make the trip a birthday present. I somehow liked the idea. For me China was like a mystery country with a lot of history and so I made up my mind and told Mr. Kranz that whenever he came over the following year, Angela and myself would join him on his way to Beijing and Wuhan. He called back to let us know that he'd most likely be going in April.

The German TV crew gave us the date for broadcasting the documentary so they were able to watch it and having watched the video, I was amazed at how different the broadcast was and the movie they made out of it.

Karl Heinz had to fly to Seattle to sign some papers for distribution of our beer to the mainland—not that we had a distributor already, but just in case someone was interested in buying our beer, the papers were signed. It was the beginning of December when Karl Heinz came back from Seattle and, getting out of the car, there were two quite nice-looking ladies with him. They were stewardesses and Karl Heinz introduced them, saying they were on their way to Maui to have their vacation, so he invited them to stay in our house instead of in a hotel. I must have looked kind of surprised as one of the ladies said, "Yes, we didn't ask—he asked us."

They turned out to be quite nice but I felt like a maid since they didn't do anything. Well, maybe that's what vacations are for—being served—but after they left I told Karl Heinz to tell me ahead next time if he was bringing people along who wanted to have their vacation in our house. I almost felt sorry for him: he looked like a little puppy which had been caught doing something wrong and he promised not to do it again, or to let me know ahead of time.

Like last year, we were planning the New Year's Eve party in the brewery. It was easier to clean up and meant our house was fine and not partly destroyed.

Another year had passed and I was actually looking forward to the trip to China. Charly gave us a discount on our tickets, which was really nice of him, and I had the feeling he wanted to get a group together but couldn't get enough people for that trip.

Karl Heinz was quite often on business trips but so far he hadn't brought any more tourists back who wanted to have their vacation in our house. I had a lot of my mind with my work, even though Thomas helped me a lot and we had two more ladies in the office and the driver to deliver the beer. I was able to sign the checks and when Karl Heinz was away, I was the only one who could do that. When I was in business school in Berlin years before, we'd learned that in a company, two signatures were required on a check. We'd somehow missed out on arranging that and I realised I had to tell Karl Heinz to make a lawyer's appointment to straighten that out.

Michael and I talked quite often whenever I was alone and he told me he was single again and intended to stay like that. We joked a lot about it and he even told me he was thinking of retiring in a few years.

Janet and her husband hadn't made it to Berlin because there was a lot of frustration between the two Germanys, the East and the West Germans. I thought about it; maybe soon the wall would come down after all and I would get my property back.

While looking at the books, I noticed the sale of the beer was a little slower than we were used to and we asked Charly if he could find out if something was wrong. Since our beer had no chemicals and was not pasteurised, there was a possibility that it might go bad if it was stored on the shelves for too long. As far as I knew, the shelf life was six months, so if it got pushed to the back and sat there for a while, it might go bad.

Karl Heinz and I talked about it but he wasn't worried and said Charly would take care of it, though I did worry a bit because our dream house was an asset at the bank. The investments from the investors weren't really enough but we hoped that with good sales, we would then be fine. In other words, if the brewery did not make it, we would lose our house, too. That night I had a panic attack, like the ones I had in Berlin after meeting Michael when I had to defend myself against being a German Fraeulein. As we had the trip to China ahead of us, I went to the doctor and told him about it and he gave me some medication like those Valerian pills, but much stronger.

I thought I was making too much of it as there are always ups and downs in a business and that it would pick up again, but I was glad I had that medication to take on the trip to China, just in case I suffered another one.

Mr. Kranz arrived at the beginning of April to check on us and found nothing wrong with the beer but told us to watch out for the shelf life. We were then getting ready for the flight from Honolulu to Tokyo, where we were supposed to have a stopover for a while before boarding for Beijing with a short stopover in Shanghai. Shortly before we left, I wrote a letter to Michael and told him that we would be leaving shortly. Thinking about the long flying hours made me tired already but I thought it was worth it as I didn't see another chance ahead of visiting China again.

As we arrived in Tokyo, we were looking for our beer but there was nothing to see so Mr. Kranz went into the store and asked for a bottle of Maui beer, to be told by the clerk that there was no more, that it was too expensive. Now we knew why the Japanese distributor hadn't ordered any more.

Our next stop was Shanghai but this one was under three hours, and we could stay on the plane, and the last leg was then from Shanghai to Beijing and quite short. Mr. Kranz had made reservations at the Intercontinental Hotel, which was quite nice for five days, and he thought that would be long enough to see a lot before leaving for Wuhan. We were happy to have Mr. Kranz with us, otherwise we would be lost. It was late when we arrived and nobody was really hungry, just tired, so we went to bed and arranged to meet in the morning for coffee. I hardly remembered how I got to bed and we must have slept like rocks.

The next morning, when we went for breakfast, Mr. Kranz was already waiting and we had an American breakfast with the best coffee I had ever had. Mr. Kranz told us there were two places we had to visit: Tiananmen Square, at that time the largest square in the world, and, of course, the Great Wall of China, both of which were day tours. It sounded great but he gave us that day off, laughing and saying the rest of the stay in Beijing would be very exhausting and on our way back from Wuhan we would only stay for a night.

We opted for the Great Wall the next day and had a great typical Chinese dish of Chow Mein noodles for a late lunch. After that, we walked to the fish market just a few minutes away from the hotel and after seeing that fish market, I didn't eat fish for quite a while.

We had three days left for sightseeing in Beijing. Tomorrow was the day for the Great Wall, then Angela's birthday, and then Tiananmen Square, so everything was nicely planned. We took a taxi to get to the Great Wall and Mr. Kranz knew his way around, so we just followed. It was amazing to see the Wall; I was not aware that it was so huge and so long—actually over 21,000 kms or over 13,000 miles. We just walked about a mile on the wall and it wasn't really easy as you had to walk a little bit up and then come down again, so we took it easy but it sure felt awesome standing on something that was erected so many hundreds of years ago and was one of the seven wonders of the world.

Angela and I had to use a restroom and we looked at the little toilets which only had a small kind of door in the middle, so looked funny: you could see the person's head and their legs. They had some beautiful souvenir shops as well, but I only bought a few postcards.

When it was already late afternoon, everyone was hungry and tired so we looked for a nice restaurant to eat a Chinese meal and since Mr. Kranz was pretty familiar with Chinese food, he told us to try Chinese duck, which was very delicious, so we decided we'd most likely go there for dinner the next day for Angela's birthday.

After seeing all that, we were really tired so went back to the hotel and Mr. Kranz told us we could do whatever we wanted the next day and that at night we'd have a birthday dinner at the restaurant. We were watching some television and I noticed Angela was quiet, looking kind of disappointed, and when I asked her about it, she told me she'd rather be with her friends on Maui and celebrate her birthday with them and not where we were, in old ruins. Well, I was pretty upset about it. Maybe she was right but we just wanted to show her the world. I told her that when we got back she could have a belated birthday party with her friends and that helped a bit.

My night wasn't the greatest—thank God I had the medication, otherwise I would have ended up with an anxiety attack. We should have thought of that—that she would have liked a birthday party on Maui with her friends, but it was too late now. With her birthday money, we went and bought little presents for her friends, so the day went by faster, and late in the afternoon we went and had her birthday dinner at the same restaurant and ordered Peking Duck, which was quite delicious as well. Mr. Kranz noticed our tenseness and said that the next day we'd go to see Tiananmen Square, so we'd better get some rest as the following day we'd leave for Wuhan. That was a great idea, so we went back to the hotel and Angela watched television and I just went to bed.

The next morning, we met at breakfast ready to see Tiananmen Square. Mr. Kranz looked tired and told us we wouldn't make it a long sightseeing trip, just the most interesting spots in the square. I understood; I guess we overdid it a bit trying to see everything in a short time.

He told us we should also see the Mausoleum of Mao Zedong, who became the founding father of the Peoples' Republic of China and the ruler of the Communist Party of China from 1949 until his death in 1976. He was embalmed and laid in the Mausoleum, where visitors from all over the world came to visit.

When we got to Tiananmen Square, we were surprised how many people were walking around, but it was Easter—though there was nothing to signal that it was Easter and, yes, we were told that Easter is only a special day for Catholics and Orthodox. We tried to get to the Mausoleum but there was a long line of people waiting to go by and we really didn't want to wait that long. It was very interesting but, for us, we'd made that mistake of trying to see too much and had seen enough for that day so we found some brochures and pictures to take along with us. We then took a taxi back to the hotel and had something to eat, then everyone tried to get some rest for the next day when we had to be at Beijing Airport for the flight to Wuhan. I wished I could have stayed a little longer because there were so many other attractions to see but I guess we saw the most important things.

We had to get up early that day to get to Beijing Airport for our flight to Wuhan. Mr. Krantz told us the flight was about two and a half hours and it was on one of the smaller planes so we were not flying very high and when I looked out of the window, I could see there were a lot of rice fields. I knew about rice and that to the Chinese rice was like potatoes are for Germany, and pizza and noodles for Italy.

We were picked up by a van from the brewery and taken to the cutest little houses in a complex. Mr. Kranz looked very serious and he later told me that he had to be like that as the brewery workers respected him more for being that way than being a happy-go-lucky fellow. From what I could see on our way from the airport to our cute hotel, Wuhan was beautiful. At that time, it was not a big city and there were little lakes and rice fields with Chinese farmers with their famous big hats working in the flooded rice fields. Apparently rice needs a lot of water to grow.

Mr. Kranz planned to stay for three days at the most and the next day he asked me to go with him to look at the brewery, which I was looking forward to. That evening, we were invited by some officials and two reporters from the local news for an interview. Everybody respected Mr. Kranz and we were interviewed as well by interviewers who spoke broken English. Then some Chinese girls came in with treats and little glasses with some kind of alcohol and one of the reporters explained that this was a famous drink in China, called Baijiu, and that you have to empty the glass in one gulp, then they lifted their arms and said, "Chin Chin," which I imagined meant "Cheers," and we had to do the same. It was a very strong-tasting drink and even though the glasses were small, I had to quit after three "Chin Chin"s. I hardly remembered what kind of snacks we were eating, but they tasted delicious. Mr. Kranz quit after five "Chin Chin"s—he was used to this procedure and told me that five were his limit. One of the reporters told us our interview would be in the newspaper and that was all I needed—I hoped nobody noticed that three "Chin Chin"s was a bit much for me.

That cute little hotel had two tiny little bedrooms, which was nice and meant that Angela and myself each had our own little room and bed and at least I had a good night's sleep. Mr. Kranz told me we would be picked up the next day and taken to the brewery.

We had a typical Chinese breakfast with soybean milk, deep fried rice, steamed buns stuffed with meat, and boiled eggs as well as some vegetables and orange juice, and the portions were huge and everything very tasty, but I could not find any coffee. We were then picked up by two very pretty Chinese girls who I believed were the same ones who had served us the "Chin Chin"s the night before. I wished them Happy Easter but they looked at me strangely, not knowing what I meant, and I then remembered what we'd been told in Beijing about them not celebrating Easter. I tried to tell them about God and Jesus on the cross but I could see I was not getting through to them, so I stopped. One girl said that Mao Zedong was their God, which reminded me very much of the Hitler Regime when Hitler was the ruler of Germany from 1933 to 1945. For us young people then, Hitler was like a God to us as well, so I understood the Chinese girls.

When we reached the brewery, I could not believe how big it was compared to ours and Mr. Kranz was already waiting to give us a tour.

Everything was pretty modern and super clean; the beer tanks were almost sparkling. I told Mr. Kranz how surprised I was and he just laughed and said it wasn't always like that—most of the time they didn't know when he was coming but this time he'd had to tell them because he had us with him.

I never actually found out how he got that job, from Germany to China, but he was treated like a VIP person there. When I looked out of the window, I saw a long line of Chinese men on their bikes with bags of empty beer bottles. I asked Mr. Kranz why they had all those empty bottles and he explained that after finishing the beer, they take the empty bottles back to the brewery and have them refilled and that way they pay less for the bottle of beer. That was a smart idea but I didn't think it would work on Maui.

I enjoyed the tour a lot and then the girls drove us back and we and Mr. Kranz decided to go for dinner and retire early, since we were flying back to Beijing the next day. There was a nice small restaurant around the corner so we had dinner there and then went back to the hotel. The bus was picking us up the next morning so I went to bed early as I had my own little room and bed.

That night I was thinking a lot, wondering if we would make it. Seeing this brewery here, everything seemed so well organised and maybe some people were right when they told us this would be a bit too big to handle, but Karl Heinz was always so optimistic that if we really tried hard, we would make it. I also thought about Michael and how my life would have been with him and his "Business Meetings," but I couldn't find an answer and I fell asleep.

We were picked up in the morning and taken to the Wuhan Airport. It had been a really interesting journey but everything was too short; we needed more time. Our flight was supposed to leave at noon but there was a slight delay for some reason, though we weren't told what. Mr. Kranz said they'd better hurry up since that kind of plane was only allowed to fly during daylight because they are not connected to a tower. I didn't know what that meant, I only understood that we had to arrive in Beijing in daylight. Finally, we were ready to take off. It was almost three in the afternoon and it was a two-and-a-half-hour flight and I had to admit that I was nervous and remembering our crash in Honolulu on our way to Manila. We were doing fine, though, and although it was almost six in the evening, it was still daylight. It was just my nerves playing tricks on me.

I guess it was all a bit much—all those impressions in such a short time—and I had to admit I was also worried about what I would find at home, even though I was only away for a short time. I thought, I always was a worrier—maybe it was left over from the war. Anyway, we made it to the hotel and I was looking forward to a good cup of coffee, so Angela stayed in the room and Mr. Kranz and myself met in the restaurant for a cup of coffee.

We talked about a lot of things and I had the feeling he was also a bit worried about our financial situation at the brewery, that we might have started out under-financed. We also talked about Berlin and he had the feeling the wall would come down sooner than we expected as the East German and East Berlin population were not happy with the government—at least the majority of the population—and there was also talk that East Germany was on the brink of bankruptcy. I remembered that long before the Berlin Wall was built, there had been rumours about building a wall until it finally happened. Now, there were rumours again about taking down the wall and maybe it would happen soon. It was so strange, sitting in China and talking about the Berlin Wall. Apparently Mr. Kranz knew more than we thought, anyway that talk made me smile. He just said, if I needed help with the brewery, to let him know. He was actually a nice man and he could almost be my father, so I enjoyed talking to him. It was getting late and the next day we would fly back home and that was a long flight, but it took me a while to fall asleep. I had happy thoughts thinking about Berlin and, yes, thinking about my property and getting it back and what to do with it: maybe build a little house. Well, I was dreaming and must have fallen asleep.

The next morning, I had a last cup of that tasty coffee and we went to the airport to start our long flight and there was enough time to think back on what we'd experienced. I noticed that most Chinese couples only had one child, or at least I only saw a few couples with just one child, and I also hadn't seen Chinese women wearing anything except long black pants: I had to ask Mr. Kranz, maybe he would know why.

We made it home safely and Karl Heinz picked us up, so we dropped Mr. Kranz off at his condominium and we had time to talk a bit as Angela was on the phone non-stop, happy to talk to her friends and planning the belated birthday party she was going to give. Maybe I shouldn't have taken her along but we thought it would be educational. Karl Heinz told me they were working on a contract with a big food chain to export our beer to the mainland. He looked tired and said, "I'm so happy you are back." And I was glad I was back.

We met Mr. Kranz for breakfast the next day and he checked out the brewery again and found everything in order. He said the beer was excellent, just the shelf-life was short because it was made without chemicals. He stayed a few more days to rest and then left again for Germany. I started to worry about Karl Heinz because he was under a lot of stress and I so hoped the contract with the food chain on the mainland would go through. I wanted to tell Karl Heinz what Mr. Kranz had told me about Berlin and that maybe the wall would come down soon, but I wasn't sure if he was really interested at that moment.

Karl Heinz and Charly decided to fly over to Los Angeles to talk to the distributor to find out how the contract was coming along and Thomas was home to help with the work, so I was not all by myself. Our friends in Jakarta kept on asking when we would be there and asking us to take some beer with us—another long trip was all I needed but they meant well; they were really nice, so I wrote back saying it wouldn't be that year after all.

Sitting alone at night while Karl Heinz and Charly were in California and sometimes listening to those two records, I just decided to call Michael—I wanted to tell him about Berlin. It was early morning in San Francisco so I called his home and not his office and the phone rang for quite a while. I was just about to give up when someone picked up the phone and a voice said, "Finally. I thought you had forgotten me." He always knew how to make me smile. I told him everything about China and Berlin as well and he was not surprised about Berlin, telling me that he had heard the rumours as well and he said, "I told you, we'll see each other again in Berlin." He asked about the brewery and I told him a bit but he heard something in my voice and he must have known my concerns because he offered help again and then said, "If you just want to run away, my house has a guest bedroom." I felt more assured then after talking to him but I didn't think I would ever ask for help. He always kept saying we would see each other again. I didn't know how; maybe it was just a phrase the way some people say, "See you again."

Charly and Karl Heinz came back and they were not that sure anymore, since the shipping cost for the beer would be expensive and that was most likely the reason the Japanese distributor sold the beer at Tokyo Airport for such a high price. We knew we had to do something and there was no chance of going back to the investors to ask for more money. The only other option we had was to sell the office building, but was it worth it? It was Charly and Karl Heinz' decision to make and it was not easy.

For the moment, we didn't want to scare Karl and Alexandra in Bavaria by telling them our exact situation, unless Mr. Kranz mentioned something. We were still operating and so far no one really noticed anything, but we didn't know how long we could hold on. Another thought came up: selling! So—we had two options, selling the office building to save the brewery, or sell the brewery and for that we would have to tell the investors that they might lose their investment, or at least part of it.

At that time, Japanese businessmen were travelling through the islands and buying anything they liked from the outside, but that was just the houses. We had an offer for our dreamhouse of over a million dollars from a Japanese investor, but we declined. I just could not move again and, anyway, our house was connected as an asset to the brewery so our hands were tied in all directions. Karl Heinz and Charly then thought of another plan—going to the bank and asking for a mortgage or line of credit put on the office building. One good thing was that I had my "stronger Valerian" pills.

I got a letter from Michael telling me how sorry he was and that he would like to talk to Karl Heinz, since they knew each other from way back when I was engaged to Michael in Berlin and Karl Heinz was the driver at the Workmen's Compensation Board where I worked, and we were all a group of friends. But I wrote back saying he would never ever, talk with him; he was too proud for that and I didn't even mention it to Karl Heinz.

Karl Heinz and Charly then got the line of credit for the office building since it was an excellent business and was always rented out, even with a waiting list, which meant we could do more advertising and even lower the price per bottle so that the shipping costs would be better and we might be able to sell to the mainland. I had to tell Michael, so one morning I called his office and his secretary answered and connected me and I was proud to tell him. We had a long conversation and, yes, our bond was still there after over thirty years. I knew it didn't make sense at all but I could not let go and neither could he.

A little of the stress was gone and we started to sell a bit more to Honolulu and the neighbour islands but it wasn't that easy to get going on the mainland. We could relax a bit but after a few serious talks with Charly we came to the conclusion that the best thing would be to improve sales and then try to sell it. The way we started out was just too complicated—underfinanced and also most likely too early for the population to accept a different kind of beer, even though there were then more different kinds on the market, even some from Europe, but somehow our beer wasn't a hit and the shelf life was too short. But, if we could sell the brewery, at least the investors wouldn't lose their money, or maybe just a little.

We had a phone call from Alexandra saying Karl had had a heart attack and was in the hospital and she almost begged Karl Heinz to go over. Well, there was nothing we could really do, so Karl Heinz had to fly over, just for a few days. While he was gone, I received another letter from our friends in Jakarta again asking when we would go over, so I told them that Karl Heinz was in Germany and we would let them know.

Angela started her last year in high school and would be finished the next year, in the summer of 1988, though she had no idea what she wanted to do afterwards. Karl Heinz called me and let me know that he'd spoken with one of the investors and more or less told them the truth and what our plan was and he understood, so that was a big help.

He also mentioned that he'd seen a Hotel Management School in one of the Bavarian Cities about fifty miles south of Munich located on a beautiful lake and he had the great idea that that might be something for Angela, especially as we were living in a tourist oriented area with hotels and Maui was expanding rapidly with more hotels being built. He got all the information and told me to think about it. Well, we still had Thomas at home; he still was not ready to get married. I didn't want to call Michael but still wanted to let him know, so I just wrote a letter. I was also wondering why I hadn't heard from Janet for a while.

After Karl Heinz' return, we discussed the idea of the school for Angela and we thought she should do it if she wanted to. It was for one year but she would have a good base for Hotel Management and when we told her that, she was all for it and we had one less worry.

We not only tried to bring sales up but we also started to get the sale going—not publicly, but just by mouth-to-mouth talk. We also knew that we wouldn't sell the brewery on Maui and maybe not even in the islands but at that moment we weren't doing too badly and sales were picking up a bit.

Karl recovered from his heart attack but said they wouldn't come over for the holidays as they had wanted to do and Karl Heinz and myself had to make a decision about Abyan and Adinda, our friends in Jakarta, as they kept on asking when we would come. Most likely they were planning on coming to Maui for a vacation and wanted a good deal for themselves and their friends on a condo for six weeks. Karl Heinz told them about our plan to sell the brewery and told them we were too busy at the moment and a week later we got a call from him telling us that he was thinking about us selling the brewery. He said he knew people on the mainland U.S.A. and also in Japan and that maybe he could help us and said that would be a reason to come over and talk about it, so Karl Heinz told him he would think about it and let him know. It sounded like a fairytale but if we were to fly over, when would we do it? Pretty soon, Advent would start and the Christmas holiday and we wanted to be home for Christmas. I also thought that people from Indonesia do not actually celebrate Christmas but because he mentioned that we could go over for Christmas, maybe they were Christians; we did not know.

We had to talk to Charly about that—maybe he could bring a group together, which would be a lot cheaper, and if we decided to go, it would be in January the next year because we had to take Angela to Germany in the summer to start the hotel school. We talked to Charly and told him everything and he was all for it since he loved to travel and if he didn't get a group together, then just he and Grace, his wife, would go. He looked up the temperature in January in Jakarta and it showed up around 85 degrees Fahrenheit or around 30 Celsius, but we were used to temperatures like that in the islands, so it looked like a "go" for the trip in January, at the most for ten days.

I was quite happy to stay home for Christmas. I remembered going to midnight celebration with my parents and Michael in Berlin and what I wanted to do on Christmas Eve that year was to go to church at midnight and if no one else wanted to go with me, I would go alone. So, Karl Heinz called Jakarta and wanted to know if it would be alright if we went in January and if two more people went along with us.

Lately, I'd found myself thinking a lot about the past—maybe my mind could not handle all the stress—and I had to work hard to get back to reality. Maybe Angela leaving the next year had something to do with it, too. I sent Irma a letter with some money, asking her to put a Christmas wreath on my parents' grave; I thought that was a bit of coming back to reality.

Michael wrote a letter saying there really were rumours going around that the Berlin Wall would come down soon—either it was true or he just wanted to make me feel better. He wrote that Janet was very busy and that her husband had been diagnosed with cancer, so that was very bad news. At the same time, Karl Heinz spoke with Jakarta and they confirmed that it was alright with them for us to go over in January.

We were busy checking out the stores to see where our beer was located on the shelves and we found some way back on the shelves behind cans and other bottles of beer and Karl Heinz and Charly even flew to Honolulu to check out the stores there, which were not as bad as on Maui. Maybe we would be lucky and get something together with Jakarta. I knew it was one of the longer flights so I talked to Charly about it and he admitted we might have two stops—one in Seoul, South Korea, and the other one in Bangkok, Thailand, but he was still working on it since it might be cheaper with a stop-over. I wasn't so sure since we might stay in a hotel for a night, but on the other hand, it would shorten the long hours of flying if we could rest for a night, but Charly was a genius in preparing things like that and we hardly paid a lot, so we let him handle it.

That year, I tried my best to decorate for Christmas and I bought little presents for my family, sent Hawaiian coffee and Hawaiian cookies to Karl and Alexandra, and then I had to think about San Francisco. It took me a while until I thought I had it right and for Janet I bought a Hawaiian Muumuu, which she could wear as a house dress, and coffee and cookies. For Michael, I sent two bottles of our beer, Maui Beer, and a T-shirt with the logo on the top of the shirt and I felt really good doing that. I got two lovely Christmas cards from Janet and Michael and in Michael's letter was an old postcard from Berlin from the time he was stationed there.

We had a nice Christmas Eve German dinner and later I told Karl Heinz that I'd like to go to Midnight celebration. He looked at me for a second and then said, "I'll come with you." It was a beautiful Christmas Eve; maybe Karl Heinz and myself needed that going to church together.

It was a great holiday season and we did not celebrate New Year's Eve at the brewery; we actually stayed home. Thomas went to his girlfriend's and Angela was with her group of friends, so it was only Karl Heinz and myself and I was almost glad about it because we finally had time to talk about our current situation. We weren't worried about the up-coming trip to Indonesia since our costs for it were almost next to nothing, or very little anyway, because of Charly's connections and "people you have to know," which he did. Of course, we hoped to get a deal together with our Jakarta friends but from my view the chances were small and I believed Karl Heinz felt the same way but wouldn't admit it.

The other problem we were facing was that if we couldn't sell the brewery and weren't going to make it, we would lose our dream house as well. I just said to him, "Then we'll have to start over again, start building houses as we did in the beginning." Well, I had the feeling he was just waiting for those words from me. He then said something which really surprised me: he said, "You are still in contact with Michael." I told him, yes, we sometimes wrote letters to each other and occasionally talked on the phone and he said, "So, he is doing alright. That's nice."

We talked almost all night until we were in 1988 and we both realised it was the best thing we ever did—being very open with each other and it cleared the air completely. We knew that whatever would happen, we would make it together.

Charly was almost ready with his plans for the trip and had arranged to have two nights in Seoul, two nights in Bangkok and five days in Jakarta, which sounded fantastic. We might return like zombies but it might also well be the last trip we would make except for the next one we still had to do—taking Angela to the Hotel School in Germany.

Because of the credit line on the office building, we lowered the price of the beer and we picked up a few more distributors on the other islands, which was helpful. Charly worked out the plan for our trip. We were supposed to leave at the end of January and I was somehow looking forward to it even thought I dreaded those long hours of flying.

Our first leg from Honolulu to Seoul was about nine hours and Charly had managed to get us business class seats, so there was more room and you could stretch your legs, but it was still a long flight. I looked out of the window while we were descending into Seoul airport and it looked almost like landing at Munich airport. At that time, Seoul was not a huge city and I saw forests and little farms, just like Munich. It was amazing but in the airport it looked different from Munich with a lot of security and soldiers.

We took a taxi to a cute little hotel. Charly had done a good job with that, but it was not their first time in Seoul. We then had the time difference to cope with as we left Honolulu on a Tuesday at 8.20 P.M. and arrived in Seoul on Wednesday at 3.20 P.M.—in other words, Seoul was 19 hours ahead of Honolulu—and although we knew about jet lag from flying to Germany from Maui, you feel the effects every time. We had a typical Korean dinner of a bowl of rice, marinated barbecue beef and vegetables, all of which tasted great, and then we called it a day.

For the next day, Charly arranged a tour to the North Korean border—there were tours available and you could look into North Korea—and after that we wanted to see one of the huge markets which are like an oversized flea market where you can buy almost anything and even very cheap designer items. If we then had some time left, we'd look at a Buddhist temple. I was really looking forward to going to the North Korean border because I was very sure we wouldn't be back there again, and after a restful night we were in the bus on our way to the border. Whilst standing there and looking over into North Korea, it almost felt like looking into East Germany when standing at the border in West Berlin. There was not much to see, just farmland but no villages.

Charly asked us if we wanted to go someplace else but I was just tired and wanted to go back to the hotel. After we had a small dinner, Karl Heinz and Charly went to get a drink but Grace and I went back to our rooms. I just went back into the past and the memories popped up; even after so many years everything was still crystal clear and I had to take one of the Valerian pills to fall asleep.

The next day, we went to that huge street market, which was overwhelming. There was everything you could think of and it was very affordable, but I actually didn't need anything at all so I just bought a T-shirt for Thomas and Angela. We really wanted to see a Buddhist Temple but Grace wasn't feeling well and wanted to go back to the hotel and she'd seen them before anyway, so Charly took her back.

It was a beautiful day and Karl Heinz and I wanted to do some walking and as there was a park nearby, we decided to go there. There were little gathering places where people could sit down and buy some treats or drinks and even a stand where you could take pictures—like a photo store with a beautiful background. We were sitting down with a drink when two very pretty girls approached us and asked if we wanted to have a picture taken with them, which I thought was a great idea since they were wearing traditional Korean clothes, like ruffled dresses, so we agreed. They took a picture and then one of them suggested having a picture taken with only Karl Heinz in the middle and one girl on each side and I saw Karl Heinz would really like it—something to show off at home. Anyway, the picture was taken with the girls holding their arms around Karl Heinz shoulders and it was a nice picture; we paid them and they left in kind of a hurry.

As it was getting late, we decided to walk back home to the hotel because we were flying out to Bangkok the next day. Karl Heinz went to get his wallet out of the back pocket of his pants, but it was gone. Now we knew why those ladies left in a hurry and that they were not working for the photo store, either. The one good thing was that he had no papers like a passport or ID in there, just dollars, and not too many of those, either. We were really lucky that it was just money they took, as if his passport had gone as well we would have been in big trouble. Karl Heinz did not tell Charly anything about it, he was too embarrassed, but we knew that in future we had to be more careful. We had a small dinner at the hotel and then got ready for the next day's flight to Bangkok—it was a so-called "short" flight, around five hours.

Grace still wasn't feeling well. In a way I was not angry because it was good to have rested those not even two days in Bangkok because that whole trip was exhausting so far. I thought Charly overdid it a bit with everything.

Arriving in Bangkok, we went to the hotel, which was a very comfortable one with a huge swimming pool and we decided not to do a lot and to just relax. There was a concert at the hotel every night which we wanted to go to and a few minutes away there was another street market, that was all. Apart from that, we wanted to make notes for the sale of the brewery as that was actually the reason we were here to talk to Abyan.

Grace and I went to a little souvenir store around the corner and I fell in love with a laughing Buddha figurine with a huge belly; it looked so funny that I bought a large one for us and a smaller one for Michael. I was very sure he would like it. The owner of the store, who sold us the figurines, told us that every morning we had to rub the Buddha's big belly for good luck. That was what we needed. That one night we went to the concert in the hotel, which was amazing and even though I couldn't understand what they were singing the voices were outstanding. We were glad we took it easy in Bangkok so all of us were ready to get going on the very short flight to Jakarta—only a little over three hours.

When we left Bangkok in the morning, I did what the store owner said and rubbed the Buddha's big belly for good luck. Indonesia for me sounded kind of mysterious. I remembered we were talking about Sumatra in school—the Indonesian island with smoking volcanos—and someone told me it had the best coffee. Now we were flying over that island and for me that trip to Indonesia was like a dream.

In some way everything felt strange to me and I'd never had that feeling before going into a different country. It was a good thing I had my smart little book with me but it didn't tell me a lot, just that Jakarta was located on the island of Java and there was a mix of cultures and languages, like Javanese, Malays, Chinese, Arabs, Indians, and even Europeans, and Jakarta was the capital of Indonesia.

It took a while to get through customs and there was also a lot of security and I noticed that nobody was actually smiling; maybe that was just my imagination. Our friends picked us up and took us to the hotel, which was pretty close to their house, and we had rented a car which had to be picked up the next day. That evening they invited us to a typical Indonesian restaurant and we had Nasi Goreng to eat, the most famous dish in Indonesia consisting of special fried rice with slices of cucumber, tomatoes and shrimps. There are different varieties but the one we had was delicious.

We arranged a meeting for the next day to start negotiations and business plans for the brewery. We had three full days left to do that and on our way back we had just a one night lay-over in Bangkok and Seoul. That was enough. It was still quite warm in the evening and must have been in the mid-90s Fahrenheit as well as being humid and after dinner I was very glad to be in that hotel room with the air-conditioner going full blast.

The next morning, Charly and Karl Heinz picked up our rental car and another hot day started. Abyan came with his car and we followed him to his house, which I liked—it was not too big but cosy with fans everywhere going full blast. His wife was nowhere in sight but another, somewhat younger, lady was present who was also very friendly. He didn't introduce her so we did not ask after his wife.

We started to talk about the plan to sell the brewery and Abyan gave us information on where to send the offers as he had friends in Canada and Japan and they were definitely interested. Of course, there had to be a commission for him worked into the plan. The lady present started to make some refreshments for us but was talking to Abyan in another language. Abyan still hadn't introduced her, but apparently she wasn't able to speak English and we were told that Indonesia was using a lot of different languages—more than 500, which was hard to understand—and that only a few, mostly business people, spoke English. It took us almost the whole afternoon to discuss price and payment information and that if there really was interest, that we would agree to the potential buyer coming over to take a look at it. That would be no problem and Abyan finally stopped discussions and invited us for dinner. He introduced us to that friendly lady as a family friend who did not speak English, but didn't mention where his wife might be. We ate another version of Nasi Goreng, which was also delicious, and were told that we should at least visit the National Monument, which was located in the centre of Jakarta.

Abyan needed some time the next day to put together an offer to send to his client or friends—we didn't know which they were—so we decided to go and visit the National Monument but had to stop on our way to give Abyan some more information about the brewery. Because it was quite humid and hot again, I just wore shorts and a short-sleeved blouse and noticed that Abyan looked at me in surprise. He then approached me and told me very nicely that I couldn't wear shorts to places like that and that I had to cover my legs. I felt very embarrassed but told Karl Heinz I had to go back and change my clothes. I should have thought about that as I hadn't seen any females wearing shorts.

That national Monument was a huge tower 132 meters, or 430 feet, high and was a symbol of Indonesia's independence from Dutch rule. It was quite interesting so I got some brochures to take along so that I could read them at home. We really were tired and it was so hot that we didn't do anything else and went straight back to the hotel and put on the air conditioning. It was a different kind of heat to what we were used to in Hawaii and it was even too hot to eat, so we just had a salad for dinner. The next day we were to meet again to look over the offer and plans and then the next day we were starting to fly home and I was glad to be going back home.

After breakfast the next day, we went to see Abyan and discussed everything. He'd done a good job in preparing the offers and had three of them—two to Canada and one to Japan—so we signed the papers and he was going to send them off as soon as possible.

Abyan was by himself without his wife or that other friendly family member around but he suggested that as all the hard work was done, we all have a glass of beer. He went to the kitchen and came back with two bottles of ice-cold beer and explained that it was Pilsener Bin Tang beer, which came from Bail. As not a real beer drinker, I didn't notice any difference in the taste of other kinds of beer but Karl Heinz and Charly really enjoyed it. Now we had made the offers and just hoped for a successful sale, even though it wasn't easy for Karl Heinz as it was his baby and he was proud of it.

When it was late afternoon, we decided to go back to the hotel and Abyan told us he would come later to have a drink with us there. I was surprised about his drinking alcohol as I thought it was a Muslim country, but I didn't ask him as after the incident with my shorts, I was careful about what I was saying. We went back to the hotel and had something to eat and when Abyan arrived, he was alone. Grace and I decided to leave the three of them alone but we had to say goodbye to him as we wouldn't see him the next day, so we thanked him for everything and mostly for his help with the offers, and I just said, "Say 'hi' to your wife." He looked at me and just smiled.

Grace had a bad headache so she went straight to her room and I was fine just being by myself. I tried to sit out on the balcony as it was a bit cooler and just looked out to the city, which looked like something out of a fairytale. I thought about Michael and I missed him talking on the phone and hoped he would like the Buddha I'd bought for him. When I went back into the room I heard Karl Heinz coming and was surprised he was there so soon. He sat down and told me that, yes, they had just had a drink and he explained that both ladies were Abyan's wives; that he was married to both of them. I didn't know that was legal, but maybe they belonged to a religion or group where it was legal.

I hadn't expected that and thought maybe it was his girlfriend, but why would his wife accept that and just not show up when the "other" wife was there. I wondered about it until Karl Heinz said, "Don't get upset about that, it's their life and they all seemed happy together," and, of course, he was right.

The next morning, we went to the airport for the first leg of our trip home. I knew I would never forget Jakarta because it was so different from the other places I'd visited. In Bangkok we stayed just one night and then to Seoul for a night and then home to the Islands. I really missed my children. Well, they weren't children anymore, of course—Thomas was almost 30 and Angela was 18, but for me they were still my children and I was really happy to be home and told Karl Heinz I needed a vacation from that vacation.

Thomas had done a good job of taking care of everything; the sales were stable and he had even got two more distributors on another island. Abyan had told us it might be a while before we got an answer so we weren't actually waiting, just doing everything we could to bring up the sales. I wrote a letter to Michael and sent him the Buddha figurine and was waiting for his answer, and Angela was preparing for her high school tests and graduation.

One day, Thomas came home with four "teenage" chickens. They were very tame brown chickens and the cutest thing ever and there was one chicken for each member of the family. We had a chicken coop built for the nights to protect them from rats and mongoose and then during the day they could run around since we had a two-acre fenced-in property which was safe for them. We could call them and they would come running and we could pick them up and carry them around. The eggs they laid were big and green. One evening I called them to put them into their coop, but only three came and there was no sign of the fourth one. Well, it was already dark, so next morning I started to look for the fourth one and found it lying dead in the pasture with a hole in its little head and next to it there was a golf ball. It had happened when Thomas was practicing his golf and I couldn't believe how he did it at such a distance. I was pretty upset and felt as if we'd lost a family member.

It was almost summer and we'd heard nothing from the investors, but Abyan told us it might take a while. In the meantime, I had a letter back from Michael with a dried rose in it. He loved the Buddha but told me to watch my health and that too much stress was not good.

We received word from Mr. Kranz, the brew master, that he would come again in the summer to check on the brewery in Wuhan and on us, but we wouldn't be there because we were taking Angela to that Hotel Management school in Germany.

I had a chance to talk to Michael—it was a while since we'd talked—and he was happy with his Buddha, at least he said he was. I told him about Angela going to school in Bavaria and he said he thought the Berlin Wall would come down soon. I asked him if he knew something and he asked if I remembered what U.S. President Ronald Reagan had said to the Soviet President Mikhail Gorbachev in June, 1987, in front of the Brandenburg Gate in Berlin. I told him I knew there was something said but with all our problems with the brewery and travelling, I must have forgotten, and Michael told me that Ronald Reagan told the Soviet leader at that time, those famous words, "Mr. Gorbachev, tear down this wall." I then vaguely remembered it but there was so much talk going on about the wall that after a while people didn't even listen anymore. However, Michael was convinced it would happen soon—if not this year, then for sure the next year. He always made me think positively; he even remembered my property and that I might then get it back.

Since Angela's school was starting in August, we were planning to leave for Germany by July. We had our first response back from Canada about the offer for the brewery and it was very low but Abyan, who also had a copy, told us not to worry—that they always do that and that he would come back with a higher offer. That was all we could hope for but we couldn't wait for that offer or for the other two which were still pending, as Angela had to be in school.

We were not planning any side trips, just straight to Munich, maybe have a few days of rest in the little village, and then back to Maui. The school was located in a beautiful setting with a lovely lake in front and the Bavarian Alps in the background and Angela seemed to be alright but it was quite emotional as it might very well be that we wouldn't see each other for a whole year. We stayed for two days until she was settled in and I really enjoyed the scenery but, at the same time, I knew I was going to miss my daughter a lot and I think I was already suffering from empty nest syndrome.

We then stayed about a week in that little village with Irma. The weather was beautiful and we walked a lot and it was a good rest. We saw Karl and Alexandra who had cut back a bit on their activities because of his heart attack, but they thought they might come to visit us the next year.

Arriving home was different and the house was kind of empty. I missed Angela a lot even though we often talked on the phone, but she seemed to like it there. At least the number of chickens was right now—three for three. Thomas told us he wanted to get married in 1990, so there was another busy time coming for us again.

The offer Abyan sent to Japan came back saying there was no interest so we only had the two offers left from Canada. We were still doing alright with the sales from the brewery but there was no chance of expanding, so even Karl Heinz now believed we were better off to sell. We then got a "no interest" report back from Canada regarding the brewery sale, so we'd made that trip to Jakarta almost for nothing, though Abyan said he was still trying with more offers to other people.

It was nice to stay home over the holidays even though my family wasn't complete without Angela there. She had her first six months of schooling behind her and I could not wait for the summer for her to be back. Michael and I talked a few times and he was quite busy since he was opening another branch of his Real Estate office in Los Angeles. I thought he was lonely and did nothing besides working but he had a good relationship with his daughter, Bianca, so that was good. I was almost ready to ask him for help with the sale of the brewery but I knew Karl Heinz would never go along with that and we had another option—if we could sell the office building and pay back the credit line, we would be able to save the brewery but it would be the last chance we had, and was it worth it?

Angela told us we didn't need to go and pick her up and that she would fly home by herself and then around the end of June, I had a call from her. She only said one sentence: "I am pregnant," and then hung up. I really didn't know what to say but I knew she had just finished her schooling and was staying with Irma, so I called Irma and Angela came on the phone. We had a few emotional moments and she said she wanted to come home. I talked to Karl Heinz about it and we were worried about her emotional state, so Karl Heinz took the next fight out to Munich to bring her back.

Somehow I was happy she was coming home but I also knew we would have a difficult time ahead of us and I realised I would be a grandmother. I didn't know if I should be happy or scared.

While Karl Heinz was on his way back with Angela, I had a chance to talk with Michael and even he didn't know the answer and just said, "Let her come home first and then you'll find out what happened." He then told me he had heard that the Berlin Wall might come down that year. I couldn't find out where he got the information from but it would be wonderful and he also asked me if I would fly over to claim my property. I didn't have an answer to that. I knew what he had in mind but it had to be a no-no; I could not risk that. I just said, "Wait and see what happens," but I had to stop the call. It was too emotional and he knew that.

Well, Angela was then home and what to do now? She didn't talk about it a lot, just saying that the father was also a student in the school. She needed a few days to think about it since she did have a few options, but otherwise she was quiet. Whatever she decided to do, she had to have a job because of having health insurance, so we hired her as a bookkeeper for the brewery so that she had insurance. What she did tell us was that if the baby was going to be born, it would be sometime in March of 1990, the next year.

Those few days were pretty tough and I was eating valerian pills like other people eat candies, and then one morning she told me that she was going to see a doctor and would let me know her decision. Those were long hours—or at least they felt like it—and when she came back I saw on her face that she had made a decision. She had tears in her eyes and said, "The baby will be born next year." I cried. I was happy. I would be a grandmother next year. It wasn't an easy time we went through with her pregnancy but we tried to get along as well as we could

There were no other offers coming in for the sale of the brewery but we were still holding on without selling the office building. I got a letter from Michael telling me he had heard that the wall would come down sometime towards the end of the year and that I should watch the news. He must have had some connection to the government or other political agencies—otherwise how would he know that—and he was right. At the beginning of November 1989, East Germany announced that from then on, East Berlin and East Germany were allowed to cross the border to West Berlin and the West could enter East Berlin and East Germany. I couldn't believe it but realised I had a decision to make. I would have to fly over right away to claim my property, since I had all the papers from the lawyer my father went to when he made his will saying that after their deaths, that property would be mine. I sat there and cried. It had taken over 25 years for the wall to end.

I talked it over with Karl Heinz and he was all for it and said that if we sold it, we might save the brewery. I did not quite agree with that but I didn't say anything. So, Angela had to take my place in the brewery for a little while so that I was able to clear that up in Berlin. I contacted Christina, Karl Heinz' sister in Berlin, because I wanted to stay with them, and I wrote a letter to Michael saying I would fly to Berlin but not saying when, and that I would contact him when I got there. Charly made the reservation and off I went.

It was another long flight and landing in Frankfurt and waiting for my flight to Berlin Tegel, I was wondering how Berlin had changed. I wondered if the pilot would have to drop altitude to get into the Berlin Corridor and if Soviet planes would still accompany us. In a way it was an eerie feeling but the pilot did not drop altitude and no other planes were in sight. As we started to descend into Berlin Tegel Airport, I looked out of the window and you could still see the wall, but of course it might take a while to tear it down.

Christina picked me up and I was so excited to be back that I thought everybody would be able to see it on my face, but actually no one looked at me. I could use their car because Christina was coming with me to the East Berlin authorities because that part of Berlin wasn't really familiar to me.

I called Karl Heinz and told him I was in Berlin and I also wanted to call Michael but it would not have been a good idea because my emotions were mixed up and I wasn't sure how I would react if he came to Berlin as well. Maybe it was not even what he wanted, maybe it was just me thinking like that, so I decided to wait a few days and then tell him I was in Berlin.

Christina's neighbours knew I was there and why, so they told me that Christina could not come with me to the authorities and that I had to use a special crossing into East Berlin because I was a foreigner, in my case an American, and that I had to go through Checkpoint Charlie, which was built by the Allies during the cold war and the existence of the wall and was almost 30 years old.

Since I could not take the car through the crossing and had to walk through, I took a taxi and then walked through the crossing into East Berlin, then took another taxi to where the authorities were located. I realised I was not the only one trying to do what I wanted to do—to get property back—and it took quite a while until it was my turn to talk and explain my reasons for being there. The official looked at all my papers and became quite friendly after seeing where I lived—at that time Hawaii was still Paradise for many people. He gave me some papers to fill out and an address in a village in East Germany which was responsible for changing the ownership of properties. That was all I wanted, so I took another taxi and went back the same way I'd got there. Now Christina could come with me to East Germany as we didn't have to cross any borders, but I needed a day of rest so we decided to drive there in two days.

That evening I was very tired but I thought I should tell Michael I was in Berlin. We had the nine-hour time difference from San Francisco so it would be early in the morning and I could call his home and not his office. The phone only rang twice before he picked up and said, "You are in Berlin," then there was a silence before he said, "I want to come over and see you where we met over thirty years ago." I had to fight very hard to say no, but I guess he understood.

Even though I was so tired, I couldn't sleep thinking about Michael and my decision to say no to him coming. Maybe it was childish to react like that as so many years had passed and we were just friends from the past. I was very sure he felt like that too and decided not to be childish and tell him that next time we talked. The next morning, I called home to see how Angela was doing and she seemed fine and in a better mood.

So, we started out to that village in East Germany to change the ownership of the property. I asked Christina to pass by the property to see how it looked as I didn't think anyone had taken care of it during those years and I was a bit shaky about what I would see. I remembered my father being so proud of it and when I got there I was surprised, of course, to find that the fruit trees were very high and the fence was damaged, but someone was using it as a vegetable garden with all kinds of vegetables growing there and it really looked pretty well organised. I wanted to know who was planting there but I thought it over and realised I had no proof I was the owner and, in fact, I could not enter the property unless I could show that I was the owner—but we were on our way right now to clear that up.

It was quite a way into the East Germany territory and the countryside was beautiful but some of the buildings needed repairs and you could see the difference between East and West. We finally made it to the office. Not a lot of people were there so I was called into one of the rooms and the employee was quite nice—of course he saw where I lived—and he finished the paperwork on quite an old typewriter and took my parents name off the title and put mine in. I had to pay a fee and he gave me an East German coin, smiled, and said, "It will be a souvenir one day." He also told me that should I later sell the property, I would have to prove that my father hadn't stolen it from a Jewish person, since there had been such an incident in that neighbourhood. That was enough for one day and we drove home without stopping at the property again.

So, my job was actually done and I could leave, but I told Karl Heinz what happened and that I would stay a few more days before going home. I also called Michael and told him that I had the property back in my name and he was really happy about it. I thought he would be angry about my decision but he wasn't at all, and he just said that I had a special place in his heart and he knew we would see each other again, and I was so glad he was not mad.

I had those few days to recover from the stress but I had to get ready to leave. I booked my flight back home, straight through and, yes, it was hard to leave Berlin again.

I had a four-hour stopover in Frankfurt and time to think. I hoped Angela would like the baby clothes I'd bought for the baby in Berlin, and since we didn't know yet whether it would be a boy or a girl, I'd bought everything in an off-white. She had a name for a little girl—Maria—already but wasn't sure about a little boy's name, but there were still a few months left.

Whatever direction I looked, we had a very uncertain future ahead of us with the brewery, maybe with our house, and also with Angela and the unborn baby but we couldn't really talk about her future as she just closed up. With all my thoughts, the time went by quickly and before I knew it, I was back in the islands.

Angela picked me up because Karl Heinz was working, and we had a nice conversation but we both avoided talking about the future and her plans for the future. Without looking at me, she asked me if I would go with her to Lamaze classes. I was surprised—I'd heard about those classes but from what I knew it was usually the husband or father of the baby that went with the woman. I said that of course I would go with her and she then told me it was for pregnant women to teach them to prepare for the birth and learn breathing techniques. She said she would register for January, her 7th month. Well, I was not so sure if I could handle that but I would definitely try. I thought that was the end of that conversation but she just briefly mentioned that I did not need to go to the hospital with her as she had two girlfriends who would stay with her during the birth, and I was really glad to hear that.

Abyan sent us an offer for the brewery from a client in Canada. The price was a bit higher but they wanted to make payments on the sale price so Karl Heinz had a talk with Abyan and he put together a counter offer and was waiting on the result of that.

Christmas passed and it was a quiet one. Michael and I had a long talk about what was happening in our families and he told me Janet's husband had recovered from his cancer. I liked those conversations and I thought he did, too. Even though we both had different lifestyles and we had different lifestyles the day we met, our connection would most likely go on for the rest of our lives. Would we really meet again, like he always said?

We then started 1990 and I was looking to become a grandmother and Thomas was going to get married; there were a lot of life changes ahead of us.

It wasn't easy to keep the brewery alive. So far we were stable but there wasn't really a future ahead, at least not for us. If some investor should come and expand it and open up branches on the other islands, it would be a good business but we didn't have the money for that—we would always be a Mom and Pap store and eventually close down.

One evening Karl Heinz started to talk to me about the property in Berlin and whether there was a chance of selling it and maybe that way we could save the brewery. I really was not ready to do that and I told him so—also we would have to look for the person who sold the property to my father and prove that he wasn't Jewish. I had to look in my father's important papers. I believed I'd seen a sales contract but hadn't paid a lot of attention to it and I knew my father mentioned something about having a younger cousin living in the next village; maybe he'd bought it from him. I tried to make Karl Heinz understand that we could not run over to Berlin now and leave Angela all alone but he was so involved in the brewery that sometimes he forgot the world around him.

Thomas told us he wanted to get married in the summer after everything was taken care of and the baby was there; also that Karl and Alexandra were invited and they had promised to come. At the end of January, we were to go to the first Lamaze meeting and about then Angela found out through ultrasound that the baby was most likely a little girl. Well, I was very sure I would be the oldest person in that meeting and most likely the only woman and that all the others would have their husbands or boyfriends with them—for sure I was the only grandmother but somehow it didn't bother Angela, so that made me feel a bit more comfortable. It was quite interesting for me to look back at the time when Thomas was born when no one was allowed to be with the pregnant mother and only the doctor and nurse were allowed in the room. Angela had told me that two of her girlfriends would be with her while she gave birth; times sure had changed. We went there twice a week through February and stopped in the middle of March when her doctor told her she should start preparing for the birth. I was quite thankful to have had the opportunity to be able to do that.

A few new restaurants were opening up on Maui so we got some new accounts, which helped a bit, but we had to sell to them more cheaply as a try-out sale. I thought back a lot to my short visit to Berlin and I started to miss it again now that everything was united and it wasn't a caged in West Berlin anymore. Maybe when we were old we could retire to Berlin, so my decision was that I wouldn't sell the property. It was the only asset we had without a mortgage or any other kind of loan against it and that thought made me feel really good.

We passed the middle of March and Angela told me she was having a few labour pains on and off, so she saw the doctor and he explained that it might take another week or things might go pretty fast. I remembered when I lost my first baby how quickly everything went, but of course that was different and Angela was a full-term baby.

She talked to her girlfriends about being prepared to go to the hospital with her soon but when she came home she looked sad and down and told me they were too busy to stay at the hospital with her. For a moment I didn't know what to do and I just said, "If you want, I can take you to the hospital when it's time." She just nodded and went to her room. Well, I saw it coming—that most likely I would stay with her until the baby was born. It was a good thing I'd bought a new supply of Valerian pills when I was in Berlin.

The next days were just spent waiting until one evening she told me she wasn't feeling well and was in pain, so we took our little suitcase and went off. The rest of the family were already sleeping, so I left a note to say where we'd gone and I think I was more scared than she was. There was no question or discussion. We both went into the hospital, checked in and got into her room where the doctor checked her out and told her it might take a while or it might go quite fast—well, we'd heard that before.

It took a while alright and the next morning we were still sitting there and the labour pains came and went again. I was just living on coffee and noon came and went and still there was nothing except that she was in a lot of pain. The doctor checked again and gave her some kind of injection. He told us he would wait a little bit longer and if nothing really happened then he would perform a Caesarean Section as otherwise it wouldn't be good for the baby, it had been far too long already.

She was in a lot of pain so I went to look for the doctor and told him he had to do something and he came with me and looked at her and just smiled and said, "The baby is coming now," and called me over to see little Maria being born. But she did not cry and the colour of her face started to turn a bit blue, so he took her and actually ran away with her. We were both exhausted but seeing a child being born is something you never forget for the whole of your life. A little later Karl Heinz stopped by together with the doctor and the doctor just said that now Grandpa was there, everything was fine. It must have been serious with little Maria as they put her in an incubator for a few hours, but then everything was alright and Angela stayed in the hospital for another two days.

We were glad that was all over and both of them were healthy. I had my first grandchild and the next day I ran to get a crib—yes, it was a bit pricey but it was for my first grandchild. Angela came home from the hospital with little Maria and it was so nice to have a baby in the house again. Now we had to concentrate on Thomas' wedding, and Karl and Alexandra had confirmed that they would come for the wedding.

I had a chance to call Michael and I told him I was a grandmother and about being at the birth. He sounded pretty excited and he said, "Now we are both grandparents," and then continued to say, "I remember when you were in the hospital and our baby did not make it." I wasn't able to talk for a few seconds and neither could he and I hadn't expected that reaction from him. We changed the subject and he asked about the brewery but there was a good feeling; maybe I still had a special place in his heart—he sure had one in mine.

Charly and Karl Heinz had a meeting to see what else we could do to stay alive and make some profit from the sale of the beer until we found a buyer, or something else for that matter. Even though Abyan did everything he could to send out offers all over, nothing really serious came back and we were looking forward to talking to Karl at Thomas' wedding. Angela worked part time in the brewery again, so I became a part-time babysitter, which I loved. Thomas' wedding was very nice and there were not too many people, but of course Karl and

Alexandra were there. Karl had changed since having his heart attack and wasn't so energetic anymore and therefore wasn't a big help.

We had more meetings and then engaged a lawyer to get advice and he advised us to go into Chapter 11 Bankruptcy in order to get re-organised. That would allow us to stop paying unsecured debts until we had a plan to start paying again, but sometimes much less. Our plan would be to sell the office building, which would most likely go faster than the brewery. The lawyer told us he knew of a lot of businesses who had done that and survived and he gave us a bit of time to think about it before letting him know.

I knew it hit Karl Heinz very hard and I felt sorry for him; he was so proud of the brewery and that's why I would not sell my property—because most likely we would lose that too and we needed that property for our old age. After a few days and quite a few beers, they decided to do it and also tried to prepare to sell the office building. It was a sad day for all of us but, as the lawyer said, we could still survive.

The Maui Brewery filing for Chapter 11 Bankruptcy became break-ing news and we more or less wished we could have left the island but it wouldn't have helped in any way and we had to keep on going if we were going to survive. I did something I had not done for quite a long time and I went to church and lit a candle. I had learned that from my grandmother who told me, "If you have a bad time, just do that and pray for strength and health, but never pray for money." My grand-mother was the wisest person I'd ever known and when I had a bad time back in Berlin, I always slept on her lap; that was what I was doing now.

It took a few days but everything then went back to normal and it was business as usual. People soon forget. Charly put a proposal to-gether for the sale of the office building as that was the plan we had to show the lawyer in order to file for Chapter 11 for the brewery.

Little Maria was almost three months old and watching her let me forget the problems we had. One evening, Angela came and wanted to talk to us, saying she intended to finish her education as there was no future for her working in the brewery. I understood that and we asked her where she wanted to go. She explained that after talking about it with some friends, she had been told that Switzerland was known for being the best in the field. I was aware of that and I also knew it was pretty expensive, but it turned out that she had found something already—the Cesar Ritz College in Le Bouveret. The campus was situated on the shores of Lake Geneva in Switzerland and she showed us some pictures which looked beautiful, showing an amazing view looking over Lake Geneva and the Swiss Alps. We told her we would talk it over.

With the savings we still had and if we sold one of our expensive cars, we could do it if we also used some of the money we would get out of the sale of the office building. The one-year college class was starting in September, so we would have to take her over. The lawyer informed the investors about our status in Chapter 11. There were not many investors and there were not too many problems, but of course they were not thrilled.

Before leaving for Switzerland, I called Michael to tell him about Angela. I didn't think he liked the idea too much but he wasn't completely against it. He just seemed a bit worried and all he said was, "Take care of yourself, little bird." Charly gave us the tickets for almost nothing. I never really understood how he could do it; maybe I understood a little, but I kept quiet.

We prepared for the trip to Switzerland to take Angela to the college in Le Bouveret and we took little Maria along. Before we left, I went to the doctor with Maria and he gave me some medication for the trip, which we knew would be tough for all of us but there was no one to look after Maria and even though Thomas and his wife were living close by, both of them were working so we couldn't leave her with them.

We went all the way through to Geneva and on to Le Bouveret and it went better than we expected, thanks to the medication from the doctor. It was the most beautiful landscape in front of Lake Geneva with the Swiss and French Alps behind. We found a small but very comfortable hotel for five days to help Angela settle at the campus. Everything looked simple but in a way it was very extraordinary; it was amazing and I enjoyed that atmosphere. The five days went by quickly and it was an emotional goodbye for a year as we knew we couldn't come and visit her during the holidays—we could not afford that as well as the tuition fees.

The flight back wasn't that great as Maria developed ear problems - most likely the flying was too much for her—but it felt good to be home again even with the problems we had. We had a few offers on the office building but they were very low since everyone knew we needed the money to bail out the brewery. Abyan somehow gave up on us after he found out we were in Chapter 11, and I really could not blame him for that.

Angela enjoyed being over there and we talked every week. They were hoping for snow for Christmas but even though we were in the Holiday season, the Christmas spirit just wasn't there. I became Grand-mother/Mother to Maria. Some days weren't easy but she became my everything. I called Michael to wish them all Happy Holidays; he was my therapist—he listened when I cried and he listened when I laughed.

Shortly after Christmas, Charly came to the brewery looking se-rious and saying he wanted to talk to us. One of the Mau investors in the brewery had filed a lawsuit against Karl Heinz and myself, claiming our visit to Switzerland was just an excuse to hide money there, money stolen from the brewery. I could not believe what I was hearing and Karl Heinz just said, "We need to see our lawyer."

It was shocking news and I believed it might stop everything, in-cluding Chapter 11 and the sale of the office building, but we had to find out for sure from the lawyer. Thinking about maybe losing our house as well made me remember to look for those important papers of my father's about the sales contract for the property in Berlin, and I did. My father had bought it in 1934 from his younger cousin, who was born in Germany and was German, not Jewish. That was great as a standby just in case we lost everything we had left.

We got an appointment with the lawyer for the first week in Janu-ary. He had heard about it but hadn't yet received any papers, though he knew who was handling the claim and that it was a famous Honolulu lawyer. He advised us to go on as usual as there was nothing we could do about it at the moment.

Nevertheless, I did ask Christina, Karl Heinz' sister, to find a Real Estate office in the village where the property was and the City Hall's address, so that I could find out prices and rules and regulations. Not that I wanted to sell the property, just to find out. Christina found all that out so I mailed a letter to the Real Estate office and what came back was not very hopeful. There was a stop, which might last a year, on selling and building on all of the properties which belonged to Western people. Maybe that was actually good, so I couldn't do anything with what was our last so-called asset. Maybe I was thinking too negatively, maybe we would still make it.

We received word from our lawyer that he was going to file a counterclaim for False Accusation and he used other sophisticated legal terms which I had never heard before, and it went to court.

I got a letter from Michael asking how we were doing and he again offered help but I didn't even tell Karl Heinz. It was even better if everything went that there would be a new beginning. There is a reason for everything, maybe that was the reason to start over again. His last words in his letter were "Take care of yourself, my little bird."

Thomas told us his wife was pregnant and the baby would arrive around August, so then I would have two grandchildren. Lately I had been wondering what would happen when Angela came back in the summer; would she take little Maria? That thought really scared me, I hadn't realised how close I'd got to that little girl.

The offers for the sale of the office building became less and it looked as if no one was really interested in doing any kind of business with us; there were too many problems involved. As some people told us, the brewery might be considered too big to handle.

Our lawyer asked for a meeting, which was not a good sign, and he tried to explain our present situation, saying we might have to prepare ourselves for being pushed into Chapter 7 Bankruptcy. He explained what that meant—that Chapter 11 is a reorganisation, while Chapter 7 is a liquidation where we would have to sell all our assets to pay back the debts we had on the brewery. In other words, if the office building was sold, most likely under value, the profits from the sale would have to go to the brewery to cover the debits there, including to the investors. And all of that under the supervision of the Court. The lawyer assured us it wasn't going to happen overnight and that we still had time to negotiate. You could see he felt sorry for us but there was not a lot to negotiate. I didn't know how long we would be able to make payments on the mortgages, loans and credit lines.

One thing I was certain of was that we would lose our dream house, and suddenly we hardly had any friends left except Charly, who did everything he could do with his connections but they were different connections and not much help either.

I was so glad my parents hadn't had to live through that—they had been so proud of us. Maria's first birthday was lovely and Angela told us she would come home at the end of July and that she had met a young man at school who would most likely come with her or follow a bit later. We didn't tell her our situation, so I hoped we would still have our house. I guess in a way we gave up fighting and prepared ourselves to lose everything.

In July Thomas and his wife had a little son and he was the cutest little thing ever. Angela came home alone in August but the young man followed a bit later and they got married shortly after he arrived and stayed with us for a while. I no longer cared about losing the house but I was afraid of losing Maria. Angela and her husband found great jobs on the other side of the Island and I needed a lot of Valerian pills until she asked me to keep Maria until they got settled. I believe two people were quite happy about her decision: her husband and myself.

As the lawyer told us, we still had time to negotiate but there was no point in dragging it out. If everything went well, I had about five months to be able to pay the bills and then we would have to leave the house. That Christmas season was sad and Karl Heinz was pretty depressed but I think he was also glad everything would soon be over. The whole family was together and we tried to still make it a Merry Christmas, mostly because of Maria. I wished Michael and his family Happy Holidays and didn't tell him the whole story but I was sure he knew.

As there wasn't enough work for Thomas, we talked it over and decided he and his family should try to leave Maui and relocate to a neighbouring island where it was cheaper to live and where he was sure he would find a job quickly, because his wife's parents had relatives there and would help out. So, our plan now was that since we knew we would lose everything, we needed to prepare to leave Maui as well so that we had Thomas there and we could help each other. Angela and I had a long discussion and the decision was that Maria would stay with us as long as they were settled in their jobs.

We then went to the lawyer and told him to go ahead with Chapter 7 as we saw no chance of recovering. There was the problem of our furniture, some of which I had bought in Asia and which was kind of antique and valuable. Charly had a friend who had a very small cottage where we could store our belongings until we could ship them over to the neighbour island, but we had to find a place to live first.

We signed the papers over to the banks and the court took over all the assets for the bank, so there was hardly anything left for us. One thing Karl Heinz took particularly badly was that we had to empty the beer tanks, so we had to open them and let the beer just flow out, and he had tears in his eyes. That day we left the empty house and left for the airport and I hardly remembered it, as though my mind just blocked it out. One thing Karl Heinz asked me while we were leaving was "Why are you staying with me?" I could not answer.

One good thing was that we could stay with Thomas and even though it was a small place, there was enough room until we got organized again. Thomas' wife found a job and so did Thomas, so I had to take care of the two children and that was a help, too. It was one of the hardest times of my life but then Karl Heinz found a job as a carpenter. It was not easy for him since it was hard work.

We eventually got word from the lawyer that there was some money left for us and most of the debtors had been paid off except for our tax liabilities, which they were still working on. We were therefore able to look for our own rental house and with Karl Heinz' paycheck we were able to buy a lot in a cheap area for less than $5,000. Well, we had to start over and I did not contact Michael to tell him where we went. I was too embarrassed.

Maybe that was a good reason to just break the bond between us— as the saying goes, there is a reason for everything, and maybe that was the reason.

We found a nice rental house and were able to get some of our furniture, so that was a start. We opened up our post-office box and also got a new telephone number but also had to inform our lawyer where we were as there was still a lot of mail coming.

It was then almost six months since we'd left Maui and it was still hard to adjust but Karl Heinz got a job offer on another Hawaiian Island as manager of a construction company. It was easier for him but he had to stay over on that island for the week and just come home on weekends, but the pay was good. Angela and her husband also came and visited us and things became a bit less stressful. I did miss my talks with Michael, but it was better this way.

I found a job delivering boxes which had to be picked up from the airport and delivered to customers and I got paid for every box. It wasn't much, but it helped, and the best thing was that I could take Maria with me. We also bought an old car, so it worked out well. We received our tax bill which included the brewery and the office building and it was outrageous but we were allowed to make monthly payments.

One afternoon, our lawyer called and I was so scared that something else had popped up, but he was kind of friendly and told me he had received a phone call from a Mr. Michael Mendez from San Francisco, claiming he was a relative of mine and wanting to know my new number as he knew we had left Maui. He asked me if he could have permission to pass on my number and I was stunned for a moment but then told the lawyer that he could. I never found out how he managed to do that but, yes, I was happy about it. I would not call him but the lawyer gave him our number, so I knew he would call.

Since Karl Heinz was working with a construction company, his boss told him that whenever there was left-over lumber, he could take it home so that we could use it to maybe start to very slowly build a little house on the property we'd bought. It might take years but we really liked that and had something to look forward to. Maybe if we were able to sell the property in Berlin, it might get done a bit faster.

It took almost a week before the phone rang and then Michael was on the line. I thought he would be happy to hear my voice but instead he scolded me for not telling him where I was. He was really mad at me but after a few minutes of me telling him what had really happened, he calmed down and understood and we were both happy that we had found each other again.

Time was passing quickly and again we were approaching the holiday season; I couldn't believe a year had already passed. With both of us working and with Karl Heinz being able to take left-over lumber and other material home, we hoped to start building our little house. I wrote Christmas cards to San Francisco and told Michael we had two post office boxes, one for business and one for private mail so that we kept the mean letters apart from the nice ones.

Shortly before Christmas Eve, I checked the nice mail and there was a little box from Michael addressed to Maria. At first, I didn't want to open it until Christmas Eve, but I didn't want to just put a box under the tree, so I opened it and there was a cute little doll and a card wrapped in foil. When I opened the card, money fell out—there was $1,000 and a little note attached, "Keep it for rainy days." I could not believe that he would send money in a letter. It could have been stolen but most likely that was the only way he could send it. Yes, I was glad to have it. I took some and bought so much food to make a big Christmas dinner for my family and I kept the rest for rainy days.

Angela and her husband flew over from Maui but I noticed a bit of tension between the two of them and then the holidays passed and it was already 1993. Little by little we cleared the lot using the left-over materials Karl Heinz had brought from the other island. It was hard work but we had a future again.

Michael and I spoke on the phone a few times and he told me he had to see a doctor since he had problems with his heart. His father had died of a heart attack and he wanted to check it out. We decided to send Maria to kindergarten in the summer, which meant I could deliver the boxes until noon and in the afternoon I would work on the lot—there was always something to do like treating the lumber with termite paint—and I remembered that was how we started out. It was hard work but you were so tired at night that you didn't need any Valerian pills. We put Maria into kindergarten and she eventually got used to it but had a hard time at first and cried every morning.

One weekend, I was reading the mail and a letter from our bank about accident insurance saying that for a small payment a month, you had accident insurance. I didn't realise it was only for car accidents but there was payment for loss of life—a good amount—and then for loss of an eye, so much percent, or loss of a leg, arm, hand, etc., and I signed up for it.

Slowly, our hectic sort of life settled down for a while. Karl Heinz' job was going well, so we could slowly continue and if everything went well, we'd be almost ready to move in by the end of the year. It was pretty small but enough for the three of us for the time being and our plan was, eventually, to build on one or two rooms. In a way I could not see myself living there for the rest of my life but it was fine for the moment. It was not actually a dream house but it was our house.

I spoke with Michael a few times during the year. He had undergone a heart operation and had two stents inserted into his body but he seemed okay. I really wished I could see him and comfort him, but of course that was just a dream. Sometimes I did miss our past life and there were days when I was suffering Rockfever—which is when you had stayed on the island for too long without leaving it. Also, of course, I missed Berlin; maybe even more than when I left after the war. Well, as the saying goes, "the grass is always greener on the other side of the fence." I was sure Karl Heinz felt the same way as I sometimes caught him staring at a plane as it flew over us.

Angela had problems with her marriage and her husband had problems adjusting to island living but they worked really hard on their relationship. I did understand his problems as I'd gone through the same thing when I arrived, being a Haole until they discovered I was a German Haole. Karl Heinz changed and was no longer the go-getter doing ten things at one time. The loss of the brewery and our house had hit him hard and there were too many empty beer bottles on the table at night sometimes.

Thank God, I had to take care of little Maria who was actually not so little anymore and very mischievous. She loved Barbie dolls and she had a lot but for some reason she loved to take their heads off while playing in the bathtub. One day she even decided to cut off one side of her hair; to her, that was funny, so there was never actually a boring day and that made me forget the past a lot.

Our plan to move into the little house was not what we expected. Since all the doors and windows had been done and the little house could be locked up, we decided to start putting in our furniture and paintings. The stuff we brought over was our most valuable—things like paintings I'd bought in Asia in art stores and furniture from Hong Kong and one painting which I bought in Bombay and which I loved.

One morning after taking Maria to Kindergarten, I went over to the little house and almost fainted. The entrance door was broken and one window smashed and all of my valuables had been stolen. As there were hardly any neighbours around, it was easy for someone to break in. I was devastated but I tried to pull myself together and went to the police station, after which two officers came along and took a report but more or less told me there wasn't much chance of getting anything back. That hit me quite hard and the idea popped into my mind: *Am I being punished for something?*

Was it because I was still in contact with Michael? I still had a special place for him, even though we were just friends now and had not seen each other for so many years. When Karl Heinz came home, I told him about the robbery and he got mad as well but wasn't really as attached to the things as I was. Well, it took me a while to get over it but I finally realised that those were just material things and the most important thing was that our family was healthy and most of the time we were together.

I did talk to Michael about it but he thought a bit differently and somehow felt sorry about it. But, for Karl Heinz and myself, it was like during the war when we had nothing left in the way of material things and just life and health were important, and that might have had something to do with it. It helped to think like that.

The police actually found out who the burglars were. They were workers with Karl Heinz who helped us out working on the little house when they had time. I had given them lunch and sat and eaten with them. We didn't know that one of them had already been in jail, which was scary, but the most scary part was that months later one of them shot another person dead while he was out on bail after his conviction of our break-in.

We had to get some protection, so we wanted a dog. Maria was all excited and we went to the Humane Society to get a female dog, which should be a good watch dog, but there were quite a few to choose from. It was terrible—all of them were standing in their cages and looking at us with their big eyes saying, "Pick me." Maria wanted them all but we had to decide right then as one of the ladies there came and showed us one of the dogs saying that it would be put down the next day because they needed the kennel and she had been there the longest. Of course, we took her. She was a mix of everything and not the prettiest but her big brown eyes looked so happy and now we had Abby, our watchdog. At least, that's what we bought her for and she was very protective of us and really cute but all the cats in the neighbourhood had to watch out.

It was nice to have an animal in the house again and she protected us as if she knew we'd saved her. We had our traditional German Christmas dinner and Angela flew over, but alone. It really didn't look as if things were too great between those two and I didn't want to ask her, but she told me anyway that they might get a divorce next year and that he would most likely go back to Europe. My first thought was *Is she going to take Maria now?* but I was too scared to ask her.

1994 arrived faster than we thought. Thomas' little son, Chris, was almost three years old and next year he could go to kindergarten as well and Maria would start her first class in two years. It was hard to believe how fast time went by and I so hoped she could stay with us. Angela filed for divorce, her husband left and she moved in with a girlfriend.

I noticed Maria kept her distance when Angela was with us and I was looking for a chance to tell her who was who. One day, she saw a pregnant woman with a big belly and she asked me if a baby was in there—somehow she must have known that already, maybe from other little girls in kindergarten—and then she asked me, "Was I in your stomach, too?" Well, there it was—the big question. I just told her that she wasn't, that she had grown in my heart. Before we adopted Angela I had bought a book called *Mother and Child Care* written by Dr. Benjamin Spock, a paediatrician, which contained almost everything you had to know. That book had advised not to force any information on your child and just to wait until she asked, and Maria was okay with that reply, so that was very good advice.

Slowly, we adjusted to the house but it was really small. Karl Heinz thought we could maybe add a master bedroom, so in our spare time he started to do that, although it took almost a year to finish. We were short of the carpet so for the time being I painted the floor and it looked really nice. I slowly started landscaping and it started to look really pretty. Sometimes I saw cars driving by and one or two just looked at our house; I assumed they looked at it because it looked nice and taken care of and although I might have been wrong, I started to become proud of it.

1994 was almost gone and I wanted to check out the status of the property in Berlin so I wrote to the real estate company to ask for new information. It took a while to get an answer, which was that yes, we would be able to sell it or build on it, but that prices were very low and all the trees and shrubbery had to be removed.

Michael called and wanted to know how we were doing, so I told him everything. He just said, "I am very proud of you, little bird, you remind me of those people after the war trying to rebuild Berlin." I was proud of that but just laughed and said, "Yes, with your help and the PX Stores." There was silence for a second and then came, "Yes, I do miss those days a lot!"

I was thinking backwards and forwards about what to do with the Berlin property. If we had to clear everything, it would cost us a lot of money and then building on it would cost as well and we were not ready to take out a mortgage after the disaster with the loans and mortgages and credit lines, so the only thing to do was to sell. But, as we were told, everything was cheap and undervalued, so we just left it for the time being.

Angela flew over with a young man she had met in a gym after she got divorced from her husband. He was a nice-looking surfer-type who was also working in a hotel on Maui. I was ready to tell Maria who she was but thinking about Dr. Spock's advice only to tell something when they asked, I kept quiet, though the fear came back that she would take her along. We had a nice time together and it looked as if he was a nice man and they asked us if we would go to Maui to visit them next time. I really was not sure if Karl Heinz was ready for it but thought it would be a great idea to leave the "rock" for a few days even though, logically, we would only leave one rock to fly to the next rock.

There was still a lot of material left so Karl Heinz had the idea of adding another room to the house, like a guestroom. I liked that idea as well as if Angela came to visit, they could stay with us. Now we were getting a pretty big house compared to the one we started out with.

One morning, I got a call from Michael, asking how we were doing. It was nice to hear from him and he told me he had a visitor from Buenos Aires. Yes, I knew right away who that was: Elena—Daniel's wife at that time—with whom Michael had a relationship. I said, "How nice; how is she doing?" and I think I "heard" him smiling. He said she was on her way to Orlando, Florida, and she had asked him to go with her as she had some business to do there. Yes, I remembered those conventions. I asked him if he would go and he said he thought he would as it was something different rather than sitting in the office all day.

Somehow, I had to cut the talk short or I would either get mad or cry and I had no reason at all to do either. I was very sure he knew how I felt but that was so childish as we were, after all, just friends and I felt very immature at that moment. All the memories which I thought I had forgotten after those many years popped up again but I could never tell him how I felt. I wouldn't mind if he was going with someone else, but not with her—that beauty from Argentina who I hated so much back so many years ago in Berlin because she had so much power over Michael and treated me like a little German nothing.

I convinced Karl Heinz we should fly to Maui and visit Angela in her new apartment and have a great time all together, and he happily agreed.

We flew over to Maui over the weekend and were able to stay in Angela's apartment and we had a nice time. The only thing we weren't able to do was to look at the brewery, the office building and our dream house, but that was alright and somehow we felt as if we were on vacation. We even visited Charly and because he wasn't as involved as us, he still had his house. He was alright and the job he had and the travel agency supported his family and him quite well. We also had our not-so-little-anymore house and I was very proud of that.

We received a letter from the church in that little village in Bavaria where my parents were buried and it said we had to dissolve the grave since it was then over ten years old and they needed the space. There was nothing I could do—those were the rules I guess, but it hit me hard that there was actually nothing left anymore—nowhere to take flowers to or just to stop and say a prayer, just gone. Even though we couldn't do it very often, it felt there was still something left of them. Karl Heinz was very understanding since he felt the same way about his mother and, of course, his father—but he had been a soldier in the war and never came home after the war and was never found.

We started adding the guestroom onto the house and it was fun doing it and when it was finished we could also use it as a family/TV room. Quite a while passed without me hearing anything from Michael but of course I expected that. It was Elena he was with so it looked like she also had a special place in his heart and I tried to see things from the funny side. Lately Karl Heinz had asked me how Michael was doing because he knew that he sometimes called, so I told him about Elena because he knew her too, and he just said, "Poor guy, she will never let him go." In a way it helped me that he said that.

Well, I then got a letter from Michael and when I opened it, out came a picture of them standing in front of a hotel in Orlando and I had to admit they looked great together—he was still that good-looking guy from San Francisco and she was still the Beauty from Argentina. It hurt a bit but it was the past and we were just friends and I was proud of myself for having my emotions under control and being able to tell them how great they both looked.

I heard from Angela that those two were getting serious and even talking about marriage. There was that fear again—what would happen to Maria. Since nobody talked about it, it looked as if we were both afraid to mention it. Michael and myself actually never talked about that subject anymore; I noticed he wanted to start a conversation about it but I changed the subject until he understood.

Lately I hadn't been feeling that great. I had lost weight, had no appetite, and had the feeling something was wrong with my intestines.

It worried me a bit because my mother had died of colon cancer and I was afraid I might have it too. It had taken me a while but when I became really tired and lost blood, Karl Heinz arranged to take me to the doctor and booked an appointment for two days later. Yes, I was pretty scared. The doctor told me he had to perform a colonoscopy, which I'd heard about from other people and wasn't really looking forward to. The nurse was very nice and told me it didn't really hurt since they used anaesthetic—not to completely anaesthetise you but just something to help. She was right. It didn't hurt and it didn't take long either. After it was done and I was completely awake again the doctor smiled and told me it was not cancer—it was ulcerative colitis, an inflammation of the digestive tract. I could have given that doctor a hug. He put me on medication, a pill a day, and that pill was almost $25.00 a day for a month but, thank God, we had good health insurance. But it was a scare for all of us.

The end of 1994 was approaching and Angela told me they had decided to wait a little longer before they got married; they wanted to save some money first. Our house was finished so they were able to come over and stay with us over Christmas.

Michael had already written two letters so I called him and we had a long talk. He started to talk about Elena and we were right back in the past. I slowly realised why I sometimes behaved so immaturely when it came to Michael and I told him all that on that day. It was because we met after the war when I had lived through very scary times during and after the war. I had still been quite young and had saved my mother's life, almost got killed by tanks, had low-flying planes aiming at me, seen people dying next to me and almost got raped. That was a lot to go through. I had even lost the only doll I ever owned and after all those bad times, I met Michael. Because of all that, he looked like a saviour to me, even though in my mind I hated him at first because his country had done all those terrible things to us. He didn't say a word, he just listened because of course he knew all that already.

Then he interrupted me and said, "Then we fell in love. Yes," he said, "that is the bond we have and will never lose." I guess he was right in that. That talk was very special to us, mostly to me, because Elena and Michael never had and never would have a bond like that. After that talk, I felt a lot better and I believe he did, too.

I was glad we had that talk on the phone. I remembered another talk like that when I met Michael's parents in Berlin and they and some friends, including Elena, started to treat me like a "German Fraeulein," even calling me that when the name wasn't a nice one for German girls, meaning "easygoing." I had fought very hard to convince them that I wasn't like that and had a meltdown and shouted at them—it was all still a very clear memory after so many years. I could remember some events from that time in my life as if it was just yesterday.

Angela and her fiancé came over to us for New Year's and I was ready to ask her about her plans for after their wedding. We needed to talk about it as Maria just living with us wasn't good enough. There was a time once when Maria all of a sudden in the evening developed a high fever. I really hadn't known what to do when she started to shake so I went to the emergency room of our hospital. After finding out that I was just her grandmother and had no papers to prove it, the doctor wouldn't touch her. I had never heard of a thing like that before because he was a doctor, but because it wasn't life threatening, he told me he would give me some medication for an allergic reaction and even then did not tell me what sort of allergy, so I was still worried. I told him that her mother lived on Maui and asked if he would talk to her and then treat her, and he agreed to that. After talking to Angela, he treated her but I really didn't want to go through that again and my idea was either adoption or to become her legal guardian. I told her what we would like to do and as she had told me before that they were thinking of maybe moving to Florida after their wedding, she promised to think about it and let me know. At least we had started to talk about it.

1995 started out quite well and Karl Heinz was asked if he would be interested in building a house for a couple who were moving to Hawaii from the mainland. It looked like a new beginning but he would have to quit his job as a carpenter. He didn't have to think about it very long and asked Thomas if he wanted to be his helper and Thomas certainly agreed as he knew he would get paid more than in his regular job. It looked so nice—that was how we had started out until the brewery messed everything up.

Slowly, our lives started to normalise. Karl Heinz gave up his job as carpenter and was working building houses with Thomas. It was slow but we got along fine. Chris, Thomas' son, was in kindergarten with Maria and the next year Maria would start regular school.

Angela came over for Easter and we discussed what she wanted to do about Maria. Her fiancé, Brian, was involved in the discussions and we came to the conclusion that we would adopt her. She was in the family anyway and we were all able to see each other any time. So, we then had to talk to a lawyer and it took all my courage to start talking to her about the paperwork. Now we had to tell Maria the truth but I had the feeling she already knew more than we thought and when I told her babies grow in women's stomachs and some grow in women's hearts and that she had grown in Angela's stomach and in my heart, she looked at me—not scared or surprised—and just said, "Well, I have two mamies then." I agreed and was just very glad that part was over. At least the basics had been laid out and now I could wait until she asked me more.

Charly called Karl Heinz and told him he had a special going on— 50% off trips to Europe on a charter flight. As he knew we had that property in Berlin, he thought it would be wise to talk to them in person and he even offered to let us make payments to them on the tickets. It would not be in the summer, more towards fall, and we talked it over and decided we couldn't refuse, especially as we could stay with Christina. I had a hard time hiding my excitement about seeing Berlin again.

In the meantime, the adoption became final, so we didn't have any problems and we told Charly to go ahead with the reservation for the fall. I called Michael to tell him our plans for the trip to Berlin because of the property and also about the adoption. The only thing he said was not to sell then because prices would eventually go up. He mentioned that he had been in New York for a week and was glad to be back home. I wanted to ask him if Elena was with him but kept quiet and he didn't say anything either.

I was surprised how quickly children adjust to new situations. Maria decided that since she had two mothers now, she was calling Angela Mom and me Mama, so she sorted that situation quite fast and I was quite relieved that we'd solved that one.

Karl Heinz got another contract to build a house but the first one wasn't finished so it would take a little time as we only had Thomas as a helper. I helped as well to save money but we hadn't hired any other workers. We still had two weeks in the fall for Berlin and that was enough. Sometimes I wondered why we never heard from the IRS (Internal Revenue Service) about the taxes I thought we owed, but assumed everything was alright.

Shortly before we left for Berlin, I received a little package from Michael with a little dream catcher—he knew I had bought one in Korea. It almost looked like a wind chime but didn't make any noise and had a lot of colourful feathers attached. A little piece of paper was attached to it, saying, "Hang it in the window in the room you'll sleep in, so it can catch beautiful dreams for you. Maybe it will catch one from our past." I had no idea how he got such ideas but they were always so lovely.

We got ready for our trip but of course, being a charter flight, it was completely booked and I had the feeling it was overbooked, though eventually everyone found their seat. It was not a comfortable flight but for us it was almost free, so we couldn't complain and when we landed at Berlin Tegel airport, I felt I was home again. We rented a car and drove to Christina's and even Karl Heinz became a bit emotional.

Since we only had a few days, we started out the next day to look at the property and try to find out what was really going on. First, we went to the County for more information but being born in Berlin, speaking German without an accent and then showing an American Passport was not a good match and neither was the information we got from them, so it seemed it might still take a while to clear everything up. We also had to prove there were no old tires or chemical buried there, which meant we had to look for my father's relatives and talk to them as they were using our property as their vegetable garden. We were also suffering from jet lag and decided that was enough for the first day.

Christina made a lovely, typically German, dinner of meat rolls, mashed potatoes and fried Pfifferlinge—a special kind of mushroom, also called Chanterelles, which people go and collect in the forest because they are quite expensive. I went to bed right away after dinner but put the dream catcher in the window hidden under the curtains. As far as I remembered the next day, the dream catcher didn't catch a dream—but I probably wouldn't have noticed it anyway and thought maybe it would the next night.

We had to find my father's relative, the one from whom he bought the property, to find out if there were any chemicals or old tires buried there. Well, I had the sales contract with me so at least we knew where to look and it was just a few streets away so we went there and met the middle-aged man who opened the door. He didn't look very friendly but came to the gate and asked us who we were, so we told him who we were and what we wanted. He just said that his family had bought the house from my father's cousin's family and he knew about my father buying our property from that family as well, but that had been many years ago before the war. That sounded correct so far but looking at the empty beer bottles lying around his house, we were not so sure anymore. Also, he did not know who planted vegetables there. After telling us the wall should not have come down, that they should have built it even higher, we left.

We only tried one more time to ask one of the neighbours if they knew who was using our property and we could feel the coldness towards us when they told us who was using it but that they were not there at the moment. The reaction of those people was so disappointing; I was under the impression people were happy to be reunited again. One lady told me she wasn't happy anymore, as she had been when it was still East Germany and some special food or clothing she was waiting for, which wasn't available for a while, finally arrived. Now, if she wanted something, she could get it whenever she wanted and there was no happy feeling.

I knew now that I could never live there and that made my decision to sell a lot easier. The only thing we could do was to see the Real Estate Company and talk to them—maybe they would have a different opinion about the united Germany. Well, at least they were more businesslike and told us it would take a long time to get the people onto one level, probably at least a generation. We left our address with them and asked them to let us know when it was a better time to sell.

I was so glad my father had not had to see what happened to his dream of retiring in his "Dream House." That evening, we talked about it with Christina and Werner and they told us the same story, that there was still a deep split between East and West, mostly in the divided Berlin. I realised that was not the Berlin I loved so much—this was the new Berlin, and the Berlin I loved was in the past, which made me sad, as though I had lost my roots. Every night, I hid the dream catcher behind the curtain but even the dream catcher was not able to catch a dream; maybe it felt like I did. We had a few days left and checked out places we used to go to but everything had changed and even our service station wasn't there anymore.

It was then time to go back and, looking out of the window when we took off from Airport Tegal, I wondered when I would see Berlin again. A song popped up in my mind which had been sung by Marlene Dietrich, a German-American actress and singer, also born in Berlin, who became famous in the movie The Blue Angel and for the song "Ich Hab Noch Einen Koffer In Berlin"—" still have a suitcase in Berlin." That's how I felt at that moment—that I still had a suitcase in Berlin and that's why I would have to go back. I looked at Karl Heinz and saw his eyes were a bit teary looking down on our Berlin.

I was surprised about Karl Heinz' emotions as he hardly showed his emotions, especially after the loss of the brewery, but it was different with Berlin as we'd lived through a lot of hardship during and after the war when we were just starting out in life, and those were happenings you never do forget.

Well, we made it back on the not-so-comfortable charter flight but we now knew it might take longer to sell the property than we had thought. At the moment, however, we were doing alright with one house almost finished and the next one waiting to start. The only problem I saw coming was that Karl Heinz sometimes had a hard time carrying lumber and doing other heavy work. I talked to him about it but he, of course, would not admit it, though he agreed to hire a helper who, together with Thomas, would do the heavy work while Karl Heinz would do the finishing touches. That worked out fine and if everything went well, we could sell the property in Berlin and that would be our retirement. We would both get our pension and we would be fine. We just had to get Maria through school but I could still find a part-time job and it now looked as if that would be our home for the rest of our lives.

That was the result of the war—our family spread all over the world. My grandparents had been pushed out of their farm in Poland and buried in Berlin and my parents left caged-in Berlin and went to Bavaria, and now we would stay where we were and most likely die there.

One evening, I sat down and listened to the two records Michael had sent me years go and thought how fast life goes by. I remembered that I had not even told Michael what was happened in Berlin but it was too late now in San Francisco, so I decided to call his office the next day. I wondered if he felt the same way. When I called and he was on the phone, I started to tell him about Berlin and how disappointed I was that it was not our Berlin anymore. He did not say anything, he just let me talk, that was the nice thing. Maybe he was bored listening to me, but he was still listening.

He then told me that a few years before, he had been in Berlin with a friend for a week on business but hadn't told me about it since he knew how it would make me feel and he had experienced the same feeling as I did. I felt better after that talk and he still insisted, "Well, we will see each other." Maybe it was wishful thinking.

1995 was almost over and we had a lovely Christmas season. Angela and Brian came over and everything was nice and peaceful. I wished Michael could be with us spending the holiday, but that was for sure wishful thinking. Maria would start school in 1996 and maybe Angela would get married in 1996, and I hoped they would stay in the islands so that I could have my whole family with me.

A young couple moved into one of the houses in the neighbourhood—he was a doctor in our hospital and she worked in an office in town and we met when I walked around the corner with Abby. I believe their grandparents had immigrated from Portugal and they seemed to be really nice and had two children—a baby and a seven-year old girl. The girl was not the problem as she was picked up by the school bus in the morning and returned on the bus at noon, but the baby needed looking after and one day the mother asked me if I would like to watch the baby until noon, just half a day, and since I loved babies, I agreed. As Maria was also in kindergarten for half a day, it was perfect.

I stayed until 2 in the afternoon when the mother, Mrs. Silva, came home and it was great with the baby but sometimes I made lunch for the seven-year old girl, Sara, who was so spoiled by her parents that it was hard to get along with her. Whatever I prepared for lunch didn't taste right or was the wrong food and when I looked at her asking her what she wanted, she just smiled and turned around and left the kitchen. I stood there remembering how it was when I was growing up—I had to clean up the plate whether I liked it or not and then after the war we were always hungry. In some families the parents had to hide the food in the pantry and put a lock on the door, not because they didn't want to give food to their children but because they had to organise it so that it would last longer because there were no refrigerators at that time. I realised times had changed drastically, but sometimes I just remembered those old times. I stayed for three months but then I spoke with Mrs. Silva about it and she understood—it was not the first time it had happened.

Instead of babysitting, I started to help with the house building again and it was already summer and Maria was preparing for her first year of school. Michael and I talked on the phone whenever we had a chance and the last time we spoke, he told me he had to take some medication for his elevated blood pressure but that it wasn't serious, though he was thinking about part-time retirement. It was hard to believe that he was already in his mid-60s. I thought he had given up the idea that we would see each other again because he hadn't mentioned it lately.

Maria started her first day of school and she was pretty excited. Her teacher was a Japanese lady and very nice but I couldn't believe Maria was going to school—I still remembered seeing her being born. The house was all done and we had an offer to build another house starting at the beginning of the next year, in 1997. Those people were going to buy all the material for the house on the mainland as it was cheaper there and since we had an enclosed garage, they asked us if they could store the material in our garage until they were ready to start and, of course, we agreed, so we already had a good beginning for the year 1997.

The old year had gone and we were already in 1997 when Angela and Brian told us they were planning to get married in the summer. Maria's first year of school would be over in the summer and Thomas' son, Chris, would start his first class in the summer as well. I liked it when everything was planned as it gives less stress, but of course it doesn't always happen like that.

I talked with Michael about his health and he felt better after taking his medication, but was thinking of maybe selling his big house and moving into the South of California and letting Janet and Bianca take over his business so that he could retire and enjoy life playing golf and maybe travelling. He was really excited about that idea and my first thought was that maybe he'd met someone, but I didn't ask him. If he had, it wasn't my business to ask him but maybe that was the reason he hadn't recently said, "We will meet again."

The people who ordered their house from the mainland got their house package and we had a completely overstocked garage, so Karl Heinz got all the permits together and was almost ready to start. I could see that he became more and more the old Karl Heinz again and it was nice to see the change and looked as though we would have a great retirement.

Because of all the building material, I had to take out and look through old papers which I had stored in the garage. There were lots of old bank statements, signed mortgage papers and credit line forms and was I ever glad that time was over. There was also that life insurance policy for accidental death in there and I was still paying for it every month. I looked at it and thought who was going to have a car accident. I had been paying for it for years now and even though the monthly amount was small, I still thought I would cancel it, so took it out and put it aside.

Finally, Karl Heinz had all the papers together to start the house and he told me that I would have to go to Church with Maria by myself because he and Thomas would be going down on Sunday morning to measure everything up so that they could start on Monday morning. He called Thomas the night before to tell him to be at our house at seven in the morning so they could all go in just one car and on Sunday morning I got up at six to make coffee and breakfast. Karl Heinz was already up and when we had coffee, he told me he hadn't slept well and that his heart was racing badly. I told him he had to see a doctor, that perhaps his blood pressure was high, and I was worried he might have a heart attack.

When Thomas arrived, I had already started to make breakfast so Karl Heinz told him to take his own car and go ahead and that he would follow a little later, after breakfast. That wasn't what had been planned but I thought maybe Karl Heinz was hungry and wanted to have breakfast before he left. In the middle of breakfast, though, he jumped up and said, "I have to go now," and didn't finish his breakfast. While he got ready for work, I asked him what time he would be home for lunch and he looked at me and said, "About 12.30," and as I looked in his eyes, I noticed they were dead-looking; I never forgot that look in all my life. He then got in his car and drove off.

I found his behaviour strange but thought he was most likely still tired but then I looked out and my car wasn't in the driveway, but instead it was in the lot next to us, which had never happened and I could not make out why. When we were getting ready to go to Church, the phone rang and it was Thomas' wife telling me there had been an accident with Dad—nothing serious, just a fender bender but asking if I could go to the next little village and meet with her. It was then I heard the ambulance siren and somehow started to get nervous.

I took Maria and drove down the road onto the highway, where I passed another accident—a car was standing sideways up on a little hill and a person was lying on the grass next to the car. When I passed, I thought how unusual it was to have two accidents at seven o'clock on a Sunday morning and then after passing, it somehow hit me that it had looked like our car and that the person on the ground had almost the same clothing that Karl Heinz wore that morning.

I was trying to turn around when I saw Thomas coming up the highway. His eyes were wide open and he was as white as a sheet. I turned around and followed him to the scene. In the meantime, they had removed the body. We were stopped by a policeman who asked that we confirm we were Thomas and his mother. He was a classmate of Thomas who had also moved over to this island, and he knew us. He told us how sorry he was but that Karl Heinz did not suffer and had died instantly. He had hydroplaned on the slippery road and lost control of the car and had been hit by an oncoming pickup truck. Only those two vehicles on the highway and they hit each other.

Thomas drove us home with Maria screaming in the back and he then called our relatives in Berlin and his brother on the mainland. I could not think at all. Angela and Brian flew over from Maui and our priest came over as well as my doctor, who brought me some tranquilizers. I did not remember a lot about that night and was just glad to have my family with me.

The next few days were like a dream. There was so much to take care of and while looking at my desk I saw that insurance policy I had wanted to cancel. At that moment I knew someone was watching over me and whoever it was must be pretty close to me—maybe it was my mother and grandmother.

My life had actually changed within ten minutes. We arranged the funeral and only his brother from the mainland was able to come, his sister could not. Then, since everyone had to go back to work, I was always busy doing something. I didn't completely realise what had happened, it just hit me after everyone was gone and normal life started again.

I started to do a little bit every day and first had to contact the people who had stored the house material in our garage. I felt I had to tell Michael what had happened but somehow I could not.

I remembered when we left Berlin after our last visit to find out about the sale of my property, that while taking off, Karl Heinz had tears in his eyes. It was his last visit to Berlin and I wondered if he felt something then: there were so many unanswered questions.

Finally, one day, I felt strong enough to call Michael. It took a while until he picked up the phone and when I heard his voice I couldn't talk, I just started to cry. He just said, "What happened to Karl Heinz?" so I told him what had happened and he immediately said, "I am coming over," but that I wasn't able to handle and I told him so. I needed time and space and he wanted to know if I was financially alright so I told him about the life insurance policy—it wasn't a lot of money but enough to get by. We talked for a long time that day and I knew then that I really needed time to think about what to do. He understood me completely and just wanted to be kept informed so we made a plan to talk twice a week.

I really didn't know how to go on and, to make it worse, twice when Maria and myself were not at home at night and Abby was sleeping in the garage, our house was broken into. Nothing was stolen so they must have been interrupted, maybe by Abby's barking, but that really scared me a lot so Thomas got us an alarm system. It was connected to the police station so at night we had to close all windows and doors and if someone on the outside tried to get in, a really loud alarm siren went off and the police would be there within ten or fifteen minutes. That was a great help but it all got me thinking that, if we sold the house, we could move closer to the city and have neighbours all around us and would be safer.

Just to check out the prices in our neighbourhood, I saw a realtor and asked him to come and have a look at our lot as I wanted to sell it. He was surprised how nice and big it was and he put a pretty good value on the house. I then really wanted to sell it, so he came over and we signed a contract. He asked if we had any liens or mortgages on it and I told him about our little mortgage and that was all. He then put his sales sign up and I somehow felt good because I had another idea, but it was one I couldn't think through until the sale of that house was final.

It took a few days before the realtor showed up and he looked kind of surprised while he told me that there was an IRS lien on the house from the brewery. I had no knowledge of it and the amount was not small—if I had to pay that, the profit from the house would be a lot smaller. Then came the next shock—no county permit had been taken out for the two rooms which we'd added to the house after it was built, which meant they were illegal and considered of no value. What was left was the little cottage for which we had the permit, which meant that the value of the house went way down. It was hard to swallow but

I just told the Realtor to drop the price; I really felt like running away and hiding.

I always wondered about the tax, but because of the time which had passed, I had relaxed, thinking it was all over and finished with. I went to our bank manager and had a talk with him about the tax lien and he was surprised and didn't know about it either. The reason wasn't clear but whatever it was, it was all now in my name and to fight it I had to get a tax attorney, which would cost me $500.00 an hour. I would have to pay it off from whatever profit I made on the sale but I still had money left from the accident insurance, so I would be fine. And then, of course, I had the Berlin property and Christina had written to me saying she'd noticed that property prices were picking up in the former East Germany.

Charly and Grace came over for a funeral and stopped by and when I told them what had happened with the tax lien, they had no idea about it either. Grace called me the next day and told me not to be too sad because Karl Heinz had told her he could have married a model but, instead, he needed someone who could work hard. I thought I wasn't hearing properly. I didn't think he would ever say a thing like that, either, and that Grace was just telling me that to make me angry. Or was it true? I never found out but whether Grace said it to make me angry or not, she did change my thinking.

My mind was now set that after selling the house and paying off all the debts, Maria and myself would leave the islands for a while and go back to Berlin—but for how long or forever, I still had to think about. After making that decision even my anxiety attacks stopped.

With everything I had to take care of, I knew it might be a while before I left the islands but my goal was set and now I could tell Michael what my plans were. When I called him and told him what I was going to do, he became serious and said, "I always had the feeling we would see each other again." Now, after so many years, I wasn't so sure anymore whether I really wanted to and I told him so. He just listened and said, "We will have our trip down memory lane in Berlin and you know it as well as I do." I had to laugh as he was usually right and the best thing was that we would be in Berlin again.

Thomas came by that night and told me he had an idea. He said he knew my plan and suggested we buy a computer for me, that we share the price and then when I left, he could use it. The idea wasn't bad but I'd never been close to a computer or used one as, while working in the brewery, our bookkeeper did that job and I just used the typewriter and a lot of composition books. However, he convinced me by telling me I could look for so many things online—like schools for Maria, apartments, etc., and could write emails to people instead of letters. Of course, no one I knew in Berlin had a computer, but Michael might have one for sure.

I agreed and we went to buy one; it wasn't cheap and it was huge, then there it was in my living room. I remember it was an IBM and I looked at it but really didn't even know how to turn it on—or off, for that matter. Thomas told me it had to be connected first and then he would show me how to use it. I felt as if I was in the dark ages but I was ready to learn and after a few days a technician came and connected it and it was ready to go. I had to admit, I was proud of myself and the next time I spoke with Michael, I asked him for his email address—I'd learnt that already and he got a kick out of that.

Angela told us they were thinking of getting married on Maui in the fall, so we started to prepare for that. It was already six months since Karl Heinz passed away but when I went to the graveyard and stood by his grave, I still had a hard time believing what had happened.

Because we lived out in the country, there were not too many people interested in buying our house. People preferred living closer to the city and we still had no actual offer so I was prepared to still be in the islands over the holiday season. I therefore told Michael that I would be in Berlin in the spring of next year and his reply was "Just in time for the blooming of the lily of the valley and the lilac trees." He still remembered that.

We flew over to Maui for Angela's wedding and it was nice. The family was together again, just one was missing.

Christmas had almost arrived and it would be the first one without Karl Heinz; well, we had to get used to it. I then really started to look forward to moving to Berlin or to just living there for a while, especially after I received a bank statement from a foreign country—but it wasn't my name on it. It was from the country where we had bought some ingredients for the brewery and I could not make out what the items were which were listed, just the balance, so I just sent it back telling them Mr. Kinds had passed away.

On Christmas Day, Michael and myself had a long talk; he had been invited to go to Bianca and her family. We were both looking forward to meeting in Berlin—of course at Airport Tegel as the Airport Gatow was not in operation anymore. We didn't talk about how long we would be in Berlin or where I would live, etc.—maybe we still didn't believe it.

Finally, we got an offer on the house. They were paying for a cottage and getting a four-bedroom house for it so the offer wasn't what I expected but it wasn't that bad either. I was told it might take about six weeks before they got their mortgage but they had enough for the down payment and there shouldn't be a problem. In one way I was happy but I was also sad as my life was about to change again and I had no idea what direction it would go; maybe it was better not to know.

I really enjoyed my computer because I finally realised that the computer didn't tell me what to do—I was the one who told the computer what to do. I found two international schools for Maria in Berlin, one of which was a boarding school, and I contacted them through email and got the information I needed. One was located pretty close to former complex Wannsee. I also found a nice two-bedroom furnished apartment, so I had almost everything under control. I just sent a few personal things over to Christina and decided to store my furniture until I knew what direction my life would go. Then the papers for the sale of the house were ready to sign and we had four weeks to leave the house.

That meant we would leave around April/May. Thomas then came over and asked me about possibly leaving Maria there until the end of the school year, when I would be settled in Berlin with an apartment and car and maybe be putting the property on the market. He would then bring her over after school was out. I knew he just wanted to come to Berlin and I had enough free airline miles that the trip would be free and I knew that booking with Charly wouldn't cost a lot of money. I even felt better about not putting her into a boarding school; she was too young for that. After talking it over with Maria, she really liked the idea of flying to Berlin with Thomas, so it looked as if everything would fall into place.

If I really met up with Michael, we would have enough time to talk about what would happen to us and whether we could have a future together—after so many years, people change. I called Michael and told him I needed about four weeks to get settled and then, if he still wanted, we could meet at the airport in Tegel. Well, knowing Michael I should have expected it and Michael told me that he was sure I could manage that in three weeks.

I told Charly to make reservations for Berlin, just one way, if possible at the end of April. I signed all the papers for the sale but left my bank account and my post office box open, so that I still had one leg in the islands. The house was emptied, the rest of the furniture put into storage, and when the last day came I went to say goodbye to Karl Heinz. I had been about a year and many thoughts went through my mind, one of which was that I was so thankful he had passed away without months of pain. I also knew that after losing the brewery, he had kind of lost his energy to go on.

Yes, we had both made mistakes but the way we started our lives together was not easy and I blamed it all on the war. We had hopes and dreams and lost most of them. While looking up, I saw a Spatz (a sparrow) sitting in a palm tree and singing. I wondered about that—we had lots of them in Berlin but I never saw a sparrow in the islands. Maybe it was Karl Heinz. Maybe it was just my imagination. But I had to smile and I felt very peaceful so whatever I saw or didn't see helped me to leave the islands more at ease.

I flew over without stopping anywhere and while taking off from J. F. Kennedy International Airport for Heathrow Airport in London, I went through a lot of flashbacks and memories. I could not get out of Europe fast enough and now it was the other way around—I couldn't get back fast enough. I promised myself just to go one day at a time and cope as well as I could with whatever was thrown at me.

Time went by quickly and while descending into Berlin Tegel, I could still see pieces of the wall and the difference between East and West Berlin but it looked more cleaned up and taken care of. Maybe I wanted to see it like that, but it wasn't only me and other people had told me the same, so it must have been true. Going through Customs and Immigration with an American passport with your birthplace Berlin was always funny, as most of them couldn't understand it and believed I was just born in Berlin and then left when I was small—until I started to speak the real Berlin slang, which you can only do if you grew up in Berlin. That made them believe, but then coming from Heavenly Hawaii was another laugh.

Christina picked me up and her huge garden had two lilac bushes and that beautiful smell reminded me of stealing branches for my mother on Mother's Day. She asked me what my plans were and I told her I really didn't know, only that I was looking for a furnished apartment and a car right away, if possible for six months. I told her Maria would come in the summer and, for the first time, I mentioned Michael, telling them that I knew him from after the war and that he was an American soldier stationed in Berlin, that Karl Heinz knew him too, and that he would come and visit me there in Berlin. They didn't pay too much attention to it.

The next day, I got a newspaper and looked for an apartment and a car, which was all I needed. I found a cute two-bedroom apartment close to Lake Wannsee and rented it for six months and the owner said I could always extend the lease. There was a phone line in the apartment and I just had to have it connected and put in my name, but the owner said he would do it for me after he found out I was an American—he always rented only to Americans. I briefly mentioned that I needed internet as well for a computer. That was a bit more money than I expected but, well, I had always been there for others and now it was my turn to be nice to myself. He also told me that if I needed a phone in the meantime, there was a public phone at the entrance. He thought everything would be ready in about fourteen days.

It was evening there in Berlin and I just wanted to tell Thomas and Michael that I had arrived safely. I called Hawaii, which wasn't too bad as it was morning there, and I spoke with Thomas telling him that I had arrived safely and would tell him more in a few days. It was very early in San Francisco but Michael answered quickly and I told him the same. Well, then I only had to find a car, a computer, and a German Bank in which to open an account.

I opened up a German account, which was easier than I thought, and the bank manager was not even impressed that I came from Hawaii. I had the feeling Berlin had become more of an international city as I heard a lot of different languages being spoken. I also found a computer. I now realised I was almost hooked on it and I was learning a lot and really enjoyed it. Finding a good car was a bit harder. I really wanted a small one, since the traffic in Berlin was a lot heavier than on our island and most likely I would drive on the Autobahn as well. Christina's husband offered to help and we found a nice-looking silver-grey Nissan Sentra which I fell in love with at first sight.

I checked with the landlord of my apartment and he told me I could move in by the middle of May. One thing I wondered about was that whenever I talked to people and they asked me where I lived, when I told them where they said, "Oh, you live in the East." For me, Germany was united again but a lot of the Berliners didn't feel that way, so where I lived it was actually the former East Germany. However, I liked the area and the apartment building was located next to the river Spree, the river which flows right through Berlin.

It was then time to tell Michael when I was moving into the apartment so one morning I called him and told him my plan that I would be in the apartment by the middle of May, or maybe a few days later. I wasn't sure what his reaction would be but he said, "Okay, I will make reservations tomorrow, maybe for May 20th," and I was sure everything would be hooked up by then and I would have a phone number as well. He said he'd call me in a few days to give me his arrival date in Berlin and by then my phone would be working.

Afterwards, I wasn't so sure if I'd done the right thing but he was the one who kept pushing me for a meeting and, well, it was too late now. Maybe he would cancel his trip. I also called Thomas to see how everything was going and he said it was fine except that Abby kept looking for us so they had got a puppy and she was now a lot better. Maybe I made a mistake by just running off like that, but I promised myself just to go day by day.

How could I have forgotten I was living in the former East Germany, but for me West Berlin was a caged-in city even though Berlin was now united and had been for quite a while. Well, I moved into my apartment and I liked it a lot I had everything I enjoyed—a car, a computer and a phone—and as soon as I got everything hooked up, I called Thomas and gave him my number and email address. The manager of the apartment did help me a bit but for all the world, I looked like an expert even though it wasn't that easy because my computer was now a "German Computer" and I had to learn to "talk" German to the computer.

I sent Michael an email with my phone number and he then called me and told me he would arrive on Wednesday, 20th May, at Airport Tegal, arriving from Frankfurt at about noon and he asked if I could pick him up or if he should take a taxi. He then started to laugh and told me he was so quiet because he didn't know if it would really happen but he had his ticket now and I had a phone and an email now and so it was going to happen. It looked like he was still his old self.

The night before he was going to arrive, I was sitting outside on my little balcony watching the River Spree and listening to the two records from Michael. A cruise ship was passing by with people singing on board and none of it felt real to me. I was sitting in the former East Germany, only a few minutes away from the former border between East Germany and West Berlin. I could even see into West Berlin in the distance and had the same feeling that I had standing at the border in South Korea looking into North Korea—you could look into it but not go there. It had been the same with Berlin, standing in West Berlin looking into East Germany but not able to go there. It was all quite emotional and the next day I would meet someone I hadn't seen for over forty years who used to be part of the winning army in World War 2—an American soldier stationed in Berlin.

I didn't sleep well that night and decided to take a taxi instead of driving my car, so I called a taxi and arrived about an hour before Michael's arrival at 12.30. I looked at the arrival board but there was no

MY LITTLE BIRD

arrival from Frankfurt at that time. There was one at 11 in the morning and the next one was at 5 in the afternoon. I was a bit confused and went into the cafeteria and ordered a coffee and looked for a newspaper. I really didn't know what to do as asking the ladies at the counter if there was a Mr. Mendez on the 11 o'clock flight wouldn't work, as they would not tell me. Maybe he had mixed up the dates and times or changed his mind and the best thing I could do was to go back hoping he would call me.

I had just about finished the coffee when I felt a touch on my shoulder. I turned around and there he was—Michael, the spoiled kid from San Francisco, with a branch of lilac flowers. All I could say was "Hi" and he just said that he had to lie about the time. He'd flown in at 11.00 but just wanted to see me and watch me for a little while. Yes, he hadn't changed.

I stood there not knowing what to do, whether to give him a hug, shake his hand, or run away. My face felt as red as a tomato and my blood pressure was over 200 for sure. He still looked quite attractive, even though his hair had started to grey and he had also added a few more pounds. Finally, he gave me a hug and said, "You haven't changed a lot, my little bird." That brought me back to reality—he was still as charming as over forty years ago and you were never quite sure if he meant it or was just being charming.

We called a taxi and drove to the apartment. Neither of us were very talkative and it felt like a fairy tale, at least for me. I didn't ask him how long he would stay and he didn't say anything. He wanted to go and have something to eat, so we went to a little Chinese restaurant around the corner—a Chinese restaurant in the former East Germany: it was so overwhelming for him as well. Slowly, we found our conversation come back. He admired my car and asked what had happened to the Mercedes and I just told him the bank had taken it.

On our way back we stopped at a grocery store and bought some snacks and a bottle of wine and he said, "Remember the PX Stores?" Who could forget the PX Stores, my whole family almost lived from them. Arriving at the apartment, the Manager came out. I guess he was waiting for us and he said hi to Michael in broken English. I guess that's what you call reunited—an American, a former East German and a former caged-in Berliner. He was so proud and invited Michael to have a German beer the next evening—at least one person who was happy about the united Germany.

We didn't talk about making plans and just sat on the balcony like I had the night before and we just started to talk about everything and nothing—mostly, of course, about the past—and the bond Michael was always talking about came back, or maybe it had never left. There was just the present and nothing of the past over-forty years. When I woke up the next morning I smelled cigarette smoke and saw Michael sitting on the balcony smoking a cigarette. When he saw me, he said, "Remember, I always did this when we stayed at Complex Wannsee or Complex Gatow?" and I had the feeling we were living half in the past and half in the present.

We went to the store to get fresh buns for breakfast, holding hands like teenagers, but we no longer walked as fast as teenagers and had to remind each other not to forget our medication in the morning—that was the present again; we hadn't had to do that in the past. I called Christina and told her that our friend had arrived and that we might stop by over the weekend. I enjoyed those first days—there were no worries, just doing what we loved to do, walking around lake Wannsee like we used to with no pressure and no tomorrow, just today.

It was a little over a week since Michael arrived but it felt like months because we were always doing something. I called Christina saying we wanted to go over but neither of them was feeling well and she said she would call us when they were better. I phoned Thomas and everything was fine, and I also told him about Michael.

One evening, sitting on the balcony, we started to talk about us and it was really emotional. The way he behaved, I believed that he had really meant everything he had said to me over the many years. It was a good feeling and he said then that he would stay until we found a decision about our future. That was a special evening for us, like so many that we had like that over forty years before.

The next day, we went to Kurfuerstendamm for dinner in quite a fancy restaurant with live music. We also danced—not that fast, but the music they played was for the little-elevated-in-age-generation. I was so proud being with him; he was the best-looking man there, but I also knew that feeling I had from over forty years ago as well. When we got home, he asked me if I would like to go on a short vacation, saying he would really like that, and I said yes, I'd love that—it would be our first proper vacation together; our vacation in the past was our special room in Daniel's house. He said he was thinking about Israel as he'd always wanted to go there but it actually wasn't where I wanted to go and I told him I'd rather go to Italy. "That will be the next trip," he said.

A little further down the street we found a travel agency and went in to try and make reservations. The girl behind the desk looked kind of surprised after she heard what we wanted. Yes, it was different from Charly's agency, but she really tried her best. She gave us an offer flying from Berlin with a stop-over in Zurich/Switzerland and then going on to Ben Gurion Airport in Tel Aviv/Israel. We also asked her if she could make a reservation for us for a hotel or bed-and-breakfast in Tel Aviv for a week. She said, "Of course," and you could see how proud she was, it must have been her first international flight reservation and she told us to come back and tell her our decision and then she would do the ticketing.

On our way home, we talked about what we would do in Israel—of course visit Jerusalem, the Dead Sea, River Jordan, maybe a walk to the Mediterranean Sea and also a visit to a Kibbutz, if that would be possible. We got so excited, we could hardly sleep and the next day we went back to the travel agency and told her we'd like to buy the tickets. She asked for identification and we just had our American passports, but in different names so I said told her we were not married. Michael must have understood that and just said, "Not yet." We all started laughing and the lady said she had a boyfriend she lived with and they were not married either; that times had changed. She found us a family hotel in Tel Aviv, so we were ready to go in four days.

I was really looking forward to that trip; it was actually the first trip we would take together. Trying to put some clothes together, I found the little smart book which I'd always used to look up what attractions to see if visiting a foreign country. I hadn't used that little book for a while as since the loss of the brewery, we had hardly travelled. Now I looked up Israel and saw a picture with a note saying whenever visiting Israel, not to forget to visit the Western Wall, also called the Wailing Wall, in Jerusalem, as it is the most religious site in the world for Jewish people. I remembered reading about it but had not paid much attention to it since I was quite sure I would never visit Israel.

I told Michael about that and he already knew about it and was planning a special trip to go there and visit the Wall. I don't know why he wanted that—maybe because of the Berlin Wall; I never found out. A memory popped up in my head and I remembered having a little girlfriend in Berlin who lived on the same street. It must have been at the beginning of World War 2 in 1939 or shortly before and we always played in the park together. Her parents had a fur coat business and lots of fancy clothes and I liked their apartment because it was so elegant looking. I was sick for a few days and could not play and after I got well and went to their apartment and store, I found everything boarded up and closed. No one was there anymore and at that time I didn't know what had happened and when I asked, nobody answered or they just turned around and went away, just saying they were Jewish. It didn't mean anything to me but later I found out why they disappeared.

I called Thomas and told him where I was going and he sounded kind of absent-minded but said everything was okay. Michael called Bianca just to tell her where he was going as well. I didn't know if she knew where he was in Germany, but I am sure he had told her. Everything for the trip was ready and we left from Tegel Airport. I was so excited, Michael just had to smile and was calm and relaxed; maybe it had something to do with the medication he took every morning. It was an enjoyable flight, mostly over the Swiss Alps, where some of the mountain tops were covered with snow. I just had to put my head on his shoulder and felt safe and secure, even while for a moment we were flying through some bad turbulence.

We made it safe and sound into Tel Aviv Airport, which was a pretty airport with lots of glassed windows, and we found a taxi and were dropped off at a cute family hotel. It was nicely decorated with a small kitchenette, a television and even a computer. The owners were very nice and told us her parents came from Russia. How small the world is. We didn't plan anything for that evening—just went to a Pizza restaurant and enjoyed being there. The next day we wanted to start with Jerusalem and as there was also a phone in the apartment, we called the travel office but they were already closed so we had to try the next day. It had been a long and exciting day and we needed to rest for the coming week.

First thing in the morning, we called the travel office but there was nothing available for that day so we made next-day reservations for Jerusalem. I was actually glad about it as we could take it easy and maybe go to the beach and walk a bit, looking at the Mediterranean Sea. We had also been told that they had beautiful art and antique shops in that area and we could sit at the beach and have lunch. Michael looked tired and he was all for it so we took a taxi and it dropped us off right at the beach.

It was a beautiful day and we walked along the beach talking about the past a lot. He asked me about my grandmother, he'd really liked her a lot, and I told him I thought she had a crush on him. He couldn't stop laughing, remembering her with her big eyes and the rosary he gave her. He asked me about Karl Heinz and I asked him about Elena and mentioned how jealous I was because she was so beautiful and I was that little nothing who just wanted to be loved and cared for. After hearing that, he just said, "Why would I be here if I hadn't loved and cared all those years and blamed myself for the mistakes I made?" Even though it was sad, I enjoyed hearing that.

After walking for quite a while, we were getting hungry and found a little open-air type of restaurant pretty close to the beach. We wanted to have a typical Israeli lunch so asked the waiter what to order and he recommended a salad, hummus and French fries—a nice, light, healthy lunch. We then went through an art gallery and admired the beautiful paintings; it was a heaven for art collectors. After that, because the next day would be hectic going to Jerusalem, we called it a day and bought a pizza to heat up at home in the little kitchenette.

The owner of the hotel met us when we got back and asked me if I could still speak German. He must have seen my nationality in my passport. I was scared at that moment and didn't know what to say, but why lie, so I said that I did and he answered me in broken German, saying, "Yes, a lot of elderly Jewish people still speak German despite what happened in the war." That surprised me.

We heated our pizza and ate it on the balcony and it felt like being back in our special room at Daniel's house. I really thanked God that night for allowing me to have that time with Michael; whatever the future held for us, no one could take that time away from me.

We had to be at the bus station quite early and, thank God, the bus wasn't all full. It was about an hour's drive and we passed a kibbutz, which looked really well taken care of and you could see people working the fields and children running around and playing. We asked the bus driver if we could visit a Kibbutz but he said not really, at least not there in the Jerusalem area, and I had the feeling he didn't like the idea.

Our first stop was the Wailing Wall located in the old city of Jerusalem, a limestone wall of which the construction started 19 B.C.—I found that in a little brochure from a newspaper stand. It was stunning and overwhelming and you felt like a little ant by comparison. Now I was glad we'd gone there. To get close to the wall you had to cover your head with a hat. Michael had a cap and I had a scarf, so we were fine and could walk slowly along the wall. We saw quite a few people kneeling on little steps, some crying, some praying, and some trying to push pieces of paper with their written wishes into cracks in the wall. I just could not help it but, holding Michael's hand, I felt unbelievably unimportant in front of this. We both kneeled down as well and both of us took a piece of paper and wrote down our wish and tried to squeeze it into a little crack. I thought Karl Heinz would have liked to see that, too. Maybe Michael knew what I was thinking as he put his arm around my shoulder while we walked away, but we were told we could only walk backwards and only face the wall. I couldn't find the reason for that.

We noticed the streets were narrow and hilly so that cars really couldn't drive through and people used bicycles and we even saw a few camels on the road. The bus driver seemed to be hungry and was looking for a restaurant to have lunch—it wasn't easy for him driving that big tourist bus through those small roads and we finally found one and had Chicken Paprika with a big bowl of salad, which was really deli-cious. The trip included a visit to one of the most holy churches in Is-rael but for some reason the bus driver wasn't feeling well and he told us we could have a refund but he wanted to drive back to Tel Aviv. How lucky could you get, but at least we'd seen something and could still go another day. Taking a taxi back, we passed by a few churches but of course only saw them from the outside. In a way, driving back wasn't too bad as we could still go to the beach in the evening and walk and have a lovely dinner, which is what we did, and it was lovely. We wanted to take another sightseeing trip the next day but if there was nothing available we could still take a taxi as the distances to different sight-seeing places wasn't that great.

We called a taxi again and went to see the Jordan River, or River Jordan. I expected to see a huge river but it was not like that and was much smaller than I thought, though it could have been that this part of the river was smaller than at other spots, since we were told the river was about 250 km long. The only thing I wanted to do was to walk down a bit and put my legs into that Jordan River but it was a bit dan-gerous as you had to walk over slippery rocks to get there and Michael refused to go. I saw quite a few people in the water being baptized. I couldn't find out what religion they were but they wore long white coats and had to dip their bodies into the water for quite a time—and the water didn't look too fresh or clean. Maybe that was the reason Michael was afraid to slip and fall in the river. A tour guide told us Christ was baptized in the Jordan River by John the Baptist and it really was quite interesting sightseeing.

We still had time and wanted to look at the Dead Sea, also called the Salt Sea, which is supposed to be the lowest point on earth. We were told that if we wanted to go into the water, we shouldn't stay in longer than ten minutes at a time. You can actually float on the lake be-cause of the high salt concentration but we didn't actually see anyone floating there, the same way we didn't see any boats, fish or plants either. The whole area looked kind of deserted but they had a nice res-taurant with delicious food. An American couple were sitting on the table next to us and we started to talk. They had just arrived from Masada, which is a fortress on a massive plateau overlooking the Dead Sea. If you want to go to the fortress, you have to take a cable car and a long winding road to get there but they were really excited to have seen it. Michael kicked me under the table—he must have been afraid they wanted to come with us and show it to us, and he was right—they said we could go together, that they would love to see it again. We told them we would really have liked that but that we were leaving in two days and they understood. Also, they were at least 20 years younger than us.

We were really glad to be back in the apartment and able to have a little snack and a glass of wine on our balcony and that balcony became almost like the special room at Daniel's house. We had actually made a mistake by going for just one week and should have taken two weeks as there were so many interesting things to see. We only had two days left and both of us decided not to go back to Jerusalem; it would just be another hectic day. I was really tired and went to bed but Michael wanted to stay up a little longer and I noticed he lit a cigarette, something he only did if he was very mad or very happy, and he didn't look mad at all. That made me happy, too.

Thinking it over, we realised we only had those two days, so we went to the beach again, enjoyed all those little stores and found a park full of exotic flowers and tropical birds, it was so peaceful there but we still had our plan to visit Italy—maybe for ten days. Thinking back, Michael said, "We would never have thought 45 years ago that we would be visiting Israel—that it was more likely we would be sitting in San Francisco with three children and maybe being grandparents." Well, I wanted to say that it was all his fault, but I didn't. We took some food home and ate on the balcony knowing that tomorrow was the day to pack things together for the flight back to Berlin. We still had the visit to Italy to look forward to and when it would be and we had to discuss that as so far we'd both avoided talking about it. Sometimes it scared me, but whatever happened, we would just have to deal with it.

Being back in Berlin was like waking up from a dream. We had really enjoyed it but it was too short. Michael called Janet and Bianca and found everything was alright, and I called Thomas. He still sounded absent-minded, so I asked him what was going on. It took a while until he answered but he then told me he had marital problems and that meant he most likely wouldn't be able to come to Berlin with Maria, which changed the whole situation a bit. I then had to discuss that with Michael as it might affect his plans as well.

It was then almost the middle of June and the idea that we had to part again was not easy, but there was still Italy there to look forward to. I called Christina as we wanted to visit her, but they were apparently still sick, so I got the feeling they didn't want to meet Michael.

To make reservations for Italy, we went to the same travel agency we had used for Israel and the lady was delighted and proud that we'd gone back to her to book for Italy. We asked for an offer for at least ten days, since Rome would take at least two days and there was also Naples and we didn't want anything hectic. For a while we forgot the future and were in the present again.

On the weekend, Michael had the idea of going to church—the one we used to go to when he was stationed there in Berlin. I'd had the thought for quite a while and didn't say anything. We went on Saturday evening and of course people weren't looking at us, not like years ago when he was wearing the American uniform and I got those rude looks, but just for old time's sake I took his hand, just as I did all those years ago, and he remembered that too and had the biggest grin. This time, I didn't have to fight for being a German Fraeulein and we enjoyed the church a lot. I was very sure that my grandmother, wherever she was, would be smiling as well.

We really enjoyed the church service and on the way home we started to make plans for the trip to Italy and also for ourselves as we now had to start facing reality and whether there was a future for us. Our bond was stronger than ever, but was it enough for the rest of our lives? At least we'd started to talk about it and we still had Italy to look forward to. I still hadn't heard from Angela, so I had to call her too.

The next week we went to the travel agency and the lady gave us an offer which looked pretty nice and which we accepted. We still had a week before departure, which was fine as we didn't want anything rushed. Michael was tired so we just took a few sightseeing tours in Berlin and enjoyed sitting in the apartment or walking around Lake

Wannsee talking a bit about the past, though some days he was still the happy-go-lucky guy I met after the war.

We finally went on the flight to Rome, just a short two-hour flight with no turbulence that time. Taking a taxi to the hotel, we noticed Italian drivers were very experienced but sometimes quite wild as well. Our driver drove through a red light and must have seen our astonished faces as he just laughed and said, "Why should I stop at the red light if there is no car in sight?" In a way it made sense but it was still illegal, though the way he explained it was funny.

Arriving at the hotel we found it wasn't a really fancy one but old-fashioned, and I liked that. As it had been a short flight, we were not tired and decided this time that we would go into local stores and just buy bread and cheese, butter and sausage and make our own sandwiches in the room with a bottle of wine. Yes, it was a crazy idea but we had so much fun trying to buy the food as we couldn't speak Italian and were mostly just using our hands to show what we wanted. They had different kinds of salami and cheese and the butcher there really had lots of fun with us as well. We tried speaking part English or German but he only spoke quite fast Italian, even though I was pretty sure he was able to speak another language. Anyway, we got what we wanted and while leaving the store, he came after us with two knives and forks so when we got to our room and prepared our sandwiches we had the best dinner ever. The next morning, we went to the front desk and got some brochures about sightseeing. So far, I liked Italy and the people we'd met so far were unique.

We talked to the front desk to ask what were the "must see" places and she said Rome was so full of history it was hard to make recommendations but we should include the Colosseum, the Trevi Fountain, Via Condotti, etc., and of course Vatican City. She gave us a brochure so we could look for ourselves and also mentioned that if we could take a private tour we would see more and the driver would be able to explain more. I looked at Michael as it might be pricey, but he agreed to a private tour and we started out to see the Trevi Fountain, supposedly the most beautiful fountain in Rome, located right in the centre of the city.

Our driver explained everything quite understandably and spoke good English. He told us there was a tradition regarding the fountain that if you throw a coin over your shoulder into the fountain, you will definitely return to Rome and so we asked the driver to look for a parking space as we wanted to walk to the fountain and throw in a coin. There were a lot of tourists around, most likely with the same thought in mind—to throw a coin in the fountain to make sure of a return to Rome, The Eternal City, and it took a while to get there and we almost had to wait in line, but it was such a beautiful summer's day that we didn't mind.

There was a tour guide standing at the fountain to answer any questions and, looking at us, he said if you throw in 1 coin, you will return but if you throw in 5 coins, you will get married here in Rome. I couldn't think how he knew we weren't married, maybe we were holding hands. Well, Michael threw in 5 American coins and I threw in 5 German coins, just to make sure, and when we returned to our taxi and told the driver what we'd done, he had to laugh about the 5 coins. He said the reason was, of course, to get more money, and that the fountain collected a lot of money every day which was used for hospitals, churches and childcare and senior homes.

Lunchtime was almost over and the driver asked where else we would like to go. Well, Vatican City was out as there wasn't a lot of time left so we'd do that the next day and use the whole day. The driver then suggested we visit Via Condotti, Rome's most famous and elegant street, for a little shopping. I really didn't feel like shopping and neither did Michael, so we asked the driver to take us to a typical Italian restaurant to have lunch. We invited the driver to join us and found one in one of the side streets—it was like being in a movie and had big bottles of wine on the table and quiet music playing in the background and, of course, lots of spaghetti and soup and salad with either pork or fish, which was so delicious. And the wine—it was a good thing we didn't have to drive as we wouldn't have been able to compete with the Italian drivers.

As that driver was very helpful, when he dropped us off we made plans for the Vatican City. We'd had a wonderful day, the sort of day you don't experience very often, and we both fell asleep on the couch.

We decided to do the Vatican City tour the next day and then we'd most likely need a rest day as there was still the Colosseum to visit and we also planned to see Naples. The taxi came and we drove to Vatican City—our driver wasn't only a good driver; he was also a good tour guide and quite good looking. When I told Michael that, he insisted our next driver was going to be a good looking Senorita and that he would sit in the front seat next to her; yes, sometimes he was still the old Michael with his charming grin.

Vatican City is a city-state surrounded by Rome and is also the head-quarters of the Roman Catholic Church and the home of the Pope. We visited St. Peter's Basilica Church which was built in renaissance style in the 1500s and has beautiful pieces of art like Michelangelo's *Pieta* sculpture. It was so quiet and peaceful in the church that you could hardly talk and we sat there for at least an hour looking at all the art pieces before lighting a candle for each of our passed-on family members.

The driver asked us what else we wanted to visit but I could see Michael was getting tired so I had the idea of visiting that same little restaurant where we'd eaten the day before, and we all agreed. We had another delicious meal and, of course, wine as well and we started talking because our driver, Marcello, had found out Michael had been an American soldier station in Berlin after World War 2. I remembered that Germany, Italy and Japan were actually Allies and signed the Tripartite Pact in 1940 in Berlin—we had talked about that in school and although we weren't really interested in learning that because we were too young to understand it all, the teacher insisted on teaching it. So, we were actually one winner against two losers; it was quite interesting how small the world was.

We told Marcello we needed a rest the next day but that we'd then like to go to Naples and he immediately said that he would give us a good price if he could drive us. Michael and I really had to laugh about his fast reaction; I enjoyed the Italian temperament and quick-wittedness and everything was set for the day after next. We had really enjoyed the day again but Michael was tired, so he lay down on the couch and slept. Sitting there and watching him, I had the strangest thoughts. I hated the war and the winner of it—because of them, we'd lost everything; my grandparents were kicked off their farm and so many people lost their lives, but without the war I never would have met Michael. Maybe it was the wine which gave me such strange thoughts.

We asked the front desk to tell Marcello to come the following day for our whole day trip to Naples, so we had a day to rest and lots of things to discuss. We still had to visit the Colosseum and had days left to do that but we decided that we would skip it if things were going to get too hectic and that we could do that on our honeymoon, because that day he asked me to marry him. He laughed and said, "I have to do that because we threw the five coins in the fountain."

There were a lot of open questions about how to tell our families, where to live, etc. He suggested I sell the Berlin property as there was no way we would live in Berlin, but that I knew. It would mean I would lose my last leg in Berlin and couldn't say, as in Marlene Dietrich's song, that I still had a suitcase in Berlin, but there was nothing except memories left for me in Berlin after the sale of the property.

Michael then told me that he would most likely have to have another operation when he got back to the States and that he had to get one or two more stents—heart problems ran in his family. Now I understood why he was getting tired easily but he wasn't concerned about the operation, saying that these days it was a simple operation. We finally seemed to have a plan and he asked me if I would accept that proposal. I stopped for a moment and then said, "What about the business meetings all over the country?" He smiled and said, "Well, since I am not employed at the real estate office anymore, there are no meetings anymore, which is really sad." I didn't need to say anything, we both knew what we wanted and it was an emotional day for us. We went out for dinner and then, coming back, we bought a bottle of champagne and talked about us—now we had a past, a present, and most likely a future together.

Since it was late in the evening for us, it was morning there and I was able to call Hawaii. The way it looked now; Maria would not be coming to Berlin to go to school because I wouldn't be staying in Berlin. I talked with Thomas and he told me that he would most likely file for divorce and I just told him there were some changes and that I would come back to Hawaii to talk it over with them. He just said, "I knew it." I also called Angela but could not reach her and because we had that trip to Naples the next day, I retired early. I was just so happy.

Marcello picked us up in the morning and told us it might take about three hours to get to Naples, depending on the traffic in Rome on the way to the Autostrada and then on to Naples. He said we would see a lot of nice scenery on the way but I had to admit that my thoughts weren't really with it, I was thinking more about the future. We were glad we had Marcello, he was a good tour guide and talked a lot about his "Napoli," you could see how proud he was to be showing us his beautiful country. He asked if we would like to go for lunch as they had the best Pizza in the world—I loved that Italian temperament— and he said the Pizza originated in Naples and we couldn't prove anything different.

When we got to Naples we saw Mount Vesuvius, an active volcano. Marcello told us the most famous eruption was when the volcano buried the city of Pompeii under volcanic ash and mentioned that it could erupt again. One thing I found very interesting was that some streets were quite narrow and there were clothes lines hanging from one side of the street to the other for the clothes to dry.

Marcello told us that when we came back to Italy, we had to visit the Island of Capri, which was the most beautiful island we would ever see, and that you could reach Capri by ferry from Naples in about 80 minutes. Then he looked at us and his look asked if we wanted to go. That was what Marcello was like—he was clever and fast but you could smile about him. He also mentioned that some famous people lived there, like Grace Kelly, Ernest Hemmingway, Sophia Loren and Giorgio Armani. He really tried everything but then Michael said, "Let's have lunch, we'd like to try your famous pizza." Marcello understood and smiled, "Maybe next time." We found a cute restaurant in the old part of the city and Marcello ordered Pizza Margherita of Neapolitan and it was really the best pizza I had ever eaten so far.

It was then time to go back to Rome because we'd most likely hit the evening traffic in Rome but it had been an amazing trip and I loved the Italian mentality. We thanked Marcello for his services and he gave us his phone number so that we could call him if we changed our minds and wanted to see more. Michael said that we really should come back and visit Capri and I had to laugh as it showed what a good tour guide Marcello had been.

That night we talked for quite a while and both agreed we'd fallen in love with "Napoli." I remembered a German song, "O Mia Bella Napoli," but we were sure there was an Italian version and wanted to get that video. I also remembered a song about Capri and we had to find that, too. Michael called Italy the most romantic country and we hadn't much time left before going back to that not-so-romantic Berlin, so we decided to just enjoy Rome and not to any more sightseeing. We decided that the next night we'd go out for dinner and listen to some live music and dance a bit.

Sometimes I caught myself just staring up in the air and not believing it was all true and thinking I was just dreaming. If Michael saw that, he just joked and said, sometimes you are still a teenager, my little bird. Maybe I never had real teenage years and had just gone from childhood to grown up; the teenage years were only war and after-war years, so the proper teenage years were missing.

The next day we walked a little on the streets of Rome and found a music store and also those two videos about Napoli and Capri, before having a light lunch. We also found quite a fancy restaurant with live music for our dinner outing that evening; another perfect day in Rome. We really dressed up that night and I felt like a little bird again; the same feeling I had so many times back in Berlin when I was out with Michael. I thought I wasn't pretty enough next to him—surely I should have outgrown that feeling by then, but most likely I never would. We had a delicious dinner with wine and a burning candle and we also danced, with Michael acting like a teenager as well, singing the song Spanish Eyes but it was "Polish" Eyes he sang into my ear. Well, I felt special and it felt good.

When we got home, he told me he wanted to ask me something and said he'd had the idea that he wanted to go to Bavaria for a few days after we got back to Berlin. He'd heard so much about that area and how beautiful it is and I could go to my parents' grave, even though their real grave wasn't there anymore, and visit where our house was and that whole area. I didn't know what to say but I loved the idea and promised to show him everything, maybe he could even say hi to Irma. I had the impression he wanted to drag things out so we didn't have to leave Germany soon, and whatever the reason, I loved the idea. Maybe I wanted to drag it on, too, frightened of facing family problems, etc., but whatever the reason, it would be great.

I woke up in the middle of the night and still had to laugh about Michael when he asked me about that trip to Bavaria—he'd looked like a puppy begging for a treat but I very well remembered that face from many years ago; he had quite a few features which never changed. I was awake for quite a while trying to think of what I would show Michael—most likely Berchtesgaden, which I knew every American was interested to see because of Hitler's regime—and maybe the Obersalzberg and, if he was interested, then Salzburg/Austria, the birthplace of Wolfgang Amadeus Mozart. I had to put my head on his shoulder, as I had always done in our room at Daniels house in Berlin if I had problems sleeping. The next day I asked him what he'd like to see and, of course, Hitler came first with Salzburg also being a great idea.

That would drag our time on for at least another four weeks but we'd come to the conclusion that we came first now. Yes, maybe it was selfish but we had about 45 years behind us where others had come first, at least in my case. Michael had more or less hidden his own life.

We had a few days left before our departure back to Berlin and I called my family just to let them know that I really wasn't sure when I would be back. Michael did the same and we felt like little runaways, but we loved it. Finally, we left Rome, that most romantic city; at least it was for us and we hoped to return one day. We had a few days to prepare for Bavaria and Michael was concerned about my little car driving on the Autobahn—he would rather use a larger one to be safer and that was up to him as he would have to rent one. I knew exactly what he would rent, so we went and rented a Mercedes—he had his charming smile again and said, "Mercedes and the Autobahn belong together."

I called Irma in the little village and told her that we were coming and that she would meet the person who had called her several times from San Francisco and she insisted that we stay at her house. I told Michael about it and he loved the idea of staying in that German Bed and Breakfast house. He told me that he'd never really seen Germany— just Berlin—as how could he have gone and visited the rest of Germany as an American soldier.

Well, of course, he drove the Mercedes on the Autobahn with no speed limit and no control stops as there had been before and he enjoyed it a lot. I told him that if we arrived in Munich while the weather was nice, we would see the Bavarian Alps in the far distance. We didn't stop at restaurants but instead stopped at the Autobahn picnic places and ate sandwiches which we'd made at home with hard boiled eggs and a thermos bottle of hot coffee; everything was kind of new for Michael and he loved every minute of it. When we arrived in Munich the weather was beautiful and we could see the Alps in the far distance.

From Munich all the way to the little village was the nicest route you could drive—you could even smell Bavaria and I'd noticed that the first time I drove the route; it smelled like cows on grassland—it smelled healthy. We stopped at a sightseeing spot at Lake Tegernsee, one of the cleanest lakes in Germany, about thirty miles south of Munich. Michael didn't quite agree with me on the smell of Bavaria but he agreed on the healthy smell mixed with cow manure. Anyway, I loved that smell, for me it was Bavaria.

On the way into the little village, we passed the cemetery where my parents were buried and I could still find the place where the grave had been, but it was now all overgrown with grass. Michael held on to me very tightly and we went into the church and lit candles for my parents and his father and he lit one more. I asked him later for whom he'd lit that candle and he said it was for Daniel, Elena's ex-husband who had always been so helpful and nice to us. Maybe at that moment he felt guilty about starting an affair with his wife. It was kind of depressing for me to be there again when all the people I was close to, like my parents and Karl Heinz, had already passed, but the feeling that I was all alone in the world wasn't there because I had Michael next to me.

We arrived at Irma's house and she had a full house. I thought she'd invited all the neighbours and her house looked like a flower shop but it was just early summer and at that time the people of Bavaria put all their pride into decorating their houses inside and out with flowers. I looked at Michael and he was speechless; I knew that custom but he did not.

They showed us to our room which was upstairs and we had to go up squeaking wooden stairs to our room. Yes, it had a balcony so we might sit outside at night and have a glass of wine and it had the nicest view of the Bavarian Alps; it was like a fairy-tale, especially for Michael rather than for me. He gave me a big hug and only said, "Thank you." They called us down into the backyard for a Bavarian style barbeque of Bratwurst, Sauerkraut and Knoedel (dumplings) and lots of beer and they also told us there was going to be a Volksfest (folk festival) in two days, which we had to go to as there would be lots of food and beer, live music and jodle—a special art of singing. It was overwhelming and we were also tired after the drive from Berlin. "What a day," we said, and that was the last we said as we ended up in Morpheus arms.

We woke up to a beautiful morning and while standing on the balcony noticed that we had the Bavarian smell all around us. After last night's barbeque and a little too much beer, we decided to spend the day in the little village and I told Michael we might go up to the little chapel; it was a beautiful walk and we could have lunch at the restaurant up there. That was the walk I used to go on quite often when we were living there; it was so peaceful and quiet and the little church which belonged to the monastery had been run by monks since the 16th century.

Well, we started to walk up and the scenery was breathtaking but I noticed Michael seemed to be having problems with the uphill walk so we just sat down and rested on benches on the side of the road. He noticed I was worried but brushed it off by saying he was fine, he just had to have that operation he'd told me about. It still worried me and maybe we shouldn't have taken that walk, but he took one of his pills and was fine again. As we always had, we walked into that little chapel and lit candles again, enjoying the view of Tegernsee. The area there was called "Marias Corner" and was a tourist attraction for many people.

We had a not-too-heavy lunch. Usually in Germany, the main meal is lunch and unlike the Americans whose main meal is at night, it is the other way around and Germans mostly eat sandwiches in the evening. Walking down the hill was a lot better for Michael and he seemed his old self again.

Irma was already waiting for us and had most likely cooked all day as there was nothing but food everywhere. When we told her we'd already eaten, she still insisted we had to eat something and reminded us about the next day's folk festival, saying that Michael had to wear Lederhosen (leather pants). I couldn't stop laughing at the thought of Michael in leather pants but I was almost certain he had to.

We told Irma we were tired and went up to our room but sat on the balcony for a while just enjoying the scenery and being together. We had a few days left for Berchtesgaden and Salzburg but all in all, time was going by quickly. Michael asked me what I thought of the idea of getting married in Hawaii and I said to him, "I thought you would never ask; that would be my dream come true." I couldn't believe how lucky I was. Karl Heinz and I had got married in Berlin, the city I loved so much, and Michael and I would be getting married in heavenly Hawaii; that made my day. It was too late to start making plans that evening so we retired and, yes, I had to put my head on his shoulder otherwise I wouldn't have been able to sleep.

There was a pretty bad thunderstorm that night and it was still pouring the next morning, so Irma said there might be a cancellation of the folk festival that night, though if we were lucky the weather might still clear up. She said the leather pants for Michael were already waiting for him and asked me if I would like to borrow a Dirndl—a Bavarian dress—for myself. As we were both the same size, I said of course I would, but "Dirndl" can also mean "young woman" and as both of us were in a kind of elevated stage of life, we both had to laugh about it. I tried it on and it fitted perfectly.

Irma was busy and although it looked as if it was clearing up a bit, there was nothing else to do just then so we went up to our room again and sat on the balcony and just talked. There was so much to talk about and we loved our conversations, which somehow always ended up in our past. He had hated being transferred to Germany but most of the young soldiers had different ideas about Germany. Of course, they were the winner of the war and we were just poor and the losers and he admitted feeling like that too until he found out there were also pretty, good-looking young women amongst the losers—then Germany was not that bad anymore. After he stopped laughing about the German girls, he changed the subject and asked me about the holocaust and if I had known about all that—a question which surprised me.

I had known a bit but not the whole story, since my parents never talked to me about it. Sometimes my parents and I went to a movie theatre to watch the news—a show called *Die Deutsche Wochenschau* (the German weekly news) which had started in 1940 and continued until the end of the war in 1945. I could see on Michael's face that he was very interested to hear that. He just said that when he got to Berlin he wasn't interested in all of that as he had other things on his mind and he smiled when I said, "Yes, I knew that." I asked him if he wanted to know more, at least about what I did remember and he definitely wanted to know everything, especially about Auschwitz Birkenau. Well, I just went a few times to see that *Deutsche Wochenschau* and horrible scenes were shown about how we, Nazi Germany, had been successful in taking over country after country and soon we were on our way to take over Russia. That was where I saw Auschwitz, the death camp, the concentration camp where I knew Jewish people were sent to die because the names Jewish People or The Jews were mentioned in the show.

Michael just gave me a hug and said, "Enough for today but another day I'd like to know more about what you remember. After seeing the *Wochenschau*, I had known what happened to my little girlfriend who I played with in our park in Berlin when she and her family disappeared overnight, and I knew that they were Jewish people."

Irma called us to say the weather was clearing up and we were able to go to the folk festival, so Michael said we'd talk later about the concentration camps. I wondered why he was so interested in them but knew I would find out later. We had a hard time fitting into our Bavarian outfits because we couldn't stop laughing, but I had to admit Michael looked quite handsome in his white shirt and the leather pants and I found myself not so bad looking either and we were sure we fitted into the Bavarian crowd. Irma suggested walking there as it was pretty close to the house, and most of the neighbours did the same.

It was in a huge hall with lots of tables and a huge dancing area in the middle. On the side was a live band playing Bavarian folk music as well as Waltz and Polka music and the music was so loud you couldn't hear yourself speak. When we entered the hall, we heard some people saying, "Das sind die Amerikaner" (These are the Americans) and it was really fun watching that happy crowd. We found a table, thank God a little away from the music, and everyone of course ordered beer, which came with huge pretzels and also radish, like Daikon. I really admired those waitresses carrying those huge beer mugs, two in each arm, and they had the cutest Dirndls too. I saw Michael having a lot of fun and flirting with them—well, that was Michael—he hadn't changed in that department and most likely never would.

Then came the performer of the Schuhplattler dance (the shoe slapper dance) which can be traced back to the 11th century and is a Bavarian and Austrian folk dance. The performers jump around and strike the soles of their shoes and thighs and knees with their hands held flat. It looked amazing, like doing a strenuous exercise, and some of them weren't that young anymore. It was great entertainment except for the cigarette smoke in the air. People were smoking and although Michael and I used to be heavy smokers when we were younger, we'd quit when it became known how dangerous it was to your health. We told Irma we were really sorry but we had to leave because we couldn't handle the smoke, especially Michael with his heart problem, and as it was just a short walk back to the house, there was no problem.

It was a beautiful evening and we sat out on the balcony and I asked him why he was so interested in the Holocaust happenings. He told me his father had a Jewish business partner in San Francisco and they had a beautiful daughter who went to school with him and he had his first crush on her when he was around 14. He had overheard talk amongst the parents about how they had left Germany in a hurry leaving everything behind after Hitler came to power in 1933, because they knew they would fear for their lives later on. Maybe that was also the reason Michael wanted to visit Israel. I promised to tell him what I could remember, but not that night as we were both too tired and we had plans to visit Berchtesgaden the next day as well as Salzburg if there was enough time.

It was a beautiful morning and we were ready for our trip to Berchtesgaden, which wasn't far away from our little village—just about 20 miles but around an hour's drive because the road was quite narrow. You actually didn't want to drive fast because the scenery was breathtaking—you were in the middle of the Bavarian Alps and close to the Austrian border, just a short distance from Salzburg/Austria. Berchtesgaden is also called the romantic corner of Germany.

Michael looked around and said, "Okay, that was Hitler's retreat, he sure found a beautiful place," and I told him Berchtesgaden was very famous for the Nazi Regime and that a lot of Americans went there to visit and he said, "And now we are here, too, Mrs. Mendez." He really enjoyed that trip. We were looking for the Kehlsteinhaus, known as the Eagles Nest for tourists, and at the train station in Berchtesgaden we bought some brochures about the area because it was difficult to find the way around and I had only been there a couple of times and that was quite a while ago.

I saw Michael was getting frustrated as all he wanted to see was where Hitler lived during about a third of his time in power and all I could offer was to take him to another little village called Markt Schellenberg, about 30 minutes south of Berchtesgaden, where there were hardly any tourists but there was a beautiful view of the Watzmann mountain, a famous mountain in the Bavarian Alps region. He was all for it and asked me how I knew about that little village and I told him about going there after the war with our church group to recuperate from the terror of the last days of the war. I still remembered almost every little corner because after coming out of bombed-flat Berlin, it had been heaven there in the country. In front of us was the Watzmann mountain and I remembered climbing up the mountain and coming down—it was beautiful but I could hardly walk the next day.

We just got a couple of sandwiches and a glass of fresh buttermilk and sat down on a bench in the town center and although we were only a few miles away from the Germany/ Austrian border, so fairly close to Salzburg, we opted to do that trip the next day because I knew at that time Salzburg would already be pretty busy. We were already looking forward to sitting on the balcony and just talking. Irma was surprised when we were back early but we told her there were too many tourists in Berchtesgaden and she agreed, mentioning that she hardly went their either because it was too crowded. She made us a nice dinner of dumplings with mushrooms collected in the forest behind her house and a big bowl of fresh lettuce from her vegetable garden, and then we sat on the balcony with a glass of wine and I tried to tell Michael what I remembered about the holocaust.

We had learned a little in school about it, that the camps were built as prisons, but they didn't tell us the real story. There were a few—one was called Dachau, which was close to Munich and erected in 1933 when Hitler came to power and about 30,000 prisoners died there; but the largest and deadliest as Auschwitz-Bikenau, built in 1940 in Poland after Hitler took over Poland. Those two I remembered clearly because they were shown in *Die Deutsche Wochenschau* every time I went to that movie house.

I was told that over a million people were killed in Auschwitz by barbaric methods and that some were even used for medical experiments—we were told those stories after the war was over and that altogether around six million people were killed. I just had to stop and felt I might have an anxiety attack coming, so I told Michael that was all I remembered and that I didn't want to talk about it anymore. Michael said, "It's enough, I don't want to hear any more."

I realised Michael had heard enough about the holocaust but I was glad I could tell him what I remembered; it was not an era you liked to remember. Anyway, that day was the day for the trip to Salzburg and we started quite early to avoid the heavy traffic crossing the border—heavy because it was summer vacation time in Germany. We had a smooth ride into Salzburg, the city divided by the Salzach River into the New City and the Old City, and we found a good parking space and then walked over to the Getreidegasse, a busy shopping street in the Old City of Salzburg and a famous and important tourist attraction. Since it was still early, not too many people were walking around so we were able to enjoy all those classy, very expensive boutiques and jewellery stores.

The most interesting attraction was the birthplace of composer Wolfgang Amadeus Mozart, who was born in 1756—the house was tiny and in fact everything was tiny including the furniture and the kitchen; it looked as though people around the 1700s must have been short. I felt like a giant next to the chairs and tables but you were not allowed to sit down as the furniture was all from the time of Mozart. I was not quite sure about that but it certainly looked old. One tourist asked the tour guide if Mozart had also died there but no, he had died of a strep infection in Vienna/Austria in 1791 at the age of 35.

I saw Michael take one of his pills and realised it was time to get out and breathe fresh air. Also that I had to tell him that night that our "gypsy life" didn't make sense anymore and even though I really liked it, we had to face reality and tidy up our situations so we could get married and he could have his operation. When we got out of the house, we saw a Fiaker—a horse-drawn carriage—passing by and that's what I wanted—a tour of Salzburg in a Fiaker, which would be really romantic. We followed the Fiaker and found a huge parking area, like a taxi carpark but there were only Fiakers for hire so we hired one with two horses and I felt like royalty and almost tried to wave to people. I thought Michael was a bit embarrassed by my behaviour, but I loved it. We rode around for a while and the driver still wanted to show us the spot where the play "Jedermann" was performed. Jedermann is a German word meaning Everyman or Anyone and is a 1911 German play. He then dropped us off close to the Mozart house and we found a store with all kinds of sweets and also "Mozartkugel," which is an Austrian specialty, a little ball with pistachio, marzipan and nougat covered with dark chocolate. It's very delicious and we bought a lot of them as Irma loved them too.

Irma really enjoyed the Mozartkugel and she wanted to start a big meal for that night but we weren't too hungry after too many Mozartkugel and said just a sandwich would be fine. When we sat on the balcony that night we knew we had to end our present situation and that meant going back home—not to Berlin now but to the places we'd run away from—so that we could start our new beginning. We decided to talk to Irma the next day telling her that we would perhaps leave in three days; time to get back to reality as it was already August and Maria was going back to school in the islands. Michael was in a better position and had no responsibility and could just pick up and go. I tried to be very positive and knew I would make it through. Then we found ourselves in the past again—there was actually a lot we had to go through but of course we were young then and times were very different.

I realised I wasn't mad at the war anymore and neither was I mad at the Allies for destroying everything we owned; if not for the war, how would I have met Michael and would I ever have left Germany. I was glad I thought like that now, even though it had taken a while. At least we had a solid plan now which made things easier. We would stay three more days and then go back to Berlin and when I told Irma our plans, she understood and commented that Michael was a good guy, just like Karl Heinz had been.

We visited the Maria Corner again, lit candles again for our loved ones, and had a delicious lunch up there. It was more of a goodbye there in that little village where my parents had been buried, even though the grave wasn't there anymore. We bought a few souvenirs to take back to the States and Irma made us sandwiches again for the drive to Berlin; as the weather was nice, we could stop and sit on the benches at the autobahn parking spaces. It was an emotional farewell since we didn't know if we would see each other again. We had a few stops on the autobahn and ate our sandwiches before getting home to Berlin, where we decided not to do any immediate calling or preparation for our return to the States and to just enjoy a nice conversation as we had experienced over the last few days—that was emotional enough. Our bond was so strong and had maybe become even stronger over the last months, so we knew we would make it, and yes, it was again a day when I had to put my head on Michael's shoulder, though even with that it took a long time for me to fall asleep.

We gave ourselves about a week to prepare to leave Berlin. Michael would fly out first and I would stay back and take care of all the things we hadn't done, like sign the papers for the sale of the property, cancel the lease on the apartment and sell the car, etc. We called home and Thomas was relieved I would be back. Angela was busy with her life and most likely going to move to Florida but as she was pregnant, they wanted to wait until the baby was born. Michael's family was alright and had no plans, so Michael could prepare for his operation.

One night we went out for dinner at a fancy restaurant close to the Brandenburg Gate, Berlin's most famous landmark and a big tourist attraction, which was built late in the 17th century and was used as a gateway entry into Berlin. While Michael opened a bottle of champagne, he also gave me a little box which I knew could only contain jewellery. He smiled and said, "It's not what you think—our wedding rings are going to be bought in the States." It was a pair of golden earrings which looked like the Edelweiss flower. I couldn't think how he had got them as we were always together and he got a kick out of telling me he'd talked to Irma one day after seeing a goldsmith in that little village and he'd asked her if she would go to the goldsmith and buy the earrings. The goldsmith was famous for those Edelweiss earrings and sold them to jewellery stores. They were tiny because they were made of gold, but just perfect for earrings. Michael had read about them in a newspaper—the flower grows way up in the mountains and can even survive cold winters. They can be very dangerous to find and stand for true love, bravery and strength.

It was a lovely evening and I was thinking that I was no longer afraid to leave Berlin and most likely not return, as after the sale of the property there was nothing in Berlin that I would miss anymore. We went to the travel agency for a one-way ticket to San Francisco for Michael and the lady—who already knew us from our trips to Israel and Italy—was surprised about that one-way ticket until we told her we were just visiting and now the good times were over. She told us she would give us a call with what she found and, yes, reality really set in. In a way it was a good feeling but also scary and although we acted happy, the memories popped up of when Michael left me behind all those years before.

We had a call from the travel agency asking us to stop by as she'd found a good connection and Michael could either fly through or have a layover in New York and after talking it over, we thought it might be better if he stopped in New York for a night to rest before flying on to San Francisco the next day. We went in and she made the reservation for Thursday, August 20th; a date I would never forget—the day Michael would leave Berlin would have been my mother's 93rd birthday if she had still been alive.

We still had over a week and although he could have flown earlier, we were still dragging it out, though we now had the ticket. I hoped to leave Berlin in four weeks and that after Michael's operation, we could make plans for our wedding in Hawaii. Michael and I went to the realtor who would sell the property and I told him my plan that he should go ahead and then send me the papers to sign to finalise the deal when he found a buyer. I would not have to go back to Berlin for that, since the only thing I'd leave behind would be my German bank account, so it looked like one thing was taken care of. I hoped Christina's husband would help me with the sale of the car and would try to contact them again after Michael had left, and I would most likely have to pay the full amount of rent for the apartment even if I left earlier.

I called Thomas to tell him my plans to return and he seemed quite stressed out, so it was time to see how everyone was going. We didn't plan anything for the last few days we had left, just concentrating on our future plans; I guess we'd have called it saying farewell to Berlin

together. Most likely we would live in California after our marriage and we would take Maria along with us—those were the talks we had most of the time while walking around Lake Wannsee. Lake Wannsee was actually the only thing that hadn't changed since Michael left over forty years before.

Christina called and wanted to know what was happening and where we were and I realised she might have thought over the situation with Michael and him being an American soldier as she asked me if we would like to go over for a barbeque on the weekend. I said I would let her know as I had to ask Michael—he was still there until the next week—but of course he agreed to go so I called Christina and said we would go. I also mentioned that Michael and Karl Heinz knew each other and she seemed surprised.

I was a bit nervous but there was nothing wrong; Michael was divorced and I was a widow. We got there and the weather was nice, so everything was perfect for a garden party and they had invited two more couples about our age. Michael soon became the center of the party with his broken German but I was used to that as Karl Heinz had been like that too, always the center of attention, and we had a lot of fun that night. Christina asked me where we met and I told her it was on a blind date and that I hated him at first because he was an American soldier, but I didn't tell her what else happened between us. Even Karl Heinz knew almost everything but he never told anybody. It looked like Michael made a good impression on everybody—there is a saying that if a person is good at communicating with people, he could sell refrigerators to Eskimos.

When we got home, we sat for a while on the balcony and Michael told me how he had enjoyed the party and, with a grin, he said, "What will happen if I lose the ticket?" I said, "Well, we would have to buy a new one," and his reply was "Does it come with a week's extension?" I knew it should be funny but in reality it was not and I wondered if there was something he wasn't telling me about why he was so against leaving. "Let's talk about it," I said, and I expected a laugh and for him to say it was just a joke but no, nothing came back except silence and then he took his pill and went to bed. I was worried as that was not like Michael and we had to have a talk the next day. Maybe we could walk around Lake Wannsee and sit down and watch the swans; maybe we would see some. I hoped I would find out what was bothering him.

After breakfast I asked Michael if we could go walking around Lake Wannsee, take some sandwiches along and sit on the benches and watch the swans as it was a beautiful summer's day. I thought it was a good place to ask him about yesterday's remark about staying another week, so we got some sandwiches and started walking and I then asked him why he wanted to stay another week. He grinned for a minute and said, "I just feel bad leaving you again like I did the first time." He said he'd like to stay a few more days in Berlin, maybe going to movies and dancing, since we hadn't done a lot in Berlin because of our travelling. I wasn't sure if he really meant it or if there were other reasons, like being afraid of the operation or maybe family problems, and when I looked at him, he again looked like a puppy begging for something.

Well, I thought it over and maybe he was right and just a week longer wouldn't make that much of a difference, so right after our walk we went to the travel agency and explained what we wanted. She only laughed and said to Michael, "Yes, our Berlin is addictive, it's hard to leave." She said she would check the flights but didn't see any problems finding a good connection by the end of August. In a way, I liked the idea as we could still enjoy Berlin for a few more days and maybe we could have another barbeque party at Christina's.

We tried to go and watch a movie but it wasn't the best idea as Michael's German wasn't good enough to completely understand it. The travel agency called us and said they had a good connection for Michael on Monday, August 31st, so we had a few days and I decided to take care of everything in three weeks and then leave Berlin as well.

We had another great party with Christina and friends and it looked as if Christina had forgotten the past and had in a way accepted Michael. They told us we should drive sightseeing up north, the former East Germany, and maybe even look at the German/Polish border as the scenery was beautiful and there were lots of little fish restaurants but we decided to only do day tours so that we could enjoyed the apartment, but that we would also go and eat at the little fish restaurants.

Bianca called Michael to find out how he was doing and when he'd be back and Michael told her he would be leaving Berlin on August 31, then he gave me the phone and said, "Please talk to her." I was not prepared for that because in a way she was the reason for our break-up 45 years before, but of course it wasn't her fault. He just nodded and said, "She knows about you." "Well," she said, "Hi!" and I said "Hi," then silence before all of a sudden she started to talk without stopping, asking how I was, how her father was, how was Berlin, etc. etc. I had no chance to say a word and Michael started to laugh saying, "That is Bianca." Bianca was still talking, saying, "Okay. Take care. See you soon," then Michael took the phone and ended the conversation. "Yes," I told Michael, "that is the Spanish and Mexican temperament," but it was nice talking to her for the first time and it showed me Michael was not going to have problems with his family about us getting married.

We started to plan a day trip up north to get to the "Ostsee," or Baltic Sea, to have a good fish lunch as Christina had suggested. It was about a three-hour drive on the Autobahn to get to Rostock, an old port city close to the German/Polish border, which was part of East Germany until Germany was united again, and Christina said we should be sure to see the University of Rostock, founded in 1419 and supposedly one of the oldest universities in the world. I was not so sure about the world, but it must at least be quite old.

The day we decided to go up north and visit Rostock, Michael asked me if I would drive on the Autobahn as he had a headache and I saw him taking two of his pills whereas usually he just took one. I didn't ask him about it and we just left and after a while he was better, or at least he told me so. It took not quite three hours to drive to Rostock and we had a picturesque view as we arrived. Christina was right, it was a MUST to see it and we didn't regret having gone.

The city was old but a really nice old and we'd been told to have lunch at the Rostocker Fish Market, which we found. We ate there and it was a real experience—they had the best fish buns ever and the fish was delicious; compared to the Pacific fish, I liked that a bit more. We could have stayed there longer but we'd decided to only do day trips so we drove back to Berlin, but thanked Christina for the tip to see Rostock. I was getting worried about Michael as he looked tired, but we still enjoyed the balcony and seeing how much Michael had enjoyed the tour made me happy.

Because we didn't have too many days left, we decided not to do any more day tours—anyway, in those three months, we'd seen more places than most people experience in their whole lives—and we spent most of the time sitting on the balcony and talking about the past. Sometimes I had the feeling he was more in the past than in the future and as much as I loved to sit on the balcony and talk about us, most of the time it was the past and I didn't really like to hear about his relationships and love affairs. I almost felt like a priest in the confessional box, so one evening I just told him that. He was quiet for a moment but replied, "I know I shouldn't, but I will tell you the reason why I think I was like that. I hated my mother for leaving us and we were pushed around from nannies to aunties and with every affair I had, I wanted to get even with my mother." I wasn't a therapist and I really did not understand that reasoning but I told him it was fine and if he felt better for telling me all of it, then it was alright, but he then stopped talking about that.

Christina called to tell us there would be a farewell party in her yard for Michael on Saturday as he was leaving on Monday, August 31st. As much as I was looking forward to the party, I wasn't looking forward to him leaving and maybe it was just me and my imagination, but he seemed distant all of a sudden even though he was still very loving and romantic.

We enjoyed every day together, walked around Lake Wannsee and drove around in the former East Germany, which was very scenic with lots of forests. Michael wanted to collect mushrooms but had no idea if they were poisonous or edible and although I collected mushrooms with my mother after the war, she knew which ones to pick and I didn't. Michael laughed and said we'd better stop—he wanted me to be his wife and we'd waited so long for that. I loved those moments; he was the old Michael again.

I had a phone call from Thomas to say his wife had moved out and for a while she was leaving their son with Thomas, so he had both children and the dogs as well; in other words "please come home." I explained to him that I'd be there in four weeks at the latest. Our last week started but we had no special plans made and there was much packing to do. We had dinner once or twice at Kurfuerstendamm, then the party at Christina's and then "ADIOS"—but not goodbye, like the Elvis Presley song.

The manager of our apartment building invited us for a drink one evening, which was good as I was able to tell him that that I'd be leaving in about four weeks. Even though my lease was still active, he only wanted two months' rent as he understood our situation. His English was pretty good, so Michael could also be part of our conversation.

"Yes," he said, "if you pull up your roots you never really feel like you're at home again. But," he went on, looking at me, "some people are different and are like gypsies, feeling at home as long as they have a place to sleep." I said that I wasn't that bad and that my home would always be Berlin and he just laughed and said he was just joking. But, thinking about it, I thought maybe he was a little bit right—I knew there was something in our family history and though I didn't know or was not supposed to know, what it was, I saw it on my grandmother's face if we talked about her past. She was so different to the rest of her family, so wise and understanding for her time and so advanced in her thinking and behaviour. There was also the happiness in her big eyes when Michael came and visited her; maybe he reminded her of someone—but again, maybe it was just my imagination because I never found anything out.

The manager told us about a friend of his who had tried to immigrate to Australia after the war, since they were looking for railroad workers, but that young man was too short—you had to be a certain height and he was just a bit too short, so he tried Canada and they let him in. I remembered while we were living in Canada that we knew a German family who had a beautiful daughter whose dream was to become a stewardess with the Canadian Airline, but there were also rules there that you must be a certain height and weight. At that time being a stewardess was a dream come true for every young woman.

Michael was very interested in those stories—he didn't have that problem in his country since there was no direct fighting involved and they didn't have to struggle from day to day like we did in order to survive—his future was set, at least for him, but maybe that upbringing made us a bit stronger. It was a late evening but quite interesting and afterwards was an evening I would have slept in my grandmother's lap, but we just fell asleep holding hands, like I used to do with Maria when she was little.

I really had to pull myself together to stop that negative thinking and convince myself that everything would be fine and that we would be getting married and live happily ever after. It was a cloudy day, so we thought a visit to Berlin Zoo would be great and that's what we did. Berlin Zoo (Berliner Zoologischer Garten) was one of the oldest in

Germany and I remembered how terrible it was at the end of the war. Michael noticed how quiet I became, so I told him about checking the zoo after the Allies stopped bombing and the German Army and the Russian Army stopped house-to-house combat. I couldn't go there but our priest and some helpers went there and told us about it—even they had a hard time seeing dead animals and dead bodies everywhere and out of about 3,500 animals, only about 100 survived. Michael then wasn't sure about going there now but I was okay—sometimes I just got those flashbacks; but it was holding hands time again.

I hadn't been to the zoo for the longest time and I was surprised how beautiful it was. It looked like a park and I had the feeling the animals were all smiling; they looked happy and well fed. When we came to the elephants, I had to laugh remembering Thomas in the Honolulu Zoo—whenever he saw an elephant, he took his slippers off and threw them into the elephant's cage. I never found out why and when I told Michael about it, he said he thought Thomas maybe thought that they needed shoes because their feet were so big. He told me a story about Bianca, that when she was little she desperately wanted high heeled shoes and when she didn't get them, she went into her room and cut off half of her hair. "She was a very lively child," he said, and you could see how proud he was.

We enjoyed the day and fed a few animals and on our way home we stopped at Christina's to find out about the garden party at the weekend—most likely that would be the last Hurrah in Berlin and, to be honest, it was about time to start getting organised again and not trying to hide some place. Arriving back at the apartment, the manager told us there had been a call from the realtor asking us to stop by; maybe there was an offer in—that would be perfect as I could then clear that up before I left and we decided to do that the next day.

We had almost everything under control and somehow it felt good. The last Sunday, we planned to go to church and then Michael would leave on Monday morning. He asked me to get a taxi to take him to Tegel Airport; I would have done that anyway. In the meantime, we went to the travel agency and asked them to start looking for flights to Hawaii for me, around the end of September, one way.

On Thursday, we went to see the realtor, who had an offer but it was so ridiculously low that I didn't accept it. Even the realtor rejected it, but at least we could see that there was some interest. It was too bad as I wished I could have finished the sale, but I wasn't going to give it away. We had three days left until departure, so there wasn't much left to do except wait, though we still had the garden party to look forward to. Bianca called again and wished her father a safe trip and I just talked to her for a few minutes; she didn't seem too excited that time, so maybe it was only the first time. I also heard from Thomas; it was time for me to get back.

Christina did a fantastic job of decorating for the garden party—she might have felt the same as I did that maybe this would be our last time together. Like always, we ended up in the past—maybe it was because of Michael but everyone had a story to tell about the war. There was an elderly gentleman who had been a very young German soldier at the Eastern frontline. They were hiding in large ditches across from the Russian Army behind trees and bushes but they knew the distance wasn't that far. In the middle of the night he wanted to smoke a cigarette so he crawled out of the ditch and because he saw another soldier smoking nearby, he joined him and lit his cigarette before he realised that the other soldier next to him was not a German one; it was a Russian soldier. They looked at each other but neither did anything so they silently smoked their cigarettes, then turned around and jumped back in their ditches. Christina said, "He tells that story to everyone, he's so proud of it," but it wasn't the first time I'd heard stories like that, so it must have happened.

It was past midnight when we got home and the next day, Sunday, was the last whole day for us in Berlin. We wanted to go around Lake Wannsee one more time and then to church in the evening, and then it was over. I felt surprisingly calm since so far we had everything under control and were looking forward to our future. After breakfast, we went around Lake Wannsee but we didn't see any swans and you felt fall was near—some leaves were already turning yellow, so the time of nature dying was there.

On Sunday evening we went to church again and lit candles for the passed ones in our family and I showed Michael the house where my mother and I lived with my aunt when the Russian army took over Berlin. Yes, it was our last evening together in Berlin; it was bittersweet but we were ready for our future together. Everything was packed ready for the next day for the flight to New York and on to San Francisco. We sat for a while on the balcony and neither of us was really tired. Michael thanked me for the time we'd spent together and for showing him all the places he wanted to see, including Berlin. He said, "We're closing this part of our lives now and starting anew and that part of my heart you were in, really grew."

Well, we must have slept a bit because Monday morning was suddenly there. Michael called a taxi to take us to Tegel Airport and we had a cup of coffee before he had to check in. A last hug while we both had tears in our eyes and then, "Adios, my little bird; stay safe; see you soon in Hawaii; I'll call you from home," and he turned and went through the gate and never turned around. I was used to that—staying behind when a person I loved left. It was Michael the first time, then Karl Heinz for Canada, then my father, and now Michael again. All I wanted then was to call a taxi and go home because that feeling was there again—of being all alone in this world.

I got home and unplugged my phone—I just didn't want to see or hear anyone and I knew Michael was not going to call me until the next day when he got home; I just wanted to sleep and not think about anything. There was a half-full bottle of wine in the kitchen and I emptied that bottle, closed the windows, pulled the curtain down and tried to sleep. When I woke up it was still light but almost Monday morning: I'd slept almost 15 hours. I felt quiet immature about what I'd done but maybe I just needed that rest. I plugged in the phone and opened the windows to let in the fresh air. I decided that when Michael called— most likely that evening when he got to San Francisco—I wouldn't tell him what I'd done, and I made myself breakfast and sat down to make a plan about what to do each day.

I called Christina's husband asking for help with the sale of the car and actually there wasn't that much to take care of and I thought I'd be ready to leave in three weeks. That night, Michael called to say he was home and that the flight was very good. He told me to hurry up and get back to the States as soon as possible and told me he'd call every second day to keep me posted about the doctor and his operation.

I was in touch with Thomas and also with Angela and with Michael on every second day. It was not easy but I knew that and was thinking a lot about my grandmother who always told me that prayers do help, but never to pray for material things, or money, just pray for guidance and strength. If I had a bad day, I went around Lake Wannsee and if the day was really bad, I went around twice. When a week had almost gone, I was doing well and I got a good deal on my flight back to the Islands on the 25th of October with a stopover in Dallas, Texas, and on to Honolulu. Our plan had been for me to stop over in San Francisco and meet Janet and Bianca and the rest of the family, but since Michael was waiting for a date for his operation, it would be a stressful time and wasn't a good idea.

Christina's husband found a buyer for my little car and I could keep it until I left so with about a week left to go I had almost everything under control and was more than ready to leave. There was another barbeque party at Christina's and the night before I left, the new owner of my car picked it up. I was then ready for the next morning and to call a taxi to go to Tegel Airport. When we took off, it was a beautiful clear fall day. I looked out of the window and my mind said not "Adios," but "Goodbye" to Berlin, the city I loved and where I had the happiest and also the saddest and most scary moments of my life. I was born there, lived there through World War 2, experienced the horror of the end of the war and its aftermath, and still loved it. But—I had a future again and maybe the end of my gypsy life.

It was a smooth flight all the way to the Islands, where Thomas picked me up with Maria. I was so happy to see my little girl again and, in a way, I now considered the Islands as being home. Thomas and I had long talks and I told him my—or, better, Michael's and my—plans and he seemed to accept it, but of course we had to wait until after the operation. I call Michael the next day and told him I was back and he was still waiting for a date for the operation.

In a way, Maria was glad to stay back in the Islands. Maybe she was scared of going to Berlin, into a new school and having to use another language as even though she was fluent in spoken German, she wasn't fluent when writing. It would have been a bilingual school with mostly English-speaking students attending, but it would not be easy for her so it might be better for her this way.

When Michael called me, he'd heard from his doctor that it might be another four weeks before his operation since it was a private hospital and a special clinic for heart problems. I had to admit that I was kind of worried about that operation and hoped and prayed that everything would be fine now that we were so far ahead with our future plans.

I received news from the Realtor in Berlin that there was another offer on my property from a family from the former West Berlin. It wasn't that great but it was better than the last one and the realtor suggested I make a counter-offer at a slightly higher price. The trend was now for former West Berliners to move to the former East Germany where the scenery was nicer. Berlin kept on growing so whoever could afford it was moving out of the city of Berlin into the outskirts, which pushed up the land and house prices. It was now chic to live in the country. So, we made the counteroffer and I waited for an answer.

In the meantime, Angela had a little boy and they were still planning on going to Florida, so my family kept on falling apart and if Michael and I were moving to California, we would hardly be in touch with anyone anymore. It sounds sad but that's life and now I could understand how my parents felt when I left for Canada and even though I was their only child, they never complained. Maybe that was also a reason why I was so happy to have Maria, my Baby.

The realtor contacted me and said my counter-offer had been accepted; yes it was nice but with that I lost my last suitcase in Berlin, there was actually no reason at all for me to return and that thought was not easy to accept. Years back I would never even have considered thinking like that.

Shortly before Michael's operation, Bianca called me, telling me she was a bit worried about her father; he was downplaying the operation but she had spoken with his doctor who said it wouldn't be that easy—that his heart was weak and that he wouldn't just put in another stent, but maybe also a pacemaker; he would decide while operating. That really scared me too, but of course he would be fine.

After talking to Michael the next day, I offered to go to San Francisco to be there while he had the operation but he didn't want me to because he was sure it just wasn't serious and that instead I should prepare everything for him to come to Hawaii after he had the operation, so there was nothing I could do except just wait.

The sale of the property in Berlin went through, so that was another worry gone, and a week went by before Michael called to let me know he'd had word from the hospital that he would have a date at the end of November. If everything went well he might be with us for Christmas, which would be wonderful. I told Thomas about it but he wasn't that interested as he was having problems of his own with his divorce. That didn't stop me from making plans for Christmas, though, and I called Angela and asked her if maybe she could come over with her family and her little boy, my grandson, and she said she would try.

Bianca phoned me to tell me her father was on his way to the hospital and he was okay but a bit nervous, and that she would keep me posted. It was a Friday; I won't forget that day. It shook me up a lot and I wasn't sure what to do, whether to go to church or listen to the two recordings—"Spanish Eyes" and "It's Now or Never"; I listened to that music whenever I was frightened or very emotional and that's what I did that night—over and over again. I knew Bianca would call me as soon as she knew what was going on and it wouldn't be that day but most likely the next day or Sunday. I was walking around like a zombie but there was nobody I could actually talk to about it.

Bianca called me on Saturday night to say the operation was over and he was in the Intensive Care Unit, but as far as I knew that was nothing out of the ordinary after an operation and Bianca felt the same way. At least it was over and most likely we would know more the next day but we both cried on the phone even though it somehow felt good to be talking to her. That night I slept a lot better and realised that yes, she would actually become my stepdaughter.

For a few days, I was only in contact with Bianca, since Michael was still in ICU, and all the doctors had told her was that Michael had a pacemaker and would have to stay in the hospital a little longer. Well, it wasn't exactly what I wanted to hear and I asked Bianca if she could ask him for his number in the hospital so that I could call him, but the next day she called me back telling me he had no phone in ICU but that she would let me know as soon as he was out. It was a nervous wait but we were glad that at least the operation was over. My hope that Michael would be with us for Christmas was fading a bit as, if the operation was that serious, I wouldn't expect him to be able to fly. If that was the case, then I would fly to San Francisco with Maria for Christmas and when I told Thomas about it and he was alright with that idea.

I was eventually allowed to talk to Michael and he sounded tired but his spirit was up; that was the Michael I knew—he would not show his weakness, in this case his illness. He said he would be out of there in a few days and on his way to Hawaii and I really hoped so much for that—to being his wife and having a whole family again with grandchildren to celebrate the holidays. The next day, I called my doctor and asked him about that pacemaker and whether it was serious and he said the only thing which can be a bit dangerous is if it is in the family—and his father had died of a massive heart attack.

The next time I talked with Bianca she said he was making progress and that if he kept on going like that, he could be released from the hospital soon. That was very good news and I started to make plans for Christmas. When I spoke with him when he was out of ICU, he was so full of life and hope again, almost the old Michael, and I was his little bird again and we laughed on the phone.

Yes, I went to church the next day and was very happy not to light another candle. We would also be spending New Year's together so I was planning to cook all German dishes, like my mother used to do on Christmas Eve, and I hoped I could remember how to do it. Well, they wouldn't know the difference anyway if it didn't turn out the same as if my mother had cooked it.

The next few days passed and I spoke with Michael almost every day. It was then almost the middle of December and I wondered if he would be well enough to travel to have Christmas with us, but he told me the doctor had said he should be able to leave the hospital in a couple of days at the most, so he would make it. He asked me if I could ask Charly to find a nonstop flight from San Francisco to Maui and then on to our Island as he wanted to avoid a big city like Honolulu, so I called Charly and asked him about it. He wasn't sure if it was possible because it was high season in Hawaii, but said he would try and he eventually found one from San Francisco to Honolulu on December 21st— but that was the only way and meant a stopover in Honolulu.

When I told Michael, he asked me to meet him in Honolulu and said we could stay overnight in Honolulu and I realised he didn't feel strong enough, and he had never visited the Islands, either. I liked the idea a lot and if he wasn't too tired, we could stay at a hotel right on Waikiki beach.

The next day, he was released from the hospital and Bianca told me he seemed to be fine but that she thought there were other problems besides his heart, which was now okay. He didn't want to talk about it and neither did his doctor, so I would ask him about it when he arrived. Charly made the reservation for Michael but left the return date open and he also arranged my flight to Honolulu and the hotel reservation.

I was relieved since I was then sure Michael would make it for the holidays and I could really start to decorate the house inside and out. We would also have a great time in Honolulu, maybe staying two nights so he could rest—it really didn't matter as long as he was out of the hospital and on his way to recovery.

The next night, I woke up in the middle of the night because I heard the phone ringing. My first thought was that something was wrong—unless it was Germany and they had forgotten the time difference. When I answered the phone, it was Bianca on the line, crying and telling me that Michael had had a stroke and was back in hospital. We both cried. He was back in ICU and she hadn't yet heard from the hospital as it had just happened a few hours before.

She knew that he was looking forward to coming to Hawaii and being with us but now we didn't know what to do because after recovering from the stroke, he would most likely have to go to a Rehabilitation Centre and that might take a while. I told Bianca to keep me posted and said that maybe I would go over to San Francisco, but it wouldn't be for Christmas, and in the meantime I would cancel his flights as it was already too close to when he was due to fly.

She promised to inform me as soon as there was any news and I sat there feeling numb; it would have been too good to be true. One thing came to my mind and that was that I was almost sure he knew he was sicker than we realised and it all made some sense now, why he had dragged out our vacation and wanted to see all the places we went to, like Italy, Israel and Berlin—maybe he knew he most likely wouldn't be able to see them in the future. Whatever happened, I would try my best to be with him and take care of him as much as I could. I thought about Karl Heinz who had a bad heart as well, but—if you can say that—his suffering was spared as he died in the car crash within minutes; maybe he was scared for a few minutes but then it was over. I hoped so and I prayed for Michael that night that he would recover or that if his time was up, he wouldn't suffer.

After thinking it through, I felt calmer and I remembered my grandmother's words that you cannot run away and hide if your time is up. Maybe she was guiding me from wherever she was. In the morning, I told Thomas the news and he told me to fly over, but it would make no sense as I didn't think I would even be able to get into the ICU and it would just be more pressure and stress for everybody. Whatever happened, no one could take away the time and the memories Michael and I had of the last few months, and that morning I called Charly, asking him to cancel everything for the time being.

I really gave up decorating the rest of the house because I knew Michael wouldn't be able to come and I just tried to get through the days. Bianca called me twice a day saying his vital signs were not stable. She had talked with his doctor, who said that when Michael told him about his trip before the operation, the doctor had advised him not to go but he went anyway—in other words, he knew very well that he was quite ill. I guess from the moment Bianca told me that, I knew there was no longer much hope and I suppose I was actually waiting for the call from Bianca to say it was over.

Angela let me know that she most like wouldn't make it to stopover for the holiday: she had a good job offer and they were preparing to maybe leave sooner. I then actually didn't care whether or not we celebrated Christmas—or Easter, for that matter.

About a week before Christmas, Bianca called me and when I picked up the phone, I knew what she was going to say; her voice told me. She was not crying but her voice was slow and she was hard to understand. "My father just passed," she said. "He had another stroke and went into a coma and didn't wake up again." And then she hung up. I waited a little while and then I called her. She felt better by then and cried and we talked for a long time; I didn't realise Michael and she had such a bond. We talked about the past and she told me that Michael had told her everything about us and, she said, she knew he really loved me all his life. I just could not cry anymore.

She asked me if I would go to the funeral and I told her I was not sure but that I would call her the next day to let her know. I don't quite remember the next hours—I had been expecting it but also hoped I was wrong. The only thing I knew was that I was not attending the funeral; I could not. When I was listening to the two records we'd heard so many times, "Spanish Eyes" and "It's Now or Never," I knew what I had to do and since that chapter of my life was over now, I would call Bianca and tell her I would not come; instead I would send those two records to her and she should put them into Michael's resting place— his Spanish Eyes were closed now and would never open up again.

Yes, the feeling of being all alone was very strong and the next chapter of my life would be very lonely....

ACKNOWLEDGMENTS & RECOGNITIONS

To the publishing company Dorrance for their exquisite help guiding me through many challenges in making my book possible. Heartfelt Thanks.

To my long time dearest friend Jane B. from New Zealand encouraging me to continue writing and to keep up my passion although through many obstacles. I will never forget this.

To my son in helping me with technical and internet relate obstacles. Thank you, my son.

To my two daughters for giving me emotional support throughout these trying times.

To my three grandchildren that are near and far, you will always be in my Heart.

And finally a special recognition to the experts of Office Max printing Division in Hilo on the Island of Hawaii for their expert guidance and advice regarding printing and Layout of pictures . I am very appreciative. ALOHA